Evolutionary Psychology

Series Editors:
Todd K. Shackelford
Viviana A. Weekes-Shackelford

For further volumes:
http://www.springer.com/series/10583

Viviana A. Weekes-Shackelford • Todd K.
Shackelford
Editors

Evolutionary Perspectives on Human Sexual Psychology and Behavior

Editors
Viviana A. Weekes-Shackelford
Todd K. Shackelford
Department of Psychology
Oakland University
Rochester, Michigan, USA

ISSN 2197-9898   ISSN 2197-9901 (electronic)
ISBN 978-1-4939-0313-9   ISBN 978-1-4939-0314-6 (eBook)
DOI 10.1007/978-1-4939-0314-6
Springer New York Heidelberg Dordrecht London

Library of Congress Control Number: 2014930340

Printed on acid-free paper

Springer is part of Springer Science+Business Media (www.springer.com)

Preface

This volume presents an outstanding collection of chapters addressing evolutionary perspectives on human sexual psychology and behavior. Not only are the chapter contributors leading researchers but also the contributors were carefully selected as gifted communicators. As a collection, the chapters in this volume provide a rich overview of historical and current empirical and theoretical work on sex differences and similarities in human psychology and behavior.

The volume is organized into three parts. In the first part, David Schmitt sets the stage for the volume with a wide-ranging review of how evolutionary scientists evaluate the evidence for mate preference adaptations. Drawing on his own extensive cross-cultural research, Schmitt provides the reader with a road map for how to *do* evolutionary psychology, with a special focus on sex differences and similarities in mate preferences.

The second and third parts of the volume focus on sexual adaptations in men and in women, respectively. The second part includes nine chapters addressing sexual adaptations in men. Joseph Camilleri and Kelly Stiver open this part with a chapter detailing recent work on sexual offending. Camilleri and Stiver review research on sexual offending and in the process provide a compelling case for the heuristic value of an evolutionary perspective for generating novel insights about rape and other sexual offenses.

David Puts and colleagues offer a stellar summary of recent research, including their own groundbreaking work, testing predictions generated from the hypothesis that sexual selection has shaped human male vocal qualities. In the past decade, evolutionary psychologists have invested significant effort unpacking individual differences in sexual psychology and behavior. This exciting work is typified by research conducted by Ben Jones and his colleagues on agreement and individual differences in men's preferences for women's facial characteristics, summarized in the next chapter. Erik Lund and Saul Miller bring the reader up to date on the accumulating evidence that human males have evolved adaptations to detect and respond to female ovulation. Lund, Miller, and their colleagues are among a new cadre of experimental social psychologists that have trained their methodological sophistication on testing hypotheses informed by an evolutionary perspective. As their chapter reveals, the empirical payoff already has been substantial.

Carin Perilloux describes some of the exciting recent research in her lab and elsewhere addressing men's perceptions—and *misperceptions*—of women's sexual interest. In the next chapter, Jaime Cloud and Carin Perilloux provide a superb review of work investigating bodily attractiveness as information processed by male psychological adaptations to assess women's fertility and reproductive value.

On average, men more than women compete for short-term and long-term romantic partners and for the expendable resources and social status that facilitate winning these mating competitions. Daniel Kruger reviews this literature, providing evidence that male mortality exceeds female mortality as a consequence of this more intense competition among men than women. In the penultimate chapter of the part on sexual adaptations in men, Gil Greengross presents a compelling argument replete with empirical evidence that male production of humor is generated by sexually selected psychological adaptations. In the final chapter of this part, Valerie Starratt and Michele Alesia summarize recent work investigating human male adaptations to retain a long-term female partner in whom they have invested time, attention, and other resources.

The second part of the volume includes eight chapters addressing sexual adaptations in women, beginning with a contribution by William McKibbin. Previous research provides evidence that human males have psychological adaptations that motivate sexual coercion and rape. According to McKibbin, an evolutionary history of male sexual coercion will have generated selection pressures on females to thwart or to avoid rape. McKibbin reviews the evidence for sexual adaptations in women motivating rape avoidance. In the next two contributions, Lisa Welling and colleagues provide thoughtful reviews of the evolutionary science addressing human female orgasm and female adaptations associated with ovulation, respectively. These linked areas of research have received increasing attention by evolutionary biologists and psychologists, and Welling and colleagues bring the reader up to date on the status of this exciting work.

Lisa DeBruine offers a comprehensive review of recent work, including her own pioneering work, investigating women's preferences for male facial features. Not only does DeBruine's review provide a superb summary of previous research in the area but also she identifies several of the most interesting and important directions for future research in this area. In the next chapter, Diana Santos Fleischman provides readers with a tour de force of empirical investigation of disgust adaptations in women, with special reference to variation in expressions of disgust as a function of ovulatory cycle status and fertility status. Bernard Fink and colleagues address variation in women's perceptions of men's body movements, particularly as a function of women's ovulatory cycle status. Summarizing their own and others' research, Fink et al. make a strong case that men's body movements, especially dance movements, are attended to by women and used by them as cues to developmental stability and "good genes."

The final two chapters of this part of the volume focus on female intrasexual competition. Norman Li and colleagues address eating restriction in women as a consequence of intrasexual competition. This work showcases the potential for evolutionary science to successfully inform human health and well-being. April Bleske-Rechek and colleagues review recent work from their own lab and from others' labs investigating rivalry in women's same-sex friendships, with particular attention to female attractiveness.

Contributions from Paul Vasey and Doug VanderLaan and from David Geary and colleagues comprise the concluding part of the volume. Vasey and VanderLaan provide a stellar review of theoretical and empirical work addressing human male androphilia—sexual attraction to men or masculinity. Geary and colleagues offer a thoughtful series of reflections on the evolution of human sex differences, with particular consideration of "social selection" and the evolution of cooperation among women.

Evolutionary Perspectives on Human Sexual Psychology and Behavior showcases the intellectual value of an interdisciplinary approach to human psychology and behavior. Guided by Darwin's insights, the contributions to this volume provide a stunningly compelling case for an evolutionary analysis of human sexual psychology and behavior.

Rochester, MI   Viviana A. Weekes-Shackelford
                                                                              Todd K. Shackelford

Contents

Contributors

Michele N. Alesia Department of Psychology, Nova Southeastern University, Fort Lauderdale, FL, USA

April Bleske-Rechek Department of Psychology, University of Wisconsin-Eau Claire, Eau Claire, WI, USA

Tiffany A. Brown Department of Psychology, Florida State University, Tallahassee, FL, USA

Joseph A. Camilleri Department of Psychology, Westfield State University, Westfield, MA, USA

Jaime M. Cloud Department of Psychology, Western Oregon University, Monmouth, OR, USA

Lisa M. DeBruine Institute of Neuroscience and Psychology, University of Glasgow, Scotland, UK

Olival Cardoso Do Lago Escola Superior de Educação Física de Jundiaí, Rua Rodrigo Soares de Oliveira, Jundiaí, Sao Paulo, Brazil

Leslie M. Doll Department of Anthropology, Pennsylvania State University, University Park, PA, USA

Bernhard Fink Courant Research Centre Evolution of Social Behavior, University of Göttingen, Göttingen, Germany

Diana Santos Fleischman Department of Psychology, University of Portsmouth, Portsmouth, UK

David C. Geary Department of Psychological Sciences, University of Missouri, Columbia, MO, USA

Gil Greengross Department of Anthropology, University of New Mexico, Albuquerque, NM, USA

Alexander K. Hill Department of Anthropology, Pennsylvania State University, University Park, PA, USA

Benedict C. Jones Institute of Neuroscience & Psychology, University of Glasgow, Lanarkshire, UK

Carolyn M. Kolb Psychology Department, University of Wisconsin-Eau Claire, Eau Claire, WI, USA

Daniel J. Kruger Institute for Social Research, University of Michigan, Ann Arbor, MI, USA

Norman P. Li School of Social Sciences, Singapore Management University, Singapore, Singapore

Erik M. Lund Department of Psychology, University of Kentucky, Lexington, KY, USA

William F. McKibbin Department of Psychology, University of Michigan-Flint, Flint, MI, USA

Saul Miller Department of Psychology, University of Kentucky, Lexington, KY, USA

Nick Neave Faculty of Health & Life Sciences, Northumbria University, Newcastle upon Tyne, UK

Carin Perilloux Department of Psychology, Union College, Schenectady, NY, USA

David Andrew Puts Department of Anthropology, Pennsylvania State University, University Park, PA, USA

Katherine Quigley Psychology Department, Ball State University, Muncie, IN, USA

Bettina Ried Escola Superior de Educação Física de Jundiaí, Jundiaí, Sao Paulo, Brazil

David P. Schmitt Department of Psychology, Bradley University, Peoria, IL, USA

April R. Smith Department of Psychology, Miami University, Oxford, OH, USA

Valerie G. Starratt Department of Psychology, Nova Southeastern University, Fort Lauderdale, FL, USA

Kelly A. Stiver Department of Psychology, Southern Connecticut State University, New Haven, CT, USA

Doug P. VanderLaan Gender Identity Service, Child, Youth and Family Service, Centre for Addiction and Mental Health, Beamish Family Wing, Intergenerational Wellness Centre, Toronto, ON, Canada

Paul L. Vasey Department of Psychology, University of Lethbridge, Lethbridge, Alberta, Canada

Bettina Weege Department of Psychology, University of Göttingen, Göttingen, Germany

Courant Research Centre Evolution of Social Behavior, University of Göttingen, Göttingen, Germany

Lisa L. M. Welling Department of Psychology, Oakland University, Rochester, MI, USA

Benjamin Winegard Department of Psychological Sciences, University of Missouri, Columbia, MO, USA

Bo Winegard Department of Psychology, Florida State University, Tallahassee, FL, USA

Jose C. Yong School of Social Sciences, Singapore Management University, Singapore, Singapore

Introduction to Evolutionary Perspectives on Human Sexual Psychology and Behavior

Evaluating Evidence of Mate Preference Adaptations: How Do We Really Know What *Homo sapiens sapiens* Really Want?

David P. Schmitt

According to Sexual Strategies Theory (Buss & Schmitt, 1993), our species comes equipped with specialized mate preference adaptations that exert a profound influence on our reproductive lives. Humans possess many psychological adaptations designed for *long-term mating*, including pair-bonding mechanisms associated with romantic love and specialized desires for choosing marital partners (Fisher, 1998). Men and women also possess psychological adaptations designed for *short-term mating*, including mechanisms that guide our desires for how often, and with whom, we prefer to engage in casual sexual encounters and extramarital affairs (Thornhill & Gangestad, 2008).

Critically, the preferences that drive men and women when pursuing long-term or short-term mating strategies differ in specialized ways. Men tend to desire easy sexual access when short-term mating and functionally relax their desires so as to obtain large numbers of sex partners, whereas women are relatively selective when short-term mating and preferentially desire men who possess cues to "good genes" as short-term mates. When long-term mating, men emphasize fertility-related cues such as youth and physical attractiveness, whereas women desire cues to a partner's ability and willingness to devote resources to her and their offspring. This basic Sexual Strategies Theory perspective was originally put forth nearly 20 years ago. In this chapter, the empirical status of Sexual Strategies Theory is evaluated along dimensions of evidentiary breadth and depth (Schmitt & Pilcher, 2004).

Women's Long-Term Mate Preferences

Evolutionary psychologists have hypothesized that women possess specially designed long-term mate preferences for cues to a man's *ability* and *willingness* to devote resources to her and their offspring (Ellis, 1992). Such cues may include a man's status and prestige which, depending on culture, may involve hunting ability, physical strength, or other locally relevant attributes, as well as his ambition and work ethic, intelligence and social dominance, and slightly older age. Several lines of evidence can be used to evaluate the existence of women's long-term mate preference adaptations, including self-reported mate preference surveys, reactions to experimental manipulations, cultural artifacts and historical records, ethnographic evidence from preindustrial cultures, examinations of actual mate choice and its marital consequences, and evidence from men's courtship effectiveness and associated fertility outcomes (see Table 1.1). Each of these sources of evidence is reviewed in turn.

D.P. Schmitt (✉)
Department of Psychology, Bradley University, Peoria, IL 61625, USA
e-mail: dps@bradley.edu

V.A. Weekes-Shackelford and T.K. Shackelford (eds.), *Evolutionary Perspectives on Human Sexual Psychology and Behavior*, Evolutionary Psychology, DOI 10.1007/978-1-4939-0314-6_1,
© Springer Science+Business Media New York 2014

Table 1.1 Examples of evidence used to evaluate mate preference adaptations postulated by Sexual Strategies Theory

	Men	Women
Short term	**Prefer easy access and large numbers of partners**	**Prefer good "sexy son" genes**
	• *Self-report surveys* – Men universally report greater activity in seeking of short-term mates, greater desire for larger numbers of sex partners, and quicker to consent to sex after brief periods of time (Schmitt et al., 2003)	• *Self-report surveys* – Women (more than men) rate and rank physical attractiveness as especially important in short-term mates (Regan, Medina, & Joshi, 2001) – Higher minimum requirements for a short-term mate's attractiveness (Kenrick, Groth, Trost, & Sadalla, 1993)
	• *Additional self-reported attitudes and behaviors* – Men have more positive attitudes toward casual sex and permissive sexuality (Petersen & Hyde, 2010) – Men have more unrestricted sociosexual attitudes and behaviors across all cultures (Schmitt, 2005c) – Men have more short-term sex fantasies (Ellis & Symons, 1990) – Men less regret for short-term sex (Paul & Hayes, 2002) – Men relax their mate preferences and are less selective when short-term mating (Buunk, Dijkstra, Fetchenhauer, & Kenrick, 2002)	– Spend more of limited budget on physical attractiveness in short-term mates (Li, 2007) – Report physical attractiveness as more important motive for short-term mating (Regan & Dreyer, 1999) • *Actual mate choice and reactions to experiments* – Women more often choose and more strongly react to physical attractiveness in actual short-term mating contexts (Wiederman & Dubois, 1998) – Women agree to sex with stranger more often if man is physically attractive (Guéguen, 2011)
	• *Actual mate choice and reactions to experiments* – Men (75 %) more often than women (0 %) consent to sex with a stranger (Clark & Hatfield, 1989) Men agree to sex with strangers whether the women is highly attractive (83 %) or average (60 %); women agree to sex with strangers only if he is highly attractive (3 %) versus average (0 %; Guéguen, 2011) – Men seek more one-night stands (Herold & Mewhinney, 1993) – Men have more extramarital affairs (Laumann, Gagnon, Michael, & Michaels, 1994) – Men more often use prostitutes for short-term sex (Burley & Symanski, 1981) – Men more often use media containing short-term sex (Salmon & Symons, 2001) – Gay men have more short-term sex partners than lesbians (Blumstein & Schwartz, 1983) – Men react positively to women who convey easy sexual access (Schmitt, Couden, & Baker, 2001)	• *Women's short-term desires across the ovulatory cycle* – Women prefer attractiveness most near ovulation (Thornhill & Gangestad, 2008), especially if husband is unattractive (Pillsworth & Haselton, 2006) – Women's sexual behaviors and attractiveness shift near ovulation (Haselton, Mortezaie, Pillsworth, Bleske-Rechek, & Frederick, 2007) • *Women who short-term mate more often* – Women who actively short-term mate especially prefer physically attractive men (Gangestad, Thornhill, & Garver-Apgar, 2005) • *Men's short-term mating success* – Physically attractive men have more sex partners (Thornhill & Gangestad, 1994), more affairs (Gangestad et al., 2004) – Men react to ovulating women (Haselton & Gildersleeve, 2011)
Long-term	**Prefer youth, fertility, and gene quality**	**Prefer ability and willingness to devote resources**
	• *Self-report surveys* – Meta-analyses of survey studies (Feingold, 1990) – Nationally representative samples (Sprecher, Sullivan, & Hatfield, 1994)	• *Self-report surveys* – Meta-analyses of survey studies (Feingold, 1992) – Nationally representative samples (Sprecher et al., 1994)

(continued)

Table 1.1 (continued)

Men	Women
– Cross-generational studies (Buss, Shackelford, Kirkpatrick, & Larsen, 2001) – Cross-cultural studies (Buss, 1989) – Trade-off decision studies (Li, 2007) – Open-ended responses (Evans & Brase, 2007)	– Cross-generational studies (Buss et al., 2001) – Cross-cultural studies (Buss, 1989) – Trade-off decision studies (Li, 2007) – Open-ended responses (Evans & Brase, 2007)
• *Reactions to experimental manipulations* – Experimental interaction effects (Feingold, 1990) – Behavioral real-world reactions (Ronay & von Hippel, 2010) – Contrast effects on cognition (Kenrick, Neuberg, Zierk, & Krones, 1994) – Contrast effects on emotion (DelPriore, Hill, & Buss, 2012)	• *Reactions to experimental manipulations* – Photo manipulations (Townsend & Levy, 1990) – Video manipulations (Sadalla, Kenrick, & Vershure, 1987) – Contrast effects on cognition (Kenrick et al., 1994) – Give number to strangers (Guéguen & Lamy, 2012)
• *Cultural artifacts, public records, and fertility outcomes* – Literary content analysis (Gottschall et al., 2003) – Internet search analysis (Ogas & Gaddam, 2011) – Meta-analysis of personal ads (Feingold, 1992) – Economic consumption analysis (Saad, 2008) – Links to higher fertility (Pflüger, Oberzaucher, Holzleitner, & Grammer, 2012)	• *Cultural artifacts, public records, and fertility outcomes* – Literary content analysis (Gottschall et al., 2003) – Meta-analysis of personal ads (Feingold, 1992) – Links to higher fertility outcomes (Pettay et al., 2007)
• *Ethnographic evidence from preindustrial cultures* – Individual ethnographies (Marlowe, 2004) – Large-scale ethnologies (Ford & Beach, 1951)	• *Ethnographic evidence from preindustrial cultures* – Individual ethnographies (Marlowe, 2004) – Large-scale ethnologies (Gregerson, 1982)
• *Actual mate choice and relationship consequences* – Dating choice studies (Lenton & Francesconi, 2010) – Online dating behavior (Hitsch et al., 2010a) – Marital choice studies (Kenrick & Keefe, 1992) – Marital outcome studies (McNulty et al., 2008) – Divorce studies (Bereczkei & Csanaky, 1996) – Mate retention effort (Buss & Shackelford, 1997) – Jealousy evocation (Buss & Haselton, 2005)	• *Actual mate choice and relationship consequences* – Dating choice studies (Lenton & Francesconi, 2010) – Online dating behavior (Hitsch, Hortaçsu, & Ariely, 2010a) – Marital choice studies (Kenrick & Keefe, 1992) – Marital outcome studies (McNulty et al., 2008) – Divorce studies (Bereczkei & Csanaky, 1996) – Mate retention effort (Buss & Shackelford, 1997) – Jealousy evocation (Buss & Haselton, 2005)
• *Women's courtship effectiveness and fertility outcomes* – Meta-analysis of courtship tactics (Schmitt, 2002) – Links to women's mate value (O'Connor et al., 2012) – Links to men's achieved fertility (Jokela, Rotkirch, Rickard, Pettay, & Lummaa, 2010)	• *Men's courtship effectiveness and fertility outcomes* – Meta-analysis of courtship tactics (Schmitt, 2002) – Actual tactic effectiveness (Renninger, Wades, & Grammer, 2004) – Links to men's mate value (Gutierres, Kenrick, & Partch, 1999) – Links to men's achieved fertility (Nettle & Pollet, 2008)

Self-Reported Mate Preference Surveys

One way to evaluate whether women possess long-term mate preferences for cues to a man's ability and willingness to devote resources is to ask people if they particularly prefer those attributes in long-term mating partners (via ratings, rankings, or nominations) and then compare the relative responses of women and men. In doing so, psychologists typically evaluate the degree of sexual differentiation using the d statistic, with an observed d of ± 0.20 being considered a small sex difference, ± 0.50 is a moderate sex difference, and ± 0.80 is a large sex difference (Cohen, 1988). Negative d values typically indicate women score more highly on a particular preference, whereas positive values indicate men score more highly.

Buss and Barnes (1986) were among the first to examine whether women (more than men) prefer cues related to a man's ability and willingness to devote resources. They found women do more strongly prefer long-term mates who have a good earning capacity (a large sex difference, $d = -0.82$), are a college graduate ($d = -0.60$), and possess intelligence ($d = -0.19$). In 1992, Feingold meta-analytically reviewed the extant literature (including 32 independent samples) on self-reported mate preferences and found sex differences were prevalent across college students and community samples with women more greatly desiring socioeconomic status ($d = -0.69$), ambition ($d = -0.67$), intelligence ($d = -0.30$), and humor ($d = -0.14$) in potential long-term mates. Numerous additional investigations have since replicated these basic sex differences in long-term mate preferences among samples of college students (Buss & Schmitt, 1993; Buunk et al., 2002; Gangestad & Simpson, 1990, 2000; Kenrick, Sadalla, Groth, & Trost, 1990; Kenrick et al., 1993; Regan & Berscheid, 1997, 1998a, 1998b; Regan, Levin, Sprecher, Christopher, & Cate, 2000; Scheib, 2001).

In 1994, Sprecher examined sex differences in mate preferences across a nationally representative sample of the United States and found women, more than men, valued a long-term mate who had a steady job ($d = -0.73$), earned more than they did ($d = -0.49$), was highly educated ($d = -0.43$), and was older by 5 years ($d = -0.67$). In a 2001 cross-generational analysis of the same mate preference questionnaire administered to Americans from 1939 to 1996, both men and women increased valuing the attribute good financial prospects and decreased valuing ambition/industriousness, though the degree of sex differences in these items largely persisted in strength across more than 50 years (Buss et al., 2001).

In 1989, Buss conducted a *cross-cultural* study of sex differences in resource-related long-term mate preferences across 37 cultures. He showed women, more than men, report desiring a slightly older long-term mate in 100 % of the cultures studied. He also documented sex differences in preferences for good financial prospects were nearly universal (97 %), and sex differences in preferences ambition/industriousness were prevalent (78 %). Others have replicated these cross-cultural findings, documenting sex differences in resource-related mate preferences as *pancultural* universals (Lippa, 2007; Zentner & Mitura, 2012). Lippa (2007) conducted an Internet sampling of 53 nations and Zentner and Mitura (2012) conducted an Internet sampling across ten nations, and both studies found *100 % of cultures* displayed the expected sex differences, with women demonstrating especially heightened long-term mate preferences for good financial prospects, social status, ambition, and older age.

Some researchers have questioned people about their long-term mate preferences using slightly modified forms of self-report methodologies. For instance, Kenrick et al. (1990) asked people what the *minimum threshold* of possessing a particular attribute would need to be to agree to marry a person. Women, on average, required men's earning capacity to be in the 70th percentile to be marriageable, whereas men required women to be in the 40th percentile (overall $d = -1.41$). Using another nuanced form of self-report, Li (2007) forced men and women to choose or engage in *trade-offs* among various cues when intentionally designing a desirable long-term mate. Women devoted the most of their limited budget toward their mates' social level (33 %), whereas for men social level was of moderate budgetary importance (17 %). Across a series of studies (Li, 2007; Li, Bailey, Kenrick, & Linsenmeier, 2002), researchers using this trade-off paradigm concluded that women, but not men, consider a long-term mate's social status a "necessity" and not a "luxury." Evans and Brase (2007) found sex differences in open-ended responses to evaluations of potential mating targets, with women mentioning ambition and intelligence of potential long-term mates significantly more than men. In summary, the relative self-report responses of men and women (via ratings, rankings, and nominations) consistently support the hypothesis that women possess long-term mate preferences for cues to a man's ability and willingness to devote resources.

Reactions to Experimental Manipulations

An additional source of evidence regarding women's hypothesized emphasis on cues to a man's ability and willingness to devote resources comes from studies involving personal reactions to randomly assigned scenarios or actual real-life interactions with randomly assigned experimental confederates. Townsend and Levy (1990) exposed samples of women (undergraduates and law students) to photographic slides of men and had the women rate how likely they would be to date, engage in short-term mating, or engage in long-term relationships with the men. Men's physical ornamentation in the slides was experimentally manipulated to provide cues to high status (i.e., men wore a blazer and a Rolex watch), moderate status (i.e., men wore a white t-shirt), or low status (i.e., men wore a Burger King outfit). The photographs further contained either a physically attractive man or a homely man. Across samples, Townsend and Levy repeatedly found women preferred to mate with homely/high-status men much more than

handsome/medium-or-low-status men, and these effects were most pronounced when women considered the men as *long-term* mates.

Sadalla et al. (1987) had participants view videos of experimental confederates (either men or women) engaging in same-sex encounters within which they were randomly assigned to act as either high in dominance (i.e., upright posture, shoulders straight, move with ease and confidence) or low in dominance (i.e., smiled a lot to appease others, averted their eyes a lot, avoid invading personal space). Women who viewed the videos found high-dominance men much more attractive than low-dominance men, whereas men did not find high-dominance women attractive (see also Ahmetoglu & Swami, 2012). Bryan et al. (2011) documented similar effects when women independently evaluate men's physical dominance, social dominance, and economic dominance.

Some investigators have found the effects of men's ability and willingness to devote resources on women's feelings of long-term desire are, in some ways, conditional. For instance, Jonason, Li, and Madson (2012) found women prefer men who *actually earned* their resources (rather than having obtained resources from other sources such as luck, inheritance, or embezzlement). Presumably, a man who has actually earned his resources possesses traits that would enable him to obtain even more resources in the future. Kruger and Fitzgerald (2011) found women prefer prestige more than dominance, with prestige being earned through meritorious actions. As noted earlier, Sexual Strategies Theory expects women prefer men as long-term mates if they are able *and willing* to devote resources. Willingness depends on cues such as a man's kindness, particularly to the woman doing the selecting (Lukaszewski & Roney, 2010). Graziano, Jensen-Campbell, Todd, and Finch (1997) found women prefer a man who is dominant as a long-term mate, but only if the man is also kind and caring to that particular woman. Chu, Farr, Muñoz, and Lycett (2011) found women like high-status men as long-term mates, but only if the woman trusts the man (again, a cue to willingness to devote resources). It is also critical to keep in mind that differing cues across the same man can sometimes convey conflicting information about his overall mate quality (Cunningham, Barbee, & Pike, 1990).

Additional sources of evidence used to evaluate the existence of mate preference adaptations include looking at the experimental side effects and logical cognitive consequences of hypothesized mate preferences. For instance, as part of a study ostensibly helping a university develop a dating service, Kenrick et al. (1994) experimentally manipulated whether already mated men and women were exposed to a target date either very high in dominance or very low in dominance. They found that women, but not men, were less committed to their current long-term mating partner after being exposed to a high-dominance individual of the opposite sex. Merely being experimentally exposed to a man with very high dominance lowered women's commitment to their current mate and did so without consciously asking women about their preferences for dominance. Dahl et al. (2009) found that women, but not men, find particularly "sexy" advertisements to be unappealing, but women found such advertisements appealing if men in the advertisements were seen as giving *commitment-related* gifts to women in the advertisements. These research methods move beyond self-report limitations by documenting the predictable experimental side effects of women's preferences for men who are able and willing to devote resources.

A compelling test of women's long-term mate preferences for men's ability and willingness to provide resources is to examine whether the preferences disappear when women have ample resources of their own. It could be that women prefer cues to men's ability and willingness to provide resources, but only because women are structurally denied access to resources in a particular culture (Buss, 1989). Addressing this alternative explanation, Townsend (1989) found women in medical school are *more* selective of a future mate's financial status, not less. Regan (1998a, 1998b) found as women's mate value goes up, so does their insistence on men's high status and resources (i.e., they "want it all"; see

also Buss & Shackelford, 2008). Having higher status and resource-related traits appears not to attenuate women's mate preferences for men's ability and willingness to provide resources.

Similarly, there are few if any links to women's achieving greater sociopolitical gender equality across cultures and their mate preferences for resource-related traits (Buss, 2008), especially after controlling for local pathogen levels (Gangestad, Haselton, & Buss, 2006). In a ten-nation analysis, Zentner and Mitura (2012) reported the magnitude of sex differences in long-term mate preferences for resource-related traits tends to shift from a large/medium effect sizes in nations with lower sociopolitical gender equality to more moderate medium/small effect sizes in nations with higher sociopolitical gender equality. For example, after placing their ten nations into three groups, they found women valued ambition/industriousness moderately more than men in low sociopolitical gender equality nation ($d = -0.65$), women valued ambition/industriousness moderately more than men in medium sociopolitical gender equality nations ($d = -0.53$), and women valued ambition/industriousness moderately more than men in high sociopolitical gender equality nations ($d = -0.48$). Thus, observed is a limited change of slightly reduced sex differences in nations with the more sociopolitical gender equality. Even in the highest sociopolitical gender equality nations, the average resource-related sex difference reported by Zentner and Mitura (2012) was moderate in size (overall $d = -0.42$), which would place it in the 81st percentile of all meta-analytically documented psychological sex differences (Hyde, 2005). Oddly, in many cases both women's and men's preferences for resource-related traits attributes were reduced in high sociopolitical gender equality nations (which seems counter to the logic of men appreciating women's resource-related traits more as women enter the workforce in high gender equality nations; Eagly & Wood, 1999). Of further interest, Eagly and Wood (1999) correlated sex differences in mate preferences for good financial prospects across nations examined by the large cross-cultural study of Buss et al. (1990). They found among four national indicators of sociopolitical gender equality that only one significantly correlated with sex differences in long-term mate preferences for good financial prospects.

In a real-world test of women's mate preferences for status, Guéguen and Lamy (2012) conducted a naturalistic experiment to evaluate whether women's reactions to a request for their phone number are affected by men's apparent status (in this case, driving different types of cars). When a potential participant was a few yards away, they had a male experimental confederate (one of six male confederates preselected for high physical attractiveness) open his car door and look the participant in the eyes and smile. Then he approached her and said, "Hello, my name's Antoine. I just want to say that I think you're really pretty. I have to go to work now, but I was wondering if you would give me your phone number. I'll call you later and we can have a drink together somewhere." Women approached by a man driving an expensive Audi A5 Ambition Luxury gave their number 23 % of the time. Women approached by a man driving a mid-priced Renault Mégane gave their number 13 % of the time. Women approached by a man driving a 15-year-old Renault 5 Super Campus (worth only a few hundred dollars) gave their number 8 % of the time. Women's preferences for resource-related cues appear to affect their real-world mating behavior.

Cultural Artifacts, Public Records, and Fertility Outcomes

Another avenue for evaluating whether women possess long-term mate preferences for men who are willing and able to provide resources is to examine cultural documents such as folktales (Carroll, 2005; Gottschall et al., 2003), personal ads (Feingold, 1992), and government records of marriage and fertility outcomes (Pettay, Helle, Jokela, & Lummaa, 2007). Gottschall et al. (2003) found mention of women's preference for cues to men's willingness and ability to provide resources in folktales across 48 cultures

(including among humans living in bands, tribes, and preindustrial cultures). Feingold (1992) meta-analytically examined what women ask for and what men advertise in public, real-life personal advertisements and found, as expected, women ask for cues to willingness and ability to provide resources (e.g., 27 % of women ask for high socioeconomic status compared to 7 % of men), and men who tend to advertise such cues actually receive more responses from women. In a study of Polish personal ads, the top four cues displayed by men that received responses from women were good education, older age, high resource levels, and tall height (Pawlowski & Slawomir, 2002).

In a study of preindustrial Finland (from the 1700s), women married to wealthier men had more children and better child survival (Pettay et al., 2007). In another study, marrying a man 4 years older was associated with maximum levels of fertility among women (Fieder & Huber, 2007). Bereczkei and Csanaky (1996) conducted a study of 1,800 Hungarians who were over 34 years of age and found that women who married older and better-educated men tended to have more children. These are important findings, as it is critical that women's mate preferences for resource-related attributes lead to reproductive success, at least in our evolutionary past (Buss, 2000). One key arena for evaluating these associations would be to examine preindustrial cultures, particularly those that still lead a foraging lifestyle prevalent among our human ancestors.

Ethnographic Evidence from Preindustrial Cultures

Gregerson (1982) found across 300 cultures that women's attraction toward men was almost invariably determined by the man's social status or culture-specific skills linked to status such as strength, bravery, and prowess. Marlowe (2004) found among the foraging Hadza people that women desire and place great import on men's hunting ability and his intelligence, key traits linked to a man's ability to provide for women and their children. Among Shuar men, those with more status and hunting ability are rated by women as more desirable husbands (Pillsworth, 2008). Ethnological studies of the links between men's status and his reproductive success in preindustrial cultures are unambiguous—men's status increases the number and survival of his offspring (Betzig, 1986; Hurtado & Hill, 1992; Smith, 2004). Although women in modern cultures typically prefer men who are taller, some studies of foraging cultures have found relative tallness is not always preferred by women (Sear & Marlowe, 2009). It is possible, however, that height and physical robustness function as important cues for men to women's physical health in especially high stress, high pathogen cultures (see also Cashdan, 2008; Pisanski & Feinberg, 2013).

Actual Mate Choice and Expected Relationship Consequences

A powerful tool for evaluating the existence of long-term mate preference adaptations is to look at the types of people who are actually chosen as marriage partners. Obviously, all of us cannot always get what we want, but real-world mate choice should to some degree reflect evolved desires. Women who explicitly state they prefer masculine mates, for example, usually end up choosing masculine men as long-term mates (Burriss, Welling, & Puts, 2011b).

Studies of dating may be related to long-term mating, though it is difficult to truly know whether the intentions of date seekers are solely for long-term marriage. Nevertheless, most speed-dating studies, especially those who use samples from the community instead of college students, find that women's (but not men's) actual dating choices are affected by a partner's status-related attributes such as his education, his income, and his intelligence (Asendorpf, Penke, & Back, 2011; Fisman, Iyengar, Kamenica, & Simonson, 2006; Todd, Penke, Fasolo, & Lenton, 2007). Some studies have failed to find significant associations between women's speed-dating choices and men's resources (Eastwick & Finkel,

2008), but these findings typically flow from college students samples at elite colleges during which the speed-dates are extremely brief (Lenton & Francesconi, 2010; Li et al., 2013). Li et al. (2013) conducted experiments using online messaging and modified speed-dating formats. They found that if a mating pool includes people low in status and physical attractiveness, real-world mate choices are sex-differentiated as expected by Sexual Strategies Theory. Men, more than women, choose mates based on physical attractiveness, and women, more than men, choose mates based on status. In addition, individuals who more greatly valued status or physical attractiveness valued these traits in their actual choices, and mate choices were most sex-differentiated when considering long-term mating (as opposed to short-term mating, within which both sexes shunned partners with low physical attractiveness). Hitsch et al. (2010a) examined 5,787 real-world online members of a dating service and found women place great emphasis on a man's educational level and "women place about twice as much weight on income than men" (p. 148). Moreover, examinations of market pressures in speed-dating contexts reveal that men, but not women, are much less selective if they have lower status (Kurzban & Weeden, 2005), whereas women are less selective if they are lower in physical attractiveness (Overbeek, Nelemans, Karremans, & Engels, 2013). Overall, resource-related traits usually matter to women more than men in studies of dating choices in the real world.

Most studies of real-world *marital* choice find that women, but not men, tend to marry partners higher than average in terms of status and resource-related traits (men with well-below average status and resources are more often shut out of the mating market altogether); and women, but not men, tend to marry partners who are older—a potential cue to his accrued status and resource levels (Kenrick & Keefe, 1992; Perusse, 1994; Trivers, 1985). Trivers (1985) found American men who marry in a given year generally earn 50 % more money than men of same age who do not marry. Lichter, Anderson, and Hayward (1995) found this effect was particularly conspicuous when men are espe-cially plentiful (due to male-biased sex ratios). Thus, women's long-term mate preferences do appear to drive their actual choices in the context of marriage.

Mate preferences are specifically designed to influence mate choice. However, the impact of mate preferences may not entirely dissipate after marriage, continuing to, in specific ways, influ-ence marital outcomes, mate retention efforts, feelings of jealousy, and divorce patterns (Blumstein & Schwartz, 1983; McNulty et al., 2008). Bereczkei and Csanaky (1996) examined marriages of 1,800 Hungarians over 34 years of age and found that women who married older and better-educated men tend to be less likely to get divorced and reported higher levels of marital satisfaction than did women who married youn-ger or less-educated men (cf. Eastwick, Luchies, Finkel, & Hunt, 2013). Using longitudinal data from National Longitudinal Study of Youth cov-ering 25 years from 1979 to 2004, Teachman (2010) found couples have less marital satisfac-tion and were more likely to experience divorce if wives were more successful at providing resources than their husbands. In a study of over 200,000 Danish people from 1997 to 2006, researchers found that married men who start to make less money than their wives tend to suffer from increased levels of erectile dysfunction, and newly breadwinner wives tend to suffer from increased insomnia and anxiety medication usage (Pierce, Dahl, & Nielsen, 2013). Women are also much more likely to divorce a partner who loses their job (Betzig, 1989).

Finally, Buss & Shackelford (1997) found men more often use retention tactics that satisfy women's long-term mate preferences (e.g., increasing resources) if their wife is younger (controlling for his age and other attributes). In this way, once married women's (and men's) mate preferences may sometimes lead to increases in the need for mate retention efforts, feelings of jealousy, and ostensibly worse rela-tionship outcomes (other than reproductive suc-cess). Men, more than women, for example, become especially jealous concerning potential interlopers if the competitors are higher in status

and resource-related traits (Buss & Haselton, 2005). Indeed, men's behaviors—how they behave in courtship and how successful they are at long-term mating—may be especially reveal-ing about women's evolved long-term mate pref-erence psychology.

Men's Courtship Effectiveness and Fertility Outcomes Can Reveal Women's Desires

In a meta-analysis of long-term mating courtship tactics, Schmitt (2002) found men are judged more effective than women in displaying status, resources, and ambition (and in derogating same-sex competitors possession of those traits). Men's status and dominance-related courtship behaviors, more so than women's, have been associated with actual courtship effectiveness (Renninger et al., 2004) and with obtaining more spouses and more children across cultures (Betzig, 1986).

Exposure to physically attractive women appears to evoke in men desires to fulfill women's evolved preferences, such as increasing men's desires to possess resources, express ambi-tion, and display creativity, independence, and risk taking (Ronay & von Hippel, 2010). In con-trast, when exposed to men who are high in dominance, men tend to rate themselves as lower in mate value (Gutierres et al., 1999). When primed with parenting (Millar & Ostlund, 2006) or mating (Ainsworth & Maner, 2012) motives, men tend to increase their mate attrac-tion effort in accordance with women's long-term mate preferences, and when showed women who possess desired traits such as youth and physical attractiveness, men increase their desires for dating (Ha, Overbeek, & Engels, 2010).

In preindustrial cultures, men's status and hunting ability, and where applicable wealth, are often linked to increased fertility (Betzig, 1986; Hurtado & Hill, 1992; Smith, 2004). Wealth is also linked to increased fertility among men, but not women, in modern cultures (Cashdan, 1996; Mealey, 1985; Nettle & Pollet,

2008). Height, a cue to physical health and inter-personal dominance, is a key factor in both women's long-term mate choice and men's long-term courtship and fertility success (Fink, Neave, Brewer, & Pawlowski, 2007; Nettle, 2002; Stulp, Buunk, & Pollet, 2013). Pawlowski, Dunbar, and Lipowicz (2000) found childless men were 1.25 in. shorter than men with chil-dren, and women rate 5'11" as ideal height for partner, but 80 % of men's personal ads list their height as 6' or more (Kenrick et al., 1990). Other masculine traits preferred by women have also been linked to increased fertility in men (e.g., deeper voice; Apicella, Feinberg, & Marlowe, 2007). Some evolutionary psychologists view men's status and dominance contests as more about intimidating other men than about fulfill-ing women's desires (Puts, 2010). Men's long-term mating psychology matters, as well, when it comes to courtship and fertility.

Men's Long-Term Mating Psychology

Across the sexually reproducing species of the natural world, males and females usually differ in the *obligatory effort* needed to produce viable offspring. For most animal species, females invest more heavily in offspring, though this is not always the case (e.g., seahorses, katydids). Trivers (1972) was among the first to point out that the intensity with which one sex invests more in offspring in a particular species can have profound influences on the mating psychol-ogy of males and females in that species. For instance, among species with observable sex differences in parental investment, the lesser-investing sex almost always has less selective mate preferences and is less restrained in mate choice compared to the heavier-investing sex.

In humans, it appears long-term mating in the form of marriage is a near-universal feature of human culture with clear adaptive benefits to the heavier-investing sex—women—in that they gain a strategic partner in their heavy-investment reproductive endeavors. However, men appear designed for marriage, too (Schmitt, 2005a). Men reap benefits from engaging in marital

relationships such as being able to provide direct investment in their personal offspring, ensuring their paternity certainty, bolstering their social status, and increasing their number of male allies via in-laws (see Buss, 2008). The extreme altriciality of human children also implies that biparental care within the marital context of long-term mating can be critical to men's per-sonal reproductive success.

Given that men are likely designed for long-term mating, they may possess specialized fitness-enhancing desires that help guide their marital mate choice. According to Sexual Strategies Theory (Buss & Schmitt, 1993), ancestral males may have evolved preferences for cues to youth, health, and genetic quality as these provide useful signals of a woman's fertil-ity status (i.e., odds of conceiving *currently*) and potential reproductive value (i.e., the number of children a woman could have *into the future*). Thus, men are expected from an evolutionary perspective to desire physical features indicative of a woman's relatively youthful age (e.g., neotenous face, full lips, clear and glowing skin, clear and wide eyes, small chin, lustrous and long hair, good muscle tone; Sugiyama, 2005), to desire physical features indicative of high-fertility estrogen levels (e.g., high feminin-ity in face, voice, finger lengths, and a 0.7 waist-to-hip ratio of body fat distribution), and to desire physical features indicative low genetic mutation load (e.g., facial and bodily symmetry). Addi-tionally, men are expected to preferentially desire attributes that would indicate a woman would not be unfaithful in a long-term partner-ship (deleteriously affecting paternity certainty), to preferentially desire women with good parent-ing skills, and to preferentially desire women who have a compatible personality (Buss & Schmitt, 1993).

Self-Reported Mate Preference Surveys

One source of evidence for evaluating these hypothesized preferences comes from self-report surveys that ask men and women to rate, rank, or nominate what they prefer in long-term mates. In

1986, Buss and Barnes were among the first to find men ranked physical attractiveness as more important in long-term mating than women do ($d = 0.92$). Feingold (1990) conducted a meta-analysis of self-reported mate preferences surveys and confirmed that men tend to prefer physical attractiveness in potential long-term mates more than women do (overall $d = 0.54$). Numerous studies since have replicated these basic sex differences in long-term mate preference for physical attractiveness (Buss & Schmitt, 1993; Buunk et al., 2002; Gangestad & Simpson, 1990, 2000; Kenrick et al., 1990, 1993; Regan & Berscheid, 1997; Regan 1998a, 1998b; Regan et al., 2000; Scheib, 2001). Buss (1989) surveyed long-term mate preferences *across 37 cultures* and found men prefer younger women as long-term mates in 100 % of cultures, and men preferred "good looks" in potential long-term mates across 34 of 37 cultures (92 %). In no cultures did women prefer physical attractiveness significantly more than men did in long-term mates.

In explaining cultural variation in sex differences in physical attractiveness, Gangestad et al. (2006) showed that women's and men's mate preferences for good looks are closely linked to local pathogen levels, with good looks being more important in high pathogen cultures, even after controlling for income, geographical region, and latitude (see also, Little, Apicella, & Marlowe, 2007). Lippa (2007) found sex differences in long-term mate preferences for good looks were a *pancultural universal*, evidenced in 100 % of 53 nations, with an average effect size of $d = 0.55$. Zentner and Mitura (2012) found sex differences in long-term mate preferences for good looks were a pancultural universal across 100 % of ten nations, and counterintuitively sex differences were *larger* as sociopolitical gender equality increased across nations, with low sociopolitical gender equality nations displaying smaller sex differences ($d = 0.24$) compared to medium ($d = 0.43$) or high sociopolitical gender equality nations ($d = 0.51$). This last finding suggests that increased sociopolitical gender equality in a nation does not reduce the size of sex differences

in mate preferences. If anything, sociopolitical gender equality increases psychological sex differences (Schmitt, Realo, Voracek, & Allik, 2008).

When asked about the *minimum level* of physical attractiveness needed for marrying a woman, the average man wanted the woman to be at least in the 60th percentile, whereas women required only the 52nd percentile; $d = 0.41$; (Kenrick et al., 1990). Unlike women, when men's mate value is increased (including being more physically attractive), their insistence on physical attractiveness in potential long-term mates is largely unaffected (so even low mate value men preferentially desire physical attractiveness in a long-term mate; Lee, Loewenstein, Ariely, Hong, & Young, 2008; Regan, 1998a, 1998b). Sprecher et al. (1994) examined long-term mate preferences in representative sample of the United States and found men, more than women, especially value good looks ($d = 0.65$) and younger age ($d = 0.99$). In a review of mate preferences changes in the United States across 57 years, Buss et al. (2001) found both men and women have increased the relative importance they place in physical attractiveness in long-term mates. However, men's increased ranking of good looks (from 14th place in 1939 to eighth place in 1996) was greater than women's increased ranking (from 17th place in 1939 to 13th place in 1996). It seems the relative emphasis that men, relative to women, place on physical attractiveness has at least persisted, if not grown, across American generations.

Many of the hypothesized sex differences in long-term mate preferences persist across developmental age, as well. As men and women get older, sex differences in age preferences become more intense. Kenrick and Keefe (1992) found men at age 25 prefer to marry a woman who is about 4 years younger, with minimum acceptable age of 20 and a maximum age of 30. Women at age 25 would marry a man who is between 25 and 35, ideally about 4 years older. At age 65, however, men would marry a woman between the ages of 50 and 60 (ideally about 10 years younger), whereas at 65 women still want an older man, between 65 and 75 years old. Similarly, Schwarz and Hassebrauck (2012) surveyed 21,245 single people between 18 and 65 (average age = 31) and found men valued physical attractiveness and relative youth more than women, regardless of age or education level. There is one revealing caveat to the youthful desires of men, however. Kenrick, Gabrielidis, Keefe, and Cornelius (1996) documented that teenage men prefer a mate who is a little older, which was explained as men's preferences being sculpted to desire the highest fertility women (women in their 20s). It is not the case that men simply want someone similar or perhaps a little younger. Men's long-term preferences for age are anchored by the actual peak fertility levels of women. Finally, studies that have examined long-term versus short-term mate preferences have documented that men's heightened preference for physical attractiveness and youth is specific to long-term mating, whereas women often emphasize physical attractiveness more than men do when evaluating short-term mates (Buss & Schmitt, 1993; Buunk et al., 2002; Confer et al., 2010; Kenrick et al., 1993).

When asked to make economic decisions (such as spending "dollars" from a limited budget), men behaviorally spend 40 % of their budget on physical attractiveness in designing an ideal long-term mate (compared to women who spend only 21 % of their budget on physical attractiveness; Li, 2007). In another study, Li et al. (2002) found that when making *trade-offs* with limited budgets, women's physical attractiveness was mentioned first by men 13 % of time but first by women only 5 % of the time. Evans and Brase (2007) found sex differences in the mentioning of physical attractiveness in open-ended responses to evaluations of potential dating targets, with men mentioning physical attractiveness significantly more than women did. In summary, the relative self-report responses of men and women (via ratings, rankings, and nominations) consistently support the hypothesis that men possess long-term mate preferences for fertility-related cues such as youth and physical attractiveness.

Reactions to Experimental Manipulations

An additional source of evidence regarding men's hypothesized emphasis on fertility-related cues such as youth and physical attractiveness in long-term mates comes from studies involving personal responses to randomly assigned scenarios or actual real-life interactions with randomly assigned experimental confederates. Meta-analyses of experimental interactions show men react more positively than women do when they personally interact with a highly attractive opposite-sex partner (effect size in men $d = 1.23$; effect size in women half as large, $d = 0.61$; Feingold, 1990). Men are also cognitively affected by physically attractive targets more than women are (Maner et al., 2003).

A particular set of cues related to relative youth and high fertility also show evidence of special design in men's mate preferences. Schaefer et al. (2006) showed men exposed to targets with feminine faces or voices react to those women with greater feelings of attraction. Johnston and Franklin (1993) had male participants morph female faces until they achieved an "ideal" face. The final female face had geometric proportions indicative of a 14-year-old girl. Many of these cues to youth and fertility are universally valued by men across cultures and time periods (Cunningham, Roberts, Barbee, Druen, & Wu, 1995; Jones, 1995; Langlois et al., 2000). Men across most cultures, for example, prefer feminized faces and body shapes indicative of high estrogen (Perrett et al., 1998; Singh & Young, 1995). Men across most cultures prefer waist-to-hip ratios in women that are linked with adaptive estrogen levels and higher fertility (Singh, 1993), a preference finding documented even among blind men feeling mannequins (Karremans, Frankenhuis, & Arons, 2010). It appears many of these specific cues to youth and fertility activate domain-specific areas of men's brains (Thornhill & Gangestad, 1999), especially in the nucleus accumbens (Aharon et al., 2001; Platek &

Singh, 2012). One caveat to this is that in cultures with frequent warfare, the need for more masculine sons may attenuate the preference for a feminine waist-to-hip ratio (Cashdan, 2008). Moreover, cultural variations in disease prevalence, paternal investment, and visual experiences can predictably moderate mate preferences for adaptive physical attributes (see Pisanski & Feinberg, 2013).

Behaviorally, when men are experimentally exposed to physically attractive women, they react by being more likely to value money, experience greater ambition, are more creative, and are willing to take more risks (Roney et al., 2006). Conversely, just holding $2,000 in one's hands elicits in men, but not women, stronger desires to mate with a physically attractive partner (Yong & Li, 2012). Men told they were making phone call to a woman lowered their voice (a feature women typically find attractive; Puts, 2005), but only if the woman was portrayed in a picture as highly physically attractive (Hughes, Farley, & Rhodes, 2010). Men also give bigger tips to women if they are physically attractive, younger, have larger breasts, and smaller body size (Lynn, 2009), buy bigger engagement rings for younger women than older women (Cronk & Dunham, 2007), and are more likely to pay for dinner if their date is physically attractive (with no such effects seen in women; Stirrat, Gumert, & Perrett, 2011).

Relationally, men (but not women) react with less commitment to their partners if exposed to highly attractive members of the opposite sex (Gutierres et al., 1999; Kanazawa & Still, 2000; Kenrick et al., 1994). Men tend to feel envy toward other men who have status and wealth or other men who have physically attractive wives, but women's envy is more intense toward other women who are physically attractive or who have wealthy husbands (DelPriore et al., 2012).

attractive women is to examine cultural documents such as folktales, personal ads, and government records of marriage and fertility. Gottschall et al. (2003) found mention of men's preference for physical attractiveness in folktales across 48 cultures (including among humans living in bands, tribes, and preindustrial cultures). Ogas and Gaddam (2011) found sex differences in physical attractiveness in actual searches conducted across several Internet search engines. Meta-analyses of personal advertisements have documented that men tend to seek long-term mates who are youthful and physically attractive, whereas women tend to advertise these traits and those who do receive more actual responses from men (Feingold, 1990; Wiederman, 1993). Content analyses of Playboy centerfolds, Miss Americas, and online escorts all revealed that a 0.7 waist-to-hip ratio—linked to adaptive estrogen levels and high fertility—is considered ideal (Saad, 2008; Singh & Young, 1995).

If men's preference for physical attractiveness in long-term mates is a psychological adaptation, physically attractive women should tend to have more children (assuming no modern confounds such as contraception use). In a study of 88 postmenopausal Austrian women from a rural community, among those who did not use contraception in their lifetime, higher objective symmetry, facial femininity, and overall physical attractiveness were linked to having more children (Pflüger et al., 2012). Attractive women also have been found to have more children among the Ache of Paraguay (Hill & Hurtado, 1996). In a retrospective study of American women in the 1950s, researchers found attractive women had 11 % more children than those who were unattractive (Jokela et al., 2010). Women who have lower testosterone (Barrett et al., 2013) and higher estrogen (Law Smith et al., 2012) tend to be more feminine and have fertility-linked traits such as wanting more children.

Cultural Artifacts, Public Records, and Fertility Outcomes

Another avenue for evaluating whether men possess long-term mate preferences for physically

Ethnographic Evidence from Preindustrial Cultures

Fieldwork by anthropologists, biologists, ethnologists, and behavioral ecologists is also relevant for evaluating men's long-term mate preferences for physical attractiveness. Marlowe (2004) found among the foraging Hadza people that men desire fertility in a partner more than women do. Ford and Beach (1951) examined 191 cultures and found that "in most societies the physical beauty of the female receives more explicit consideration than does the handsomeness of the male" (p. 86). Jones (1995) replicated American studies linking facial neoteny with attractiveness in women (but not men) across preindustrial cultures such as the Ache of Paraguay and the Hiwi of Venezuela. Lightness of skin color may be associated with relative youth within a culture, and van den Berghe and Frost (1986) found that in 47 of 51 cultures (92 %) men express preferences for lighter skin women.

Actual Mate Choice and Expected Relationship Consequences

Most studies of dating behavior in "speed-dating" events find men's choices, more than women's, are influenced by desires for physical attractiveness (Asendorpf et al., 2011; Fisman et al., 2006; Kurzban & Weeden, 2007; Lenton & Francesconi, 2010; Todd et al., 2007). A few have found both men's and women's choices are influenced by physical attractiveness (e.g., Kurzban & Weeden, 2005), but subsequent research has revealed that this tends to occur when people are forced to make choices based on especially brief interactions (Lenton & Francesconi, 2010) and when researchers fail to distinguish between short-term and long-term mating contexts (Li et al., 2013). Hitsch et al. (2010a) and Hitsch, Hortaçsu, and Ariely (2010b) examined 5,787 real-world online members of a dating service and found that "men consistently display stronger looks preferences than women" (Hitsch et al., 2010b, p. 15). Responses to personal advertisements also reflect long-term mate preferences, as generally women receive more responses than men do

when they advertise youth and physical attractiveness (Baize & Schroeder, 1995).

Perhaps the strongest test of the existence of long-term mate preference adaptations comes from analyzing actual marriages, especially who marries whom and how reproductively valuable those choices are over the long run. Most studies have found that men, more than women, tend to marry younger partners who are closer to peak fertility (Kenrick & Keefe, 1992; Perusse, 1994). As men age, this mate preference mechanism results in newly married men marrying younger and younger women (Kenrick et al., 1990). In the United States, the average man's first marriage is to a woman who is 3 years younger, the average man's second marriage is to a woman who is 5 years younger, and the average man's third marriage is to a woman who is 8 years younger (Guttentag & Secord, 1983). In a study of the wealthiest 400 people in the United States, wealthy men tend to be married to someone 7 years younger, and among second marriages wealthy men are married to someone 22 years younger, on average (Pollet, Pratt, Edwards, & Stulp, 2013). Wealthy women's spouses, in contrast, did not differ in age from the general population of the United States. In Sweden, a retrospective look at marriages in the 1800s found that the average man's second marriage was to a woman 11 years younger (Guttentag & Secord, 1983). Also in Sweden, men who marry first wives who are 6 years younger have the highest levels of lifetime fertility (Fieder & Huber, 2007). Long-term mate preferences for youth appear to pay men actual dividends in the currency of reproductive success.

Historically, men with high status across all studied cultures have tended to seek out wives who were younger and especially high physical attractiveness (Betzig, 1986). Several researchers have documented that men with higher status tend to successfully satisfy their long-term mating desires and marry women who are more particularly physically attractive (Elder, 1969; Lipowicz, 2003; Pawlowski & Dunbar, 1999;

Udry & Eckland, 1984). A man's status is in some cases the biggest predictor of his wife's physical attractiveness. Elder (1969) documented a strong positive correlation ($r = 0.46$) between a woman's physical attractiveness in high school and her husband's job status 10 years after graduating from high school. Udry and Eckland (1984) found that physically attractive women in high school end up married to men with higher education and income, and high physical attractiveness also reduces the probability that women remain unmarried. Lipowicz (2003) found that in the United States, where being overweight is considered unattractive, men who have less education have wives who are more overweight.

If men's long-term mate preferences for youth and physical attractiveness exist, whether men's wives satisfy (or not) men's desires may affect some aspects relationship quality once married (Buss, 2000). McNulty, Neff, and Karney (2008) examined marital couples' relative levels of physical attractiveness and found that both spouses behaved more positively in relationships in which wives were more attractive than their husbands, and both spouses behaved more negatively in relationships in which husbands were more attractive than their wives. In terms of satisfaction, it seems *relative* levels of fertility-related attributes are most operative. Meltzer, McNulty, Novak, Butler, and Karney (2011) found that marital quality is higher if women are thinner than their husbands, and several studies have found that men's sexual satisfaction in marriage is higher if his wife in younger (Buss & Shackelford, 1997; Zhang, Parish, Huang, & Pan, 2012). Again, though, mate preferences are designed to influence mate choice, not satisfaction or happiness across all possible relationship outcomes. It may be that obtaining one's ideal mate choice leads to subjective distress once mated, a finding that is not at odds with an evolutionary perspective as long as reproductive success is enhanced by the mate choice. Men, for example, tend to need to use more mate retention tactics (such as giving more resources) if their wife is younger (controlling for his age and other factors; Buss & Shackelford, 1997).

Women's Courtship Effectiveness and Fertility Outcomes Can Reveal Men's Desires

In a meta-analysis of long-term mating courtship tactics, Schmitt (2002) found that women are judged more effective than men when displaying youth and physical attractiveness and when derogating their competitor's youth and physical attractiveness. Women also feel more anxiety around physical attractiveness than men do (Etcoff, 1999), spending more time and money on physical attractiveness enhancement, especially when mating motivations are active or when in a low resource environment (Griskevicius, Tybur, Delton, & Robertson, 2011). Highly physically attractive women appear to know they possess valued traits, requiring of potential long-term mating partners higher levels of wealth and more masculinity in voices and faces (Buss & Shackelford, 2008; O'Connor et al., 2012). Women with the most desirable waist-to-hip ratios also tend to have more pronounced mate preferences for men with resources (Pawlowski & Jasienska, 2008).

Women who, in their grade school photos, are judged more physically attractive have higher lifetime fertility (Jokela et al., 2010) and are more likely to be married (Harper, 2000). Hill and Hurtado (1996) found that physically attractive women among the foraging Ache foragers also have higher lifetime fertility. In a study of women who do not use contraception, physically attractive women were found to have more children (Pflüger et al., 2012). These results provide supportive evidentiary breadth for viewing men's preferences for long-term mates who are physically attractive as evolved psychological adaptations.

Other Supportive Evidence

As noted earlier, men who have higher social status tend to emphasize physical attractiveness more in potential long-term mates. Researchers have found that men with more masculine or male-typical psychologies tend to prefer feminized female faces (Smith, Jones, & DeBruine, 2010), as do men who consider themselves more attractive to the opposite sex (Burriss, Welling, & Puts, 2011a; Kandrik & DeBruine, 2013) and those who have high testosterone (Welling et al., 2008). When men can afford to, they insist on physically attractive mates. Gay men and heterosexual men show very similar long-term mate preferences with physical attractiveness being critical to both (Bailey et al., 1994), suggesting that mate preference adaptations for physical attractiveness are specific to the psychology of the desirer (men), not the biological sex of the target of desire (whether men or women).

When it comes to preferences for physical attractiveness, it is critical to distinguish between long-term and short-term mating. A few studies show no evidence of sex differences in preferences for physical attractiveness (Eastwick & Finkel, 2008), but these studies fail to clearly distinguish between long-term and short-term mating when examining men's and women's preferential mating desires (see Li et al., 2013). In short-term mating, as described in the next part, women do indeed desire physical attractiveness in potential mates. Big time.

Women's Short-Term Mating Psychology

Although most heterosexual women want as good a mate as possible, they cannot all marry the best available man (especially in legally imposed monogamous cultures). Women may, however, gain brief sexual access to especially high-quality men by engaging in casual sex with them. In doing so, women may reap the adaptive benefit of acquiring "good genes" from these high-quality men. That is, she may obtain genes that underlie the men's ability to achieve high status, good health, and enhanced reproductive success, with such genes being especially fruitful for the women's own sons. Indeed, Sexual Strategies Theory (Buss & Schmitt, 1993)

hypothesized that because gaining access to good genes is a key benefit women obtain from short-term mating, women will possess evolved desires for cues to good genes in potential short-term mates such as symmetry, masculinity, and overall physical attractiveness.

Self-Reported Mate Preference Surveys

One piece of evidence in support of the Sexual Strategies Theory perspective on women's short-term mating psychology comes from surveys that ask women how important physical cues to good genes are when they are choosing a short-term mate compared to a long-term mate. When asked, women tend to particularly prefer physical attractiveness in short-term mates compared to long-term mates (Buss & Schmitt, 1993; Buunk et al., 2002; Gangestad & Simpson, 1990, 2000; Kenrick et al., 1990, 1993; Regan & Berscheid, 1997, 1998a, 1998b; Regan et al., 2000, 2001; Scheib, 2001). Regan et al. (2001) found that women rated physical attractiveness 7.80 on importance in short-term mate choice, but only 6.32 in long-term mating (on a 9-point scale). Castro and Lopes (2011) found that women prefer a "pretty face" 3.42 in short-term mates, but only 2.17 in long-term mates (on a 5-point scale), and women prefer a "beautiful body" 3.08 in short-term mates, but only 1.83 in long-term mates.

When asked about the *minimum level* of physical attractiveness needed for engaging in casual sex with a man, the average women wanted the man to be at least in the 69th percentile, whereas they required a man of the 62nd percentile for a man as long-term mate (Kenrick et al., 1993). Regan (1998a) found similar results, with women wanting men to be at least 71st percentile of attractiveness as a short-term mate, whereas they required a man of 60th percentile of attractiveness as long-term mate. Regan (1998b) also found that women, but not men, are unwilling to compromise on attractiveness in their *ideal* short-term mate.

When asked to make economic decisions (such as spending "dollars" from a limited budget), women behaviorally spend 51 % of their budget on physical attractiveness in designing an ideal short-term mate (but only 21 % of their budget in long-term mating; Li, 2007). In another cross-cultural study, American women spent 46 % of their budget on physical attractiveness in short-term mating, but only 23 % of their budget on physical attractiveness in long-term mating (Li, Valentine, & Patel, 2011), and the differences were more intense at 43 % versus 15 % in Singapore. When asked to rate physical attractiveness among a list of traits, women's mean rating of physical attractiveness placed it as the eighth most important trait in short-term mating, but only 15th in long-term mating (Stewart, Stinnett, & Rosenfeld, 2000).

Women emphasize specific physical attributes much more in short-term mating than long-term mating, such as facial symmetry, facial masculinity, large muscles, and other testosterone-related cues (Johnston, 2006; Mueller & Mazur, 1998; Roney et al., 2006; Waynforth, Delwadia, & Camm, 2005). Women also report physical attractiveness-related motives for short-term mating 24 % of the time (in men it is only 10 %; Regan & Dreyer, 1999).

Actual Mate Choice and Reactions to Experimental Manipulations

Women tend to more often choose and more strongly react to physical attractiveness in their *actual* behavior within short-term mating contexts (Wiederman & Dubois, 1998). For instance, women tend to have affairs with especially symmetrical men (Gangestad et al., 2005) and women have more frequent and consistent copulatory orgasms with physically attractive men (Puts, Welling, Burriss, & Dawood, 2012; Shackelford et al., 2000; Thornhill, Gangestad, & Comer, 1995). Women are judged more likely to consent to short-term mating with a male stranger if he is high in physical attractiveness (7 %), compared to only moderate physical attractiveness (3 %) or low physical attractiveness (2 %; Schützwohl et al., 2009). When approached by *actual* strangers in real-life situations, women

tend to say "yes" to a real stranger's query "will you go to bed with me?" if the man is high in physical attractiveness (3 %) versus only average in physical attractiveness (0 %; Guéguen, 2011). In a Danish study, whether women said yes to an actual stranger's asking for sex was influenced by the physical attractiveness of experimental confederates (Danish men were not so influenced; Hald & Høgh-Olesen, 2010). Men's physical attractiveness matters to women in their real-life casual sex experiences involving short-term mating.

Comparing Women's Short-Term Preferences Across Ovulatory Cycles

If women are to maximally gain the "good genes" benefits of selective short-term mating, they would be most effective at choosing attractive men for casual sex when the women are nearing ovulation (the time interval during which the odds of conceptive sex are maximized). Several studies have found, perhaps not coincidentally, that women's preference for physical attractiveness in potential mates peaks around ovulation (Thornhill & Gangestad, 2008). Interestingly, this is especially true if women are of low mate value (Millar, 2013) and if a woman's husband is physically unattractive (hence, her adaptive need for "good genes" is intensified; Gangestad et al., 2010; Larson, Pillsworth, & Haselton, 2012; Pillsworth & Haselton, 2006).

Women around ovulation also prefer men whose faces and bodies are highly symmetrical (Gangestad & Thornhill, 1998; Johnston, Hagel, Franklin, Fink, & Grammer, 2001), a finding linked directly to shifts in women's hormones (Garver-Apgar, Gangestad, & Thornhill, 2008). Women's preferences for men who have facial or bodily masculinity (Anderson et al., 2010; DeBruine, Jones, Frederick, et al., 2010; Little, Jones, & Burriss, 2007), vocal masculinity (Feinberg et al., 2006; Puts, 2005), and social dominance (Gangestad, Simpson, Cousins, Garver-Apgar, & Christensen, 2004) all peak around ovulation (see DeBruine, Jones, Tybur,

Lieberman, & Griskevicius, 2010), and again these shifts appear likely tied to hormonal variations (Puts, 2006). Many of these shifts are most pronounced within the context of women explicitly evaluating men as short-term mates (Lukaszewski & Roney, 2009). Women's preference for tall men peaks around ovulation (Pawlowski & Jasienska, 2005), as does their preference for creatively intelligent men (Haselton & Miller, 2006). In one study, women preferred not only physically attractive men but just the sight or thought of a man with a highly attractive body aroused women and they were more willing to have sex with a physically attractive man (Gangestad, Thornhill, & Garver-Apgar, 2010).

Women's manifest behaviors also shift around ovulation, at which time they tend to be more provocative (Haselton et al., 2007) and attractive (Oberzaucher et al., 2012), especially if sociosexually unrestricted and chronically interesting in short-term mating (Durante, Li, & Haselton, 2008). Women feel more attractive and are perceived as more attractive when approaching ovulation (Durante et al., 2008). Women want to go to dance clubs more when approaching ovulation (Haselton & Miller, 2006), speak at a higher frequency when approaching ovulation (Fischer et al., 2011), and have a warmer personality when approaching ovulation (Markey & Markey, 2011). Women nearing ovulation tend to over-perceive sexy men (i.e., cads) as being super dads (Durante, Griskevicius, Simpson, Cantú, & Li, 2012), are more likely to interact extensively with masculine men (Flowe, Swords, & Rockey, 2012), and are more likely to say "yes" to a dance request at bar (59 %) compared to when women are in nonfertile stages of their ovulatory cycle (36 %; $d = 0.73$, Guéguen, 2009). Ovulating women's pupils tend to dilate when viewing their favorite celebrity, whereas they do not if not ovulating, viewing another person's favorite celebrity, or if women are on the pill (Laeng & Falkenberg, 2007).

Women approaching ovulation are better at identifying men's (but not women's) sexual orientation (Rule, Rosen, Slepian, & Ambady, 2011), exhibit higher out-group bias and prejudice (McDonald et al., 2011), and are able to categorize men's gender more quickly and access aspects of masculine semantics better (Macrae et al., 2002). Finally, women approaching ovulation are touched more in bars (Grammer, Renninger, & Fischer, 2004), dress more provocatively when going out (Haselton et al., 2007), receive better tips as exotic dancers ($335 versus $260; $d = 0.75$, Miller et al., 2007), are more attractive to men generally (Roberts et al., 2004), and feel more desirable and want more sex (Röder, Brewer, & Fink, 2009). The psychological shifts that seem to occur in women's affect, cognition, and behavior suggest that their short-term mating psychology—designed to obtain good genes from symmetrical, masculine, and healthy men—is heightened when nearing ovulation.

Comparing Preferences of Women Who Short-Term Mate Versus Women Who Only Long-Term Mate

Another useful tool for evaluating women's short-term mate preferences is to compare women who engage in a lot of short-term mating to women who are exclusively long-term maters. From a Sexual Strategies Theory perspective, it is unsurprising that women who engage in more short-term mating during their lifespan tend to emphasize physical attractiveness, masculinity, and interpersonal dominance more in mate choice (Gangestad et al., 2005; Little, Jones, Penton-Voak, Burt, & Perrett, 2002; Provost, Kormos, Kosakoski, & Quinsey, 2006; Quist et al., 2012; Simpson, Gangestad, Christensen, & Niels, 1999; Wilbur & Campbell, 2010).

Women high in unrestricted sociosexuality (i.e., short-term-oriented women) tend to perceive smiles as flirting (much like most men do; Howell, Etchells, & Penton-Voak, 2012). If single, women high in sociosexuality prefer especially masculine men (whereas already mated women do not; Sacco, Jones, DeBruine, &

Hugenberg, 2012). Women who are more likely to engage in short-term mating tend to prefer men who possess masculine attributes (Frederick & Haselton, 2007; Little et al., 2002) even including the way masculine men walk (Provost, Troje, & Quinsey, 2008). Some of these associations are more pronounced if the women are physically unattractive themselves (Penton-Voak et al., 2003). Overall, it appears women who engage in short-term mating are more likely to exhibit the short-term mate preferences hypothesized by Sexual Strategies Theory.

Men's Courtship Effectiveness in Short-Term Mating Can Reveal Women's Short-Term Desires

If women do possess evolved desires for particular kinds of short-term mating partners, these desires may be revealed in the kinds of men who are especially successful at short-term mating. Men who are higher in physical attractiveness compete more and are chosen more often by women as short-term mates (but not as long-term mates; Simpson et al., 1999). Physically attractive and masculine men tend to have more sex (Gallup et al., 2007; Puts, 2005; Shoup & Gallup, 2008), have more sex partners (Bogaert & Fisher, 1995; Rhodes, Simmons, & Peters, 2005; Thornhill & Gangestad, 1994), are considered more attractive by women as short-term mates (Gangestad et al., 2004), are more successful at engaging in extra-pair copulations (i.e., having affairs) and mate poaching (Gangestad & Thornhill, 1997; Schmitt et al., 2004), have more children (Apicella et al., 2007; Waynforth, 1999), are seen as more dominant (Simpson, Gangestad, Christensen, & Niels, 1999), are actually stronger in grip strength (Gallup et al., 2007; Shoup & Gallup, 2008), and have better quality sperm (Scheib, 1994; Soler et al., 2003). Overall, it appears men's physical attractiveness and masculinity are at least somewhat reliable indicators of his genetic quality and hence his desirability as a short-term mate.

Men also react to women's ovulatory status in ways consistent with women's short-term mating strategy being designed to obtain high-quality genes, such as men reacting to women's near-ovulation status in strip clubs by giving bigger tips ($d = 0.75$, Miller, Tybur, & Jordan, 2007), men's testosterone tending to go up when smelling ovulating women's scent ($d = 0.75$, Miller & Maner, 2010), and men exposed to ovulating women more easily access sex-related concepts in cognitive tests and make riskier decisions (Miller & Maner, 2011). Generally, men find a woman's voice, body odor, waist-to-hip ratio, skin tone, and facial features especially attractive when she is ovulating (e.g., Bryant & Haselton, 2009; Oberzaucher et al., 2012; Roberts et al., 2004). Men also spend more effort mate guarding when their partners ovulate ($d = 0.87$, Gangestad, Thornhill, & Garver, 2002; see also Thornhill & Gangestad, 2008).

Other Functions of Short-Term Mating in Women

Women may engage in short-term mating for a variety of adaptive reasons (Greiling & Buss, 2000), not just to obtain good genes from physically attractive men. Women can benefit from confusing their partners about paternity, from directly obtaining resources, from obtaining physical protection of multiple males, from evaluating their own mate value, and from the potential of a short-term mating experience to lead to a long-term mateship. Evidence for these functions is not as robust as is the evidence for good genes acquisition. For instance, women engaged in short-term mating tend to prefer men who provide immediate resources (especially as opposed to men who just have future resource *potential*; Buss & Schmitt, 1993), and men are typically judged more effective in short-term contexts when they provide immediate resources (Schmitt, 2002). Resource levels are closely related to age, and in a study of 25-year-olds (Buunk et al., 2001), researchers found that women tend to prefer short-term mates who are older than themselves by about 4

years (age 29, with an average maximum acceptable age of 38), whereas men prefer women of
about 1 year younger as short-term mates (age
24, with an average maximum acceptable age of
31).

Women prefer short-term mates who are muscular (Frederick & Haselton, 2007), have a
V-torso (Braun & Bryan, 2006), and demonstrate
attributes indicative of good fighting ability and
grip strength (Gallup, White, & Gallup, 2007;
Sell et al., 2010). Not surprisingly, men who are
successful at short-term mating and mate
poaching tend to have a V-torso (Hughes &
Gallup, 2003). The typical findings in studies of
prostitution (e.g., Bonnerup et al., 2000) and pornography consumption (Hald, 2006) also support
the view that women more often than men engage
in short-term mating in exchange for resources.

Another possible function of short-term mating for women is using short-term mating as a
means of successfully navigating out of and into
long-term mateships. For example, women view
short-term mating as a good way to end past
relationships and for finding a good replacement
long-term mate (Greiling & Buss, 2000). Using
short-term mating to achieve a long-term partnership is the second most popular reason women
give for short-term mating (Li & Kenrick, 2006).
Women also view hookups, booty calls, or
"friends with benefits" as hopeful pathways to
long-term mating more than men do (Reiber &
Garcia, 2010). Women, more so than men, tend to
engage in extramarital affairs if they are dissatisfied with their current long-term relationship,
with 77 % of women viewing "love" as an acceptable reason for extramarital affairs, compared to
only 43 % of men (Glass & Wright, 1985). About
3 % of single women over 30 years of age desire
short-term mating, whereas about 8 % of single
men over 30 desire short-term mates (Tadinac &
Hromatko, 2006). Among mated women over 30,
18 % report they desire an extramarital affair,
whereas about 35 % of men do (Tadinac &
Hromatko, 2006). Compared to women, men's
short-term mating is thought to be driven by a
different mate preference psychology.

Men's Short-Term Mating Psychology

Evolutionary psychologists expect that men can
reap strong reproductive benefits from engaging
in short-term mating. Indeed, as the lesser-
investing sex in terms of gametes (Bateman,
1948) and obligatory parental investment
(Trivers, 1972), men should be more eager than
women for opportunistic short-term mateships
and should be less discriminating than women
in their selections of casual sex partners. Several
sources of evidence have confirmed these fundamental features of men's short-term mating psychology (see Schmitt et al., 2012).

Self-Reported Mate Preference Surveys

One source of evidence comes from surveys that
ask men and women the degree to which they
eagerly desire short-term mating. In 1993, Buss
and Schmitt asked a college student sample the
extent to which they were *currently seeking*
short-term mates, the *number of sex partners*
they ideally desired at limited time intervals
into the future, and whether they would *consent
to sex* with someone they viewed as desirable if
they had known the person for limited amounts
of time. In nearly every instance, men more
eagerly desired and more quickly consented to
short-term sex than women did. Several studies
have since replicated these basic findings
(Fenigstein & Preston, 2007; Kennair, Schmitt,
Fjeldavli, & Harlem, 2009; McBurney, Zapp, &
Streeter, 2005; Wilcox, 2003). Schmitt et al.
(2003) replicated these findings across more
than 10,000 college students representing ten
major regions of the world. Sex differences in -
self-reported desires for short-term mating
are likely a pancultural universal (see also,
Lippa, 2009).

An important caveat to these findings, however, is that many men report they are relatively
uninterested in short-term mating. Evolutionary
psychologists do not expect all men to be eager
for short-term mating at all times. Instead, only

some men eagerly pursue short-term mating strategies, especially those who can successfully pursue the strategy given their own physical attractiveness, status, and overall mate value (Gangestad & Simpson, 2000). Early attachment experiences, local pathogen levels and sex ratios, and heritable differences also influence the degree to which men pursue short-term mating as a sexual strategy (Bailey, Kirk, Zhu, Dunne, & Martin, 2000; Garcia et al., 2010; Schmitt, 2005b; Walum et al., 2008; Zion et al., 2006). Still, the logic of Sexual Strategies Theory suggests that *when* men pursue short-term mating, they do so guided by evolved desires that are different from the desires of women who pursue short-term mating. Namely, men who short-term mate are expected to desire more numerous mating partners, be quicker to consent to sex, and more eagerly engage in brief sexual encounters compared to women who short-term mate. A wide variety of data sources supports this view (Buss & Schmitt, 2011).

Additional Self-Reported Attitudes and Behaviors

Beyond simply asking men and women the extent to which they eagerly desire short-term mating, per se, sex differences exist in numerous sex-related attitudes and behaviors closely associated with short-term mating. For instance, men have significantly more positive attitudes than women toward casual sex, permissive sexuality, and emotion-free sexual experiences (Hendrick, Hendrick, Slapion-Foote, & Foote, 1985; Oliver & Hyde, 1993; Petersen & Hyde, 2010). Carroll, Volk, and Hyde (1985) asked men and women if they always needed to be emotionally close in order to have sex with someone, with 45 % of women and only 8 % of men responding they required emotion for sex. Also asked was the somewhat awkward question of whether they would *never refuse a sexual offer*, with 46 % of men saying they would never refuse a sexual offer, but not a single woman (0 %) reporting she would never refuse a sexual offer. In the context of short-term

mating, evidence suggests that *all* women are at least somewhat selective, whereas about half of men apparently have no minimum standards at all.

In a meta-analysis of 30 sexuality-related attitudes and behaviors, Petersen and Hyde (2010) found that men had more positive attitudes toward casual sex ($d = 0.45$) and toward sexual permissiveness ($d = 0.21$). Men were also more likely to engage in extramarital sex ($d = 0.33$) and casual sex ($d = 0.28$). Petersen and Hyde (2010) reported that "most gender differences in sexual attitudes and behaviors were small" (p. 21), but this was not true for sex differences in eagerness for short-term mating nor is it true for evolutionary psychology's many predictions concerning mate preferences (which were empirically ignored by Petersen and Hyde). Indeed, many sex differences in mate preferences hypothesized by Sexual Strategies Theory are rather large in size (as noted above).

Sociosexuality

In 1991, Simpson and Gangestad developed a measure of a trait called sociosexuality. This measure was specifically designed to assess whether someone is willing to have sex without commitment (i.e., is sociosexually unrestricted). Across every sample that has ever been studied, men report more unrestricted sociosexual attitudes and behaviors than women (De Jong et al., 2012; Schmitt, 2005c; Simpson et al., 2004). Schmitt (2005c) assessed the sociosexuality of men and women across 48 nations and found that men were more unrestricted than women in every culture (average $d = 0.74$). In 2009, Lippa replicated Schmitt's results across a larger sample of 53 nations, including exactly replicating the overall sex difference of $d = 0.74$.

Sexual Fantasies

Men are more likely than women are to have sexual fantasies and desires involving short-term sex with multiple opposite-sex partners (Hughes, Harrison, & Gallup, 2004; Leitenberg & Henning, 1995; Stone, Goetz, & Shackelford, 2005). Hunt (1974) found 33 % of men and only

18 % of women have sex fantasies involving multiple partners of the opposite sex. Davidson (1985) found 42 % of men and only 17 % of women have sex fantasies involving multiple partners of the opposite sex. Hessellund (1976) found 37 % of men and only 7 % of women have sex fantasies involving multiple partners of the opposite sex. There are also sex differences in sex fantasies involving group sex, with 31 % of men and 15 % of women reporting such fantasies (Wilson, 1987). Ellis and Symons (1990) found 32 % of men (but only 8 % of women) have had sexual fantasies involving over 1,000 partners in their lifetime. Hughes et al. (2004) found 78 % of men, but only 32 % of women, reported they would engage in a threesome.

Regret and Sexual Desires

Emotionally, men tend to experience less regret than women do after engaging in short-term sex or "hookups" (instead men particularly regret *missed opportunities* for short-term mating; Roese et al., 2006; Bradshaw, Kahn, & Saville, 2010; Campbell, 2008; de Graaf & Sandfort, 2004; Galperin et al., 2013; Paul & Hayes, 2002; Townsend, 1995). Men also tend to over-perceive sexual interest from opposite-sex strangers more than women do (Abbey, 1982; Haselton & Buss, 2000; Henningsen, Henningsen, & Valde, 2006; Perilloux, Easton, & Buss, 2012; Sigal, Gibbs, Adams, & Derfler, 1988), men tend to want, initiate, and enjoy a wider variety of sex practices than women do (Baumeister, Catanese, & Vohs, 2001; Laumann et al., 1994; Purnine, Carey, Jorgensen, & Randall, 1994), and men tend to have higher general sex drives in all cultures that have been studied (Lippa, 2009).

Relaxed Mate Preferences

Men generally relax their mate preferences in short-term mating, whereas women *increase* their selectivity in short-term mating, especially for physical attractiveness (Bryan, Webster, & Mahaffey, 2011; Buunk et al., 2002; Confer, Perilloux, & Buss, 2010; Fisher & Cox, 2009;

Gangestad & Simpson, 2000; Greitemeyer, 2005; Kenrick et al., 1990, 1993; Landolt, Lalumiere, & Quinsey, 1995; Li et al., 2002; Li & Kenrick, 2006; Regan, 1998a, 1998b; Regan & Berscheid, 1997; Regan et al., 2000; Scheib, 2001; Schützwohl, Fuchs, McKibbin, & Shackelford, 2009; Simpson & Gangestad, 1992; Stewart et al., 2000; Wiederman & Dubois, 1998). Indeed, although men's perceptions of women's physical attractiveness become biased as evenings get late in bars, women continue to perceive men's physical attractiveness with high accuracy (controlling for alcohol consumption; Gladue & Delaney, 1990). Men, but not women, also prefer short-term mates who are easily sexually accessible. In an experimental study, men found that women who give cues to "easy sexual access" as more attractive for short-term mating but not for long-term mating, and women showed no increased attraction toward easily sexually accessible men in any mating context (Schmitt et al., 2001).

Actual Mate Choice and Reactions to Experimental Manipulations

Although men self-report that they value and desire large numbers of short-term sex partners more than women do, it is possible that such findings do not reflect what men actually do when offered short-term sex. In studies of actual mating behavior, however, men are more likely than women to consent to sex with a stranger (Clark, 1990; Clark & Hatfield, 1989; Greitemeyer, 2005; Hald & Høgh-Olesen, 2010; Schützwohl et al., 2009; Surbey & Conohan, 2000; Voracek, Fisher, Hofhansl, Rekkas, & Ritthammer, 2006; Voracek, Hofhansl, & Fisher, 2005). In 1989, Clark and Hatfield had experimental confederates approach college students across various campuses and ask if they would like to have sex. Around 75 % of men agreed to have sex with a complete stranger, whereas no women (0 %) agreed to sex with a complete stranger. Twenty years later, Hald and Høgh-Olesen (2010) largely replicated these findings in Denmark, with 59 % of single men and 0 % of single women agreeing to the proposition, "Would you go to bed with me?" Interestingly, they also asked participants who were already in relationships, finding 18 % of men and 4 % of women currently in a relationship responded positively to the request.

Schützwohl et al. (2009) asked participants to judge what men and women would do in a similar situation, but they also manipulated the physical attractiveness of the confederate. For men, they were thought to agree to sex with a stranger if she was highly attractive 54 % of the time, whereas women were thought to agree to sex with a stranger if he was highly attractive 8 % of the time. Guéguen (2011) had confederates of various levels of physical attractiveness *actually* approach real-life strangers and ask if they would have sex, finding 83 % of men agreed to have sex with a highly attractive woman and 60 % of men agreed to sex with a woman of average attractiveness. For women, 3 % agreed to have sex with a highly attractive man, but no woman (0 %) agreed to have sex with a man of average attractiveness. As noted earlier, men of high physical attractiveness are most able to successfully pursue a short-term sexual strategy. For the average-looking man, short-term mating may not represent a viable reproductive option.

In 2011, Conley conducted a version of the "ask for sex" methodology using hypothetical requests from strangers and celebrities. Although her theoretical portrayal of evolutionary psychology was highly flawed (see Schmitt et al., 2012), her results were quite interesting. Conley (2011) found that women were much more likely to agree to a brief sexual encounter with a high-profile celebrity (e.g., Brad Pitt, Johnny Depp) compared with an unknown stranger and that sex differences in the reactions to celebrities were minimal (men were hypothetically asked for sex by Angelina Jolie or Jennifer Lopez). In the unknown stranger condition, there will still large sex differences, but not with the highly attractive celebrities condition. However, these findings with celebrity requests for sex do not disconfirm Sexual Strategies Theory. The findings quite likely resulted from women's (but not men's) short-term mating psychology being

specially designed to obtain good genes from physically attractive short-term partners (Thornhill & Gangestad, 2008). Indeed, given the findings on women's short-term psychology noted earlier, women who were nearing ovulation and were already in relationships with asymmetrical and submissive partners would be *even more* likely to consent to sex with Brad Pitt or Johnny Depp (Pillsworth & Haselton, 2006). A further problem with the study was the use of participants who were only 22 years old on average to consider sex with much older celebrities, celebrities who also were married. Women in their 20s generally prefer older partners as short-term mates than men do (Buunk, Dijkstra, Kenrick, & Warntjes, 2001), and women tend to find already mated prospective partners especially attractive (Parker & Burkley, 2009). Brad Pitt and Johnny Depp (highly attractive, more than 10 years older, married) are among the most adaptively designed humans when it comes to fulfilling women's (but not men's) short-term mate preferences as outlined by Sexual Strategies Theory.

One-Night Stands

In studies of the psychology of one-night stands, men have been found to intentionally seek out and initiate short-term sex more than women do (Herold & Mewhinney, 1993; Maticka-Tyndale, Herold, & Mewhinney, 1998; Spanier & Margolis, 1983). Maticka-Tyndale et al. (1998) examined intentions to engage in casual sex among college students on spring break and found 76 % of men and 19 % of women *intended* to have sex with someone they just met on vacation. Herold and Mewhinney (1993) asked 169 bar patrons if they had engaged in a one-night stand after meeting a person at a bar, with 72 % of men and only 49 % of women reporting they had done so. About 63 % of men (versus 28 % of women) had *expected* to end up in a one-night stand, with 25 % of men reporting they had always enjoyed one-night stands and only 2 % of women having always enjoyed one-night stands. In another study involving bar patrons, Hendrie, Mannion, and Godfrey (2009) found that men approached women 83 % of the time, and of those women approached 50 % were wearing revealing clothes (whereas only 20 % of all women in the bar were wearing revealing clothes).

Extramarital Affairs

Numerous studies have confirmed that men are more likely than women to engage in extramarital sex (Atkins, Baucom, & Jacobson, 2001; Blow & Hartnett, 2005; Blumstein & Schwartz, 1983; Brand, Markey, & Hodges, 2007; Druckerman, 2007; Glass & Wright, 1985; Laumann et al., 1994; Oliver & Hyde, 1993; Petersen & Hyde, 2010; Schmitt et al., 2004; Seal, Agostinelli, & Hannett, 1994; Thompson, 1983; Træen & Martinussen, 2008; Wiederman, 1997; Wiederman & Hurd, 1999). As presented in Table 1.2, most studies in the United States find that men are about twice as likely as women to have engaged in extramarital sex. Cross-culturally, the differences are often much greater, with men in many cultures being much more likely than women to engage in short-term mating while married (see Table 1.2, international data from Druckerman, 2007).

Moreover, when men are unfaithful, they tend more than women do to be unfaithful multiple times with *different* sexual partners (Blumstein & Schwartz, 1983; Hansen, 1987; Laumann et al., 1994; Lawson & Samson, 1988; Spanier & Margolis, 1983), and men who engage in extramarital sex are not especially unhappy with their marriages (whereas women are; Brand et al., 2007). Men are also more likely to seek short-term sex partners who are already mated (i.e., engage in short-term *mate poaching*; Davies, Shackelford, & Hass, 2007, 2010; Jonason, Li, Webster, & Schmitt, 2009; Parker & Burkley, 2009; Schmitt et al., 2004; Schmitt & Buss, 2001).

Prostitution and Pornography

Behaviorally, men are more likely than women to pay for short-term sex with (male or female) prostitutes (Burley & Symanski, 1981; Symons, 1979). In a 2010 representative sample of the United States, 13.5 % of men and only 2.2 % of women reported having "ever paid for sex?"

(General Social Survey, 2013). In a Danish study, 16 % of men and no women (0 %) reported that they had "ever had sex with a prostitute?" (Bonnerup et al., 2000). Men are also more likely than women to enjoy sexual magazines and videos containing themes of short-term sex and sex with multiple partners (Giotakos, 2004; Koukounas & McCabe, 1997; Malamuth, 1996; Murnen & Stockton, 1997; Salmon & Symons, 2001; Youn, 2006). In a large study of married couples across five cultures, husbands were universally more likely than their wives to report enjoying sexy books and videos (Weisfeld et al., 2011). About 39 % of men masturbate more than three times per week using pornography, whereas only 7 % of women do (Hald, 2006). Furthermore, men are more likely than women to masturbate while thinking about short-term sex and multiple opposite-sex partners (Ellis & Symons, 1990; Hald, 2006; Jones & Barlow, 1990).

Sexual Orientation

An interesting test case for men's greater eagerness for short-term mating is to examine the sexual differences between gay men and lesbians. Gay men tend to have more unrestricted sociosexuality, engage in more extra-dyadic sex, and relax their short-term mate preferences more than lesbians do (Bailey, Gaulin, Agyei, & Gladue, 1994; Bell & Weinberg, 1978; Blumstein & Schwartz, 1983; Schmitt, 2005c; Symons, 1979). Blumstein and Schwartz (1983) found that 76 % of gay couples had experienced an affair, whereas only 11 % of lesbian couples had. As noted by Schmitt (2005c), gay men have identical levels of unrestricted sociosexual *attitudes* compared to heterosexual men, but because their mating pool consists of other men who possess relatively unrestricted sociosexuality, gay men tend to *behaviorally* engage in more short-term mating than heterosexual men. Bell and Weinberg (1978) found that 75 % of gay men have had more than 100 sex partners, with 18 % claiming to have had more than 1,000 partners (while no lesbians claimed this number of short-term sex partners). To the degree that gay men's and lesbians mating

Table 1.2 Sex differences in infidelity rates across nations, samples, and time periods

Nation/sample	Men's infidelity prevalence (%)	Women's infidelity prevalence (%)
Ever engaged in extramarital sex?		
Finland (1993)	44	19
Japan (1975)	73	4
The Netherlands (1980)	28	18
United States (1948–2010)		
Kinsey, Pomeroy, and Martin (1948) and Kinsey, Pomeroy, Martin, and Gebhard (1953)	50	26
Hunt Report (1974)	41	18
Laumann et al. (1994)	25	10
General Social Survey (1994)	23	12
General Social Survey (2000)	25	13
General Social Survey (2002)	24	16
General Social Survey (2004)	23	13
General Social Survey (2006)	23	18
General Social Survey (2008)	23	13
General Social Survey (2010)	22	16
Zimbabwe (1990)	67	3
Engaged in extramarital sex in the past year?		
Australia (2002)	3	2
Bolivia (2003)	9	<1
Brazil (1996)	12	1
Philippines (2003)	5	<1
China (2000)	18	3
Ethiopia (2000)	7	<1
France (2004)	4	2
Great Britain (2003; includes married and cohabiting)	9	5
Italy (1998)	4	1
Kenya (2003)	12	2
Nigeria (2003)	15	1
Norway (1997)	11	7
Peru (1996)	14	<1
Switzerland (1997)	3	1
Tanzania (2005)	29	3
United States: General Social Survey (1994)	4	2
Zimbabwe (1999)	14	1

markets represent the outcomes of sex-specific sexual desires, it appears men's short-term mate preferences are decidedly different from women's.

Conclusion

According to Sexual Strategies Theory (Buss & Schmitt, 1993), our species comes equipped with specialized adaptations (or mate preferences) that profoundly influence on our desire, pursuit, and selection of mates. The evolved mate preferences that drive men and women when pursuing long-term or short-term mating strategies differ in fundamental ways. When short-term mating, men preferentially desire easy sexual access and relax their desires so as to obtain large numbers of sex partners, whereas women are relatively selective and especially desire "good genes" when short-term mating. When long-term mating, men emphasize fertility-related cues such as youth and physical attractiveness, whereas women desire cues to a partner's ability and willingness to devote resources to herself and their offspring. Much remains to be explored in the evolutionary psychology of human mating, but at present the evidentiary status of most mate preference adaptations postulated by Sexual Strategies Theory, evaluated using multiple lines of evidence as advocated by Schmitt and Pilcher (2004), is both broad and deep.

References

Abbey, A. (1982). Sex differences in attributions for friendly behavior: Do males misperceive females' friendliness? *Journal of Personality and Social Psychology, 42*, 830–838.

Aharon, I., Etcoff, N., Ariely, D., Chabris, C. F., O'Connor, E., & Breiter, H. C. (2001). Beautiful faces have variable reward value: fMRI and behavioral evidence. *Neuron, 32*, 537–551.

Ahmetoglu, G., & Swami, V. (2012). Do women prefer 'nice guys'? The effect of male dominance behavior on women's ratings of sexual attractiveness. *Social Behavior and Personality, 40*, 667–672.

Ainsworth, S. E., & Maner, J. K. (2012). Sex begets violence: Mating motives, social dominance, and physical aggression in men. *Journal of Personality and Social Psychology, 103*, 819–829.

Anderson, U. S., Perea, E. F., Becker, D. V., Ackerman, J. M., Shapiro, J. R., Neuberg, S. L., et al. (2010). I only have eyes for you: Ovulation redirects attention (but not memory) to attractive men. *Journal of Experimental Social Psychology, 46*, 804–808.

Apicella, C., Feinberg, D. R., & Marlowe, F. W. (2007). Voice pitch predicts reproductive success in male hunter-gatherers. *Biology Letters, 3*, 682–684.

Asendorpf, J. B., Penke, L., & Back, M. D. (2011). From dating to mating and relating: Predictors of initial and long-term outcomes of speed-dating in a community sample. *European Journal of Personality, 25*, 16–30.

Atkins, D. C., Baucom, D. H., & Jacobson, N. S. (2001). Understanding infidelity: Correlates in a national random sample. *Journal of Family Psychology, 15*, 735–749.

Bailey, J. M., Gaulin, S., Agyei, Y., & Gladue, B. A. (1994). Effects of gender and sexual orientation on evolutionary relevant aspects of human mating psychology. *Journal of Personality and Social Psychology, 66*, 1081–1093.

Bailey, J. M., Kirk, K. M., Zhu, G., Dunne, M. P., & Martin, N. G. (2000). Do individual differences in sociosexuality represent genetic or environmentally contingent strategies? Evidence from the Australian twin registry. *Journal of Personality and Social Psychology, 78*, 537–545.

Baize, H. R., & Schroeder, J. E. (1995). Personality and mate selection in personal ads: Evolutionary preferences in a public mate selection process. *Journal of Social Behavior and Personality, 10*, 517–536.

Barrett, E. S., Van Thurston, T., Jasienska, S., Furberg, G., Ellison, P. T., & Thune, I. (2013). Marriage and motherhood are associated with lower testosterone concentrations in women. *Hormones and Behavior, 63*(1), 72–79.

Bateman, A. J. (1948). Intra-sexual selection in Drosophila. *Heredity, 2*, 349–368.

Baumeister, R. F., Catanese, K. R., & Vohs, K. D. (2001). Are there gender differences in strength of sex drive? Theoretical views, conceptual distinctions, and a review of relevant evidence. *Personality and Social Psychology Review, 5*, 242–273.

Bell, A. P., & Weinberg, M. S. (1978). *Homosexualities: A study of diversity among men and women.* New York: Simon and Schuster.

Bereczkei, T., & Csanaky, A. (1996). Mate choice, marital success, and reproduction in a modern society. *Ethology and Sociobiology, 17*, 17–35.

Betzig, L. (1986). *Despotism and differential reproduction: A Darwinian view of history.* New York: Aldine.

Betzig, L. (1989). Causes of conjugal dissolution: A cross-cultural study. *Current Anthropology, 30*, 654–676.

Blow, A. J., & Hartnett, K. (2005). Infidelity in committed relationships II: A substantive review. *Journal of Marital and Family Therapy, 31*, 217–233.

Blumstein, P., & Schwartz, P. (1983). *American couples.* New York: William Morrow.

Bogaert, A. F., & Fisher, W. A. (1995). Predictors of university men's number of sexual partners. *The Journal of Sex Research, 32*, 119–130.

Bonnerup, J. A., Gramkow, A., Sorensen, P., Melbye, M., Adami, H.-O., Glimelius, B., et al. (2000). Correlates of heterosexual behavior among 23–87 year olds in Denmark and Sweden, 1992–1998. *Archives of Sexual Behavior, 29*, 91–106.

Bradshaw, C., Kahn, A. S., & Saville, B. K. (2010). To hook up or date: Which gender benefits? *Sex Roles, 62*, 661–669.

Brand, R. J., Markey, C. M., & Hodges, S. D. (2007). Sex differences in self-reported infidelity and its correlates. *Sex Roles, 57*, 101–109.

Braun, M. F., & Bryan, A. (2006). Female waist-to-hip and male waist-to-shoulder ratios as determinants of romantic partner desirability. *Journal of Social and Personal Relationships, 23*, 805–819.

Bryan, A. D., Webster, G. D., & Mahaffey, A. L. (2011). The big, the rich, and the powerful: Physical, financial, and social dimensions of dominance in mating and attraction. *Personality and Social Psychology Bulletin, 37*, 365–382.

Bryant, G. A., & Haselton, M. G. (2009). Vocal cues of ovulation in human females. *Biology Letters, 5*, 12–15.

Burley, N., & Symanski, R. (1981). Women without: An evolutionary and cross-cultural perspective on prostitution. In R. Symanski (Ed.), *The immoral landscape: Female prostitution in western societies* (pp. 239–274). Toronto: Butterworth.

Burriss, R. P., Welling, L. L. M., & Puts, D. A. (2011a). Men's attractiveness predicts their preference for female facial femininity when judging for short-term, but not long-term partners. *Personality and Individual Differences, 50*, 542–546.

Burriss, R. P., Welling, L. L. M., & Puts, D. A. (2011b). Mate-preference drives mate-choice: Men's self-rated masculinity predicts their female partner's preference for masculinity. *Personality and Individual Differences, 51*, 1023–1027.

Buss, D. M. (1989). Sex differences in human mate preferences: Evolutionary hypotheses tested in 37 cultures. *Behavioral and Brain Sciences, 12*, 1–49.

Buss, D. M. (2000). *The dangerous passion: Why jealousy is as necessary as love and sex.* New York: The Free Press.

Buss, D. M. (2008). *Evolutionary psychology. The new science of the mind* (3rd ed.). Boston: Allyn and Bacon.

Buss, D. M., Abbott, M., Angleitner, A., Asherian, A., Biaggio, A., Blanco-Villasenor, A., et al. (1990). International preferences in selecting mates: A study of 37 cultures. *Journal of Cross-Cultural Psychology, 21*, 5–47.

Buss, D. M., & Barnes, M. L. (1986). Preferences in human mate selection. *Journal of Personality and Social Psychology, 50*, 559–570.

Buss, D. M., & Haselton, M. G. (2005). The evolution of jealousy. *Trends in Cognitive Sciences, 9*, 506–507.

Buss, D. M., & Schmitt, D. P. (1993). Sexual strategies theory: An evolutionary perspective on human mating. *Psychological Review, 100*, 204–232.

Buss, D. M., & Schmitt, D. P. (2011). Evolutionary psychology and feminism. *Sex Roles, 64*, 768–787.

Buss, D. M., & Shackelford, T. K. (1997). From vigilance to violence: Mate retention tactics in married couples. *Journal of Personality and Social Psychology, 72*, 346–361.

Buss, D. M., & Shackelford, T. K. (2008). Attractive women want it all: Good genes, economic investment, parenting proclivities, and emotional commitment. *Evolutionary Psychology, 6*, 134–146.

Buss, D. M., Shackelford, T. K., Kirkpatrick, L. A., & Larsen, R. J. (2001). A half century of mate preferences: The cultural evolution of values. *Journal of Marriage and Family, 63*, 491–503.

Buunk, A. P., Dijkstra, P., Kenrick, D. T., & Warntjes, A. (2001). Age preferences for mates as related to gender, own age, and involvement level. *Evolution and Human Behavior, 22*, 241–250.

Buunk, B. P., Dijkstra, P., Fetchenhauer, D., & Kenrick, D. T. (2002). Age and gender differences in mate selection criteria for various involvement levels. *Personal Relationships, 9*, 271–278.

Campbell, A. (2008). The morning after the night before: Affective reactions to one-night stands among mated and unmated women and men. *Human Nature, 19*, 157–173.

Carroll, J. (2005). Literature and evolutionary psychology. In D. M. Buss (Ed.), *The handbook of evolutionary psychology* (pp. 931–952). New York: Wiley.

Carroll, J. L., Volk, K. D., & Hyde, J. S. (1985). Differences between males and females in motives for engaging in sexual intercourse. *Archives of Sexual Behavior, 14*, 131–139.

Cashdan, E. (1996). Women's mating strategies. *Evolutionary Anthropology, 5*, 134–143.

Cashdan, E. (2008). Waist-to-hip ratio across cultures: Trade-offs between androgen- and estrogen-dependent traits. *Current Anthropology, 49*, 1099–1107.

Castro, F. N., & Lopes, F. A. (2011). Romantic preferences in Brazilian undergraduate students. *Journal of Sex Research, 48*, 479–485.

Chu, S., Farr, D., Muñoz, L. C., & Lycett, J. E. (2011). Interpersonal trust and market value moderates the bias in women's preferences away from attractive high-status men. *Personality and Individual Differences, 51*, 143–147.

Clark, R. D. (1990). The impact of AIDS on gender differences in willingness to engage in casual sex. *Journal of Applied Social Psychology, 20*, 771–782.

Clark, R. D., & Hatfield, E. (1989). Gender differences in receptivity to sexual offers. *Journal of Psychology and Human Sexuality, 2*, 39–55.

Cohen, J. (1988). *Statistical power analysis for the behavioral sciences* (2nd ed.). Hillsdale, NJ: Erlbaum.

Confer, J. C., Perilloux, C., & Buss, D. M. (2010). More than just a pretty face: Men's priority shifts toward bodily attractiveness in short-term versus long-term mating contexts. *Evolution and Human Behavior, 31* (2205), 348–353.

Conley, T. D. (2011). Perceived proposer personality characteristics and gender differences in acceptance of casual sex offers. *Journal of Personality and Social Psychology, 100*, 309–329.

Cronk, L., & Dunham, D. (2007). Amounts spent on engagement rings reflect aspects of male and female mate quality. *Human Nature, 18*, 329–333.

Cunningham, M., Barbee, A. P., & Pike, C. L. (1990). What do women want? Facialmetric assessment of multiple motives in the perception of male facial physical attractiveness. *Journal of Personality and Social Psychology, 59*, 61–72. 1991-01192-00110.1037.

Cunningham, M. R., Roberts, R., Barbee, A. P., Druen, P. B., & Wu, C. (1995). Their ideas of attractiveness are, on the whole, the same as ours: Consistency and variability in the cross-cultural perception of female attractiveness. *Journal of Personality and Social Psychology, 68*, 261–279.

Dahl, D. W., Sengupta, J., & Vohs, K. D. (2009). Sex in advertising: Gender differences and the role of relationship commitment. *Journal of Consumer Research, 36*(2), 215–231.

Davidson, J. K. (1985). The utilization of sexual fantasies by sexually experienced university students. *Journal of American College Health, 34,* 24–32.

Davies, A. P. C., Shackelford, T. K., & Hass, R. G. (2007). When a 'poach' is not a poach: Re-defining human mate poaching and reestimating its frequency. *Archives of Sexual Behavior, 36,* 702–716.

Davies, A. P. C., Shackelford, T. K., & Hass, R. G. (2010). Sex differences in perceptions of benefits and costs of mate poaching. *Personality and Individual Differences, 49,* 441–445.

de Graaf, H., & Sandfort, T. G. M. (2004). Gender differences in affective responses to sexual rejection. *Archives of Sexual Behavior, 33,* 395–403.

DeBruine, L. M., Jones, B. C., Frederick, D. A., Haselton, M. G., Penton-Voak, I. S., & Perrett, D. I. (2010). Evidence for menstrual cycle shifts in women's preferences for masculinity: A response to Harris (in press) "Menstrual Cycle and Facial Preferences Reconsidered". *Evolutionary Psychology, 8,* 768–775.

DeBruine, L. M., Jones, B. C., Tybur, J. M., Lieberman, D., & Griskevicius, V. (2010). Women's preferences for masculinity in male faces are predicted by pathogen disgust, but not by moral or sexual disgust. *Evolution and Human Behavior, 31,* 69–74.

De Jong, M. G., Pieters, R., & Stremersch, S. (2012). Analysis of sensitive questions across cultures: An application of multigroup item randomized response theory to sexual attitudes and behavior. *Journal of Personality and Social Psychology, 103*(3), 543.

DelPriore, D. J., Hill, S. E., & Buss, D. M. (2012). Envy: Functional specificity and sex-differentiated design features. *Personality and Individual Differences, 53*(3), 317–322. http://dx.doi.org/10.1016/j.paid.2012.03.029.

Druckerman, P. (2007). *Lust in translation: The rules of infidelity from Tokyo to Tennessee.* New York: Penguin Press.

Durante, K. M., Griskevicius, V., Simpson, J. A., Cantú, S. M., & Li, N. P. (2012). Ovulation leads women to perceive sexy cads as good dads. *Journal of Personality and Social Psychology, 103,* 292–305.

Durante, K. M., Li, N. P., & Haselton, M. G. (2008). Changes in women's choice of dress across the ovulatory cycle: Naturalistic and laboratory task-based evidence. *Personality and Social Psychology Bulletin, 34,* 1451–1460.

Eagly, A. H., & Wood, W. (1999). The origins of sex differences in human behavior: Evolved dispositions versus social roles. *American Psychologist, 54,* 408–423.

Eastwick, P. W., & Finkel, E. J. (2008). Sex differences in mate preferences revisited: Do people know what they initially desire in a romantic partner? *Journal of Personality and Social Psychology, 94,* 245–264.

Eastwick, P. W., Luchies, L. B., Finkel, E. J., & Hunt, L. L. (2013, April 15). The predictive validity of ideal partner preferences: A review and meta-analysis.

Psychological Bulletin. Advance online publication. doi:10.1037/a0032432.

Elder, G. (1969). Appearance and education in marriage mobility. *American Sociological Review, 34,* 519–533.

Ellis, B. J. (1992). The evolution of sexual attraction: Evaluative mechanisms in women. In J. H. Barkow, L. Cosmides, & J. Tooby (Eds.), *The adapted mind* (pp. 267–288). New York: Oxford University Press.

Ellis, B. J., & Symons, D. (1990). Sex differences in sexual fantasy: An evolutionary psychological approach. *Journal of Sex Research, 27,* 527–556.

Etcoff, N. (1999). *Survival of the prettiest: The science of beauty.* New York: Doubleday.

Evans, K., & Brase, G. L. (2007). Assessing sex differences and similarities in mate preferences: Above and beyond demand characteristics. *Journal of Social and Personal Relationships, 24,* 781–791.

Feinberg, D. R., Jones, B. C., Law Smith, M. J., Moore, F. R., DeBruine, L. M., Cornwell, R. E., et al. (2006). Menstrual cycle, trait estrogen level, and masculinity preferences in the human voice. *Hormones and Behavior, 49,* 215–222.

Feingold, A. (1990). Gender differences in effects of physical attractiveness on romantic attraction: A comparison across five research paradigms. *Journal of Personality and Social Psychology, 59,* 981–993.

Feingold, A. (1992). Gender differences in mate selection preferences: A test of the parental investment model. *Psychological Bulletin, 112,* 125–139.

Fenigstein, A., & Preston, M. (2007). The desired number of sexual partners as a function of gender, sexual risks, and the meaning of 'ideal'. *Journal of Sex Research, 44,* 89–95.

Fieder, M., & Huber, S. (2007). The effects of sex and childlessness on the association between status and reproductive output in modern society. *Evolution and Human Behavior, 28,* 392–398.

Fink, B., Neave, N., Brewer, G., & Pawlowski, B. (2007). Variable preferences for sexual dimorphism in stature (SDS): Further evidence for an adjustment in relation to own height. *Personality and Individual Differences, 43,* 2249–2257.

Fischer, J., Semple, S., Fickenscher, G., Jurgens, R., Kruse, E., Heistermann, M., et al. (2011). Do women's voices provide cues of the likelihood of ovulation? The importance of sampling regime. *PLoS One, 6,* e24490. doi:10.1371/journal.pone.0024490.

Fisher, H. E. (1998). Lust, attraction, and attachment in mammalian reproduction. *Human Nature, 9,* 23–52.

Fisher, M., & Cox, A. (2009). The influence of male facial attractiveness on women's receptivity. *The Journal of Social, Evolutionary, and Cultural Psychology, 3,* 49–61.

Fisman, R., Iyengar, S. S., Kamenica, E., & Simonson, I. (2006). Gender differences in mate selection: Evidence from a speed dating experiment. *Quarterly Journal of Economics, 121,* 673–697.

Flowe, H. D., Swords, E., & Rockey, J. C. (2012). Women's behavioural engagement with a masculine male heightens during the fertile window: Evidence for the cycle shift hypothesis. *Evolution and Human Behavior, 33*, 285–290.

Ford, C. S., & Beach, F. A. (1951). *Patterns of sexual behavior*. New York: Harper & Row.

Frederick, D. A., & Haselton, M. G. (2007). Why is muscularity sexy? Tests of the fitness indicator hypothesis. *Personality and Social Psychology Bulletin, 33*, 1167–1183.

Gallup, A. C., White, D. D., & Gallup, G. G., Jr. (2007). Handgrip strength predicts sexual behavior, body morphology, and aggression in male college students. *Evolution and Human Behavior, 28*, 423–429.

Galperin, A., Haselton, M. G., Frederick, D. A., von Hippel, W., Poore, J. C., Buss, D. M., et al. (2013). Sexual regret: Evidence for evolved sex differences. *Archives of Sexual Behavior, 42*(7), 1145–1161.

Gangestad, S. W., Haselton, M. G., & Buss, D. M. (2006). Evolutionary foundations of cultural variation: Evoked culture and mate preferences. *Psychological Inquiry, 17*, 75–95.

Gangestad, S. W., & Simpson, J. A. (1990). Toward an evolutionary history of female sociosexual variation. *Journal of Personality, 58*(69), 96.

Gangestad, S. W., & Simpson, J. A. (2000). The evolution of human mating: Trade-offs and strategic pluralism. *The Behavioral and Brain Sciences, 23*, 573–644.

Gangestad, S. W., Simpson, J. A., Cousins, A. J., Garver-Apgar, C. E., & Christensen, P. N. (2004). Women's preferences for male behavioral displays change across the menstrual cycle. *Psychological Science, 15*, 203–207.

Gangestad, S. W., & Thornhill, R. (1997). The evolutionary psychology of extrapair sex: The role of fluctuating asymmetry. *Evolution and Human Behavior, 18*, 69–88.

Gangestad, S. W., & Thornhill, R. (1998). Menstrual cycle variation in women's preferences for the scent of symmetrical men. *Proceedings of the Royal Society of London B, 265*, 927–933.

Gangestad, S. W., Thornhill, R., & Garver, C. E. (2002). Changes in women's sexual interests and their partners' mate retention tactics across the menstrual cycle: Evidence for shifting conflicts of interest. *Proceedings of the Royal Society of London B, 269*, 975–982.

Gangestad, S. W., Thornhill, R., & Garver-Apgar, C. E. (2005). Women's sexual interests across the ovulatory cycle depend on primary partner developmental instability. *Proceedings of the Royal Society of London B, 272*, 2023–2027.

Gangestad, S. W., Thornhill, R., & Garver-Apgar, C. E. (2010). Men's facial masculinity predicts changes in their female partners' sexual interests across the cycle, whereas men's intelligence does not. *Evolution and Human Behavior, 31*, 412–424.

Garcia, J. R., MacKillop, J., Aller, E. L., Merriwether, A. M., Wilson, D. S., & Lum, J. K. (2010). Associations between dopamine D4 receptor gene variation with both infidelity and sexual promiscuity. *PLoS One, 5*, e14162. doi:10.1371/journal.pone.0014162.

Garver-Apgar, C. E., Gangestad, S. W., & Thornhill, R. (2008). Hormonal correlates of women's mid-cycle preference for the scent of symmetry. *Evolution and Human Behavior, 29*, 223–232.

General Social Survey. (2013). 1972–2010. Retrieved March 4, 2013, from http://www3.norc.org/gss+website/

Giotakos, O. (2004). Gender differences in the perceptions for the ideal sex partner. *Sexual and Relationship Therapy, 19*, 373–378.

Gladue, B. A., & Delaney, H. J. (1990). Gender differences in perception of attractiveness of men and women in bars. *Personality and Social Psychology Bulletin, 16*, 378–391.

Glass, S. P., & Wright, T. L. (1985). Sex differences in type of extramarital involvement and marital dissatisfaction. *Sex Roles, 12*, 1101–1120.

Gottschall, J. B., Berkey, R. C., Mitchell, D. C., Fleischner, M., Glotzbecker, M., Kernan, K., et al. (2003). Patterns of characterization in folktales across geographic regions and levels of cultural complexity: Literature as a neglected source of quantitative data. *Human Nature, 14*(3), 365–382.

Grammer, K., Renninger, L., & Fischer, B. (2004). Disco clothing, female sexual motivation, and relationship status: Is she dressed to impress? *Journal of Sex Research, 41*, 66–74.

Graziano, W. G., Jensen-Campbell, L. A., Todd, M., & Finch, J. F. (1997). Interpersonal attraction from an evolutionary perspective: Women's reactions to dominant and prosocial men. In J. A. Simpson & D. T. Kenrick (Eds.), *Evolutionary social psychology* (pp. 141–167). Mahwah, NJ: Lawrence Erlbaum.

Gregerson, E. (1982). *Sexual practices: The story of human sexuality*. London: Mitchell Beazley.

Greiling, H., & Buss, D. M. (2000). Women's sexual strategies: The hidden dimension of short-term mating. *Personality and Individual Differences, 28*, 929–963.

Greitemeyer, T. (2005). Receptivity to sexual offers as a function of sex, socioeconomic status, physical attractiveness, and intimacy of the offer. *Personal Relationships, 12*, 373–386.

Griskevicius, V., Tybur, J. M., Delton, A. W., & Robertson, T. E. (2011). The influence of mortality and socioeconomic status on risk and delayed rewards: A life history theory approach. *Journal of Personality and Social Psychology, 100*, 1015–1026.

Guéguen, N. (2009). Menstrual cycle phases and female receptivity to a courtship solicitation: An evaluation in a nightclub. *Evolution and Human Behavior, 30*, 351–355.

Guéguen, N. (2011). Gender differences in receptivity to sexual offers: A field study testing the impact of the attractiveness of the solicitor. *Archives of Sexual Behavior, 40*, 915–919. doi:10.1007/s10508-011-9750-4.

Guéguen, N., & Lamy, L. (2012). Men's social status and attractiveness: Women's receptivity to men's date requests. *Swiss Journal of Psychology, 71*, 157–160.

Gutierres, S. E., Kenrick, D. T., & Partch, J. J. (1999). Beauty, dominance, and the mating game: Contrast effects in self-assessment reflect gender differences in mate selection. *Personality and Social Psychology Bulletin, 25*, 1126–1134.

Guttentag, M., & Secord, P. (1983). *Too many women?* Beverly Hills, CA: Sage.

Ha, T., Overbeek, G. E., & Engels, R. C. M. E. (2010). Effects of attractiveness and social status on dating desire in heterosexual adolescents: An experimental study. *Archives of Sexual Behavior, 39*, 1063–1071.

Hald, G. M. (2006). Gender differences in pornography consumption among young heterosexual Danish adults. *Archives of Sexual Behavior, 35*, 577–585.

Hald, G. M., & Høgh-Olesen, H. (2010). Receptivity to sexual invitations from strangers of the opposite gender. *Evolution and Human Behavior, 31*, 453–458.

Hansen, G. L. (1987). Extradyadic relations during courtship. *The Journal of Sex Research, 22*(3), 382–390.

Harper, B. (2000). Beauty, stature and the labour market: A British cohort study. *Oxford Bulletin of Economics and Statistics, 62*, 771–800.

Haselton, M. G., & Buss, D. M. (2000). Error management theory: A new perspective on biases in cross-sex mind reading. *Journal of Personality and Social Psychology, 78*, 81–91.

Haselton, M. G., & Gildersleeve, K. (2011). Can men detect ovulation? *Current Directions in Psychological Science, 20*, 87–92.

Haselton, M. G., & Miller, G. F. (2006). Women's fertility across the cycle increases the short-term attractiveness of creative intelligence. *Human Nature, 17*, 50–73.

Haselton, M. G., Mortezaie, M., Pillsworth, E. G., Bleske-Rechek, A., & Frederick, D. A. (2007). Ovulatory shifts in human female ornamentation: Near ovulation, women dress to impress. *Hormones and Behavior, 51*, 40–45.

Hendrick, S., Hendrick, C., Slapion-Foote, M. J., & Foote, F. H. (1985). Gender differences in sexual attitudes. *Journal of Personality and Social Psychology, 48*, 1630–1642.

Hendrie, C. A., Mannion, H. D., & Godfrey, G. K. (2009). Evidence to suggest that nightclubs function as human sexual display grounds. *Behaviour, 146*, 1331–1348.

Henningsen, D. D., Henningsen, M. L. M., & Valde, K. S. (2006). Gender differences in perceptions of women's sexual interest during cross-sex interactions: An application and extension of cognitive valence theory. *Sex Roles, 54*, 821–829.

Herold, E. S., & Mewhinney, D. M. K. (1993). Gender differences in casual sex and AIDS prevention: A survey of dating bars. *Journal of Sex Research, 30*, 36–42.

Hessellund, H. (1976). Masturbation and sexual fantasies in married couples. *Archives of Sexual Behavior, 5*, 133–147.

Hill, K., & Hurtado, A. M. (1996). *Ache life history: The ecology and demography of a foraging people*. Hawthorne, NY: Aldine de Gruyter.

Hitsch, G. J., Hortaçsu, A., & Ariely, D. (2010a). Matching and sorting in online dating. *American Economic Review, 100*, 130–163.

Hitsch, G. J., Hortaçsu, A., & Ariely, D. (2010b). *What makes you click? Mate preferences in online dating.* Retrieved February 17, 2012, from http://home. uchicago.edu/~ghitsch/Hitsch-Research/Guenter_Hitsch_files/Mate-Preferences.pdf

Howell, E. C., Etchells, P. J., & Penton-Voak, I. S. (2012). The sexual overperception bias is associated with sociosexuality. *Personality and Individual Differences, 53*, 1012–1016.

Hughes, S. M., Farley, S. D., & Rhodes, B. C. (2010). Vocal and physiological changes in response to the physical attractiveness of conversational partners. *Journal of Nonverbal Behavior, 34*, 155–167.

Hughes, S. M., & Gallup, G. G., Jr. (2003). Sex differences in morphological predictors of sexual behavior: Shoulder to hip and waist to hip ratios. *Evolution and Human Behavior, 24*, 173–178.

Hughes, S. M., Harrison, M. A., & Gallup, G. G., Jr. (2004). Sex differences in mating strategies: Mate guarding, infidelity and multiple concurrent sex partners. *Sexualities, Evolution & Gender, 6*, 3–13.

Hunt, M. (1974). *Sexual behavior in the 1970s*. Chicago: Playboy Press.

Hurtado, A. M., & Hill, K. (1992). Paternal effect on offspring survivorship among Ache and Hiwi hunter-gatherers: Implications for modeling pair-bond stability. In B. S. Hewlett (Ed.), *Father–child relations: Cultural and biosocial contexts* (pp. 31–55). New York: Aldine De Gruyter.

Hyde, J. S. (2005). The gender similarities hypothesis. *American Psychologist, 60*, 581–592.

Johnston, V. S. (2006). Mate choice decisions: The role of facial beauty. *Trends in Cognitive Sciences, 10*, 9–13.

Johnston, V. S., & Franklin, M. (1993). Is beauty in the eye of the beholder? *Ethology and Sociobiology, 14*, 183–199.

Johnston, V. S., Hagel, R., Franklin, M., Fink, B., & Grammer, K. (2001). Male facial attractiveness: Evidence for hormone-mediated adaptive design. *Evolution and Human Behavior, 22*, 251–267.

Jokela, M., Rotkirch, A., Rickard, I. J., Pettay, J., & Lummaa, V. (2010). Serial monogamy increases reproductive success in men but not in women. *Behavioral Ecology, 21*, 906–912.

Jonason, P. K., Li, N. P., & Madson, L. (2012). It's not all about the Benjamins: Understanding preferences for mates with resources. *Personality and Individual Differences, 52*, 306–310.

Jonason, P. K., Li, N. P., Webster, G. D., & Schmitt, D. P. (2009). The dark triad: Facilitating a short-term mating strategy in men. *European Journal of Personality, 23*, 5–18.

Jones, D. (1995). Sexual selection, physical attractiveness, and facial neoteny: Cross-cultural evidence and implications. *Current Anthropology, 36*, 723–748.

Jones, J. C., & Barlow, D. H. (1990). Self-reported frequency of sexual urges, fantasies and masturbatory fantasies in heterosexual males and females. *Archives of Sexual Behavior, 19*, 269–279.

Kanazawa, S., & Still, M. C. (2000). Teaching may be hazardous to your marriage. *Evolution and Human Behavior, 21*, 185–190.

Kandrik, M., & DeBruine, L. M. (2013). Self-rated attractiveness predicts preferences for opposite-sex faces, while self-rated sex-typicality predicts preferences for same-sex faces. *Journal of Evolutionary Psychology, 10*(4), 177–186.

Karremans, J. C., Frankenhuis, W. E., & Arons, S. (2010). Blind men prefer a low waist-to-hip ratio. *Evolution and Human Behavior, 31*, 182–186.

Kennair, L. E. O., Schmitt, D. P., Fjeldavli, Y. L., & Harlem, S. K. (2009). Sex differences in sexual desires and attitudes in Norwegian samples. *Interpersona, 3*, 1–32.

Kenrick, D. T., Gabrielidis, C., Keefe, R. C., & Cornelius, J. S. (1996). Adolescents' age preferences for dating partners: Support for an evolutionary model of life-history strategies. *Child Development, 67*, 1499–1511.

Kenrick, D. T., Groth, G. E., Trost, M. R., & Sadalla, E. K. (1993). Integrating evolutionary and social exchange perspectives on relationships: Effects of gender, self-appraisal, and involvement level on mate selection criteria. *Journal of Personality and Social Psychology, 64*, 951–969.

Kenrick, D. T., & Keefe, R. C. (1992). Age preferences in mates reflect sex differences in human reproductive strategies. *Behavioral and Brain Sciences, 15*, 75–133.

Kenrick, D. T., Neuberg, S. L., Zierk, K. L., & Krones, J. M. (1994). Evolution and social cognition: Contrast effects as a function of sex, dominance, and physical attractiveness. *Personality and Social Psychology Bulletin, 20*, 210–217.

Kenrick, D. T., Sadalla, E. K., Groth, G., & Trost, M. R. (1990). Evolution, traits, and the stages of human courtship: Qualifying the parental investment model. *Journal of Personality, 58*, 97–116.

Kinsey, A. C., Pomeroy, W. B., & Martin, C. E. (1948). *Sexual behavior in the human male*. Philadelphia: Saunders.

Kinsey, A. C., Pomeroy, W. B., Martin, C. E., & Gebhard, P. H. (1953). *Sexual behavior in the human female*. Philadelphia: Saunders.

Koukounas, E., & McCabe, M. (1997). Sexual and emotional variables influencing sexual response to erotica. *Behaviour Research and Therapy, 35*, 221–230.

Kruger, D. J., & Fitzgerald, C. J. (2011). Reproductive strategies and relationship preferences associated with prestigious and dominant men. *Personality and Individual Differences, 50*, 365–369.

Kurzban, R., & Weeden, J. (2005). HurryDate: Mate preferences in action. *Evolution and Human Behavior, 26*, 227–244.

Kurzban, R., & Weeden, J. (2007). Do advertised preferences predict the behavior of speed daters? *Personal Relationships, 14*, 623–632.

Laeng, B., & Falkenberg, L. (2007). Women's pupillary responses to sexually significant others during the hormonal cycle. *Hormones and Behavior, 52*, 520–530.

Landolt, M. A., Lalumiere, M. L., & Quinsey, V. L. (1995). Sex differences in intra-sex variations in human mating tactics: An evolutionary approach. *Ethology and Sociobiology, 16*, 3–23.

Langlois, J. H., Kalakanis, L., Rubenstein, A. J., Larson, A., Hallam, M., & Smoot, M. (2000). Maxims or myths of beauty? A meta-analytic and theoretical review. *Psychological Bulletin, 126*, 390–423.

Larson, C. M., Pillsworth, E. G., & Haselton, M. G. (2012). Ovulatory shifts in women's attractions to primary partners and other men: Further evidence of the importance of primary partner sexual attractiveness. *PLoS One, 7*, e44456. doi:10.1371/journal.pone.0044456.

Laumann, E. O., Gagnon, J. H., Michael, R. T., & Michaels, S. (1994). *The social organization of sexuality*. Chicago: University of Chicago Press.

Law Smith, M. J., Deady, D. K., Moore, F. R., Jones, B. C., Cornwell, R. E., Stirrat, M., et al. (2012). Maternal tendencies in women are associated with estrogen levels and facial femininity. *Hormones and Behavior, 61*, 12–16.

Lawson, A., & Samson, C. (1988). Age, gender and adultery. *The British Journal of Sociology, 39*, 409–440.

Lee, L., Loewenstein, G., Ariely, D., Hong, J., & Young, J. (2008). If I'm not hot, are you hot or not? Physical-attractiveness evaluations and dating preferences as a function of one's own attractiveness. *Psychological Science, 19*, 669–677.

Leitenberg, H., & Henning, K. (1995). Sexual fantasy. *Psychological Bulletin, 117*, 469–496.

Lenton, A. P., & Francesconi, M. (2010). How humans cognitively manage an abundance of mate options. *Psychological Science, 21*, 528–533.

Li, N. (2007). Mate preference necessities in long- and short-term mating: People prioritize in themselves what their mates prioritize in them. *Acta Psychologica Sinica, 39*, 528–535.

Li, N. P., Bailey, J. M., Kenrick, D. T., & Linsenmeier, J. A. W. (2002). The necessities and luxuries of mate preferences: Testing the tradeoffs. *Journal of Personality and Social Psychology, 82*(6), 947–955.

Li, N. P., & Kenrick, D. T. (2006). Sex similarities and differences in preferences for short-term mates: What, whether, and why. *Journal of Personality and Social Psychology, 90*, 468–489.

Li, N. P., Valentine, K. A., & Patel, L. (2011). Mate preferences in the US and Singapore: A cross-cultural test of the mate preference priority model. *Personality and Individual Differences, 50*, 291–294.

Li, N. P., Yong, J. C., Tov, W., Sng, O., Fletcher, G. J. O., Valentine, K. A., et al. (2013). Mate preferences do predict attraction and choices in the early stages of mate selection. *Journal of Personality and Social Psychology, 105*(5), 757–776.

Lichter, D. T., Anderson, R. N., & Hayward, M. D. (1995). Marriage markets and marital choice. *Journal of Family Issues, 16*, 412–431.

Lipowicz, A. (2003). Effect of husbands' education on fatness of wives. *American Journal of Human Biology, 15*(1), 1–7.

Lippa, R. A. (2007). The preferred traits of mates in a cross-national study of heterosexual and homosexual men and women: An examination of biological and cultural influences. *Archives of Sexual Behavior, 36*(2), 193–208.

Lippa, R. A. (2009). Sex differences in sex drive, sociosexuality, and height across 53 nations: Testing evolutionary and social structural theories. *Archives of Sexual Behavior, 38*, 631–651.

Little, A. C., Apicella, C. L., & Marlowe, F. W. (2007). Preferences for symmetry in human faces in two cultures: Data from the UK and the Hadza, and isolated group of hunter-gatherers. *Proceedings of the Royal Society of London B, 274*, 3113–3117.

Little, A. C., Jones, B. C., & Burriss, R. P. (2007). Preferences for masculinity in male bodies change across the menstrual cycle. *Hormones and Behavior, 52*, 633–639.

Little, A. C., Jones, B. C., Penton-Voak, I. S., Burt, D. M., & Perrett, D. I. (2002). Partnership status and the temporal context of relationships influence human female preferences for sexual dimorphism in male face shape. *Proceedings of the Royal Society of London B, 269*, 1095–1103.

Lukaszewski, A. W., & Roney, J. R. (2009). Estimated hormones predict women's mate preferences for dominant personality traits. *Personality and Individual Differences, 47*, 191–196.

Lukaszewski, A. W., & Roney, J. R. (2010). Kind toward whom? Mate preferences for personality traits are target specific. *Evolution and Human Behavior, 31*, 29–38.

Lynn, M. (2009). Determinants and consequences of female attractiveness and sexiness: Realistic tests with restaurant waitresses. *Archives of Sexual Behavior, 38*, 737–745.

Macrae, C. N., Alnwick, K. A., Milne, A. B., & Schloerscheidt, A. M. (2002). Person perception across the menstrual cycle: Hormonal influences on social-cognitive functioning. *Psychological Science, 13*(6), 532–536.

Malamuth, N. M. (1996). Sexually explicit media, gender differences, and evolutionary theory. *The Journal of Communication, 46*, 8–31.

Maner, J. K., Kenrick, D. T., Becker, D. V., Delton, A. W., Hofer, B., Wilbur, C. J., et al. (2003). Sexually selective cognition: Beauty captures the mind of the beholder. *Journal of Personality and Social Psychology, 85*, 1107–1120.

Markey, P., & Markey, C. (2011). Changes in women's interpersonal styles across the menstrual cycle. *Journal of Research in Personality, 45*, 493–499.

Marlowe, F. W. (2004). Mate preferences among Hadza huntergatherers. *Human Nature, 15*, 365–376.

Maticka-Tyndale, E., Herold, E. S., & Mewhinney, D. (1998). Casual sex on spring break: Intentions and behaviors of Canadian students. *Journal of Sex Research, 35*, 254–264.

McBurney, D. H., Zapp, D. J., & Streeter, S. A. (2005). Preferred number of sexual partners: Tails of distributions and tales of mating systems. *Evolution and Human Behavior, 26*, 271–278.

McDonald, M. M., Asher, B. D., Kerr, N. L., & Navarrete, C. D. (2011). Fertility and intergroup bias in racial and minimal-group contexts evidence for shared architecture. *Psychological Science, 22*(7), 860–865.

McNulty, J. K., Neff, L. A., & Karney, B. R. (2008). Beyond initial attraction: Physical attractiveness in newlywed marriage. *Journal of Family Psychology, 22*, 135–143.

Mealey, L. (1985). The relationship between social status and biological success: A case study of the Mormon religious hierarchy. *Ethology and Sociobiology, 6*, 249–257.

Meltzer, A. L., McNulty, J. K., Novak, S. A., Butler, E. A., & Karney, B. R. (2011). Marriages are more satisfying when wives are thinner than their husbands. *Social Psychological and Personality Science, 2*, 416–424.

Millar, M. (2013). Menstrual cycle changes in mate preferences for cues associated with genetic quality: The moderating role of mate value. *Evolutionary Psychology, 11*(1), 18–35.

Millar, M. G., & Ostlund, N. M. (2006). The effects of a parenting prime on sex differences in mate selection criteria. *Personality and Social Psychology Bulletin, 32*, 1459–1468.

Miller, S. L., & Maner, J. K. (2010). Scent of a woman: Men's testosterone responses to olfactory ovulation cues. *Psychological Science, 21*, 276–283.

Miller, S. L., & Maner, J. K. (2011). Ovulation as a male mating prime: Subtle signs of women's fertility influence men's mating cognition and behavior. *Journal of Personality and Social Psychology, 100*, 295–308.

Miller, G., Tybur, J., & Jordan, B. D. (2007). Ovulatory cycle effects on tip earnings by lap dancers. *Evolution and Human Behavior, 28*, 375–381.

Mueller, U., & Mazur, A. (1998). Facial dominance in Homo sapiens as honest signaling of male quality. *Behavioral Ecology, 8*, 569–579.

Murnen, S. K., & Stockton, M. (1997). Gender and self-reported sexual arousal in response to sexual stimuli: A meta-analytic review. *Sex Roles, 37*, 135–153.

Nettle, D. (2002). Height and reproductive success in a cohort of British men. *Human Nature, 13*, 473–491.

Nettle, D., & Pollet, T. V. (2008). Natural selection on male wealth in humans. *American Naturalist, 172*, 658–666.

O'Connor, J. J. M., Feinberg, D. R., Fraccaro, P. J., Borak, D. J., Tigue, C. C., Re, D. E., et al. (2012). Female preferences for male vocal and facial masculinity in videos. *Ethology, 118*, 321–330.

Oberzaucher, E., Katina, S. T., Schmehl, S. F., Holzleitner, I. J., Mehu-Blantar, I., & Grammer, K. (2012). The myth of hidden ovulation. Shape and texture changes in the face during the menstrual cycle. *Journal of Evolutionary Psychology, 10*(4), 163–175. doi:10.1556/JEP.10.2012.4.1.

Ogas, O., & Gaddam, S. (2011). *A billion wicked thoughts: What the world's largest experiment reveals about human desire*. New York: Dutton/Penguin Books.

Oliver, M. B., & Hyde, J. S. (1993). Gender differences in sexuality: A meta-analysis. *Psychological Bulletin, 114*, 29–51.

Overbeek, G., Nelemans, S. A., Karremans, J., & Engels, R. C. (2013). The malleability of mate selection in speed-dating events. *Archives of Sexual Behavior, 42*(7), 1163–1171.

Parker, J., & Burkley, M. (2009). Who's chasing whom? The impact of gender and relationship status on mate poaching. *Journal of Experimental Social Psychology, 45*, 1016–1019.

Paul, E. L., & Hayes, K. A. (2002). The causalities of 'casual' sex: A qualitative exploration of the phenomenology of college students' hookups. *Journal of Social and Personal Relationships, 19*, 639–661.

Pawlowski, B., & Dunbar, R. I. M. (1999). Impact of market value on human mate choice decisions. *Proceedings of the Royal Society of London B, 266*, 281–285.

Pawlowski, B., Dunbar, R. I. M., & Lipowicz, A. (2000). Tall men have more reproductive success. *Nature, 403*, 156.

Pawlowski, B., & Jasienska, G. (2005). Women's preferences for sexual dimorphism in height depend on menstrual cycle phase and expected duration of relationship. *Biological Psychology, 70*, 38–43.

Pawlowski, B., & Jasienska, G. (2008). Women's body morphology and preferences for sexual partners' characteristics. *Evolution and Human Behavior, 29*, 19–25.

Pawlowski, B., & Slawomir, K. (2002). The impact of traits offered in personal advertisements on response rates. *Evolution and Human Behavior, 23*, 139–149.

Penton-Voak, I. S., Little, A. C., Jones, B. C., Burt, D. M., Tiddeman, B. P., & Perrett, D. I. (2003). Female condition influences preferences for sexual dimorphism in faces of male humans (Homo sapiens). *Journal of Comparative Psychology, 117*, 264–271.

Perilloux, C., Easton, J. A., & Buss, D. M. (2012). The misperception of sexual interest. *Psychological Science, 23*, 146–151.

Perrett, D. I., Lee, K. J., Penton-Voak, I. S., Rowland, D., Yoshikawa, S., Burt, D. M., et al. (1998). Effects of sexual dimorphism on facial attractiveness. *Nature, 394*, 884–887.

Perusse, D. (1994). Mate choice in modern societies: Testing evolutionary hypotheses with behavioral data. *Human Nature, 5*, 256–278.

Petersen, J. L., & Hyde, J. S. (2010). A meta-analytic review of research on gender differences in sexuality, 1993–2007. *Psychological Bulletin, 136*, 21–38.

Pettay, J. E., Helle, S., Jokela, J., & Lummaa, V. (2007). Wealth class-specific natural selection on female life-history traits in historical human populations. *PLoS One, 2*, e606.

Pflüger, L. S., Oberzaucher, E. K., Holzleitner, I. J., & Grammer, K. (2012). Cues to fertility: Perceived attractiveness and facial shape predict reproductive success. *Evolution and Human Behavior, 33*, 708–714.

Pierce, L., Dahl, M. S., & Nielsen, J. (2013). In sickness and in wealth: Psychological and sexual costs of income comparison in marriage. *Personality and Social Psychology Bulletin., 39*(3), 359–374.

Pillsworth, E. G. (2008). Mate preferences among the Shuar of Ecuador: Trait rankings and peer evaluations. *Evolution and Human Behavior, 29*, 256–267.

Pillsworth, E. G., & Haselton, M. G. (2006). Male sexual attractiveness predicts differential ovulatory shifts in female extra-pair attraction and male mate retention. *Evolution and Human Behavior, 27*, 247–258.

Pisanski, K., & Feinberg, D. R. (2013). Cross-cultural variation in mate preferences for averageness, symmetry, body size, and masculinity. *Cross-Cultural Research, 47*, 162–197.

Platek, S. M., & Singh, D. (2012). Optimal waist-to-hip ratios in women activate neural reward centers in men. *PLoS One, 5*, e9042.

Pollet, T. V., Pratt, S. E., Edwards, G., & Stulp, G. (2013). The golden years: Men from the Forbes 400 have much younger wives when remarrying than the general US population. *Letters on Evolutionary Behavioral Science, 4*, 5–8.

Provost, M. P., Kormos, C., Kosakoski, G., & Quinsey, V. L. (2006). Sociosexuality in women and preference for facial masculinization and somatotype in men. *Archives of Sexual Behavior, 35*, 305–312.

Provost, M. P., Troje, N. F., & Quinsey, V. L. (2008). Short-term mating strategies and attraction to masculinity in point-light walkers. *Evolution and Human Behavior, 29*, 65–69.

Purnine, D. M., Carey, M. P., Jorgensen, R. S., & Randall, S. (1994). Gender differences regarding preferences for specific heterosexual practices. *Journal of Sex & Marital Therapy, 20*, 271–287.

Puts, D. A. (2005). Mating context and menstrual phase affect women's preferences for male voice pitch. *Evolution and Human Behavior, 26*, 388–397.

Puts, D. A. (2006). Cyclic variation in women's preferences for masculine traits: Potential hormonal causes. *Human Nature, 17*, 114–127.

Puts, D. A. (2010). Beauty and the beast: Mechanisms of sexual selection in humans. *Evolution and Human Behavior, 31*, 157–175. doi:10.1016/j.evolhumbehav.2010.02.005.

Puts, D. A., Welling, L. L. M., Burriss, R. P., & Dawood, K. (2012). Men's masculinity and attractiveness predict their female partners' reported orgasm frequency and timing. *Evolution and Human Behavior, 33*(1), 1–9. doi:10.1016/j.evolhumbehav.2011.03.003.

Quist, M. C., Watkins, C. D., Smith, F. G., Little, A. C., DeBruine, L. M., & Jones, B. C. (2012).

Sociosexuality predicts women's preferences for symmetry in men's faces. *Archives of Sexual Behavior, 41*, 1415–1421.

Regan, P. C. (1998a). Minimum mate selection standards as a function of perceived mate value, relationship context, and gender. *Journal of Psychology and Human Sexuality, 10*, 53–73.

Regan, P. C. (1998b). What if you can't get what you want? Willingness to compromise ideal mate selection standards as a function of sex, mate value, and relationship context. *Personality and Social Psychology Bulletin, 24*, 1294–1303.

Regan, P. C., & Berscheid, E. (1997). Gender differences in characteristics desired in a potential sexual and marriage partner. *Journal of Psychology and Human Sexuality, 9*, 25–37.

Regan, P. C., & Dreyer, C. S. (1999). Lust? Love? Status? Young adults' motives for engaging in casual sex. *Journal of Psychology and Human Sexuality, 11*, 1–24.

Regan, P. C., Levin, L., Sprecher, S., Christopher, F. S., & Cate, R. (2000). Partner preferences: What characteristics do men and women desire in their short-term and long-term romantic partners? *Journal of Psychology and Human Sexuality, 12*, 1–21.

Regan, P. C., Medina, R., & Joshi, A. (2001). Partner preferences among homosexual men and women: What is desirable in a sex partner is not necessarily desirable in a romantic partner. *Social Behavior and Personality, 29*, 625–633.

Reiber, C., & Garcia, J. R. (2010). Hooking up: Gender differences, evolution, and pluralistic ignorance. *Evolutionary Psychology, 8*, 390–404.

Renninger, L. A., Wades, T. J., & Grammer, K. (2004). Getting that female glance: Patterns and consequences of male nonverbal behavior in courtship contexts. *Evolution and Human Behavior, 25*(6), 416–431.

Rhodes, G., Simmons, L. W., & Peters, M. (2005). Attractiveness and sexual behavior: Does attractiveness enhance mating success? *Evolution and Human Behavior, 26*, 186–201.

Roberts, S. C., Havlicek, J., Flegr, J., Hruskova, M., Little, A. C., Jones, B. C., et al. (2004). Female facial attractiveness increases during the fertile phase of the menstrual cycle. *Proceeding of the Royal Society of London B, 271*(Suppl. 5), S270–S272.

Röder, S., Brewer, G., & Fink, B. (2009). Menstrual cycle shifts in women's self-perception and motivation: A daily report method. *Personality and Individual Differences, 47*, 616–619.

Roese, N. J., Pennington, G. L., Coleman, J., Janicki, M., Li, N. P., & Kenrick, D. T. (2006). Sex differences in regret: All for love or some for lust? *Personality and Social Psychology Bulletin, 32*, 770–780.

Ronay, R., & von Hippel, W. (2010). The presence of an attractive woman elevates testosterone and physical risk taking in young men. *Social Psychological and Personality Science, 1*, 57–64.

Roney, J. R., Hanson, K. N., Durante, K. M., & Maestripieri, D. (2006). Reading men's faces: Women's mate attractiveness judgments track men's testosterone and interest in infants. *Proceedings of the Royal Society B: Biological Sciences, 273*(1598), 2169–2175.

Rule, N. O., Rosen, K. S., Slepian, M. L., & Ambady, N. (2011). Mating interest improves women's accuracy in judging male sexual orientation. *Psychological Science, 22*, 881–886.

Saad, G. (2008). Advertised waist-to-hip ratios of online female escorts: An evolutionary perspective. *The International Journal of e-Collaboration, 4*, 40–50.

Sacco, D. F., Jones, B. C., DeBruine, L. M., & Hugenberg, K. (2012). The roles of sociosexual orientation and relationship status in women's face preferences. *Personality and Individual Differences, 53*, 1044–1047.

Sadalla, E. K., Kenrick, D. T., & Vershure, B. (1987). Dominance and heterosexual attraction. *Journal of Personality and Social Psychology, 52*, 730–738.

Salmon, C., & Symons, D. (2001). *Warrior lovers: Erotic fiction, evolution, and female sexuality*. London: Weidenfeld & Nicolson.

Schaefer, K., Fink, B., Grammer, K., Mitteroecker, P., Gunz, P., & Bookstein, F. L. (2006). Female appearance: Facial and bodily attractiveness as shape. *Psychology Science, 48*, 187–204.

Scheib, J. E. (1994). Sperm donor selection and the psychology of female mate choice. *Ethology and Sociobiology, 15*, 113–129.

Scheib, J. E. (2001). Context-specific mate choice criteria: Women's trade-offs in the contexts of long-term and extra-pair mateships. *Personal Relationships, 8*, 371–389.

Schmitt, D. P. (2002). A meta-analysis of sex differences in romantic attraction: Do rating contexts affect tactic effectiveness judgments? *British Journal of Social Psychology, 41*, 387–402.

Schmitt, D. P. (2005a). Fundamentals of human mating strategies. In D. M. Buss (Ed.), *The evolutionary psychology handbook* (pp. 258–291). New York: Wiley.

Schmitt, D. P. (2005b). Is short-term mating the maladaptive result of insecure attachment? A test of competing evolutionary perspectives. *Personality and Social Psychology Bulletin, 31*, 747–768.

Schmitt, D. P. (2005c). Sociosexuality from Argentina to Zimbabwe: A 48-nation study of sex, culture, and strategies of human mating. *The Behavioral and Brain Sciences, 28*, 247–275.

Schmitt, D. P., Alcalay, L., Allik, J., Angleiter, A., Ault, L., Austers, I., et al. (2004). Patterns and universals of mate poaching across 53 nations: The effects of sex, culture, and personality on romantically attracting another person's partner. *Journal of Personality and Social Psychology, 86*, 560–584.

Schmitt, D. P., Alcalay, L., Allik, J., Ault, L., Austers, I., Bennett, K. L., et al. (2003). Universal sex differences in the desire for sexual variety: Tests from 52 nations, 6 continents, and 13 islands. *Journal of Personality and Social Psychology, 85*, 85–104.

Schmitt, D. P., & Buss, D. M. (2001). Human mate poaching: Tactics and temptations for infiltrating existing mateships. *Journal of Personality and Social Psychology, 80*, 894–917.

Schmitt, D. P., Couden, A., & Baker, M. (2001). Sex, temporal context, and romantic desire: An experimental evaluation of Sexual Strategies Theory. *Personality and Social Psychology Bulletin, 27*, 833–847.

Schmitt, D. P., Jonason, P. K., Byerley, G. J., Flores, S. D., Illbeck, B. E., O'Leary, K. N., et al. (2012). A reexamination of sex differences in sexuality: New studies reveal old truths? *Current Directions in Psychological Science, 21*, 135–139.

Schmitt, D. P., & Pilcher, J. J. (2004). Evaluating evidence of psychological adaptation: How do we know one when we see one? *Psychological Science, 15*, 643–649.

Schmitt, D. P., Realo, A., Voracek, M., & Allik, J. (2008). Why can't a man be more like a woman? Sex differences in Big Five personality traits across 55 cultures. *Journal of Personality and Social Psychology, 94*, 168–182.

Schützwohl, A., Fuchs, A., McKibbin, W. F., & Shackelford, T. K. (2009). How willing are you to accept sexual requests from slightly unattractive to exceptionally attractive imagined requestors? *Human Nature, 20*, 282–293.

Schwarz, S., & Hassebrauck, M. (2012). Sex and age differences in mate-selection preferences. *Human Nature, 23*, 447–466.

Seal, D. W., Agostinelli, G., & Hannett, C. A. (1994). Extradyadic romantic involvement: Moderating effects of sociosexuality and gender. *Sex Roles, 31*, 1–22.

Sear, R., & Marlowe, F. W. (2009). How universal are human mate choices? Size does not matter when Hadza foragers are choosing a mate. *Biology Letters, 5*, 606–609.

Sell, A., Bryant, G. A., Cosmides, L., Tooby, J., Sznycer, D., von Rueden, C., et al. (2010). Adaptations in humans for assessing physical strength from the voice. *Proceedings of the Royal Society of London B, 277*, 3509–3518.

Shackelford, T. K., Weekes, V. A., LeBlanc, G. J., Bleske, A. L., Euler, H. A., & Hoier, S. (2000). Female coital orgasm and male attractiveness. *Human Nature, 11*, 299–306.

Shoup, M. L., & Gallup, G. G., Jr. (2008). Men's faces convey information about their bodies and their behavior: What you see is what you get. *Evolutionary Psychology, 6*, 469–479.

Sigal, J., Gibbs, M. S., Adams, B., & Derfler, R. (1988). The effect of romantic and nonromantic films on perception of female friendly and seductive behavior. *Sex Roles, 19*, 545–554.

Simpson, J. A., & Gangestad, S. W. (1991). Individual differences in sociosexuality: Evidence for convergent and discriminant validity. *Journal of Personality and Social Psychology, 60*, 870–883.

Simpson, J. A., & Gangestad, S. W. (1992). Sociosexuality and romantic partner choice. *Journal of Personality, 60*, 31–51.

Simpson, J. A., Gangestad, S. W., Christensen, P., & Niels, K. (1999). Fluctuating asymmetry, sociosexuality, and intrasexual competitive tactics. *Journal of Personality and Social Psychology, 76*, 159–172.

Simpson, J. A., Wilson, C. L., & Winterheld, H. A. (2004). Sociosexuality and romantic relationships. In J. H. Harvey, A. Wenzel, & S. Sprecher (Eds.), *The handbook of sexuality in close relationships* (pp. 87–112). Mahwah, NJ: Erlbaum.

Singh, D. (1993). Adaptive significance of female physical attractiveness: Role of waist-to-hip ratio. *Journal of Personality and Social Psychology, 65*, 293–307.

Singh, D., & Young, R. K. (1995). Body weight, waist-to-hip ratio, breast, and hips: Role of judgments of female attractiveness and desirability for relationships. *Ethology and Sociobiology, 16*, 483–507.

Smith, E. A. (2004). Why do good hunters have higher reproductive success? *Human Nature, 15*, 343–364.

Smith, F. G., Jones, B. C., & DeBruine, L. M. (2010). Individual differences in empathizing and systemizing predict variation in face preferences. *Personality and Individual Differences, 49*, 655–658.

Soler, C., Nunez, M., Gutierrez, R., Núñez, J., Medina, P., Sancho, M., et al. (2003). Facial attractiveness in men provides clues to semen quality. *Evolution and Human Behavior, 24*, 199–207.

Spanier, G. B., & Margolis, R. L. (1983). Marital separation and extramarital sexual behavior. *Journal of Sex Research, 19*, 23–48.

Sprecher, S., Sullivan, Q., & Hatfield, E. (1994). Mate selection preferences: Gender differences examined in a national sample. *Journal of Personality and Social Psychology, 66*, 1074–1080.

Stewart, S., Stinnett, H., & Rosenfeld, L. B. (2000). Sex differences in desired characteristics of short-term and long-term relationship partners. *Journal of Social and Personal Relationships, 17*, 843–853.

Stirrat, M., Gumert, M., & Perrett, D. (2011). The effect of attractiveness on food sharing preferences in human mating markets. *Evolutionary Psychology, 9*, 79–91.

Stone, E. A., Goetz, A. T., & Shackelford, T. K. (2005). Sex differences and similarities in preferred mating arrangements. *Sexualities, Evolution & Gender, 7*, 269–276.

Stulp, G., Buunk, A. P., & Pollet, T. V. (2013). Women want taller men more than men want shorter women. *Personality and Individual Differences, 54*, 877–883.

Sugiyama, L. (2005). Physical attractiveness in adaptationist perspective. In D. M. Buss (Ed.), *The handbook of evolutionary psychology* (pp. 292–342). New York: Wiley.

Surbey, M. K., & Conohan, C. D. (2000). Willingness to engage in casual sex: The role of parental qualities and perceived risk of aggression. *Human Nature, 11*, 367–386.

Symons, D. (1979). *The evolution of human sexuality.* New York: Oxford University Press.

Tadinac, M., & Hromatko, I. (2006). Strangers in the night or love forever: Characteristics and preferences of short vs. long-term relationship seekers. *Psihologijske Teme, 15,* 261–276.

Teachman, J. (2010). Wives' economic resources and risk of divorce. *Journal of Family Issues, 31,* 1305–1323.

Thompson, A. P. (1983). Extramarital sex: A review of the research literature. *Journal of Sex Research, 19,* 1–22.

Thornhill, R., & Gangestad, S. W. (1994). Human fluctuating asymmetry and sexual behavior. *Psychological Science, 5,* 297–302.

Thornhill, R., & Gangestad, S. W. (1999). The scent of symmetry: A human sex pheromone that signals fitness? *Evolution and Human Behavior, 20,* 175–201.

Thornhill, R., & Gangestad, S. W. (2008). *The evolutionary biology of human female sexuality.* New York: Oxford University Press.

Thornhill, R., Gangestad, S. W., & Comer, R. (1995). Human female orgasm and mate fluctuating asymmetry. *Animal Behaviour, 50,* 1601–1615.

Todd, P. M., Penke, L., Fasolo, B., & Lenton, A. P. (2007). Different cognitive processes underlie human mate choices and mate preferences. *Proceedings of the National Academy of Sciences of the United States of America, 104,* 15011–15016.

Townsend, J. M. (1989). Mate selection criteria: A pilot study. *Ethology and Sociobiology, 10,* 241–253.

Townsend, J. M. (1995). Sex without emotional involvement: An evolutionary interpretation of sex differences. *Archives of Sexual Behavior, 24,* 173–205.

Townsend, J. M., & Levy, G. D. (1990). Effects of potential partners' physical attractiveness and socioeconomic status on sexuality and partner selection. *Evolution and Human Behavior, 19,* 149–164.

Træen, B., & Martinussen, M. (2008). Extradyadic activity in a random sample of Norwegian couples. *Journal of Sex Research, 45,* 319–328.

Trivers, R. (1972). Parental investment and sexual selection. In B. Campbell (Ed.), *Sexual selection and the descent of man: 1871–1971* (pp. 136–179). Chicago: Aldine.

Trivers, R. (1985). *Social evolution.* Menlo Park, CA: Benjamin/Cummings.

Udry, J. R., & Eckland, B. K. (1984). Benefits of being attractive: Differential payoffs for men and women. *Psychological Reports, 54,* 47–56.

van den Berghe, P. L., & Frost, P. (1986). Skin color preference, sexual dimorphism, and sexual selection: A case of gene-culture co-evolution? *Ethnic and Racial Studies, 9,* 87–113.

Voracek, M., Fisher, M. L., Hofhansl, A., Rekkas, P. V., & Ritthammer, N. (2006). 'I find you to be very attractive...' Biases in compliance estimates to sexual offers. *Psicothema, 18,* 384–391.

Voracek, M., Hofhansl, A., & Fisher, M. L. (2005). Clark and Hatfield's evidence of women's low receptivity to male strangers' sexual offers revisited. *Psychological Reports, 97,* 11–20.

Walum, H., Westberg, L., Henningsson, S., Neiderhiser, J. M., Reiss, D., Igl, W., et al. (2008). Genetic variation in the vasopressin receptor 1a gene (AVPR1A) associates with pair-bonding behavior in humans. *Proceedings of the National Academy of Sciences, 105*(37), 14153–14156.

Waynforth, D. (1999). Differences in time use for mating and nepotistic effort as a function of male attractiveness in rural Belize. *Evolution and Human Behavior, 20,* 19–28.

Waynforth, D., Delwadia, S., & Camm, M. (2005). The influence of women's mating strategies on preference for masculine facial architecture. *Evolution and Human Behavior, 26,* 409–416.

Weisfeld, C. C., Dillon, L. M., Nowak, N. T., Mims, K. R., Weisfeld, G. E., Imamoğlu, E. O., et al. (2011). Sex differences and similarities in married couples: Patterns across and within cultures. *Archives of Sexual Behavior, 40,* 1165–1172.

Welling, L. L. M., Jones, B. C., DeBruine, L. M., Smith, F. G., Feinberg, D. R., Little, A. C., et al. (2008). Men report stronger attraction to femininity in women's faces when their testosterone levels are high. *Hormones and Behavior, 54,* 703–708.

Wiederman, M. W. (1993). Evolved gender differences in mate preferences: Evidence from personal advertisements. *Ethology and Sociobiology, 14,* 331–352.

Wiederman, M. W. (1997). Extramarital sex: Prevalence and correlates in a national survey. *Journal of Sex Research, 34,* 167–174.

Wiederman, M. W., & Dubois, S. L. (1998). Evolution and sex differences in preferences for short-term mates: Results from a policy capturing study. *Evolution and Human Behavior, 19,* 153–170.

Wiederman, M. W., & Hurd, C. (1999). Extradyadic involvement during dating. *Journal of Social and Personal Relationships, 16*(2), 265–274.

Wilbur, C. J., & Campbell, L. (2010). What do women want? An interactionist account of women's mate preferences. *Personality and Individual Differences, 49,* 749–754.

Wilson, G. D. (1987). Male–female differences in sexual activity, enjoyment, and fantasies. *Personality and Individual Differences, 8,* 125–127.

Wilcox, R. R. (2003). *Applying contemporary statistical techniques.* San Diego, CA: Academic.

Yong, J. C., & Li, N. P. (2012). Cash in hand, want better looking mate: Significant resource cues raise men's mating standards. *Personality and Individual Differences, 53,* 55–58.

Youn, G. (2006). Subjective sexual arousal in response to erotica: Effects of gender, guided fantasy, erotic stimulus, and duration of exposure. *Archives of Sexual Behavior, 35,* 87–97.

Zentner, M., & Mitura, K. (2012). Stepping out of the caveman's shadow: Nations' gender gap predicts degree of sex differentiation in mate preferences. *Psychological Science, 23*, 1176–1185.

Zhang, N., Parish, W. L., Huang, Y., & Pan, S. (2012). Sexual infidelity in China: Prevalence and gender-specific correlates. *Archives of Sexual Behavior, 41*, 861–873.

Zion, I. B., Tessler, R., Cohen, L., Lerer, E., Raz, Y., Bachner-Melman, R., et al. (2006). Polymorphisms in the dopamine D4 receptor gene (DRD4) contribute to individual differences in human sexual behavior: Desire, arousal and sexual function. *Molecular Psychiatry, 11*, 782–786.

Part II

Sexual Adaptations in Men

Adaptation and Sexual Offending

Joseph A. Camilleri and Kelly A. Stiver

Sexual Offending

Sexual behavior towards non-consenting individuals is a challenging topic for theoretical and empirical inquiry because there are many related terms that are inconsistently used. Generally, sexual offending is the broadest term that refers to a sexual act that that may cause unwanted physical or psychological harm to the victim. Sexual aggression and sexual assault typically refer to physical and more severe forms of sexual offending. Sexual coercion is also a broad term but refers to forceful or manipulative tactics people use to obtain sex from a reluctant person that may result in either psychological or physical harm (Camilleri, Quinsey, & Tapscott, 2009). Some terms specify the relationship between perpetrator and victim, such as child molestation, incest, and partner sexual coercion. These distinctions are important because different types of sexual offending require different explanations (see Camilleri, 2012). Among nonhuman animals, analogous behaviors are referred to as forced copulation, resisted mating, and sexual coercion, or sometimes are discussed as a lack of female control over fertilization (see Box 2.1). Our review will involve a typology of sexual offending that allows for theoretical consistency

across these varieties of sexual offending. We will refrain from using the term "rape" more generally because (1) it is legally defined, which changes across times and jurisdictions, and (2) it is a severe form of sexual offending. Thus, our discussion will follow Camilleri's (2012) typology to understand various types of sexual offending behavior by considering how they could function as an adaptation.

Throughout this chapter, we will also draw parallels from research on nonhuman animals, particularly examining work that involves sexual conflict over reproduction. Behavior of nonhuman animals is often studied using life history theory: the idea that natural selection has shaped the schedule and duration of key events in an animal's life (e.g., age at first reproduction, investment in care for offspring) so as to maximize reproductive success (Stearns, 1992). Examination of behavior from a life history perspective often involves consideration of the flexibility (plasticity) of behavioral investment; for example, are animals fixed or flexible in their reproductive behaviors once they are set upon a particular life history trajectory? Also considered is the mechanism underlying development along a particular trajectory (e.g., the role of genetic and environmental factors on the development of adult reproductive behavior). Note that members of a species may differ in their life histories depending on variation in these factors. Here, we focus primarily on male alternative reproductive tactics (discrete variation in reproductive behavior; Boxes 2.1–2.3) and additionally discuss disordered sexual behavior among

J.A. Camilleri (✉)
Department of Psychology, Westfield State University, Westfield, MA 01085, USA
e-mail: jcamilleri@westfield.ma.edu

V.A. Weekes-Shackelford and T.K. Shackelford (eds.), *Evolutionary Perspectives on Human Sexual Psychology and Behavior*, Evolutionary Psychology, DOI 10.1007/978-1-4939-0314-6_2,
© Springer Science+Business Media New York 2014

animals (Box 2.4) and examples of alternative reproductive tactics and sexual aggression among primates (Box 2.5).

Box 2.1: Introduction to Forced Copulation and Fertilization Among Nonhuman Animals: Alternative Reproductive Tactics

Among animals, there are clear examples of sexual violence and aggression, particularly directed at females from males, and in some cases, this behavior can take extreme forms, involving direct male coercion and control of female reproduction and even forced copulation (see Muller, Kahlenberg, & Wrangham, 2009a; Palmer, 1989). As outlined in the discussion of variation in the behavior of human males, forcible copulation may be the result of selection as a mating tactic or an exaptation or by-product resulting from prior selection for increased male dominance and aggression. In some species, forced copulation is the standard form of mating (e.g., in some species of waterfowl; McKinney, Derrickson, & Mineau, 1983). Additionally, intra-male cooperation may also be involved in female-directed aggression and forced copulation, as when groups of males act collaboratively with one another to control or coerce a female (e.g., dolphin male alliances; see Connor & Vollmer, 2009). When females are at risk of forced matings, they may evolve counteradaptations to minimize harm and decrease the chance of fertilization resulting (e.g., cryptic female choice; Eberhard, 1996). Thus, the existence of male attempts to control female mating, and paternity of young results in a situation of sexual conflict between males and females.

However, in some species, coercive or forced sex is only carried out by some males in the population, while others engage in courtship and access mating only through female choice (Boxes 2.2–2.5). Therefore, there are differences in the degree to which males and females have differing preferences over fertilization (and therefore in the role male control and of female

counteradaptations) in any specific mating event. Some of the clearest examples of conflict over mating and fertilization between females and some males are in species that show discrete variation in male reproductive behavior, a phenomenon that is termed alternative reproductive tactics (Oliveira, Taborsky, & Brockmann, 2008). Alternative reproductive tactics are observed in many taxa and are defined by discrete variation in reproductive phenotype (behavior and often also morphology and physiology; see Oliveira et al., 2008 for recent review). Research has primarily focused on these tactics in males: while females also appear to show discrete variation in reproductive behaviors, it is unclear whether alternative female tactics are a rarer phenomenon or simply a less-examined one (see Henson & Warner, 1997; Neff & Svensson, 2013). For this reason and in the interests of drawing parallels with human variation, we focus here on examples from males, treating individual species as case studies that highlight the variation in reproductive conflict between males and females.

When examining alternative reproductive tactics, one important question that arises is whether tactics are flexible: that is, once reproductively mature, are individuals restricted to only one or a few of the potential tactics within a species or do they maintain the potential to engage in any of the tactics, given the correct situation? Alternative reproductive tactics may reflect fixed alternative life histories (see Box 2.2) that may result from a genetic polymorphism (obligate tactic) or be developmentally facultative (e.g., arising through epigenetic changes among individuals that share a common genome). The result of this fixed life history pathway is that individuals are, by the point of reproductive maturity, excluded from engaging in one or more of the tactics that exist in a species. Alternatively, tactics

(continued)

Box 2.1 (continued)

may show developmental flexibility, across the lifespan of the individual, such that individuals can switch between tactics facultatively on a long-term (e.g., based on growth) or short-term (e.g., based social environment) basis (see Box 2.3). While it can be debated whether these latter cases of short-term flexibility truly represent alternative reproductive tactics (as they may not demonstrate the discrete variation that typically defines alternative tactics; see Taborsky, Oliviera, & Brockmann, 2008), we nonetheless include such examples from nonhuman animals here, due to the parallels to the possible underlying mechanisms of rape and coercive sexual behavior in humans.

Among animals, the issues of coercive or forced sexual encounters can become challenging in terms of definition. First, there is an issue of external fertilization. While this eliminates the potential for unwanted copulation, females in many species may experience unwanted fertilization. Perhaps the clearest such examples come from fishes: in several species, some males engage in a sneaking tactic where they join in a spawning event and add their gametes to those of the actively spawning male and female (see Taborsky, 1994, 1998, 2001; note that in such species, sneaker males tend to be more successful when they are of a smaller size or engage in female mimicry and therefore decrease their likelihood of being noticed by the dominant male and spawning female). Although females in these species may not risk physical harm from sneaker males, there is the experience of conflict arising from these alternative male reproductive tactics, as females are unable to control fertilization of their eggs. When considering here the similarities between alternative mating strategies among human males and among animal species, we take a broad approach in the animal examples, discussing general variations in reproductive phenotype associated with conflict over fertilization. Below we identify specific examples from nonhuman animals that generally involve male and female conflict, highlighting cases where such conflict also involves potential harm to females (see particularly Box 2.5 for specific examination of control and forcible copulation among primates).

Finally, a note on the mechanisms and physiological correlates of alternative reproductive tactics. While a popular topic of discussion in the examination of the underlying mechanisms and associated physiology, we do not go into detail on this point here. Rather, we note known and potential mechanisms when appropriate and direct curious readers to read more extensive examinations of these topics (see Oliveira et al., 2008). It is clear that as our understanding of variation in human reproductive behavior increases, drawing these specific parallels to similar animal behaviors will be of importance, and we encourage readers to consider the value of understanding mechanisms when examining the potential evolutionary basis of behavioral variation.

Psychological and Behavioral Adaptations

The adaptationist program in evolutionary psychology identifies how psychological phenotypes (i.e., thoughts, feelings, or behaviors) could have been naturally or sexually selected to overcome barriers to fitness. Generally, a trait is adaptive if it has specialized design features that function to increase the organism's fitness and if they are complex, precise, efficient, reliable, and economical (Williams, 1966). Fitness benefits can be tested by observing how variations in the trait are related to variations in reproductive success. Investigating psychological adaptations with humans poses unique challenges because there are obvious limits to manipulating traits and in measuring fitness. This does not mean adaptationist approaches to human psychology are impossible—it just means the methods need to be more comprehensive.

Evidentiary standards for adaptations have been elaborated in great detail. Schmitt and Pilcher (2004) reviewed how evidence for adaptations requires both theoretical and empirical support, and because psychologists study constructs that are not always directly observable and are noisy, they look for convergent evidence from theoretical, psychological, medical, physiological, genetic, phylogenetic, anthropological, and cross-cultural research. Andrews, Gangestad, and Matthews (2002) identified six standards for identifying adaptations: comparative evidence, fitness maximization, benefits in ancestral environments, optimization models, tight fit between design features and its function, and inferring a trait's function from its form. Our review of the literature on sexual coercion will review evidence for these standards in varying degrees by considering the fit between theory and research data that support such hypotheses and by looking to other species for analogous behaviors to understand how sexual coercion could have evolved among humans.

Early Adaptive Explanations

The earliest evolutionary explanations focused on rape more generally by treating it as a homogenous behavior with a single ultimate explanation. Symons (1979) provided one of the first evolutionary accounts of rape by suggesting that due to a male mating psychology that is oriented towards high frequency mating, force is used with a non-consenting person when the costs of engaging in such behavior are low. The concept of costs and benefits was elaborated by Shields and Shields (1983), who suggested that because of differences in sexual strategies, deceitful and manipulative courtship, in addition to forcible rape, could have evolved.

A popular hypothesis, the mate deprivation hypothesis, has been proposed in different forms for over 30 years (Alexander & Noonan, 1979;

Lalumière, Chalmers, Quinsey, & Seto, 1996; Thornhill, 1980; Thornhill & Thornhill, 1983). This hypothesis posits that men are more likely to engage in sexually coercive behavior when the probability of mating through consensual means is low. Consistent with such an evolutionary approach were data indicating this behavior was mostly committed by younger men (since reproductive success is more strongly related to mate number among men) and is associated with lower socioeconomic status (Perkins & Klaus, 1996; Thornhill & Thornhill, 1983) and higher rates of pregnancy resulting from rape than from consenting sex (Gottschall & Gottschall, 2003). Also, analogous behaviors are found in nonhuman species, including other primates (Box 2.5). Another condition for adaptation is that the behavior must be universal—indeed, sexual offending is certainly found in all documented cultures and times (Brown, 1991; Lalumière et al., 2005), and evolutionary-minded researchers are also studying variability in rape prevalence rates across nations (e.g., Barber, 2000).

Accumulation of empirical tests of evolutionary hypotheses indicated more complexity in explaining sexual offending. In a non-forensic sample, Lalumière, Chalmers, Quinsey, and Seto (1996) found that sexually coercive men were not different from men who were not sexually coercive in terms of self-perceived mating sexual success and reported more instances of sexual experiences. These results were at odds with the mate deprivation model, and so Lalumière et al. proposed the micro-mate deprivation hypothesis—that men who are typically successful at mating resort to coercive sex when faced with refusal. Also in this time, individual difference characteristics were being associated with sexual offending, such as sexual preference for coercive sex (e.g., Lalumière & Quinsey, 1996), and conditions where sexual coercion could not have resulted in reproductive success emerged as counterarguments to evolutionary explanations, such as sexual offending against children (Coyne, 2003). More sophisticated evolutionary explanations were forwarded to account for these other types of offending behavior (Quinsey & Lalumière, 1995).

Table 2.1 Evolutionary typology of sexual offending

	Adaptation (Boxes 2.1 and 2.5)	By-product (Box 2.4)	Disorder (Box 2.4)
Obligate (Box 2.2)	Psychopathy	Sexual homicide	Developmentally disabled; incest
Facultative—developmentally fixed (Box 2.2)	Competitively disadvantaged	Sexual homicide	Paraphilias (pedophilia, zoophilia, gerontophilia)[a]
Facultative—developmentally flexible (Boxes 2.3 and 2.5)	Young male syndrome	Sexual homicide	Paraphilias (exhibitionism, voyeurism, toucherism, frotteurism)
	Cuckoldry risk		Pathological jealousy
	Sexual bullying		

See appropriate boxes where noted for analogous examples from nonhuman animals
[a]This type was included as an obligate disorder in Camilleri (2012), but considering the organizational effects of hormones on sexual preferences, these paraphilias can be thought of as disorders of developmentally fixed traits

Evolutionary Typology

Camilleri (2012) extended Lalumière et al.'s (2005) application of obligate and facultative adaptations towards sexual offending to account for differences in sexual offender types. This typology recognizes that any behavior can fall into one of nine categories by considering two dimensions: adaptive-maladaptive traits (adaptation, by-product, disorder) and obligate-facultative behavioral patterns (obligate and facultative developmentally fixed, which can be considered to be associated with fixed life history trajectories, and facultative developmentally flexible, which shows greater plasticity within individuals; see Table 2.1). This typology provides a theoretically meaningful way to categorize sexual offenders by suggesting etiological paths to sexual offending represents different types. Similar behavioral patterns are seen across nonhuman animals (see Box 2.1). Previous attempts at sexual offender typologies have treated traits or mechanisms as separate types. This is problematic because these traits or mechanisms may be descriptive of many sexual offender types, not diagnostic of any particular one (see Camilleri, 2012 for a review). Also, most typologies of sexual offenders lack theoretical reasons for including some traits and not others, as is found in the Massachusetts Treatment Center Rapist Typology (Knight, 1999). The types as presented here are based on our current understanding of the phenomena but can change depending on theoretical and research developments.

Obligate

Obligate traits, unlike facultative ones, are due to genetic differences between organisms, and so differences in behavioral patterns can be attributed to differences in genes. Although most psychological traits are considered facultative, there are some characteristics of people that may be considered obligate (i.e., heritable alternative strategy)—a likely candidate is personality (Buss, 1991). By definition, personality refers to individual differences in patterns of thoughts, feelings, and behaviors. Genes appear to account for stability in personality traits (McGue, Bacon, & Lykken, 1993) because particular genes may lead to decreased plasticity in personality development.[1]

One path to sexual offending that may be obligate in its structure is *psychopathy* (Kinner, 2003; Mealey, 1995). Characteristics of psychopaths, such as leading a parasitic lifestyle and being manipulative, suggest their behavior is oriented towards exploiting others. Psychopaths are well known in forensic settings because they comprise approximately 15 % of prison populations (reviewed in Ogloff, 2006). Although there is substantial literature on psychopathy assessments, types, characteristics, and consequences (see Patrick, 2008), there is little agreement on the etiology of psychopathy. Understanding the causes of

---

[1] Although the explanation is more nuanced than simply "genes cause personality" (see Caspi, Roberts, & Shiner, 2005).

psychopathy is important for research on sexual offending because coercive sexuality appears to be a core factor (Harris, Rice, Hilton, Lalumière, & Quinsey, 2007), and there is a positive relationship between psychopathy and sexual arousal to non-consenting sexual scenarios (as cited in Harris, Lalumière, Seto, Rice, & Chaplin, 2012). Men who sexually molested children had significantly lower psychopathy scores than rapists and a combined group rapists who also molested children (Porter et al., 2000).

Evolutionary-derived explanations have suggested that psychopaths are a discrete class of individuals and that psychopathy as an obligate trait is maintained through frequency-dependent selection (Mealey, 1995)—particular trait or traits are optimal only when they exist as a certain percentage in a population. Selection favors the traits when they are rare and disfavors them when they are common. There are several lines of research that address this hypothesis, including taxometric analyses and behavioral genetics.

Psychopathy and taxometric analyses. Taxometric analyses are used to identify whether one or more discrete groups underlie a continuously measured construct (see Boxes 2.1–2.3 and 2.5 for discussion of an analogous phenomenon in animals—alternative reproductive tactics that show discrete variation in reproductive behavior). This method is useful to identify whether there are categorical differences between psychopaths and nonpsychopaths, because measurements on this construct vary on a continuous scale. Evidence of a taxon is consistent with viewing psychopathy as an obligate trait because taxa represent different types of people. To date, there are many studies that have looked at the taxometric structure of psychopathy: although early studies found support for a taxon (Harris et al., 2007; Harris, Rice, & Quinsey, 1994; Skilling, Quinsey, & Craig, 2001; Vasey, Kotov, Frick, & Loney, 2005), a larger number of studies are now indicating psychopathy varies on a dimensional scale (e.g., Edens, Marcus, Lilienfeld, & Poythress, 2006; Guay, Ruscio, Knight, & Hare, 2007; Marcus, John, & Edens, 2004; Walters, Brinkley, Magaletta, & Diamond, 2008). Explanations for these conflicting findings include methodological differences and the suggestion that current measures of psychopathy are confounded because they include antisocial traits of nonpsychopathic criminals. Harris et al. (2007) identified a third factor of psychopathy, labeled coercive and precocious sexuality, and found that it also clustered into a taxon. This result was not replicated by Walters et al. (2011); however, their methods differed in that they did not run taxometric analyses on the precocious/coercive sex factor alone, but included those items in the PCL-R before running the analysis. Thus, this analysis included items that would appear among both psychopathic and nonpsychopathic offenders, making it difficult to discriminate between the two.

Finally, an important consideration when sampling from non-forensic populations is that there may not be a sufficient number of true psychopaths in the sample to detect a taxon because it is estimated they comprise only 3 % of the population. Because true base rates are unknown, we are unsure how long psychopaths may escape detection by the justice system; if the majority of psychopaths are identified and therefore typically incarcerated, this decreases our ability to sample them among a purportedly normal population.

Psychopathy and genetics. The most convincing evidence in support of psychopathy as an obligate trait is the extensive research on genetic contributions to psychopathy. If psychopathy is an obligate trait sustained through frequency-dependent selection, then genetic differences should account for a substantial proportion of variation in psychopathy. There have been several studies looking at the behavior genetics of both psychopathy and a related construct—antisocial personality. Not only have studies generally found robust genetic contributions to these constructs (Burt, 2009; Ferguson, 2010); a study found a strong genetic contribution to variation in psychopathic traits among 7-year-olds (callous, unemotional, and antisocial), with no effects of shared environmental effects (Viding, Blair, Moffitt, & Plomin, 2005). Longitudinal research also shows that early signs of psychopathy in adolescence are related to psychopathy later in life (Lynam, Caspi, Moffitt, Loeber, & Stouthamer-Loeber, 2007).

There are some suggestions that a common factor underlies psychopathy and antisocial personality disorder (e.g., Skilling, Harris, Rice, & Quinsey, 2002). Larsson et al. (2007) found that a common genetic factor was related to both psychopathy and antisocial personality disorder and that a common shared environment was related to only antisocial personality disorder. Similar findings showed weaker genetic effects, compared to environmental effects, when considering antisocial behavior (Rhee & Waldman, 2002). These results are intriguing because they suggest greater environmental influence on nonpsychopathic offenders and greater genetic influence on psychopathic offenders. Similar to nonhuman species, it is difficult to tease apart different etiologies when the phenotypes are the same (see Boxes 2.1 and 2.2).

With genetic contributions to psychopathy established, researchers are now focusing their attention to exactly which genes may be associated with this disposition. Although no single gene has emerged as a primary candidate, investigations are now piecing together the complex impact genes, metabolic pathways, transporters, and neural receptors have on both antisocial behavior and psychopathy (reviewed in Gunter, Vaughn, & Philibert, 2010).

These results do not mean experiences have no impact on the development of psychopathy—epigenetics show some early promise (Gunter et al., 2010), and there are some early development factors that might impact psychopathy (Marshall & Cooke, 1999). The complexity of obligate traits suggests that changes in tactics are still possible (see Box 2.2), that a life history that is fixed does not mean that all behaviors associated with it are unchanging. Longitudinal research is still needed to get a better sense of the developmental trajectory of psychopathy. Not surprisingly, Blonigen, Hicks, Krueger, Patrick, and Iacono (2006) found stronger genetic contributions to stability of psychopathy traits over time and greater non-shared environment effects on psychopathic traits that changed over time. Interestingly, Harris, Rice, and Lalumière (2001) found the independent effects of psychopathy and neurodevelopment (i.e., environmental impact early in development) on criminality.

Considering the extent to which there are variable findings on psychopaths, the nature and

etiology of psychopathy have yet to be confirmed. Research that includes criminal and noncriminal populations using improved measures of psychopathy that include items only relevant to their diagnosis may help. Still, consistent with psychopathy as an obligate strategy, there are considerable data to suggest strong genetic contributions to its expression. If further confirmatory findings emerge, then implications for treatment suggest supervision and management may work best (Camilleri, 2012; Quinsey, Harris, Rice, & Cormier, 2006). Future research should consider the reproductive costs and benefits of psychopathy—data and models are needed to see whether psychopathy is reproductively viable and is indeed preserved through frequency-dependent selection.

Facultative: Developmentally Fixed

Behavioral phenotypes that are facultative but developmentally fixed mean the probability of its expression is consistently high across the lifespan once the mechanism is activated (which can also be conceptualized as fixed alternative life history pathways; see Box 2.2). These responses are still considered facultative because their expression depends on responses to certain environments. These mechanisms assist with explaining the smaller proportion of men who start their antisocial behavior at an early age, including sexual offending, and fail to desist. There are many examples where reproductive behaviors appear to change in response to environmental conditions early in development. As an example, precocious sexuality is related to poorer social conditions, such as socioeconomic status, life expectancy, neighborhood resources, and absence of a father, suggesting early-onset sexuality is a facultative reproductive response to lower probability of survival and mating success (reviewed in Thornhill & Palmer, 2004). Competitively disadvantaged men appear to fit this category.

In addition to finding that offenders clustered into adolescent-limited offenders (see "Young Male Syndrome"), Moffitt (1993) found another cluster they identified as life-course persistent—antisocial behavior starts early in development and persists. The evolutionary typology proposed suggests that life-course persistent offenders could result either from a developmentally fixed path or an obligate path. One type, labeled the *competitively disadvantaged*, falls within the developmentally fixed path. According to Lalumière et al. (2005), this path includes men who experience either social or neural adversity early in development, resulting in lowered embodied capital whereby the benefits of adopting a high mating effort, risk taking, and antisocial reproductive strategies outweigh their costs. Theoretically, the reason why such a response becomes fixed is because poor environmental conditions early in development reliably signal poor mating opportunities later in life. We see such phenotypic adjustments in other species (see Box 2.2). In humans, there are many early social and neurodevelopmental correlates of crime that are consistent with this explanation.

Competitive disadvantage and social adversity. Much research has demonstrated a link between poverty and crime more generally and with rape more specifically. Variables associated with poor living conditions appear to be a fairly robust correlate of crime, such as income inequality (Daly, Wilson, & Vasdev 2001), antisocial parenting (Harris et al., 2001), and abuse victimization (Jespersen, Lalumière, & Seto, 2009). Interestingly, Ingoldsby and Shaw (2002), studying the effects of early environments on antisocial behaviors, found that middle of childhood may be a critical period where such environmental experiences might have longer-term consequences. SES has been linked to crime in general and sexual offending as well. In a meta-analysis, poverty was related to rape with a moderate effect size of 0.38 (Hsieh & Pugh, 1993). Although income inequality was not significantly related to rape in this meta-analysis, the effect size was strong and it was based on only two studies. A more recent study found that the Gini coefficient was related to rape, not other violent crimes (Choe, 2008).[2] These results suggest that conditions

indicative of competition, such as poverty or larger income disparity, are related to higher rates of sexual violence.

An assumption of each path to sexual offending being proposed here is that it is sex-specific—that is, the paths should be more strongly related to sexual offending among men than among women. Because sexual coercion promotes reproduction by increasing mate number, this strategy would not increase fitness among women. Tittle and Meier's (1990) review found that, more often than not, the relationship between SES and crime was more pronounced among men than women. The problem with this study was that it was a narrative review of the literature—meta-analytic reviews are therefore still needed. Another setback is that these studies focused on delinquency as the dependent variable. It is also possible that SES may have more similar impacts on the sexes for crime in general but greater effects on men for sexual offending.

The exact mechanisms through which poor conditions impact behavior are not well understood. There is emerging evidence, however, that social adversity experienced in childhood, such as socioeconomic status, effects regions of the brain that are related to social information processing (Noble, Houston, Kan, & Sowell, 2012), but it should be noted that links between neural processes and behavior, such as risk taking, require further work (Steinberg, 2007).

The timing of early experiences appears to be important to consider. In their review, Ingoldsby and Shaw (2002) argued that exposure to neighborhood stressors by middle childhood, such as economic disadvantage, violence, and deviant peer groups, may impact the trajectory of early-onset antisociality. Subsequent research were consistent with this model whereby some support was found for early childhood exposure to parent–child conflict and neighborhood problems were related to early signs of antisocial behavior, and that antisocial peer groups later in childhood seems to maintain antisocial behaviors (Ingoldsby et al., 2006). Still, there were a group of children who had these early exposures yet their antisocial behavior declined with age, so there may be other factors that contribute to

---

[2] How poor regions within a location are clustered does not appear to matter. Poverty clustering was not found to be related to rape (Stretesky, Schuck, & Hogan, 2004).

life-course persistent antisociality. For example, there appears to be additive effects of early risk factors on adolescent antisocial behavior, and peer relationships might mediate the relationship between early experiences and antisociality in adolescence (Criss, Shaw, Moilanen, Hitchings, & Ingoldsby, 2009). It also appears that the *amount* of exposure to poverty, such as time in poverty and percent of youth spent in poverty, is related to delinquent behavior—being poor in the short term was not related to delinquency (Jarjoura, Triplett, & Brinker, 2002). They also found that exposure to poverty in the first 5 years of life was related to delinquency—after controlling for the effects of poverty from ages 0 to 5, poverty from ages 6 to 10 was unrelated to delinquency. Each of these results suggests not just temporal sensitivity to social adversity, but the amount and timing are important in determining the risk of antisocial behavior, which are consistent with the competitive disadvantage hypothesis.

Competitive disadvantage and neurodevelopment. In addition to social adversity, neurodevelopmental incidents may also lead to competitive disadvantage, resulting in sexually coercive behaviors as a facultative-fixed response. For example, Rylands et al. (2012) found that not only were men who were different in impulsive aggression, a trait associated with sexual offending, showed differences in terms of childhood adversity, they were also different in terms of brainstem serotonin transporter (SERT). Interestingly, brainstem SERT was strongly related to experiencing childhood trauma ($r = 0.76$).

One method for investigating neural adversity early in development is to consider physical perturbations that are indicative of such experiences. Arseneault, Tremblay, Boulerice, Séguin, and Saucier (2000) found that minor physical anomalies were predictive of violent behavior in adolescence after controlling for family adversity in childhood. This is important because it suggests that physical or neurological variables could be independent from childhood environmental effects. Specific to sexual offending, atypical early neurological development, such as that related to prenatal alcohol

exposure, is related to sexual offenses (reviewed in Baumbach, 2002). Psychometric research is therefore needed for early assessment of competitive disadvantage and for factor analyses to determine whether neural and social adversity are independent paths.

Another work has suggested that early experiences may have consequences to adult social development by revealing how phenotypic markers of developmental stressors relate to violent criminal behavior. Lalumière, Harris, and Rice (2001) found that nonpsychopathic offenders (including rapists and non-rapists) had higher fluctuating asymmetry than non-offenders (higher fluctuating asymmetry indicates developmental incidents). Similarly, nonpsychopathic offenders scored higher than psychopathic offenders on obstetrical problems, indicating complications in early development and suggesting a possible role of such complications in the development of antisocial behavior in adults.

Although we can think of social and neural adversity as being separate factors that trigger competitive disadvantage, there may be additive or interaction effects between them. Raine's review of the literature suggests that experiencing both biological and social risk factors exponentially increased the risk of antisocial and violent behavior, and Arseneault et al. (2002) found that obstetrical problems had an impact on adolescent violent behavior only if they had grown up in adverse social environments.

Box 2.2: Alternative Tactics as Fixed Alternative Life Histories (Analogue to "Obligate" and "Facultative Developmentally Fixed")

In contrast to the facultative developmentally flexible tactics described in Box 2.3, some alternative reproductive tactics are associated with fixed alternative life histories. Variation in life history may result from genetic polymorphisms underlying the alternative phenotypes (resulting in so-called "obligate" tactics) or to

(continued)

Box 2.2 (continued)

differences in early development among individuals that share a common genome, leading to a phenotype that is facultative but developmentally fixed by reproductive age (see Emlen, 2008). These two potential origins of fixed alternative tactics can be difficult to distinguish from one another by simply examining phenotype, as both can result in certain tactics being unavailable to certain males once their life history course is set (see below). As discussed in Box 2.1, determining the organizational mechanisms underlying these set of life history pathways can be challenging, and they are therefore often best considered to be the likely result of some gene by environment interactions (e.g., as when early growth is a determining factor: early growth can be influenced both by genes and by environmental factors such as resource availability at time of birth).

One clear example of a genetically based alternative tactics that vary in degree of conflict over fertilization is found in the pygmy swordtail *Xiphophorus nigrensis*, an internally fertilizing fish with female pregnancy (Zimmerer & Kallman, 1989). Males in this species show Y-linked variation (the *P*-locus) with four alleles that result in size and color variation. This variation in male size and color results in discrete variation in male reproductive behavior: specifically, small males show a broader range of reproductive behavior than the other male types (Zimmerer & Kallman, 1989). Of particular interest to us, small males are the only ones that perform "sneak-chases," which involve darting towards the female and a gonopodial thrust and copulation attempts (Zimmerer & Kallman, 1989). Thus, this single-gene variant is associated with the level of conflict over fertilization between males and females.

Salmon shows male variation in reproductive tactic which is fixed across the timespan on the basis of both condition (early growth) and frequency dependence (i.e., the relative frequency of each tactic in the environment; Gross, 1985). The large dominant "hooknose" males show slower early growth and take longer to reach reproductive maturity but are the only morph females will spontaneously spawn with. The "jack" or "sneaker" morph develops more quickly and has frequency-dependent reproductive success (high success when jacks is rare in the population due to decreased hooknose vigilance; Gross, 1985) based on their ability to get close to spawning females. This period of early growth determines the lifetime tactic of a male salmon: once matured as a jack, the "hooknose" pathway is no longer available to him (Gross, 1985).

However, tactics based on alternative life histories do not preclude changes in tactic across the lifespan. Male ocellated wrasse (*Symphodus ocellatus*, a fish species native to the Mediterranean) engage in three different reproductive tactics. Dominant territorial "nesting males" are the largest and most colorful males and are the only male phenotype that females choose to spawn with and that perform parental care (Taborsky, Hudde, & Wirtz, 1987; Warner & Lejeune, 1985). The other two male phenotypes "satellite" and "sneaker males" are the medium and smallest of the reproductive males and are respectively the moderately and least dominant and colorful (Taborsky et al., 1987; Warner & Lejeune, 1985). Sneakers and satellites spawn parasitically at the nests of nesting males and are not preferred by females; thus, their spawning is a form of reproductive conflict in this species (Alonzo & Warner, 2000; van den Berghe, Wernerus, & Warner, 1989). The three male ocellated wrasse types are the product of three alternative life history pathways

(continued)

Box 2.2 (continued)

that relate to the amount of pre-reproductive growth (although the ultimate mechanism of differentiation remains unknown; see Alonzo, Taborsky, & Wirtz, 2000). All possible male life histories involve a change in reproductive phenotype between their first and second reproductive year (sneaker to satellite, satellite to nesting male, or nonreproductive to nesting male; Alonzo et al., 2000). Therefore, some males spend their entire lives in reproductive conflict with females (never becoming the preferred phenotype), while others experience this conflict only in their first reproductive year, or not at all (Alonzo et al., 2000). Similar change in reproductive tactic occurs in other fish species, although these may not involve a change in conflict over fertilization with females. For example, bluegill sunfish (*Lepomis macrochirus*) shows fixed life histories that can involve a change in reproductive tactics (Gross & Charnov, 1980), but individual bluegill males either always breed as a phenotype that is preferred by females (nesting males) or they never do (sneakers who become satellites).

Facultative: Developmentally Flexible

Facultative psychological mechanisms are defined as traits that are responsive to environmental conditions and would have evolved in response to unpredictable environments (Alcock, 2001). Most psychological traits are considered to be facultative, but little attention has considered the ontogeny of these mechanisms. Some mechanisms are flexible, meaning its occurrence is not permanent, but responds to both the presence and absence of a particular condition. For example, being hungry depends on how satiated an organism is—hunger subsides after eating. Other responses are fixed, meaning its occurrence persists once turned on. An example of

this is the organizational effects hormones have on sex-typical behavior (see Quinsey, 2003). There are many examples of sexually coercive behaviors in nonhuman species that are facultative (Box 2.3). What is common among facultative adaptations is that their expression depends on variations in environmental conditions. Several paths to sexual offending may fall into either of these categories.

Box 2.3: Long- and Short-Term Flexible Alternative Tactics (Analogue to "Developmentally Flexible")

In some species, investment in particularly reproductive tactics is facultative and developmentally flexible: individuals of reproductive age can engage in any of the possible tactics, provided the proper context (see also Box 2.4 for more such examples from primates). Often, the major factor involved in the reproductive tactic used is an individual's social status, such as when the most dominant male has controlled access to females. In these situations, subordinate males may resort to a tactic of forced copulation of unguarded females (see Box 2.4). Individual dominance can vary over the long term (such as when the alpha male in a group has a distinctly different morphology, e.g., elephant seals, described below) or short term (when tactic is based on a specific relative characteristic, such as size, e.g., garter snakes and water dragons, described below). Other social factors may play a role in tactic determination: for example, relative sex ratio of reproductive individuals in the population (the operational or adult sex ratio; see Kokko & Jennions, 2008) can change reproductive behavior specifically with regard to conflict over fertilization (and can also lead to other forms of male–female reproductive conflict, such as overinvestment in parental care; see also Apicella & Marlowe, 2007; Kokko & Jennions, 2008).

(continued)

Box 2.3 (continued)

In elephant seals, large dominant "beachmasters" guard and attempt to control the reproduction of female seals, while smaller, subordinate "satellite" males attempt to sneak copulation (Hoelzel, LeBoeuf, Reiter, & Campagna, 1999; Le Boeuf, 1974); reproductive success of males generally correlates with their copulation success (Hoelzel et al., 1999). Females are generally more receptive to males who are more dominant (Cox, 1981). Variation male aggressive behavior during mating results in females experiencing greater risk of injury or mortality from satellite than they do from beachmasters (Mesnick & Le Boeuf, 1991). Thus, females attempt to evade copulation with subordinate males, although they decrease potential costs of mating by showing increased receptivity when they are unable to evade satellites (Mesnick & Le Boeuf, 1991). As male dominance is based on physical ability, and therefore on size, all males have the potential to achieve dominance provided they survive for long enough (Le Boeuf, 1974).

Clear examples of the role of short-term variability in reproductive strategy can be seen in garter snakes (Shine, Langkilde, & Mason, 2003) and eastern Australian water dragons (Baird, Baird, & Shine, 2012). Garter snakes show variation in reproductive behavior based on body size (larger males show more courtship behavior; Shine et al., 2003). They also change relative investment in reproductive behaviors based on the number of male competitors present (shifting investment from inducing female receptivity to increasing the likelihood of mating when more male competitors are present; Shine et al., 2003). Eastern Australian water dragons also show alternative tactics that are moderated by social context and thus can show high short-term plasticity: larger dominant males are territorial, while smaller males act as opportunistic satellite males (Baird et al., 2012). An experimental removal of territorial males confirmed that when a territory vacancy arises, satellite males quickly move up in status and adopt the strategy of a dominant territorial male (Baird et al., 2012).

Cuckoldry risk. Sexual offending in relationships has recently been given considerable attention by evolutionists. Traditional evolutionary explanations that rape evolved in response to limited mating opportunities do not apply in this context because presumably the person is (or at least was) in a mutually consensual mating relationship. An alternative explanation was posed to suggest that partner sexual coercion overcomes a fitness barrier posed by cuckoldry risk. That is, a way men could have minimized cuckoldry risk was by forcing copulation when faced with a reluctant sexual partner who had engaged in an extra-pair mating within the last reproductive cycle (Buss, 2003; Camilleri & Quinsey, 2009a; Goetz & Shackelford, 2006; Lalumière et al., 2005; Thornhill & Palmer, 2000; Wilson & Daly, 1992).

Camilleri and Quinsey (2012) embedded this idea in the context of sexual conflict, which is when a trait is adaptive in one sex while posing fitness costs to the other sex. First, there may be fitness benefits of extra-pair copulations among women, including mating with males with better genes, gaining resources from an extra-pair partner, paternity confusion leading to greater investment in offspring, status enhancement, diversifying genes, and potentially "trading up" to a better quality mate (reviewed in Mulder & Rauch, 2009; Wilson & Daly, 1992). Being cuckolded certainly poses reproductive costs to men, and so we would expect adaptations to identify and minimize this risk. Sexually coercing one's partner was hypothesized to function by minimizing cuckoldry risk. Sexual conflict is a powerful middle-level theory because in addition to accounting for partner sexual coercion, it may account for a wide variety of aggressive behaviors in sexual relationships, including harassment, intimidation, social isolation, punishment, and infanticide. For partner sexual coercion to be considered a cause or consequence of sexual conflict, harm in one sex must be adaptive in the other sex, harm must not be a by-product of the trait, called *collateral harm* or *collateral cost*, and indirect benefits to the harmed sex must be ruled out, such as having sexually coercive sons. Addressing these criteria is difficult with humans because coevolutionary trajectories are methodologically difficult to ascertain—since genetic and fitness experimental designs are not possible, alternative methods have been proposed to answer some of the questions posed by the sexual conflict theory (see Camilleri & Quinsey, 2012, for a more detailed review of this topic).

The relationship between cuckoldry risk and partner sexual coercion appears to be a robust finding. Goetz and Shackelford (2006) found a significant relationship between infidelity and partner sexual coercion, as reported by both perpetrators and victims. Starratt, Goetz, Shackelford, McKibbin, and Stewart-Williams (2008) found that more insults of partner infidelity were related to more instances of partner sexual coercion. Goetz and Shackelford (2009) replicated these effects in another sample. Reanalyzing Camilleri and Quinsey's (2009a) data, there was a significant correlation between cues to partner infidelity and self-reported propensity for partner sexual coercion among men, $r(140) = 0.30, p < 0.001$, not among women, $r(142) = 0.12, p = 0.16$ (i.e., women did not show a greater propensity for partner sexual coercion when their partner had an increased risk of infidelity). Across these six studies, effect sizes narrowly ranged from 0.23 to 0.32 ($M = 0.28$, SD $= 0.04$, 95 % CI 0.24–0.31), suggesting cuckoldry risk has a moderate impact on partner sexual coercion and that other factors contribute to this behavior, such as psychopathy (Camilleri & Quinsey, 2009b). Using a forensic sample, Camilleri and Quinsey (2009) found that among incarcerated partner rapists, 27 % suspected, knew, or were threatened with infidelity prior to committing their offense. Considering these results

have been replicated across students, communities, forensic samples, potential perpetrators, and victims using multiple operationalizations, these data suggest a robust relationship between cuckoldry risk and partner sexual coercion.

These relationships indicate partner sexual coercion may be in response to partner infidelity, but they do not identify whether such a facultative response is developmentally flexible or fixed. There is some preliminary evidence that cuckoldry risk is developmentally flexible. In a non-forensic sample, Camilleri and Quinsey (2009a) found that the relationship between partner sexual coercion and cuckoldry risk was strongest when risk events took place recently. As the average time since cuckoldry risk events took place increased, the relationship between cuckoldry risk and partner sexual coercion weakened. The response, as predicted, also appears to be sex-specific because these effects were found only among men.

Also, Camilleri and Quinsey (2009a) did not find a relationship between an indirect proxy of cuckoldry risk—proportion of time away from partner since last having intercourse—and propensity for partner sexual coercion. They argued that more direct cues to infidelity are needed for someone to take the risks associated with coercive behaviors. Interestingly, McKibbin, Starratt, Shackelford, and Goetz (2011) found that proportion of time was related to partner sexual coercion but only when men's suspicion of partner infidelity was higher. Methodologically, these studies have setbacks because they are correlational and self-report. Thus, further work using experimental designs and research with forensic samples and the use of mathematical models would assist with providing a more comprehensive understanding of how cuckoldry risk is facultatively related to partner sexual coercion. For example, it is possible that one instance of infidelity might permanently increase a partner's sensitivity to cuckoldry risk.

The young male syndrome. Two of the most robust predictors of antisocial behavior, including sexual offending, are age and sex. Known as the fundamental data of criminology, a large proportion of crimes are committed by younger males (reviewed in Quinsey, Skilling, Lalumière, & Craig, 2004). Evolutionary explanations account for these data by suggesting that younger males are more willing to tolerate risks due to higher fitness variance, and thus higher competition, for establishing mateships (Wilson & Daly, 1985). Selection would have favored traits associated with taking risks for resources, status, and mateships during this developmental period of high competition. Lalumière et al. (2005) proposed that these risky behaviors, which include sexual coercion, subside as men age because they eventually form long-term mateships and switch to parental investment, making such risky behaviors too costly. Consistent with this view is that marriage is a protective factor for violent recidivism (reviewed in Laub & Sampson, 2001). This path to sexual offending would therefore be considered a *developmentally flexible facultative mechanism*, because conditions turn these behaviors on and off.

This path to sexually coercive behavior in humans might account for a large proportion of both sexual and nonsexual crimes (Lalumière et al., 2005). Data patterns show an increase in the frequency of sexual crimes committed by males into young adulthood then a decline as men age. A similar curve is found among women, but the frequency does not peak to the same extent as men. Using US data, both forcible rape and all sexual offenses follow this pattern (higher rates among women are due to including prostitution; FBI Uniform Crime Reports, 1993–2001).

Moffitt's longitudinal research on criminal populations identified *adolescent-limited* offenders as a discrete category and is consistent with the Young Male Syndrome. That is, unlike life-course-persistent offenders, men who fall into the adolescent-limited category are not characterized by unfavorable traits to the same degree, including certain personality traits, psychopathology, interpersonal/familial conflict, and neurocognitive deficits, among others (Moffitt, 1993; Moffitt, Caspi, Harrington, & Milne, 2002).

Despite the pervasiveness of the age-sex-crime curve, not all young men commit sexual offenses. There are still individual differences in one's likelihood to engage in such behavior. To account for this, Lalumière et al. (2005) suggested there are younger men whose environmental conditions increase the benefits of risk behaviors, including

living in areas where competition is high as indicated by higher homicide rates. Moffitt et al.'s adolescent-limited group, although generally better off than life-course-persistent offenders, scored lower on economic life variables than other antisocial men (Moffitt et al., 2002). So, younger men who face environments or conditions that promote competition might have a more temporary response because the conditions may not be as entrenched or severe as those experienced by LCP.

Individual differences in young male syndrome are consistent with Wilson and Daly's (1998) hypothesis that men's sexual proprietariness and violence should correlate with higher intrasexual competition. Some evidence in support of this idea is that domestic violence is positively related to higher male-to-female sex ratio (D'Alessio & Stolzenberg, 2010); however, not all studies find such a clear relationship. Barber (2000) found a *negative* correlation between male-to-female sex ratio and rape rates across nations, but only among 15–64-year-olds (no relationship was found among 15–19-year-olds), suggesting that in regions where there is high competition, measured by more men relative to women, there are fewer rates of sexual violence. An issue with these data is that regions where there are more women relative to men could be a consequence of high competition (due to male-male homicide), not a cause of it. Sex ratio is an important variable in determining competition (see Box 2.3), but future work in this area will need to control for life expectancy and homicide rates to provide a more accurate understanding of its relationship to sexual violence in humans.

Although younger males account for a large proportion of sexual crimes, and are likely to desist as they age, there is a smaller number of sexual offenders who start earlier in development and persist well into adulthood. These offenders may fall into either the facultative fixed or obligate categories described above.

By-Products and Disorders

By-Products. Although this volume is focused on adaptive explanations of behavior, there may be either unintended outcomes of these adaptations, known as by-products, or these adaptations may not be functioning in the way they were designed, known as disorders. The typology of sexual offenders outlined by Camilleri (2012) also recognizes that sexual offending could also be understood in these ways. Rape has been considered a by-product of men's sexual interest in impersonal sex (Symons, 1979) or arousal to visual stimuli, sex drive, and sexual variety (Palmer, 1991). There are several considerations, however, with by-product explanations. The first is that because by-products come from adaptations, it is not clear exactly which of the cited traits are adaptive. Arousal to visual stimuli, for example, certainly seems to correlate with men's sexual psychology, but its adaptive function has not been established. This is not to say these characteristics are not adaptations, but if sexual offending is indeed their by-products, researchers need to establish the adaptive function of those initial traits, then empirically link those traits to sexual offending.

There has not been a systematic method to test the links between sexual offending as a by-product and their associated adaptations. Camilleri (2012) proposed a way to test for this link with the assumption that the degree to which sexes differ on adaptations should match the degree to which the sexes differ on their by-products. Effect size differences between the sexes varied from 0.3 to 1.2 in terms of partners desired, sexual consent after knowing someone for a month, and interest in short-term mating (Schmitt et al., 2003), whereas the effect size for rape was 15.2—a massive effect size that does not match the range of sexual psychological traits. If by-product hypotheses are true, then they need to explain why such a discrepancy exists. Another way to match by-products with adaptations is to see if patterns of sexual homicide correspond with patterns of sexual offending that does not result in homicide. Two studies found that sexual homicide matches the age-sex-crime curve found in general sexual offending (Shackelford, 2002; Wilson, Daly, & Scheib, 1997). These methods represent a starting point for more direct and thorough tests of by-product hypotheses for sexual offending.

Furthermore, we would expect, following Camilleri's (2012) typology, that sexual homicide offenders cluster into adaptive types (i.e., since there are five types of sexual offenders listed under adaptations, we expect sexual homicide to cluster into the same five categories). Although this approach is not a direct test of by-products, it does suggest that sexual homicide is not a homogenous behavior with one etiological path. Further support for the notion that sexual homicide is a by-product of adaptive paths to sexual offending comes from Sewall, Krupp, and Lalumière's (2013) cluster analysis—they found sexual homicide perpetrators clustered into sadistic, competitively disadvantaged, and slashers (i.e., mutilates victim's body). However, one category that did not emerge was psychopathic offenders. Their results may not be generalizable to all sexual offenders because they included serial sexual homicide perpetrators, and a thorough assessment of constructs was not always possible (e.g., PCL-R). Further work following their approach would assist with understanding the etiology of sexual homicide.

Providing support for by-product hypotheses involves more than just ruling out adaptation predictions. More systematic investigations of the adaptations from which rape is hypothesized to be a by-product from, in addition to better ways to empirically test for by-products, are needed. That is, by-product explanations need to be held to the same standards that are used to establish adaptations.

Disorders. The disordered path to sexual offending is different from men who are competitively disadvantaged—competitive disadvantage suggests adopting a coercive reproductive strategy as an adaptive response to atypical development that poses a barrier to reproduction. Disorders are gross abnormalities to one's psychology and behavior that impair adaptive sexual behaviors. Despite such explanations being around for quite some time (e.g., Palmer, 1991; Quinsey & Lalumière, 1995), very few studies have tested them. Similar to by-products, a disorder needs to be linked to particular psychological adaptations, and theoretical and empirical evidence needs to be accrued to suggest that the adaptation is not functioning in the way it was designed. Candidates for disordered forms of sexual offending include developmentally disabled offenders, paraphilias, and pathological jealousy (see Box 2.4 for similar disorder among nonhuman animals).

Initial evidence that sexual offending by developmentally disabled men is more likely a result of a disordered psychology, as opposed to being a form of competitive disadvantage, comes from finding that these men are more likely to sexually prefer nonreproductive stimuli (Rice, Harris, Lang, & Chaplin, 2008). It is not clear which mechanisms are malfunctioning, but cognitive decision making (i.e., ability to weigh costs and benefits) is a likely candidate. Some offender groups, such as incest offenders, may have a malfunctioning kin recognition mechanism, although some may also result from deviant sexual interests (Seto, Lalumière, & Kuban, 1999).

Some paraphilias could be a disorder of possibly developmentally fixed mechanisms: disordered age preferences could result in pedophilia or gerontophilia and disordered species recognition could result in zoophilia. Other paraphilias might result from flexible mechanisms: disorders of the courtship process might result in voyeurism, exhibitionism, frotteurism, and toucherism (Freund, Scher, & Hucker, 1983). Although very little research currently exists for paraphilias generally, pedophilia has been given considerable attention, particularly its link to various neurological impairments in offenders (Seto, 2008). Lastly, pathological jealousy might result from disordered mechanisms associated with minimizing cuckoldry risk, since these men are persistently jealous, even without any indication that a partner has been unfaithful.

Similar to by-product explanations, more extensive research on the initial adaptations are needed, with appropriate methodologies to identify which mechanism is malfunctioning. There are many studies that link sexual offending with other disorders or neuropsychological impairments, such as the fraternal birth order effect (Lalumière, Harris, Quinsey, & Rice, 1998), handedness (Bogaert, 2001), comorbid psychiatric disorders (Långström et al., 2004), and brain injury (Blanchard et al., 2002), but

how these factors lead to specific sexual offending types is still unknown.

Box 2.4: Evidence of By-Product and Disorder in Animal Reproductive Behavior

As in humans, animals can show a striking breadth of reproductive responding, including behaviors that could be considered errors, as they would result in nonproductive sexual behavior, such as mating with the wrong species or inanimate objects or with killing a sexual partner.

Low selectivity of sexual response of males has been documented in many species, and this erroneous behavior of males likely persists because the cost of such errors is sufficiently low as to "escape" selection pressure for high selectivity or as a by-product of selection for other sexual behaviors. For example, the head and neck of female birds, even if static in motion, are sufficient stimuli to elicit copulation by males (Domjan, Greene, & North, 1989; Schein & Hale, 1959). Similarly, there are several documented examples of male animals copulating with static (deceased) members of their species (termed "Davian behavior"; Dickerman, 1960; e.g., Costa et al., 2010; Moeliker, 2001; Russell, Sladen, & Ainley, 2012; Sinovas, 2009). Additionally, there are many anecdotal examples of males of many species copulating with objects that have even a passing similarity to females, be they other species or inanimate objects. In species where reproduction can involve male control of females and forcible copulation, females may occasionally be killed during sex (e.g., Le Boeuf & Mesnick, 1990).

Unlike research with humans, the etiology of disordered sexual behavior in nonhumans is often unknown, due to the complexity and difficulty of such research. As animal examples are often found serendipitously, researchers generally lack information about the parentage or developmental experiences of individuals displaying unusual

(continued)

Box 2.4 (continued)

behavior. There is, however, some indication that early experiences can play a role in shaping male response to focus on inappropriate targets. These typically arise in species where species recognition is based on early exposure: individuals, particularly those raised by other species, may misidentify accordingly when choosing reproductive partners (see reviews by Bolhuis, 1991; Irvin & Price, 1999), and experience can play a role in development of sexual response to objects (e.g., male turkey response to the human hand; Schein & Hale, 1959). Note that "reverse imprinting" has been suggested to play a role in human inbreeding avoidance (based on co-residency; Westermarck effect—Westermarck, 1891; Lieberman & Smith, 2012; and observation of association between own mother and other children; see Lieberman & Smith, 2012), and the role of imprinting in the development of paraphilias has been debated (for a recent review of learning and sexual response in humans and nonhuman animals, see Hoffmann (2012)).

Box 2.5: Primates and Sexual Aggression

Our closest genetic relatives, primates (particularly apes) show clear differences among males both within and among species in terms of reproductive behaviors (Smuts & Smuts, 1993). Differences in male reproductive tactics generally involve variation in degree of sexual aggression and coercion. While forced copulation is rare when looking across species, many primates show a bias in female-directed aggression by males, such that they more frequently target females when they are in estrus, suggesting that such aggression functions as sexual coercion and control (Smuts & Smuts, 1993). Infanticide is another form of aggression-based sexual

conflict often studied in primates (see Smuts & Smuts, 1993), but whether it should be considered a form of sexual coercion, due to the influence on female receptivity, has been debated (see discussion in Palombit, 2009). Although there are several examples of indirect coercion and control among primates (see Muller & Wrangham, 2009), we focus specifically on examples of forced copulation and direct coercion (aggression to overcome female mating resistance; Muller, Kahlenberg, & Wrangham, 2009a) and include only species for which there is clear information on these behaviors.

The examples outlined below largely fall into the category of short- and long-term facultative developmentally flexible tactics and, in some cases, mirror examples among humans (particularly "young male syndrome" and "cuckoldry risk"). This does not necessarily rule out the possibility of obligate or developmentally fixed tactics, although given the traits of the suggested examples of these tactics in humans (e.g., the rarity of psychopaths in the general population), detecting such patterns of behavior among primates would be challenging, given our decreased instances and duration of contact compared to our contact with our own species.

Chimpanzees

Common chimpanzee (Pan troglodytes): Male aggression directed at females is rather frequently biased towards cycling females, and performance of such aggression is not isolated to males of a particular social status (Muller, 2007; Muller, Emery Thompson, & Wrangham, 2006). This male aggression represents high costs to females, who can suffer extreme damage during these interactions (Muller, Kahlenberg, & Wrangham, 2009b). However, the most extreme form of direct coercion, forced copulation, is relatively rare (Tutin, 1979). It has been suggested that this is because of

(continued)

Box 2.5 (continued)

the high levels of female promiscuity and low resistance to male courtship (Muller, Kahlenberg, & Wrangham, 2009b). The few instances of forced copulation recorded have generally been cases of brothers or sons forcing copulation on sister/mother (Goodall, 1986), suggesting that it may be used only when females resist males who they are averse to mating with (due to the potential costs of inbreeding; e.g., Ralls, Ballou, & Templeton, 1988).

Bonobo (Pan paniscus): In striking contrast to the common chimpanzee, there is a clear lack of male aggression towards females and little evidence of instances of indirect or direct coercion and forced copulation among bonobos. This reflects the general pattern of low aggression in this species (where sexual activity, rather than aggression, is used to resolve conflicts) and codominance between males and females. See Paoli (2009) for a full review of these points, and of bonobo sexual behavior.

Gorillas

Forced copulation by lowland gorillas has been observed in captivity, but only when the female could not escape (Smuts & Smuts, 1993), and forced copulation has been only rarely reported in wild-living gorillas (Robbins, 2009). Female-directed aggression among gorillas seems to act to control female group affiliation, as well being a form of sexual coercion, and females typically receive aggression only from dominant silverback males (Robbins, 2009). There is more female-directed aggression in multi-silverback groups that receive more aggression, but this is a result of the greater number of dominant males, rather than increased aggression by individual males (Robbins, 2009). Thus, mountain gorilla (*Gorilla beringei beringei*) females, which are more frequently in multi-male groups, generally receive more aggression than western

gorillas (*Gorilla gorilla gorilla*) females (Robbins, 2009). Sexual coercion through aggression is implied by mating patterns; for example, among mountain gorillas in multi-male groups, the male who directs more aggression towards a female also copulates more frequently with her (Robbins, 2009; Smuts & Smuts, 1993). Levels of aggression and harm to females are also often less than in other species (e.g., chimpanzees, Muller, Kahlenberg, & Wrangham, 2009b), and male gorilla aggression often takes the form of threats rather than direct physical contact (Robbins, 2009).

Orangutans

Forced copulation is common among orangutans (see extensive review in Knott, 2009), although these copulations generally result in less lasting physical damage to females, and male orangutans generally show lower levels of physical violence towards females relative to other primates such as chimpanzees (see Knott, 2009; Muller, Kahlenberg, & Wrangham, 2009b). Orangutans offer the clearest examples of alternative tactics among primates, as the propensity of males to engage in forcible copulation is associated with clear morphological variation in facial ornamentation (Knott, 2009). "Flanged" males are the older (and thus typically most dominant), preferred by females, and have prominent fleshy cheek ornamentations that more younger "unflanged" males lack. While both types engage in forced copulation, across sites, unflanged males are more likely to engage in forcible sex (see overview in Knott, 2009). The variation in rate of forced copulations by flanged males may reflect their dominance (or prime) status—the oldest flanged males which are past-prime and less preferred by females are also more likely to engage in forced copulation (Knott, 2009; Mitani, 1985). Thus, it

(continued)

Box 2.5 (continued)

seems that female preference correlates with likelihood of engaging in forced copulation and that it is in fact a strategy of non-preferred (and less dominant) male orangutans (Knott, 2009). In agreement with this idea, the size of unflanged males is generally predictive of their likelihood of forcing copulation, and those large unflanged males who are closest to becoming dominant (and therefore flanged) are less likely to force copulation, perhaps reflecting a female ability to assess status within male phenotypes (Utami Atmoko, 2000).

Baboons

Among baboon species, forced copulation does not appear to occur in the wild (Smuts, 1985/2007). There is interspecies variation in the level of male aggression and control of females, and such aggression can function as a form of coercion or control, although it also occurs outside of a sexual context (Smuts & Smuts, 1993). Chacma baboon (*Papio hamadryas griseipes*) males show a generally high level of female-directed aggression, which appears to be multimodal in function: it can serve as male coercion, but there is also a clear role of male–male competition (e.g., signaling to rivals; Kitchen et al., 2009). Aggression by dominant males hamadryas baboons (*Papio hamadryas*) appears to condition females to remain close to him, as it is particularly frequent during and immediately following a change in leadership (Swedell & Schreier, 2009).

Social coalitions as female counteradaptations to male aggression

In several baboon species, male–female interactions termed "friendships" appear to in part be a method of female defense against aggression from other males directed towards themselves and their offspring (Smuts, 1985/2007). Similar

preferences of females for particular males based on social benefits have been noted in several other species including gorillas, chimpanzees, and macaques (Smuts & Smuts, 1993). These positive associations may function as a female counteradaptation to male aggression and sexual conflict among primates, and even females in haremic species show preferences for group membership based on the protection from aggression and infanticide that the dominant male provides (Smuts & Smuts, 1993).

Female-female interactions may also function to decrease the amount of aggression and reproductive control females experience from males. Bonds between female bonobos appear to strongly contribute to the notably low levels of aggression in this species generally (Paoli, 2009). Additionally, there is evidence that female coalitions among common chimpanzees may function to reduce exposure to male aggression (Newton-Fisher, 2006).

The selection pressure that rape places on human women is understudied relative to the potential selective benefits and mechanisms underlying male rape behavior. Rape presents considerable physical risk to women and can result in additional potential costs by decreasing her control over her reproduction decisions. Thus, it stands to reason that women may have evolved counteradaptations to mitigate these costs, both in terms of physiological mechanisms, and biases towards particular social interactions and behaviors. Increased attention to rape-avoidance behaviors, as well as mechanisms that may allow for rape-cost reduction in women would be valuable, in terms of better understanding both the fitness consequences of rape and the potential adaptive function of how women respond to rape and sexual control/coercion.

Conclusions

The purpose of this chapter was to review research and theory on sexual offending from an evolutionary framework. Evolutionary approaches towards behavior and psychology suggest the evolution of these traits could function as an adaptation, by-product of adaptations, or disordered adaptations. Although we focused on adaptive explanations, alternatives should be given equal empirical and theoretical attention. We also reviewed how in other species, forced copulation could function as either an obligate, facultative-fixed, or facultative flexible behavioral tactic. A larger puzzle is that humans appear to present multiple contexts, functions, and malfunctions under which sexual offending occurs. We could identify no other example of a species that shows such diversity in coercive/nonconsensual sexual behaviors or in any specific reproductive behavior. This contrast may be a product of insufficient research with nonhuman animals (e.g., lack of attention to or constraints on our ability observe such individual variation), a generally greater emphasis on these behaviors and their subtle variations in humans, or some unique feature of humans as a species that has lead to greater elaboration of the associated behaviors. Overall, we recognize that sexual offending is a complex act, occurring under different contexts, against different types of victims, and with different underlying motivations and potential fitness consequences to the perpetrator. Further research using this theoretical model as a guide might assist with untangling this complexity.

References

Alcock, J. (2001). *Animal behavior: An evolutionary approach* (7th ed.). Sunderland, MA: Sinauer Associates.

Alexander, R. D., & Noonan, K. M. (1979). Concealment of ovulation, parental care, and human social evolution. In N. A. Chagnon & W. Irons (Eds.), *Evolutionary biology and human social behavior* (pp. 436–453). North Scituate, MA: Duxbury Press.

Alonzo, S. H., Taborsky, M., & Wirtz, P. (2000). Male alternative reproductive behaviors in a Mediterranean wrasse, *Symphodus ocellatus*: Evidence from otoliths for separate life-history pathways. *Evolutionary Ecology Research, 2*, 997–1007.

Alonzo, S. H., & Warner, R. R. (2000). Dynamic games and field experiments examining intra- and intersexual conflict: Explaining counter-intuitive mating behavior in a Mediterranean wrasse, *Symphodus ocellatus. Behavioral Ecology, 11*, 56–70.

Andrews, P. W., Gangestad, S. W., & Matthews, D. (2002). Adaptationism—How to carry out an exaptationist program. *Behavioral and Brain Sciences, 25*, 489–504.

Apicella, C. L., & Marlowe, F. W. (2007). Men's reproductive investment decisions: Mating, parenting *and* self-perceived mate value. *Human Nature, 18*, 22–34.

Arseneault, L., Tremblay, R. E., Boulerice, B., Séguin, J. R., & Saucier, J. F. (2000). Minor physical anomalies and family adversity as risk factors for violent delinquency in adolescence. *The American Journal of Psychiatry, 157*(6), 917–923.

Arseneault, L., Tremblay, R. E., Boulerice, B., & Saucier, J. F. (2002). Obstetrical complications and violent delinquency: Testing two developmental pathways. *Child Development, 73*(2), 496–508.

Baird, T. A., Baird, T. D., & Shine, R. (2012). Aggressive transition between alternative male social tactics in a long-lived Australian dragon (*Physignathus lesueurii*) living at high density. *PLoS One, 7*(8), e418–e419.

Barber, N. (2000). The sex ratio as a predictor of cross-national variation in violent crime. *Cross-Cultural Research, 34*, 264.

Baumbach, J. (2002). Some implications of prenatal alcohol exposure for the treatment of adolescents with sexual offending behaviors. *Sexual Abuse: A Journal of Research and Treatment, 14*(4), 313–327.

Blanchard, R., Christensen, B. K., Strong, S. M., Cantor, J. M., Kuban, M. E., Klassen, P., Dickey, R., & Blak, T. (2002). Retrospective self-reports of childhood accidents causing unconsciousness in phallometrically diagnosed pedophiles. *Archives of Sexual Behavior, 31*, 511–526.

Blonigen, D. M., Hicks, B. M., Krueger, R. F., Patrick, C. J., & Iacono, W. G. (2006). Continuity and change in psychopathic traits as measured via normal-range personality: A longitudinal-biometric study. *Journal of Abnormal Psychology, 115*(1), 85–95.

Bogaert, A. F. (2001). Handedness, criminality, and sexual offending. *Neuropsychologia, 39*(5), 465–469.

Bolhuis, J. J. (1991). Mechanisms of avian imprinting: A review. *Biological Reviews of the Cambridge Philosophical Society, 66*, 303–345.

Brown, D. E. (1991). *Human universals*. Boston: McGraw-Hill.

Burt, S. A. (2009). Are there meaningful etiological differences within antisocial behavior? Results of a meta-analysis. *Clinical Psychology Review, 29*(2), 163–178.

Buss, D. M. (1991). Evolutionary personality psychology. *Annual Review of Psychology, 42*, 459–491.

Buss, D. M. (2003). *The evolution of desire: Strategies of human mating* (2nd ed.). New York: Basic Books.

Camilleri, J. A. (2012). Evolutionary psychological perspectives on sexual offending: From etiology to intervention. In T. K. Shackelford & V. A. Weekes-Shackelford (Eds.), *The Oxford handbook of evolutionary perspectives on violence, homicide, and war* (pp. 173–196). New York: Oxford University Press.

Camilleri, J. A., & Quinsey, V. L. (2009a). Testing the cuckoldry risk hypothesis of partner sexual coercion in community and forensic samples. *Evolutionary Psychology, 7*, 164–178.

Camilleri, J. A., & Quinsey, V. L. (2009b). Individual differences in the propensity for partner sexual coercion. *Sexual Abuse: A Journal of Research and Treatment, 21*, 111–129.

Camilleri, J. A., & Quinsey, V. L. (2012). Sexual conflict and partner rape. In A. T. Goetz & T. K. Shackelford (Eds.), *Oxford handbook of sexual conflict in humans* (pp. 257–268). New York: Oxford University Press.

Camilleri, J. A., Quinsey, V. L., & Tapscott, J. L. (2009). Assessing the propensity for sexual coaxing and coercion in relationships: Factor structure, reliability, and validity of the tactics to obtain sex scale. *Archives of Sexual Behavior, 38*(6), 959–973. doi:10.1007/s10508-008-9377-2.

Caspi, A., Roberts, B. W., & Shiner, R. L. (2005). Personality development: Stability and change. *Annual Review of Psychology, 56*, 453–484.

Choe, J. (2008). Income inequality and crime in the United States. *Economics Letters, 101*(1), 31–33.

Connor, R. C., & Vollmer, N. L. (2009). Sexual coercion in dolphin courtships: A comparison with chimpanzees. In M. N. Muller & R. W. Wrangham (Eds.), *Sexual coercion in primates: An evolutionary perspective on male aggression against females* (pp. 218–243). Cambridge, MA: Harvard University Press.

Costa, H. C., da Silva, E. T., Campos, P. S., da Cunha Oliveira, M. P., Nunes, A. V., & da Silva Santos, P. (2010). The Corpse Bride: A case of Davian behaviour in the Green Ameiva (*Ameiva ameiva*) in southeastern Brazil. *Herpetology Notes, 3*, 79–83.

Cox, C. R. (1981). Agonistic encounters among male elephant seals: Frequency, context, and the role of female preference. *American Zoologist, 21*, 197–209.

Coyne, J. A. (2003). Of vice and men: A case study in evolutionary psychology. In S. B. Travis (Ed.), *Evolution, gender, and rape* (pp. 172–189). Cambridge, MA: MIT Press.

Criss, M. M., Shaw, D. S., Moilanen, K. L., Hitchings, J. E., & Ingoldsby, E. M. (2009). Family, neighborhood, and peer characteristics as predictors of child adjustment: A longitudinal analysis of additive and mediation models. *Social Development, 18*(3), 511–535.

Daly, M., Wilson, M., & Vasdev, S. (2001). Income inequality and homicide rates in Canada and the United States. *Canadian Journal of Criminology, 43*, 219–236.

D'Alessio, S. J., & Stolzenberg, L. (2010). The sex ratio and male-on-female intimate partner violence. *Journal of Criminal Justice, 38*(4), 555–561.

Dickerman, R. W. (1960). "Davian Behaviour Complex" in ground squirrels. *Journal of Mammology, 41*, 403.

Domjan, M., Greene, P., & North, N. C. (1989). Contextual conditioning and the control of copulatory behavior by species-typical sign stimuli in male Japanese quail. *Journal of Experimental Psychology: Animal Behavior Processes, 15*, 147–153.

Eberhard, W. G. (1996). *Female control: Sexual selection by cryptic female choice*. Princeton, NJ: Princeton University Press.

Edens, J. F., Marcus, D. K., Lilienfeld, S. O., & Poythress, N. G. (2006). Psychopathic, not psychopath: Taxometric evidence for the dimensional structure of psychopathy. *Journal of Abnormal Psychology, 115*, 131–144.

Emlen, D. J. (2008). The role of genes and the environment in the expression and evolution of animal alternative tactics. In R. Oliveira, M. Taborsky, & H. J. Brockmann (Eds.), *Alternative reproductive tactics: An integrative approach* (pp. 85–108). Cambridge, MA: Cambridge University Press.

Ferguson, C. J. (2010). Genetic contributions to antisocial personality and behavior: A meta-analytic review from an evolutionary perspective. *The Journal of Social Psychology, 150*, 160–180.

Freund, K., Scher, H., & Hucker, S. (1983). The courtship disorders. *Archives of Sexual Behavior, 12*, 369–379.

Goetz, A. T., & Shackelford, T. K. (2006). Sexual coercion and forced in-pair copulation as sperm competition tactics in humans. *Human Nature, 17*(3), 265–282.

Goetz, A. T., & Shackelford, T. K. (2009). Sexual coercion in intimate relationships: A comparative analysis of the effects of women's infidelity and men's dominance and control. *Archives of Sexual Behavior, 38*, 226–234.

Goodall, J. (1986). *The chimpanzees of Gombe: Patterns of behavior*. Cambridge, MA: Harvard University Press.

Gottschall, J. A., & Gottschall, T. A. (2003). Are per-incident rape-pregnancy rates higher than per-incident consensual pregnancy rates? *Human Nature, 14*(1), 1–20.

Gross, M. R. (1985). Disruptive selection for alternative life histories in salmon. *Nature, 313*, 47–48.

Gross, M. R., & Charnov, E. L. (1980). Alternative male life histories in bluegill sunfish. *Proceeding of the National Academy of Sciences of the United States of America, 77*, 6937–6948.

Guay, J., Ruscio, J., Knight, R. A., & Hare, R. D. (2007). A taxometric analysis of the latent structure of psychopathy: Evidence for dimensionality. *Journal of Abnormal Psychology, 116*(4), 701.

Gunter, T. D., Vaughn, M. G., & Philibert, R. A. (2010). Behavioral genetics in antisocial spectrum disorders and psychopathy: A review of the recent literature. *Behavioral Sciences and the Law, 28*, 148–173.

Harris, G. T., Lalumière, M. L., Seto, M. C., Rice, M. E., & Chaplin, T. C. (2012). Explaining the erectile responses of rapists to rape stories: The contributions of sexual activity, non-consent, and violence with injury. *Archives of Sexual Behavior, 41*(1), 221–229.

Harris, G. T., Rice, M. E., Hilton, N. Z., Lalumière, M. L., & Quinsey, V. L. (2007). Coercive and precocious sexuality as a fundamental aspect of psychopathy. *Journal of Personality Disorders, 21*(1), 1–27.

Harris, G. T., Rice, M. E., & Lalumière, M. L. (2001). Criminal violence: The roles of psychopathy, neurodevelopmental insults, and antisocial parenting. *Criminal Justice and Behavior, 28*(4), 402–426.

Harris, G. T., Rice, M. E., & Quinsey, V. L. (1994). Psychopathy as a taxon: Evidence that psychopaths are a discrete class. *Journal of Consulting and Clinical Psychology, 62*(2), 387–397.

Henson, S. A., & Warner, R. R. (1997). Male and female alternative reproductive behaviors in fishes: A new approach using intersexual dynamics. *Annual Review of Ecology and Systematics, 28*, 571–592.

Hoelzel, A. R., LeBoeuf, B. J., Reiter, J., & Campagna, C. (1999). Alpha-male paternity in elephant seals. *Behavioural Ecology and Sociobiology, 46*, 298–306.

Hoffmann, H. (2012). Considering the role of conditioning in sexual orientation. *Archives of Sexual Behavior, 41*, 63–72.

Hsieh, C. C., & Pugh, M. D. (1993). Poverty, income inequality, and violent crime: A meta-analysis of recent aggregate data studies. *Criminal Justice Review, 18*(2), 182–202.

Ingoldsby, E. M., & Shaw, D. S. (2002). Neighborhood contextual factors and early-starting antisocial pathways. *Clinical Child and Family Psychology Review, 5*(1), 21–55.

Ingoldsby, E. M., Shaw, D. S., Winslow, E., Schonberg, M., Gilliom, M., & Criss, M. M. (2006). Neighborhood disadvantage, parent-child conflict, neighborhood peer relationships, and early antisocial behavior problem trajectories. *Journal of Abnormal Child Psychology, 34*(3), 303–319.

Irvin, D. E., & Price, T. (1999). Sexual imprinting, learning and speciation. *Heredity, 82*, 347–354.

Jarjoura, G. R., Triplett, R. A., & Brinker, G. P. (2002). Growing up poor: Examining the link between persistent childhood poverty and delinquency. *Journal of Quantitative Criminology, 18*(2), 159–187.

Jespersen, A. F., Lalumière, M. L., & Seto, M. C. (2009). Sexual abuse history among adult sex offenders and non-sex offenders: A meta-analysis. *Child Abuse & Neglect, 33*, 179–192.

Kinner, S. (2003). Psychopathy as an adaptation: Implications for society and social policy. In R. W. Bloom & N. Dess (Eds.), *Evolutionary psychology and violence: A primer for policymakers and public policy advocates* (pp. 57–81). Westport, CT: Praeger.

Kitchen, D. M., Beehner, J. C., Bergman, J. T., Cheney, D. L., Crockford, C., Engh, A. L., et al. (2009). The causes and consequences of male aggression directed at female chacma baboons. In M. N. Muller & R. W. Wrangham (Eds.), *Sexual coercion in primates: An evolutionary perspective on male aggression against females* (pp. 128–156). Cambridge, MA: Harvard University Press.

Knight, R. A. (1999). Validation of a typology for rapists. *Journal of Interpersonal Violence, 14*(3), 303–330.

Knott, C. D. (2009). Orangutans: Sexual coercion without sexual violence. In M. N. Muller & R. W. Wrangham (Eds.), *Sexual coercion in primates: An evolutionary perspective on male aggression against females* (pp. 81–111). Cambridge, MA: Harvard University Press.

Kokko, H., & Jennions, M. D. (2008). Parental investment, sexual selection and sex ratios. *Journal of Evolutionary Biology, 21*, 919–948.

Lalumière, M. L., Chalmers, L. J., Quinsey, V. L., & Seto, M. C. (1996). A test of the mate deprivation hypothesis of sexual coercion. *Ethology and Sociobiology, 17*(5), 299–318.

Lalumière, M. L., Harris, G. T., Quinsey, V. L., & Rice, M. E. (1998). Sexual deviance and number of older brothers among sexual offenders. *Sexual Abuse: A Journal of Research and Treatment, 10*(1), 5–15.

Lalumière, M. L., Harris, G. T., & Rice, M. E. (2001). Psychopathy and developmental instability. *Evolution and Human Behavior, 22*(2), 75–92.

Lalumière, M., & Quinsey, V. (1996). Sexual deviance, antisociality, mating effort, and the use of sexually coercive behaviors. *Personality and Individual Differences, 21*, 33–48.

Lalumière, M. L., Harris, G. T., Quinsey, V. L., & Rice, M. E. (2005). *The causes of rape: Understanding individual differences in male propensity for sexual aggression.* Washington, DC: American Psychological Association.

Långström, N., Sjöstedt, G., & Grann, M. (2004). Psychiatric disorders and recidivism in sexual offenders. *Sexual Abuse: A Journal of Research and Treatment, 16*(2), 139–150.

Larsson, H., Tuvblad, C., Rijsdijk, F. V., Andershed, H., Grann, M., & Lichtenstein, P. (2007). A common genetic factor explains the association between psychopathic personality and antisocial behavior. *Psychological Medicine, 37*, 15–26.

Laub, J. H., & Sampson, R. J. (2001). Understanding desistance from crime. *Crime and Justice, 28*, 1–69.

Le Boeuf, B. J. (1974). Male-male competition and reproductive success in elephant seals. *American Zoologist, 14*, 163–176.

Le Boeuf, B. J., & Mesnick, S. L. (1990). Sexual behavior of male northern elephant seals: I. Lethal injuries to adult females. *Behaviour, 116*(1–2), 143–162.

Lieberman, D., & Smith, A. (2012). It's all relative: Sexual aversions and moral judgments regarding sex among siblings. *Current Directions in Psychological Science, 21*, 243–247.

Lynam, D. R., Caspi, A., Moffitt, T. E., Loeber, R., & Stouthamer-Loeber, M. (2007). Longitudinal evidence that psychopathy scores in early adolescence predict adult psychopathy. *Journal of Abnormal Psychology, 116*, 155–165.

Marcus, D. K., John, S. L., & Edens, J. F. (2004). A taxometric analysis of psychopathic personality. *Journal of Abnormal Psychology, 113*, 626–635.

Marshall, L. A., & Cooke, D. J. (1999). The childhood experiences of psychopaths: A retrospective study of familial and societal factors. *Journal of Personality Disorders, 13*(3), 211–225.

McGue, M., Bacon, S., & Lykken, D. T. (1993). Personality stability and change in early adulthood: A behavioral genetic analysis. *Developmental Psychology, 29*, 96–109.

McKibbin, W. F., Starratt, V. G., Shackelford, T. K., & Goetz, A. T. (2011). Perceived risk of female infidelity moderates the relationship between objective risk of female infidelity and sexual coercion in humans (Homo sapiens). *Journal of Comparative Psychology, 125*(3), 370–373.

McKinney, F., Derrickson, S. R., & Mineau, P. (1983). Forced copulation in waterfowl. *Behaviour, 86*, 250–294.

Mealey, L. (1995). The sociobiology of sociopathy: An integrated evolutionary model. *Behavioral and Brain Sciences, 18*, 523–599.

Mesnick, S. L., & Le Boeuf, B. J. (1991). Sexual behavior of male northern elephant seals: II. Female response to potentially injurious encounters. *Behaviour, 117*(3–4), 262–280.

Mitani, J. C. (1985). Mating behavior of male orangutans in the Kutai Game Reserve, Indonesia. *Animal Behaviour, 33*, 392–402.

Moeliker, C. W. (2001). The first case of homosexual necrophilia in the mallard Anas platyrhynchos (Aves: Anatidae). *Deinsea, 8*, 243–247.

Moffitt, T. E. (1993). Adolescence-limited and life-course-persistent antisocial behavior: A developmental taxonomy. *Psychological Review, 100*(4), 674.

Moffitt, T. E., Caspi, A., Harrington, H., & Milne, B. J. (2002). Males on the life-course-persistent and adolescence-limited antisocial pathways: Follow-up at age 26 years. *Development and Psychopathology, 14*(1), 179–207.

Mulder, M. B., & Rauch, K. L. (2009). Sexual conflict in humans: Variations and solutions. *Evolutionary Anthropology, 18*, 201–214.

Muller, M. N. (2007). Chimpanzee violence: Femmes fatales. *Current Biology, 17*, 365–366.

Muller, M. N., Emery Thompson, E., & Wrangham, R. W. (2006). Male chimpanzees prefer mating with old females. *Current Biology, 16*, 2234–2238.

Muller, M. N., Kahlenberg, S., & Wrangham, R. W. (2009a). Male aggression and sexual coercion of females in primates. In M. N. Muller & R. W. Wrangham (Eds.), *Sexual coercion in primates: An evolutionary perspective on male aggression against females* (pp. 3–22). Cambridge, MA: Harvard University Press.

Muller, M. N., Kahlenberg, S., & Wrangham, R. W. (2009b). Male aggression against females in chimpanzees. In M. N. Muller & R. W. Wrangham (Eds.), *Sexual coercion in primates: An evolutionary perspective on male aggression against females* (pp. 184–217). Cambridge, MA: Harvard University Press.

Muller, M. N., & Wrangham, R. W. (Eds.). (2009). *Sexual coercion in primates: An evolutionary perspective on male aggression against females*. Cambridge, MA: Harvard University Press.

Neff, B. D., & Svensson, E. I. (2013). Polyandry and alternative mating tactics. *Philosophical Transactions of the Royal Society B, 368*, 20120045. doi:10.1098/rstb.2012.0045.

Newton-Fisher, N. E. (2006). Wild female chimpanzees form coalitions against male aggression. *International Journal of Primatology, 2*, 1589–1599.

Noble, K. G., Houston, S. M., Kan, E., & Sowell, E. R. (2012). Neural correlates of socioeconomic status in the developing human brain. *Developmental Science, 15*(4), 516–527.

Ogloff, J. R. P. (2006). Psychopathy/antisocial personality disorder conundrum. *The Australian and New Zealand Journal of Psychiatry, 40*, 519–528.

Oliveira, R., Taborsky, M., & Brockmann, H. J. (2008). *Alternative reproductive tactics: An integrative approach*. Cambridge, MA: Cambridge University Press.

Palmer, C. T. (1989). Rape in nonhuman animal species: Definitions, evidence, and implications. *Journal of Sex Research, 3*, 355–374.

Palmer, C. (1991). Human rape: Adaptation or by-product? *Journal of Sex Research, 28*, 365–386.

Palombit, R. (2009). "Friendship" with males: A female counterstrategy to infanticide in chacma baboons of the Okavango Delta. In M. N. Muller & R. W. Wrangham (Eds.), *Sexual coercion in primates: An evolutionary perspective on male aggression against females* (pp. 377–409). Cambridge, MA: Harvard University Press.

Paoli, T. (2009). The absence of sexual coercion in bonobos. In M. N. Muller & R. W. Wrangham (Eds.), *Sexual coercion in primates: An evolutionary perspective on male aggression against females* (pp. 410–423). Cambridge, MA: Harvard University Press.

Patrick, C. J. (Ed.). (2008). *Handbook of psychopathy*. New York: Guilford.

Perkins, C., & Klaus, P. (1996). *Criminal victimization 1994* (Bureau of Justice Statistics Special Series No. NCJ-163069). Washington, DC: US Department of Justice.

Porter, S., Fairweather, D., Drugge, J., Herve, H., Birt, A., & Boer, D. P. (2000). Profiles of psychopathy in incarcerated sexual offenders. *Criminal Justice and Behavior, 27*(2), 216–233.

Quinsey, V. L. (2003). The etiology of anomalous sexual preferences in men. *Annals of the New York Academy of Sciences, 989*, 105–117.

Quinsey, V. L., Harris, G. T., Rice, M. E., & Cormier, C. A. (2006). *Violent offenders: Appraising and managing risk* (2nd ed.). Washington, DC: American Psychological Association.

Quinsey, V. L., & Lalumière, M. L. (1995). Evolutionary perspectives on sexual offending. *Sexual Abuse: A Journal of Research and Treatment, 7*(4), 301–315.

Quinsey, V. L., Skilling, T. A., Lalumière, M. L., & Craig, W. M. (2004). *Juvenile delinquency: Understanding the origins of individual differences*. Washington, DC: American Psychological Association.

Ralls, K., Ballou, J. D., & Templeton, A. (1988). Estimates of lethal equivalents and the cost of inbreeding in mammals. *Conservation Biology, 2,* 185–193.

Rhee, S. H., & Waldman, I. D. (2002). Genetic and environmental influences on antisocial behavior: A meta-analysis of twin and adoption studies. *Psychological Bulletin, 128*(3), 490–529.

Rice, M. E., Harris, G. T., Lang, C., & Chaplin, T. C. (2008). Sexual preferences and recidivism of sex offenders with mental retardation. *Sexual Abuse: A Journal of Research and Treatment, 20*(4), 409–425.

Robbins, M. M. (2009). Male aggression against females in mountain gorillas: Courtship or coercion? In M. N. Muller & R. W. Wrangham (Eds.), *Sexual coercion in primates: An evolutionary perspective on male aggression against females* (pp. 112–127). Cambridge, MA: Harvard University Press.

Russell, D. G. D., Sladen, W. J. L., & Ainley, D. G. (2012). Dr. George Murray Levick (1876–1956): Unpublished notes on the sexual habits of the Adélie penguin. *Polar Record, 48,* 387–393.

Rylands, A., Hinz, R., Jones, M., Holmes, S. E., Feldmann, M., Brown, G., et al. (2012). Pre- and postsynaptic serotonergic differences in males with extreme levels of impulsive aggression without callous unemotional traits: A positron emission tomography study using C-DASB and C-MDL100907. *Biological Psychiatry, 72,* 1004–1011.

Schein, M. W., & Hale, E. B. (1959). The effect of early social experience on male sexual behaviour of androgen injected turkeys. *Animal Behaviour, 7,* 189–192.

Schmitt, D. P., & 118 Members of the International Sexuality Description Project. (2003). Universal sex differences in the desire for sexual variety: Tests from 52 nations, 6 continents, and 13 islands. *Journal of Personality and Social Psychology, 85,* 85–104.

Schmitt, D. P., & Pilcher, J. J. (2004). Evaluating evidence of psychological adaptation. *Psychological Science, 15*(10), 643–649.

Seto, M. C. (2008). Pedophilia: Psychopathology and theory. In D. R. Laws & W. T. O'Donohue (Eds.), *Sexual deviance: Theory, assessment, and treatment* (2nd ed., pp. 164–182). New York: Guilford.

Seto, M. C., Lalumière, M. L., & Kuban, M. (1999). The sexual preferences of incest offenders. *Journal of Abnormal Psychology, 108*(2), 267–272.

Sewall, L. A., Krupp, D. B., & Lalumière, M. L. (2013). A test of two typologies of sexual homicide. *Sexual Abuse: A Journal of Research and Treatment, 25,* 82–100.

Shackelford, T. K. (2002). Are young women the special targets of rape-murder? *Aggressive Behavior, 28*(3), 224–232.

Shields, W., & Shields, L. (1983). Forcible rape: An evolutionary perspective. *Ethology and Sociobiology, 4,* 115–136.

Shine, R., Langkilde, T., & Mason, R. T. (2003). The opportunistic serpent: Male garter snakes adjust courtship tactics to mating opportunities. *Behaviour, 140,* 1509–1526.

Sinovas, P. (2009). Bombina variegata (yellow fire-bellied toad). Mating behaviour. *Herpetology Review, 40,* 199.

Skilling, T. A., Harris, G. T., Rice, M. E., & Quinsey, V. L. (2002). Identifying persistently antisocial offenders using the Hare Psychopathy Checklist and DSM antisocial personality disorder criteria. *Psychological Assessment, 14,* 27–38.

Skilling, T. A., Quinsey, V. L., & Craig, W. M. (2001). Evidence of a taxon underlying serious antisocial behavior in boys. *Criminal Justice and Behavior, 28,* 450–470.

Smuts, B. B. (1985/2007). *Sex and friendship in baboons*. New York: Aldine Publishing.

Smuts, B. B., & Smuts, R. W. (1993). Male aggression and sexual coercion of females in nonhuman primates and other mammals: Evidence and theoretical implications. *Advances in the Study of Behavior, 22,* 1–63.

Starratt, V. G., Goetz, A. T., Shackelford, T. K., McKibbin, W. F., & Stewart-Williams, S. (2008). Men's partner-directed insults and sexual coercion in intimate relationships. *Journal of Family Violence, 23,* 315–323.

Steinberg, L. (2007). Risk taking in adolescence new perspectives from brain and behavioral science. *Current Directions in Psychological Science, 16*(2), 55–59.

Stearns, S. C. (1992). *The evolution of life histories*. London: Oxford University Press.

Stretesky, P. B., Schuck, A. M., & Hogan, M. J. (2004). Space matters: An analysis of poverty, poverty clustering, and violent crime. *Justice Quarterly, 21,* 817–841.

Swedell, L., & Schreier, A. (2009). Male aggression towards females in hamadryas baboons: Conditioning, coercion, and control. In M. N. Muller & R. W. Wrangham (Eds.), *Sexual coercion in primates: An evolutionary perspective on male aggression against females* (pp. 244–270). Cambridge, MA: Harvard University Press.

Symons, D. (1979). *The evolution of human sexuality*. New York: Oxford University Press.

Taborsky, M. (1994). Sneakers, satellites and helpers: Parasitic and cooperative behaviour in fish reproduction. *Advances in the Study of Behavior, 23,* 1–100.

Taborsky, M. (1998). Sperm competition in fish: 'Bourgeois' males and parasitic spawning. *Trends in Ecology and Evolution, 13,* 222–227.

Taborsky, M. (2001). The evolution of parasitic and cooperative reproductive behaviors in fishes. *Journal of Heredity, 92,* 100–110.

Taborsky, M., Hudde, B., & Wirtz, P. (1987). Reproductive behaviour and ecology of *Symphodus (Crenilabrus) ocellatus,* a European Wrasse with four types of male behaviour. *Behaviour, 102,* 82–118.

Taborsky, M., Oliviera, R. F., & Brockmann, H. J. (2008). The evolution of alternative reproductive tactics: Concepts and questions. In R. Oliveira, M. Taborsky, & H. J. Brockmann (Eds.), *Alternative reproductive tactics: An integrative approach* (pp. 1–21). Cambridge, MA: Cambridge University Press.

Thornhill, R. (1980). Rape in Panorpa scorpionflies and a general rape hypothesis. *Animal Behaviour, 28,* 52–59.

Thornhill, R., & Palmer, C. T. (2000). *A natural history of rape.* London: MIT Press.

Thornhill, R., & Palmer, C. T. (2004). Evolutionary life history perspective on rape. In C. Crawford & C. Salmon (Eds.), *Evolutionary psychology, public policy and personal decisions* (pp. 249–274). Mahwah, NJ: Lawrence Erlbaum.

Thornhill, R., & Thornhill, N. W. (1983). Human rape: An evolutionary analysis. *Ethology and Sociobiology, 4,* 137–173.

Tittle, C. R., & Meier, R. F. (1990). Specifying the SES/delinquency relationship. *Criminology, 28*(2), 271–300.

Tutin, C. G. E. (1979). Mating patterns and reproductive strategies in a community of wild chimpanzees (*Pan troglodytes schweinfurthii*). *Behavioral Ecology and Sociobiology, 6,* 29–38.

Utami Atmoko, S. S. (2000). *Bimaturism in orangutan males: Reproductive and ecology strategies.* PhD dissertation, Utrecht University, Utrecht.

van den Berghe, E., Wernerus, F., & Warner, R. R. (1989). Female choice and the mating cost of peripheral males. *Animal Behaviour, 38,* 875–884.

Vasey, M. W., Kotov, R., Frick, P., & Loney, B. R. (2005). The latent structure of psychopathy in youth: A taxometric investigation. *Journal of Abnormal Child Psychology, 33,* 411–429.

Viding, E., Blair, R. J. R., Moffitt, T. E., & Plomin, R. (2005). Evidence for substantial genetic risk for psychopathy in 7-year-olds. *Journal of Child Psychology and Psychiatry, 46*(6), 592–597.

Walters, G. D., Marcus, D. K., Edens, J. F., Knight, R. A., & Sanford, G. M. (2011). In search of the psychopathic sexuality taxon: Indicator size does matter. *Behavioral Sciences and the Law, 29,* 23–39.

Walters, G. D., Brinkley, C. A., Magaletta, P. R., & Diamond, P. M. (2008). Taxometric analysis of the Levenson self-report psychopathy scale. *Journal of Personality Assessment, 90*(5), 491–498.

Warner, R. R., & Lejeune, P. (1985). Sex change limited by parental care: A test using four Mediterranean labrid fishes genus *Symphodus. Marine Biology, 87,* 89–99.

Westermarck, E. (1891). *A short history of human marriage.* London: Macmillan.

Williams, G. C. (1966). *Adaptation and natural selection.* Princeton, NJ: Princeton University Press.

Wilson, M., & Daly, M. (1985). Competitiveness, risk taking, and violence: The young male syndrome. *Ethology and Sociobiology, 6,* 59–73.

Wilson, M., & Daly, M. (1992). The man who mistook his wife for a chattel. In J. H. Barkow, L. Cosmides, & J. Tooby (Eds.), *The adapted mind: Evolutionary psychology and the generation of culture* (pp. 289–322). New York: Oxford University Press.

Wilson, M., & Daly, M. (1998). Lethal and nonlethal violence against wives and the evolutionary psychology of male sexual proprietariness. In R. E. Dobash & R. P. Dobash (Eds.), *Rethinking violence against women* (pp. 199–230). Thousand Oaks, CA: Sage.

Wilson, M., Daly, M., & Scheib, J. E. (1997). Femicide: An evolutionary psychological perspective. In P. A. Gowaty (Ed.), *Feminism and evolutionary biology* (pp. 431–465). New York: Chapman & Hall.

Zimmerer, E. J., & Kallman, K. D. (1989). Genetic basis for alternative reproductive tactics in the pygmy swordtail, *Xiphophorus nigrensis. Evolution, 43,* 1298–1307.

Sexual Selection on Human Voices

3

David A. Puts, Leslie M. Doll, and Alexander K. Hill

Introduction

Vocal communication plays important roles in mediating social relationships across diverse species (Hopp, Owren, & Evans, 1997), including many primates (Clarke et al., 2006; Crockford et al., 2004; de la Torre & Snowdon, 2009; Hauser, 1992; Hauser & Marler, 1993a, 1993b; Owren et al., 1993; Seyfarth et al., 1980). Despite the relevance of communication to both sexes, the acoustic properties of adult vocalizations are often sexually differentiated. In primates, vocalizations are sexually differentiated in such species as Japanese macaques (*Macaca fuscata*: Green, 1981), lion-tailed macaques (*Macaca silenia*: Green, 1981), chacma baboons (*Papio hamadryas ursinus*: Fischer, Hammerschmidt, Cheney, & Seyfarth, 2002; Rendall, Kollias, Ney, & Lloyd, 2005; Rendall, Owren, Weerts, & Hienz, 2004), orangutans (*Pongo pygmaeus*: Delgado, 2006), chimpanzees (*Pan troglodytes*: Mitani & Gros-Louis, 1995), and bonobos (*Pan paniscus*: Mitani & Gros-Louis, 1995).

Sex differences can evolve for a variety of reasons, but sexual selection is often implicated (Andersson, 1994). Sexual selection (Darwin, 1859, 1871) favors traits that help win mating opportunities and operates through multiple mechanisms, including mate choice, favoring sexual displays and ornaments for attracting mates, and contest competition, favoring size, strength, aggression, anatomical weapons, and threat displays for winning mates by force or threat of force. Darwin (1871) noted the pubertal enlargement of male vocal structures in many mammals and males' use of vocalizations chiefly, and sometimes exclusively, during the breeding season. These facts suggest the influence of sexual selection on male vocalizations. Yet, Darwin concluded that females were not generally attracted to male vocalizations and that, while the roaring of a male lion or stag might intimidate adversaries, this benefit would have been insufficient to account for changes in male vocal structures. Rather, Darwin hypothesized that such vocalizations were byproducts of intense nervous excitement under strong emotion, such as when preparing to fight. He suggested that the frequent use of the voice in this manner may, in Lamarckian fashion over many generations, "at last have produced an inherited effect on the vocal organs of the stag, as well as other male mammals" (Darwin, 1882, p. 527).

Subsequent researchers have generally not shared this view, and recent evidence strongly implicates sexual selection in producing sex differences in numerous acoustic signals and their anatomical substrates (Charlton, Reby, & McComb, 2007; Reby et al., 2005; Ryan & Rand, 1995), including those of many primates

D.A. Puts (✉)
Department of Anthropology, Pennsylvania State University, University Park, PA 16802, USA
e-mail: dap27@psu.edu

V.A. Weekes-Shackelford and T.K. Shackelford (eds.), *Evolutionary Perspectives on Human Sexual Psychology and Behavior*, Evolutionary Psychology, DOI 10.1007/978-1-4939-0314-6_3,
© Springer Science+Business Media New York 2014

(Delgado, 2006; Snowdon, 2004). In some primates, vocalizations may function in male contest competition. For example, among orangutans, lower-ranking males avoid long calls given by higher-ranking males (Mitani, 1985), indicating that acoustic cues suggest threat potential to conspecifics. High dominance rank may be advertized partly by the fundamental and formant frequencies of vocalizations. Vocal fundamental frequency relates negatively to body size across primates (Hauser, 1993; Mitani & Stuht, 1998), and among rhesus macaques, formant frequencies indicate body size and age (Ghazanfar et al., 2007), both potential correlates of dominance. In addition, mantled guereza males possess a subhyoid air sac causing them to display lower formant spacing than would be expected given their vocal tract length (Harris, Fitch, Goldstein, & Fashing, 2006). This suggests that vocalizations may have been selected to exaggerate apparent body size among males of this species (Harris et al., 2006). Research thus indicates that, especially in males, vocalizations may serve as signals of dominance, a predictor of mating and reproductive success across primates (Cowlishaw & Dunbar, 1991). Mate choice by females has also likely been an important influence in shaping the vocalizations of male primates. Among gibbons, for instance, there is evidence that male calls signal fitness, with call quality suffering during times when food is unavailable or energy must be allocated to thermoregulation (Cowlishaw, 1996).

Sex Differences in the Human Voice

The human voice is also highly sexually differentiated (Childers & Wu, 1991; Fitch & Holbrook, 1970; Wu & Childers, 1991). Men speak at a lower fundamental frequency (F_0), the rate of vocal fold vibration during phonation and the acoustic parameter closest to what we perceive as pitch. Men also speak with lower, more closely spaced formants (e.g., Childers & Wu, 1991), frequencies of high energy that affect the perceived timbre of a vocalization. In addition, some evidence suggests that men tend to speak in a more monotone voice, that is, F_0 varies less across an utterance in men than it does in women (Daly & Warren, 2001; Puts, Apicella, & Cárdenas, 2012), although the ubiquity of this sex difference is debated (Simpson, 2009).

These sex differences are very large, ranging from around three standard deviations in the case of monotonicity to nearly six standard deviations in the case of fundamental frequency (Puts, Apicella, et al., 2012). In a sample of 630 US university undergraduate students, there was no overlap between men's and women's mean speaking fundamental frequency when reading a standard passage (D. A. Puts, unpublished data, Fig. 3.1). In the same data set, this sex difference exceeded those of many commonly studied sexually differentiated traits, including waist-to-hip ratio, height, weight, and handgrip strength (Fig. 3.2). Vocal sex differences also do not merely reflect the sex difference in body size. Fundamental frequency and formant position (a measure of formant structure) correlate only modestly with stature within sexes—in men, these correlations are approximately -0.2 and -0.3, respectively—and remain highly sexually differentiated after controlling for stature (Puts, Apicella, et al., 2012).

With the exception of F_0 variation (monotonicity) (Daly & Warren, 2001), the proximate anatomical and physiological substrates for these vocal sex differences are well understood. Men's vocal tracts and vocal folds are 15 % and 60 % longer, respectively, than are women's (Fant, 1960; Titze, 2000), several times the 7–8 % sex difference in stature (Gaulin & Boster, 1985). At puberty, elevated testosterone levels (Tossi, Postan, & Bianculli, 1976) acting through androgen receptors in the vocal folds (Aufdemorte, Sheridan, & Holt, 1983; Newman, Butler, Hammond, & Gray, 2000; Saez & Sakai, 1976) cause males' vocal folds to grow longer and thicker than those of females, both absolute and relative to overall body growth (Harries, Hawkins, Hacking, & Hughes, 1998; Harries, Walker, Williams, Hawkins, & Hughes, 1997; Hollien, Green, & Massey, 1994). Men's larger vocal folds consequently vibrate at an F_0

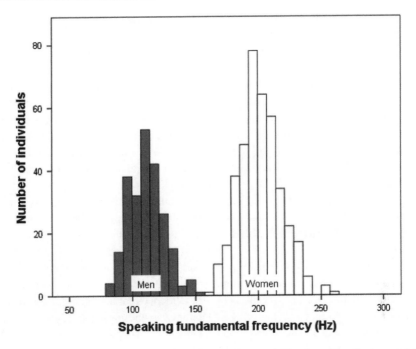

Fig. 3.1 There is almost no overlap between men's and women's mean habitual speaking fundamental frequency

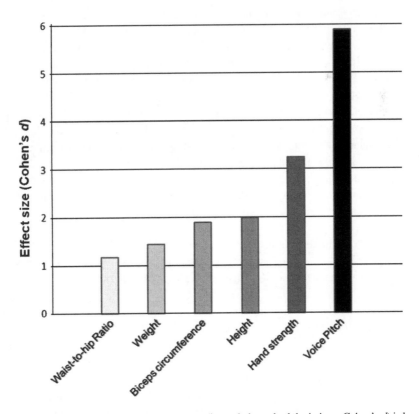

Fig. 3.2 The difference between male and female means (in pooled standard deviations, Cohen's *d*) is larger for voice pitch (measured by F_0) than for other putative targets of sexual selection

approximately half that of females during phonation. Similarly, males' larynges descend at puberty (Fitch & Giedd, 1999), producing a longer vocal tract and resulting in lower, more closely spaced formant frequencies. Although the proximate causes of the sex difference in vocal monotonicity are unclear, the apparent cross-cultural prevalence of this sex difference (Henton, 1995) suggests that sex hormones may be involved in producing its underlying neuropsychology (Puts, Apicella, et al., 2012).

Sexual Selection and Human Voices

Vocal communication may be important for primate species generally, but in none is it more important than in humans. We are a supremely communicative species, so much so that spoken language may be regarded as *the* defining human characteristic (Pinker, 1994). It is conspicuous that men's and women's voices are so different when vocal communication is so important to both sexes. For those interested in understanding the social dynamics of human sexuality, such acoustic sexual dimorphisms are particularly relevant. As we will see, these traits affect attractiveness and perceptions of dominance and predict mate preferences and behavior related to competition for mates. Therefore, clarifying why men and women sound different will elucidate how the voice mediates vocal communication and interpersonal relationships in general, and more specifically, such relationships as dominance hierarchies, social status, and romantic relationships.

Darwin (1882) attributed human sex differences in the voice and vocal anatomy to phylogenetic inertia: humans inherited these differences from ancestral species, and ancestral sex differences evolved due to the "the long-continued use of the vocal organs by the male under the excitement of love, rage and jealousy" (p. 566). Although we now know that heredity works differently, to Darwin, it was the repeated (largely functionless) use of vocalizations by males that eventually resulted in heritable sex differences in the voice and vocal anatomy.

Humans merely inherited these sex differences. By contrast, Ellis (1905, p. 125) noted that, when one considers the development of vocal sex differences at puberty, "it is difficult not to believe that this change has an influence on sexual selection and sexual psychology." In Ellis' view, because women's voices change far less than do men's at puberty, it is unlikely that women's voices evolved to attract men. Instead, men's vocal changes at puberty make the "deeper masculine voice" a secondary sexual trait in men, a conclusion further suggested to Ellis by the fact that male mammals are generally more vocal during the rutting season.

These writers worked over a century ago and had a paucity of information at their disposal. In what follows, we review the comparative wealth of evidence that has accumulated since that time, largely in the past couple of decades. We find evidence in support of the hypothesis than sexual selection has played a major role in producing sex differences in the human voice. Ancestral men and women likely competed with their same-sex rivals for mates via both mate choice and contest competition. However, in general, mate choice appears to have been relatively more important than contests in shaping women's traits (Barber, 1995; Buss & Dedden, 1990; Cashdan, 1996, 1998; Low, Alexander, & Noonan, 1987; Schmitt & Buss, 1996), and contests appear to have been more important than mate choice in shaping men's traits (Archer, 2009; Daly & Wilson, 1988, 1990; Puts, 2010). These generalities also seem to apply to voices, as we will see.

Sexual Selection on Women's Voices: Male Mate Choice

Male mate choice for feminine voices may partly account for the evolution of sex differences in these phenotypic characters. Although he ultimately rejected sexual selection on men as the cause of sex differences in the human voice, Darwin (1882, p. 695) proposed that women acquired "sweeter" voices as a sexual ornament. Laboratory studies have shown that men indeed prefer feminine voices (Apicella & Feinberg, 2009; Collins & Missing, 2003; Feinberg, DeBruine, Jones, & Perrett, 2008; Jones, Feinberg, Debruine, Little, & Vukovic, 2008, 2010; Puts, Barndt, Welling, Dawood, & Burriss, 2011), particularly for short-term, purely sexual relationships (Puts et al., 2011) and when the woman's voice indicates positive social interest (Jones et al., 2008).

The relative importance of women's voices in short-term contexts may reflect associations with current fertility (Puts et al., 2011). For example, a high voice pitch partly reflects age, with voice pitch decreasing as women senesce (Awan, 2006; Decoster & Debruyne, 1997; Nishio & Niimi, 2008). Accordingly, Röder, Fink, and Jones (2013) found that women of peak reproductive ages had more attractive voices than did either pubescent girls or postmenopausal women. In addition, Bryant and Haselton (2009) found that women's voices were higher in pitch during the fertile phase of the ovulatory cycle, although Fischer et al. (2011) found a slight decline in pitch near ovulation, and Puts, Bailey, et al. (2012) found no significant change in pitch with estradiol or progesterone levels over women's cycles. Men also find women's voices least attractive during menstruation, a time of lowered fertility (Pipitone & Gallup, 2011), and most attractive during the late follicular (fertile) phase of the cycle (Pipitone & Gallup, 2008). These changes appear to be driven by fluctuating ovarian hormones: normally cycling women's voices were most attractive when their progesterone levels were low and their estradiol levels were high, again corresponding with peak fertility in their cycles (Puts, Bailey, et al., 2012).

Consistent with the hypothesis that attractive, feminine voices increase women's competitiveness for mates, other women perceive feminine voices as more attractive to men and more flirtatious (Puts et al., 2011), that is, attractive, feminine women's voices are perceived as greater threats in competition for mates. Similarly, women perceive other women's voices to be more attractive to men when the speakers' progesterone levels are low, indicative of greater fertility in their cycles (Puts, Bailey, et al.,

2012). Feminine voices could not have evolved to help women exclude competitors from mates by force or force threat, however, because femininity in women's voices decreases the appearance of physical threat (Jones et al., 2010; Main, Jones, DeBruine, & Little, 2009; Perrett et al., 1998).

Sexual Selection on Men's Voices

Despite evidence that sexual selection has shaped women's voices, there are several reasons to expect that sexual selection operating on men, rather than on women, played a larger role in the evolution of vocal sexual dimorphisms. First, sexual selection tends to be stronger in the sex that invests less in offspring (Trivers, 1972), is capable of reproducing at a faster rate (Clutton-Brock & Vincent, 1991), and has a higher variance in reproductive success (Bateman, 1948). In humans, males invest less in offspring than females do (Eibl-Eibesfeldt, 1989; Geary, 2000; Hewlett, 1992), can reproduce at a faster rate (e.g., Chagnon, 1992; Salzano, Neel, & Maybury-Lewis, 1967), and have higher reproductive variance (Chagnon, 1990; Hewlett, 1988; Howell, 1979; Salzano et al., 1967). Thus, sexual selection has almost certainly been stronger in shaping men's traits than it has been in shaping women's. Second, sexually selected traits tend to emerge at sexual maturity, and males, much more than females, exhibit dramatic pubertal changes in vocal characteristics (Barber, 1995; Ellis, 1905). Finally, as we will see, considerable evidence indicates that masculine voices increase men's success in competition for mates.

Female Mate Choice

Men might have evolved deeper voices partly because women prefer these traits. Some correlational studies report that women prefer a more masculine than average vocal pitch (Collins, 2000; Hodges-Simeon, Gaulin, & Puts, 2010), monotonicity (Hodges-Simeon et al., 2010), and timbre (Hodges-Simeon et al., 2010, but not Collins, 2000). Women also prefer an experimentally masculinized, relative to feminized, mean pitch (Feinberg, DeBruine, Jones, & Little, 2008; Feinberg et al., 2006; Feinberg, Jones, Little, Burt, & Perrett, 2005; Jones et al., 2010; Riding, Lonsdale, & Brown, 2006, but see Apicella & Feinberg, 2009). Additionally, women's visual object memory improves after hearing masculine male voices but not after hearing feminine male voices or female voices, suggesting that women may be particularly attuned to masculine voices (Smith, Jones, Feinberg, & Allan, 2012). However, Riding et al. (2006) did not find women to prefer men's voices masculinized (increased) in monotonicity, and Feinberg et al. (2005) did not find that masculinizing timbre increased the attractiveness of men's voices. Yet, at least three studies have found that male voices masculinized in both pitch and timbre simultaneously were more attractive to women than the same voices with these acoustic parameters feminized (Feinberg et al., 2005, 2006; Puts, 2005).

Much of the variation across studies likely results from differences in the type of study (correlational vs. experimental), manipulation sizes, the rating task (e.g., sexual attractiveness vs. attractiveness for a committed relationship), stimulus presentation (e.g., paired masculinized/feminized stimuli vs. no rater hearing the same stimulus twice), and other methodological and sampling details. In general, women appear to prefer voices slightly more masculine than average, particularly in pitch. These results suggest that if female preferences influenced the evolution of masculine voices, then men's voices are now near the optimum under this form of sexual selection.

Why does vocal masculinity matter in a mate? A related question concerns why women's preferences for masculine voices have evolved and been maintained by selection. That is, what fitness benefits, if any, are associated with mating with deep-voiced males? Given evidence for heritability in the acoustic properties of both human and nonhuman vocalizations (e.g., Debruyne, Decoster, Van Gijsel, & Vercammen, 2002; Forstmeier, Burger, Temnow, & Deregnaucourt, 2009) and that putative biomarkers for genetic quality may predict vocal attractiveness (Hughes, Harrison, & Gallup, 2002), a logical possibility is that men's vocal traits signal heritable fitness benefits. These benefits may partly relate to heritable dominance, social status, and associated perquisites. Evidence detailed below in the part "Male Contest Competition" suggests that a masculine voice predicts dominance in men, and the offspring (perhaps especially male offspring) might benefit from inheriting whatever alleles contributed to their fathers' dominance.

Other evidence suggests that androgen-dependent traits, such as a deep voice (Bruckert, Lienard, Lacroix, Kreutzer, & Leboucher, 2006; Dabbs & Mallinger, 1999; Evans, Neave, Wakelin, & Hamilton, 2008; Puts, Apicella, et al., 2012), signal heritable immune system efficiency (Folstad & Karter, 1992; Tybur & Gangestad, 2011). There are two possible reasons for this. First, androgens may be immunosuppressant (Grossman, 1985), and compromising the immune system by producing high androgen levels may be feasible only for otherwise healthy individuals (Folstad & Karter, 1992). Although some evidence indicates that sex steroids suppress immune function in humans (Bouman, Heineman, & Faas, 2005), a meta-analysis found that testosterone treatment had little such effect in birds (Roberts, Buchanan, & Evans, 2004). Other evidence suggests that the immunosuppressive effects of testosterone are condition-dependent, with testosterone suppressing immune function to a greater degree in males in poor condition (Moore, Al Dujaili, et al., 2011; Moore, Cornwell, et al., 2011; Roberts & Peters, 2009). If heritable immunocompetence mitigates the immunosuppressive costs of high testosterone production, then testosterone-dependent male traits such as masculine voices should signal underlying genes that would confer disease resistance to offspring.

Second, immune system activation may suppress testosterone production. A recent meta-analysis found strong support for this hypothesis across mammals and birds (Boonekamp, Ros, & Verhulst, 2008). If a male's immune system more quickly and efficiently dealt with immune threats, then testosterone production might be suppressed less frequently, less severely, and/or for shorter durations, and a more masculine phenotype would develop. To the extent that such immune efficiency was heritable, ancestral women may have produced healthier offspring by mating with masculine men.

Thus, women's preferences for men's voices may have been shaped in part to extract heritable benefits such as dominance and immunocompetence for offspring. However, testosterone is positively correlated with male infidelity, violence, divorce, low investment in mates and offspring, and interest in extra-pair sex (Booth & Dabbs, 1993; Burnham et al., 2003; Gray, Kahlenberg, Barrett, Lipson, & Ellison, 2002; McIntyre et al., 2006). Indeed, women perceive more masculine male voices as indicating a lower likelihood of male investment in relationships (O'Connor, Fraccaro, & Feinberg, 2012). Additionally, the extent to which women associate low trustworthiness with masculine voices predicts individual variation in preference for such voices (Vukovic et al., 2011). Women's preferences for masculine vs. feminine men in general, and for masculine voices in particular, may reflect this trade-off between the costs and benefits associated with choosing a masculine partner. At least three factors seem to affect how women respond to this trade-off: the type of relationship sought (especially in terms of commitment level), women's own mate value, and changes in fertility across the ovulatory cycle.

Mating context. The fitness benefits of mate choice likely depend upon the type of mating relationship under consideration (Kenrick, Groth, Trost, & Sadalla, 1993; Kenrick, Sadalla, Groth, & Trost, 1990). When the prospective relationship is purely sexual, a woman does not obtain sustained male investment, but she may obtain genetic benefits for her offspring. However, when the prospective relationship involves commitment of time and resources to a mate and mutual offspring, mate choice is expected to depend on substantially more than signs of a mate's heritable fitness. Often this distinction is discussed in terms of the temporal context of the relationship (long-term vs. short-term), but it may be more accurate to conceptualize it in terms of commitment level, as, for example, a

couple could have a long-term relationship that is nevertheless purely sexual, with no male investment.

Because women can expect to obtain little beyond genetic benefits from a purely sexual (generally short-term) relationship and because of the typically lower investment associated with masculine traits, several authors have predicted that women's preferences for masculine men will be stronger when judging men's attractiveness for a short-term, uncommitted relationship than for a long-term, committed one (e.g., Gangestad & Simpson, 2000; Little, Jones, Penton-Voak, Burt, & Perrett, 2002; Penton-Voak et al., 2003; Puts, 2005). In fact, women show stronger preferences for masculine voices when judging men's attractiveness as short-term partners than when judging men's attractiveness as long-term partners (Puts, 2005). The temporal context of the imagined relationship thus affects women's masculinity preferences in ways consistent with trade-off theories of women's mate preferences. One study also revealed a correlation between women's reported openness to short-term relationships and their preferences for masculine characteristics in men's voices (Jones, Boothroyd, Feinberg, & DeBruine, 2010).

Women's own attractiveness. Women higher in mate value may be able to recruit and/or retain investment from more masculine men than can women lower in mate value. Indeed, several studies have shown that women's own attractiveness and beliefs about their attractiveness positively predict their preferences for masculine male voices (O'Connor, Feinberg, et al., 2012; Vukovic et al., 2008, 2010), and as one would predict, this appears to be true particularly for women's preferences in long-term, committed relationship contexts (Feinberg et al., 2012). Conversely, women's self-rated health negatively predicted their short-term vocal masculinity preferences (Feinberg et al., 2012). This preference pattern may function to promote mating with masculine males, who putatively possess heritable immunity, when the benefit is greatest, as when women have poor health themselves (Feinberg et al., 2012).

Changes across the ovulatory cycle. Other evidence indicates that women also resolve the trade-off between good genes and investment partly by preferring men with masculine voices more strongly around ovulation (when conception risk is highest) than during other cycle phases (Feinberg et al., 2006; Puts, 2005; see also Puts, 2006). Puts (2005) also found a significant interaction between imagined mating context (short-term, purely sexual vs. long-term, committed) and cycle phase, such that women significantly preferred masculinized male voices only during the fertile phase and for short-term, sexual relationships. These results complement a broader literature in which women's preferences for other male traits, such as masculine faces and bodies, are highest during the fertile phase of the cycle and in short-term mating contexts (Gangestad & Thornhill, 2008). In one study, hormone levels estimated from women's self-reported ovulatory cycle position suggested that changes in progesterone levels may drive these cyclic preference shifts (Puts, 2006). Studies of cyclic changes in women's preferences for men's faces have also implicated testosterone (Welling et al., 2007) and estradiol (Roney & Simmons, 2008; Roney, Simmons, & Gray, 2011). Similar studies measuring hormones in relation to cyclic variation in women's voice preferences have not yet been reported.

The hormonal and psychological mechanisms that drive correlations between masculinity preferences and female fertility remain poorly understood. Nevertheless, this well-established relationship constitutes evidence that women's preferences for masculine voices function at least partly in recruiting high-quality genes for their offspring. The fact that these preferences are also most pronounced for short-term, purely sexual relationships further suggests that women's mating preferences may have been shaped by selection to increase the likelihood of producing fit offspring while maintaining a relationship with an investing long-term partner. This explanation emphasizes the importance of extra-pair sex for the evolution of fertility-contingent masculinity preferences.

Women's interest in extra-pair mating is seemingly greater around ovulation than it is during other phases of the ovulatory cycle. Women report more frequent sexual fantasies about men other than their primary partner (Gangestad, Thornhill, & Garver, 2002; see also Haselton & Gangestad, 2006; Pillsworth & Haselton, 2006) and less commitment to their romantic partner (Jones, Little, et al., 2005) during the fertile phase of their cycle than they do at other times. Women are also more receptive to men's courtship invitations (Guéguen, 2009a, 2009b), more likely to dress attractively and express interest in revealing clothing (Durante, Griskevicius, Hill, Perilloux, & Li, 2011; Durante, Li, & Haselton, 2008; Grammer, Renninger, & Fischer, 2004; Haselton, Mortezaie, Pillsworth, Bleske-Rechek, & Frederick, 2007), more likely to attend social gatherings where they might meet men (Haselton & Gangestad, 2006), and report both greater extra-pair flirtation and mate guarding by their primary partner (Gangestad et al., 2002; Haselton & Gangestad, 2006) during the late follicular phase of the ovulatory cycle. Importantly, recent studies have found that women with more masculine romantic partners show smaller changes in their sexual interests during the ovulatory cycle (Gangestad, Thornhill, & Garver-Apgar, 2010).

While the extra-pair mating account of cyclic preference shifts predominates in the literature, a different, but not mutually exclusive, explanation focuses on the potential benefits of increased commitment and attraction to relatively feminine men when raised progesterone prepares the body for pregnancy (Puts, 2006). As mentioned above, women report greater commitment to their primary romantic partner during the luteal phase of the ovulatory cycle when the body prepares for pregnancy (Jones, Little, et al., 2005). Analyses of other aspects of women's behavior, such as their dress, sexual fantasy about extra-pair men, and extra-pair flirtation, also suggest that women's bonds with their partner are strengthened during the luteal phase of the cycle (Durante et al., 2008; Gangestad et al., 2002; Haselton & Gangestad, 2006). This strengthened bond, together with increased preferences for men displaying cues of pro-sociality and commitment when progesterone levels are raised (DeBruine, Jones, & Perrett, 2005; Jones, Little, et al., 2005), may reflect adaptations designed to increase the amount of care and support available to women during pregnancy. Importantly, both the extra-pair mating and "care-during-pregnancy" accounts of cyclic shifts in women's mate preferences may reflect the two sides of the trade-off between the costs and benefits of mating with relatively more masculine men.

Male Contest Competition

Sex differences in voices may also have evolved through male contest competition. Hypertrophic growth of male vocal folds and the descent of the larynx at puberty produce deep, resonant vocalizations that exaggerate apparent size (Fitch, 1997). Studies investigating the role of male contests have explored relationships between vocal masculinity and dominance (social influence through force or threat of force, Henrich & Gil-White, 2001). Although dominance may be less relevant to men's mating success in modern life than it has been during most of human evolution (Puts, 2010), the underlying logic of these studies is that past contest competition would have favored signals of threat potential and deference to these signals. Indeed, men's voices masculinized in pitch and/or timbre are perceived as emanating from men who are more dominant than are the feminized versions (Feinberg et al., 2005, 2006; Jones et al., 2010; Puts, Gaulin, & Verdolini, 2006; Puts, Hodges, Cárdenas, & Gaulin, 2007; Watkins et al., 2010; Wolff & Puts, 2010). Correlational studies have also found that more masculine (lower) within-utterance pitch variation (greater monotonicity) predicts dominance perceptions (Aronovich, 1976; Hodges-Simeon et al., 2010; but see Tusing & Dillard, 2000), and people are more likely to choose male leaders with more masculine voices (Klofstad, Anderson, & Peters, 2012), especially in wartime scenarios (Tigue, Borak, O'Connor, Chandl, & Feinberg, 2012).

Masculinity predicts dominance. Masculine voices thus convey the impression of dominance, but deference to masculine voices would not be maintained by selection unless masculinity was a reliable signal of formidability. In fact, vocal masculinity seems to indicate potential for aggressive behavior. For example, people accurately assess men's fighting ability and physical strength from their voices (Sell et al., 2010), though it is not presently clear which acoustic variables communicate this information. Although some studies have found relationships between vocal pitch and men's height (Graddol & Swann, 1983) and weight (Evans, Neave, & Wakelin, 2006), most have not (Bruckert et al., 2006; Collins, 2000; Kunzel, 1989; Lass & Brown, 1978; Rendall et al., 2005; Sell et al., 2010; van Dommelen & Moxness, 1995). Similarly, some studies have found relationships between vocal timbre and men's height (Evans et al., 2006; Greisbach, 1999; Rendall et al., 2005; Sell et al., 2010), but others have not (Collins, 2000; Gonzalez, 2004), and some have found relationships between vocal timbre and weight (Evans et al., 2006; Gonzalez, 2004), but most have not (Bruckert et al., 2006; Collins, 2000; Rendall et al., 2005; Sell et al., 2010).

Puts, Apicella, et al. (2012) present evidence that mean standardized formant frequency ("formant position") is a superior measure of masculinity in vocal timbre to mean spacing between consecutive formant frequencies ("formant dispersion"), the measure used by most previous studies. In this study, formant position was more sexually dimorphic than formant dispersion in both a US sample and a sample of Hadza foragers from Tanzania. Puts, Apicella, et al. (2012) found that masculine formant position was related to handgrip strength and height, but formant dispersion was related to neither. Masculine pitch (measured by mean fundamental frequency) was related to height and testosterone levels, and masculine vocal dynamics (measured by monotonicity, or low within-utterance variation in fundamental frequency) was related to physical aggression.

Voice pitch may also be modulated in relation to perceived relative dominance. For example,

men who perceived themselves to be better
fighters than their competitor lowered their
voice pitch when addressing him, whereas men
who believed they were less dominant raised
their pitch (Puts et al., 2006). Similarly, Ohala
(1983, 1984) reviewed evidence that high pitch
tends to be used to indicate deference (as when
asking a question), and low pitch tends to be used
to indicate assertiveness (as when making a state-
ment) across languages. Additionally, when male
observers witness a man speaking aggressively
with another man, they perceive him as being
more dominant (Jones, DeBruine, Little,
Watkins, & Feinberg, 2011).

Also consistent with the idea that men use
vocal masculinity to assess other men's competitive abilities, Watkins et al. (2010) observed that
low-dominance men were particularly sensitive
to the masculinity of other men's voices. However, these findings should be treated cautiously,
as Wolff and Puts (2010) observed no similar
relationships in two studies between men's own
dominance and their sensitivity to the masculinity of other men's voices. Although more
research is required to clarify discrepant findings,
exploring individual differences in men's dominance sensitivity may provide important insights
into the role of masculine cues in communicating
dominance to potential rivals.

Female Choice Versus Male Contests

Given evidence that vocal masculinity in men
has been shaped both by female choice and
male contests, it is reasonable to ask which
mode of sexual selection played a larger role in
the evolution of these traits. Do masculine voices
appear to be sexual ornaments or threat displays?
As discussed above, male traits such as vocal
masculinity are closer to the optimum under
female choice than under male contests. Thus,
on the one hand, female choice may appear more
influential if it won out against male contests in
moving the mean closer to the optimum under
female choice.

On the other hand, many additional factors
might shift masculine traits nearer the optimum
under mate choice, including ecological costs

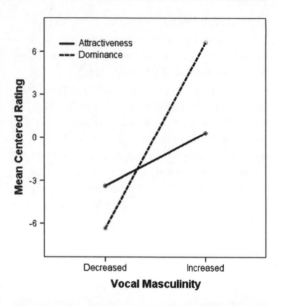

Fig. 3.3 Manipulating men's fundamental and formant
frequencies has much larger effects on how other men rate
the speaker's fighting ability than on how women, even
those in the fertile phase of their cycles, rate his sexual
attractiveness. The interaction between vocal masculinity
and attribute rated is $F_{1,106} = 20.8$, $p < 0.0001$,
$\eta^2 = 0.16$ (Data from Puts, 2005; Puts et al., 2006)

and benefits of producing and maintaining masculine traits and, importantly, the costs of advertising more dominance than one can back up
(Rowher, 1977; Rowher & Ewald, 1981). Moreover, this reasoning based on the optimum trait
value under mate choice assumes that modern
female preferences are comparable to those that
shaped men's voices over human evolution.
Making a similar assumption, one can ask about
the effect of masculinity on attractiveness to
mates compared to the effect on perceptions
of dominance. In other words, how well does
masculinity serve the alternative (but not mutually exclusive) putative functions of mate attraction vs. dominance signaling? The answer is that
across studies, masculine traits are more
effective at signaling dominance (Puts, 2010),
and this is particularly true of vocal masculinity.
Experiments that have compared masculinized to
feminized male voices have found larger positive
effects on the appearance of dominance than on
attractiveness (Feinberg et al., 2005, 2006; Puts
et al., 2006, Fig. 3.3).

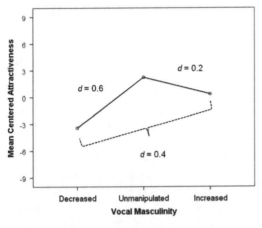
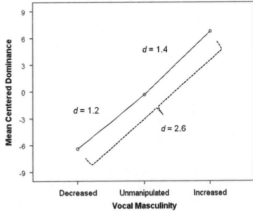

Fig. 3.4 Vocal masculinity has larger effects (measured in standard deviations, Cohen's *d*) on perceptions of dominance than on attractiveness. Voices were rated by women in the fertile phase of their cycle for attractiveness in a short-term, purely sexual relationship and by men for physical dominance (e.g., fighting ability). See Puts (2005) and Puts et al. (2006) for additional methodological details. Figure redrawn from Puts, Jones, and DeBruine (2012)

However, the effect of masculinity on dominance may be more linear near the male average, and the effect on attractiveness may be more curvilinear. If so, then comparing effects on attractiveness vs. dominance using only two levels of masculinization/feminization might be misleading because such a linear comparison would adequately describe the effect of masculinity/femininity on dominance, but not the curvilinear effect on attractiveness. Figure 3.4 illustrates how the effect of masculinity on attractiveness might be underestimated by a comparison of only masculinized and feminized stimuli (data from Puts, 2005; Puts et al., 2006). In this case, it is more appropriate to compare the feminized and masculinized versions of the male trait to the unmanipulated condition. Again, however, the result is that, over the normal range of male voices, masculinity has larger effects on dominance than it does on attractiveness. Therefore, although additional research is needed, deep voices appear better designed by selection for winning male contests than for attracting mates.

Men's Voices, Mating, and Reproductive Success

If sexual selection shaped men's voices, then vocal masculinity must have contributed to male mating and reproductive success over human evolution. Evidence that masculine voices contribute to mating opportunities in modern samples would support the possibility that these conditions held ancestrally. In fact, several studies have demonstrated that men with masculine or attractive voices report more sexual partners, and more short-term and extra-pair sexual relationships in particular, than their relatively feminine peers report (Hodges-Simeon, Gaulin, & Puts, 2011; Hughes, Dispenza, & Gallup, 2004; Puts, 2005). Complementing these findings, Apicella, Feinberg, and Marlowe (2007) observed a positive correlation between men's vocal masculinity and their reported reproductive success in a natural fertility sample of African hunter-gatherers; men with lower-pitched voices reported more children born to them and a greater number of currently living children than did men with relatively higher-pitched voices. As men's voice pitch was unrelated to the mortality rate of their children, this correlation may reflect a positive effect of masculine voice pitch on men's mating opportunities. Collectively, these findings suggest that voices evolved because they elevated reproductive success through increasing mating opportunities.

Conclusions and Directions for Future Research

In several ways, the voice represents an ideal model trait for studying human sexual selection. It is highly sexually differentiated, and vocal sex differences develop mainly at sexual maturity and are not plausibly due to ecological selection (e.g., sexual division of labor). The voice is also eminently quantifiable and highly salient due to its association with verbal communication. Evidence reviewed above indicates that sexual selection has shaped both men's and women's voices and that male contests, female mate choice, and male mate choice all played roles in the evolution of human vocal sexual dimorphisms. Feminine voices in women increase attractiveness to men, may signal fertility, and are thus likely to have been shaped by male mate choice. Masculine voices in men also affect attractiveness to women, perhaps because a masculine voice signals heritable benefits such as dominance and immune system efficiency. Consistent with the hypothesis that masculine voices signal heritable benefits, women prefer more masculine voices for purely sexual relationships and during the fertile phase of the ovulatory cycle. Thus, female mate choice is likely to have shaped men's voices over human evolution. However, masculine voices function more efficiently in signaling dominance to other men than they do in increasing attractiveness to women. Indeed, several contest-relevant traits such as size, strength, and aggressiveness can be accurately, if not precisely, assessed from men's voices, and men appear to modulate their voices in relation to their dominance relative to a competitor. Masculine voices thus appear primarily to be dominance signals.

A number of important and unresolved questions await future research. Among these are how vocal characteristics affect mating and reproductive success. For example, do masculine voices increase men's sexual opportunities, as some research suggests? If

so, to what extent are these mating advantages due to increased dominance among men and to what extent are they due to greater attractiveness to women? Because the mating environments of many modern societies are likely to differ in important ways from those in which human mating adaptations evolved, it will be essential to examine these questions cross-culturally, especially among more traditional peoples.

Future research should also determine how voice preferences and dominance perceptions relate to actual mate choices and contest outcomes. Work so far on these issues is sparse, but encouraging. Another unanswered question regards how people integrate information from cues in different domains (e.g., facial and vocal masculinity) with information about attitudes and intentions (e.g., emotional content and movement). Our understanding of social perception would also be enriched by further work exploring how familiarity with potential mates and competitors (e.g., past performance in competitive encounters with rivals or previous behavior in romantic relationships) figures in contest- and mating-related perceptions.

Although the research described above provides evidence for the ultimate functions of perceptions of men's vocal masculinity, the proximate mechanisms for individual differences in these perceptions remain unclear. Steroid hormones such as progesterone, estradiol, and testosterone (Jones, Perrett, et al., 2005; Puts, 2006; Roney & Simmons, 2008; Roney et al., 2011; Welling et al., 2007) are likely to mediate shifts in women's masculinity preferences over the ovulatory cycle, but more work is needed. Studies of social learning suggest that experience produces individual variation in voice preferences. Such studies have generally focused on mate choice (reviewed in Little, Jones, Debruine, & Caldwell, 2011), but social learning can also influence perceptions of men's dominance (Jones et al., 2011). Additionally, experience with voices can recalibrate judgments of masculinity and associated attributions (Buckingham et al., 2006), and conditioning and associative learning can contribute to preferences and perceptions (e.g., Jones, DeBruine, Little, & Feinberg, 2007). Establishing how such relatively simple socio-cognitive processes interact to provide rich and colorful preferences and perceptions is essential to more fully understand social perception, mate preferences, and perceptions of rivals.

Future research should also continue to employ cross-species comparison to investigate the predictors of resonant and low-pitched vocalizations across primates and the possible influence of sexual selection. In addition, it will be important to utilize such data to establish whether men have particularly low voices or women have particularly high voices after controlling for these predictors, as this will help clarify whether sexual selection in men or women was more important in producing present vocal sexual dimorphisms. The identification of genetic polymorphisms associated with variation in vocal masculinity/femininity will also facilitate the search for signatures of recent selection on these traits in the human lineage.

References

Andersson, M. (1994). *Sexual selection*. Princeton, NJ: Princeton University Press.

Apicella, C. L., & Feinberg, D. R. (2009). Voice pitch alters mate-choice-relevant perception in hunter-gatherers. *Proceedings of the Royal Society B: Biological Sciences, 276*, 1077–1082.

Apicella, C. L., Feinberg, D. R., & Marlowe, F. W. (2007). Voice pitch predicts reproductive success in male hunter-gatherers. *Biology Letters, 3*, 682–684.

Archer, J. (2009). Does sexual selection explain human sex differences in aggression? *Behavioral and Brain Sciences, 32*, 249–266.

Aronovich, C. D. (1976). The voice of personality: Stereotyped judgments and their relation to voice quality and sex of speaker. *Journal of Social Psychology, 99*, 207–220.

Aufdemorte, T. B., Sheridan, P. J., & Holt, G. R. (1983). Autoradiographic evidence of sex steroid receptors in laryngeal tissues of the baboon (Papio cynocephalus). *Laryngoscope, 93*, 1607–1611.

Awan, S. N. (2006). The aging female voice: Acoustic and respiratory data. *Clinical Linguistics & Phonetics, 20*, 171–180.

Barber, N. (1995). The evolutionary psychology of physical attractiveness: Sexual selection and human morphology. *Ethology and Sociobiology, 16*, 395–424.

Bateman, A. J. (1948). Intra-sexual selection in Drosophila. *Heredity, 2*, 349–368.

Boonekamp, J. J., Ros, A. H., & Verhulst, S. (2008). Immune activation suppresses plasma testosterone level: A meta-analysis. *Biology Letters, 4*, 741–744.

Booth, A., & Dabbs, J. M. (1993). Testosterone and men's marriages. *Social Forces, 72*, 463–477.

Bouman, A., Heineman, M. J., & Faas, M. M. (2005). Sex hormones and the immune response in humans. *Human Reproduction Update, 11*, 411–423.

Bruckert, L., Lienard, J. S., Lacroix, A., Kreutzer, M., & Leboucher, G. (2006). Women use voice parameters to assess men's characteristics. *Proceedings of the Royal Society B: Biological Sciences, 273*, 83–89.

Bryant, G. A., & Haselton, M. G. (2009). Vocal cues of ovulation in human females. *Biology Letters, 5*, 12–15.

Buckingham, G., DeBruine, L. M., Little, A. C., Welling, L. L. M., Conway, C. A., Tiddeman, B. P., et al. (2006). Visual adaptation to masculine and feminine faces influences generalized preferences and perceptions of trustworthiness. *Evolution and Human Behavior, 27*, 381–389.

Burnham, T. C., Chapman, J. F., Gray, P. B., McIntyre, M. H., Lipson, S. F., & Ellison, P. T. (2003). Men in committed, romantic relationships have lower testosterone. *Hormones and Behavior, 44*, 119–122.

Buss, D. M., & Dedden, L. A. (1990). Derogation of competitors. *Journal of Social and Personal Relationships, 7*, 395–422.

Cashdan, E. (1996). Women's mating strategies. *Evolutionary Anthropology, 5*, 134–143.

Cashdan, E. (1998). Are men more competitive than women? *British Journal of Social Psychology, 37* (Pt 2), 213–229.

Chagnon, N. (1990). On Yanomamo violence: Reply to Albert. *Current Anthropology, 31*, 49–53.

Chagnon, N. A. (1992). *Yanomamo* (4th ed.). Fort Worth, TX: Harcourt Brace.

Charlton, B. D., Reby, D., & McComb, K. (2007). Female red deer prefer the roars of larger males. *Biology Letters, 3*, 382–385.

Childers, D. G., & Wu, K. (1991). Gender recognition from speech. Part II: Fine analysis. *Journal of the Acoustical Society of America, 90*, 1841–1856.

Clarke, E., Reichard, U. H., & Zuberbuhler, K. (2006). The syntax and meaning of wild gibbon songs. *PLoS ONE, 1*, e73.

Clutton-Brock, T. H., & Vincent, A. C. (1991). Sexual selection and the potential reproductive rates of males and females. *Nature, 351*, 58–60.

Collins, S. A. (2000). Men's voices and women's choices. *Animal Behaviour, 60*, 773–780.

Collins, S. A., & Missing, C. (2003). Vocal and visual attractiveness are related in women. *Animal Behaviour, 65*, 997–1004.

Cowlishaw, G. U. Y. (1996). Sexual selection and information content in gibbon song bouts. *Ethology, 102*, 272–284.

Cowlishaw, G., & Dunbar, R. I. (1991). Dominance rank and mating success in male primates. *Animal Behaviour, 41*, 1045–1056.

Crockford, C., Herbinger, I., Vigilant, L., & Boesch, C. (2004). Wild chimpanzees produce group-specific calls: A case for vocal learning? *Ethology, 110*(3), 221–243.

Dabbs, J. M., & Mallinger, A. (1999). High testosterone levels predict low voice pitch among men. *Personality and Individual Differences, 27*, 801–804.

Daly, N., & Warren, P. (2001). Pitching it difference in New Zealand English: Speaker sex and intonation patters. *Journal of Sociolinguistics, 5*, 85–96.

Daly, M., & Wilson, M. (1988). *Homicide*. New York: Aldine de Gruyter.

Daly, M., & Wilson, M. (1990). Killing the competition. *Human Nature, 1*, 81–107.

Darwin, C. (1859). *On the origin of species by means of natural selection*. London: John Murray.

Darwin, C. (1871). *The descent of man, and selection in relation to sex*. London: John Murray.

Darwin, C. (1882). *The descent of man, and selection in relation to sex* (2nd ed.). London: John Murray.

DeBruine, L. M., Jones, B. C., & Perrett, D. I. (2005). Women's attractiveness judgments of self-resembling faces change across the menstrual cycle. *Hormones and Behavior, 47*, 379–383.

Debruyne, F., Decoster, W., Van Gijsel, A., & Vercammen, J. (2002). Speaking fundamental frequency in monozygotic and dizygotic twins. *Journal of Voice, 16*, 466–471.

Decoster, W., & Debruyne, F. (1997). The ageing voice: Changes in fundamental frequency, waveform stability and spectrum. *Acta Oto-Rhino-Laryngologica Belgica, 51*, 105–112.

de la Torre, S., & Snowdon, C. T. (2009). Dialects in pygmy marmosets? Population variation in call structure. *American Journal of Primatology, 71*(4), 333–342.

Delgado, R. A. (2006). Sexual selection in the loud calls of male primates: Signal content and function. *International Journal of Primatology, 27*, 5–25.

Durante, K. M., Griskevicius, V., Hill, S. E., Perilloux, C., & Li, N. P. (2011). Ovulation, female competition, and product choice: Hormonal influences on consumer behavior. *The Journal of Consumer Research, 37*, 921–934.

Durante, K. M., Li, N. P., & Haselton, M. G. (2008). Changes in women's choice of dress across the ovulatory cycle: Naturalistic and laboratory task-based evidence. *Personality and Social Psychology Bulletin, 34*, 1451–1460.

Eibl-Eibesfeldt, I. (1989). *Human ethology*. New York: Aldine de Gruyter.

Ellis, H. (1905). *Studies in the psychology of sex: Sexual selection in man*. Philadelphia: F.A. Davis Company.

Evans, S., Neave, N., & Wakelin, D. (2006). Relationships between vocal characteristics and body size and shape in human males: An evolutionary explanation for a deep male voice. *Biological Psychology, 72*, 160–163.

Evans, S., Neave, N., Wakelin, D., & Hamilton, C. (2008). The relationship between testosterone and vocal frequencies in human males. *Physiology and Behavior, 93*, 783–788.

Fant, G. (1960). *Acoustic theory of speech production*. The Hague: Mouton.

Feinberg, D. R., DeBruine, L. M., Jones, B. C., & Little, A. C. (2008). Correlated preferences for men's facial and vocal masculinity. *Evolution and Human Behavior, 29*, 233–241.

Feinberg, D. R., DeBruine, L. M., Jones, B. C., Little, A. C., O'Connor, J. J. M., & Tigue, C. C. (2012). Women's self-perceived health and attractiveness predict their male vocal masculinity preferences in different directions across short- and long-term relationship contexts. *Behavioral Ecology and Sociobiology, 66*, 413–418.

Feinberg, D. R., DeBruine, L. M., Jones, B. C., & Perrett, D. I. (2008). The role of femininity and averageness of voice pitch in aesthetic judgments of women's voices. *Perception, 37*, 615–623.

Feinberg, D. R., Jones, B. C., Law Smith, M. J., Moore, F. R., DeBruine, L. M., Cornwell, R. E., et al. (2006). Menstrual cycle, trait estrogen level, and masculinity preferences in the human voice. *Hormones and Behavior, 49*, 215–222.

Feinberg, D. R., Jones, B. C., Little, A. C., Burt, D. M., & Perrett, D. I. (2005). Manipulations of fundamental and formant frequencies affect the attractiveness of human male voices. *Animal Behaviour, 69*, 561–568.

Fischer, J., Hammerschmidt, K., Cheney, D. L., & Seyfarth, R. M. (2002). Acoustic features of male baboon loud calls: Influences of context, age, and individuality. *Journal of the Acoustical Society of America, 111*, 1465–1474.

Fischer, J., Semple, S., Fickenscher, G., Jurgens, R., Kruse, E., Heistermann, M., et al. (2011). Do women's voices provide cues of the likelihood of ovulation? The importance of sampling regime. *PLoS One, 6*, e24490.

Fitch, W. T. (1997). Vocal tract length and formant frequency dispersion correlate with body size in rhesus macaques. *Journal of the Acoustical Society of America, 102*, 1213–1222.

Fitch, W. T., & Giedd, J. (1999). Morphology and development of the human vocal tract: A study using magnetic resonance imaging. *Journal of the Acoustical Society of America, 106*, 1511–1522.

Fitch, J. L., & Holbrook, A. (1970). Modal vocal fundamental frequency of young adults. *Archives of Otolaryngology, 92,* 379–382.

Folstad, I., & Karter, A. J. (1992). Parasites, bright males and the immuno-competence handicap. *American Naturalist, 139,* 603–622.

Forstmeier, W., Burger, C., Temnow, K., & Deregnaucourt, S. (2009). The genetic basis of zebra finch vocalizations. *Evolution, 63,* 2114–2130.

Gangestad, S. W., & Simpson, J. A. (2000). On the evolutionary psychology of human mating: Trade-offs and strategic pluralism. *Behavioral and Brain Sciences, 23,* 573–587.

Gangestad, S. W., & Thornhill, R. (2008). Human oestrus. *Proceedings of the Royal Society B: Biological Sciences, 275,* 991–1000.

Gangestad, S. W., Thornhill, R., & Garver, C. E. (2002). Changes in women's sexual interests and their partners' mate-retention tactics across the menstrual cycle: Evidence for shifting conflicts of interest. *Proceedings of the Royal Society B: Biological Sciences, 269,* 975–982.

Gangestad, S. W., Thornhill, R., & Garver-Apgar, C. E. (2010). Men's facial masculinity predicts changes in their female partners' sexual interests across the ovulatory cycle, whereas men's intelligence does not. *Evolution and Human Behavior, 31,* 412–424.

Gaulin, S. J. C., & Boster, J. S. (1985). Cross cultural differences in sexual dimorphism: Is there any variance to be explained. *Ethology and Sociobiology, 6,* 193–199.

Geary, D. C. (2000). Evolution and proximate expression of human paternal investment. *Psychological Bulletin, 126,* 55–77.

Ghazanfar, A. A., Turesson, H. K., Maier, J. X., Van Dinther, R., Patterson, R. D., & Logothetis, N. K. (2007). Vocal-tract resonances as indexical cues in rhesus monkeys. *Current Biology, 17*(5), 425–430.

Gonzalez, J. (2004). Formant frequencies and body size of speaker: A weak relationship in adult humans. *Journal of Voice, 32,* 277–287.

Graddol, D., & Swann, J. (1983). Speaking fundamental frequency: Some physical and social correlates. *Language and Speech, 26,* 351–366.

Grammer, K., Renninger, L., & Fischer, B. (2004). Disco clothing, female sexual motivation, and relationship status: Is she dressed to impress? *Journal of Sex Research, 41,* 66–74.

Gray, P. B., Kahlenberg, S. M., Barrett, E. S., Lipson, S. F., & Ellison, P. T. (2002). Marriage and fatherhood are associated with lower testosterone in males. *Evolution and Human Behavior, 23,* 193–201.

Green, S. M. (1981). Sex differences and age gradations in vocalizations of Japanese and lion-tailed monkey. *American Zoologist, 21,* 165–184.

Greisbach, R. (1999). Estimation of speaker height from formant frequencies. *Forensic Linguistics, 6,* 265–277.

Grossman, C. J. (1985). Interactions between the gonadal steroids and the immune system. *Science, 227,* 257–261.

Guéguen, N. (2009a). Menstrual cycle phase and female receptivity to a courtship solicitation: An evaluation in a nightclub. *Evolution and Human Behavior, 30,* 351–355.

Guéguen, N. (2009b). The receptivity of women to courtship solicitation across the menstrual cycle: A field experiment. *Biological Psychology, 80,* 321–324.

Harries, M., Hawkins, S., Hacking, J., & Hughes, I. (1998). Changes in the male voice at puberty: Vocal fold length and its relationship to the fundamental frequency of the voice. *Journal of Laryngology and Otology, 112,* 451–454.

Harries, M. L., Walker, J. M., Williams, D. M., Hawkins, S., & Hughes, I. A. (1997). Changes in the male voice at puberty. *Archives of Disease in Childhood, 77,* 445–447.

Harris, T. R., Fitch, W. T., Goldstein, L. M., & Fashing, P. J. (2006). Black and white colobus monkey (Colobus guereza) roars as a source of both honest and exaggerated information about body mass. *Ethology, 112,* 911–920.

Haselton, M. G., & Gangestad, S. W. (2006). Conditional expression of women's desires and men's mate guarding across the ovulatory cycle. *Hormones and Behavior, 49,* 509–518.

Haselton, M. G., Mortezaie, M., Pillsworth, E. G., Bleske-Rechek, A., & Frederick, D. A. (2007). Ovulatory shifts in human female ornamentation: Near ovulation, women dress to impress. *Hormones and Behavior, 51,* 40–45.

Hauser, M. D. (1992). Articulatory and social factors influence the acoustic structure of rhesus monkey vocalizations: A learned mode of production? *Journal of the Acoustical Society of America, 91*(4), 2175–2179.

Hauser, M. D. (1993). The evolution of nonhuman primate vocalizations: Effects of phylogeny, body weight and social-context. *American Naturalist, 142,* 528–542.

Hauser, M. D., & Marler, P. (1993a). Food-associated calls in rhesus macaques (*Macaca mulatta*) I: Socioecological factors. *Behavioral Ecology, 4*(3), 194–205.

Hauser, M. D., & Marler, P. (1993b). Food-associated calls in rhesus macaques (*Macaca mulatta*) II: Costs and benefits of call production and suppression. *Behavioral Ecology, 4*(3), 206–212.

Henrich, J., & Gil-White, F. J. (2001). The evolution of prestige: Freely conferred deference as a mechanism for enhancing the benefits of cultural transmission. *Evolution and Human Behavior, 21,* 165–196.

Henton, C. (1995). Pitch dynamism in female and male speech. *Language and Communication, 15,* 43–61.

Hewlett, B. S. (1988). Sexual selection and parental investment among Aka pygmies. In L. Betzig, M. Borgerhoff Mulder, & P. Turke (Eds.), *Human reproductive behavior: A Darwinian perspective* (pp. 263–276). New York: Cambridge University Press.

Hewlett, B. S. (1992). Husband-wife reciprocity and the father-infant relationship among Aka pygmies. In B.

S. Hewlett (Ed.), *Father-child relations: Cultural and biosocial contexts* (pp. 153–176). New York: Aldine de Gruyter.

Hodges-Simeon, C. R., Gaulin, S. J., & Puts, D. A. (2010). Different vocal parameters predict perceptions of dominance and attractiveness. *Human Nature, 21*, 406–427.

Hodges-Simeon, C. R., Gaulin, S. J., & Puts, D. A. (2011). Voice correlates of mating success in men: Examining "contests" versus "mate choice" modes of sexual selection. *Archives of Sexual Behavior, 40*, 551–557.

Hollien, H., Green, R., & Massey, K. (1994). Longitudinal research on adolescent voice change in males. *Journal of the Acoustical Society of America, 96*, 2646–2654.

Hopp, S. L., Owren, M. J., & Evans, C. S. (1997). *Animal acoustic communication: Sound analysis and research methods.* Berlin: Springer.

Howell, N. (1979). *Demography of the Dobe! Kung.* New York: Academic.

Hughes, S. M., Dispenza, F., & Gallup, G. G. (2004). Ratings of voice attractiveness predict sexual behavior and body configuration. *Evolution and Human Behavior, 25*, 295–304.

Hughes, S. M., Harrison, M. A., & Gallup, G. G., Jr. (2002). The sound of symmetry: Voice as a marker of developmental instability. *Evolution and Human Behavior, 23*, 173–180.

Jones, B. C., Boothroyd, L. G., Feinberg, D. R., & DeBruine, L. M. (2010). Age at menarche predicts individual differences in women's preferences for masculinized male voices in adulthood. *Personality and Individual Differences, 48*, 860–863.

Jones, B. C., DeBruine, L. M., Little, A. C., & Feinberg, D. R. (2007). The valence of experience with faces influences generalized preferences. *Journal of Evolutionary Psychology, 5*, 119–129.

Jones, B. C., DeBruine, L. M., Little, A. C., Watkins, C. D., & Feinberg, D. R. (2011). 'Eavesdropping' and perceived male dominance rank in humans. *Animal Behaviour, 81*, 1203–1208.

Jones, B. C., Feinberg, D. R., Debruine, L. M., Little, A. C., & Vukovic, J. (2008). Integrating cues of social interest and voice pitch in men's preferences for women's voices. *Biology Letters, 4*, 192–194.

Jones, B. C., Feinberg, D. R., DeBruine, L. M., Little, A. C., & Vukovic, J. (2010). A domain-specific opposite-sex bias in human preferences for manipulated voice pitch. *Animal Behaviour, 79*, 57–62.

Jones, B. C., Little, A. C., Boothroyd, L., Debruine, L. M., Feinberg, D. R., Smith, M. J., et al. (2005). Commitment to relationships and preferences for femininity and apparent health in faces are strongest on days of the menstrual cycle when progesterone level is high. *Hormones and Behavior, 48*, 283–290.

Jones, B. C., Perrett, D. I., Little, A. C., Boothroyd, L., Cornwell, R. E., Feinberg, D. R., et al. (2005). Menstrual cycle, pregnancy and oral contraceptive use alter attraction to apparent health in faces.

Proceedings of the Royal Society B: Biological Sciences, 272, 347–354.

Kenrick, D., Groth, G., Trost, M., & Sadalla, E. (1993). Integrating evolutionary and social exchange perspectives on relationships: Effects of gender, self-appraisal, and involvement level on mate selection criteria. *Journal of Personality and Social Psychology, 64*, 951–969.

Kenrick, D. T., Sadalla, E. K., Groth, G., & Trost, M. R. (1990). Evolution, traits, and the stages of human courtship: Qualifying the parental investment model. *Journal of Personality, 58*, 97–116.

Klofstad, C. A., Anderson, R. C., & Peters, S. (2012). Sounds like a winner: Voice pitch influences perception of leadership capacity in both men and women. *Proceedings of the Royal Society B, 279*, 2698–2704.

Kunzel, H. J. (1989). How well does average fundamental frequency correlate with speaker height and weight? *Phonetica, 46*, 117–125.

Lass, N. J., & Brown, W. S. (1978). Correlational study of speakers' heights, weights, body surface areas, and speaking fundamental frequencies. *Journal of the Acoustical Society of America, 63*, 1218–1220.

Little, A. C., Jones, B. C., Debruine, L. M., & Caldwell, C. A. (2011). Social learning and human mate preferences: A potential mechanism for generating and maintaining between-population diversity in attraction. *Philosophical Transactions of the Royal Society of London B Biological Sciences, 366*, 366–375.

Little, A. C., Jones, B. C., Penton-Voak, I. S., Burt, D. M., & Perrett, D. I. (2002). Partnership status and the temporal context of relationships influence human female preferences for sexual dimorphism in male face shape. *Proceedings of the Royal Society B: Biological Sciences, 269*, 1095–1100.

Low, B. S., Alexander, R. D., & Noonan, K. M. (1987). Human hips, breasts and buttocks: Is fat deceptive? *Ethology and Sociobiology, 8*, 249–257.

Main, J. C., Jones, B. C., DeBruine, L. M., & Little, A. C. (2009). Integrating gaze direction and sexual dimorphism of face shape when perceiving the dominance of others. *Perception, 38*, 1275–1283.

McIntyre, M., Gangestad, S. W., Gray, P. B., Chapman, J. F., Burnham, T. C., O'Rourke, M. T., et al. (2006). Romantic involvement often reduces men's testosterone levels—But not always: The moderating role of extrapair sexual interest. *Journal of Personality and Social Psychology, 91*, 642–651.

Mitani, J. C. (1985). Sexual selection and adult male orangutan long calls. *Animal Behavior, 33*, 272–283.

Mitani, J. C., & Gros-Louis, J. (1995). Species and sex differences in the screams of chimpanzees and bonobos. *International Journal of Primatology, 16*, 393–411.

Mitani, J. C., & Stuht, J. (1998). The evolution of nonhuman primate loud calls: Acoustic adaptation for long-distance transmission. *Primates, 39*, 171–182.

Moore, F. R., Al Dujaili, E. A., Cornwell, R. E., Smith, M. J., Lawson, J. F., Sharp, M., et al. (2011). Cues to sex- and stress-hormones in the human male face: Functions of glucocorticoids in the immunocompetence handicap hypothesis. *Hormones and Behavior, 60*, 269–274.

Moore, F. R., Cornwell, R. E., Smith, M. J., Al Dujaili, E. A., Sharp, M., & Perrett, D. I. (2011). Evidence for the stress-linked immunocompetence handicap hypothesis in human male faces. *Proceedings of the Royal Society B: Biological Sciences, 278*, 774–780.

Newman, S. R., Butler, J., Hammond, E. H., & Gray, S. D. (2000). Preliminary report on hormone receptors in the human vocal fold. *Journal of Voice, 14*, 72–81.

Nishio, M., & Niimi, S. (2008). Changes in speaking fundamental frequency characteristics with aging. *Folia Phoniatrica et Logopaedica, 60*, 120–127.

O'Connor, J. J. M., Feinberg, D. R., Fraccaro, P. J., Borak, D. J., Tigue, C. C., Re, D. E., et al. (2012). Female preferences for male vocal and facial masculinity in videos. *Ethology, 118*, 321–330.

O'Connor, J. J. M., Fraccaro, P. J., & Feinberg, D. R. (2012). The influence of male voice pitch on women's perceptions of relationship investment. *Journal of Evolutionary Psychology, 10*, 1–13.

Ohala, J. J. (1983). Cross-language use of pitch: An ethological view. *Phonetica, 40*, 1–18.

Ohala, J. J. (1984). An ethological perspective on common cross-language utilization of F0 of voice. *Phonetica, 41*, 1–16.

Owren, M. J., Dieter, J. A., Seyfarth, R. M., & Cheney, D. L. (1993). Vocalizations of rhesus (*Macaca mulatta*) and Japanese (*M. fuscata*) macaques cross-fostered between species show evidence of only limited modification. *Developmental Psychobiology, 26*(7), 389–406.

Penton-Voak, I. S., Little, A. C., Jones, B. C., Burt, D. M., Tiddeman, B. P., & Perrett, D. I. (2003). Female condition influences preferences for sexual dimorphism in faces of male humans (Homo sapiens). *Journal of Comparative Psychology, 117*, 264–271.

Perrett, D. I., Lee, K. J., Penton-Voak, I., Rowland, D., Yoshikawa, S., Burt, D. M., et al. (1998). Effects of sexual dimorphism on facial attractiveness. *Nature, 394*, 884–887.

Pillsworth, E. G., & Haselton, M. G. (2006). Male sexual attractiveness predicts differential ovulatory shifts in female extra-pair attraction and male mate retention. *Evolution and Human Behavior, 27*, 247–258.

Pinker, S. (1994). *The language instinct*. New York: William Morrow and Company.

Pipitone, N. R., & Gallup, G. G., Jr. (2008). Women's voice attractiveness varies across the menstrual cycle. *Evolution and Human Behavior, 29*, 268–274.

Pipitone, N. R., & Gallup, G. (2011). The unique impact of menstruation on the female voice: Implications for the evolution of menstrual cycle cues. *Ethology, 118*, 281–291.

Puts, D. A. (2005). Mating context and menstrual phase affect women's preferences for male voice pitch. *Evolution and Human Behavior, 26*, 388–397.

Puts, D. A. (2006). Cyclic variation in women's preferences for masculine traits: Potential hormonal causes. *Human Nature, 17*, 114–127.

Puts, D. A. (2010). Beauty and the beast: Mechanisms of sexual selection in humans. *Evolution and Human Behavior, 31*, 157–175.

Puts, D. A., Apicella, C. L., & Cárdenas, R. A. (2012). Masculine voices signal men's threat potential in forager and industrial societies. *Proceedings of the Royal Society B: Biological Sciences, 279*, 601–609.

Puts, D. A., Bailey, D. H., Cárdenas, R. A., Burriss, R. P., Welling, L. L., Wheatley, J. R., et al. (2012). Women's attractiveness changes with estradiol and progesterone across the ovulatory cycle. *Hormones and Behavior, 63*, 13–19.

Puts, D. A., Barndt, J. L., Welling, L. L. M., Dawood, K., & Burriss, R. P. (2011). Intrasexual competition among women: Vocal femininity affects perceptions of attractiveness and flirtatiousness. *Personality and Individual Differences, 50*, 111–115.

Puts, D. A., Gaulin, S. J. C., & Verdolini, K. (2006). Dominance and the evolution of sexual dimorphism in human voice pitch. *Evolution and Human Behavior, 27*, 283–296.

Puts, D. A., Hodges, C., Cárdenas, R. A., & Gaulin, S. J. C. (2007). Men's voices as dominance signals: Vocal fundamental and formant frequencies influence dominance attributions among men. *Evolution and Human Behavior, 28*, 340–344.

Puts, D. A., Jones, B. C., & DeBruine, L. M. (2012). Sexual selection on human faces and voices. *Journal of Sex Research, 49*, 227–243.

Reby, D., McComb, K., Cargnelutti, B., Darwin, C., Fitch, W. T., & Clutton-Brock, T. (2005). Red deer stags use formants as assessment cues during intrasexual agonistic interactions. *Proceedings of the Biological Sciences, 272*, 941–947.

Rendall, D., Kollias, S., Ney, C., & Lloyd, P. (2005). Pitch (F0) and formant profiles of human vowels and vowel-like baboon grunts: The role of vocalizer body size and voice-acoustic allometry. *Journal of the Acoustical Society of America, 117*, 944–955.

Rendall, D., Owren, M. J., Weerts, E., & Hienz, R. D. (2004). Sex differences in the acoustic structure of vowel-like grunt vocalizations in baboons and their perceptual discrimination by baboon listeners. *Journal of the Acoustical Society of America, 115*, 411–421.

Riding, D., Lonsdale, D., & Brown, B. (2006). The effects of average fundamental frequency and variance of fundamental frequency on male vocal attractiveness to women. *Journal of Nonverbal Behavior, 30*, 55–61.

Roberts, M. L., Buchanan, K. L., & Evans, M. R. (2004). Testing the immunocompetence handicap hypothesis:

A review of the evidence. *Animal Behavior, 68*(2), 227–239.

Roberts, M., & Peters, A. (2009). Is testosterone immuno-suppressive in a condition-dependent manner? An experimental test in blue tits. *Journal of Experimental Biology, 212*, 1811–1818.

Röder, S., Fink, B., & Jones, B. C. (2013). Facial, olfactory, and vocal cues to female reproductive value. *Evolutionary Psychology, 11*(2), 392–404.

Roney, J. R., & Simmons, Z. L. (2008). Women's estradiol predicts preference for facial cues of men's testosterone. *Hormones and Behavior, 53*, 14–19.

Roney, J. R., Simmons, Z. L., & Gray, P. B. (2011). Changes in estradiol predict within-women shifts in attraction to facial cues of men's testosterone. *Psychoneuroendocrinology, 36*, 742–749.

Rowher, S. (1977). Status signaling in Harris' sparrows: Some experiments in deception. *Behaviour, 61*, 107–129.

Rowher, S., & Ewald, P. W. (1981). The cost of dominance and advantage of subordination in a badge signaling system. *Evolution, 35*, 441–454.

Ryan, M. J., & Rand, A. S. (1995). Female responses to ancestral advertisement calls in tungara frogs. *Science, 269*, 390–392.

Saez, S., & Sakai, F. (1976). Androgen receptors in human pharyngo-laryngeal mucosa and pharyngo-laryngeal epithelioma. *Journal of Steroid Biochemistry, 7*, 919–921.

Salzano, F. M., Neel, J. V., & Maybury-Lewis, D. (1967). I. Demographic data on two additional villages: Genetic structure of the tribe. *American Journal of Human Genetics, 19*, 463–489.

Schmitt, D. P., & Buss, D. M. (1996). Strategic self-promotion and competitor derogation: Sex and context effects on the perceived effectiveness of mate attraction tactics. *Journal of Personality and Social Psychology, 70*, 1185–1204.

Sell, A., Bryant, G. A., Cosmides, L., Tooby, J., Sznycer, D., von Rueden, C., et al. (2010). Adaptations in humans for assessing physical strength from the voice. *Proceedings of the Royal Society B: Biological Sciences, 277*, 3509–3518.

Seyfarth, R., Cheney, D. L., & Marler, P. (1980). Vervet monkey alarm calls: Semantic communication in a free-ranging primate. *Animal Behaviour, 28*, 1070–1094.

Simpson, A. P. (2009). Phonetic differences between male and female speech. *Language and Linguistics Compass, 3*, 621–640.

Smith, D. S., Jones, B. C., Feinberg, D. R., & Allan, K. (2012). A modulatory effect of male voice pitch on long-term memory in women: Evidence of adaptation for mate choice? *Memory and Cognition, 40*, 135–144.

Snowdon, C. T. (2004). Sexual selection and communication. In P. Kappeler & C. P. van Schaik (Eds.), *Sexual selection in primates: New and comparative perspectives* (pp. 57–70). Cambridge, UK: Cambridge University Press.

Tigue, C. C., Borak, D. J., O'Connor, J. J. M., Chandl, C., & Feinberg, D. R. (2012). Voice pitch influences voting behavior. *Evolution and Human Behavior, 33*, 210–216.

Titze, I. R. (2000). *Principles of voice production*. Iowa City, Iowa: National Center for Voice and Speech.

Tossi, O., Postan, D., & Bianculli, C. (1976). *Longitudinal study of children's voice at puberty*. Paper presented at the XVIth International Congress of Logopedics and Phoniatrics.

Trivers, R. L. (1972). Parental investment and sexual selection. In B. Cambell (Ed.), *Sexual selection and the descent of man, 1871–1971* (pp. 136–179). London: Heinemann.

Tusing, K. J., & Dillard, J. P. (2000). The sounds of dominance: Vocal precursors of perceived dominance during interpersonal influence. *Human Communication Research, 26*, 148–171.

Tybur, J. M., & Gangestad, S. W. (2011). Mate preferences and infectious disease: Theoretical considerations and evidence in humans. *Philosophical Transactions of the Royal Society of London B Biological Sciences, 366*, 3375–3388.

van Dommelen, W. A., & Moxness, B. H. (1995). Acoustic parameters in speaker height and weight identification: Sex-specific behaviour. *Language and Speech, 38*(Pt 3), 267–287.

Vukovic, J., Feinberg, D. R., Jones, B. C., DeBruine, L. M., Welling, L. L. M., Little, A. C., et al. (2008). Self-rated attractiveness predicts individual differences in women's preferences for masculine men's voices. *Personality and Individual Differences, 45*, 451–456.

Vukovic, J., Jones, B. C., DeBruine, L. M., Feinberg, D. R., Smith, F. G., Little, A. C., et al. (2010). Women's own voice pitch predicts their preferences for masculinity in men's voices. *Behavioral Ecology, 21*, 767–772.

Vukovic, J., Jones, B. C., Feinberg, D. R., Debruine, L. M., Smith, F. G., Welling, L. L., et al. (2011). Variation in perceptions of physical dominance and trustworthiness predicts individual differences in the effect of relationship context on women's preferences for masculine pitch in men's voices. *British Journal of Psychology, 102*, 37–48.

Watkins, C. D., Fraccaro, P. J., Smith, F. G., Vukovic, J., Feinberg, D. R., DeBruine, L. M., et al. (2010). Taller men are less sensitive to cues of dominance in other men. *Behavioral Ecology, 21*, 943–947.

Welling, L. L., Jones, B. C., DeBruine, L. M., Conway, C. A., Law Smith, M. J., Little, A. C., et al. (2007). Raised salivary testosterone in women is associated with increased attraction to masculine faces. *Hormones and Behavior, 52*, 156–161.

Wolff, S. E., & Puts, D. A. (2010). Vocal masculinity is a robust dominance signal in men. *Behavioral Ecology and Sociobiology, 64*, 1673–1683.

Wu, K., & Childers, D. G. (1991). Gender recognition from speech. Part I: Coarse analysis. *Journal of the Acoustical Society of America, 90*, 1828–1840.

Agreement and Individual Differences in Men's Preferences for Women's Facial Characteristics

4

Benedict C. Jones

Men's Face Preferences and Cues of Health

Judgments of facial attractiveness are thought to play a critical role in social interaction in general and may play an important role in human mate choices (Little, Jones, & DeBruine, 2011; Rhodes, 2006). Consistent with this claim, recent work has revealed assortative mating for facial appearance in romantic couples (Burriss, Roberts, Welling, Puts, & Little, 2011; Little, Burt, & Perrett, 2006) and suggests that individual differences in face preferences predict individual differences in actual romantic partner characteristics (Burriss, Welling, & Puts, 2011; DeBruine, 2013; DeBruine et al., 2006). These findings potentially link face preferences to actual partner choice.

Identifying healthy, fertile mates is key to male reproductive success in many species. Consequently, many researchers have suggested that heterosexual men's judgments of women's facial attractiveness may reflect psychological adaptations that evolved, at least in part, to identify healthy women (i.e., high-quality potential mates; Fink & Penton-Voak, 2002; Little, Jones, et al., 2011; Miller & Todd, 1998; Thornhill & Gangestad, 1999). Consistent with this proposal, several studies have demonstrated that women's

B.C. Jones (✉)
Institute of Neuroscience & Psychology, University of Glasgow, Scotland, UK
e-mail: ben.jones@glasgow.ac.uk

faces contain cues to aspects of their underlying health, such as longevity (Henderson & Anglin, 2003; Reither, Hauser, & Swallen, 2009), fertility (Law Smith et al., 2006; Roberts et al., 2004), and past health problems (Kalick, Zebrowitz, Langlois, & Johnson, 1998; Thornhill & Gangestad, 2006). Moreover, these traits are often ones that men, on average, consider attractive (Fink & Penton-Voak, 2002; Little, Jones, et al., 2011; Miller & Todd, 1998; Thornhill & Gangestad, 1999) and that are positively correlated with measures of women's reproductive potential (e.g., Rhodes, Simmons, & Peters, 2005). The first part of this chapter will discuss some of the evidence for the suggestion that men, on average, consider women's faces displaying cues of health and/or fertility to be relatively attractive. By contrast with this focus on what men *on average* consider attractive in women's faces, the second part of my chapter will then discuss evidence that variation in men's preferences for health cues in women's faces is systematic, rather than arbitrary, and may also be adaptive.

Femininity and Women's Facial Attractiveness

Studies investigating the relationships between ratings of women's facial attractiveness and either facial-metric measures of sexually dimorphic aspects of their face shape or ratings of their facial femininity have typically reported relatively strong

Fig. 4.1 Examples of
female faces with
exaggerated and reduced
sex-typical shape cues. The
feminized faces are shown
on the *left* and the
masculinized faces are
shown on the *right*

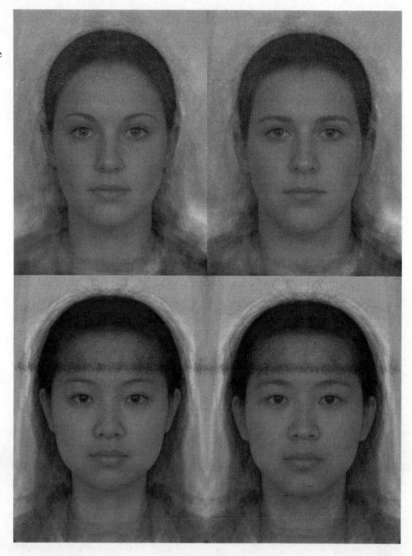

positive correlations between these measures (e.g., Cunningham, Roberts, Barbee, Druen, & Wu, 1995; Koehler, Simmons, Rhodes, & Peters, 2004; Rhodes, Chan, Zebrowitz, & Simmons, 2003; Rhodes et al., 2007). Consistent with these findings from correlational studies of women's facial attractiveness, studies in which feminine (i.e., female sex typical) shape characteristics were either exaggerated or reduced in digital images of women's faces (Fig. 4.1) have reported that both men and women show strong preferences for women's faces displaying feminine shape characteristics (e.g., Little, DeBruine, & Jones, 2011; Perrett et al., 1998; Welling, Jones, DeBruine, Smith, et al., 2008). These experimental

results suggest that femininity is not simply a correlate of women's facial attractiveness but is also a visual cue (e.g., Perrett et al., 1998). While some researchers have suggested that the strength of women's preferences for exaggerated sex-typical shape characteristics in men's faces can differ (sometimes quite markedly) according to whether shape cues were manipulated in composite (i.e., prototype) face images or in individual (i.e., exemplar) face images (Rhodes, 2006; but see also Scott & Penton-Voak, 2011), strong preferences for feminine characteristics in women's faces have been observed using both composite (e.g., Perrett et al., 1998) and individual face stimuli (e.g., Welling, Jones, DeBruine, Smith, et al., 2008). These relatively strong preferences for feminine characteristics in women's faces, which appear to be very consistent across stimulus type, complement preferences for feminine characteristics that have been reported in men's studies of women's vocal (e.g., Jones, Feinberg, DeBruine, Little, & Vukovic, 2010) and body shape (Tovee et al., 1999) attractiveness. There is also evidence that men's preferences for feminine characteristics in women's faces can be similar across cultures. For example, both UK and Japanese men show strong preferences for feminine characteristics in women's faces (Perrett et al., 1998).

That men show relatively strong preferences for feminine characteristics in women's faces, voices, and body shapes is consistent with the proposal that feminine characteristics in women's faces advertise information about their underlying mate quality that men prefer and that is also advertised by feminine characteristics in other domains (Cornwell et al., 2004; Fraccaro et al., 2010). Further evidence for this proposal comes from research suggesting that men's preferences for cues of women's femininity in multiple domains tend to be positively correlated. For example, positive correlations between individual differences in men's preferences for feminine characteristics in women's faces and their preferences for feminine characteristics in recordings of women's voices (Fraccaro et al., 2010) support the proposal that these different aspects of women's femininity advertise common information about their underlying mate quality. Correlations between individual differences in men's preferences for feminine characteristics in women's faces and their preferences for putative "female" pheromones (Cornwell et al., 2004) also suggest that these different aspects of women's femininity advertise common information about their underlying mate quality. Results such as these raise the potentially important question of what aspects of women's mate quality are advertised by feminine physical characteristics.

Findings from several studies suggest that women displaying particularly feminine facial characteristics also tend to be in relatively good health. For example, Thornhill and Gangestad (2006) reported that women with particularly feminine face shapes, assessed from an analysis of facial proportions that were shown to be sexually dimorphic, reported having experienced fewer respiratory infections in the preceding 3 years than did women with relatively masculine face shapes. Furthermore, women with particularly feminine face shapes reported recovering more quickly when they developed respiratory infections than did women with relatively masculine face shapes. Consistent with these findings linking respiratory health to feminine face shapes in women, other work has reported similar correlations between respiratory health and ratings of women's facial femininity (Gray & Boothroyd, 2012), while several other studies have reported that women displaying feminine facial characteristics are perceived to be particularly healthy (e.g., Rhodes et al., 2007). Although findings such as these suggest that health and facial femininity may be correlated in women, Rhodes et al. (2003) found no significant correlation between ratings of women's facial femininity and a measure of their actual health derived from analyses of their medical records. Nonetheless, the positive correlation between femininity and perceived health in that sample remained significant when the possible effects of attractiveness were controlled for using a partial correlation analysis, demonstrating that the tendency for feminine women to be perceived to be particularly healthy is not solely an attractiveness halo effect.

While the studies discussed above focused primarily on investigating the possible links between facial femininity and measures of women's general health, other research has investigated possible correlations between facial femininity and measures of women's reproductive health. For example, Law Smith et al. (2006) reported a positive correlation between ratings of women's facial femininity and their estrogen levels (measured from urine samples collected during the late follicular phase of the menstrual cycle to control for cyclic shifts in hormone levels). Law Smith et al. (2006) also reported a positive relationship that approached significance between ratings of women's facial femininity and their progesterone levels (measured from urine samples collected during the luteal phase of the menstrual cycle to control for cyclic shifts in hormone levels). Given the importance of estrogen and progesterone levels for women's reproductive health (see Law Smith et al., 2006 for a review), these results suggest that facial femininity may also be a cue of women's reproductive health. Findings such as these linking facial femininity to indices of women's reproductive health complement those reporting links between feminine characteristics in women's body shapes and measures of their reproductive health (e.g., Jasienska, Ziomkiewicz, Ellison, Lipson, & Thune, 2004).

The research described in the preceding paragraphs outlined some of the evidence that feminine characteristics in women's faces advertise information about health-related aspects of their mate quality. However, findings from other studies have suggested that feminine facial characteristics may also advertise information about women's personalities that is likely to be important in the context of mate choice. For example, women with more feminine facial characteristics report greater levels of maternal desire (i.e., greater interest in reproducing) than do relatively masculine women (Law Smith et al., 2012). Additionally, women with more feminine facial characteristics are perceived as likely to provide others with greater levels of social support than are relatively masculine women (Watkins et al., 2012). Indeed, increasing feminine characteristics in women's faces makes them appear more trustworthy, emotionally warm, and cooperative (Perrett et al., 1998). Collectively, these findings suggest that feminine facial characteristics in women advertise personality traits and dispositions that may be valued in romantic and social partners.

Symmetry, Averageness, and Women's Facial Attractiveness

Although often treated as discrete characteristics, multiple lines of evidence indicate that facial symmetry and averageness (i.e., prototypicality) are positively correlated (see Rhodes, 2006). For example, unless deliberate steps are taken to prevent them being confounded, increasing the averageness of face images using computer graphic techniques increases the symmetry of the images (e.g., Jones, DeBruine, & Little,

2007). Consequently, this chapter will consider the roles of these traits together.

Studies that have measured the symmetry and/or averageness of face shapes have typically reported that both measures are somewhat weakly correlated with ratings of women's facial attractiveness (e.g., Grammer & Thornhill, 1994). Studies that have assessed facial symmetry or averageness using perceptual ratings have also observed positive correlations between these dimensions and women's facial attractiveness that are typically stronger than those observed in studies that have relied on facial measurements (e.g., Lie, Rhodes, & Simmons, 2008; Rhodes et al., 2001). These stronger correlations in studies using perceptual judgments to assess symmetry and averageness are thought to occur because the relatively small number of measurements used in traditional facial metric methods captures perceptually salient aspects of facial stimuli quite poorly (Rhodes, 2006). Indeed, when symmetry and averageness are experimentally manipulated in images of women's faces using computer graphic methods (Fig. 4.2), evidence that symmetry and averageness are attractive in women's faces is more compelling (Little & Jones, 2003, 2006; Perrett, May, & Yoshikawa, 1994, 1999; Rhodes et al., 2001), particularly when men assess the attractiveness of women's faces (Little & Jones, 2006). Moreover, symmetry and averageness preferences have been observed in diverse cultures, suggesting that they may serve a function that is fundamental to human social behavior (Apicella, Little, & Marlowe, 2007; Little, Apicella, & Marlowe, 2007).

Although I am not aware of any studies that have manipulated symmetry independently of averageness, studies that have compared the effects of averageness of women's facial attractiveness when the possible effects of symmetry were and were not controlled for have concluded that symmetry contributes significantly to the appeal of averageness in women's faces but that the difference in averageness preferences between conditions is relatively subtle (e.g., Jones et al., 2007). Other studies have also demonstrated that the appeal of averaged faces cannot be explained by the removal of blemishes and texture details in

Fig. 4.2 Examples of face images subtly manipulated in symmetry (*top row*) and averageness (*bottom row*). The original (i.e., less symmetric or less average) images are shown on the *right* and the manipulated (i.e., more symmetric or more average) images are shown on the *left*

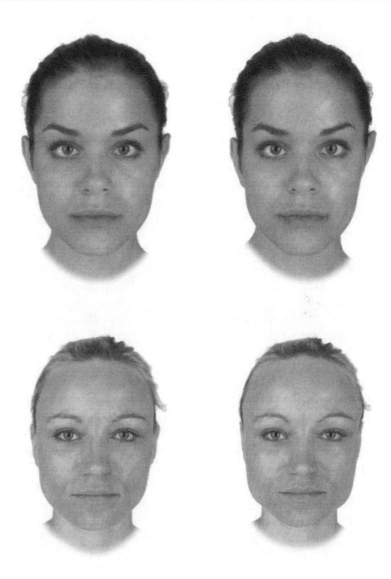

the skin, which was a by-product of the computer graphic methods used to manipulate averageness in early studies. Increasing averageness in face images while holding skin texture constant still yields preferences for averageness (Little & Hancock, 2002; O'Toole, Price, Vetter, Bartlett, & Blanz, 1999; Penton-Voak & Perrett, 2001; Rhodes & Tremewan, 1996). If averageness and symmetry preferences are not due to these potential artifacts, why then do men prefer women's faces showing these traits?

In addition to influencing perceptions of women's attractiveness, increasing symmetry and averageness in face images increases perceptions of women's health (Rhodes et al., 2001). Thus, symmetry and averageness appear to function as cues to apparent health (Rhodes et al., 2001; see also Jones et al., 2001; Rhodes et al., 2007). Indeed, correlational studies suggest that the links between attractiveness and both averageness and symmetry are mediated, at least in part, by health perceptions; the correlations between attractiveness perceptions of both averageness and symmetry weaken significantly when the effects of health ratings are controlled for using a partial correlation design (Rhodes et al., 2007; see also Jones et al., 2001).

Consistent with the proposal that facial symmetry and averageness communicate potentially important information about women's health, some studies have reported positive correlations between these facial characteristics and measures of women's health derived from relatively detailed analyses of their medical records (Rhodes et al., 2001). Moreover, other work suggests that facial symmetry is correlated with genetic heterozygosity in women (Lie et al., 2008). This is potentially noteworthy, since it suggests a correlation between facial symmetry and a known biomarker for good immunity to infectious disease in women (see Lie et al., 2008 for discussion).

While the findings described above (and the results of the partial correlation analyses in particular) raise the possibility that symmetry and averageness are preferred in women's faces because they are (or appear to be) particularly healthy, other researchers have proposed alternative explanations for the attractiveness of symmetric and average faces. For example, some researchers have suggested that average and symmetric faces are judged to be relatively attractive, not because they are associated with health or any other desirable traits, but because symmetric and average stimuli of any kind can be processed most easily by the visual system (see, e.g., Enquist, Ghirlanda, Lundqvist, & Wachtmeister, 2002; Halberstadt & Rhodes, 2000; Winkielman, Halberstadt, Fazendeiro, & Catty, 2006). Under this view, preferences for symmetric and average faces are a functionless by-product of the perceptual system, rather than potentially adaptive preferences for healthy mates (Enquist et al., 2002; Halberstadt & Rhodes, 2000; Winkielman et al., 2006). While this view has received some empirical support, particularly from studies of preferences for average faces (see, e.g., Halberstadt & Rhodes, 2000; Winkielman et al., 2006), other work suggests that processing efficiency alone cannot fully explain preferences for symmetric and average faces. For example, inverting faces (i.e., turning them upside down) weakens men's preferences for symmetry in women's faces, despite not altering the actual symmetry of the faces or symmetry detection (Little & Jones, 2003, 2006). This finding suggests that ease

of processing alone cannot explain men's preferences for symmetry in women's faces and suggests that symmetry preferences and symmetry detection can, to some extent, be dissociated (Little & Jones, 2006). Similarly, the opposite-sex bias in symmetry preferences observed in some studies, in which men show stronger preferences for symmetry in women's faces while women show stronger preferences for symmetry in men's faces, is also difficult to explain in terms of processing efficiency alone (Little & Jones, 2006; see also Jones et al., 2001).

There is compelling evidence that averageness and symmetry are positively correlated with women's facial attractiveness. However, it is also important to note that several studies now have shown that highly attractive female faces typically possess many non-average (i.e., distinctive) traits that contribute significantly to their high attractiveness (e.g., Perrett et al., 1994). For example, caricaturing the shape of highly attractive female faces against an average female face shape increases their attractiveness while simultaneously shifting the face shape away from average (e.g., Perrett et al., 1994). Findings such as these demonstrate that although averageness may well contribute to female attractiveness, it does not fully explain it.

Perceived Facial Adiposity and Women's Facial Attractiveness

Several studies of women's facial attractiveness have reported that perceived facial adiposity (ratings of weight from the face) is negatively correlated with women's facial attractiveness, at least within the normal range of body weight[1] (e.g., Coetzee et al., 2009). This pattern of results has been reported in UK and African samples (see, e.g., Coetzee et al., 2012). Moreover, ratings of facial adiposity are highly correlated with

---

[1] As is also the case for body attractiveness (e.g., Tovee et al., 1999), appearing to be very underweight is also unattractive, however (Coetzee, Perrett, & Stephen, 2009).

Fig. 4.3 Averages of the 15 faces with the highest bioelectrical impedance (*left image*) and the 15 faces with the lowest bioelectrical impedance (*right image*) from a sample of 50 young adult women

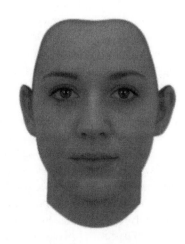

measures of body weight, such as body mass index, indicating that the ratings are somewhat accurate (Coetzee et al., 2009; Tinlin et al., 2013; see also Fig. 4.3). Indeed, recent work has shown that ratings of women's facial adiposity are more strongly correlated with body mass index than they are with other body parameters that are known to be important for women's attractiveness (e.g., waist-to-hip ratio, Tinlin et al., 2013).

Ratings of facial adiposity are also correlated with a wide range of measures of poor health in women, including greater frequency of illness (Coetzee et al., 2009; Tinlin et al., 2013); greater levels of stress, anxiety, and depression (Tinlin et al., 2013); and poorer cardiovascular health (Coetzee et al., 2009). Other work suggests that ratings of women's facial adiposity are negatively correlated with longevity (Reither et al., 2009). The link between facial adiposity and health is not limited to studies of women's general medical health, however. Tinlin et al. (2013) reported that women's facial adiposity was negatively correlated with their estrogen levels, suggesting that high levels of facial adiposity may be associated with poor reproductive health. Findings such as these linking facial adiposity to aspects of health suggest that men's preferences for women displaying facial cues associated with relatively low (but not too low, Coetzee et al., 2009) body weight may be adaptive.

A potentially important, but currently unresolved, issue is what specific facial parameters people use to gauge adiposity from facial cues. Some recent work has suggested that facial

width-to-height ratio may be an important facial cue for accurate perception of women's weight (Coetzee, Chen, Perrett, & Stephen, 2010). However, other work has suggested that the utility of this cue for judging others' weight during social interactions is limited by the fact that it is extremely susceptible to distortions related to viewing angle (i.e., tilting the head back or forward can dramatically alter both the perceived width-to-height ratio and apparent adiposity of a face, Schneider, Hecht, & Carbon, 2012). While the evidence that facial adiposity is related to women's attractiveness, perceived health, and actual health is compelling, the specific facial cues that people use to assess adiposity during social interactions remain very unclear.

Skin Characteristics and Women's Facial Attractiveness

While the findings described in the previous parts emphasize the effects of shape cues on women's facial attractiveness, other research has highlighted the importance of surface characteristics of the face for women's attractiveness. For example, Jones et al. (2005) demonstrated that even relatively subtle manipulations of color and texture cues associated with health ratings of women's faces had pronounced effects on their facial attractiveness. Increasing color and texture associated with high perceived health increased the attractiveness of women's faces dramatically. Moreover, Law

Smith et al. (2006) reported positive correlations between women's hormone levels and facial attractiveness among women who were not wearing makeup, but not among women who were wearing makeup. This finding also suggests that color and/or texture cues in women's faces may communicate information about their underlying condition. Although results such as these show that perceived skin condition is potentially an important component of women's facial attractiveness and a cue to their mate quality, the specific characteristics of women's facial skin that contribute to these effects have only recently begun to be investigated.

One aspect of women's facial skin that appears to be particularly important for their facial attractiveness is the evenness of their skin coloration; women with more even (i.e., homogenous) skin coloration tend to be rated as more attractive (e.g., Fink, Grammer, & Thornhill, 2001). Homogeneity is not the only surface characteristic that is attractive in women's faces, however. Studies of variation in skin color cues within races have reported preferences for women's faces displaying lighter skin tones and yellower skin coloration (e.g., Coetzee et al., 2012). These patterns of results are not unique to white faces (see, e.g., Coetzee et al., 2012), and preferences for these aspects of women's skin color may be adaptive; lighter skin tone appears to be a feminine facial characteristic in humans that may be associated with fertility in women, and yellowness in faces is associated with good perceived health and healthy diet (reviewed in Coetzee et al., 2012).

The work described above suggests that skin characteristics influence perceptions of women's faces. Other research suggests that color and texture cues associated with a healthy appearance can also modulate men's preferences for feminine shape characteristics in faces; Smith, Jones, DeBruine, and Little (2009) found that men showed stronger preferences for feminine shape characteristics in women's faces when they displayed healthy-looking color and texture cues than when they displayed unhealthy-looking color and texture cues. These findings suggest that men integrate information from shape and surface characteristics when assessing women's attractiveness and, potentially, mate quality. This integration may be important for mate choice if shape and surface characteristics in faces communicate different aspects of women's health, such as short-term and long-term health, and/or if it allows men to more accurately gauge the health of potential mates (Smith et al., 2009).

Variability in Women's Facial Attractiveness

While some prior research suggests that between-subjects differences in women's facial attractiveness are related to changes in their hormone levels, other work has suggested that within-subject changes in women's hormone levels might also drive within-subject changes in their facial attractiveness. For example, Roberts et al. (2004) found, in two different samples, that photographs of women's faces taken during the late follicular phase of the menstrual cycle were, on average, rated as being more attractive than photographs of women's faces taken during the luteal phase of the menstrual cycle. This difference was greatest when clothing and hairstyle were visible in the images but was also apparent when they were not, suggesting that cyclic variation in women's grooming and clothing choices (see also, e.g., Haselton, Mortezaie, Pillsworth, Bleske-Recheck, & Frederick, 2007 for further evidence of these types of cyclic shifts in women's behavior) contributes to cyclic sifts in women's facial attractiveness but does not explain it. While these results challenged the assumption that women do not display cues to ovulation (see Haselton & Gildersleeve, 2011 for detailed discussion of this issue), Roberts et al.'s (2004) study has been criticized for treating raters, rather than face images, as the primary unit of analysis (Haselton & Gildersleeve, 2011). Moreover, Bleske-Rechek et al. (2011) were unsuccessful in a recent attempt to replicate Roberts et al.'s (2004) findings for cyclic shifts in women's facial attractiveness, although the method used to collect attractiveness judgments in this latter study (projection of images onto classroom screens) is, perhaps, suboptimal for detecting what may be fairly subtle differences in appearance.

While the criticisms and null result described above appear to raise doubt about Roberts et al.'s (2004) suggestion that women's facial attractiveness increases around ovulation, findings from two other recent studies paint a quite different picture. In a study with over 200 women, Puts et al. (2013) found that changes in women's facial attractiveness were negatively correlated with changes in their progesterone level during the menstrual cycle. Since progesterone levels are highest during the luteal (low fertility) phase of the menstrual cycle, this suggests that changes in progesterone level during the menstrual cycle may underpin cyclic changes in women's facial attractiveness. Similarly, Bobst and Lobmaier (2012) recently found that men responded more positively to female faces transformed to have the average characteristics of a sample of female face images collected during the follicular phase of the menstrual cycle. Collectively, these results support Roberts et al.'s proposal that women's facial attractiveness is increased during the follicular phase of the menstrual cycle and suggest that concerns about Roberts et al.'s analyses may be misguided. That women's facial attractiveness is greater around ovulation is consistent with the proposal that perceptions of women's facial attractiveness at least partly reflect perceptual responses to fertility cues.

Gaze Direction, Emotional Expressions, and Women's Facial Attractiveness

Most research into women's facial attractiveness has focused on investigating the effects of parameters that are generally relatively stable over hours, days, and, in some cases, even weeks, such as shape characteristics and skin condition (but see also part "Variability in Women's Facial Attractiveness"). However, other work has investigated the effects of more changeable characteristics in faces, such as gaze direction and emotional expressions, which can change rapidly in a split second.

Men generally prefer direct gaze, a potential signal of social interest, when assessing the attractiveness of women's faces than averted gaze (e.g., Conway, Jones, DeBruine, & Little, 2008; Mason, Tatkow, & Macrae, 2005). However, this preference for eye contact (i.e., direct gaze) can be modulated by other characteristics of the faces. For example, men show stronger preferences for direct versus averted gaze in physically attractive women's faces than in physically unattractive women's faces (Conway, Jones, DeBruine, Little, Hay, et al., 2008) and in women's faces displaying positive emotional expressions (e.g., smiles) than in women's faces displaying negative emotional expressions (e.g., neutral or disgusted expressions, Conway, Jones, DeBruine, & Little, 2008). Moreover, some studies have reported that these context-sensitive preferences for direct gaze are greater when men assess women's attractiveness than when other women assess women's attractiveness, suggesting adaptive design in women's gaze preferences (Conway, Jones, DeBruine, & Little, 2008). Similar interactions between changeable social cues and physical attractiveness have also been reported in neuroimaging studies; eye contact elicits greater activation in reward centers when viewing attractive than unattractive faces, for example (Kampe, Frith, Dolan, & Frith, 2001). Importantly, both neuroimaging and behavioral studies have shown that this integration of cues to the direction of others' attention and their physical attractiveness depends on viewer-referenced coding of gaze direction (i.e., the coding of gaze direction in relation to the viewer), rather than target-referenced coding of gaze direction (i.e., the coding of gaze direction in relation to the target), suggesting that viewers use gaze cues primarily to assess others' intentions towards them specifically, rather than to assess others' intentions more generally (Main, DeBruine, Little, & Jones, 2010; see also Kampe et al., 2001). Indeed, integrating information about the direction and valence of others' attention with information about their attractiveness and mate quality may serve an important function during social interaction by allowing people to allocate more of their own social and mating effort to the most desirable (i.e., highest quality) individuals who are willing to reciprocate (see Jones, DeBruine, Little, Conway, & Feinberg, 2006 for discussion). These effects of changeable aspects of faces (together with variability in attractiveness relating to, e.g., menstrual cycle phase and grooming) may explain why attractiveness ratings of women can be variable across face images of the same individuals (see Jenkins et al., 2011).

Individual Differences in Men's Face Preferences

As mentioned earlier in this chapter, men's preferences for feminine characteristics in women's faces are positively correlated with their preferences for feminine characteristics in other types of female stimuli (e.g., women's voices and putative female pheromones, Cornwell et al., 2004; Fraccaro et al., 2010). While these correlated preferences demonstrate that at least some of the variation in men's preferences for feminine characteristics in women's faces is systematic, rather than arbitrary, they do not identify any specific factors that might contribute to individual differences in men's preferences for feminine women. Indeed, while identifying sources of individual differences in women's preferences for men's faces has been the focus of a considerable amount of empirical research in the attractiveness literature (see Little, Jones, et al., 2011 for a recent review), relatively few studies have sought to identify sources of individual differences in men's face preferences. However, recent work has attempted to explore this issue. The remainder of this chapter will review some of this research.

Concern About Pathogens and Men's Face Preferences

There is now good evidence linking feminine characteristics to aspects of women's health, including infrequent illness (Gray & Boothroyd, 2012; Thornhill & Gangestad, 2006). These findings complement other research suggesting that women with more feminine body shapes also tend to be healthier (see Jasienska et al.,

2004 for discussion). Among women, concerns about pathogens are known to predict the strength of preferences for men displaying exaggerated sex-typical features (i.e., masculine men, DeBruine, Jones, Crawford, Welling, & Little, 2010; DeBruine, Jones, Tybur, Lieberman, & Griskevicius, 2010; Little, DeBruine, et al., 2011). Evidence for this relationship between mate preferences and women's concerns about pathogens has come from studies of population-level and individual-level differences in mate preferences and from priming experiments (DeBruine, Jones, Crawford, et al., 2010; DeBruine, Jones, Tybur, et al., 2010; Jones, Feinberg, et al., 2013; Little, DeBruine, et al., 2011). These relationships and effects are thought to occur because women who are particularly concerned about pathogens prioritize health cues when assessing potential mates' attractiveness, potentially minimizing the consequences of their vulnerability to disease for their reproductive success (DeBruine, Jones, Crawford, et al., 2010; DeBruine, Jones, Tybur, et al., 2010; Little, DeBruine, et al., 2011). While pathogen-related variation in women's preferences for masculine men is now very well established in the literature on human mate preferences, several recent studies have presented evidence that concerns about pathogens also figure in men's face preferences.

Jones, Fincher, et al. (2013) reported that men's pathogen disgust, a putative measure of individual differences in concern about pathogens (Tybur, Lieberman, & Griskevicius, 2009), was positively correlated with the strength of men's preferences for feminine shape characteristics in women's faces in two different samples of men (each of whom judged the attractiveness of a different set of face stimuli). By contrast with these findings for pathogen disgust and men's judgments of women's facial attractiveness, neither sexual disgust nor moral disgust predicted men's preferences for feminine women. This suggests that the link between pathogen disgust and mate preferences is not simply a consequence of individual differences in disgust sensitivity in general but is specific to disgust in one relatively narrow domain (Jones, Fincher, et al., 2013; see also DeBruine, Jones, Tybur, et al., 2010). Additionally, no significant relationships between pathogen disgust and femininity preferences were observed for men's judgments of other men's facial attractiveness, suggesting that the link between pathogen disgust and femininity preferences occurs primarily for mating-related attractiveness judgments. Consistent with the proposal that these findings reflect adaptations that function, at least in part, to reduce the consequences of vulnerability to disease on men's reproductive success, men with high average (i.e., trait) levels of salivary cortisol, a biomarker for immunosuppression (see Martin, 2009; Sapolsky, Romero, & Munck, 2000 for comprehensive reviews), also showed stronger preferences for feminine characteristics in women's faces (Jones, Fincher, et al., 2013). Together these findings implicate individual differences in vulnerability to disease in men's faces preferences and, potentially, their mate preferences. Indeed, Jones et al. (2013) found that partnered men (i.e., men in romantic relationships) who scored higher on pathogen disgust, but not sexual or moral disgust, reported having particularly feminine partners.

While the correlational findings described above suggest that individual differences in men's concerns about pathogens are positively correlated with their preferences for feminine characteristics in women's faces, they do not allow strong conclusions to be made about the extent to which concerns about pathogens directly influence men's face preferences. However, a recent experiment by Little, DeBruine, et al. (2011) investigated precisely this issue. Little, DeBruine, et al. (2011) used a priming paradigm in which men viewed either pathogen-related images (images depicting possible sources of pathogens) or a set of matched control images (similar images that did not depict possible sources of pathogens). These priming stimuli have previously been shown to elicit strong disgust responses across diverse cultures (i.e., people from diverse cultures rated the pathogen-related images to be more disgusting than the control images, Curtis, Aunger, & Rabie, 2004). Men randomly allocated to the pathogen-related

priming condition subsequently showed stronger preferences for women's faces with feminine characteristics than did men randomly allocated to the control condition. By contrast with these findings for pathogens and women's faces, viewing the pathogen-related images did not increase men's perceptions of men's faces, complementing the sex specificity observed in the correlational studies of men's pathogen disgust described in the preceding paragraph.

Although these findings suggest that men who are (or perceive themselves to be) particularly vulnerable to disease show stronger preferences for feminine characteristics in women's faces, a previous study by Scott, Swami, Josephson, and Penton-Voak (2008) does not support this proposal. In a study of 25 men living in rural Malaysia, Scott et al. (2008) found that those men who reported having missed a day of work in the previous year because of illness showed *weaker* preferences for women's faces displaying feminine characteristics than did men who reported not having missed a day of work in the previous year because of illness. Although this finding could be interpreted as evidence against the proposal that men who are particularly vulnerable to disease show stronger preferences for feminine characteristics in women's faces or that the link between vulnerability to disease and face preferences in preindustrialized regions is different to that in more developed regions, I would argue that such conclusions may be premature, however, for several reasons. First, de Barra, DeBruine, Jones, Mahmud, and Vurtis (2013) recently found that men and women who experienced more bouts of diarrhea in childhood showed stronger preferences for exaggerated sex-typical characteristics in opposite-sex, but not own-sex, faces, particularly if they reported also having been ill in the last year. These data support the proposal that increased preferences for exaggerated sex-typical characteristics in opposite-sex faces function, at least partly, to offset the costs of increased vulnerability to disease. They also suggest that vulnerability to disease may predict face preferences in very similar ways across ecological conditions. Second, the sample size in Scott et al.'s study was relatively small and the measure of health (reported number of days of work missed due to illness) may tap personality factors, such as diligence, or social factors, such as status, rather than health, per se. That pathogens appear to have been an important factor in the evolution of men's face preferences (i.e., men's face preferences, like women's, appear to have evolved to be sensitive to pathogen-related factors and concerns) is consistent with recent work in population genetics that has concluded that, among a range of local environmental factors, pathogens have been the critical selective pressure for human evolution (Fumagalli et al., 2011).

Testosterone, Sexual Desire, and Men's Face Preferences

While much of the recent work on systematic variation in men's face preferences has focused on investigating whether concerns about pathogens contribute to both between-subjects and within-subject differences in men preferences for feminine characteristics in women's faces, other work has explored the relationship between men's femininity preferences and factors relating to their sexual motivation (e.g., men's testosterone levels and reported sexual desire).

Sexual desire may be a generalized energizer of attractiveness judgments, functioning, at least in part, to strengthen existing sexual preferences and promote mating with high-quality mates (e.g., Welling, Jones, & DeBruine, 2008). Consistent with both this proposal and the proposal that men's preferences for feminine women are linked to their sexual motivation (Miller & Todd, 1998; Thornhill & Gangestad, 1999), heterosexual men who score higher on a sexual desire inventory show stronger preferences for feminine characteristics in women's, but not men's, faces (Jones, Little, Watkins, Welling, & DeBruine, 2011). These findings complement other work showing that reported sexual desire is positively correlated with homosexual men's preferences for masculine characteristics in men's faces (Welling et al., 2013). Additionally, the relationship between sexual desire and heterosexual

men's preferences for feminine women in this study was driven by individual differences in men's scores on the dyadic sexual desire subscale, which assesses desire to engage in sexual behaviors with a partner, rather than men's scores on the solitary sexual desire subscale, which assesses desire to engage in sexual behaviors without a partner (Jones, unpublished analyses of data reported in Jones et al., 2011). These latter analyses suggest that men's preferences for facial cues associated with quality in potential mates are stronger among men who are more motivated to engage in sexual behavior with women. Thus, the relationship between sexual desire and men's face preferences may function to increase their reproductive success by increasing the likelihood of men associating, and potentially mating, with healthy women when mating is more likely to occur (Jones et al., 2011).

The studies described above suggest that between-subjects differences in men's sexual desire are positively correlated with their preferences for feminine characteristics in women's faces. However, other research suggests that within-subject changes in men's sexual desire may also be associated with their preferences for feminine characteristics in women's faces (Welling, Jones, DeBruine, Smith, et al., 2008). Men's testosterone levels are positively correlated with measures of their sexual motivation (see Welling, Jones, DeBruine, Smith, et al., 2008 for a review), and men show stronger preferences for feminine characteristics in women's faces when their own testosterone levels are high than when their own testosterone levels are relatively low (Welling, Jones, DeBruine, Smith, et al., 2008). By contrast with these findings for men's judgments of women's faces, men's judgments of the attractiveness of other men's faces were not associated with changes in their own testosterone levels (Welling, Jones, DeBruine, Smith, et al., 2008). This null result for testosterone levels and men's attractiveness judgments of other men's faces may be noteworthy, since it supports the proposal that sexual desire (and related factors) predicts men's judgments of the attractiveness of potential mates, but not other men. While some researchers have recently expressed skepticism that face preferences necessarily reflect mate preferences more generally (e.g., Penton-Voak, 2011; Scott, Clark, Boothroyd, & Penton-Voak, 2013), findings like these linking aspects of sexual desire to men's face preferences implicate mating motivations in men's preferences for feminine characteristics in women's faces.

Closing Remarks

Studies of men's perceptions of the attractiveness of women's faces suggest that characteristics associated with good health and fertility, such as femininity, symmetry/averageness, and cues associated with relatively low levels of body fat, tend to be considered attractive by men. However, men's preferences for attractive, healthy-looking facial characteristics in women's faces can also vary systematically among (and even within) individuals; men's preferences for women's faces displaying feminine characteristics appear to be linked to men's own sexual motivation and hormone levels, as well as responding to environmental factors, such as changes in exposure to potential sources of pathogens. Importantly, this systematic variation in men's face preferences occurs in ways that may function, at least in part, to increase men's reproductive success by maximizing the benefits of their mate choices and/or promoting attraction to high-quality mates when mating is likely to occur (e.g., when sexual desire is high).

Individual differences in women's mate preferences are well established in the literature on human mate preferences and are generally thought to be driven by differences among women in how they resolve putative trade-offs between the costs and benefits associated with choosing particular types of mate (Fink & Penton-Voak, 2002; Little, Jones, et al., 2011). It is unclear how trade-offs figure in men's assessments of the attractiveness of women as potential mates, however. For example, feminine women possess both attractive physical characteristics, such as health and fertility, and attractive personality characteristics, such as maternal desire and emotional warmth. One interpretation of these findings is that they imply that individual differences in mate preferences occur even in the absence of explicit trade-offs. An alternative view is that men are faced with a trade-off between the benefits of mating with a high-quality partner and the cost in terms of the mating effort they will need to expend in order to attract a high-quality, attractive mate. While recent studies have highlighted the existence of systematic variation in men's mate preferences, the trade-offs that may drive this variation are poorly understood. Investigating this issue in future work is likely to be a fruitful line of inquiry, which would have the potential to clarify the processes that underpin systematic variation in men's mate preferences.

Acknowledgment BCJ's research on human mate preferences is supported by European Research Council Starting Grant 282655 (OCMATE).

References

Apicella, C. L., Little, A. C., & Marlowe, F. W. (2007). Facial averageness and attractiveness in an isolated population of hunter-gatherers. *Perception, 36*, 1813–1820.

Bleske-Rechek, A., Harris, H. D., Denkinger, K., Webb, R. M., Erickson, L., & Nelson, L. A. (2011). Physical cues of ovulatory status: A failure to replicate enhanced facial attractiveness and reduced waist-to-hip ratio at high fertility. *Evolutionary Psychology, 9*, 336–353.

Bobst, C., & Lobmaier, J. S. (2012). Men's preference for the ovulating female is triggered by subtle face shape differences. *Hormones & Behavior, 62*(4), 413–417.

Burriss, R. P., Roberts, S. C., Welling, L. L. M., Puts, D. A., & Little, A. C. (2011). Heterosexual romantic couples mate assortatively for facial symmetry, but not masculinity. *Personality and Social Psychology Bulletin, 37*, 601–613.

Burriss, R. P., Welling, L. L. M., & Puts, D. A. (2011). Mate preference drives mate-choice: Men's self-rated masculinity predicts their female partner's preference for masculinity. *Personality and Individual Differences, 51*, 1023–1027.

Coetzee, V., Chen, J., Perrett, D. I., & Stephen, I. D. (2010). Deciphering faces: Quantifiable visual cues to weight. *Perception, 39*, 51–61.

Coetzee, V., Faerber, S. J., Greeff, J. M., Lefevre, C. E., Re, D. E., & Perrett, D. I. (2012). African perceptions of female attractiveness. *PLoS One, 7*, e48116.

Coetzee, V., Perrett, D. I., & Stephen, I. D. (2009). Facial adiposity: A cue to health? *Perception, 38*, 1700–1711.

Conway, C. A., Jones, B. C., DeBruine, L. M., & Little, A. C. (2008). Evidence for adaptive design in human gaze preference. *Proceedings of the Royal Society of London B, 275*, 63–69.

Conway, C. A., Jones, B. C., DeBruine, L. M., Little, A. C., Hay, J., Welling, L. L. M., et al. (2008). Integrating physical and social cues when forming face preferences: Differences among low and high anxiety individuals. *Social Neuroscience, 3*, 89–95.

Cornwell, R. E., Boothroyd, L. G., Burt, D. M., Feinberg, D. R., Jones, B. C., Little, A. C., et al. (2004). Concordant preferences for opposite-sex signals? Human pheromones and facial characteristics. *Proceedings of the Royal Society of London B, 271*, 635–640.

Cunningham, M. R., Roberts, A. R., Barbee, A. P., Druen, P. B., & Wu, C.-H. (1995). Their ideas of beauty are, on the whole, the same as ours: Consistency and variability in the cross-cultural perception of female physical attractiveness. *Journal of Personality and Social Psychology, 68*, 261–279.

Curtis, V., Aunger, R., & Rabie, T. (2004). Evidence that disgust evolved to protect from risk of disease. *Proceedings of the Royal Society of London B, 271*, S131–S133.

de Barra, M., DeBruine, L. M., Jones, B. C., Mahmud, Z. H., & Vurtis, V. A. (2013). Illness in childhood predicts face preferences in adulthood. *Evolution and Human Behavior, 34*(6), 384–389.

DeBruine, L. M. (2013). Evidence versus speculation on the validity of methods for measuring masculinity preferences: Comment on Scott et al. *Behavioral Ecology, 24*(3), 591–593.

DeBruine, L. M., Jones, B. C., Crawford, J. R., Welling, L. L. M., & Little, A. C. (2010). The health of a nation predicts their mate preferences: Cross-cultural variation in women's preferences for masculinized male faces. *Proceedings of the Royal Society of London B, 277*, 2405–2410.

DeBruine, L. M., Jones, B. C., Little, A. C., Boothroyd, L. G., Perrett, D. I., Penton-Voak, I. S., et al. (2006). Correlated preferences for facial masculinity and ideal or actual partner's masculinity. *Proceedings of the Royal Society of London B, 273*, 1355–1360.

DeBruine, L. M., Jones, B. C., Tybur, J. M., Lieberman, D., & Griskevicius, V. (2010). Women's preferences for masculinity in male faces are predicted by pathogen disgust, but not by moral or sexual disgust. *Evolution and Human Behavior, 31*, 69–74.

Enquist, M., Ghirlanda, S., Lundqvist, D., & Wachtmeister, C. A. (2002). An ethological theory of attractiveness. In G. Rhodes & L. A. Zebrowitz (Eds.), *Facial attractiveness: Evolutionary, cognitive and social perspectives* (pp. 27–153). Westport, CT: Ablex.

Fink, B., Grammer, K., & Thornhill, R. (2001). Human (Homo sapiens) facial attractiveness in relation to skin texture and color. *Journal of Comparative Psychology, 115*, 92–99.

Fink, B., & Penton-Voak, I. S. (2002). Evolutionary psychology of facial attractiveness. *Current Directions in Psychological Science, 11*, 154–158.

Fraccaro, P. J., Feinberg, D. R., DeBruine, L. M., Little, A. C., Watkins, C. D., & Jones, B. C. (2010). Correlated male preferences for femininity in female faces and voices. *Evolutionary Psychology, 8*, 447–461.

Fumagalli, M., Sironi, M., Pozzoli, U., Ferrer-Admettla, A., Pattini, L., & Nielsen, R. (2011). Signatures of environmental genetic adaptation pinpoint pathogens as the main selective pressure through human evolution. *PLoS Genetics, 7*, e1002355.

Grammer, K., & Thornhill, R. (1994). Human (Homo sapiens) facial attractiveness and sexual selection: The role of symmetry and averageness. *Journal of Comparative Psychology, 108*, 233–242.

Gray, A. W., & Boothroyd, L. G. (2012). Female facial appearance and health. *Evolutionary Psychology, 10*, 66–77.

Halberstadt, J., & Rhodes, G. (2000). The attractiveness of non-face averages: Implications for an evolutionary explanation of the attractiveness of average faces. *Psychological Science, 11*, 285–289.

Haselton, M. G., & Gildersleeve, K. (2011). Can men detect ovulation? *Current Directions in Psychological Science, 20*, 87–92.

Haselton, M. G., Mortezaie, M., Pillsworth, E. G., Bleske-Recheck, A. E., & Frederick, D. A. (2007). Ovulation and human female ornamentation: Near ovulation, women dress to impress. *Hormones and Behavior, 51*, 40–45.

Henderson, J. J. A., & Anglin, J. M. (2003). Facial attractiveness predicts longevity. *Evolution and Human Behavior, 24*, 351–356.

Jasienska, G., Ziomkiewicz, A., Ellison, P. T., Lipson, S. F., & Thune, I. (2004). Large breasts and narrow waists indicate reproductive potential in women. *Proceedings of the Royal Society of London B, 271*(1545), 1213–1217.

Jenkins, R., White, D., Van Montfort, X., & Burton, A. M. (2011). Variability in photos of the same face. *Cognition, 121*, 313–323.

Jones, B. C., DeBruine, L. M., & Little, A. C. (2007). The role of symmetry in attraction to average faces. *Perception & Psychophysics, 69*, 1273–1277.

Jones, B. C., DeBruine, L. M., Little, A. C., Conway, C. A., & Feinberg, D. R. (2006). Integrating gaze direction and expression in preferences for attractive faces. *Psychological Science, 17*, 588–591.

Jones, B. C., Feinberg, D. R., DeBruine, L. M., Little, A. C., & Vukovic, J. (2010). A domain-specific opposite-sex bias in human preferences for manipulated voice pitch. *Animal Behaviour, 79*, 57–62.

Jones, B. C., Feinberg, D. R., Watkins, C. D., Fincher, C. L., Little, A. C., & DeBruine, L. M. (2013). Pathogen disgust predicts women's preferences for masculinity in men's voices, faces, and bodies. *Behavioral Ecology, 24*, 373–379.

Jones, B. C., Fincher, C. L., Welling, L. L. M., Little, A. C., Feinberg, D. R., Watkins, C. D., et al. (2013). Salivary cortisol and pathogen disgust predict men's preferences for feminine shape cues in women's faces. *Biological Psychology, 92*(2), 233–240.

Jones, B. C., Little, A. C., Penton-Voak, I. S., Tiddeman, B. P., Burt, D. M., & Perrett, D. I. (2001). Facial symmetry and judgements of apparent health: Support for a 'good genes' explanation of the attractiveness-symmetry relationship. *Evolution and Human Behavior, 22*, 417–429.

Jones, B. C., Little, A. C., Watkins, C. D., Welling, L. L. M., & DeBruine, L. M. (2011). Reported sexual desire predicts men's preferences for sexually dimorphic cues in women's faces. *Archives of Sexual Behavior, 40*, 1281–1285.

Jones, B. C., Perrett, D. I., Little, A. C., Boothroyd, L. G., Cornwell, R. E., Feinberg, D. R., et al. (2005). Menstrual cycle, pregnancy and oral contraceptive use alter attraction to apparent health in faces. *Proceedings of the Royal Society of London B, 272*, 347–354.

Kalick, S. M., Zebrowitz, L. A., Langlois, J. H., & Johnson, R. M. (1998). Does human facial attractiveness honestly advertise health? Longitudinal data on an evolutionary question. *Psychological Science, 9*, 8–13.

Kampe, K. K., Frith, C. D., Dolan, R. J., & Frith, U. (2001). Reward value of attractiveness and gaze. *Nature, 413*, 589.

Koehler, N., Simmons, L. W., Rhodes, G., & Peters, M. (2004). The relationship between sexual dimorphism in human faces and fluctuating asymmetry. *Proceedings of the Royal Society of London B, 271*, S233–S236.

Law Smith, M. J., Deady, D. K., Moore, F. R., Jones, B. C., Cornwell, R. E., Stirrat, M. R., et al. (2012). Maternal tendencies in women are associated with estrogen levels and facial femininity. *Hormones and Behavior, 61*, 12–16.

Law Smith, M. J., Perrett, D. I., Jones, B. C., Cornwell, R. E., Moore, F. R., Feinberg, D. R., et al. (2006). Facial appearance is a cue to oestrogen levels in women. *Proceedings of the Royal Society of London B, 273*, 135–140.

Lie, H. C., Rhodes, G., & Simmons, L. W. (2008). Genetic diversity revealed in human faces. *Evolution, 62*, 2473–2486.

Little, A. C., Apicella, C. L., & Marlowe, F. W. (2007). Preferences for symmetry in human faces in two cultures: Data from the UK and the Hadza, an isolated group of hunter-gatherers. *Proceedings of the Royal Society of London B, 274*, 3113–3117.

Little, A. C., Burt, D. M., & Perrett, D. I. (2006). Assortative mating for perceived personality in faces. *Personality and Individual Differences, 40*, 973–984.

Little, A. C., DeBruine, L. M., & Jones, B. C. (2011). Exposure to visual cues of pathogen contagion changes preferences for masculinity and symmetry in opposite-sex faces. *Proceedings of the Royal Society of London B, 278*, 2032–2039.

Little, A. C., & Hancock, P. J. (2002). The role of masculinity and distinctiveness on the perception of attractiveness in human male faces. *British Journal of Psychology, 93*, 451–464.

Little, A. C., & Jones, B. C. (2003). Evidence against perceptual bias views for symmetry preferences in human faces. *Proceedings of the Royal Society of London B, 279*, 1759–1763.

Little, A. C., & Jones, B. C. (2006). Attraction independent of detection suggests special mechanisms for symmetry preferences in human face perception. *Proceedings of the Royal Society of London B, 273*, 3093–3099.

Little, A. C., Jones, B. C., & DeBruine, L. M. (2011). Facial attractiveness: Evolutionary based research. *Philosophical Transactions of the Royal Society B, 366*, 1638–1659.

Main, J. C., DeBruine, L. M., Little, A. C., & Jones, B. C. (2010). Interactions among the effects of head orientation, emotional expression and physical attractiveness on face preferences. *Perception, 39*, 62–71.

Martin, L. B. (2009). Stress and immunity in wild vertebrates: Timing is everything. *General and Comparative Endocrinology, 163*, 70–76.

Mason, M. F., Tatkow, E. P., & Macrae, C. N. (2005). The look of love—Gaze shifts and person perception. *Psychological Science, 16*, 236–239.

Miller, G. F., & Todd, P. M. (1998). Mate choice turns cognitive. *Trends in Cognitive Sciences, 2*, 190–198.

O'Toole, A. J., Price, T., Vetter, T., Bartlett, J. C., & Blanz, V. (1999). 3D shape and 2D surface textures of human faces: The role of "averages" in attractiveness and age. *Image & Vision Computing, 18*, 9–19.

Penton-Voak, I. S. (2011). In retreat from nature? Successes and concerns in Darwinian approaches to facial attractiveness. *Journal of Evolutionary Psychology, 1*, 1–21.

Penton-Voak, I. S., & Perrett, D. I. (2001). Male facial attractiveness: Perceived personality and shifting female preferences for male traits across the menstrual cycle. *Advances in Animal Behaviour, 30*, 219–259.

Perrett, D. I., Burt, D. M., Penton-Voak, I. S., Lee, K. J., Rowland, D. A., & Edwards, R. (1999). Symmetry and human facial attractiveness. *Evolution and Human Behavior, 20*, 295–307.

Perrett, D. I., Lee, K. J., Penton-Voak, I. S., Rowland, D. R., Yoshikawa, S., Burt, D. M., et al. (1998). Effects of sexual dimorphism on facial attractiveness. *Nature, 394*, 884–887.

Perrett, D. I., May, K. A., & Yoshikawa, S. (1994). Facial shape and judgments of female attractiveness. *Nature, 368*, 239–242.

Puts, D. A., Bailey, D. H., Cárdenas, R. A., Burriss, R. P., Welling, L. L. M., Wheatley, J. R., et al. (2013). Women's attractiveness changes with estradiol and progesterone across the ovulatory cycle. *Hormones and Behavior, 63*(1), 13–19.

Reither, E. N., Hauser, R. M., & Swallen, K. C. (2009). Predicting adult health and mortality from adolescent facial characteristics in yearbook photographs. *Demography, 46*, 27–41.

Rhodes, G. (2006). The evolutionary psychology of facial beauty. *Annual Review of Psychology, 57*, 199–226.

Rhodes, G., Chan, J., Zebrowitz, L. A., & Simmons, L. W. (2003). Does sexual dimorphism in human faces signal health? *Proceedings of the Royal Society of London B, 270*, S93–S95.

Rhodes, G., Simmons, L. W., & Peters, M. (2005). Attractiveness and sexual behaviour: Does attractiveness enhance mating success? *Evolution and Human Behavior, 26*, 186–201.

Rhodes, G., & Tremewan, T. (1996). Averageness, exaggeration and facial attractiveness. *Psychological Science, 7*, 105–110.

Rhodes, G., Yoshikawa, S., Palermo, R., Simmons, L. W., Peters, M., Lee, K., et al. (2007). Perceived health contributes to the attractiveness of facial symmetry, averageness, and sexual dimorphism. *Perception, 36*, 1244–1252.

Rhodes, G., Zebrowitz, L., Clark, A., Kalick, S. M., Hightower, A., & McKay, R. (2001). Do facial averageness and symmetry signal health? *Evolution and Human Behavior, 22*, 31–46.

Roberts, S. C., Havlíček, J., Flegr, J., Hruskova, M., Little, A. C., Jones, B. C., et al. (2004). Female facial attractiveness increases during the fertile phase of the menstrual cycle. *Proceedings of the Royal Society of London B, 271*, 270–272.

Sapolsky, R. M., Romero, L. M., & Munck, A. U. (2000). How do glucocorticoids influence stress responses? Integrating permissive, suppressive, stimulatory, and preparative actions. *Endocrine Reviews, 21*, 55–89.

Schneider, T. M., Hecht, H., & Carbon, C.-C. (2012). Judging body weight from faces: The height-weight illusion. *Perception, 41*, 12–124.

Scott, I. M. L., Clark, A. P., Boothroyd, L. G., & Penton-Voak, I. S. (2013). Do men's faces really signal heritable immunocompetence? *Behavioral Ecology, 24*(3), 596–597.

Scott, I. M., & Penton-Voak, I. S. (2011). The validity of composite photographs for assessing masculinity preferences. *Perception, 40*, 323–331.

Scott, I. M., Swami, V., Josephson, S. C., & Penton-Voak, I. S. (2008). Context-dependent preferences for facial dimorphism in a rural Malaysian population. *Evolution and Human Behavior, 29*, 289–296.

Smith, F. G., Jones, B. C., DeBruine, L. M., & Little, A. C. (2009). Interactions between masculinity-femininity

and apparent health in face preferences. *Behavioral Ecology, 20*, 441–445.

Thornhill, R., & Gangestad, S. W. (1999). Facial attractiveness. *Trends in Cognitive Sciences, 3*, 452–460.

Thornhill, R., & Gangestad, S. W. (2006). Facial sexual dimorphism, developmental stability, and susceptibility to disease in men and women. *Evolution and Human Behavior, 27*, 131–144.

Tinlin, R. M., Watkins, C. D., Welling, L. L. M., DeBruine, L. M., Al-Dujaili, E. A. S., & Jones, B. C. (2013). Perceived facial adiposity conveys information about women's health. *British Journal of Psychology, 104*(2), 235–248.

Tovee, M. J., Maisey, D. S., Emery, J. L., & Cornelissen, P. L. (1999). Visual cues to female physical attractiveness. *Proceedings of the Royal Society London B, 266*, 211–2118.

Tybur, J. M., Lieberman, D., & Griskevicius, V. (2009). Microbes, mating, and morality: Individual differences in three functional domains of disgust. *Journal of Personality and Social Psychology, 97*, 103–122.

Watkins, C. D., DeBruine, L. M., Little, A. C., & Jones, B. C. (2012). Social support influences preferences for feminine facial cues in potential social partners. *Experimental Psychology, 59*, 340–347.

Welling, L. L. M., Jones, B. C., & DeBruine, L. M. (2008). Sex drive is positively associated with women's preferences for sexual dimorphism in men's and women's faces. *Personality and Individual Differences, 44*, 161–170.

Welling, L. L. M., Jones, B. C., DeBruine, L. M., Smith, F. G., Feinberg, D. R., Little, A. C., et al. (2008). Men report stronger attraction to femininity in women's faces when their testosterone levels are high. *Hormones and Behavior, 54*, 703–708.

Welling, L. L. M., Singh, K., Puts, D. A., Jones, B. C., & Burriss, R. P. (2013). Self-reported sexual desire in homosexual men and women predicts preferences for sexually dimorphic facial cues. *Archives of Sexual Behavior, 42*, 785–791.

Winkielman, P., Halberstadt, J., Fazendeiro, T., & Catty, S. (2006). Prototypes are attractive because they are easy on the mind. *Psychological Science, 17*, 799–807.

Male Adaptations to Female Ovulation

5

Erik M. Lund and Saul L. Miller

As the other chapters in this book point out, no domain of behavior is more central to the evolution of our species than mating. Reproductive success is the sine qua non of biological evolution. Consequently, the human body and mind are equipped with powerful psychological and biological mechanisms that aim to boost our reproductive success.

While many factors may influence reproductive success or failure, arguably one of the most important factors is fertility. Across many sexually reproducing species, females are only fertile during the brief period of time surrounding estrus or ovulation. This period of peak fertility is crucial from an evolutionary perspective as sexual intercourse is unlikely to lead to conception at other times in a female's reproductive cycle.

In this chapter, we review research that has examined the implications of shifting levels of women's fertility for men's mating psychology (see Chap. 15 by Puts and Welling for a discussion of female adaptations to shifting levels of fertility). We begin with a review of the physiology of female fertility and the history of its study in psychology. We then provide an overview of hypotheses generated from an evolutionary perspective pertaining to male psychological adaptations designed to detect and respond to fertility cues. We review evidence supporting the notion that men are capable of detecting women's fertility cues and that exposure to those cues functionally shapes men's mate-seeking and relationship maintenance psychology and behavior. Last, we outline important directions for future research in this area.

Female Fertility and the Concealment of Estrus

Women experience distinct and dramatic shifts in their fertility level across the menstrual cycle. In humans, a female's menstrual cycle lasts 28 days on average. Ovulation typically occurs approximately halfway through the menstrual cycle (e.g., 14 days after the start of menstruation), at which point an egg leaves the ovary and travels down the fallopian tube. The vast majority of pregnancies occur when intercourse takes place during the 5-day period leading up to or on the day of ovulation. The probability of conception from sexual intercourse ranges from 10 % five days before ovulation to 33 % on the day of ovulation (Wilcox, Weinberg, & Baird, 1995). In contrast, the likelihood of conception occurring outside this fertile window is practically nil. By definition then, there is a small and critical window in which fertilization can occur.

Similar shifts in female fertility occur in a wide array of mammalian species. In some animals, such as sheep, goats, and horses, females are only fertile during certain seasons. In other species, like cats,

E.M. Lund (✉)
Department of Psychology, University of Kentucky,
Lexington, KY 40506, USA
e-mail: e.m.lund@uky.edu

V.A. Weekes-Shackelford and T.K. Shackelford (eds.), *Evolutionary Perspectives on Human Sexual Psychology and Behavior*, Evolutionary Psychology, DOI 10.1007/978-1-4939-0314-6_5,
© Springer Science+Business Media New York 2014

cows, and pigs, females experience peak fertility levels several times a year. Those periods of peak fertility are known as estrus. With respect to behavior, estrus is often characterized by heightened proceptivity and receptivity to sexual activity. In many nonhuman primates, for example, females display the highest degree of sexual activity in the ovulatory or estrus phase of the cycle (Nadler, 1981; Saayman, 1970). With respect to physiology, estrus is often characterized by overt changes in physical appearance. For example, in chimpanzees (Wallis, 1982, 1992), baboons (Saayman, 1972), and macaques (Higham et al., 2012), females experience anogenital swelling during their period of peak fertility. Those large sexual swellings provide a clear, explicit signal to males that the female is fertile.

Unlike many other species, human females do not display highly overt physical signals of their fertility such as the sexual swelling of hindquarters occurring among nonhuman primates. Moreover, in contrast to other species in which sexual behavior is often restricted to estrus, human females have an extended sexuality—they are sexually proceptive and receptive across the menstrual cycle. A recent study of over 20,000 women demonstrated that, aside from a reduction in sexual activity during menses, women display no systematic changes in sexual activity with partners over their menstrual cycle (Brewis & Meyer, 2005). Because of these distinct differences between humans and other mammals, there was considerable consensus among researchers for nearly half a century that estrus was concealed in human females (Alexander & Noonan, 1979; Symons, 1979). This was hypothesized to be the case because, in a species in which biparental care is an important component to successful reproduction (such as humans), concealment of fertility status would have been selected for in order to maintain male investment throughout the ovulatory cycle (Etkin, 1954), reduce intrasexual competition among males (Daniels, 1983), promote paternal care (Strassmann, 1981), increase the likelihood of women acquiring greater quantities of protein through male hunting (Hill, 1982; Parker, 1987; Symons, 1979), confuse paternity (Benshoof & Thornhill, 1979), and reduce the risk of infanticide (Hrdy, 1981).

Within the past two decades, however, a cascade of empirical studies has come to a different conclusion. While women may experience an extended sexuality, there is now abundant evidence suggesting that women's mating motives and behavior differ between the fertile phase of the cycle and the non-fertile phases (Gangestad & Thornhill, 2008; see also Chap. 15 in this book). Moreover, and more central to this chapter, an emerging body of evidence indicates that, despite a lack of overt physical signals to women's fertility, men may still be attuned to more subtle cues to female fertility. Before discussing evidence for men's attunement to women's fertility, we first outline why this attunement may exist.

Male Counteradaptations to Concealed Estrus

As mentioned previously, there are several reasons why women may have evolved to conceal ovulation. In brief, women would have gained significant advantages by concealing their fertility status from men (e.g., they would have increased the probability of maintaining male investment). Thus, why should women signal their reproductive state to men? The answer to this question is that women most likely did *not* evolve to signal their reproductive state to men. Rather women probably evolved to conceal their estrus (given the reasons stated earlier). Thus, a different question emerges: If women evolved to conceal estrus, why is it that they display cues to fertility that men are attuned to?

In order to elicit ovulation, certain physiological changes are required (e.g., changes in hormones like estrogen and FSH). While many of those changes may be concealed to some extent, it is unlikely that they could be completely concealed. Internal physiological changes are likely to have some effect externally, even if only very subtly. Thus, suppression of external cues to fertility is constrained by the internal changes needed for reproduction. As a result, the physiological changes required for increasing fertility may produce some physiological by-products—external changes that "leak" information about fertility status (Gangestad & Thornhill, 2008). Males may therefore be attuned not to intentional signals of ovulation, but rather to "leaky" by-products of internal changes associated with ovulation.

Why should males have evolved to be sensitive to such leaky fertility cues? Males spend an extraordinary amount of time and energy attempting to gain sexual access to females. They not only have to attract a female but also need to outcompete other male rivals. All of this effort, however, may be for naught if sexual intercourse is unlikely to lead to conception. For example, it would be very costly for a male to engage in intrasexual competition (which in many species is violent in nature and thus not only requires energy but can also lead to physical harm) in order to gain access to a female low in fertility. As a result, males who were capable of directing those efforts toward securing a fertile mate would have had a significant advantage over males who did not base mating-related efforts (particularly for short-term mating opportunities) upon probability of conception. Thus, in order to reduce the costs of competing for mates who are unlikely to be fertile, men may have evolved to be sensitive to even very subtle cues to a heightened fertility level. Consistent with this perspective, in numerous species, male intrasexual competition is at its highest during times when females peak in fertility (Cox & Le Boeuf, 1977).

In sum, in the coevolutionary arms race that characterizes relations between the sexes, women would have gained a significant advantage by concealing fertility, while men would have gained an advantage by an awareness of fertility. The result of this intersexual competition may be that women evolved to conceal overt signals to ovulation, in turn forcing men to develop a sensitivity to the more subtle, leaky fertility cues.

Evidence of Male Attunement to Female Fertility

An emerging literature reveals that men may indeed be sensitive to cues to ovulation. In a study receiving widespread attention, Miller, Tybur, and Jordan (2007) examined professional lap dancers' earnings over the course of their menstrual cycle. They found that, for a 5-h shift, female lap dancers who were not taking hormonal contraceptives (i.e., normally cycling) made, on average, $135 more in tips during the fertile phase of their cycle (days 9–15) than during the non-fertile phases of their cycle (days 1–5 and 18–28). That is, women at high fertility garnered significantly more money from male patrons than did women at low fertility. These results support the notion that men are attuned to shifts in women's fertility. However, they also suggest much more: Men may not only be able to detect ovulatory cues, but they may functionally attune their behavior in response to those ovulatory cues. Women high in fertility pay particular attention to indicators of status (Lens, Driesmans, Pandelaere, & Janssens, 2012). Thus, men may increase displays of wealth and status (e.g., by giving more money), thereby promoting the attraction of a mate high in fertility.

Other recent studies have come to a similar conclusion: Exposure to ovulatory cues may cause men to behave in ways that make them more sexually appealing to women. For example, Coyle and Kaschak (2012) investigated the types of linguistic patterns men use when in the presence of a woman. In their study, normally cycling female confederates described to male participants a picture using one of two types of syntactic structures—a double object construction (e.g., The captain sent the first mate a message) or a prepositional object construction (e.g., The captain sent a message to the first mate). The male participants then described another picture to those same women. Coyle and Kaschak found that men who interacted with a woman high in fertility (as compared to a woman low in fertility) were more likely to display unique, nonconforming types of linguistic patterns (i.e., the men were more likely to use a different syntactic structure than the one used previously by the female confederate). Women high in fertility are attracted to indicators of creative intelligence when pursing short-term relationships (Haselton & Miller, 2006). Consequently, men may display unique, nonconforming language patterns around women high in fertility as a way of highlighting their creativity.

Although nonconformity may increase a man's sexual appeal when it signals creative intelligence, conformity can also heighten one's value when it signals unity. For example, behavioral mimicry (conforming to another person's subtle behaviors) suggests cohesiveness between individuals and is associated with increased social liking (i.e., people tend to evaluate positively others who mimic them; Lakin, Jefferis, Cheng, & Chartrand, 2003). Consequently, as a way of increasing one's sexual appeal, a mating motive may lead one to behaviorally mimic a potential romantic partner. Indeed, increases in men's short-term mating desires are associated with increases in men's tendency to mimic attractive women (van Straaten, Engels, Finkenauer, & Holland, 2008). To assess the effect of female fertility on men's behavioral mimicry, Miller and Maner (2011, Study 3) videotaped male undergraduate students interacting with a normally cycling female confederate on different days of her cycle. While the male participant and female confederate worked on a cooperative task, the female confederate touched her face while resting an elbow on the table. Consistent with predictions, men were more likely mimic the woman's behavior (i.e., touch their face while resting an elbow on the table) during those days when the woman was high in fertility (as indicated by a heightened probability of conception; Wilcox et al., 1995).

In this same study, Miller and Maner (2011, Study 3) also examined men's tendency to engage in risky behavior when in the presence of the female confederate. Male risk-taking is a signal of ambition and confidence, traits that women often find desirable in a romantic partner (Baker & Maner, 2008, 2009; Daly & Wilson, 2001). Thus, in the second part of this study, men performed a blackjack gambling task with the female confederate present. Findings revealed that men were more likely to make riskier gambling decisions when the confederate was high in fertility. It is important to note that the female confederate was rigorously trained to keep eye contact and conversation to a minimum, wear similar clothing each time, and behave in an introverted, non-flirtatious way. Independent observers verified that those guidelines were followed. Therefore, the findings are strong indicators that even subtle cues to fertility are strong predictors of changes in men's behavior—behavior that women tend to find particularly attractive among men.

While these studies suggest that men are attuned to shifts in women's fertility and change their mating-related behavior accordingly when exposed to fertility cues, these studies also leave unanswered an important question: What are the specific cues to fertility that men are detecting? Several emerging lines of research suggest three broad types of discernible ovulatory cues that men may use to focus their mating effort toward women high in fertility. They are olfactory cues, auditory cues, and visual cues.

Olfactory Cues

In many animals, olfaction is a principal vehicle by which female fertility shapes male-mating behavior (e.g., Pankevich, Baum, & Cherry, 2004). In ring-tailed lemurs, a social species like humans, males' display heightened vigilance to a female's odor when she is likely to conceive (Scordato & Drea, 2007). In marmosets, males display increased investigative behaviors and arousal after being exposed to the scent of an ovulating female (Ziegler, Schultz-Darken, Scott, Snowdon, & Ferris, 2005). Thus, in several nonhuman primate species, males appear capable of discerning female fertility levels via olfaction.

Whether a similar mechanism operates in humans has been a topic of interest in recent years. Some researchers have hypothesized that scent does *not* serve as a cue to fertility in humans (Roney & Simmons, 2012). This is because in many nonhuman species, female scents influence male behavior via an effect on the vomeronasal organ (VNO). For example, in rodents, lesions to the VNO reduce male behavioral and physiological reactions to female pheromones (Coquelin, Clancy, Macrides, Noble, & Gorski, 1984; Pfeiffer & Johnston, 1994). Evidence suggests that the human analog to the VNO is nonfunctioning (Bhatnagar &

Smith, 2010; Frasnelli, Lundström, Boyle, Katsarkas, & Jones-Gotman, 2011). Thus, without a functioning equivalent to the VNO, humans may lack the ability to discern fertility levels simply from scent cues.

However, there are other reasons to suspect that scent *does* play a role in the detection of women's fertility. First, despite human noses having fewer mucosa receptor cells than those in other mammals, humans produce olfactory substances in a quantity that is almost the largest of all the primates (Schaal & Porter, 1991; Stoddart, 1990). Indeed, when one considers the number, size, and production of sebaceous and apocrine glands, humans may be considered one of most odorous of primate species (Pawłowski, 1999). Second, those glands are concentrated in areas central to reproduction (e.g., the areola mammae, and pubic and anogenital areas, Stoddart, 1990), suggesting that the odors produced from those glands contain information about one's reproductive state. Third, those glands are also concentrated in the armpit—a part of the body that, once our species began walking upright, became situated close to the nose of conspecifics during social interaction. Indeed, humans, chimpanzees, and gorillas have axillary organs in the armpits marked with hair that when mixed with sweat and other microorganisms has been suggested as a source of chemosensory signaling (Montagna, 1985; Spielman, Zeng, Leyden, & Preti, 1995). Last, the size of those axillary glands has been found to fluctuate across the menstrual cycle in women, which may indicate their importance in the chemosensory signaling of fertility (Mykytowycz, 1985). In sum, despite the lack of a functioning VNO, there is reason to hypothesize that humans still use olfaction to secure important reproductive information about potential mates.

Following this reasoning, several studies have begun to examine whether men are capable of detecting shifts in women's fertility via scent. In an early study on olfaction and fertility, Doty and colleagues (1975) asked men to smell human vaginal odors from women at different points in their cycle. They observed that men rated the scents as less intense and more pleasant the

closer a woman was to ovulation. In another study, Singh and Bronstad (2001) asked women to wear T-shirts to bed for three consecutive nights during the high-fertility phase of their cycle (close to ovulation) and another three nights during the low-fertility phase (mid-luteal phase). Men then smelled the T-shirts and rated them for attractiveness. Findings revealed that men judged the scent of the T-shirts worn during high fertility to be most attractive. This finding that men subjectively evaluate the body odors of women close to ovulation as more pleasant smelling than the odors of women far from ovulation has been replicated several times (Havlíček, Dvořáková, Bartoš, & Flegr, 2006; Kuukasjärvi et al., 2004; Miller & Maner, 2010b; Thornhill et al., 2003) and verified in studies using rigorous physiological methods for determining ovulation (Gildersleeve, Haselton, Larson, & Pillsworth, 2012). Taken together, these studies demonstrate that scent may be one means by which men are sensitive to shifts in female fertility.

To serve as a functional chemosensory signaling device, scent cues to ovulation should have effects in men well beyond subjective assessments of odor pleasantness. Indeed, olfactory cues to female ovulation might be expected to promote specific physiological processes in men that are linked with mating behavior. For example, the neuroendocrine system is a key component of mating. In many species, including humans, heightened testosterone levels facilitate male-mating behavior (Batty, 1978; Roney, Lukaszewski, & Simmons, 2007). Thus, scent cues to fertility may be expected to heighten male testosterone levels as a way of facilitating the pursuit of a fertile romantic partner. Indeed, in other primate species, chemosensory cues to female ovulation cause increases in male testosterone (Ziegler et al., 2005).

Given this, Miller and Maner (2010b) hypothesized that women's fertility cues would influence men's testosterone levels. The researchers used the same paradigm used by Singh and Bronstad (2001), mentioned previously. In brief, men smelled T-shirts worn by women during high-fertility and low-fertility phases. The effect of extraneous odors was rigorously controlled for; women were instructed not to eat anything, wear any perfumes, smoke cigarettes, drink alcohol, or engage in a variety of other behaviors that could have influenced their scent. Men provided saliva samples prior to and 15 min post-smelling the T-shirt. As hypothesized, testosterone levels in the saliva were substantially higher among men who smelled the T-shirts worn by women high in fertility than among men who smelled T-shirts worn by women low in fertility or T-shirts not worn by anyone. Although testosterone did not significantly increase above baseline in response to ovulatory cues, exposure to the odor of a woman close to ovulation enervated the pattern of testosterone decrease evident in the control conditions. Thus, olfactory scent cues appear to have physiological effects on men associated with heightened mating behavior.

In addition to physiological reactions, men may have evolved cognitive responses to female ovulatory cues that encouraged mating behavior. In humans, scents have been shown to influence decision-making, thought accessibility, and behavioral intentions associated with specific goals (Bone & Ellen, 1999; Holland, Hendriks, & Aarts, 2005; Mitchell, Kahn, & Knasko, 1995). Thus, Miller and Maner (2011, Study 1) predicted that scent cues to fertility would enhance thoughts among men associated with the goal of mating. After smelling a T-shirt worn by a woman high in fertility (close to ovulation), a T-shirt worn by a woman low in fertility (during the luteal phase), or a control T-shirt not worn by anyone, men completed ten word fragments (s _ x; _ _ ck; _ ips; _ i _ k; _ ak _ d; _um; _ l _ t; _ ouch; p _ n _ s; o _ al). Each word fragment could be completed with either a sexual word or a neutral word (e.g., s_x could be sex or six). Consistent with predictions, men exposed to the scent of a woman high in fertility completed more words in a sexual manner than men in the other conditions. Thus, scent cues to fertility may prime mating motives in men by making sexual concepts more cognitively accessible.

In order to facilitate mating with a woman high in fertility, olfactory fertility cues may also influence men's perception of a woman's sexual desire. In another study by Miller & Maner, 2011, Study 2), men rated the emotional state (angry, happy, scared, or sexually aroused) of a female T-shirt supplier. An effect of T-shirt supplier's fertility was only evident for perceptions of sexual arousal. Men who reported a heightened sensitivity to odors judged the woman to be more sexually aroused if they had smelled a T-shirt worn close to ovulation as opposed to a T-shirt worn far from ovulation. Perceiving sexual interest in a woman may further facilitate men's sexual pursuit as men find attractive signs that a woman might be sexually accessible (Buss & Schmitt, 1993; Maner et al., 2005).

An important methodological aspect of many of the studies just reviewed is that male participants were aware that they were smelling odors from women. In a recent study, Roney and Simmons (2012) failed to find evidence of an increase in testosterone among men exposed to the odor of an ovulating woman (in comparison to exposure to the neutral odor of water). Men in that study were not told that odors came from women. Roney and Simmons concluded that an awareness of who or what the odor comes from (a man, a woman, an animal, etc.) might be an important boundary condition to the effects of olfactory fertility cues on men's mating processes. Their research highlights the important fact that there likely exist several (as of yet unexplored) factors that moderate effects of women's scent on men's behavior and physiology. Nevertheless, while certain boundary conditions are likely to exist, taken as a whole, the majority of research to date supports the notion that olfaction is one means by which men are attuned to shifts in women's fertility.

Auditory Cues

Auditory cues are another way that males of other species may ascertain the fertility status of a potential mate. For example, during estrus, female baboons elicit distinct vocal calls—vocal calls that are not sounded among non-fertile females and vocal calls that males recognize as cues to fertility (Moos-Heilen & Sossinka, 1990). Similarly, male macaques' behavioral responses to female copulation calls depend upon the female's fertility status, with stronger behavioral responses observed when the female is likely to conceive (Semple & McComb, 2000).

There is reason to suspect that vocal cues to fertility may exist in humans as well. Receptors for estrogen and progesterone—hormones involved in the regulation of women's fertility—have been identified in laryngeal tissue. Thus, the larynx and surrounding vocal tract tissues are likely to be affected by cyclical hormone changes (Abitbol, Abitbol, & Abitbol, 1999; Caruso et al., 2000). In other words, internal hormonal changes associated with peak fertility may be leaked out to men via their effects on women's voice. Indeed, hormonal changes associated with puberty, menopause, pregnancy, and hormone replacement therapy, all influence vocal acoustics (Caruso et al., 2000; Firat et al., 2009).

Consistent with such findings, an emerging line of research suggests that women's vocal acoustics do shift throughout the cycle and, moreover, men are attuned to those shifts (Fischer et al., 2011; Pipitone & Gallup, 2012). In one study, Bryant and Haselton (2009) recorded women speaking the same sentence during high- and low-fertility phases of their cycle (confirmed by hormone levels). Acoustical analyses revealed that the vocal pitch was higher the closer the woman was to ovulation. Combining this finding with research indicating that men tend to prefer women with higher-pitched voices (Feinberg, DeBruine, Jones, & Perrett, 2008; Feinberg et al., 2005; Pipitone & Gallup, 2012) suggests that the pitch of a woman's voice may serve as a cue to fertility and cause men to be attracted to women displaying that vocal cue. Following this hypothesis, Pipitone and Gallup (2008) assessed men's attraction to women's voices at different points in the menstrual cycle. They found that men rated the women's voices as most attractive when the speaker was closest to ovulation. While the research on auditory cues to fertility is only in its infancy, the existing data provide support for the idea that vocal acoustics serve as another cue to shifts in women's fertility.

Visual Cues

In many species, some of the most overt cues to female fertility are visual in nature (e.g., the reddening and swelling of the hindquarters in nonhuman primates). However, as mentioned previously, it is unlikely that women evolved to exhibit such unambiguous, overt physical indicators of fertility. Nevertheless, women may still experience more subtle changes in physical qualities due to the internal physiological changes required for ovulation.

Consistent with this perspective, several studies indicate that women's physical features do change slightly across the menstrual cycle. For example, in the days leading up to ovulation, body parts composed of soft tissue (e.g., ears, fingers, breasts) become more symmetrical (Manning, Scutt, Whitehouse, Leinster, & Walton, 1996; Scutt & Manning, 1996). Additionally, women's skin coloration becomes lighter during high-fertility days (van den Berghe & Frost, 1986), and women's waist-to-hip ratio may decrease around ovulation (Kirchengast & Gartner, 2002). Such subtle changes may serve as visual cues to women's fertility. In a study assessing this hypothesis, Roberts and colleagues (2004) had male and female participants view facial photographs of women during high-fertility (days 8–14) and low-fertility (days 17–25) phases of their cycle. Both men and women indicated that they found women to be more attractive during the fertile than non-fertile days of the cycle, suggesting that women, like the females of nonhuman primate species, do display some visual cues to fertility.

In addition to physiological changes, women may also leak their fertility status to men via behavioral changes (e.g., Fink, Hugill, & Lange, 2012; Guéguen, 2009). In particular, several recent studies suggest that women's choice of clothing varies across the menstrual cycle. For example, when asked to draw an outfit they might wear to a party, women close to ovulation (confirmed by hormone tests) were more likely to draw revealing outfits (e.g., short skirts, sleeveless tops) than women far from ovulation (Durante, Li, & Haselton, 2008). Indeed, when actually going out to bars and parties, women do wear more provocative and revealing clothing during high-fertility than low-fertility days of the cycle (Grammer, Renninger, & Fischer, 2004; Haselton, Mortezaie, Pillsworth, Bleske-Rechek, & Frederick, 2007). This tendency for enhanced ornamentation around ovulation is likely a consequence of heightened female intrasexual competition around ovulation (for a review, see Rosvall, 2011; also see Chap. 15 in this book). While the motivation for such changes in ornamentation may be based in intrasexual competition, those changes may still act as visual cues to fertility for men seeking fertile mates.

Thus, several physical and behavioral changes may serve as visual cues to heightened female fertility. While those cues are not as overt (e.g., changes in symmetry are very subtle) nor as unambiguous (e.g., a woman might wear a sleeveless top for a variety of reasons) as the reddening and swelling of the hindquarters in other primate species, they may nevertheless still provide information about women's fertility.

When one considers the range of possible olfactory, auditory, and visual cues that may alert men to a woman's fertility, it is perhaps not as surprising that men are more likely to give large sums of money to ovulating lap dancers or to take risks in front of a woman high in fertility. Indeed, in real-life situations, those cues probably work in conjunction to increase men's mating behavior. In sum, several lines of evidence suggest that men are attuned to shifts in women's fertility and, in the presences of those cues, display changes in psychology and behavior that promote the procurement of fertile mates.

Relationship Maintenance

In the previous parts of this chapter, we highlighted the importance of women's fertility for men's mate-seeking behavior. However, shifts in women's fertility may also have consequences for other aspects of men's mating psychology—in particular, men's mate-guarding and relationship maintenance.

Evolutionary theories posit that people possess adaptive mate-guarding mechanisms designed to help prevent dire costs associated with a partner's infidelity. For men, one of the greatest potential costs of a partner's sexual infidelity is genetic cuckoldry, which could lead the man to devote years of effort and resources to raising another man's offspring. Given the shifts in women's fertility across their menstrual cycle, cuckoldry would be most likely to occur as a result of a woman's unfaithfulness when she is close to ovulation. Moreover, some research suggests that women may be motivated to seek out extra-pair mates (i.e., sexual partners outside their current romantic relationship) when high in fertility (see Chap. 15 in this book). Consequently, men may have evolved psychological mechanisms designed to protect against a partner's sexual infidelity, especially when their partner is close to ovulation.

Consistent with this hypothesis, in many species, males' display enhanced mate-guarding when females are high in fertility. For example, male house martins ensure that when their female partners are fertile they spend little time alone in the nest and dogmatically follow them in flight (Riley, Bryant, Carter, & Parkin, 1995). Similar increases in male mate-guarding behavior during periods of female peak fertility has been observed in kestrels (Korpimäki et al., 1996), Montagu's harrier (Arroyo, 1999), Seychelles warblers (Komdeur, Kraaijeveld-Smit, Kraaijeveld, & Edelaar, 1999), seabirds (Birkhead & Møller, 1992), and other species (Birkhead, 1982; Lumpkin, 1981).

Some evidence suggests that a similar enhancement in male mate-guarding occurs in humans when women are close to ovulation. In a study by Gangestad, Thornhill, and Garver (2002), women reported that their male partners engaged in more mate-guarding and mate-retention behaviors, such as calling and inquiring about their whereabouts more frequently and monopolizing their time, when the women were high in fertility as compared to low in fertility. During the high-fertility phase of the cycle, women also report that their male partners are more possessive, jealous, and likely to express feelings of love and desire. This is particularly true when the men are low in physical attractiveness, and thus their female partners are more interested in seeking out sexual opportunities with other men (Haselton & Gangestad, 2006; Pillsworth & Haselton, 2006). These findings suggest that men are attuned to the heightened risks of sexual infidelity when a partner is close to ovulation and increase their mate-guarding behaviors accordingly.

In addition to behaving differently toward their romantic partners, men may also behave differently toward other men when their romantic partner is high in fertility. To prevent infidelity, one needs to monitor not only one's romantic partner but also same-sex others who might tempt one's partner away. Thus, when their partner is high in fertility, men may be wary of other men who display characteristics that their partner finds attractive. Based on this logic, Burriss and Little (2006) hypothesized and found that when their partner's conception risk was high men perceived an increased romantic threat from male dominant faces—faces displaying dominant characteristics that women high in fertility find sexually appealing. This suggests that men have a functional, biased attunement to rivals who pose the biggest risk of cuckoldry when their partners are at peak fertility.

Intrasexual rivals are only some of the threats that people face when attempting to maintain their relationship. Another pervasive obstacle to the maintenance of long-term relationships is the existence of attractive relationship alternatives. Long-term relationships provide numerous social and reproductive benefits. Consequently, when faced with a potential, attractive alternative to one's current partner, people often display a devaluation of the positive characteristics (e.g., physical attractiveness) of that romantic alternative (Gonzaga, Haselton, Smurda, Davies, & Poore, 2008; Karremans & Verwijmeren, 2008; Maner, Gailliot, & Miller, 2009; Plant, Kunstman, & Maner, 2010). By devaluing the alternative, people are less tempted to stray from their current relationship.

Integrating this research on relationship maintenance with research on men's attraction to female fertility cues, Miller and Maner (2010a) hypothesized that, while single men would report increased liking of a woman close to ovulation (i.e., mate-seeking behaviors), men in committed relationships would report decreased liking of a woman (who is not their current partner) close to ovulation (i.e., relationship maintenance behaviors). This devaluation of the fertile woman would allow committed men to reduce the temptation to stray from their current relationship and thus maintain the reproductive benefits that relationship provides. To test this hypothesis, the researchers had male participants rate the attractiveness of a female confederate at different points in her cycle. Consistent with previous findings indicating that men are attuned to and find attractive cues to fertility, single men in the current study rated the confederate as more attractive when her fertility level (indicated by probability of conception) was high. In contrast, committed men indicated that they found the female confederate *less* attractive as fertility level increased. Thus, men in relationships may attenuate their attraction to a fertile woman when that woman is not their current partner.

Research examining the moderating effects of relationship status on men's responses to female fertility cues is only just beginning, and much more research is needed to fully understand the effect of female fertility cues on men's mate-guarding and relationship maintenance processes. Nevertheless, the handful of studies reviewed above suggest that whether the female is a partner or stranger and whether the male is paired or single may play important roles in shaping men's responses to fertility cues.

Future Directions

The studies discussed in this chapter provide a glimpse into the ways in which men have evolved to respond to fluctuating female fertility. While these studies provide converging evidence for a male attunement to subtle female fertility cues, there are still many questions yet to be answered. Here, we raise two questions that future research might profitably address: Do fertility cues affect nonconsensual male-mating tactics such as sexual coercion? Are the effects of fertility cues on men's mating behavior moderated by men's sexuality?

Fertility Cues and Sexual Coercion

Nonconsensual intercourse (i.e., rape) has been a persistent occurrence throughout evolutionary history. By definition, rape circumvents female mate choice and represents a threat to female reproductive success. Rape has been proposed both as a specific adaptation to increase male reproductive success and as strictly a by-product of other tendencies, with the verdict still very much undecided (for a discussion, see Ellsworth & Palmer, 2011; Thornhill & Palmer, 2000).

Recently, researchers have begun to investigate whether women display adaptive anti-rape mechanisms that are linked with their fertility status. While rape always carries psychological, physical, and social costs, a rape occurring when a woman is close to ovulation adds the possibility of impregnation and thus circumvention of female sire choice. To date, studies investigating fertility effects on women's anti-rape adaptations have all converged on a similar conclusion—women display heightened vigilance of potential rapists when high in fertility (Bröder & Hohmann, 2003; Garver-Apgar, Gangestad, & Simpson, 2007; Navarrete, Fessler, Fleischman, & Geyer, 2009; Petralia & Gallup, 2002).

While rape may pose significant reproductive costs to women, for men rape may provide potential reproductive advantages—the main advantage being an ability to impregnate a woman and thus pass on his genes. Of course, even for men, rape may also come with serious costs. Historically, rapists could have been the targets of aggression by a rape victim's family members or romantic partner. Rapists may have also been perceived as untrustworthy, promoting exclusion from the group. In today's society, rape is a serious felony that can lead to a lifetime in prison. Because of the severe costs associated with rape, an evolutionary perspective suggests that a man's decision to rape should be highly dependent upon the probability of gaining reproductive benefits from that rape (i.e., dependent

upon the probability of the sexual intercourse leading to conception). Therefore, it has been proposed that male rapists may target ovulating women who have the greatest likelihood of siring offspring (Gottschall & Gottschall, 2003). Consistent with this hypothesis, Gotschall and Gotschall noted that based upon a national survey from the Center of Disease Control, a higher incidence of pregnancies resulted from acts of rape (6–8 %) versus consensual intercourse (3–4 %). Although consistent with the hypothesis that fertility cues influence rape decisions, this finding is far from conclusive. Empirical, controlled studies are needed to further test the hypothesis that male rapists are more likely to target women high in fertility. The findings from such studies would have important theoretical and practical implications.

Homosexual Responses to Fertility Cues

The overwhelming majority of psychological research on female fertility has used heterosexual participants. This restriction to heterosexuals is not unwarranted. Successful reproduction can only occur when the romantic partners are of the opposite sex. Consequently, an evolutionary perspective suggests that reproductive adaptations (including those related to shifting levels of fertility) should be evidenced in heterosexual relationships. Nevertheless, exploring potential effects of female fertility cues among homosexual men can provide important information about the processes involved in both the expression of sexuality and the factors shaping men's responses to fertility cues.

Two possible alternative hypotheses may be generated. One hypothesis is that all men, including homosexual men, are attuned to shifts in women's fertility. This would make sense if such adaptations are "hardwired"—they are passed on through genes and unlikely to be affected by proximate factors such as sexuality. All living men are alive because their ancestors were successful at reproducing. Thus, the male ancestors of both heterosexual and homosexual men likely possessed similar reproductive adaptations, including those for detecting shifts in female fertility. Consequently, those adaptations might have been passed down to their offspring, regardless of the sexuality of those offspring. Consistent with this perspective, studies indicate that although homosexual and heterosexual men target different mates, they still value similar characteristics in those mates (e.g., young, physically attractive mates; Kenrick, Keefe, Bryan, Barr, & Brown, 1995).

An alternative hypothesis is that only heterosexual men are attuned to shifts in women's fertility. This is possible if male adaptations are flexible and dependent upon proximate factors, such as the individual's sexuality. Indeed, a variety of psychological adaptations appear to be highly flexible, depending both upon proximate individual differences and situational factors. In other words, many adaptations are available for use but are only activated when certain proximate conditions are met. If heterosexuality is a necessary proximate prerequisite for activating psychological adaptations to female fertility, then homosexual men may not be sensitive to shifts in women's fertility. Consistent with such a perspective that focuses on differences between homosexual and heterosexual mating processes, prior research has found that homosexual men prefer the scent of testosterone—a preference that is absent in heterosexual men (Pause, 2004).

We are only aware of one study to date that has examined the moderating effect of male sexuality on men's sensitivity to female fertility cues. Trouton et al., (2012) had male participants smell T-shirts worn by women during high- and low-fertility phases of the cycle. Consistent with prior findings, heterosexual men indicated that the T-shirts worn during high fertility were more pleasant smelling than the T-shirts worn during low fertility. While homosexual men displayed a similar pattern of means (higher ratings of pleasantness for T-shirts worn during high fertility than T-shirts worn during low fertility), the effect of cycle phase did not reach statistical significance. While this may suggest that homosexual men are not attuned to shifts in women's fertility, it should be noted that the study was highly underpowered—the sample

size for homosexual males was very small (less than 15). Thus, findings from this study need to be interpreted with caution. Still, the study itself laid the methodological foundation for future research to investigate fertility-related mating processes in heterosexual and homosexual individuals. Findings from such future studies may shed light on how biological, cultural, and situational forces shape men's mating responses to female fertility cues.

Conclusion

From an evolutionary perspective, no domain of animal behavior has more importance than reproduction. Battling for status, seeking out resources, and detecting predators are all behaviors that ultimately serve to enable human beings to acquire mates and produce offspring. Thus, understanding the factors shaping reproduction is crucial to understanding social behavior more broadly.

As is the case with many other species, shifts in female fertility play an important role in human reproduction. An evolutionary perspective, therefore, suggests that female fertility cues may have important consequences for male physiology, cognition, and behavior. Indeed, the studies reviewed in this chapter suggest that men are attuned to myriad olfactory, auditory, and visual cues to female fertility. Moreover, when exposed to those cues, men display functional behaviors associated with mate-seeking, mate-guarding, and relationship maintenance. By considering the importance of reproductive factors such as female fertility and by integrating theories from evolutionary psychology, comparative animal behavior research, anthropology, and biology, we seek to gain a truly robust understanding of romantic relationships.

References

Abitbol, J., Abitbol, P., & Abitbol, B. (1999). Sex hormones and the female voice. *Journal of Voice, 13*(3), 424–446.
Alexander, R. D., & Noonan, K. M. (1979). Concealment of ovulation, parental care, and human social evolution. In N. A. Chagnon & W. G. Irons (Eds.),

Evolutionary biology and human social behavior: An anthropological perspective (pp. 436–453). Scituate, MA: North Duxbury Press.

Arroyo, B. E. (1999). Copulatory behavior of semi-colonial Montagu's Harriers. *Condor, 101*, 340–346.

Baker, M. D., & Maner, J. K. (2008). Risk-taking as a situationally sensitive male mating strategy. *Evolution and Human Behavior, 29*(6), 391–395.

Baker, M. D., & Maner, J. K. (2009). Male risk-taking as a context-sensitive signaling device. *Journal of Experimental Social Psychology, 45*(5), 1136–1139.

Batty, J. (1978). Acute changes in plasma testosterone levels and their relation to measures of sexual behaviour in the male house mouse (Mus musculus). *Animal Behaviour, 26*(2), 349–357.

Benshoof, L., & Thornhill, R. (1979). The evolution of monogamy and concealed ovulation in humans. *Journal of Social and Biological Structures, 2*(2), 95–106.

Bhatnagar, K. P., & Smith, T. D. (2010). The human vomeronasal organ: Part VI: A nonchemosensory vestige in the context of major variations of the mammalian vomeronasal organ. *Current Neurobiology, 1*, 1–9.

Birkhead, T. R. (1982). Timing and duration of mate guarding in magpies, Pica pica. *Animal Behaviour, 30*(1), 277–283.

Birkhead, T. R., & Møller, A. P. (1992). *Sperm competition in birds: Evolutionary causes and consequences.* New York: Academic Press.

Bone, P. F., & Ellen, P. S. (1999). Scents in the marketplace: Explaining a fraction of olfaction. *Journal of Retailing, 75*, 243–262.

Brewis, A., & Meyer, M. (2005). Marital coitus across the life course. *Journal of Biosocial Science, 37*(04), 499–518.

Bröder, A., & Hohmann, N. (2003). Variations in risk taking behavior over the menstrual cycle: An improved replication. *Evolution and Human Behavior, 24*(6), 391–398.

Bryant, G. A., & Haselton, M. G. (2009). Vocal cues of ovulation in human females. *Biology Letters, 5*(1), 12–15.

Burriss, R. P., & Little, A. C. (2006). Effects of partner conception risk phase on male perception of dominance in faces. *Evolution and Human Behavior, 27*(4), 297–305.

Buss, D. M., & Schmitt, D. P. (1993). Sexual strategies theory: An evolutionary perspective on human mating. *Psychological Review, 100*(2), 204–232.

Caruso, S., Roccasalva, L., Sapienza, G., Zappalá, M., Nuciforo, G., & Biondi, S. (2000). Laryngeal cytological aspects in women with surgically induced menopause who were treated with transdermal estrogen replacement therapy. *Fertility and Sterility, 74*(6), 1073–1079.

Coquelin, A., Clancy, A., Macrides, F., Noble, E., & Gorski, R. (1984). Pheromonally induced release of luteinizing hormone in male mice: Involvement of the vomeronasal system. *The Journal of Neuroscience, 4*(9), 2230–2236.

Cox, C. R., & Le Boeuf, B. J. (1977). Female incitation of male competition: A mechanism in sexual selection. *The American Naturalist, 111*(978), 317–335.

Coyle, J. M., & Kaschak, M. P. (2012). Female fertility affects men's linguistic choices. *PLoS ONE, 7*(2), e27971.

Daly, M., & Wilson, M. (2001). Risk-taking, intrasexual competition, and homicide. In J. A. French, A. C. Kamil, & D. W. Leger (Eds.), *Evolutionary psychology and motivation* (pp. 1–36). Lincoln, NE: University of Nebraska Press.

Daniels, D. (1983). The evolution of concealed ovulation and self-deception. *Ethology and Sociobiology, 4*(2), 69–87.

Doty, R. L., Ford, M., Preti, G., & Huggins, G. R. (1975). Changes in the intensity and pleasantness of human vaginal odors during the menstrual cycle. *Science, 190*(4221), 1316–1318.

Durante, K. M., Li, N. P., & Haselton, M. G. (2008). Changes in women's choice of dress across the ovulatory cycle: Naturalistic and laboratory task-based evidence. *Personality and Social Psychology Bulletin, 34*, 1451–1460.

Ellsworth, R. M., & Palmer, C. T. (2011). The search for human rape and anti-rape adaptations: Ten years after a natural history of rape. In K. M. Beaver & A. Walsh (Eds.), *The Ashgate research companion to biosocial theories of crime* (pp. 349–368). Burling, VT: Ashgate Publishing Company.

Etkin, W. (1954). Social behavior and the evolution of man's mental faculties. *The American Naturalist, 88*(840), 129–142.

Feinberg, D. R., DeBruine, L. M., Jones, B. C., & Perrett, D. I. (2008). The role of femininity and averageness of voice pitch in aesthetic judgments of women's voices. *Perception, 37*(4), 615–623.

Feinberg, D. R., Jones, B. C., DeBruine, L. M., Moore, F. R., Law Smith, M. J., Cornwell, R. E., et al. (2005). The voice and face of woman: One ornament that signals quality? *Evolution and Human Behavior, 26*(5), 398–408.

Fink, B., Hugill, N., & Lange, B. P. (2012). Women's body movements are a potential cue to ovulation. *Personality and Individual Differences, 53*(6), 759–763.

Firat, Y., Engin-Ustun, Y., Kizilay, A., Ustun, Y., Akarcay, M., Selimoglu, E., et al. (2009). Effect of intranasal estrogen on vocal quality. *Journal of Voice, 23*(6), 716–720.

Fischer, J., Semple, S., Fickenscher, G., Jürgens, R., Kruse, E., Heistermann, M., et al. (2011). Do women's voices provide cues of the likelihood of ovulation? The importance of sampling regime. *PLoS ONE, 6*(9), e24490.

Frasnelli, J., Lundström, J. N., Boyle, J. A., Katsarkas, A., & Jones-Gotman, M. (2011). The vomeronasal organ is not involved in the perception of endogenous odors. *Human Brain Mapping, 32*(3), 450–460.

Gangestad, S. W., & Thornhill, R. (2008). Human oestrus. *Proceedings of the Royal Society of London, B, 275* (1638), 991–1000.

Gangestad, S. W., Thornhill, R., & Garver, C. E. (2002). Changes in women's sexual interests and their partner's mate-retention tactics across the menstrual cycle: Evidence for shifting conflicts of interest. *Proceedings of the Royal Society of London, B, 269* (1494), 975–982.

Garver-Apgar, C. E., Gangestad, S. W., & Simpson, J. A. (2007). Women's perceptions of men's sexual coerciveness change across the menstrual cycle. *Acta Psychologica Sinica, 39*(3), 536–540.

Gildersleeve, K. A., Haselton, M. G., Larson, C. M., & Pillsworth, E. G. (2012). Body odor attractiveness as a cue of impending ovulation in women: Evidence from a study using hormone-confirmed ovulation. *Hormones and Behavior, 61*(2), 157–166.

Gonzaga, G. C., Haselton, M. G., Smurda, J., Davies, M. S., & J. C., P. (2008). Love, desire, and the suppression of thoughts of romantic alternatives. *Evolution and Human Behavior, 29*(2), 119–126.

Gottschall, J., & Gottschall, T. (2003). Are per-incident rape-pregnancy rates higher than per-incident consensual pregnancy rates? *Human Nature, 14*(1), 1–20.

Grammer, K., Renninger, L., & Fischer, B. (2004). Disco clothing, female sexual motivation, and relationship status: Is she dressed to impress? *Journal of Sex Research, 41*(1), 66–74.

Guéguen, N. (2009). Menstrual cycle phases and female receptivity to a courtship solicitation: An evaluation in a nightclub. *Evolution and Human Behavior, 30*(5), 351–355.

Haselton, M. G., & Gangestad, S. W. (2006). Conditional expression of women's desires and men's mate guarding across the ovulatory cycle. *Hormones and Behavior, 49*(4), 509–518.

Haselton, M. G., & Miller, G. F. (2006). Women's fertility across the cycle increases the short-term attractiveness of creative intelligence compared to wealth. *Human Nature, 17*, 50–73.

Haselton, M. G., Mortezaie, M., Pillsworth, E. G., Bleske-Rechek, A., & Frederick, D. A. (2007). Ovulatory shifts in human female ornamentation: Near ovulation, women dress to impress. *Hormones and Behavior, 51*(1), 40–45.

Havlíček, J., Dvořáková, R., Bartoš, L., & Flegr, J. (2006). Non-advertized does not mean concealed: Body odour changes across the human menstrual cycle. *Ethology, 112*(1), 81–90.

Higham, J. P., Heistermann, M., Saggau, C., Agil, M., Perwitasari-Farajallah, D., & Engelhardt, A. (2012). Sexual signalling in female crested macaques and the evolution of primate fertility signals. *BMC Evolutionary Biology, 12*, 89.

Hill, K. (1982). Hunting and human evolution. *Journal of Human Evolution, 11*(6), 521–544.

Holland, R. W., Hendriks, M., & Aarts, H. (2005). Smells like clean spirit: Nonconscious effects of scent on cognition and behavior. *Psychological Science, 16* (9), 689–693.

Hrdy, S. B. (1981). *The woman that never evolved.* Cambridge, MA: Harvard University Press.

Karremans, J. C., & Verwijmeren, T. (2008). Mimicking attractive opposite-sex others: The role of romantic relationship status. *Personality and Social Psychology Bulletin, 34*(7), 939–950.

Kenrick, D. T., Keefe, R. C., Bryan, A., Barr, A., & Brown, S. (1995). Age preferences and mate choice among homosexuals and heterosexuals: A case for modular psychological mechanisms. *Journal of Personality and Social Psychology, 69*(6), 1166–1172.

Kirchengast, S., & Gartner, M. (2002). Changes in fat distribution (WHR) and body weight across the menstrual cycle. *Collegium Antropologicum, 26*(Suppl), 47–57.

Komdeur, J., Kraaijeveld-Smit, F., Kraaijeveld, K., & Edelaar, P. (1999). Explicit experimental evidence for the role of mate guarding in minimizing loss of paternity in the Seychelles warbler. *Proceedings of the Royal Society of London, B, 266*(1433), 2075–2081.

Korpimäki, E., Lahti, K., May, C. A., Parkin, D. T., Powell, G. B., Tolonen, P., et al. (1996). Copulatory behaviour and paternity determined by DNA fingerprinting in kestrels: Effects of cyclic food abundance. *Animal Behaviour, 51*(4), 945–955.

Kuukasjärvi, S., Eriksson, C. J. P., Koskela, E., Mappes, T., Nissinen, K., & Rantala, M. J. (2004). Attractiveness of women's body odors over the menstrual cycle: The role of oral contraceptives and receiver sex. *Behavioral Ecology, 15*(4), 579–584.

Lakin, J. L., Jefferis, V. E., Cheng, C. M., & Chartrand, T. L. (2003). The chameleon effect as social glue: Evidence for the evolutionary significance of non-conscious mimicry. *Journal of Nonverbal Behavior, 27*(3), 145–162.

Lens, I., Driesmans, K., Pandelaere, M., & Janssens, K. (2012). Would male conspicuous consumption capture the female eye? Menstrual cycle effects on women's attention to status products. *Journal of Experimental Social Psychology, 48*(1), 346–349.

Lumpkin, S. (1981). Avoidance of cuckoldry in birds: The role of the female. *Animal Behaviour, 29*(1), 303–304.

Maner, J. K., Gailliot, M. T., & Miller, S. L. (2009). The implicit cognition of relationship maintenance: Inattention to attractive alternatives. *Journal of Experimental Social Psychology, 45*(1), 174–179.

Maner, J. K., Kenrick, D. T., Becker, D. V., Robertson, T., Hofer, B., Neuberg, S. L., et al. (2005). Functional projection: How fundamental social motives can bias interpersonal perception. *Journal of Personality and Social Psychology, 88*, 63–78.

Manning, J. T., Scutt, D., Whitehouse, G. H., Leinster, S. J., & Walton, J. M. (1996). Asymmetry and the menstrual cycle in women. *Ethology and Sociobiology, 17*(2), 129–143.

Miller, S. L., & Maner, J. K. (2010a). Evolution and relationship maintenance: Fertility cues lead committed men to devalue relationship alternatives. *Journal of Experimental Social Psychology, 46*(6), 1081–1084.

Miller, S. L., & Maner, J. K. (2010b). Scent of a woman: Men's testosterone responses to olfactory ovulation cues. *Psychological Science, 21*(2), 276–283.

Miller, S. L., & Maner, J. K. (2011). Ovulation as a male mating prime: Subtle signs of women's fertility influence men's mating cognition and behavior. *Journal of Personality and Social Psychology, 100*(2), 295–308.

Miller, G., Tybur, J. M., & Jordan, B. D. (2007). Ovulatory cycle effects on tip earnings by lap dancers: Economic evidence for human estrus? *Evolution and Human Behavior, 28*(6), 375–381.

Mitchell, D. J., Kahn, B. E., & Knasko, S. C. (1995). There's something in the air: Effects of congruent and incongruent ambient odor on consumer decision-making. *Journal of Consumer Research, 22,* 229–238.

Montagna, W. (1985). The evolution of human skin(?). *Journal of Human Evolution, 14*(1), 3–22.

Moos-Heilen, R., & Sossinka, R. (1990). The influence of oestrus on the vocalization of female gelada baboons (Theropithecus gelada). *Ethology, 84*(1), 35–46.

Mykytowycz, R. (1985). Olfaction—A link with the past. *Journal of Human Evolution, 14*(1), 75–90.

Nadler, R. D. (1981). Laboratory research on sexual behavior of the great apes. In C. E. Graham (Ed.), *Reproductive biology of the great apes* (pp. 191–238). New York: Academic Press.

Navarrete, C. D., Fessler, D. M. T., Fleischman, D. S., & Geyer, J. (2009). Race bias tracks conception risk across the menstrual cycle. *Psychological Science, 20*(6), 661–665.

Pankevich, D. E., Baum, M. J., & Cherry, J. A. (2004). Olfactory sex discrimination persists, whereas the preference for urinary odorants from estrous females disappears in male mice after vomeronasal organ removal. *The Journal of Neuroscience, 24*(42), 9451–9457.

Parker, S. (1987). A sexual selection model for hominid evolution. *Human Evolution, 2*(3), 235–253.

Pause, B. M. (2004). Are androgen steroids acting as pheromones in humans? *Physiology & Behavior, 83*(1), 21–29.

Pawłowski, B. (1999). Loss of oestrus and concealed ovulation in human evolution: The case against the sexual-selection hypothesis. *Current Anthropology, 40*(3), 257–275.

Petralia, S. M., & Gallup, G. G., Jr. (2002). Effects of a sexual assault scenario on handgrip strength across the menstrual cycle. *Evolution and Human Behavior, 23*(1), 3–10.

Pfeiffer, C. A., & Johnston, R. E. (1994). Hormonal and behavioral responses of male hamsters to females and female odors: Roles of olfaction, the vomeronasal system, and sexual experience. *Physiology and Behavior, 55*(1), 129–138.

Pillsworth, E. G., & Haselton, M. G. (2006). Male sexual attractiveness predicts differential ovulatory shifts in female extra-pair attraction and male mate retention. *Evolution and Human Behavior, 27*(4), 247–258.

Pipitone, R. N., & Gallup, G. G. (2008). Women's voice attractiveness varies across the menstrual cycle. *Evolution and Human Behavior, 29*(4), 268–274.

Pipitone, R. N., & Gallup, G. G., Jr. (2012). The unique impact of menstruation on the female voice: Implications for the evolution of menstrual cycle cues. *Ethology, 118*(3), 281–291.

Plant, E. A., Kunstman, J. W., & Maner, J. K. (2010). You do not only hurt the one you love: Self-protective responses to attractive relationship alternatives. *Journal of Experimental Social Psychology, 46*(2), 474–477.

Riley, H. T., Bryant, D. M., Carter, R. E., & Parkin, D. T. (1995). Extra-pair fertilizations and paternity defence in house martins, Delichon urbica. *Animal Behaviour, 49*(2), 495–509.

Roberts, S. C., Havlicek, J., Flegr, J., Hruskova, M., Little, A. C., Jones, B. C., et al. (2004). Female facial attractiveness increases during the fertile phase of the menstrual cycle. *Proceedings of the Royal Society of London, B, 271,* S270–S272.

Roney, J. R., Lukaszewski, A. W., & Simmons, Z. L. (2007). Rapid endocrine responses of young men to social interactions with young women. *Hormones and Behavior, 52*(3), 326–333.

Roney, J. R., & Simmons, Z. L. (2012). Men smelling women: Null effects of exposure to ovulatory sweat on men's testosterone. *Evolutionary Psychology, 10*(4), 703–713.

Rosvall, K. A. (2011). Intrasexual competition in females: Evidence for sexual selection? *Behavioral Ecology, 22*(6), 1131–1140.

Saayman, G. S. (1970). The menstrual cycle and sexual behaviour in a troop of free ranging chacma baboons [Papio ursinus]. *Folia Primatologica, 12*(2), 81–110.

Saayman, G. S. (1972). Effects of ovarian hormones upon the sexual skin and mounting behaviour in the free-ranging chacma baboon (Papio ursinus). *Folia Primatologica, 17,* 297–303.

Schaal, B., & Porter, R. H. (1991). "Microsmatic Humans" revisited: The generation and perception of chemical signals. In J. S. R. Peter, J. B. Slater, C. Beer, & M. Milinski (Eds.), *Advances in the study of behavior* (Vol. 20, pp. 135–199). San Diego, CA: Academic Press.

Scordato, E. S., & Drea, C. M. (2007). Scents and sensibility: Information content of olfactory signals in the ringtailed lemur, Lemur catta. *Animal Behaviour, 73*(2), 301–314.

Scutt, D., & Manning, J. T. (1996). Ovary and ovulation: Symmetry and ovulation in women. *Human Reproduction, 11*(11), 2477–2480.

Semple, S., & McComb, K. (2000). Perception of female reproductive state from vocal cues in a mammal species. *Proceedings of the Royal Society of London, B, 267*(1444), 707–712.

Singh, D., & Bronstad, P. M. (2001). Female body odour is a potential cue to ovulation. *Proceedings of the Royal Society of London, B, 268*(1469), 797–801.

Spielman, A. I., Zeng, X. N., Leyden, J. J., & Preti, G. (1995). Proteinaceous precursors of human axillary odor: Isolation of two novel odor-binding proteins. *Experientia, 51*(1), 40–47.

Stoddart, D. M. (1990). *The scented ape: The biology and culture of human odour*. Cambridge, MA: Cambridge University Press.

Strassmann, B. I. (1981). Sexual selection, paternal care, and concealed ovulation in humans. *Ethology and Sociobiology, 2*(1), 31–40.

Symons, D. (1979). *The evolution of human sexuality*. New York: Oxford University Press.

Thornhill, R., Gangestad, S. W., Miller, R., Scheyd, G., McCollough, J. K., & Franklin, M. (2003). Major histocompatibility complex genes, symmetry, and body scent attractiveness in men and women. *Behavioral Ecology, 14*(5), 668–678.

Thornhill, R., & Palmer, C. T. (2000). *A natural history of rape: Biological bases of human sexual coercion*. Cambridge, MA: MIT Press.

Trouton, G. T., Guitar, A. E., Carmen, R. A., Geher, G., & Grandis, T. L. (2012). Olfactory ability to detect ovulatory cues: A function of biological sex, sexual orientation, or both? *Journal of Social, Evolutionary, and Cultural Psychology, 6*(4), 469–479.

van den Berghe, P. L., & Frost, P. (1986). Skin color preference, sexual dimorphism and sexual selection: A case of gene culture co-evolution? *Ethnic and Racial Studies, 9*(1), 87–113.

van Straaten, I., Engels, R., Finkenauer, C., & Holland, R. (2008). Sex differences in short-term mate preferences and behavioral mimicry: A semi-naturalistic experiment. *Archives of Sexual Behavior, 37*(6), 902–911.

Wallis, J. (1982). Sexual behavior of captive chimpanzees (Pan troglodytes): Pregnant versus cycling females. *American Journal of Primatology, 3*(1–4), 77–88.

Wallis, J. (1992). Chimpanzee genital swelling and its role in the pattern of sociosexual behavior. *American Journal of Primatology, 28*(2), 101–113.

Wilcox, A. J., Weinberg, C. R., & Baird, D. D. (1995). Timing of sexual intercourse in relation to ovulation—Effects on the probability of conception, survival of the pregnancy, and sex of the baby. *New England Journal of Medicine, 333*(23), 1517–1521.

Ziegler, T. E., Schultz-Darken, N. J., Scott, J. J., Snowdon, C. T., & Ferris, C. F. (2005). Neuroendocrine response to female ovulatory odors depends upon social condition in male common marmosets, Callithrix jacchus. *Hormones and Behavior, 47*(1), 56–64.

(Mis)reading the Signs: Men's Perception of Women's Sexual Interest

Carin Perilloux

A History of Sexual Misperception Research

Evidence that men misperceive women's sexual interest has accumulated for the last 30 years, ever since Abbey (1982) began investigating the phenomenon in an effort to understand whether men's misperception plays a key role in the critical issue of men's sexually coercive behavior. In Abbey's original study, one opposite sex pair of subjects engaged in a neutral conversation while a second pair of subjects observed through a one-way mirror. Men, regardless of whether they were part of the conversation or simply observing it, subsequently rated the female conversation partner as more flirtatious, attractive, and sexually interested than the woman rated herself—and, perhaps more importantly, higher than the female observer rated the female conversation partner on the same traits. These results have repeatedly been replicated (Harnish, Abbey, & DeBono, 1990; Henningsen & Henningsen, 2010; Levesque, Nave, & Lowe, 2006).

Additional studies using methodological variations have yielded similar patterns. For instance, men rate female targets in photographs or videos as more sexually interested than

women rate the same female targets (Abbey, Cozzarelli, McLaughlin, & Harnish, 1987; Abbey & Melby, 1986; Farris, Treat, Viken, & McFall, 2008a). Vignette studies—which, despite their own drawbacks, have the fortunate property of eliminating the potentially distracting visual elements of photographs and videos—generate similar results (Abbey & Harnish, 1995; Bostwick & DeLucia, 1992; Muehlenhard, 1988). Further, having participants recall instances from their own lives in which they were sexually misperceived, or in which they misperceived someone's sexual interest, reproduces the basic finding of men overestimating women's interest (Abbey, 1987; Haselton, 2003).

Finally, the recent emergence of "speed dating"—in which a large number of adults talk briefly (1–5 min) in dyads—has made possible a novel method for studying sexual interest perception in action (e.g., Kurzban & Weeden, 2005). Speed-dating events allow researchers to compare participants' estimates of targets' interest with the level of interest actually reported by those targets and also allow for calculating multiple such comparisons for a single participant to generate a more accurate estimate of his or her average tendency to misperceive. In these (relatively) naturalistic settings, men again report believing that the women with whom they interact are more sexually interested in them than the women claim to be (Back, Penke, Schmukle, & Asendorpf, 2011; Perilloux, Easton, & Buss, 2012).

C. Perilloux (✉)
Department of Psychology, Union College, 807 Union Street, Schenectady, NY 12308, USA
e-mail: carinp@gmail.com

V.A. Weekes-Shackelford and T.K. Shackelford (eds.), *Evolutionary Perspectives on Human Sexual Psychology and Behavior*, Evolutionary Psychology, DOI 10.1007/978-1-4939-0314-6_6,
© Springer Science+Business Media New York 2014

While this sex-differentiated pattern of overperception occurs reliably across a variety of experimental designs, there is also substantial variation within men's tendencies toward overperception. Individual difference variables that have been shown to predict overperception include drinking habits (Abbey, McAuslan, & Ross, 1998; Jacques-Tiura, Abbey, Parkhill, & Zawacki, 2007), masculinity (Fisher & Walters, 2003; Levesque et al., 2006), and, especially, history of sexual aggression and rape-supportive beliefs (Abbey et al., 1998; Abbey & Harnish, 1995; Abbey, Zawacki, & Buck, 2005; Bondurant & Donat, 1999; Fisher & Walters, 2003; Jacques-Tiura et al., 2007; Kowalski, 1993; Shea, 1993; Vrij & Kirby, 2002). More recently, researchers studying sociosexuality have found that men who are more interested in casual sex are also more likely to overperceive women's sexual interest and to attribute greater sexuality to female targets (Howell, Etchells, & Penton-Voak, 2012; Jacques-Tiura et al., 2007; Lenton, Bryan, Hastie, & Fischer, 2007; Perilloux et al., 2012).

In addition to showing individual variation, men's degree of sexual overperception shows contextual variation, though studies of these contextual effects have produced inconsistent results. For example, cues such as eye contact, close interpersonal distance, and physical touch increased estimates of a female target's interest in one study (Koukounas & Letch, 2001) but produced no effect in another (Abbey & Melby, 1986). One context, however, consistently increases misperception: intoxication. When men drink alcohol, they attend to women's approach cues more than avoidance cues (Abbey et al., 2005), are less sensitive to women's facial expressions (Farris, Treat, & Viken, 2010), and, perhaps due to these cognitive effects, are more likely to identify women as being sexually interested (Abbey, Zawacki, & McAuslan, 2000).

In sum, there is abundant evidence that men perceive women's sexual interest differently from how women perceive their own sexual interest; the mechanisms underlying this phenomenon, however, remain the subject of debate.

The next two parts review the range of existing explanations for men's overperception. Afterwards, a new framework is introduced that challenges the predominant view that these findings are best explained with respect to a cognitive bias. Finally, the chapter ends with suggestions for arbitrating between competing explanations and further elucidating the nuances of sexual intent perception.

Explanations of Men's Sexual Misperception

One of the first explanations for sexual misperception was the *oversexualization hypothesis* (Abbey, 1982): the idea that men are socialized to pay more attention to sexual stimuli, value sex more, and seek sex more often than women. According to Abbey, these tendencies color men's perceptions—including perceptions of women—in a sexual way, leading men to assume greater sexuality and sexual interest on the part of female targets. Abbey (1991) later appended a *media effects* component to her original hypothesis, adding that the media portrays women as hiding their true sexual desires beneath a veil of chastity such that men are taught to persist so that the woman will eventually reveal her true level of interest. Despite the intuitive appeal of the hypothesis, Abbey's proposal left much unexplained, including individual differences and contextual effects on men's perceptions of women's interest, neither of which are easily accommodated by the theory.

A related proposal, the *projection hypothesis* (Shotland & Craig, 1988), begins with Abbey's original assertion that men are socialized to seek sex more than women and adds that when men are estimating women's sexual interest, they assume that women's sex drives are similar to their own; this projection is what causes men to overestimate women's sexual intent. This hypothesis is consistent with evidence that short-term mating interest predicts overperception of sexual interest (Howell et al., 2012). More recently, this hypothesis has been reformulated as the *mediation hypothesis*

(Koenig, Kirkpatrick, & Ketelaar, 2007), which suggests that if an individual is attracted to a target, then this attraction is projected onto—and assumed to be mirrored by—the target. Therefore, this model predicts that statistically controlling for the degree to which an individual is sexually interested in the target should cause the relationship between gender and overperception to disappear, a prediction that has received some initial support (Koenig et al., 2007).

Finally, the *cue insensitivity hypothesis* proposes that men are simply unable to discern indicators of sexual interest from those of friendliness (e.g., Farris, Treat, Viken, & McFall, 2008b), unlike women who are relatively accurate. Indeed, men perform worse than women at assessing whether a photograph of a woman is depicting sexual interest or friendliness (Farris et al., 2008b; Farris, Viken, & Treat, 2010). In addition, Kowalski (1993) documented that while men and women were equally able to identify *sexual* cues from the opposite sex, men performed worse than women in identifying *mundane* or *romantic* cues. These results reinforce that men err, but specifically they err when faced with ambiguous or subtle sexual cues; this distinction plays a key role in explanations for misperception from an evolutionary perspective.

An Evolutionary Approach to Sexual Misperception

Based on signal detection logic (Green & Swets, 1966), error management theory (EMT) was proposed to account for various cognitive biases when making inferences under uncertainty (Haselton & Buss, 2000). For example, because others' beliefs and desires are not directly perceivable, and thus uncertain, EMT would apply to cognitive mechanisms that function to infer or estimate other individuals' mental states. If inferences about mental states were a recurrent feature of human social life throughout evolutionary history—as they no doubt were—and the outcome of these inferences in some way influenced reproductive success, then selection

should be expected to shape decision-making processes to maximize the net expected benefits less the costs of judgments—to the extent possible. That last part is key: when inferring information about others' mental states, there is often much ambiguity or even misleading information (Byrne & Whiten, 1988; Pinker, Nowak, & Lee, 2008), thus making perfect accuracy very difficult to achieve. In such cases, there are, inevitably, errors. EMT is relevant specifically when the different types of errors have consistently different associated costs. In such instances, EMT proposes that decision-making systems should be expected to embody the asymmetrical costs of the different types of errors.

To make the logic of EMT concrete, consider an example in which a hiker encounters a long, stick-like object in his path. He must make a rapid decision as to whether to treat this object as a stick or a snake. His decision will determine his behavior (i.e., continue walking over the object or alter his current route to walk around the object), and he does not have the time to gather all of the necessary information to know for sure whether the object is a stick or snake. There are two possible errors he can make. First, he could incorrectly conclude that the stick is a snake and alter his course (a false alarm), which carries the cost of the marginal time and energy expended. Second, he could incorrectly conclude that the snake is a stick and tread over it, carrying the potentially large cost of a snake bite. Given that the fitness consequences of these outcomes was likely recurrent over evolutionary time, selection should, according to EMT, be expected to give rise to a bias to treat stick-like objects as snakes, more often than the converse, even though—given the relative rarity of snakes to sticks—this bias leads to a greater number of errors.

There are many domains like the hiking example in which decisions must be made under uncertainty, such as making inferences about sexual interest. Humans, unlike most non-human animals, do not clearly signal their sexual interest and instead rely on subtle cues such as flirting (Eibl-Eibesfeldt, 1971; Henningsen, 2004; Moore, 2002; Pinker et al., 2008). Indeed, women might have adaptations specifically designed to maintain ambiguity regarding their level of sexual interest (e.g., laughter; Grammer, 1990), or women might be unsure of their interest in a man at the early stages of interaction because they require more information—often difficult or impossible to ascertain during a short interaction—to determine their level of interest (Pillsworth & Haselton, 2006). If women's cues are thus unreliable and only somewhat diagnostic of underlying interest, male adaptations to assess women's interest and women's adaptations to conceal it would have coevolved, resulting in imperfect accuracy on the part of men and imperfect concealment on the part of women. As a consequence, just as in the hiking example, men must make a decision about whether or not to pursue a woman based on uncertain and incomplete information, and here men also face two types of errors: inferring sexual interest on the part of an uninterested women—a false alarm—or failing to identify when a woman is actually sexually interested—a miss.

The costs of false alarms and misses in the context of sexual intent perception are clarified through the logic of Parental Investment Theory (Trivers, 1972; for a comprehensive review of sex differences in mating strategies in humans, see Schmitt, 2014, Chap. 1). According to Parental Investment Theory, the sex with the larger obligatory investment in reproduction is the limiting resource for the sex with the smaller investment; this asymmetry causes the lower-investing sex to compete for access to the higher-investing sex, who will in turn exhibit greater selectiveness in mate choice (Kokko & Jennions, 2008; Trivers, 1972). In humans, women's minimum obligatory parental investment is the time and caloric costs of at least 9 months of gestation and 2 or more years of lactation (at least ancestrally). Men's minimum obligatory parental investment, however, consists of a much shorter time investment (i.e., the time necessary to complete copulation) and essentially zero energetic expenditure toward fetal or infant development (of course, in our species, men's typical investment is much greater than the minimum). This asymmetry in minimum obligations produces downstream effects in the form of sex-differentiated mating strategies in humans. For example, men can increase their reproductive success with each additional mating opportunity whereas women's reproductive success will be based to a much greater degree on finding the best possible mate and securing future investment for her and her offspring during the time period of her high opportunity costs (i.e., pregnancy and lactation). This fact of our reproductive biology results in sex differences in the type of mating behavior that is most adaptive; for instance, men are, on average, more likely to pursue a short-term mating strategy than are women (Buss & Schmitt, 1993).

Given the large benefits to men of each additional mating, missing such opportunities carries a substantial cost. Given that there is some degree of uncertainty in estimating women's sexual interest, one adaptive solution could be to alter the perceptual threshold, reducing the chance of making the more costly type of error—missing mating opportunities—even if doing so means making a larger number of the less costly errors. So, while over-inferring women's interest (false alarm) might result in the reputational damage that can accompany a romantic rejection, under-inferring women's interest (miss) carries the much greater costs of passing up a reproductive opportunity. EMT applies this analysis of the relative costliness of errors to propose that selection would favor adaptations in men that bias perception toward the less costly error, false alarms (Haselton & Buss, 2000).

In addition to explaining the robust overall sex difference in perceptions of sexual interest, EMT leads to specific predictions about how changes in the costliness of the errors can produce adaptive changes in men's overall bias. One way in which the cost asymmetry can be altered is by changing the target. In one experiment, men rated the extent to which various behaviors (e.g., kissing, hand-holding, saying "I love you") performed by a hypothetical woman would indicate that she wanted to have sex (Haselton & Buss, 2000). As predicted by EMT, and in line with previous research, men rated these behaviors directed toward them to indicate greater sexual interest relative to female participants' ratings of a hypothetical woman performing these behaviors. However, when the target female was changed from a hypothetical potential date to one's sister interacting with a hypothetical man, men's estimates of the target female's level of sexual interest dropped. This pattern of results is consistent with EMT because the genetic and social costs and benefits of overestimating one's sister's sexual interest have been recurrently different, over our evolutionary history, from the costs and benefits of overestimating female non-relatives' sexual interest (Lieberman, 2008; Westermarck, 1921), and would thus not favor a bias toward over-inference.

The sister effect is not the only application of EMT to predict adjustment of cognitive biases to target-based changes in the costliness of errors. One such feature that has been proposed to alter error costs would be the female target's physical attractiveness (Perilloux et al., 2012). The costs associated with a false alarm do not seem likely to differ as a function of the woman's attractiveness, but the costs associated with misses do. Missing out on a sexual opportunity with an unattractive woman is a costly error in the currency of reproductive success, but missing out on a sexual opportunity with an attractive woman is even more costly: women are perceived as physically attractive to the extent that they exhibit observable traits that have been reliably correlated with unobservable qualities of health, youth, and fertility (e.g., Sugiyama, 2005). Therefore, mating opportunities with an attractive woman would have been more likely to result in reproduction (due to her higher fertility) and healthy offspring (due to her youth and health) than an unattractive woman, all else equal. So EMT would predict, and studies have documented, that men's overperception of women's interest is positively correlated with the attractiveness of the target (Koenig et al., 2007; Perilloux et al., 2012).

Similarly, the cost asymmetry between misses and false alarms is hypothesized to be even more extreme to the extent that a man is pursuing a short-term mating strategy. Men pursuing a long-term mating strategy certainly experience

opportunity costs when missing a mating opportunity, but the social costs of the false alarm may be less trivial for these men. Earning a reputation as a "cad" who pursues uninterested women would damage a man's chances of attracting a high-quality long-term mate because women's long-term mate preferences generally prioritize traits such as loyalty (e.g., Bereczkei, Voros, Gal, & Bernath, 1997; Vigil, Geary, & Byrd-Craven, 2006). The asymmetry between false alarms and misses, then, would be smaller for long-term-oriented men. Therefore, the sexual overperception bias should be particularly pronounced among short-term-oriented men, as is indeed the case (Howell et al., 2012; Jacques-Tiura et al., 2007; Lenton et al., 2007; Perilloux et al., 2012).

EMT, then, is consistent with previously documented results, provides a functional explanation for the existence of such biases, and proposes theory-driven predictions of modifications in men's misperception. Earlier hypotheses of sexual misperception— *oversexualization, media effects, and projection*—are, in contrast, unable to effectively explain how individual differences and situational effects predict the degree to which men perceive greater sexual interest from women. The *oversexualization hypothesis* would predict that simply being male would cause one to overperceive (Abbey, 1982), but this general sex difference approach is clearly inconsistent with trait-level predictors of men's misperception, as presented above. The *media effects* hypothesis cannot account for target-related effects on misperception (Abbey, 1991), such as the tendency for attractive women to elicit higher levels of misperception than unattractive women (Perilloux et al., 2012). The original *projection hypothesis* relies on overall differences in sex drive between men and women (Shotland & Craig, 1988), which also sits uneasily with data regarding individual differences within men's misperception rates. Finally, the *cue insensitivity hypothesis* has only limited empirical support for its proposal that men are unable to distinguish between cues of sexual interest and those of friendliness (Farris et al., 2008b) and faces a serious challenge from findings that men show significantly lower levels of sexual misperception if the target is their sister (Haselton & Buss, 2000).

Only two of these hypotheses appear currently viable: EMT's hypothesis of a specialized cognitive bias in men and Koenig et al.'s (2007) more domain-general *mediation hypothesis*. These two accounts make many similar predictions because the targets to whom men find themselves highly attracted are the very targets representing more costly misses, resulting in both hypotheses predicting that men will overperceive high-quality target females more. The *mediation hypothesis*, however, does not make predictions about individual differences between men, except for differences which would directly affect the degree to which they are attracted to female targets (e.g., men's short-term mating motivation). For example, men's own attractiveness does not appear to predict the degree to which they are attracted to women (i.e., men, regardless of their own attractiveness, express similar judgments of beauty in women; Lee, Loewenstein, Ariely, Hong, & Young, 2008), and thus the *mediation hypothesis* would not predict that men's attractiveness should affect their misperception rates. One study, however, reveals that men's attractiveness might in fact predict the degree to which men infer women's interest (Perilloux et al., 2012), though this effect requires replication. This pattern of results is problematic for the *mediation hypothesis*, whereas target-specific and perceiver-specific traits are automatically incorporated in EMT. Compared to the *mediation hypothesis* and earlier hypotheses of men's misperception, EMT has the advantage in parsimony and explanatory power, making it the most prominent theory to date for explaining the evolutionary origins and facultative operations of men's sexual misperception.

The Nature of the Bias: Cognitive or Behavioral

EMT proposes that evolution has shaped psychological biases to minimize the costliness of inferential errors, given certain preconditions (Haselton & Buss, 2000). Recently, however, theorists have pointed out that there are actually two ways in which such errors can be managed. The first is the route originally proposed by EMT—*biasing beliefs*—in which men have an incorrect representation about the state of the world (e.g., a woman's degree of sexual interest) and act on the basis of the biased belief (Haselton & Buss, 2000). The second way is to maintain correct representations about the state of the world but to *bias behavior* in the direction of the action with the less costly error (Kurzban, 2010; McKay & Dennett, 2009; McKay & Efferson, 2010). This second route entails maintaining priors that are as accurate as possible while making decisions based on the expected value of the choices of action; this model will be referred to here, for lack of a better term, as Bayesian expected value maximization (BEVM). The BEVM model of managing errors has considerable overlap with the original EMT model in that both focus attention on the asymmetry in the cost-benefit matrix in producing biases (McKay & Efferson, 2010). However, unlike EMT, BEVM proposes that individuals maintain accurate beliefs and maximize expected value *given* those beliefs about outcomes and likelihoods. BEVM thus accounts for the existence of biases, but at the level of behavior rather than at the level of belief, thereby preserving accurate information about the state of the world for use by other psychological mechanisms.

BEVM suggests that if the beliefs in question can be used by other psychological mechanisms, then having false beliefs about the state of the world affects not only the functioning of one particular perceptual mechanism but also the decision-making capabilities of many other mechanisms which may not benefit from incorrect information (Kurzban, 2010; Pinker, 2011). Consider the following pair of examples, which contrasts the BEVM and EMT perspectives, respectively:

> Thom works as a waiter at an expensive restaurant. One evening he waits on an attractive woman who is eating alone, working on some documents. During his break, he goes to the woman's table and begins talking to her. As their conversation

progresses, the woman is polite but appears to be romantically uninterested in Thom. He estimates her level of interest relatively accurately (i.e., not high) but persists in talking to her because this strategy maximizes expected value. *His evolved decision-making mechanisms calculate that the costs of missing out on a potential mating opportunity with her are sufficiently larger than the opportunity costs incurred, weighted by his best estimate of the probability of incurring each cost.* In the midst of this conversation, Thom notices his manager watching him pointedly, alerting Thom that his fraternizing with the customer might be inappropriate. Thom must now reevaluate his decision to persist in talking to the woman in light of the possibility that he might lose his job. Given his unbiased estimate of the woman's interest, he could aptly decide to cease interacting with her because although the costs of missing out on a mating opportunity with her are high, he has accurately estimated the likelihood that she is interested to be quite low, whereas the costs of a false alarm now include the possible loss of his job.

Emmett works as a waiter at an expensive restaurant. One evening he waits on an attractive woman who is eating alone, working on some documents. During his break, he goes to the woman's table and begins talking to her. As their conversation progresses, the woman is polite but appears to be romantically uninterested in Emmett. He overestimates her level of interest and thus persists in talking to her. *His evolved perceptual mechanisms cause him to bias his beliefs toward greater interest because the costs of missing out on a potential mating opportunity were recurrently larger than the costs of acting on inaccurately high estimates of interest.* In the midst of this conversation, Emmett notices his manager watching him pointedly, alerting Emmett that his fraternizing with the customer might be inappropriate. Emmett must now reevaluate his decision to persist in talking to the woman in light of the possibility that he might lose his job. Given his biased overestimate of the woman's interest, he would likely decide to continue to pursue her because he perceives the likelihood of obtaining sexual access as higher than it truly is, even though the costs of a false alarm now include the possible loss of his job.

These examples highlight the fact that BEVM and EMT approaches explain men's apparent sexual misperception in similar but distinct ways. Both approaches minimize the more costly error, missing a potential sexual opportunity. The BEVM approach posits that men maintain accurate priors of a woman's interest and bias behavior toward pursuing low probability outcomes,

rather than minimizing misses through false beliefs. The result is that men's perceptual mechanisms could optimize accuracy in estimating the probability that a woman is interested in them and yet still appear biased by setting a low threshold for behaving as though the woman were interested. Importantly, under the BEVM approach, if the information about the probability is then accessed by another psychological system, this separate system will have access to the most accurate possible estimate. This estimate allows for adaptively biased behavior in one domain while maintaining accuracy in information that can be accessed by mechanisms in other domains. Retaining these estimates also allows for individual differences and contextual cues to influence a man's estimates of the costs, benefits, and probabilities in the expected value function, consistent with recent evidence reviewed above.

Comparing the EMT and BEVM Models

The systems implied by the BEVM model and the EMT model, under most circumstances, lead to the same outcomes, causing men to make the less costly error. The BEVM model, however, entails retaining accurate representations while the EMT model entails retaining false ones, making the BEVM model, everything else equal, a more adaptive solution. Everything might not, however, always be equal. A cognitive bias could be favored over a behavioral one in the service of persuasion: having a false belief might help one to influence others by creating a self-fulfilling prophecy (James, 1890). For example, because people are attracted to others with whom attraction is mutual (Buss, Shackelford, Kirkpatrick, & Larsen, 2001), if a man were to hold a false belief that a woman is more interested in him than she really is, then this false belief might cause him to be more attracted to her than he otherwise would be. Subsequently, if he behaves in a way that advertises his (upwardly biased) attraction, then this behavior—via the same mutual attraction process—could elicit higher levels of interest from that woman, fulfilling the false-belief-induced prophecy. While maintaining the false belief and simultaneously acting as though the false belief were true might have the same effect, Trivers (2000) argued that genuinely accepting the false beliefs could make the false belief's bearer more persuasive.

The beneficial effect of these false beliefs about a woman's interest would, of course, have to outweigh the costs of maintaining false beliefs that might be used by other psychological systems (as illustrated in the Thom and Emmett scenarios above). Further, the value of broadcasting such false beliefs in the service of persuasion is limited by skepticism on the part of receivers. False-belief-generating systems designed to benefit men can be expected to lead to selection for skepticism as a counter-strategy on the part of women. So, while "self-deception" might result in men being more convincing (Trivers, 2000; von Hippel & Trivers, 2011), women can be expected to have evolved systems that result in reciprocal skepticism.

Haselton and Buss (2000), in their original formulation of EMT, proposed that "decision-making adaptations have evolved through natural or sexual selection to commit predictable errors," locating EMT's explanatory power in *cognitive belief systems* (p. 81). More recently, Haselton and Buss (2009) have endorsed the line of argument above that false beliefs might function to persuade rather than, or in addition to, guiding decision-makers' behavior. This addition resonates with recent proposals that, indeed, the only reason false-belief-generating systems should be expected to evolve are in the strategic contexts of influencing others (Kurzban, 2010; Kurzban & Aktipis, 2007), which would certainly include mating.

Because the BEVM model similarly takes into account the expected value of the benefits of the persuasive value of false beliefs, the BEVM model and the more recent EMT model with the added element of persuasion are difficult to tease apart. However, Haselton and Buss (2009) also point out that even if biasing behavior toward the less costly error—as opposed to maintaining a false belief—would be maximally effective in principle, constraints might have prevented

selection from designing such mechanisms. This worry about the BEVM account comprises two concerns, one computational, the other evolutionary. First, the computational concern is that estimating the priors involved in the requisite calculations requires an extensive amount of time and energy, costs which are postulated to be larger than the losses inherent in instead implementing a heuristic that generates appropriate false beliefs. Second, the evolutionary concern is that a BEVM instantiation might not have been able to be selected due to some historical constraint, for instance, that a BEVM mechanism was not possible, given the structure of related mechanisms. In either case, the suggestion is that because a BEVM mechanism cannot be selected, a biased belief system like EMT is the most adaptive alternative.

Evidence from other domains of psychology speaks to these constraints arguments, which lose traction to the extent that Bayesian calculations are seen throughout the human computational system (Cosmides & Tooby, 1996). For instance, even 12-month-olds demonstrate reasoning that is equivalent to a Bayesian ideal observer (Teglas et al., 2011). When observing novel simulations of moving objects, infants' surprise at physically unlikely movements follows a Bayesian model of expectations. Similar results have been documented among adults: when asked to make conditional predictions about uncertain events in the world (e.g., "How long is this poem likely to be if you've read 10 lines of it already?"), human performance is equivalent to Bayesian model predictions given the same priors (Griffiths & Tenenbaum, 2006). Research has further uncovered optimal Bayesian design in various cognitive mechanisms ranging from perceptual processing of motion (Weiss, Simoncelli, & Adelson, 2002) to sensorimotor learning (Kording & Wolpert, 2004) to memory (Anderson & Milson, 1989). If the human mind instantiates Bayesian processes in these domains, then it seems reasonable to suppose that Bayesian processes could have evolved within domains associated with large reproductive consequences, such as perception of sexual interest.

The EMT and BEVM accounts stand opposed in their proposals of which type of bias—cognitive or behavioral—adaptively manages error asymmetries. Haselton and Buss (2009) argue that the question of whether a particular bias is cognitive or behavioral must be arbitrated on a case-by-case basis because there is not necessarily a reason to suppose that cognitive biases are always more or less effective than behavioral biases. The BEVM account, however, proposes that behavioral biases are, all else equal, better solutions than cognitive biases, with persuasion being the sole exception.

Moving forward, empirically distinguishing between these models will become necessary to gain a clearer understanding of whether a cognitive or behavioral bias better characterizes men's sexual intent perception. Although the EMT model and the BEVM model bear a certain similarity to one another, distinguishing between them represents a challenge, but not an insurmountable one. One important avenue of research is to investigate the proposed persuasive value of false beliefs. For example, if men who have unreasonably positive beliefs about women's sexual interest in them are not more successful in their courtship compared to men who show no such bias or who underestimate women's interest, then the persuasive argument would be undermined to some extent.

There is some recent evidence along these lines in the domain of perceived competence and status: people who are dispositionally overconfident (i.e., have overestimated their abilities on the task in question) or were manipulated into being overconfident are rated by others as having higher status (Anderson, Brion, Moore, & Kennedy, 2012). This pattern held regardless of whether participants were interacting in a one-shot task with another participant or in the context of a year-long group project. Further, observers were shown to rely on false cues (i.e., cues not statistically related to actual competence in the task) rather than reliable cues (i.e., cues statistically linked to competence in the task) when estimating competence. Other research,

however, documents that while overconfident individuals are rated more positively by others of minimal acquaintance, these beneficial effects disappear as the relationship is extended, even though overconfident individuals maintain their inflated self-perceptions (Paulhus, 1998). If men's overperception of women's interest were found to lead to propitious interpersonal outcomes—even in the short term—it would provide evidence that false beliefs about women's sexual interest can indeed function as persuasive tools.

A second way in which the models differ is that the BEVM model predicts that men have a correct (or at least unbiased) representation of women's interest while the EMT view predicts that men's view is systematically incorrect. Although no research to date has directly addressed this potential divergence in predictions, techniques that can assess men's beliefs might illuminate the distinction. For example, if the "true" belief about women's interest were available to men, then incentivizing them to tell the truth about their beliefs, using techniques from behavioral economics, might productively advance the debate.

The body of evidence that seems to show that men have *incorrect* beliefs about women's interest poses a challenge to the BEVM model. In most studies, men self-report their (over) estimates of women's level of interest, thus presumably accessing the beliefs directly rather than *behaving as if* the woman had a high level of interest (e.g., Haselton & Buss, 2000; Perilloux et al., 2012; Shotland & Craig, 1988). But motivation toward deceptive or, at least, ambiguous self-presentation in the realm of sexual interest makes its measurement imprecise at best and misleading at worst. Because experimenters do not know the actual level of sexual interest a woman has in a man, but only her report of it, the fact that men's perceptions are incorrect cannot be distinguished from the possibility that women's reports are inaccurate. For instance, women might be motivated to underreport their own sexual interest in these studies to appear less promiscuous (Haselton & Buss, 2000). Alternatively, women might not have decided how interested they are in a man at the time of the assessment (Haselton & Galperin, 2013). Therefore, from the sex differences one sees in the data between men and women, it can be difficult to know if men are actually misperceiving or women consistently underreporting or some combination of the two.

Another potential means of distinguishing between the two proposals is that while both models predict that men will be more likely to behave as though women are interested, the EMT account predicts that the key mediator of men's behavior is the magnitude of asymmetry between the errors. In contrast, the BEVM account predicts that the key mediator would be expected value—a calculation that includes not only the error costs but also the probability they will occur. For this reason, the two models could be distinguished by manipulating men's beliefs about the relevant probabilities, perhaps through a manipulation of perceived base rates (see Future Directions, below).

Another challenge to the BEVM model is that men overestimate sexual interest when no information has been provided and there is zero probability that sex could occur, such as when judging photographs of strangers' faces (Maner et al., 2005). Further, men show a *greater* bias when estimating the sexual interest of hypothetical female targets than real female targets with whom they are acquainted (Lindgren, George, & Shoda, 2007). The BEVM model does not predict a difference in accuracy based on real or hypothetical targets, but does predict reasonable accuracy from male perceivers; therefore, such findings might be difficult for the BEVM model to explain.

The BEVM model appears, on first principles, to propose a better solution to the management of errors, but the EMT model is consistent with much empirical work to date and can provide a heuristically valuable theoretical framework for understanding biases in the service of persuasion. In short, many questions remain, and additional work is needed to carefully and systematically distinguish between the BEVM and EMT models with regard to men's sexual intent perception.

Future Directions

Many avenues of future research on men's sexual interest perception remain underexplored: there are likely still important individual difference and contextual predictors of sexual interest perception to document; the debate between cognitive biases and behavioral biases must be directly addressed; and there is still uncertainty about the best way to actually measure (mis)perception because all parties involved might be motivated to mislead in self-reports (Haselton & Buss, 2000).

This lack of true benchmarks with which to compare estimates of sexual interest is arguably the largest limitation in sexual intent perception research. To address this question, researchers have adopted multiple approaches that point toward men as the misperceivers. In one approach, Haselton and Buss (2000) assessed men's estimates, women's self-ratings, and estimates of other women's interest and argued that if men's estimates were higher than both sets of female ratings, that would be considered overperception. A possible difficulty with this line of reasoning is that if men really are more accurate and women unknowingly underreport, men would still be observed to rate sexual interest higher than both groups of women—appearing as though men overperceived. Studies of naturally occurring mistakes of inference also implicate men as incorrectly identifying women as sexually interested when they are not (Abbey, 1987; Haselton, 2003). However, even if men were accurate and behaved based on their correct estimation, women might more frequently rebuff them as a form of reputation management (Muehlenhard & Hollabaugh, 1988), thus resulting in men experiencing more false alarms than misses. All of these points stress that measurement of actual sexual interest is exceedingly difficult and an entire line of future research could be devoted strictly to establishing more accurate measures.

An aspect of the mechanism that has received very little attention thus far is the degree to which it is under conscious control or awareness. When asked which type of error would be worse to make when estimating a woman's level of interest, men report that false alarms are more costly (Henningsen & Henningsen, 2009), contrary to the proposed asymmetries in both EMT and BEVM models. Neither model requires conscious awareness of the operation of the underlying decision-making processes, but if men's behavior were motivated by their perception of false alarms as more costly, the result would presumably be greater conservatism in men estimating women's interest.[1] Yet research clearly documents that although men perceive false alarms as more costly, they consistently behave as though misses are more costly (e.g., Abbey, 1987; Haselton, 2003). This discrepancy between conscious perceptions of costliness and nonconscious calculations of costliness could be an interesting avenue of future research in highlighting obstacles in conscious strategies to prevent misperception.

Individual differences such as mating strategy and rape-relevant attitudes are significant predictors of men's perception of sexual interest, as described above. These results are unsurprising insofar as decision-making systems should be expected to take an individual's traits as inputs when they are relevant in that decision domain. For instance, in the same way that men's formidability alters the likelihood they will decide to use aggression (Sell, Tooby, & Cosmides, 2009), a man's physical attractiveness could adjust the probability component of a BEVM model of sexual perception. That is, for instance, if very attractive men have a higher expected probability of succeeding in approaching a woman than

unattractive men, then this advantage should express itself in the decision rule. Similarly, an EMT model could propose that the error asymmetry—the cost of reputational damage associated with false alarms—would have been recurrently higher for less attractive men, leading to a more pronounced overperception bias in more attractive men (Perilloux et al., 2012).

Interestingly, preliminary work on men's attractiveness indicated that self-ratings positively correlated with sexual intent perceptions, but that third-party rated attractiveness was not (Perilloux et al., 2012). This pattern of results suggests that men whose probability of success is higher (e.g., more attractive men) are less likely to encounter uninterested women and thus do not *appear* to overperceive as much. In contrast, less attractive men seem to overestimate both their own attractiveness and women's interest, perhaps reflecting persuasion-based biases. These results do not, however, directly address the underlying mechanism nor whether it is based on biased beliefs or biased decision thresholds. Clearly more work is needed to first replicate the attractiveness results and then to tease apart the proposed underlying mechanisms.

Similarly, because women prefer men of higher status (Buss, 1989; Li, Bailey, Kenrick, & Linsenmeier, 2002), a man's status level might influence expectations of success and thereby willingness to infer sexual interest. Indeed, preliminary experimental evidence indicates that when a man is interacting with a woman, increases in testosterone—a hormone associated with status in men (Mazur, 1985)—predicts subsequent overestimation of her sexual interest (Perilloux & Buss, 2011). In the same experiment, however, winning or losing a competition against a same-sex competitor did not similarly impact subsequent sexual interest estimations; additional work is needed in this area to clarify these issues.

Individual differences matter not only as they pertain to the men estimating sexual interest but also as they pertain to the female targets. Attractiveness may be easy for male participants to observe in superficial lab interactions (and easy for researchers to assess through objective

---

[1] Alternative accounts that invoke socialization or general learning models as explanations for men's overperception claim that men learn that women often express less sexual intent than they actually feel (e.g., Abbey, 1982; Abbey, 1991). Following this same logic, then, if men have "learned" that false alarms are more costly than misses, then these same accounts would have to explain why men continue to err more toward false alarms than misses.

ratings), but other components of mate value should be explored as they may also influence the costs and benefits associated with assessing a particular woman's sexual interest. As indicated above, men might be expected to bias their estimation of a woman's sexual interest to the extent that she has high mate value because these women represent higher-cost misses and higher-benefit hits. Attractiveness, given its tremendous importance in determining women's mate value, may represent an extreme example of this effect (Perilloux et al., 2012), but further examples are expected for the myriad of other traits that comprise women's mate value. By this reasoning, men should be more likely to assess a woman as sexually interested if she appears to have a good sense of humor (Li et al., 2002), if she appears to be kind (Buss, 1989; Evans & Brase, 2007) and, perhaps counterintuitively, if she appears to be faithful (Buss, 1989; Buss et al., 2001). This last prediction would be particularly interesting because a relationship between perceptions of a woman's fidelity and heightened inferences of sexual interest should only occur among men oriented toward long-term mating; higher levels of commitment are *not* viewed as desirable among men oriented toward short-term mating.

Another potential avenue of research, alluded to above, derives from the fact that the BEVM model predicts that men will not change their reports of women's sexual interest when incentivized for accuracy because they already presumably have access to their best estimate; money, as it is irrelevant to the calculation in the inference task at hand, should not change that estimate. The prediction, according to the EMT account, is less clear with regard to men, but the account does make a prediction when it comes to women. According to EMT, the true level of women's sexual interest should fall between women's self-ratings and their ratings of other women's sexual intent (because the former may reflect underreporting to appear chaste, and the latter may reflect over-reporting to derogate competitors; Haselton & Buss, 2000). Therefore, providing monetary incentives to women to correctly estimate other women's sexual interest should motivate them to lower their

third-party estimates toward this correct middle value. If, instead, women adopt men's pattern of results when incentivized, this could imply that men's ratings of women's sexual interest were more accurate.

The two models also make different predictions with regard to the types of information that will influence a man's decision about whether a woman is interested in him. The EMT model relies solely on the error asymmetry, thus altering the relative costs of misses and false alarms should—and apparently does (e.g., target female attractiveness; Koenig et al., 2007; Perilloux et al., 2012)—alter men's decisions to treat a woman as sexually interested, just as the BEVM model would also predict. But the BEVM model further accounts for the probability that each type of error will occur, whereas the EMT model does not. Therefore, only BEVM predicts that experimentally manipulating men's access to information about error probabilities—perhaps by providing biased feedback on sexual interest perception tasks—should influence men's subsequent decisions about women's sexual interest in the direction that would, given the false information, maximize expected value.

Another potentially important line of research is to investigate the persuasive account whereby men, by overestimating women's interest, actually attain better mating outcomes than men who do not overestimate women's interest. One promising route is to identify signals that men broadcast to indicate their (exaggerated) beliefs of a woman's interest and manipulate these signals to measure their effect on women. If women indicate greater interest in men displaying signals associated with overperception, then the revised EMT account of misperception that identifies persuasion as the function of the system would receive support. Speed dating represents another interesting method for investigating the self-fulfilling prophecy model of overperception. If men's beliefs about their partners' sexual interest were assessed—and compared to women's expressed interest—the value of overperception could be measured in the real-world currency of subsequent mating opportunities compared between overperceivers and unbiased perceivers.

Conclusions

That men perceive greater sexual interest from women than women perceive in themselves or other women is now well established. However, the phenomenon is more complex than it seemed to be in the 1980s. Misperception does not appear to depend solely upon one's sex but also depends in potentially complex ways upon one's traits and cues from one's environment. Early theories of men's sex drive as the culprit have given way to more comprehensive theories, such as the EMT and BEVM models that take advantage of what we know of our evolved psychology to provide richer backgrounds from which to explore the nuances of this phenomenon. The recent debate between cognitive bias models and behavioral bias models is likely to generate important new avenues of research that hold the promise of illuminating this important aspect of men's mating behavior.

References

Abbey, A. (1982). Sex differences in attributions for friendly behavior: Do males misperceive females' friendliness? *Journal of Personality and Social Psychology, 42*, 830–838.

Abbey, A. (1987). Misperceptions of friendly behavior as sexual interest: A survey of naturally occurring incidents. *Psychology of Women Quarterly, 11*, 173–194.

Abbey, A. (1991). Misperception as an antecedent of acquaintance rape: A consequence of ambiguity in communication between men and women. In A. Parrot & L. Bechhofer (Eds.), *Acquaintance rape: The hidden crime* (pp. 96–111). New York: Wiley.

Abbey, A., Cozzarelli, C., McLaughlin, K., & Harnish, R. J. (1987). The effects of clothing and dyad sex composition on perceptions of sexual intent: Do women and men evaluate these cues differently. *Journal of Applied Social Psychology, 17*, 108–126.

Abbey, A., & Harnish, R. J. (1995). Perception of sexual intent: The role of gender, alcohol consumption, and rape supportive attitudes. *Sex Roles, 32*, 297–313.

Abbey, A., McAuslan, P., & Ross, L. T. (1998). Sexual assault perpetration by college men: The role of alcohol, misperception of sexual intent, and sexual beliefs and experiences. *Journal of Social and Clinical Psychology, 17*, 167–195.

Abbey, A., & Melby, C. (1986). The effects of nonverbal cues on gender differences in perceptions of sexual intent. *Sex Roles, 15*, 283–298.

Abbey, A., Zawacki, T., & Buck, P. O. (2005). The effects of past sexual assault perpetration and alcohol consumption on men's reactions to women's mixed signals. *Journal of Social and Clinical Psychology, 24*, 129–155.

Abbey, A., Zawacki, T., & McAuslan, P. (2000). Alcohol's effects on sexual perception. *Journal of Studies on Alcohol, 61*, 688–697.

Anderson, C., Brion, S., Moore, D. A., & Kennedy, J. A. (2012). A status-enhancement account of overconfidence. *Journal of Personality and Social Psychology, 103*, 718–735.

Anderson, J. R., & Milson, R. (1989). Human memory: An adaptive perspective. *Psychological Review, 96*, 703–719.

Back, M. D., Penke, L., Schmukle, S. C., & Asendorpf, J. B. (2011). Knowing your own mate value: Sex-specific personality effects on the accuracy of expected mate choices. *Psychological Science, 22*, 984–989.

Bereczkei, T., Voros, S., Gal, A., & Bernath, L. (1997). Resources, attractiveness, family commitment: Reproductive decisions in human mate choice. *Ethology, 103*, 681–699.

Bondurant, B., & Donat, P. L. N. (1999). Perceptions of women's sexual interest and acquaintance rape: The role of sexual overperception and affective attitudes. *Psychology of Women Quarterly, 23*, 691–705.

Bostwick, T. D., & DeLucia, J. L. (1992). Effects of gender and specific dating behaviors on perceptions of sex willingness and date rape. *Journal of Social & Clinical Psychology, 11*, 14–25.

Buss, D. M. (1989). Sex differences in human mate preferences: Evolutionary hypotheses tested in 37 cultures. *Behavioral & Brain Sciences, 12*, 1–49.

Buss, D. M., & Schmitt, D. P. (1993). Sexual Strategies Theory: A contextual evolutionary analysis of human mating. *Psychological Review, 100*, 204–232.

Buss, D. M., Shackelford, T. K., Kirkpatrick, L. A., & Larsen, R. J. (2001). A half century of mate preferences: The cultural evolution of values. *Journal of Marriage and Family, 63*, 491–503.

Byrne, R. W., & Whiten, A. (1988). *Machiavellian intelligence: Social expertise and the evolution of intellect in monkeys, apes, and humans.* New York, NY: Clarendon Press/Oxford University Press.

Cosmides, L., & Tooby, J. (1996). Are humans good intuitive statisticians after all? Rethinking some conclusions of the literature on judgment under uncertainty. *Cognition, 58*, 1–73.

Eibl-Eibesfeldt, I. (1971). *Love and hate: The natural history of behavior patterns.* New York, NY: Aldine de Gruyter.

Evans, K., & Brase, G. L. (2007). Assessing sex differences and similarities in mate preferences: Above and beyond demand characteristics. *Journal of Social and Personal Relationships, 24*, 781–791.

Farris, C., Treat, T. A., & Viken, R. J. (2010). Alcohol alters men's perceptual and decisional processing of women's sexual interest. *Journal of Abnormal Psychology, 119*, 427–432.

Farris, C., Treat, T. A., Viken, R. J., & McFall, R. M. (2008a). Sexual coercion and the misperception of sexual intent. *Clinical Psychology Review, 28*, 48–66.

Farris, C., Treat, T. A., Viken, R. J., & McFall, R. M. (2008b). Perceptual mechanisms that characterize gender differences in decoding women's sexual interest. *Psychological Science, 19*, 348–354.

Farris, C., Viken, R., & Treat, T. (2010). Perceived association between diagnostic and non-diagnostic cues of women's sexual interest: General Recognition Theory predictors of risk for sexual coercion. *Journal of Mathematical Psychology, 54*, 137–149.

Fisher, T. D., & Walters, A. S. (2003). Variables in addition to gender that help to explain differences in perceived sexual interest. *Psychology of Men & Masculinity, 4*, 154–162.

Grammer, K. (1990). Strangers meet: Laughter and non-verbal signs of interest in opposite-sex encounters. *Journal of Nonverbal Behavior, 14*, 209–236.

Green, D. M., & Swets, J. A. (1966). *Signal detection and psychophysics.* New York: Wiley.

Griffiths, T. L., & Tenenbaum, J. B. (2006). Optimal predictions in everyday cognition. *Psychological Science, 17*, 767–773.

Harnish, R. J., Abbey, A., & DeBono, K. G. (1990). Toward an understanding of 'the sex game': The effects of gender and self-monitoring on perceptions of sexuality and likability in initial interactions. *Journal of Applied Social Psychology, 20*, 1333–1344.

Haselton, M. G. (2003). The sexual overperception bias: Evidence of a systematic bias in men from a survey of naturally occurring events. *Journal of Research in Personality, 37*, 34–47.

Haselton, M. G., & Buss, D. M. (2000). Error management theory: A new perspective on biases in cross-sex mind reading. *Journal of Personality and Social Psychology, 78*, 81–91.

Haselton, M. G., & Buss, D. M. (2009). Error management theory and the evolution of misbeliefs. *Behavioral and Brain Sciences, 32*, 522–523.

Haselton, M. G., & Galperin, A. (2013). Error management in relationships. In J. Simpson & L. Campbell (Eds.), *Oxford handbook of close relationships* (pp. 234–254). Oxford: Oxford University Press.

Henningsen, D. (2004). Flirting with meaning: An examination of miscommunication in flirting interactions. *Sex Roles, 50*, 481–489.

Henningsen, D. D., & Henningsen, M. L. M. (2009). *Testing error management theory: Two tests of the commitment skepticism bias and the sexual overperception bias.* Paper presented at the international communication association conference, Chicago, IL.

Henningsen, D. D., & Henningsen, M. L. M. (2010). Testing error management theory: Exploring the commitment skepticism bias and the sexual overperception bias. *Human Communication Research, 36*, 618–634.

Howell, E. C., Etchells, P. J., & Penton-Voak, I. S. (2012). The sexual overperception bias is associated with sociosexuality. *Personality and Individual Differences, 53*, 1012–1016.

Jacques-Tiura, A., Abbey, A., Parkhill, M., & Zawacki, T. (2007). Why do some men misperceive women's sexual intentions more frequently than others do? An application of the confluence model. *Personality and Social Psychology Bulletin, 33*, 1467–1480.

James, W. (1890). *The principles of psychology.* New York: Holt.

Koenig, B. L., Kirkpatrick, L. A., & Ketelaar, T. (2007). Misperception of sexual and romantic interests in opposite-sex friendships: Four hypotheses. *Personal Relationships, 14*, 411–429.

Kokko, H., & Jennions, M. D. (2008). Parental investment, sexual selection and sex ratios. *Journal of Evolutionary Biology, 21*, 919–948.

Kording, K., & Wolpert, D. M. (2004). Bayesian integration in sensorimotor learning. *Nature, 427*, 244–247.

Koukounas, E., & Letch, N. M. (2001). Psychological correlates of perception of sexual intent in women. *Journal of Social Psychology, 141*, 443–456.

Kowalski, R. M. (1993). Inferring sexual interest from behavioral cues: Effects of gender and sexually relevant attitudes. *Sex Roles, 29*, 13–36.

Kurzban, R. (2010). *Why everyone (else) is a hypocrite: Evolution and the modular mind.* Princeton, NJ: Princeton University Press.

Kurzban, R., & Aktipis, C. A. (2007). Modularity and the social mind: Are psychologists too self-ish? *Personality and Social Psychology Review, 11*, 131–149.

Kurzban, R., & Weeden, J. (2005). HurryDate: Mate preferences in action. *Evolution and Human Behavior, 26*, 227–244.

Lee, L., Loewenstein, G., Ariely, D., Hong, J., & Young, J. (2008). If I'm not hot, are you hot or not? Physical-attractiveness evaluations and dating preferences as a function of one's own attractiveness. *Psychological Science, 19*, 669–677.

Lenton, A., Bryan, A., Hastie, R., & Fischer, O. (2007). We want the same thing: Projection in judgments of sexual intent. *Personality and Social Psychology Bulletin, 33*, 975–988.

Levesque, M. J., Nave, C. S., & Lowe, C. A. (2006). Toward an understanding of gender differences in inferring sexual interest. *Psychology of Women Quarterly, 30*, 150–158.

Li, N. P., Bailey, J. M., Kenrick, D. T., & Linsenmeier, J. A. W. (2002). The necessities and luxuries of mate preferences: Testing the tradeoffs. *Journal of Personality and Social Psychology, 82*, 947–955.

Lieberman, D. (2008). Moral sentiments relating to incest: Discerning adaptations from by-products. In W. Sinnott-Armstrong (Ed.), *Moral psychology* (The evolution of morality: Adaptations and innateness, Vol. 1, pp. 165–190). Cambridge, MA: MIT Press.

Lindgren, K. P., George, W. H., & Shoda, Y. (2007). Sexual intent perceptions: The role of perceiver experience and the real-person reduction. *Journal of Applied Social Psychology, 37*, 346–369.

Maner, J. K., Kenrick, D. T., Neuberg, S. L., Becker, D. V., Robertson, T., Hofer, B., et al. (2005). Functional projection: How fundamental social motives can bias interpersonal perception. *Journal of Personality and Social Psychology, 88*, 63–78.

Mazur, A. (1985). A biosocial model of status in face-to-face primate groups. *Social Forces, 64*, 377–402.

McKay, R. T., & Dennett, D. C. (2009). The evolution of disbelief. *Behavioral and Brain Sciences, 32*, 493–561.

McKay, R., & Efferson, C. (2010). The subtleties of error management. *Evolution and Human Behavior, 31*, 309–319.

Moore, M. M. (2002). Courtship communication and perception. *Perceptual & Motor Skills, 94*, 97–105.

Muehlenhard, C. L. (1988). Misinterpreted dating behaviors and the risk of date rape. *Journal of Social and Clinical Psychology, 6*, 20–37.

Muehlenhard, C. L., & Hollabaugh, L. C. (1988). Do women sometimes say no when they mean yes? The prevalence and correlates of women's token resistance to sex. *Journal of Personality and Social Psychology, 54*, 872–879.

Paulhus, D. L. (1998). Interpersonal and intrapsychic adaptiveness of trait self-enhancement: A mixed blessing? *Journal of Personality and Social Psychology, 74*, 1197–1208.

Perilloux, C., & Buss, D. M. (2011). *Testosterone and men's sexual overperception*. Paper presented at the 23rd annual conference of the Human Behavior and Evolution Society, Montpellier, France.

Perilloux, C., Easton, J. A., & Buss, D. M. (2012). The misperception of sexual interest. *Psychological Science, 23*, 146–151.

Pillsworth, E. G., & Haselton, M. G. (2006). Women's sexual strategies: The evolution of long-term bonds and extra-pair sex. *Annual Review of Sex Research, 17*, 59–100.

Pinker, S. (2011). Representations and decision rules in the theory of self-deception. *Behavioral and Brain Sciences, 34*, 35–37.

Pinker, S., Nowak, M. A., & Lee, J. J. (2008). The logic of indirect speech. *Proceedings of the National Academy of Sciences of the United States of America, 105*, 833–838.

Schmitt, D. P. (2014). Evaluating evidence of mate preference adaptations: How do we really know what Homo sapiens sapiens really want? In V. A. Weekes-Shackelford & T. K. Shackelford (Eds.), *Evolutionary perspectives on human sexual psychology and behavior*. New York: Springer.

Sell, A., Tooby, J., & Cosmides, L. (2009). Formidability and the logic of human anger. *Proceedings of the National Academy of Sciences of the United States of America, 106*, 15073–15078.

Shea, M. E. C. (1993). The effects of selective evaluation on the perception of female cues in sexually coercive and noncoercive males. *Archives of Sexual Behavior, 22*, 415–433.

Shotland, R. L., & Craig, J. M. (1988). Can men and women differentiate between friendly and sexually interested behavior? *Social Psychology Quarterly, 51*, 66–73.

Sugiyama, L. S. (2005). Physical attractiveness in adaptationist perspective. In D. M. Buss (Ed.), *The handbook of evolutionary psychology* (pp. 292–343). Hoboken, NJ: Wiley.

Teglas, E., Vul, E., Girotto, V., Gonzalez, M., Tenenbaum, J. B., & Bonatti, L. L. (2011). Pure reasoning in 12-month-old infants as probabilistic inference. *Science, 332*, 1054–1059.

Trivers, R. L. (1972). Parental investment and sexual selection. In B. Campell (Ed.), *Sexual selection and the descent of man: 1871–1971* (pp. 136–179). Chicago: Aldine.

Trivers, R. L. (2000). The elements of a scientific theory of self-deception. *Annals of the New York Academy of Sciences, 907*, 114–131.

Vigil, J. M., Geary, D. C., & Byrd-Craven, J. (2006). Trade-offs in low-income women's mate preferences: Within-sex differences in reproductive strategy. *Human Nature, 17*, 319–336.

von Hippel, W., & Trivers, R. (2011). The evolution and psychology of self-deception. *Behavioral and Brain Sciences, 34*, 1–56.

Vrij, A., & Kirby, E. (2002). Sex differences in interpreting male-female dyad interactions: Males' predominance in perceiving sexual intent. *International Review of Victimology, 9*, 289–297.

Weiss, Y., Simoncelli, E. P., & Adelson, E. H. (2002). Motion illusions as optimal percepts. *Nature Neuroscience, 5*, 598–604.

Westermarck, E. A. (1921). *The history of human marriage* (5th ed.). London: Macmillan.

Bodily Attractiveness as a Window to Women's Fertility and Reproductive Value

Jaime M. Cloud and Carin Perilloux

Dedicated to the memory of Devendra Singh (1938–2010)

Intellectual debate regarding the universality of standards of beauty has waned in recent years. An unprecedented number of researchers now embrace the evolutionary perspective that components of physical attractiveness reflect individuals' health and reproductive condition, rather than arbitrary cultural norms (e.g., Singh & Singh, 2011; Sugiyama, 2005) (cf. Wolf, 1991). An increasing amount of attention has instead been placed on the relative strength with which morphological traits predict perceptions of overall attractiveness. For instance, variations in body mass index (BMI) are frequently compared to those in waist-to-hip ratio (WHR) to determine whether BMI or WHR is the more salient index of a woman's bodily attractiveness (Singh, 1993; Tovée, Maisey, Emery, & Cornelissen, 1999). Studies consistently find that both measures affect perceptions of attractiveness (e.g., Furnham, Petrides, & Constantinides, 2005; Furnham, Swami, & Shah, 2006); however, the specific values associated with maximum levels of attractiveness appear to depend on the availability of local resources. For example, in subsistence-based societies, greater priority is given to body weight (BMI) than body shape (WHR), as the former indicates the availability of sufficient

resources to support the metabolic costs of reproduction (Marlowe & Wetsman, 2001; Sugiyama, 2004; Wetsman & Marlowe, 1999). Nearly every morphological trait imaginable—from head (e.g., hair color; Swami, Furnham, & Joshi, 2008) to toe (e.g., foot size; Fessler, Haley, & Lal, 2005)—has received some empirical attention. In order to make the process of drawing inferences from this data more tractable, a line is often drawn at the neck, separating facial and bodily components of attractiveness (e.g., Confer, Perilloux, & Buss, 2010). The primary focus of the current chapter is the argument that bodily components of attractiveness convey certain information about a woman's reproductive profile that cannot be gleaned as easily from facial components of attractiveness.

We begin this chapter by integrating evidence that various bodily traits predict a woman's health, hormonal profile, and reproductive status with empirical findings that demonstrate systematic preferences for optimal levels within those traits. We then consider the plasticity of attractiveness judgments across cultures and time periods. In this part, we present new evidence challenging the popular belief that Baroque ideals of attractiveness (e.g., high BMI) are vastly different from modern ideals. We conclude with evidence showing that

J.M. Cloud (✉)
Department of Psychology, Western Oregon University,
Monmouth, OR 97361, USA
e-mail: jaimemcloud@gmail.com

V.A. Weekes-Shackelford and T.K. Shackelford (eds.), *Evolutionary Perspectives on Human Sexual Psychology and Behavior*, Evolutionary Psychology, DOI 10.1007/978-1-4939-0314-6_7,
© Springer Science+Business Media New York 2014

men preferentially attend to women's bodies in short-term mating contexts (e.g., one-night stand). These results are discussed in light of the hypothesis that fertility cues may be better gleaned from a woman's body than her face.

Components of Bodily Attractiveness

Aspects of physical attractiveness are experienced as "attractive" because they have been reliably associated with individuals' health, hormonal profile, and reproductive status throughout human evolutionary history (Symons, 1979; Williams, 1975). These traits are said to be *honest*, meaning the integrity of their signaling value is maintained by the inability of individuals with decreased fitness to imitate such cues (Zahavi, 1975). Bilateral symmetry, for example, reflects an individual's ability to withstand environmental (e.g., parasitic) and genetic perturbations during development (Thornhill & Gangestad, 1994). Individuals with lower-quality immune systems are more susceptible to developmental insults and are therefore less likely to maintain symmetrical features. Consequently, individuals with symmetrical faces and bodies are preferentially sought as mates (Gangestad & Thornhill, 1997; Thornhill & Gangestad, 1994).

Although attended to by individuals of both sexes, men place relatively greater priority than women on a potential mate's physical attractiveness (Buss, 1989; Li, Bailey, Kenrick, & Linsenmeier, 2002). This is because men's reproductive success, more so than women's, was primarily limited by access to healthy, fertile mates over human evolutionary history (Sugiyama, 2005; Symons, 1979). Consequently, men's mating psychology is designed to attend to cues of a woman's *reproductive value* (a measure of future reproductive potential that is strongly correlated with a woman's age) and *fertility* (i.e., fecundability, a measure of a woman's current ability to become pregnant) and find women who possess high levels of both especially attractive. Although these two dimensions are partially dissociable (e.g., a young pregnant woman is likely to have high reproductive value despite a current fertility of zero), many

bodily traits simultaneously convey information pertaining to both. In this first part, we review various bodily features, detailing their health and reproductive correlates, as well as empirical evidence showing systematic preferences for specific variations in each trait.

Leg Length

One of the more recent empirical developments over the past decade has been the identification of leg length as a determinant of attractiveness. This trait is frequently operationalized as a leg-to-body ratio (LBR), representing the proportion of an individual's height (usually including the head) that is accounted for by the legs (Swami, Einon, & Furnham, 2006; Swami, Gray, & Furnham, 2006). Before its application in evolutionary psychology, LBR was primarily used as a measure of childhood nutritional status, with lower LBRs representing periods of interrupted growth (Davey Smith et al., 2001). LBR has also been associated with various indices of health, including lower BMI, blood pressure, and cholesterol, as well as a reduced risk of coronary heart disease, diabetes, and cancer (Davey Smith et al., 2001; Gunnell, May, Ben-Shlomo, Yarnell, & Davey Smith, 2003; Gunnell, Whitley, et al., 2003). Importantly, childhood environmental conditions have been shown to influence leg length more strongly than any other component of stature (e.g., trunk length; Gunnell, May, et al., 2003), rendering LBR an especially powerful marker of resource availability and health during development.

In addition to functioning as an honest signal of health, Swami, Einon, et al. (2006) propose that women have a slightly higher LBR than men, and thus, LBR is used to differentiate masculine from feminine body types. To test this possibility, Swami et al. presented men and women with line drawings of male and female figures that varied in LBR. They hypothesized that if high LBRs are attractive because they indicate genetic quality, high LBRs should be considered more attractive than low LBRs regardless of sex. If, on the other hand, high LBRs signal femininity, high LBRs should be considered more attractive only within female figures. The results supported the latter relationship between LBR and femininity: as LBR increased, attractiveness ratings increased for female figures, but decreased for male figures. This pattern of results also replicated in a cross-cultural sample of British and Malaysian participants (Swami, Einon, & Furnham, 2007). Other studies eschew the explanation provided by Swami, Gray, et al. (2006), given research that shows no sexual dimorphism in LBR (for relevant citations, see Sorokowski & Pawlowski, 2008). These studies instead find a curvilinear, rather than linear, preference for LBR, with attractiveness assessments peaking at average (approximately 0.50) to slightly above-average (elongated by 5–10 %) LBRs for both male and female stimuli (Frederick, Hadji-Michael, Furnham, & Swami, 2010; Sorokowski, Sorokowska, & Mberira, 2012; Sorokowski & Pawlowski, 2008). Most notably, Sorokowski et al. (2011) surveyed the LBR preferences of men and women from 27 nations and found average LBRs to be maximally attractive across figures of both sexes. Clearly more research is needed to resolve the discrepancy between these findings and those of Swami, Einon, et al. (2006, 2007); however, hypotheses that LBR signals femininity (Swami, Einon, et al., 2006) or health (Frederick et al., 2010; Sorokowski et al., 2012; Sorokowski & Pawlowski, 2008) need not be mutually exclusive. Higher than average LBRs may be selected for up until the point at which long legs become biomechanically inefficient (e.g., in running or jumping; Sorokowski et al., 2012). Thus, leg length may serve as a cue of health and possibly, femininity.

Foot Size

Foot size is another bodily trait hypothesized to act as a sexually dimorphic signal. Women have smaller feet proportionate to their stature compared to men (Fessler et al., 2005; Voracek, Fisher, Rupp, Lucas, & Fessler, 2007), thereby posing a biomechanical challenge of maintaining body stability, particularly during pregnancy (Fessler et al., 2005). If women have been

selected toward smaller foot size, counteracting evolutionary pressures (e.g., an increase in perceived attractiveness) must have outweighed costs associated with small feet. In women, foot size gradually increases with age and parity (for relevant citations, see Fessler et al., 2005); thus, small feet may be considered attractive because they indicate high reproductive value. Indeed, women with relatively large feet are judged to be older (Fessler et al., 2012) and less attractive (Fessler et al., 2005, 2012; Voracek et al., 2007) than those with relatively small feet. As would be expected in light of biomechanical efficiencies, women prefer men with average-to-large-sized feet (Fessler et al., 2012; Voracek et al., 2007), although, consistent with unidirectional sexual selection for foot size, women are less interested in men's feet than men are in women's feet (Fessler et al., 2012; Voracek et al., 2007). Foot size may therefore indicate a woman's reproductive value and has been recognized (albeit not for the ultimate reasons indicated here) as an important component of female attractiveness as evidenced by practices such as historical Chinese foot binding (Fessler et al., 2005).

Breast Size

Human females are unique among primates because their breasts are perennially enlarged even when they are not pregnant or lactating (Marlowe, 1998). This, bolstered by the lack of evidence to suggest that breast size is directly related to reproductive capabilities (e.g., milk production; Anderson, 1983), suggests that prominent breasts are maintained by a process of sexual selection (Symons, 1979). The majority of research on the issue of preferred breast size shows medium- to large-sized breasts to be maximally attractive (Dixson, Grimshaw, Linklater, & Dixson, 2011; Zelazniewicz & Pawlowski, 2011; but see Furnham & Swami, 2007), especially in combination with other desirable bodily traits (e.g., low WHR; Furnham, Dias, & McClelland, 1998; Furnham et al., 2006; Singh & Young, 1995). Members of both sexes generally agree that women with large breasts are particularly attractive (e.g., Furnham et al., 1998; cf. Gitter, Lomranz, Saxe, & Bar-Tal, 1983); however, a preference for large breasts is exaggerated in men with a stronger proclivity toward casual sex (i.e., men with an unrestricted sociosexual orientation; Penke & Asendorpf, 2008; Zelazniewicz & Pawlowski, 2011). Guéguen (2007) showed that men were more likely than women to offer assistance to large-breasted women, despite the sexes' general agreement in attractiveness ratings, indicating an instrumental motivation behind assistance patterns.

A number of hypotheses have been proposed to explain the function of perpetually enlarged breasts in women. It was originally thought that large breasts signaled the availability of fat reserves necessary for reproduction (Cant, 1981; Gallop, 1982). This conjecture is supported by research showing that ovarian function ceases in women with too little body fat (amenorrhea; Ellison, 1990; Frisch, 1987). Still this hypothesis only explains why a certain amount of body fat is attractive; it does not explain why fat reserves would be localized around the mammary glands. Other research suggests that large breasts signal fecundity. Jasieńska, Ziomkiewicz, Ellison, Lipson, and Thune (2004) found that women with large breasts have higher estrogen levels then women with small breasts. This finding is given practical significance in combination with research showing women to be more likely to conceive during cycles with higher estrogen concentrations (Lipson & Ellison, 1996; Venners et al., 2006). Thus, an attraction to large-breasted women might function to preferentially direct mating effort toward women who are especially fecund.

Some researchers have also proposed a "good genes" hypothesis, in which breasts are purported to function as honest signals of phenotypic quality. Manning, Scutt, Whitehouse, and Leinster (1997), for instance, showed that large breasts were less asymmetrical than expected allometrically, in spite of the associated increase in estrogen (Jasieńska et al., 2004), which Manning et al. argue suppresses the immune system. Other research has shown breast symmetry to positively predict number of offspring, indicating that women with symmetrical breasts may be preferentially sought after as mates because they offer direct (i.e., high fecundity) and

indirect (i.e., highly fecund daughters) fitness benefits (Møller, Soler, & Thornhill, 1995). Combined, these pieces of evidence suggest that symmetrical breasts indicate high phenotypic quality because they signal the ability to withstand the associated immunosuppressing costs of estrogen (Manning et al., 1997) while larger breasts allow for easier detection of asymmetry, increasing their signaling value.

The nubility hypothesis, proposed by Marlowe (1998), provides a complementary explanation. In this explanation, large breasts provide two key pieces of information. First, large breasts are only present in women who have passed puberty and are thus of reproductive age; prepubescent girls have small, non-protruding breasts (Marlowe, 1998). Second, large breasts serve as a more honest indication of a woman's age than small breasts because their greater weight stretches and slackens fibrous breast tissue over time, leading to more obvious age-related changes in firmness. Thus, large breasts—a signal of sexual maturity (Sugiyama, 2005)—begin to sag and signal declining reproductive value (Barber, 1995). For large breasts, relative to small breasts, the difference between firm breasts and sagging breasts is more pronounced. Hence, men's preference for ample breasts (and women's desire for breasts larger than their current size; Thompson & Tantleff, 1992) can be accounted for by the ability of large breasts to better signal fertility (i.e., sexual maturity) via their size and reproductive value via their firmness.

Body Shape and Size

A woman's body is subjected to what Singh (1993) refers to as a "wide first-pass filter," identifying women who exhibit cues of poor reproductive condition. WHR, for example, is affected by three factors directly relating to a woman's ability to conceive: (1) her hormonal profile, (2) her pregnancy status, and possibly, (3) her ovulatory status. First, a woman's WHR provides information regarding her hormonal profile, indicating whether she is within the reproductive window of her lifespan and, if she is, the ease with which she can conceive. Supporting this point, the WHR of young boys and girls is remarkably similar until puberty, at which time a bimodal distribution emerges with minimal overlap (Marti et al., 1991). In women, the increase in estrogen that accompanies puberty inhibits fat deposition in the abdominal region and stimulates fat deposition in the gluteofemoral region (hips, buttocks, and thighs), generating WHR values that typically fall between 0.67 and 0.80. In men, the increase in testosterone causes the reverse pattern of fat deposition, generating significantly higher WHR values that range from 0.85 to 0.95. At menopause, decreased estrogen levels increase WHR, thereby reducing the disparity between men and women's WHRs. Because sex differences in WHR are manifested most prominently during the reproductive window of a woman's life-span, a low WHR probabilistically indicates that a woman is both post-pubescent and premenopausal (Singh, 1993, 2006; Singh & Singh, 2011).

Furthermore, women with low WHRs have more optimal hormone profiles (i.e., higher estrogen levels; Jasieńska et al., 2004), have fewer irregular menstrual cycles, ovulate more frequently, and have less difficulty conceiving than women with abnormally high WHRs (for relevant citations, see Singh & Singh, 2011). This is further evidenced in women with polycystic ovarian syndrome, a condition marked by impaired estrogen production, who have higher WHRs and experience greater difficulty conceiving and an increased risk of miscarriage (Jakubowicz, Iuorno, Jakubowicz, Roberts, & Nestler, 2002; Singh & Singh, 2011). Lower WHRs also advertise reproductive quality beyond conception: gluteofemoral fat appears to be a special store of neurodevelopmental resources such that women with lower WHRs (greater gluteofemoral fat storage) produce children who score higher on cognitive tests (Lassek & Gaulin, 2008).

Second, as a woman progresses through pregnancy, her WHR increases dramatically (vastly exceeding 1.0), a clear indication that she is currently incapable of conceiving. As copulations with a pregnant woman cannot increase a man's reproductive success, it would be adaptive to find women with very high WHRs to be unattractive. Finally, preliminary evidence suggests that WHR decreases at ovulation (Kirchengast & Gartner, 2002). Thus, a woman's figure might also reveal whether she is at peak cycle fertility; however, these results should be interpreted with caution, as Bleske-Rechek et al. (2011) failed to replicate this effect. Clearly, a bounty of information pertaining to a woman's fertility and reproductive value can be estimated from just a brief glimpse of her WHR.

Research over the past two decades has supported these ultimate explanations for why WHR is associated with women's attractiveness. Women with WHR values that fall at the low end of the typical female range (0.68–0.72) are considered more attractive than women with masculine WHRs (>0.80). In the study that pioneered the investigation of WHR and physical attractiveness, Singh (1993) provided participants with line drawings of women that varied only by weight and WHR. Within each body weight category—underweight (90 lbs.), normal weight (120 lbs.), and overweight (150 lbs.)—were four values of WHR: 0.70, 0.80, 0.90, and 1.0 (see Fig. 7.1). Results indicated that, within each weight class, attractiveness ratings increased as WHR decreased in a linear fashion. N7, a normal weight figure with a WHR of 0.70, was rated as most attractive and was associated with sexiness and good health more so than any other figure.

Singh's (1993) results have been systematically replicated using various methodologies, including line drawings (e.g., Furnham, McClelland, & Omer, 2003; Schmalt, 2006; Singh, 1994a, 1994b, 2004), actual photographs (Henss, 2000; Singh, 1994b; Wilson, Tripp, & Boland, 2005), online advertisements of female escorts (Saad, 2008), archival data from the sixteenth- to eighteenth-century British literature (Singh, Renn, & Singh, 2007), and ancient Indian, Egyptian, Greco-Roman, and African sculptures (Singh, 2002) (for a review, see Singh, 2006). A preference for low WHR has also been demonstrated by evaluating modifications made by plastic surgeons to Singh's original line drawings with the goal of making them more attractive. As expected, the normal weight figure with a WHR of 0.70 (N7) was altered the least (Singh, 2006).

Fig. 7.1 The stimuli used in Singh (1993) represent three body weights—underweight (I), normal weight (II), and overweight (III)—and four levels of WHR. From Singh, D. (1993), "Adaptive significance of female physical attractiveness: Role of waist-to-hip ratio," *Journal of Personality and Social Psychology, 65,* 293–307. Copyright 1993 by the American Psychological Association. Reproduced with permission

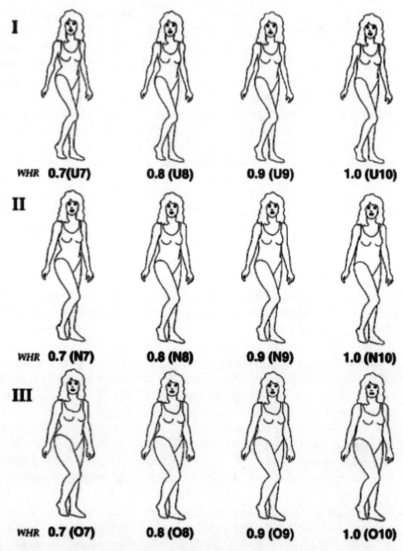

Several studies have shown cross-cultural agreement in the preference for low WHR with participants representing ethnicities from the Azore Islands, Cameroon, Guinea-Bissau, Greece, Indonesia, Kenya, Samoa, Uganda, the United Kingdom, the United States, and New Zealand (Furnham, Moutafi, & Baguma, 2002; Furnham et al., 2003; Singh, 2004; Singh, Dixson, Jessop, Morgan, & Dixson, 2010; Singh & Luis, 1995). Other studies, particularly those involving inhabitants of subsistence-based societies, show a less consistent preference for low WHR (Marlowe & Wetsman, 2001; Wetsman & Marlowe, 1999; Yu & Shepard, 1998) (cf. Sugiyama, 2004). For instance, Wetsman and Marlowe (1999) found that men from a foraging population (Hadza) in Tanzania were not differentially attracted to women with feminine (e.g., 0.70) or masculine (e.g., 0.90) WHRs. These researchers later showed a preference among Hadza men for women with WHRs at or above 0.80 (Marlowe & Wetsman, 2001); however, this result was subsequently shown to be a mere artifact of frontal-view stimuli (Marlowe, Apicella, & Reed, 2005). Unlike stimuli presented in profile, frontal-view stimuli do not account for the protrusion of the buttocks. Marlowe et al. (2005) found that Hadza men prefer a relatively low-profile WHR (more protruding buttocks) and relatively high frontal WHR (thicker waist), whereas the opposite is true for American men. Thus, cross-cultural disparity may be less extreme than originally thought for preferences of *actual* WHRs, where both the width of the waist and the protrusion of the buttocks are taken into account (Marlowe et al., 2005). This cross-cultural evidence indicates that men's preferences for hourglass shapes were not invented by Western media, a point made even clearer by the finding that congenitally blind individuals—who cannot have been inundated with media images of models and celebrities—show a similar preference for women with low WHR when assessing female body shapes through touch (Karremans, Frankenhuis, & Arons, 2010).

Some researchers allege that the preference for low WHR is actually driven by a preference for women with low body weight (Tassinary & Hansen, 1998; Tovée & Cornelissen, 1999). By narrowing the waist, critics argue, abdominal fat is eliminated, decreasing the perceived overall weight of the target stimuli (Tovée & Cornelissen, 1999). The goal of recent research has been to adjudicate between adaptationist (Singh, 1993) and by-product (Tassinary & Hansen, 1998) explanations of WHR preferences by controlling for the effects of BMI. Some researchers have done so statistically (Streeter & McBurney, 2003), others by increasing the thickness of arms and legs in line drawings to compensate for thinner waists (Furnham et al., 2005). In all cases, WHR remains a significant predictor of attractiveness, with assessments peaking at approximately 0.70. A particularly compelling set of studies utilized pre- and post-operational photographs of women who underwent micro-fat grafting surgery (Singh et al., 2010; Singh & Randall, 2007). In this procedure, fat cells are removed from the circumference of the waist and transplanted into the buttocks. Body size thus remains unchanged: Only the *distribution* of fat is altered. For every pair of photographs, men and women judged the postoperative photographs (lower WHR) to be more attractive than the preoperative photographs (higher WHR), a pattern of results that replicated across diverse racial groups (Singh et al., 2010).

Much of the research that tests body *shape* preferences (WHR) also tests body *weight* preferences (BMI) (Faries & Bartholomew, 2012; Furnham et al., 2003; Henss, 1995; Singh, 1993; Sugiyama, 2004). Fairly consistently, WHR and BMI both show robust effects on perceptions of attractiveness; however, debate continues over which is the more influential factor (e.g., Singh, 1993, 2006; Tovée & Cornelissen, 2001; Tovée, Hancock, Mahmoodi, Singleton, & Cornelissen, 2002; Tovée et al., 1999; Tovée, Reinhardt, Emery, & Cornelissen, 1998). Effect sizes produced by BMI are frequently larger than those produced by WHR, leading researchers to conclude that BMI is a greater determinant of female physical attractiveness (e.g., Tovée et al., 1998).

We caution against such an inference. For one, there is little practical value in determining whether BMI or WHR is the more influential determinant of attractiveness when it is already known that both body size and body shape affect attractiveness judgments. There are also several methodological problems in this line of research that limit the ability to draw conclusions from a comparison of effect sizes. First, greater variance accounted for by one factor (e.g., BMI) might simply be the result of stimuli varying more widely on that factor than the other (Singh, personal communication; Streeter & McBurney, 2003). Indeed, the figures used in several studies vary widely in weight (emaciated to obese) but very little in WHR (0.68–0.98; Tovée & Cornelissen, 2001; Tovée et al., 1998). When the effect of WHR is evaluated within an ancestrally valid range of body weights (which eliminates obesity as a category because resources were likely never in surplus), WHR more strongly influences perceptions of attractiveness (Furnham et al., 2002, 2005; Furnham, Tan, & McManus, 1997; Singh, 1993). Likewise, WHR would affect attractiveness judgments to a greater extent if the range of WHR values more accurately represented ancestral conditions, where young women were often pregnant and thus possessing WHRs greater than 1.00 (Strassmann, 1997). Finally, clothing might obscure the view of female targets' WHR more so than their BMI in studies that use images of real women as stimuli (Perilloux, Cloud, & Buss, 2013; Tovée & Cornelissen, 2001; Tovée et al., 1998). Needless to say, if neither WHR nor BMI can be readily assessed, these variables can exert little effect on attractiveness judgments.

Plasticity of Attractiveness Judgments

In spite of mounting evidence that components of physical attractiveness are in large part defined by their health and fertility correlates (for a review, see Sugiyama, 2005), some scholars maintain that standards of beauty are guided by arbitrary dictates of culture (e.g., Wolf, 1991). For instance, in their discussion of changing trends in body size, Voracek and Fisher (2002) diagrammed three women who epitomized female beauty in their respective time periods, each notably thinner than the previous: Hélène Fourment (1636–1638, the wife of Peter Paul Rubens), Marilyn Monroe (1926–1962), and finally supermodel, Eva Herzigova (1973–present). Other examples include research showing a trend toward slenderness for Miss America pageant winners and Playboy centerfolds between the 1960s and 1980s (Garner, Garfinkel, Schwartz, & Thompson, 1980; Mazur, 1986). Fluctuations in ideal body weight (such as those in the examples above) are often used as evidence against evolutionary explanations for attractiveness preferences. These researchers reason that if specific body morphologies are associated with greater reproductive potential, evolution should have shaped attractiveness judgments to be stable across cultures and time periods (e.g., Swami, Gray, et al., 2006).

Such an argument misconstrues the nature of humans' evolved psychology. Universality is expected at the level of the evolved mechanism, *not* at the level of its output (Tooby & Cosmides, 1992). In other words, while the algorithms that underlie attractiveness judgments are predicted to be cross-culturally and cross-generationally stable, the *output* of those algorithms can vary as a function of environmental input. This point is illustrated by the decision rules that underlie trade-offs. When

making decisions to optimize one trait over another—as a given woman rarely possesses indicators of good genes, high fertility, *and* high reproductive value simultaneously—men do not downregulate their preferences for all of the relevant traits. Rather, they systematically adjust certain preferences based on environmental conditions.

For example, in societies where food is scarce or the energetic costs of work are high, a preference for heavy women would direct mating effort toward those who have sufficient fat stores to maintain pregnancy and lactation during times of resource scarcity (Marlowe & Wetsman, 2001). There would be little benefit to mating with women who do not have the fat reserves to support pregnancy, no matter how fit they otherwise appear to be. Consistent with this, studies have demonstrated a preference for overweight women in non-Western samples (Furnham et al., 2002; Sugiyama, 2004; Wetsman & Marlowe, 1999; Yu & Shepard, 1998; but see Singh, 2004). This pattern differs dramatically from the preference for underweight to normal weight women in Western samples (Faries & Bartholomew, 2012; Furnham et al., 2003; Henss, 1995; Schmalt, 2006; Singh, 1993; Singh & Young, 1995; Wilson et al., 2005), where resource streams are so reliable that women can "afford" a lower average body weight. When resources are plenty, women do not need to store excess fat on their bodies to support future pregnancies. As a result, they are able to avoid the negative health outcomes associated with being overweight (e.g., cardiovascular disease; Must et al., 1999). These results demonstrate how environmental circumstances can serve as input to algorithms that generate attractiveness judgments, recalibrating the desired values of various traits based on adaptive trade-offs.

Secondly, environmental input can factor into the attractiveness assessment algorithms of some traits more heavily than others. In particular, preferences for traits that are distally related to fitness consequences might be more permeable to environmental influences than those that are more strongly associated with health and fertility. In the case of BMI and WHR, the results of several studies suggest that the former are more culturally malleable than the latter. In his original study,

Singh (1993) reanalyzed the dimensions of Miss America pageant winners and Playboy centerfolds to assess whether preferences for WHR changed over time as they did for BMI (Garner et al., 1980; Mazur, 1986). Replicating the findings of Garner et al. (1980) and Mazur (1986), Singh found a trend for increased thinness in both groups, but despite this reduction in body size, WHR values remained consistent ranging between 0.68 and 0.72. Freese and Meland (2002) further replicated this finding, showing Miss America pageant winners and Playboy centerfolds to have WHR values that consistently fell within the feminine range over a multi-decade span (despite finding a wider range of WHR values than those calculated by Singh). These results, showing BMI preferences to be less cross-culturally and cross-generationally stable than WHR preferences, do not necessarily imply that the former is less a product of evolution than the latter. Algorithms that underlie judgments of optimal body size (i.e., BMI) may simply be designed to incorporate more environmental input than those that underlie judgments of optimal body shape (i.e., WHR). It is likely that the fitness payoffs associated with various body sizes vary more as a function of environment than those associated with various body shapes, which may be more constant across environments.

A common argument used to support the claim that standards of beauty vary across cultures and time periods is the assertion that Europeans considered plump women to be attractive in the sixteenth and seventeenth centuries. Almost exclusively, the evidence presented to justify this widely held belief contrasts Peter Paul Rubens' (1577–1640) paintings of fat women with present-day idealization of thin women. Swami, Gray, et al. (2006), for example, challenge previous research showing a WHR of 0.70 to be universally attractive, citing as evidence a mean WHR of 0.77 across 30 nude women depicted in paintings by Rubens. We argue that this conclusion is unwarranted for two reasons: (1) An analysis comparing the fatness of women depicted by Rubens and other Baroque artists suggests that Rubens was unusual in his predilection for heavy women (detailed below) and (2) there is nothing special about a

WHR of exactly 0.70. Other than the fact that 0.70 happens to fall at the low end of the distribution of feminine WHR values in many modern cultures, there is no systematic reason to expect this WHR to be more attractive than other feminine WHRs. The key point is simply that because WHR distributions overlap very little between the sexes, WHRs that are more clearly in the female distribution should be perceived as optimally attractive (Singh, personal communication).

One of us (J.M.C.), in collaboration with Singh, empirically tested the validity of the claim that plump women were considered attractive in the Baroque era by assessing the proportion of Baroque artists who shared Rubens' penchant for fat women (Confer & Singh, 2009). If Rubens' paintings represent a sixteenth- and seventeenth-century European ideal of beauty, a significant proportion of Baroque artists should have also portrayed women as heavyset. If, instead, Rubens portrayals of women were atypical for that era, his paintings may simply reflect his personal taste rather than an overall societal trend. To examine this issue, independent judges (23 men, 29 women) compared 30 European paintings from 1500 to 1650 with a classic Rubens painting (*Die drei Grazien*; 1639) to determine whether his contemporaries painted women as fat as or fatter than Rubens did. The WHR of the women in each painting was also measured to assess whether Baroque artists preferred a body shape different from an hourglass figure (Singh, 1993).

Figure 7.2 presents the percentages of paintings depicting women with varying degrees of fatness relative to the women depicted in *Die drei Grazien* (ranging from *definitely less fat* to *definitely more fat*). For each 50-year interval between 1500 and 1650, the majority of artists depicted women as less fat than those in *Die drei Grazien*. These findings indicate that like Picasso's (1881–1973) unusual depictions of the human form, Rubens portrayed atypical characterizations of women for the Baroque era. The fact that the preponderance of Baroque artists did not idealize a female figure as considerably different from the figure preferred today calls into question the most prevalent example for the argument that standards of beauty are culturally defined.

Fig. 7.2 The percentage of paintings by the sixteenth- and seventeenth-century European artists who depicted women with varying degrees of fatness relative to the women depicted in Rubens's classic *Die drei Grazien* (1639)

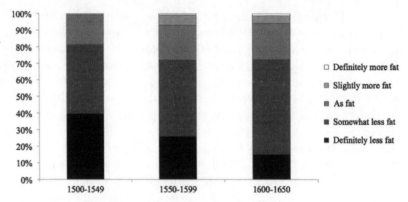

Fig. 7.3 The mean WHR of women depicted in the sixteenth- and seventeenth-century European paintings by Rubens (*right column*) and other contemporary artists (*leftmost three columns*)

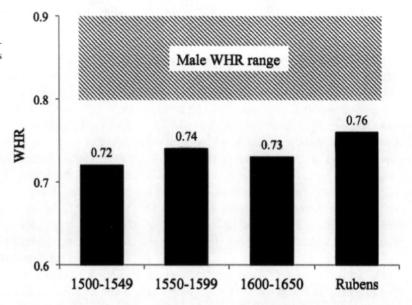

In addition, this analysis corroborates the research described above documenting a preference for women with low WHR. Every portrait selected, including the women depicted in Rubens' paintings, exhibited WHR values within the feminine range (<0.80; see Fig. 7.3). Thus, despite idiosyncrasies with regard to a woman's body size (weight), women were never depicted as possessing a masculine body shape (WHR). The results of this study provide further evidence that preferences for some traits (i.e., BMI) may be more culturally malleable than preferences for others (i.e., WHR). Yet even for BMI, a trait that shows relatively high levels of cultural dependency, the disparity between Baroque ideals of

body weight and those of modern day appears to be less extreme than originally thought.

One final point regarding the plasticity of attractiveness judgments is simply that minor fluctuations in the optimum value of a trait (e.g., 0.68 vs. 0.70 WHR; Freese & Meland, 2002) do not provide *prima facie* evidence against evolutionary explanations of attractiveness. As stated earlier, there is nothing "magical" about a 0.70 WHR (Singh, personal communication). Indeed, there is no evidence to suggest that WHR values of 0.68 or 0.72 are any more or less strongly associated with health and reproductive outcomes than a WHR of 0.70. A much more relevant comparison is between two starkly different WHRs, one from a female distribution and the other from a male distribution. Women with WHRs closer to the male range should be predicted to experience more adverse health and fertility effects than women with WHRs more solidly in the female range. After all, many variations in a woman's health and reproductive status cause dramatic (not minor) fluctuations from a feminine baseline (except for the possibility that WHR slightly decreases at ovulation; Kirchengast & Gartner, 2002). For example, soon after a woman becomes pregnant, her WHR increases not from 0.70 to 0.72, but from 0.70 to well above 1.00. A similar change in WHR occurs after a woman enters menopause (Singh, 1993, 2006; Singh & Singh, 2011). It is no surprise then that extreme fluctuations in WHR influence judgments of attractiveness more strongly than minor fluctuations, and thus small differences in preferred WHRs across time and space should not be considered incompatible with an evolutionary explanation.

Relative Importance of Facial and Bodily Attractiveness

An enormous amount of research has been devoted to identifying the specific features that make some individuals more physically attractive than others (for a review, see Sugiyama, 2005). Some of these features pertain exclusively to facial attractiveness (e.g., averageness; Langlois & Roggman, 1990), others to bodily attractiveness (e.g., WHR; Singh, 1993), while still others pertain to both facial *and* bodily attractiveness (e.g., symmetry; Perrett et al., 1999; Thornhill & Gangestad, 1994). Thus far, we have exclusively discussed bodily components of attractiveness; Chaps 4 and 14 of this volume discuss facial components of attractiveness in detail. Recent research has shifted focus away from identifying subcomponents of facial and bodily attractiveness toward evaluating the face and body as whole units of attractiveness (Confer et al., 2010; Currie & Little, 2009; Jonason, Raulston, & Rotolo, 2012; Lu & Chang, 2012). Of particular interest is the relative importance of the face and body in judgments of overall

attractiveness, and whether the prioritization of facial or bodily attractiveness is dependent upon mating context (short-term vs. long-term mating; Buss & Schmitt, 1993). Confer et al. (2010) argue that the differential efficacy with which the face and body can convey cues of fertility and reproductive value is of key importance in addressing this issue.

As reviewed above both dimensions of a woman's reproductive profile—fertility and reproductive value—can be assessed through a number of her bodily features. The same is also true of a woman's facial features. Fluctuations in facial asymmetry, for example, might indicate whether a woman is ovulating (Scutt & Manning, 1996), an event associated with increased fertility. Other facial features, especially those that are age dependent (e.g., wrinkles and sagginess; Fink, Grammar, & Thornhill, 2001), better indicate a woman's reproductive value. The face and body, therefore, convey cues of fertility and reproductive value with substantial overlap (Thornhill & Grammer, 1999), as evidenced by a high correlation between facial and bodily attractiveness ratings in real women (Peters, Rhodes, & Simmons, 2007). Even with this high degree of overlap, one component—the face or the body—may convey relatively richer information about a woman's reproductive condition than the other (Confer et al., 2010). A woman's body, for example, may better convey information regarding fertility because WHR advertises pregnancy status to a degree that facial features cannot (Singh, 1993). In contrast, information regarding a woman's reproductive value might be gleaned more effectively from her face where age-dependent features (e.g., full lips; Cunningham, 1986) are most densely concentrated and can be easily observed (e.g., wrinkles, Fink et al., 2001).

Although a man's reproductive success seems best served by selecting a maximally fertile mate with maximum residual reproductive value, men typically prioritize cues associated with one dimension over the other. This is because the two dimensions peak at different ages—reproductive value at approximately age 17 and fertility at approximately age 24 (Symons, 1979; Williams,

1975)—necessitating a trade-off between women who are at the pinnacle of fertility and others who are at the pinnacle of reproductive value. One factor that influences the priority men place on each dimension is the intended duration of the mateship (short term vs. long term; Buss & Schmitt, 1993). The reproductive success of men pursuing casual sexual dalliances is more directly affected by a potential mate's current fertility than her future reproductive potential (Buss & Schmitt, 1993). Theoretically then, men should prioritize cues of fertility over cues of reproductive value when evaluating a woman as a short-term mate. The opposite should be true for men evaluating a woman as a long-term mate because transient fluctuations in fertility are less consequential to men's reproductive success, given the probability of future reproductive opportunities. This is indeed what research has shown (Confer et al., 2010; Currie & Little, 2009; Jonason et al., 2012; Lu & Chang, 2012). Confer et al. (2010) presented men with a picture of a woman whose face was occluded by a "face box" and whose body was occluded by a "body box" (see Fig. 7.4). Men were instructed to evaluate the woman behind the boxes as either a short-term mate or long-term mate; however, they could only remove one box—the face box *or* the body box—to inform their decision about whether they would engage in the designated relationship with the occluded individual. As predicted, significantly more men assigned to the short-term condition than the long-term condition chose to remove the body box.[1] In a follow-up analysis, men in this study who were dispositionally oriented more toward short-term mating showed an even stronger preference in the predicted direction, providing additional evidence for the overall pattern. These results are consistent with the hypothesis that indices of fertility, which are of particular importance to men pursuing a short-term relationship, are better assessed through a woman's body than her face.

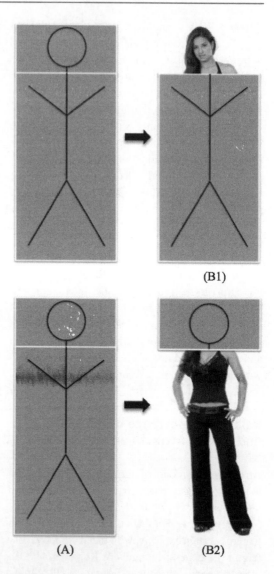

Fig. 7.4 Box choice procedure used in Confer et al. (2010). Column A represents the image that is first presented to participants: an opposite-sex individual occluded by a "face box" and a "body box." Column B represents the image that is presented to participants upon removal of the "face box" (B1) or "body box" (B2). Copyright 2010 by Elsevier

Similar context-dependent shifts in the prioritization of a woman's bodily attractiveness have been demonstrated through a variety of methodologies. Currie and Little (2009) showed ratings of a woman's bodily attractiveness to better predict ratings of her overall attractiveness when she was evaluated as a short-term mate

---

[1] Women's box choice was also evaluated. Significantly more women chose to remove the face box than the body box, and this did not differ based on mating context.

than as a long-term mate. Likewise, Perilloux et al. (2013) found that bodily traits (i.e., BMI) better predicted self-perceptions of overall attractiveness among women who pursue casual sexual opportunities (compared to women who pursue long-term, committed relationships), suggesting that women are, at some level, aware of men's greater prioritization of bodily attractiveness in short-term mating contexts.

Further replicating these results, Jonason et al. (2012) showed men to be more desirous of bodily attractiveness than facial attractiveness in a potential mate, particularly within the context of a short-term relationship. Jonason et al. also conducted a budget allocation study in which participants designed a short-term and long-term mate by distributing a finite number of "mate dollars" across various traits. Men allocated more "mate dollars" to a potential mate's bodily attractiveness than facial attractiveness, an effect that again was particularly strong within the context of a short-term relationship. Because this procedure requires participants to make trade-offs in their mate preferences—each mate dollar spent on one trait reduces the amount left to spend on other traits—it more accurately represents real-life decision-making processes.

Most recently, Lu and Chang (2012) explored how the prioritization of a woman's bodily attractiveness in short-term mating contexts affects lower-level attentional processes. In their first experiment, the authors used a visual dot-probe methodology and found that men attended to the waist/hip region of a woman more frequently than her facial region after a short-term mating prime but attended to both regions with equal frequency after a long-term mating prime. A similar pattern of results was found using a change blindness paradigm. Participants were instructed to indicate whether a feature (e.g., clothing accessories) in the waist/hip region or the facial region differed across two otherwise identical images. Preferential attention to one region was inferred from how quickly participants were able to identify the difference. Results indicated that men noticed a change to a woman's waist/hip region more quickly than a change to her facial region following a short-term mating prime, whereas the opposite was true

following a long-term mating prime. Finally, the authors presented participants with an image of a woman's waist/hip region or an image of a woman's facial region. Participants were instructed to identify the letter that appeared alongside either image, with response latency indicating participants' degree of distraction by the image. Men assigned to the short-term mating condition identified the letter more slowly when it was presented alongside a woman's waist/hip region than alongside her facial region. Men assigned to the long-term mating condition showed no difference in response latency across conditions. Taken together, these results show robust evidence of an adaptive perceptual shift in men to preferentially attend to women's bodies in short-term mating contexts. Remarkably, this increase in the importance of a woman's bodily attractiveness occurs in spite of research showing the face to be a better predictor of overall attractiveness than the body *generally* (i.e., when no differentiation is made between short-term and long-term mating contexts; Furnham & Reeves, 2006; Peters et al., 2007; Riggio, Widaman, Tucker, & Salinas, 1991).

Even as studies that investigate faces and bodies as whole units of attractiveness grow in popularity, much remains to be explored. For instance, does women's assessment of intrasexual (same-sex) competitors coincide with men's greater prioritization of bodily attractiveness in short-term mating contexts? Perhaps a mated woman would preferentially attend to the body of an intrasexual competitor, relative to her face, when the competitor in question approaches her partner with a short-term mating opportunity. Doing so would allow women to better simulate the decision-making processes that influence their partners' desire to take advantage of the mating opportunity and react accordingly. Other research might explore how cross-cultural differences in the availability of short-term mating opportunities predict attitudes regarding the relative importance of a woman's facial and bodily attractiveness. For example, in populations with a female-biased sex ratio, there are more opportunities for men to engage in short-term relationships (Pedersen, 1991; Schmitt, 2005). Consequently, women may experience greater pressure (e.g., in the media, from peers) to enhance their bodily attractiveness in female-biased populations than in male-biased populations. The approach of examining faces and bodies as whole units of attractiveness does not detract from the study of individual traits, but rather complements it by introducing testable hypotheses to fine-tune our understanding of how attractiveness is assessed.

Conclusions

The bodily traits reviewed in this chapter influence judgments of attractiveness precisely *because* they communicate fitness-relevant information. (If other bodily traits—such as the elbow—functioned as honest signals of a woman's health and reproductive status, they too would be sexually arousing.) A high degree of informational overlap is predicted and documented both between and within many bodily traits (Thornhill & Grammer, 1999). For example, fertility can be assessed through the size of a woman's breasts as well as her WHR because both traits are estrogen-dependent (Jasieńska et al., 2004). This redundancy has been argued to increase the reliability of fitness assessments (Johnstone, 1996). By cross-referencing information conveyed by individual traits—each only probabilistically associated with relevant fitness outcomes—one can triangulate on a more accurate fitness assessment.

Some classes of fitness-relevant information (i.e., indices of fertility vs. reproductive value) may be especially pertinent to the reproductive goals of a short-term or long-term relationship. In such cases, we expect men's perceptual systems to bias attention toward traits that most effectively convey that information. A growing body of research supports this basic premise. Men attend to a woman's bodily attractiveness with particular frequency in short-term mating contexts (Confer et al., 2010), where cues of fertility are of greater importance than cues of reproductive value (Buss & Schmitt, 1993). This effect is unlikely to be the result of arbitrary cultural norms or media effects, as even lower-level attentional processes have been shown to manifest the same systematic bias toward bodily attractiveness in short-term relationships (Lu & Chang, 2012). The algorithms that underlie judgments of attractiveness, and the prioritization of various morphological traits, are instead products of evolution. The adaptationist perspective applied throughout this chapter is a powerful theoretical framework that provides functional explanations for why standards of beauty exist in the form that they do. Through a careful consideration of adaptive problems, specialized mechanisms that constitute human mating psychology have been, and will continue to be, discovered.

References

Anderson, P. (1983). The reproductive role of the human breast. *Current Anthropology, 24*, 25–45.

Barber, N. (1995). The evolutionary psychology of physical attractiveness: Sexual selection and human morphology. *Ethology and Sociobiology, 16*, 395–424.

Bleske-Rechek, A., Harris, H. D., Denkinge, K., Webb, R. M., Erickson, L., & Nelson, L. A. (2011). Physical cues of ovulatory status: A failure to replicate enhanced facial attractiveness and reduced waist-to-hip ratio at high fertility. *Evolutionary Psychology, 9*, 336–353.

Buss, D. M. (1989). Sex differences in human mate preferences: Evolutionary hypotheses tested in 37 cultures. *Behavioral & Brain Sciences, 12*, 1–49.

Buss, D. M., & Schmitt, D. P. (1993). Sexual strategies theory: A contextual evolutionary analysis of human mating. *Psychological Review, 100*, 204–232.

Cant, J. (1981). Hypotheses for the evolution of human breasts and buttocks. *American Naturalist, 117*, 199–204.

Confer, J. C., & Singh, D. (2009). *Did Europeans in the sixteenth and seventeenth centuries really idealize fat (Rubenesque) women? Examining the widely held belief*. Poster presented at the 10th annual meeting of the Society for Personality and Social Psychology, Tampa, FL.

Confer, J. C., Perilloux, C., & Buss, D. M. (2010). More than just a pretty face: Men's priority shifts toward bodily attractiveness in short-term versus long-term mating contexts. *Evolution and Human Behavior, 31*, 348–353.

Cunningham, M. (1986). Measuring the physical in physical attractiveness: Quasi-experiments on the sociobiology of female facial beauty. *Journal of Personality and Social Psychology, 50*, 925–935.

Currie, T. E., & Little, A. C. (2009). The relative importance of the face and body in judgments of human physical attractiveness. *Evolution and Human Behavior, 30*, 409–416.

Davey Smith, G., Greenwood, R., Gunnell, D., Sweetnam, P., Yarnell, J., & Elwood, P. (2001). Leg length, insulin resistance, and coronary heart disease risk: The Caerphilly Study. *Journal of Epidemiology and Community Health, 55*, 867–872.

Dixson, B. J., Grimshaw, G. M., Linklater, W. L., & Dixson, A. F. (2011). Eye tracking of men's preferences for female breast size and areola pigmentation. *Archives of Sexual Behavior, 40*, 51–58.

Ellison, P. (1990). Human ovarian function and reproductive ecology: New hypotheses. *American Anthropologist, 92*, 933–952.

Faries, M. D., & Bartholomew, J. B. (2012). The role of body fat in female attractiveness. *Evolution and Human Behavior, 33*, 672–681.

Fessler, D. M. T., Haley, K. J., & Lal, R. D. (2005). Sexual dimorphism in foot length proportionate to stature. *Annals of Human Biology, 32*, 44–59.

Fessler, D. M. T., Stieger, S., Asaridou, S. S., Bahia, U., Cravalho, M., de Barros, P., et al. (2012). Testing a postulated case of intersexual selection in humans: The role of foot size in judgments of physical attractiveness and age. *Evolution and Human Behavior, 33*, 147–164.

Fink, B., Grammar, K., & Thornhill, R. (2001). Human (*Homo sapiens*) facial attractiveness in relation to skin texture and color. *Journal of Comparative Psychology, 115*, 92–99.

Frederick, D. A., Hadji-Michael, M., Furnham, A., & Swami, V. (2010). The influence of leg-to-body ratio (LBR) on judgments of female physical attractiveness: Assessments of computer-generated images varying in LBR. *Body Image, 7*, 51–55.

Freese, J., & Meland, S. (2002). Seven tenths incorrect: Heterogeneity and change in the waist-to-hip ratio of Playboy centerfold models and Miss America pageant winners. *The Journal of Sex Research, 39*, 133–138.

Frisch, R. E. (1987). Body fat, menarche, fitness and fertility. *Human Reproduction, 2*, 521–533.

Furnham, A., Dias, M., & McClelland, A. (1998). The role of body weight, waist-to-hip ratio, and breast size in judgments of female attractiveness. *Sex Roles, 39*, 311–326.

Furnham, A., McClelland, A., & Omer, L. (2003). A cross-cultural comparison of ratings of perceived fecundity and sexual attractiveness as a function of body weight and waist-to-hip ratio. *Psychology, Health, and Medicine, 8*, 219–230.

Furnham, A., Moutafi, J., & Baguma, P. (2002). A cross-cultural study on the role of weight and waist-to-hip ratio on female attractiveness. *Personality and Individual Differences, 32*, 729–745.

Furnham, A., Petrides, K. V., & Constantinides, A. (2005). The effects of body mass index and waist-to-hip ratio of ratings of female attractiveness, fecundity, and health. *Personality and Individual Differences, 38*, 1823–1834.

Furnham, A., & Reeves, E. (2006). The relative influence of facial neoteny and waist-to-hip ratio on judgments

of female attractiveness and fecundity. *Psychology, Health & Medicine, 11*, 129–141.

Furnham, A., & Swami, V. (2007). Perception of female buttocks and breast size in profile. *Social Behavior and Personality, 35*, 1–8.

Furnham, A., Swami, V., & Shah, K. (2006). Body weight, waist-to-hip ratio and breast size correlates of ratings of attractiveness and health. *Personality and Individual Differences, 41*, 443–454.

Furnham, A., Tan, T., & McManus, C. (1997). Waist-to-hip ratio and preferences for body shape: A replication and extension. *Personality and Individual Differences, 22*, 539–549.

Gallop, G. G. (1982). Permanent breast enlargement in human females: A sociobiological analysis. *Journal of Human Evolution, 11*, 597–601.

Gangestad, S. W., & Thornhill, R. (1997). The evolutionary psychology of extra-pair sex: The role of fluctuating asymmetry. *Evolution and Human Behavior, 18*, 69–88.

Garner, D. M., Garfinkel, P. E., Schwartz, D., & Thompson, M. (1980). Cultural expectations of thinness in women. *Psychological Reports, 47*, 183–191.

Gitter, G., Lomranz, J., Saxe, L., & Bar-Tal, Y. (1983). Perceptions of female physique characteristics by American and Israeli students. *The Journal of Social Psychology, 121*, 7–13.

Guéguen, N. (2007). Bust size and hitchhiking: A field study. *Perceptual and Motor Skills, 105*, 1294–1298.

Gunnell, D., May, M., Ben-Shlomo, Y., Yarnell, J., & Davey Smith, G. (2003). Height, leg length, and cancer: The Caerphilly Study. *Nutrition and Cancer, 47*, 34–39.

Gunnell, D., Whitley, E., Upton, M. N., McConnachie, A., Davey Smith, G., & Watt, G. C. M. (2003). Associations of height, leg length and lung function with cardiovascular risk factors in the Midspan Family Study. *Journal of Epidemiology and Community Health, 57*, 141–146.

Henss, R. (1995). Waist-to-hip ratio and attractiveness: Replication and extension. *Personality and Individual Differences, 19*, 479–488.

Henss, R. (2000). Waist-to-hip ratio and female attractiveness. Evidence from photographic stimuli and methodological considerations. *Personality and Individual Differences, 28*, 501–513.

Jakubowicz, D. J., Iuorno, M. J., Jakubowicz, S., Roberts, K. A., & Nestler, J. E. (2002). Effects of Metformin on early pregnancy loss in the polycystic ovary syndrome. *The Journal of Clinical Endocrinology and Metabolism, 87*, 524–529.

Jasieńska, G., Ziomkiewicz, A., Ellison, P. T., Lipson, S. F., & Thune, I. (2004). Large breasts and narrow waists indicate high reproductive potential in women. *Proceedings of the Royal Society of London B, 271*, 1213–1217.

Johnstone, R. A. (1996). Multiple displays in animal communication: 'Backup signals' and 'multiple messages'. *Philosophical Transactions of the Royal Society of London B, 351*, 329–338.

Jonason, P. K., Raulston, T., & Rotolo, A. (2012). More than just a pretty face and a hot body: Multiple cues in mate choice. *The Journal of Social Psychology, 152,* 174–184.

Karremans, J. C., Frankenhuis, W. E., & Arons, S. (2010). Blind men prefer low waist-to-hip ratio. *Evolution and Human Behavior, 31,* 182–186.

Kirchengast, S., & Gartner, M. (2002). Changes in fat distribution (WHR) and body weight across the menstrual cycle. *Collegium Antropologicum, 26,* 47–57.

Langlois, J. H., & Roggman, L. A. (1990). Attractive faces are only average. *Psychological Science, 1,* 115–121.

Lassek, W. D., & Gaulin, S. J. C. (2008). Waist-hip ratio and cognitive ability: Is gluteofemoral fat a privileged store of neurodevelopmental resources? *Evolution and Human Behavior, 29,* 26–34.

Li, N. P., Bailey, J. M., Kenrick, D. T., & Linsenmeier, J. A. W. (2002). The necessities and luxuries of mate preferences: Testing the tradeoffs. *Journal of Personality and Social Psychology, 82,* 947–955.

Lipson, S. F., & Ellison, P. T. (1996). Comparison of salivary steroid profiles in naturally occurring conception and non-conception cycles. *Human Reproduction, 11,* 2090–2096.

Lu, H. J., & Chang, L. (2012). Automatic attention towards the face or body as a function of mating motivation. *Evolutionary Psychology, 10,* 120–135.

Manning, J. T., Scutt, D., Whitehouse, G. H., & Leinster, S. J. (1997). Breast asymmetry and phenotypic quality in women. *Evolution and Human Behavior, 18,* 223–236.

Marlowe, F. (1998). The nubility hypothesis: The human breast as an honest signal of residual reproductive value. *Human Nature, 9,* 263–271.

Marlowe, F., Apicella, C., & Reed, D. (2005). Men's preferences for women's profile waist-to-hip ratio in two societies. *Evolution and Human Behavior, 26,* 458–468.

Marlowe, F., & Wetsman, A. (2001). Preferred waist-to-hip ratio and ecology. *Personality and Individual Differences, 30,* 481–489.

Marti, B., Tuomilehto, J., Soloman, V., Kartovaara, L., Korhonen, H. J., & Pietinen, P. (1991). Body fat distribution in the Finnish population: Environmental determinants and predictive power for cardiovascular risk factor levels. *Journal of Epidemiology and Community Health, 45,* 131–137.

Mazur, A. (1986). U.S. trends in feminine beauty and overadaptation. *Journal of Sex Research, 22,* 281–303.

Møller, A. P., Soler, M., & Thornhill, R. (1995). Breast asymmetry, sexual selection, and human reproductive success. *Ethology and Sociobiology, 16,* 207–219.

Must, A., Spadano, J., Coakley, E. H., Field, A. E., Colditz, G., & Dietz, W. H. (1999). The disease burden associated with overweight and obesity. *The Journal of the American Medical Association, 282,* 1523–1529.

Pedersen, F. A. (1991). Secular trends in human sex ratios: Their influence on individual and family behavior. *Human Nature, 2,* 271–291.

Penke, L., & Asendorpf, J. B. (2008). Beyond global sociosexual orientations: A more differentiated look at sociosexuality and its effects on courtship and romantic relationships. *Journal of Personality and Social Psychology, 95,* 1113–1135.

Perilloux, C., Cloud, J. M., & Buss, D. M. (2013). Women's physical attractiveness and short-term mating strategies. *Personality and Individual Differences, 54,* 490–495.

Perrett, D. I., Burt, M., Penton-Voak, I. S., Lee, K. J., Rowland, D. A., & Edwards, R. (1999). Symmetry and human facial attractiveness. *Evolution and Human Behavior, 20,* 295–307.

Peters, M., Rhodes, G., & Simmons, L. W. (2007). Contributions of the face and body to overall attractiveness. *Animal Behavior, 73,* 937–942.

Riggio, R. E., Widaman, K. F., Tucker, J. S., & Salinas, C. (1991). Beauty is more than skin deep: Components of attractiveness. *Basic and Applied Social Psychology, 12,* 423–439.

Saad, G. (2008). Advertised waist-to-hip ratios of online female escorts: An evolutionary perspective. *International Journal of e-Collaboration, 4,* 40–50.

Schmalt, H. D. (2006). Waist-to-hip ratio and female physical attractiveness: The moderating role of power motivation and the mating context. *Personality and Individual Differences, 41,* 455–465.

Schmitt, D. P. (2005). Sociosexuality from Argentina to Zimbabwe: A 48-nation study of sex, culture, and strategies of human mating. *Behavioral and Brain Sciences, 28,* 247–311.

Scutt, D., & Manning, J. T. (1996). Symmetry and ovulation in women. *Human Reproduction, 11,* 2477–2480.

Singh, D. (1993). Adaptive significance of female physical attractiveness: Role of waist-to-hip ratio. *Journal of Personality and Social Psychology, 65,* 293–307.

Singh, D. (1994a). Ideal female body shape: Role of body weight and waist-to-hip ratio. *International Journal of Eating Disorders, 16,* 283–288.

Singh, D. (1994b). Is thin really beautiful and good? Relationship between waist-to-hip ratio (WHR) and female attractiveness. *Personality and Individual Differences, 16,* 123–132.

Singh, D. (2002). Female mate value at a glance: Relationship of waist-to-hip ratio to health, fecundity, and attractiveness. *Neuroendocrinology Letters, 23,* 81–91.

Singh, D. (2004). Mating strategies of young women: Role of physical attractiveness. *The Journal of Sex Research, 41,* 43–54.

Singh, D. (2006). Universal allure of the hourglass figure: An evolutionary theory of female physical attractiveness. *Clinics in Plastic Surgery, 33,* 359–370.

Singh, D., Dixson, B. J., Jessop, T. S., Morgan, B., & Dixson, A. F. (2010). Cross-cultural consensus for waist-hip ratio and women's attractiveness. *Evolution and Human Behavior, 31,* 176–181.

Singh, D., & Luis, S. (1995). Ethnic and gender consensus for the effect of waist-to-hip ratio on judgment of women's attractiveness. *Human Nature, 6,* 51–65.

Singh, D., & Randall, P. (2007). Beauty is in the eye of the plastic surgeon: Waist-to-hip ratio (WHR) and women's attractiveness. *Personality and Individual Differences, 43*, 329–340.

Singh, D., Renn, P., & Singh, A. (2007). Did the perils of abdominal obesity affect depiction of feminine beauty in the sixteenth to eighteenth century British literature? Exploring the health and beauty link. *Proceedings of the Royal Society B, 274*, 891–894.

Singh, D., & Singh, D. (2011). Shape and significance of feminine beauty: An evolutionary perspective. *Sex Roles, 64*, 723–731.

Singh, D., & Young, R. K. (1995). Body weight, waist-to-hip ratio, breasts, and hips: Role in judgments of female attractiveness and desirability for relationships. *Ethology and Sociobiology, 16*, 483–507.

Sorokowski, P., & Pawlowski, B. (2008). Adaptive preferences for leg length in a potential partner. *Evolution and Human Behavior, 29*, 86–91.

Sorokowski, P., Sorokowska, A., & Mberira, M. (2012). Are preferences for legs length universal? Data from a semi-nomadic Himba population from Namibia. *The Journal of Social Psychology, 152*, 370–378.

Sorokowski, P., Szmajke, A., Sorokowska, A., Cunen, M. B., Fabrykant, M., Zarafshani, K., et al. (2011). Attractiveness of leg length: Report from 27 nations. *Journal of Cross-Cultural Psychology, 42*, 131–139.

Strassmann, B. I. (1997). The biology of menstruation in *Homo sapiens*: Total lifetime menses, fecundity, and nonsynchrony in a natural-fertility population. *Current Anthropology, 38*, 123–129.

Streeter, S. A., & McBurney, D. H. (2003). Waist-to-hip ratio and attractiveness: New evidence and a critique of "a critical test". *Evolution and Human Behavior, 24*, 88–98.

Sugiyama, L. S. (2004). Is beauty in the context-sensitive adaptations of the beholder? Shiwiar use of waist-to-hip ratio in assessments of female mate value. *Evolution and Human Behavior, 25*, 51–62.

Sugiyama, L. S. (2005). Physical attractiveness in adaptationist perspective. In D. M. Buss (Ed.), *The handbook of evolutionary psychology* (pp. 292–343). Hoboken, NJ: Wiley.

Swami, V., Einon, D., & Furnham, A. (2006). The leg-to-body ratio as a human aesthetic criterion. *Body Image, 3*, 317–323.

Swami, V., Einon, D., & Furnham, A. (2007). Cultural significance of leg-to-body ratio preferences? Evidence from Britain and rural Malaysia. *Asian Journal of Social Psychology, 10*, 265–269.

Swami, V., Furnham, A., & Joshi, K. (2008). The influence of skin tone, hair length, and hair colour on ratings of women's physical attractiveness, health, and fertility. *Scandinavian Journal of Psychology, 49*, 429–437.

Swami, V., Gray, M., & Furnham, A. (2006). The female nude in Rubens: Disconfirmatory evidence of the waist-to-hip ratio hypothesis of female physical attractiveness. *Imagination, Cognition, and Personality, 26*, 139–147.

Symons, D. (1979). *The evolution of human sexuality.* New York: Oxford University Press.

Tassinary, L. G., & Hansen, K. A. (1998). A critical test of the waist-to-hip ratio hypothesis of female physical attractiveness. *Psychological Science, 9*, 150–155.

Thompson, J. K., & Tantleff, S. (1992). Female and male ratings of upper torso: Actual, ideal, and stereotypical conceptions. *Journal of Social Behavior and Personality, 7*, 345–354.

Thornhill, R., & Gangestad, S. W. (1994). Human fluctuating asymmetry and sexual behavior. *Psychological Science, 5*, 297–302.

Thornhill, R., & Grammer, K. (1999). The body and face of woman: One ornament that signals quality? *Evolution and Human Behavior, 20*, 105–120.

Tooby, J., & Cosmides, L. (1992). The psychological foundations of culture. In J. Barkow, L. Cosmides, & J. Tooby (Eds.), *The adapted mind: Evolutionary psychology and the generation of culture.* New York: Oxford University Press.

Tovée, M. J., & Cornelissen, P. L. (1999). The mystery of female beauty. *Nature, 399*, 215–216.

Tovée, M. J., & Cornelissen, P. L. (2001). Female and male perceptions of female physical attractiveness in front-view and profile. *British Journal of Psychology, 92*, 391–402.

Tovée, M. J., Hancock, P. J. B., Mahmoodi, S., Singleton, B. R. R., & Cornelissen, P. L. (2002). Human female attractiveness: Waveform analysis of body shape. *Proceedings of the Royal Society of London B, 269*, 2205–2213.

Tovée, M. J., Maisey, D. S., Emery, J. L., & Cornelissen, P. L. (1999). Visual cues to female sexual attractiveness. *Proceedings of the Royal Society of London B, 266*, 211–218.

Tovée, M. J., Reinhardt, S., Emery, J. L., & Cornelissen, P. L. (1998). Optimum body-mass index and maximum sexual attractiveness. *The Lancet, 352*, 548.

Venners, S. A., Liu, X., Perry, M. J., Korrick, S. A., Li, Z., Yang, F., et al. (2006). Urinary estrogen and progesterone metabolite concentrations in menstrual cycles of fertile women with non-conception, early pregnancy loss or clinical pregnancy. *Human Reproduction, 21*, 2272–2280.

Voracek, M., & Fisher, M. L. (2002). Shapely centerfolds? Temporal change in body measures: Trend analysis. *British Medical Journal, 325*, 1447–1448.

Voracek, M., Fisher, M. L., Rupp, B., Lucas, D., & Fessler, D. M. T. (2007). Sex differences in relative foot length and perceived attractiveness of female feet: Relationships among anthropometry, physique, and preference ratings. *Perceptual and Motor Skills, 104*, 1123–1138.

Wetsman, A., & Marlowe, F. (1999). How universal are preferences for female waist-to-hip ratios? Evidence from the Hadza of Tanzania. *Evolution and Human Behavior, 20*, 219–228.

Williams, G. C. (1975). *Sex and evolution*. Princeton, NJ: Princeton University Press.

Wilson, J. M. B., Tripp, D. A., & Boland, F. J. (2005). The relative contributions of waist-to-hip ratio and body mass index to judgments of attractiveness. *Sexualities, Evolution, and Gender, 7*, 245–267.

Wolf, N. (1991). *The beauty myth: How images of female beauty are used against women*. New York: William Morrow.

Yu, D. W., & Shepard, G. H. (1998). Is beauty in the eye of the beholder? *Nature, 396*, 321–322.

Zahavi, A. (1975). Mate selection: A selection for a handicap. *Journal of Theoretical Biology, 53*, 205–214.

Zelazniewicz, A. M., & Pawlowski, B. (2011). Female breast size attractiveness for men as a function of sociosexual orientation (restricted vs. unrestricted). *Archives of Sexual Behavior, 40*, 1129–1135.

Social and Environmental Conditions Intensifying Male Competition for Resources, Status, and Mates Lead to Increased Male Mortality

8

Daniel J. Kruger

Introduction

Being male is the single most prominent demographic risk factor for early mortality in technologically advanced societies (Kruger & Nesse, 2006a). In previous decades, the women's health movement has made considerable advances in improving health outcomes by promoting the notion that men and women differ in physiology and in health promotion needs. Perhaps surprisingly, there is no complementary movement so substantial in scope promoting the examination of health issues specific to men. Men's health advocates and researchers may be gaining momentum in recent years, yet we still see pleas echoing the notion that men's health has not yet reached a critical mass as a topic of systematic research. A recent editorial in a leading public health journal calls for a better comprehension of men's health and health disparities, emphasizing the lack of a comprehensive framework for understanding men's health issues (Treadwell & Young, 2013). The authors suggest that social structure and differential access to health care services may be responsible for differential health outcomes between women and men, and list "social and systemic forces" (p. 5) such as incarceration, poverty,

erosion of public education, labor market collapse, and food insecurity that jeopardize the health of some men more than others. Notably, the factors influencing men's health disparities are considered extrinsic to the men themselves. The framework the authors wish for "will consider what is known to matter, the substance of social norms...this awareness will be inscribed and fully articulated in a report that examines men and where jeopardy enters their lives" (Treadwell & Young, 2013, p. 5). This line of thinking may have impeded the progress of the men's health movement, compiling a hodgepodge collection of risk factors driven by social expectations. In fact, there already exists a systematic and comprehensive theoretical framework explaining why men take more risks than women do, and why some men take more risks than others do. It even goes beyond purely behavioral differences to address those related to physiology. This framework underlies the study of all other forms of life, yet somehow eludes most of those who research our own species.

Evolution by natural and sexual selection is the most powerful explanatory framework in the life sciences and provides a powerful foundation for understanding sexual psychology and behavior. The processes of sexual selection, intrasexual competition and intersexual selection, have shaped sex differences in human physiology, psychology, and behavior. Men have higher variation and skew in reproductive success compared to women, and this selected for higher

8

D.J. Kruger (✉)
Institute for Social Research, University of Michigan, Ann Arbor, MI 48109, USA
e-mail: kruger@umich.edu

V.A. Weekes-Shackelford and T.K. Shackelford (eds.), *Evolutionary Perspectives on Human Sexual Psychology and Behavior*, Evolutionary Psychology, DOI 10.1007/978-1-4939-0314-6_8, © Springer Science+Business Media New York 2014

investments in mating effort and competition relative to somatic efforts of building and maintaining one's body, compared to investments by women. Men have both physiological and behavioral systems designed to focus more so on competition at the expense of longevity compared to women, and this leads to higher male mortality rates from behavioral, behaviorally mediated, and other internal causes of death. Sex differences in mortality are influenced by a complex interaction of genetic heritage and developmental environment, incorporating genetic, physiological, psychological, social, and environmental factors. The increasing content and complexity of these research areas and growing sophistication of research methods have led researchers to adopt increasing degrees of specialization. This chapter uses the foundation of evolutionary life history theory to integrate topical areas and research techniques and reduce disciplinary and subdisciplinary fragmentation in the understanding of human patterns of risky behavior and mortality.

Sexual Reproduction

Differences in average male and female life expectancies were recognized as early as 1662 (Lopez & Ruzicka, 1983). Sex differences are shaped by sexual selection, including sex differences in human psychology and behavior. Darwin (1871) noted that mammalian males are significantly more physically aggressive than females and considered male intrasexual competition to be the best explanation for why this was the case. Ornaments such as the peacock's tail and armaments such as a deer's antlers are costly to produce, but they confer advantages in intersexual selection and intrasexual competition. More than a century after Darwin's insights, many explanations of sex differences in human aggression and mortality are still based only on proximate factors (e.g., Rogers, Hummer, & Nam, 2000). Yet, there has also been a revival of the recognition that sex differences emerge from an interaction of characteristics shaped by sexual selection and environmental conditions

(e.g., Daly & Wilson, 1978). There are multiple levels of influences responsible for differences between men and women, including psychological and social factors, all of which occur in the fundamental context of the basic biological properties of sex and sexual reproduction. Continuous reproduction sustains all life on earth. The original form of reproduction was likely asexual, where some portion of the organism broke off to create a genetic clone (Boyden, 1954). This form of reproduction is still with us and within us; all of the cells in our bodies created after fertilization are products of asexual reproduction.

Sexual reproduction was a major evolutionary innovation; it involves the combination of genetic material with another compatible organism. This process results in considerably more genetic variation than would occur from asexual reproduction and mutation. Most mutations are either neutral or harmful to reproductive success, and sexual reproduction may have initially been successful because sexual recombination of genes can purge harmful mutations, which may accumulate in a cloned lineage. Although sexual reproduction reduces the proportion of a parent's genes represented in offspring compared to asexual cloning, the increased genetic variability facilitates adaptation to challenges from both changes in environmental conditions (Williams, 1975) and the coevolutionary arms race with other species, including threats from predators and parasites (Williams, 1975), competition from other species (Bell, 1982), countering the adaptations of prey to predation, and starvation (Bell, 1982).

Sexual reproduction involves the combination of gametes (sex cells) from compatible organisms. Gametes have two basic functions, to find compatible gametes to pair with and to invest their genetic material and cytoplasm in a fertilized zygote. The more somatic investment of cytoplasm a parent makes in a gamete, the greater the viability of the resulting zygote. Although smaller gametes are less physiologically costly to produce, zygotes created by pairs of smaller gametes are less viable than those created by larger gametes. However, smaller gametes will out-compete medium-sized gametes when large gametes with sufficient cytoplasm to produce a more viable zygote are available, because they are less costly to produce and greater production increases the chance of fertilization. These contrasting selection pressures create anisogamy, the divergence in size of gametes (Bulmer & Parker, 2002). By definition, parents who invest more cytoplasm and create larger gametes are females and parents that invest less cytoplasm and create smaller gametes are males.

These fundamental biological properties of sex are the foundation for sex differences at higher levels of complexity. Starting from the most basic organisms, female parental investment is usually greater than male parental investment (Bateman, 1948). As they have greater obligatory investment, females are generally more selective in choosing mating partners than males, and males exert more effort in mating competition for reproductive access to females (Trivers, 1972). Male competition can include direct physical fights for social rank and/or control of territories, as well as developing elaborate traits and displays that females prefer in their mates (Darwin, 1871). Sex differences in parental investment, and the resulting difference in the intensity of mating competition, are responsible for other sexually dimorphic characteristics. This fact is reinforced by the handful of species where males make a greater parental contribution to females, such as in seahorses, the Mormon cricket, and certain birds. In these species, the females are the ones that compete for males and have brighter coloration (Berglund & Rosenqvist, 2003). Sexual selection explains some sex differences in human psychology and behavioral tendencies, including tendencies for risk-taking, competitiveness, and sensitivity to position in social hierarchies that are stronger in men than in women (Cronin, 1991).

Senescence

We are the products of nearly four billion years of natural and sexual selection. Yet our lifespans are very brief on geological timescales and even short compared to some other species. Why has such a long period of evolution not endowed us with capabilities to persist indefinitely? Natural selection maximizes survival of genes rather than the survival of individuals (Williams, 1957), and building and maintaining our bodies is in the service of reproduction—promoting the survival of genes. Genes that benefit their own survival earlier in the host individual's lifespan will spread faster than genes whose self-benefits occur later because unavoidable sources of mortality will reduce the cohort size, and thus potential selection pressure, as the host organisms age (Medawar, 1952). Many genes have multiple (pleiotropic) effects, and genes with early benefits but later costs will be selected for because younger individuals have a higher reproductive value (Williams, 1957). Again, selection pressure was greater at younger ages because few people survived to old age in ancestral environments. The resulting decline of physiological function over a lifespan is known as senescence (Williams, 1957).

Sex and Life History Trade-Offs

Life history theory describes how organisms allocate effort towards specific aspects of survival and reproduction across the lifespan (Roff, 1992; Stearns, 1992). Organisms face trade-offs between different possible allocations of investment because the total amount of effort is limited. Organisms must make trade-offs between somatic effort and reproductive effort, between mating effort and parenting effort, between current and future reproduction, and between the quantity of offspring produced and the amount invested in each offspring. These inherent trade-offs in investment are influenced by the environmental conditions in which organisms live. Individual physiological and behavioral strategies generally reflect adaptations to developmental conditions (for reviews, see Roff, 1992; Stearns, 1992).

Early in an organisms' lifespan, the somatic effort of building and maintaining a body takes precedence over reproduction. Once an organism reaches sexual maturity, a greater portion of the organisms' resources becomes devoted to reproduction. For some species, reproductive effort is predominantly mating effort; however, many animal species also exhibit parental care of offspring. Humans have a substantially longer developmental period than other primates do (Low, 1998), which is associated with the very large somatic investment in human brain development. The large investment in mental functioning may have enabled the ecological dominance attained by our hominid ancestors, which reduced predation pressure (Alexander, 1979).

Males have higher variance in reproductive success compared to females, and male reproductive success may benefit more from greater investments in reproductive competition compared to reproductive success for females. The greater variation and skew in male reproductive success selected for higher investments in mating effort and competition relative to somatic effort (building and maintaining one's body) promoting longevity than for females. Increased male mortality from sexual competition early in life would also decrease selection against senescence in males relative to females. On average, men have greater height and weight, more upper-body strength, higher metabolic rates, higher juvenile mortality, and later sexual maturity compared to women (see Miller, 1998).

Mechanisms Underlying Mortality Differences

The male biases towards reproduction at the expense of somatic effort, growth at the expense of maintenance, and mating at the expense of parenting result in physiological and behavioral strategies are both riskier than those of women's strategies. Males' riskier strategies will lead to higher levels of mortality from behavioral and most non-behavioral causes across the lifespan. There are several levels of mechanisms serving as proximate causes of differences in mortality rates between men and women, ranging in scale from microscopic to macroeconomic.

Many are familiar with the chromosomal differences between men and women, where men have an "incomplete set" of sex chromosomes, XY compared to XX for women. Because men have only one full X chromosome, deleterious recessive genes on their X chromosome are more likely to be expressed because there are no corresponding genes on a paired chromosome as there are for XX females (Smith & Warner, 1989). Many people may believe that these chromosomal differences are what ultimately defines male and female (rather than differences in gametic investment) and drives differences between men and women. However, among birds and many other animal species, males are the homogametic sex (e.g., ZZ), whereas while females are the heterogametic sex (e.g., ZW). In birds, the Z chromosome is larger and has more genes than the W, mimicking the relationship between the X and Y chromosomes in humans (Smith, Roeszler, Hudson, & Sinclair, 2007). Thus, differences in mortality between males and females across species cannot be due solely to a truncated set of genes.

Males also have a set of increased physiological susceptibilities that reflect their greater bias towards reproductive effort compared to females, who allocate relatively more to somatic maintenance. Men are more vulnerable to infectious diseases, injuries, physical challenges, degenerative diseases, and stress (Kraemer, 2000). Some of these differences stem from divergence between male and female structural, physiological, endocrine, and immunological systems (Hazzard, 1990). Men's larger body sizes are more costly physiologically (Owens, 2002) and men typically have greater loads of parasites (Moore & Wilson, 2002). Men generally have much higher levels of testosterone than women do, and testosterone has deleterious effects on immune system functioning (Hazzard, 1990; Owens, 2002). Men also lack the beneficial effects of female sex hormones, such as estrogen (Lawlor, Ebrahim, & Smith, 2001). Increased dietary fat consumption has led to epidemic cardiovascular disease in Western nations in recent decades. This has disproportionately affected men in part because they are more susceptible to atherosclerosis at any given level of fat intake (Lawlor et al., 2001).

In the medical and public health literatures, mortality related to the factors above is typically classified as "internal" causes of death. In addition to these internal causes of death, external causes of death resulting from behavior also contribute to the human sex differential in mortality. Some of these are immediate, such as mortality from accidents and violence. Across human history, potentially lethal violence in conflicts both within and between groups was a feature of male mating competition (Chagnon, 1988). Accidental deaths rank fourth in mortality causes for men and seventh for women in the USA (Anderson, 2001). Men's substantially higher rate of accidents is typically attributed to poor motor and cognitive regulation by those focusing on proximate causes (e.g., Kraemer, 2000). Men have a higher rate of motor vehicle mortality even when controlling for driving distances (Jonah, 1986). Men tend to be more likely to work in hazardous occupations (Hazzard, 1986) and have higher suicide rates than women (McClure, 2000). Males also have considerably higher rates of violent behaviors (Daly & Wilson, 1997) as well as consumption of alcohol, tobacco, and other drugs (Kraemer, 2000). Sex differences for such behaviorally moderated internal causes, such as the consequences of smoking tobacco, peak in mid-to-late adulthood, consistent with the lag in the impact of health-related behaviors on mortality (Kruger & Nesse, 2004, 2006a).

Sex differences in risk-taking behavior may also be a product of specific selection pressures for women. Child survival is threatened more by maternal than paternal death, so more cautious behavioral tendencies may have protected women's reproductive success (Campbell, 1999). Social psychologists have proposed that women respond to threats by tending and befriending in order to cultivate strong social bonds and protect the vulnerable, in contrast to the male-biased "fight or flight" response (Taylor

et al., 2000). This argument is also based on sex differences in parental investment. The relative roles of male risk-taking and female risk aversion are debatable (Campbell, 1999); though considering differential selection pressures on women and men will enable a more holistic understanding of sex differences in behavior and mortality patterns.

Modern evolutionists recognize the "nature vs. nurture" debate as presenting a false dichotomy. Our developmental processes are a complex interaction between the evolutionary heritage represented in our genes and the environmental conditions that we live in. Risky male behavior is likely encouraged by social norms encouraging boys to be tough and adventurous and discouraging the expression of feelings such as anxiety and shame (Kindlon & Thompson, 1999; Kraemer, 2000). Social norms expecting the inverse from girls and raising expectations for nurturing behavior would also contribute to divergence in behaviors. Thus, some environmental conditions exacerbate higher mortality risk for males.

Other social factors have more complex or inverse effects. Preferences for male offspring in some cultures lead to higher mortality rates for females in infancy and childhood from both infanticide and neglect (Hrdy, 1999; Rahaman, Aziz, Munshi, Patwari, & Rahman, 1982). In 1979, the Chinese government implemented the so-called single-child law to limit population growth. Urban residents were allowed one child and rural residents were allowed a second child after 5 years, but generally only if the firstborn child was a female (Hesketh, Lu, & Xing, 2005). Wealthy Chinese could also give birth internationally; children of these births are not counted towards the quota. In traditional Chinese culture, sons ensure the well-being of their elderly parents, whereas daughters live with their husband's family. Family names are perpetuated through the patriline, resulting in general preferences for sons over daughters (Hesketh et al., 2005). Although illegal, sex-specific abortions increased after population control was implemented (Chan, Blyth, & Chan, 2006), and the ratio of males to females at birth increased from 1.08 in 1982 to 1.11 in 1990 and to 1.17 in 2000 (Wei, 2007). Higher rates of female infant mortality also contributed to a surplus of men, especially in rural areas where the ratio reaches 1.30 (Ding & Hesketh, 2006; Zhu, Lu, & Hesketh, 2009).

Sex Differences in Mortality Across the Life Course Follow the Intensity of Mating Competition

Being male is associated with higher mortality risk across the entire human life course. This trend is consistent even before birth, as miscarriage rates are higher for male pregnancies than for female pregnancies (MacDorman, Hoyert, Martin, Munson, & Hamilton, 2007). This may be related to the greater extraction of maternal resources by male fetuses compared to females, which also leads to greater risks of premature labor. At just over a year in age, boys are generally more assertive than girls are (Goldberg & Lewis, 1969) and between 2 and 4 years of age are more aggressive and destructive towards people and objects than girls are (Koot & Verhulst, 1991). Rough and tumble forms of play such as chasing, capturing, wrestling, and restraining are three to six times more frequent in boys than in girls (DiPietro, 1981). This type of play may be a mechanism for establishing social dominance, considered more important by boys than by girls (Jarvinen & Nicholls, 1996). Such sex differences in childhood behavior may reflect preparation for the male status contests of adolescence (Campbell, 2005). The dominance hierarchies that emerge by 6 years of age predict social rank at age 15 (Weisfeld, 1999).

Tendencies for risky behaviors peak with sexual maturity, consistent with the notion that the risky behavioral strategies of young males were selected for because they facilitate mating competition (Wilson & Daly, 1993). Male mating effort may also peak in young adulthood in part because young men may not yet have a trade-off with parenting effort, as they have no partners or offspring to invest in (Hill & Kaplan, 1999). Returns on mating effort may also be relatively

higher because young men may not have committed their resources to partners or offspring, and are thus more attractive to potential partners (Hill & Kaplan, 1999). Males may also have greater returns on mating effort, especially for brief sexual relationships, because of the observable physiological correlates of senescence that increase with age. Younger men fathered most offspring resulting from extra-pair sexual affairs among Ache foragers, whereas older men tended to father most of their offspring within long-term relationships (Hill & Hurtado, 1996).

The physical transformation to adulthood, marking the life history transition from the somatic effort of building and maintaining the body towards reproductive effort, is initiated by a steady rise in adrenal androgens. The male reproductive neuroendocrine system acts as a negative feedback loop. If the hypothalamus detects testosterone or estradiol in the bloodstream during childhood, it shuts off production of gonadotropin-releasing hormone to curtail production of testosterone and estradiol (Bribiescas, 2006). By ages 12 and 13, the hypothalamus becomes more tolerant of male sex hormones, enabling adrenarche. Testosterone and estradiol help regulate the allocation of body tissue to energy-storing fat and lean muscle tissue (Bribiescas, 2001). The increasing proportions of lean muscle tissue signals the allocation of energy towards reproductive effort.

Testosterone levels are associated with the intensity of male competition, rising when men anticipate athletic and social status challenges (Booth, Shelley, Mazur, Tharp, & Kittok, 1989; Cohen, Nisbett, Bowdle, & Schwarz, 1996; Gladue, Boechler, & McCaul, 1989). Testosterone levels are associated with social dominance in adolescent boys (Schaal, Tremblay, Soussignan, & Susman, 1996). Production of testosterone is physiologically costly because of its detrimental impact on other somatic systems, including the immune and digestive systems (Folstad & Karter, 1992). Thus, there is a trade-off between reproductive and somatic effort in regulating testosterone levels and male secondary sexual characteristics.

These features, such as prominent brow ridges and large jaws, are dependent on testosterone levels and difficult to fake. Highly masculine features signal a good match between the genotype and developmental environment, as well as a stable developmental trajectory free of debilitating injury or disease. Women use these features to evaluate prospective mates (Zahavi, 1975) and having highly masculine features is associated with male reproductive success across species (see Andersson, 1994).

The degree of male facial masculinity is related to both perceptions of social dominance (Berry & Brownlow, 1989; McArthur & Apatow, 1983) and actual social status (Mazur, Mazur, & Keating, 1984; Mueller & Mazur, 1997). Men with higher facial masculinity become sexually active at younger ages (Mazur, Halpern, & Udry, 1994). People are aware of the relationship between males with high testosterone features and high mating effort reproductive strategies; they associate highly masculine male faces with riskier and more competitive behavioral strategies, greater mating competition, and lesser parental investment in comparison with less masculine faces (Kruger, 2006). Consistent with these accurate perceptions, women prefer men with more masculine faces for sexual affairs, but they prefer men with more feminine faces for marriage (Kruger, 2006). These preferences follow the type of investment, genetic and paternal care, respectively, which is the most important for each type of relationship. Highly masculine men who have higher mate value because of social dominance and/or physiological quality may have higher returns on mating effort and thus would invest relatively less effort to long-term relationships and parenting.

As indicated above, mating and mortality patterns are interrelated (Hill & Hurtado, 1996), and are likely mediated by adrenal androgens such as testosterone. High testosterone levels are associated with higher rates of infidelity, violence, and divorce in men (Booth & Dabbs, 1993). Male testosterone levels fall when men marry (Mazur & Michalek, 1998) and when they engage in substantial infant care (Gettler, McDade, Feranil, & Kuzawa, 2011), reflecting the life history shift from mating to parenting. When a man's marriage ends in divorce, his testosterone levels increase (Mazur & Michalek, 1998). In industrialized countries, the male testosterone peak coincides with peaks in male mortality from behavioral causes, including intentional violence and accidents (Kruger & Nesse, 2004, 2006a). Sex differences in mortality peak in early adulthood from behavioral causes and decline rapidly afterwards. Male testosterone levels peak just after age 20 in industrialized countries, declining gradually until more rapid drops after age 40 (Mazur & Michalek, 1998). Sex differences in mortality rates follow this trend, although sex differences in suicide rates rise dramatically after age 65 (Kruger & Nesse, 2004, 2006). Sex differences in mortality from behaviorally moderated internal causes peak in mid-to-late adulthood in industrialized countries, consistent with the delayed impact of health-related behaviors on mortality (Kruger & Nesse, 2004, 2006a).

External causes of death account for 35 % of excess male life years lost (beyond female mortality rates), including non-automobile accidents (10 %), suicide and auto-accidents (both 9 %), and homicide (7 %; Kruger & Nesse, 2004). Internal causes of death are both the largest source of mortality and life years lost from excess male mortality during middle to late adulthood. Cardiovascular disease accounts for about one-quarter of excess male life years lost, followed by cancer (malignant neoplasms, 8 %), liver disease and cirrhosis 3 %, congenital abnormalities 2 %, and 1 % each for stroke (cerebrovascular disease), pneumonia and influenza, and diabetes mellitus (Kruger & Nesse, 2004).

Historical Changes Affecting Sex Differences in Mortality

Life expectancies are very high and mortality rates are very low in modern technologically advanced societies compared to those in the environments of recent human ancestors. The ecological dominance achieved by hunter-gatherers reduced mortality from predation (Alexander, 1979). Mortality from infectious diseases rose with the origins of agriculture and the growing settled populations it enabled (Diamond, 1997). Historical records show that in the late Middle Ages, British men had lower life expectancies than women (Hollingsworth, 1957). Modern sanitation, public health measures, and other features of scientific medicine such as vaccination and antibiotics have dramatically reduced infectious disease mortality (Lopez, 1998). Once the leading cause of death (Diamond, 1997), infectious diseases have largely given way to lifestyle factors and novel mortality risks from advanced technology. Mortality from childbirth is still substantial (UNICEF, 2003), yet rates have declined an order of magnitude in modernized countries over the past century (Guyer, Freedman, Strobino, & Sondik, 2000), reducing the mortality risk of young adult women.

The fatal effects of consuming excess dietary fats, tobacco, alcohol, and other drugs are more pronounced in men, as are mortality risks from weapons, automobiles, and other machinery. The increase in dietary fat consumption in industrialized countries led to the male-biased heart disease epidemic, not so much from greater male fat intake, but from higher male susceptibility to atherosclerosis at any given level of fat intake (Lawlor et al., 2001). Consistent with these trends, the gap between male and female mortality rates has steadily increased in developed nations in the last century (Lopez, 1998; Zhang, Sasaki, & Kesteloot, 1995). Most recently, the sex differences in mortality rates for lung cancer and stroke are becoming less pronounced because of decreases in male smoking rates (Lopez, 1998) and increases in female smoking rates (Pampel, 2002).

In non-industrialized populations, male testosterone levels do not decline as rapidly in later adulthood (Ellison et al., 2002), reflecting differences in life history patterns. For example, the forest dwelling Ache of Paraguay had a flexible marital system allowing for easy remarriage and most adult women had children by several different fathers. Women evaluated mates during organized club fighting and new partnerships would often begin after these fights (Hill & Hurtado, 1996). Understandably, sex differences in mortality remained high throughout adulthood (Kruger & Nesse, 2006a). Before contact with modernized populations, homicide accounted for about half of all Ache deaths. Illness and disease (mostly gastrointestinal) accounted for 25 % of all deaths and accidents accounted for 12 % of deaths. Cardiovascular disease, the most prominent cause of adult mortality in industrialized countries, was notably absent (Hill & Hurtado, 1996).

These patterns indicate that sex differences in mortality rates are not just an artifact of modernity, although the sources of these sex differences have shifted along with the general reduction of behavioral (or external) causes of mortality and the increase in internal causes related to features of modern lifestyles. Foragers commonly use opportunistic raiding and ambushes more so than formally organized battles (Ember, 1978; Keeley, 1996). The functions of these conflicts include retaliation for previous killings, elevation of personal prestige, and the acquisition of resources and women. Yanomamo men gain higher social status and more wives by killing other men, about 40 % of Yanomamo males have killed other men (Chagnon, 1988). Archeological research shows that a much higher proportion of individuals died from violence in ancient than modern societies (e.g., Schulting, 2006).

Contrary to contemporary depictions in modern media, contact with modern societies typically decreases the frequency of warfare in tribal groups (Keeley, 1996). Half a thousand individuals died violently in a single incident around 1325 CE in the American Dakotas, notably none of the remains found were of young women (Keeley, 1996).

Phylogenetic Comparisons

Tracing phylogenetic patterns of behaviors helps reconstruct evolutionary origins and histories of attributes (Tinbergen, 1963). Comparisons across species document the relationships between reproductive systems and strategies, the intensity of male mating competition, and the sex differences in mortality rates. Trade-offs that increase male reproductive success even at the expense of longevity (Møller, Christe, & Lux, 1999) lead to shorter average lifespans across most animal species (Hazzard, 1990). There is also variation in the magnitude in sex differences in mortality, as reproductive patterns influence the intensity of sexual selection for each sex.

Polygyny is a common mating system in mammals, because of the relative male specialization in mating effort and female specialization in infant care and nutritional provisioning (Low, 2003, 2007; Reichard & Boesch, 2003). In highly polygynous species, a few males produce most of the offspring, creating powerful selection for traits that lead to success in mating competition. The degree of polygyny, related to the degree of inequality in male reproductive success, drives sex differences in physiology and behavior, including traits that are also detrimental to the health and longevity of high proportions of individuals (Kirkwood & Rose, 1991; Stearns, 1992; Williams, 1957). The intensity of male competition in highly polygynous species results in riskier patterns of male behavior (Plavcan, 2000; Plavcan & van Schaik, 1997; Plavcan, van Schaik, & Kappeler, 1995), larger sizes and more bodily armor in males (Promislow, 1992), higher male mortality rates (Leutenegger & Kelly, 1977), and shorter lifespans compared to females (Clutton-Brock & Isvaran, 2007). The gap in longevity between the sexes is predominantly for polygynous species across vertebrates (Clutton-Brock & Isvaran, 2007).

Elephant seals are a common example of a highly polygynous mammal species. Male elephant seal reproductive success is highly skewed, as males compete for control of harems of about 30 females. The vast majority of matings are by males who control these harems (Harvey & Clutton-Brock, 1985). Male development takes twice as long as female development, males reach three to four times the size of females, and 80 % of males die before reproducing (Harvey & Clutton-Brock, 1985). All of these features demonstrate the powerful effects of intense mating competition; the variance in male lifetime reproductive success is over four times that of females (Le Boeuf & Reiter, 1988). New Zealand fur seals have a more moderate degree of polygyny. Some males compete to control territories where they monopolize mates, whereas other males are not territorial. Territorial males are more aggressive in interactions with other males, have more matings with females, have higher testosterone levels, and have increased parasite burden compared to non-territorial males (Negro, Caudron, Dubois, Delahaut, & Gemmell, 2010).

Humans have a moderate degree of polygyny, below the average among primates, though the vast majority of cultures (84 % of those documented by anthropologists) allow for polygyny (Ember, Ember, & Low, 2007) and the variation in male reproductive success is substantially higher than in female reproductive success. Mating competition is a potent selection force in humans because a few males are responsible for a disproportionately high number of matings (Betzig, 1986). Women are on average 80 % as large as men (Clutton-Brock, 1985), and this physiological dimorphism is directly related to the level of male mating competition (see Bribiescas, 2006).

Patterns of mating behavior among the species that are our closest living relatives are informative in understanding mating-related behavior in humans. Across most primates, males compete to gain access to desirable mates, making displays of status, establishing territorial dominance through loud warning calls, provisioning resources, demonstrating strength, and fighting with other males (Buss, 2005). Females favor males with abundant access to resources and phenotypic cues of gene quality as mating partners (Buss & Schmitt, 1993; Gangestad & Thornhill, 1997; Lancaster, 1989). There is also considerable variation in behaviors related to mating dynamics among primates.

Males in some species may actively avoid one another. Male orangutans are mostly solitary and use long distance calls to keep lower-ranking males away, though fellow dominant males may actually be attracted and may attempt to displace the resident male (Galdikas, 1979). Interactions between male orangutans are rare; they consist of intense physical aggression with consequences for social ranking and/or possession of a desired mate (Mitani, 1990). Orangutans have a one-male mating system, as do most mountain gorillas (Harcourt, 1981). The majority of mountain gorilla males do not have to engage in male competition with other resident males for fecund females, physical aggression occurs in encounters with out-group males and to prevent local females from joining a different group (Sicotte, 1993). About 40 % of mountain gorilla groups have more than one male (Weber & Vedder, 1983); these males may benefit from the advantage in forming coalitions against out-group males and also lower rates of infanticide caused by other adult males (Robbins, 1995). In multi-male groups, social dominance hierarchies formed and dominant males accounted for 83 % of the matings observed (Robbins, 1999). When mountain gorilla males do compete aggressively, their behaviors include grunting, screaming, chest beating, hits, kicks, and bites (Harcourt, Stewart, & Hauser, 1993; Robbins, 1999).

Male Japanese macaques use physical aggression to establish a social dominance ranking system and dominant males are more likely to mate with females during their fertile periods. Yet independent of social dominance, males favored in female mate choice sired more offspring (Soltis et al., 1997). There is a very large positive correlation between male dominance rank achieved through successful fights with rival males and mating success in savannah baboons (Alberts, Watts, & Altmann, 2003). Coalition formation occurs between male yellow and Anubis baboons, and the dominance hierarchy does not determine mating opportunities (Bulger, 1993) as is does in non-coalitional Chacma baboons (Bulger, 1993).

Male langur monkeys compete viciously for control of harems, resulting in high levels of male mortality (Hrdy, 1977). Barbary macaque males engage in scream fights when two or more are near an estrous female (Kuester & Paul, 1992). Males approach each other within 10 m and begin screaming at each other; this may escalate into true fighting, including hitting, thrashing, and biting (Kuester & Paul, 1992). The rate of male langur monkey physical injury caused by other males increases sharply during mating season, demonstrating the relationship between mating competition and aggression (Kuester & Paul, 1992).

Our closest living primate relatives are bonobo and common chimpanzees, who share many parallels with human social behavior. Male common chimpanzees demonstrate both intragroup and intergroup male aggression and killings (Boesch et al., 2007; Fawcett & Muhumuza, 2000). Chimpanzees form social groups to protect themselves from out-group members, so intragroup killings are extremely rare and may be a result of extreme intrasexual competition among males (Wilson & Wrangham, 2003). Males killed another male group member when the number of cycling females in their group was extremely low (Fawcett & Muhumuza, 2000). More frequently, male chimp coalitions raid neighboring territories, killing the resident males and expand into their territories (Mitani, Watts, & Amsler, 2010). Higher-ranking chimpanzee males have both higher testosterone levels and increased parasite burden than lower-ranking males (Muehlenbein & Watts, 2010). Male mortality rates are higher than for females in both wild (Goodall, 1986; Hill et al., 2001; Nishida, 1990) and captive chimpanzee populations (Dyke, Gage, Alford, Swenson, & Williams-Blangero, 1995).

In recent decades, bonobo chimpanzees have gained recognition as a model of behavior in a close human relative, and are noted for having very little violence or overt intrasexual competition compared to common chimpanzees (de Waal & Lantig, 1998). Matrilineal groups with strong female alliances that may have led to low levels of aggression and sexual coercion among bonobos (Wrangham, 1993). Yet the number of estrous females predicts the frequency and intensity of male–male aggression, and aggressors mated more often than their targets (Hohmann & Fruth, 2003).

Human Life History Variation and Sex Differences in Mortality

The relationship between male mortality risk and factors shaping of the distribution of male reproductive success across species is mirrored by variation within our own species. Mortality patterns are an integral part of life history, along with size at birth, patterns of growth, age and size at maturity, allocation of reproductive effort, age schedules of birth, and the number and sex ratio of offspring (Low, 1998). The male to female mortality ratio (M:F MR) may also be an important indicator of population life history, serving as a heuristic for the intensity of male competition, the relative male allocation to mating and parenting effort, and future discounting in male behavioral and physiological strategies (Kruger, 2008). Species living in environments with resource instability and unpredictability of future events (due to high predation rates, for example) will tend to evolve clusters of traits associated with rapid and prolific breeding with relatively low investment in offspring (MacArthur & Wilson, 1967; Pianka, 1970). Species living in stable and predictable environments instead have a long-term strategy of investing more so in somatic and parental effort with lower reproductive rates and longer intergenerational times than those in less predictable and stable environments. There are individual differences in life history strategies within species, contingent upon environmental conditions, parallel to differences between species (Rushton, 1985).

There are considerable differences in life history patterns across human populations. In the modern area, there has been a dramatic shift from high mortality and fertility rates to low mortality and fertility rates (Thompson, 1929). The "demographic transition" describes a shift from a triangular population pyramid, where young individuals represent the largest segments and proportions decline with age, to one that was more rectangular, indicating higher rates of survival. This occurred first in industrial Europe during the nineteenth century and in other industrializing countries in the twentieth century. Some of the less developed areas of the world have yet to make or complete this transition, and the national degree of demographic transition may partially underlie the cross-national variation in life history patterns. Some of the most developed countries, especially those with restrictive immigration policies, now have fertility rates below the replacement rate (Luttbeg, Borgerhoff Mulder, & Mangel, 2000). Access to modern contraception, progressive social norms, and the increasing importance of and extent of tertiary education are resulting in the delay or avoidance of reproduction in postindustrial nations. Sex differences in mortality rates are related to multiple other features of life history across the life course.

The optimal age at which women first give birth is the result of trade-offs in fertility and mortality; the greater the adult mortality rate, the earlier the age at first birth (Low, Simon, & Anderson, 2002). Those who grow up in contexts with high risks of violent death begin reproducing at an earlier age and have more children during their reproductive lifespan than do women who grow up in low-risk, high resource ecologies (Wilson & Daly, 1997). Higher levels of male mating effort correspond with higher levels of male competition, and the degree of male competition over limited resources is related to the risks of violent death (Kruger & Nesse, 2006a, 2007; Wilson & Daly, 1997). These strategies reflect an emphasis on maximizing returns from current opportunities and a discounting of the value of future possibilities. There may be a feedback loop between male risk-taking and mortality, as men with less certain future prospects may focus more so on mating effort as they may have more to gain from increasing the immediate quantity of offspring than more long-term paternal effort investing in the quality of offspring. Controlling for gross national income per capita, the overall sex difference in mortality rates is inversely related to the average mother's age at birth of her first child and directly related to the adolescent fertility rate (Kruger, 2008).

Patterns of maternal somatic investment, as indicated by the sum of offspring biomass in each reproductive bout, vary substantially among mammalian species (Low et al., 2002). Offspring size at birth is considered a central a life history trait (Low, 1998). Women typically give single births, but when twins are occasionally born they each weigh less than single-birth individuals, following from trade-offs in finite investment. When adult mortality rates are high, the ability to invest parentally is low or uncertain, and maternal somatic investment in each offspring declines (Low et al., 2002). Higher maternal somatic investment may reflect greater expectations for paternal investment (Kruger, Clark, & Vanas, 2013). The sex difference in mortality rates predicts the percentage of newborns with low birth weight (Kruger, 2008). Expectations for paternal investment may be related to both expectations for male mortality and the relative male allocations to mating and parenting effort.

As noted above, males grow more slowly and have a longer overall development period than females in species with greater male-male competition (Harvey & Clutton-Brock, 1985). Across human societies, the degree of male competition predicts sex differences in the age of first reproduction (Low, 1998). The intensity of competition for social status and resources will result in corresponding delays in men's reproductive opportunities beyond the age of physical maturation, as older men with more asset accumulation will fare better in both female choice and male-male competition (Geary, 2002). The sex difference in mortality rates predicts the difference between the average age of males and females at first marriage across nations (Kruger, 2008). These results indicate that the sex difference in mortality reflects the degree of male competition for resources, social status, and mates. There appears to be some convergence between male and female strategies, as women's maternal somatic investment in a developing fetus is strongly related to male somatic investment, as indicated by male mortality rates from internal causes, and the adolescent female fertility rate was strongly related to male mortality rates from behavioral causes (Kruger, 2008).

Social Position, Social Inequality, and Sex Difference in Mortality Within Populations

Although life history strategies are partially inherited, the way strategies unfold in humans is likely shaped by environmental circumstances including socioeconomic factors, cultural conditions, and physical constraints (Heath & Hadley, 1998). Greater sex differences in mortality rates may reflect greater degrees of male competition for resources, social status, and mates. Both individual level factors (e.g., social status) and population level factors (e.g., the degree of inequality in social status) likely influence individual risk-taking and mortality outcomes. During recent human evolution, males who did not have substantial resources or status may have been unable to establish long-term relationships. Men with relatively low social status and resources may have riskier behavioral strategies, with less to lose and facing the prospect of being without a partner. Consistent with this notion, sex differences in mortality rates are higher among those lower in income and education in the USA (Kruger & Nesse, 2006a). Across human history, men who had low standings in their social context became warriors, adventurers, and explorers (Daly & Wilson, 1988, 2001). The death rate from assaults is ten times higher in Scottish routine laborers than managers and professionals (Leyland & Dundas, 2010). Poverty is a risk factor for exposure to violence (Sampson & Lauritsen, 1994), and such exposure is associated with individuals' own tendencies for violent behavior (Salzinger, Feldman, Stockhammer, & Hood, 2002). In one study, neighborhood poverty at the Census Tract level explained over two-thirds of the variance in violent crime (Coulton, Korbin, Su, & Chow, 1995).

Why would these risk-taking tendencies be sustained over evolutionary time if they are so frequently detrimental? Wilson and Daly (1997) argue that men with high uncertainty in outcomes may be rational in their response of risk-taking and discounting of future prospects. In unpredictable environments, there may be a convex-upward association between proximate outcomes of risk-taking and reproductive success. Not all men will benefit from risky strategies, but some men will benefit enough for these tendencies to be maintained, even if they are also generally detrimental on an individual basis. The skew in reproductive benefits to some proportion of individuals would make the average outcomes sufficient for selection. Individuals developing in relatively less predictable environments may develop riskier behavioral strategies because they need to take advantage of possibly fleeting opportunities (Chisholm, 1999). Those who live in chronically risky and uncertain environments, including significant family conflict, have earlier menarche, earlier ages of reproduction, and higher reproductive rates (Chisholm, 1999; Kim, Smith, & Palermiti, 1997). In ancestral environments, one of the most pressing adaptive problems was avoiding death before being able to reproduce. In areas where mortality rates were low and more predictable, long-term strategies were optimal because there were fewer urgent adaptive problems. Students who believe the future is more predictable and estimate relatively longer lifespans for themselves take risks less frequently (Hill, Ross, & Low, 1997).

Unmarried men also have higher mortality rates across the adult lifespan than married men, sex differences in mortality do not decline as substantially as among those who are married (Kruger & Nesse, 2006a). This demonstrates the hazards associated with a life history where the transition from mating effort to parenting effort does not occur. Excess male mortality may be directly related to male mating effort and inversely related to paternal investment. Across anthropoid primates, the degree to which males invest in offspring is directly related to their longevity (Allman, Rosin, Kumar, & Hasenstaub, 1998).

Men often provide considerable parental investment, much more compared to males in most other primate species (Buss & Schmitt, 1993; Geary & Flinn, 2001; Low, 1998). Women prefer men who are more likely to provide paternal investment as long-term relationship partners (Kruger, 2006; Kruger & Fisher, 2005). In addition to the direct physical conflicts found across male primates, men also compete with each other for resources and social status not from physical domination in order to attract and retain mates. In ancestral human populations, men who controlled more resources married younger women, married more women, and produced offspring earlier (Low, 1998). Contemporary foraging societies have some degree of status hierarchy, even those noted to be relatively egalitarian, and men with higher social status have more mates (Chagnon, 1992; Hill & Hurtado, 1996). Variance in male wealth and power increased through sociopolitical arrangements and intergenerational transfers over the course of human genetic and cultural coevolution (Smuts, 1995). Cross-culturally, women evaluate prospective partners in terms of social status and economic power (e.g., Ardener, Ardener, & Warmington, 1960; Buss, 1989; Feingold, 1992; Kenrick & Simpson, 1997; Townsend, 1987; Townsend & Roberts, 1993; Wiederman & Allgeier, 1992). Across a wide variety of societies with considerable differences in the definitions of wealth, men with higher social status and greater economic power have greater reproductive success (Hopcroft, 2006).

The famous Whitehall studies of white-collar British government office employees were initially based on the assumption that top-level office workers were under more stress and thus would die more frequently of heart attacks than their subordinates. A steep status gradient in health and mortality outcomes was found; however, it ran in the other direction (Marmot, 2004). Even in a population that was relatively affluent by global economic standards and had universal access to state supported health care, social status was inversely related to mortality risk and the impact of the status gradient was stronger for men than it was for women.

The degree of inequality in outcomes historically related to male reproductive success will drive male competition and sex differences in mortality. As the benefits become more concentrated among a smaller number of elite men, there will be greater incentives to get into positions of high status and greater reproductive costs for not doing so. Echoing the pattern observed across species, the degree of polygyny in human populations is associated with the degree of excess male mortality, even when controlling for socioeconomic factors (Kruger, 2010). Greater variation and skew in male social status and resource control creates greater competition for positions of power and status, leading to higher male mortality rates. Socioeconomic position relative to others has a stronger influence on mortality rates for males than for females (Bopp & Minder, 2003; Kruger & Nesse, 2006a; Martikainen, Makela, Koskinen, & Valkonen, 2001).

The degree of economic inequality predicts homicide rates at the neighborhood level (Wilson & Daly, 1997) and sex differences in mortality across modern nation states (Kruger, 2010). Across nations, economic inequality and polygyny explain the majority of the variance in sex differences in mortality rates (Kruger, 2010). Men that need to compete more vigorously for social status and resources may show higher mortality rates, as a reflection of riskier behavioral strategies and physiological susceptibility to the stress of competition.

Changes that increase economic uncertainty and variation and skew in social status and economic power within societies, even on a relatively short time scale, may also lead to higher male mortality rates from riskier behavioral strategies and the physiological embodiment of stress. The economic transitions from state planned to market economies in Central and Eastern Europe in the 1990s provide a naturalistic demonstration. During the socialist period, social status and material wealth variations were relatively small for most of the population, and employment was guaranteed. Risky male strategies were less prevalent because of the relatively low payoffs for aggressive competition. The variance and skew in social status and resources increased tremendously during the rapid transition market economies (United Nations Development Program, 1998). Sex differences in mortality rates increased substantially for Eastern European nations, most prominently during early adulthood (Kruger & Nesse, 2007). The increase in male mortality rates was due both to external causes, reflecting risky behavioral strategies, and internal causes, reflecting the impact of stress on physiological susceptibility. These trends contrasted with a minimal increase in mortality disparities across Western European countries in the same time period. A similar pattern occurred during the Croatian War of Independence in 1991–1995. Evolved facultative adaptations responding to adverse and unstable environments apparently led to riskier behavioral strategies in the civilian population. Sex differences in violence and accidents (excluding those directly related to combat) peaked 1 year after the military conflict climaxed in intensity and the male homicide rate was considerably higher for several years following the conflict compared to before the war began (Kruger & Nesse, 2006b).

The Sex Ratio and Sex Differences in Mortality

The relative proportions of potentially reproductive males and females in a population exert a powerful influence on reproductive patterns across species. Because the reproductive strategies of men and women are somewhat divergent, imbalances produce different outcomes in female-biased and male-biased populations. When there are more men than women, there is greater male competition for signals of relationship commitment and paternal investment (Pedersen, 1991), and higher expectations for paternal care of offspring (Guttentag & Secord, 1983). Women are better able to marry partners higher in socioeconomic status than themselves (Lichter, Anderson, & Hayward, 1995) and men who have lower social status and less abundant resources have even greater difficulties getting married (Pollet & Nettle, 2007). A relative population surplus of men increases mortality risk for men, but not women (Jin, Elwert, Freese, & Christakis, 2010). Across the 50 US states and Washington, DC, the population sex ratio of men to women predicts sex differences in mortality rates, a relationship that becomes even stronger when controlling for total area population and population density. In China, the general demographic trend is for higher survival for both men and women, however since the adult male population has become increasingly male biased, the improvements for adult male survival has lagged behind the improvements for women (Kruger & Polanski, 2011). The increasing trend in excess male mortality occurs in young adulthood, the typical years of peak male mating competition.

Female-biased populations, where men are scarce, can also exhibit relatively higher rates of male risk-taking than more balanced populations. When the population includes relatively more women than men, women have more difficulty in marrying (Kruger, Fitzgerald, & Peterson, 2010; Lichter, Kephart, McLaughlin, & Landry, 1992) and are more likely to be sexually active outside marriage (Schmitt, 2005). Men are more likely to compete directly with each other for sex partners, thus increasing levels of male violence. There is an association between violent crime rates and the scarcity of men across nations which is not accounted for by level of economic development, income inequality, urbanization, population density, number of police, or prevalence of illegal drug trafficking. Remarkably, there is also an association between the scarcity of adult men and young adult violence at the census tract level across a small US city noted for its high violent crime rates (Kruger, 2012).

Conclusion

Evolutionary life history theory offers a powerful framework for understanding human risk-taking and mortality patterns. Although there are multiple mechanisms underlying differences in mortality risks for men and women, operating at different levels and interacting with each other, life history theory integrates these into a unified coherent picture. Those studying human health patterns and seeking to improve health outcomes may greatly benefit from an understanding of how our genetic heritage and developmental environment interact to shape health outcomes. Although adverse factors such as economic inequality may be difficult to eliminate, interventions to reduce male risk-taking and mortality levels will be more effective when integrating the insights of how male psychology has been shaped by relatively more intense mating completion compared to women.

References

Alberts, S. C., Watts, H. E., & Altmann, J. E. (2003). Queuing and queue-jumping: Long-term patters of reproductive skew in male savannah baboons, *Papio cynocephalus*. *Animal Behaviour, 65*, 821–840.

Alexander, R. D. (1979). *Darwinism and human affairs*. Seattle, WA: University of Washington Press.

Allman, J., Rosin, A., Kumar, R., & Hasenstaub, A. (1998). Parenting and survival in anthropoid primates, caretakers live longer. *Proceedings of the National Academy of Sciences of the United States of America, 95*, 6866–6869.

Anderson, R. (2001). *National vital statistics reports, 49 (11), Deaths: Leading causes for 1999*. Hyattsville, MD: Center for Disease Control.

Andersson, M. (1994). *Sexual selection*. Princeton, NJ: Princeton University Press.

Ardener, E., Ardener, S., & Warmington, W. A. (1960). *Plantation and village in the Cameroons: Some economic and social studies*. London: Oxford University Press.

Bateman, A. J. (1948). Intra-sexual selection in Drosophila. *Heredity, 2*, 349–368.

Bell, G. (1982). *The masterpiece of nature: The evolution and genetics of sexuality*. London: Croom Helm.

Berglund, A., & Rosenqvist, G. (2003). Sex role reversal in pipefish. *Advances in the Study of Behavior, 32*, 131–167.

Berry, D. S., & Brownlow, S. (1989). Were the physiognomists right? Personality correlates of facial babyishness. *Personality and Social Psychology Bulletin, 15*, 266–279.

Betzig, L. (1986). *Despotism and differential reproduction: A Darwinian view of history*. Hawthorne, NY: Aldine de Gruyter.

Boesch, C., Head, J., Tagg, N., Arandjelovic, M., Vigilant, L., & Robbins, M. M. (2007). Fatal chimpanzee attack in Loango National Park, Gabon. *International Journal of Primatology, 28*, 1025–1034.

Booth, A., & Dabbs, J. (1993). Testosterone and men's marriages. *Social Forces, 72*, 463–477.

Booth, A., Shelley, G., Mazur, A., Tharp, G., & Kittok, R. (1989). Testosterone, and winning and losing in human competition. *Hormones and Behavior, 23*, 556–571.

Bopp, M., & Minder, C. (2003). Mortality by education in German speaking Switzerland, 1990–1997: Results from the Swiss National Cohort. *International Journal of Epidemiology, 32*, 346–354.

Boyden, A. (1954). The significance of asexual reproduction. *Systematic Zoology, 3*, 26–37.

Bribiescas, R. G. (2001). Reproductive ecology and life history of the human male. *Yearbook of Physical Anthropology, 44*, 148–176.

Bribiescas, R. G. (2006). *Men: Evolutionary and life history*. Cambridge, MA: Harvard University Press.

Bulger, J. B. (1993). Dominance rank and access to estrous females in male savanna baboons. *Behaviour, 127*, 67–103.

Bulmer, M. G., & Parker, G. A. (2002). The evolution of anisogamy: A game-theoretic approach. *Proceedings of the Royal Society of London Series B, 269*, 2381–2388.

Buss, D. M. (1989). Sex difference in human mate preferences: Evolutionary hypotheses tested in 37 cultures. *Behavioural and Brain Sciences, 12*, 1–49.

Buss, D. M. (2005). *The murderer next door: Why the mind is designed to kill*. New York: Penguin Press.

Buss, D. M., & Schmitt, D. P. (1993). Sexual strategies theory: An evolutionary perspective on human mating. *Psychological Review, 100*, 204–232.

Campbell, A. (1999). Staying alive: Evolution, culture, and women's intrasexual aggression. *Behavioural and Brain Sciences, 22*, 203–252.

Campbell, A. (2005). Aggression. In D. M. Buss (Ed.), *The handbook of evolutionary psychology* (pp. 628–675). Hoboken, NJ: Wiley.

Chagnon, N. (1988). Life histories, blood revenge, and warfare in atribal population. *Science, 239*, 985–992.

Chagnon, N. A. (1992). *Yanomamo*. New York: Holt, Rinehart, & Winston.

Chan, C. L. W., Blyth, E., & Chan, C. H. Y. (2006). Attitudes to and practices regarding sex selection in China. *Prenatal Diagnosis, 26*, 610–613.

Chisholm, J. S. (1999). *Death, hope and sex: Steps to an evolutionary ecology of mind and morality*. Cambridge, UK: Cambridge University Press.

Clutton-Brock, T. H. (1985). Size, sexual dimorphism and polygamy in primates. In W. L. Jungers (Ed.), *Size and scaling in primate biology* (pp. 211–237). New York: Plenum.

Clutton-Brock, T. H., & Isvaran, K. (2007). Sex differences in ageing in natural populations of vertebrates. *Proceedings of the Royal Society of London, Series B: Biological Sciences, 274*, 3097–3104.

Cohen, D., Nisbett, R. E., Bowdle, B. F., & Schwarz, N. (1996). Insult, aggression, and the southern culture of honor: An "experimental ethnography". *Journal of Personality and Social Psychology, 70*, 945–960.

Coulton, C., Korbin, J., Su, N., & Chow, J. (1995). Community level factors and child maltreatment rates. *Child Development, 66*, 1262–1276.

Cronin, H. (1991). *The ant and the peacock: Altruism and sexual selection from Darwin to today*. New York: Cambridge University Press.

Daly, M., & Wilson, M. (1978). *Sex, evolution, and behavior: Adaptations for reproduction*. North Scituate, MA: Duxbury Press.

Daly, M., & Wilson, M. (1988). *Homicide*. New York: Aldine de Gruyter.

Daly, M., & Wilson, M. (1997). Crime and conflict: Homicide in evolutionary perspective. *Crime and Justice, 22*, 251–300.

Daly, M., & Wilson, M. (2001). Risk-taking, intrasexual competition, and homicide. *Nebraska Symposium on Motivation, 47*, 1–36.

Darwin, C. (1871). *The descent of man and selection in relation to sex*. London: Murray.

de Waal, F. B. M., & Lantig, F. (1998). *Bonobo: The forgotten ape*. Berkeley, CA: University of California Press.

Diamond, J. (1997). *Guns, germs, and steel: The fates of human societies* (1st ed.). New York: W.W. Norton.

Ding, Q. J., & Hesketh, T. (2006). Family size, fertility preferences, and sex ratio in China in the era of the one child family policy: Results from national family planning and reproductive health survey. *British Medical Journal, 333*, 371–373.

DiPietro, J. A. (1981). Rough and tumble play: A function of gender. *Developmental Psychology, 17*, 50–58.

Dyke, B., Gage, T. B., Alford, P. L., Swenson, B., & Williams-Blangero, S. (1995). Model life table for captive chimpanzees. *American Journal of Primatology, 37*, 25–37.

Ellison, P. T., Bribiescas, R. G., Bentley, G. R., Campbell, B. C., Lipson, S. F., Panter-Brick, C., et al. (2002). Population variation in age-related decline in male salivary testosterone. *Human Reproduction, 17*, 3251–3253.

Ember, C. R. (1978). Myths about hunter-gatherers. *Ethnology, 17*, 439–448.

Ember, M., Ember, C. R., & Low, B. S. (2007). Comparing explanations of polygyny. *Cross-Cultural Research, 41*, 428–440.

Fawcett, K., & Muhumuza, G. (2000). Death of a wild chimpanzee community member: Possible outcome of intense sexual competition. *American Journal of Primatology, 51*, 243–247.

Feingold, A. (1992). Gender differences in mate selection preferences: A test of the parental investment model. *Psychological Bulletin, 112*, 125–139.

Folstad, I., & Karter, A. J. (1992). Parasites, bright males, and the immunocompetence handicap. *American Naturalist, 139*, 603–622.

Galdikas, B. (1979). Orangutan adaptation at Tanjung Puting Reserve: Mating and ecology. In D. Hamburg

& E. McCown (Eds.), *The great apes* (pp. 194–233). Menlo Park, CA: Benjamin Cummings.

Gangestad, S. W., & Thornhill, R. (1997). Human sexual selection and developmental stability. In J. A. Simpson & D. T. Kenrick (Eds.), *Evolutionary social psychology* (pp. 169–195). Mahwah, NJ: Erlbaum.

Geary, D. C. (2002). Sexual selection and human life history. In R. Kail (Ed.), *Advances in child development and behavior* (pp. 41–101). San Diego, CA: Academic.

Geary, D. C., & Flinn, M. V. (2001). Evolution of human parental behavior and the human family. *Parenting: Science and Practice, 1*, 5–61.

Gettler, L. T., McDade, T. W., Feranil, A. B., & Kuzawa, C. W. (2011). Longitudinal evidence that fatherhood decreases testosterone in human males. *Proceedings of the National Academy of Sciences of the United States of America, 108*, 16194–16199.

Gladue, B. A., Boechler, M., & McCaul, K. D. (1989). Hormonal responses to competition in human males. *Aggressive Behavior, 15*, 409–422.

Goldberg, S., & Lewis, M. (1969). Play behavior in the year-old infant: Early sex differences. *Child Development, 40*, 21–31.

Goodall, J. (1986). *The chimpanzees of Gombe.* Boston: Houghton Mifflin Publishing.

Guttentag, M., & Secord, P. F. (1983). *Too many women? The sex ratio question.* Beverly Hills, CA: Sage.

Guyer, B., Freedman, M. A., Strobino, D. M., & Sondik, E. J. (2000). Annual summary of vital statistics: Trend in the health of Americans during the 20th century. *Pediatrics, 106*, 1307–1317.

Harcourt, A. H. (1981). Intermale competition and the reproductive behavior of the great apes. In C. E. Graham (Ed.), *Reproductive biology of the great apes* (pp. 301–318). New York: Academic.

Harcourt, A. H., Stewart, K., & Hauser, M. (1993). Functions of wild gorilla 'close' calls. I. Repertoire, context, and interspecific comparison. *Behaviour, 124*, 91–122.

Harvey, P. H., & Clutton-Brock, T. H. (1985). Life history variation in primates. *Evolution, 39*, 559–581.

Hazzard, W. (1986). Biological basis of the sex differential in longevity. *Journal of the American Geriatrics Society, 34*, 455–471.

Hazzard, W. (1990). The sex differential in longevity. In W. Hazzard, R. Endres, E. Bierman, & J. Blass (Eds.), *Principles of geriatric medicine and gerontology* (2nd ed., pp. 37–47). New York: McGraw-Hill.

Heath, K., & Hadley, C. (1998). *Dichotomous male reproductive strategies in a polygynous human society: Mating versus parental effort.* Report from The Wenner-Gren Foundation for Anthropological Research.

Hesketh, T., Lu, L., & Xing, Z. W. (2005). The effect of China's one-child family policy after 25 years. *The New England Journal of Medicine, 353*, 1171–1176.

Hill, K., Boesch, C., Goodall, J., Pusey, A., Williams, J., & Wrangham, R. (2001). Mortality rates among wild chimpanzees. *Journal of Human Evolution, 40*, 437–450.

Hill, K., & Hurtado, M. (1996). *Ache life history: The ecology and demography of a foraging people.* Hawthorne, NY: Aldine de Gruyter.

Hill, K., & Kaplan, H. (1999). Life history traits in humans: Theory and empirical studies. *Annual Review of Anthropology, 28*, 397–438.

Hill, E. M., Ross, L. T., & Low, B. S. (1997). The role of future unpredictability in human risk-taking. *Human Nature, 8*, 287–325.

Hohmann, G., & Fruth, B. (2003). Intra- and inter-sexual aggression by bonobos in the context of mating. *Behaviour, 140*, 1389–1413.

Hollingsworth, T. H. (1957). A demographic study of the British ducal families. *Population Studies, 9*, 4–26.

Hopcroft, R. L. (2006). Sex, status and reproductive success in the contemporary U.S. *Evolution and Human Behavior, 27*, 104–120.

Hrdy, S. B. (1977). *The langurs of Abu: Female and male strategies of reproduction.* Cambridge, MA: Harvard University Press.

Hrdy, S. (1999). Mother Nature: A history of mothers, infants and natural selection. New York: Pantheon.

Jarvinen, D. W., & Nicholls, J. G. (1996). Adolescents' social goals, beliefs about the causes of social success and dissatisfaction in peer relations. *Developmental Psychology, 32*, 435–441.

Jin, L., Elwert, F., Freese, J., & Christakis, N. A. (2010). Preliminary evidence regarding the hypothesis that the sex ratio at sexual maturity may affect longevity in men. *Demography, 47*, 579–586.

Jonah, B. A. (1986). Accident risk and risk-taking behavior among young drivers. *Accident Analysis & Prevention, 18*, 255–271.

Keeley, L. H. (1996). *War before civilization.* New York: Oxford University Press.

Kenrick, D. T., & Simpson, J. A. (1997). Why social psychology and evolutionary psychology need one another. In J. Simpson & D. Kenrick (Eds.), *Evolutionary social psychology* (pp. 1–20). Mahwah, NJ: Lawrence Erlbaum.

Kim, K., Smith, P. K., & Palermiti, A. L. (1997). Conflict in childhood and reproductive development. *Evolution and Human Behavior, 18*, 109–142.

Kindlon, D., & Thompson, M. (1999). *Raising Cain: Protecting the emotional life of boys.* London: Michael Joseph.

Kirkwood, T. B., & Rose, M. R. (1991). Evolution of senescence: Late survival sacrificed for reproduction. *Philosophical Transactions of the Royal Society of London, Series B: Biological Sciences, 332*, 15–24.

Koot, H. M., & Verhulst, F. C. (1991). Prevalence of problem behavior in Dutch children aged 2–3. *Acta Psychiatrica Scandinavica, 83*, 1–37.

Kraemer, S. (2000). The fragile male. *British Medical Journal, 321*, 1609–1612.

Kruger, D. J. (2006). Male facial masculinity influences attributions of personality and reproductive strategy. *Personal Relationships, 13*, 451–463.

Kruger, D. J. (2008). Human life history variation and sex differences in mortality rates. *Journal of Social, Evolutionary, and Cultural Psychology, 2*, 281–288.

Kruger, D. J. (2010). Socio-demographic factors intensifying malemating competition exacerbate male mortality rates. *Evolutionary Psychology, 8*, 194–204.

Kruger, D. J. (2012, August). *The health impact of male scarcity in modern human populations*. Oral presentation, International Society for Human Ethology, Vienna.

Kruger, D. J., Clark, J., & Vanas, S. (2013). Male scarcity is associated with higher prevalence of premature gestation and low birth weight births across the USA. *American Journal of Human Biology, 25*(2), 225–227.

Kruger, D. J., & Fisher, M. (2005). Males identify and respond adaptively to the mating strategies of other men. *Sexualities, Evolution, and Gender, 7*, 233–244.

Kruger, D. J., Fitzgerald, C. J., & Peterson, T. (2010). Female scarcity reduces women's marital ages and increases variance in men's marital ages. *Evolutionary Psychology, 8*, 420–431.

Kruger, D. J., & Nesse, R. M. (2004). Sexual selection and the male:female mortality ratio. *Evolutionary Psychology, 2*, 66–77.

Kruger, D. J., & Nesse, R. M. (2006a). An evolutionary life-history framework for understanding sex differences in human mortality rates. *Human Nature, 17*, 74–97.

Kruger, D. J., & Nesse, R. M. (2006b). Understanding sex differences in Croatian mortality with an evolutionary framework. *Psychological Topics, 15*, 351–364.

Kruger, D. J., & Nesse, R. M. (2007). Economic transition, male competition, and sex differences in mortality rates. *Evolutionary Psychology, 5*, 411–427.

Kruger, D. J., & Polanski, S. P. (2011). Sex differences in mortality rates have increased in China following the single-child law. *Letters on Evolutionary Behavioral Science, 2*, 1–4.

Kuester, J., & Paul, A. (1992). Influence of mate competition and female choice on male mating success in Barbary macaques. *Behaviour, 120*, 192–217.

Lancaster, J. B. (1989). Evolutionary and cross-cultural perspectives on single-parenthood. In R. W. Bell & N. J. Bell (Eds.), *Interfaces in psychology* (pp. 63–72). Lubbock, TX: Texas Tech University Press.

Lawlor, D. A., Ebrahim, S., & Smith, G. D. (2001). Sex matters: Secular and geographical trends in sex differences in coronary heart disease mortality. *British Medical Journal, 323*, 541–545.

Le Boeuf, B. J., & Reiter, J. (1988). Lifetime reproductive success in northern elephant seals. In T. Clutton-Brock (Ed.), *Reproductive success* (pp. 344–362). Chicago: University of Chicago Press.

Leutenegger, W., & Kelly, J. T. (1977). Relationship of sexual dimorphism in canine size and body size to social, behavioral, and ecological correlates in anthropoid primates. *Primates, 18*, 117–136.

Leyland, A. H., & Dundas, R. (2010). The social patterning of deaths due to assault in Scotland, 1980–2005: Population-based study. *Journal of Epidemiology and Community Health, 64*, 432–439.

Lichter, D. T., Anderson, R. N., & Hayward, M. D. (1995). Marriage markets and marital choice. *Journal of Family Issues, 16*, 412–431.

Lichter, D. T., Kephart, G., McLaughlin, D. K., & Landry, D. J. (1992). Race and the retreat from marriage: A shortage of marriageable men. *American Sociological Review, 57*, 781–799.

Lopez, A. D. (1998). Morbidity and mortality, changing patterns in the twentieth century. In P. Armitage & T. Colton (Eds.), *Encyclopedia of biostatistics* (pp. 2690–2701). New York: Wiley.

Lopez, A. D., & Ruzicka, L. T. (1983). *Sex differentials in mortality*. Canberra: Australian National University Press.

Low, B. (1998). The evolution of human life histories. In C. Crawford & D. Krebs (Eds.), *Handbook of evolutionary psychology: Issues, ideas, and applications* (pp. 131–161). Mahwah, NJ: Lawrence Erlbaum.

Low, B. (2003). Ecological and social complexities in monogamy. In U. Reichard & C. Boesch (Eds.), *Monogamy: Mating strategies and partnerships in birds, humans, and other mammals* (pp. 161–176). Cambridge, UK: Cambridge University Press.

Low, B. (2007). Ecological and socio-cultural impacts on mating and marriage systems. In R. Dunbar & L. Barrett (Eds.), *The Oxford handbook of evolutionary psychology* (pp. 449–462). Oxford, UK: Oxford University Press.

Low, B. S., Simon, C. P., & Anderson, K. G. (2002). An evolutionary ecological perspective on demographic transitions, modeling multiple currencies. *American Journal of Human Biology, 14*, 149–167.

Luttbeg, B., Borgerhoff Mulder, M., & Mangel, M. S. (2000). To marry or not to marry? A dynamic model of marriage behavior and demographic transition. In L. Cronk, N. A. Chagnon, & W. Irons (Eds.), *Human behavior and adaptation: An anthropological perspective* (pp. 345–368). New York: Aldine de Gruyter.

MacArthur, R., & Wilson, E. O. (1967). *The theory of island biogeography*. Princeton, NJ: Princeton University Press.

MacDorman, M. F., Hoyert, D. L., Martin, J. A., Munson, M. L., & Hamilton, B. E. (2007). Fetal and perinatal mortality, United States, 2003. *National Vital Statistics Reports, 55*(6), 1–17.

Marmot, M. (2004). *Status syndrome—How your social standing directly affects your health and life expectancy*. London: Bloomsbury.

Martikainen, P., Makela, P., Koskinen, S., & Valkonen, T. (2001). Income differences in mortality: A register-based follow-up study of three million men and women. *International Journal of Epidemiology, 30*, 1397–1405.

Mazur, A., Halpern, C., & Udry, J. (1994). Dominant looking male teenagers copulate earlier. *Ethology and Sociobiology, 15*, 87–94.

Mazur, A., Mazur, J., & Keating, C. (1984). Military rank attainment of a West Point class: Effects of cadets' physical features. *American Journal of Sociology, 90*, 125–150.

Mazur, A., & Michalek, J. (1998). Marriage, divorce, and male testosterone. *Social Forces, 77*, 315–330.

McArthur, L. Z., & Apatow, K. (1983). Impressions of baby-faced adults. *Social Cognition, 2*, 315–342.

McClure, G. (2000). Changes in suicide in England and Wales, 1960–1997. *British Journal of Psychiatry, 176*, 64–67.

Medawar, P. B. (1952). *An unsolved problem of biology*. London: H.K. Lewis.

Miller, G. F. (1998). How mate choice shaped human nature: A review of sexual selection and human evolution. In C. Crawford & D. Krebs (Eds.), *Handbook of evolutionary psychology: Ideas, issues, and applications* (pp. 87–129). Mahwah, NJ: Lawrence Erlbaum.

Mitani, J. C. (1990). Experimental field studies of Asian ape social systems. *International Journal of Primatology, 11*, 103–126.

Mitani, J. C., Watts, D. P., & Amsler, S. J. (2010). Lethal intergroup aggression leads to territorial expansion in wild chimpanzees. *Current Biology, 20*, R507–R508.

Møller, A. P., Christe, P., & Lux, E. (1999). Parasitism, host immune function, and sexual selection. *Quarterly Review of Biology, 74*, 3–20.

Moore, S. L., & Wilson, K. (2002). Parasites as a viability cost of sexual selection in natural populations of mammals. *Science, 297*, 2008–2009.

Muehlenbein, M. P., & Watts, D. P. (2010). The costs of dominance: Testosterone, cortisol and intestinal parasites in wild male chimpanzees. *BioPsychoSocial Medicine, 4*, 21.

Mueller, U., & Mazur, A. (1997). Facial dominance in Homo sapiens as honest signaling of male quality. *Behavioral Ecology, 8*, 569–579.

Negro, S. S., Caudron, A. K., Dubois, M., Delahaut, P., & Gemmell, N. J. (2010). Correlation between male social status, testosterone levels, and parasitism in a dimorphic polygynous mammal. *PLoS One, 5*, 9.

Nishida, T. (1990). *The chimpanzees of the Mahale mountains*. Tokyo: University of Tokyo Press.

Owens, I. P. F. (2002). Sex differences in mortality rate. *Science, 297*, 2015–2018.

Pampel, F. (2002). Cigarette use and the narrowing sex differential in mortality. *Population and Development Review, 28*, 77–104.

Pedersen, F. A. (1991). Secular trends in human sex ratios: Their influence on individual and family behavior. *Human Nature, 2*, 271–291.

Pianka, E. R. (1970). On r and K selection. *American Naturalist, 104*, 592–597.

Plavcan, J. M. (2000). Inferring social behavior from sexual dimorphism in the fossil record. *Journal of Human Evolution, 39*, 327–344.

Plavcan, J. M., & van Schaik, C. P. (1997). Interpreting hominid behavior on the basis of sexual dimorphism. *Journal of Human Evolution, 32*, 345–374.

Plavcan, J. M., van Schaik, C. P., & Kappeler, P. M. (1995). Competition, coalitions and canine size in primates. *Journal of Human Evolution, 28*, 245–276.

Pollet, T. V., & Nettle, D. (2007). Driving a hard bargain: Sex ratio and male marriage success in a historical US population. *Biology Letters, 4*, 31–33.

Promislow, D. E. (1992). Costs of sexual selection in natural populations of mammals. *Proceedings of the Royal Society of London Series B, 247*, 203–210.

Rahaman, M. M., Aziz, K. M. S., Munshi, M. H., Patwari, Y., & Rahman, M. (1982). A diarrhea clinic in rural Bangladesh: Influence of distance, age, and sex on attendance and diarrheal mortality. *American Journal of Public Health, 72*, 1124–1128.

Reichard, U., & Boesch, C. (2003). *Monogamy: Mating strategies and partnerships in birds, humans, and other mammals*. Cambridge, UK: Cambridge University Press.

Robbins, M. M. (1995). A demographic analysis of male life history and social structure of mountain gorillas. *Behaviour, 132*, 21–47.

Robbins, M. M. (1999). Male mating patterns in wild multimale mountain gorilla groups. *Animal Behaviour, 57*, 1013–1020.

Roff, D. A. (1992). *The evolution of life histories: Theory and analysis*. New York: University of Chicago Press.

Rogers, R. G., Hummer, R. A., & Nam, C. B. (2000). *Living and dying in the USA: Behavioral, health, and social differences of adult mortality*. San Diego, CA: Academic.

Rushton, J. P. (1985). Differential K theory, the sociobiology of individual and group differences. *Personality & Individual Differences, 6*, 441–452.

Salzinger, S., Feldman, R. S., Stockhammer, T., & Hood, J. (2002). An ecological framework for understanding risk for exposure to community violence and the effects of exposure on children and adolescents. *Aggression and Violent Behavior, 7*, 423–451.

Sampson, R. J., & Lauritsen, J. (1994). Violent victimization and offending: Individual, situational and community-level risk factors. In A. J. Reiss & J. A. Roth (Eds.), *Understanding and preventing violence: Social influences* (Vol. 3, pp. 1–114). Washington, DC: National Academy Press.

Schaal, B., Tremblay, R. E., Soussignan, R., & Susman, E. J. (1996). Male testosterone linked to high social dominance but low physical aggression in early adolescence. *Journal of the American Academy of Child and Adolescent Psychiatry, 35*, 1322–1330.

Schmitt, D. P. (2005). Sociosexuality from Argentina to Zimbabwe: A 48-nation study of sex, culture, and strategies of human mating. *Behavioral and Brain Sciences, 28*, 247–311.

Schulting, R. J. (2006). Skeletal evidence and contexts of violence in the European mesolithic and neolithic. In R. Gowland & C. Knüsel (Eds.), *The social archaeology of funerary remains* (pp. 224–237). Oxford, UK: Oxbow Books.

Sicotte, P. (1993). Inter-group encounters and female transfer in mountain gorillas: Influence of group composition on male behavior. *American Journal of Primatology, 30*, 21–36.

Smith, C. A., Roeszler, K. N., Hudson, Q. J., & Sinclair, A. H. (2007). Avian sex determination: What, when and where? *Cytogenetic and Genome Research, 117*, 165–173.

Smith, D. W., & Warner, H. R. (1989). Does genotypic sex have a direct effect on longevity. *Experimental Gerontology, 24*, 277–288.

Smuts, B. B. (1995). The evolutionary origins of patriarchy. *Human Nature, 6*, 1–32.

Soltis, J., Mitsunaga, F., Shimizu, K., Nozaki, M., Yanagihara, Y., Domingo-Roura, X., et al. (1997). Sexual selection in Japanese macaques II: Female mate choice and male-male competition. *Animal Behaviour, 54*, 737–746.

Stearns, S. C. (1992). *The evolution of life histories*. Oxford: Oxford University Press.

Taylor, S. E., Klein, L. C., Lewis, B. P., Gruenewald, T. L., Gurung, R. A., & Updegraff, J. A. (2000). Biobehavioral responses to stress in females: Tend-and-befriend, not fight-or-flight. *Psychological Review, 107*, 411–429.

Thompson, W. S. (1929). Population. *American Journal of Sociology, 34*, 959–975.

Tinbergen, N. (1963). On aims and methods in ethology. *Zeitschrift für Tierpsychologie, 20*, 410–433.

Townsend, J. M. (1987). Sex differences in sexuality among medical students: Effects of increasing socioeconomic status. *Archives of Sexual Behavior, 16*, 427–446.

Townsend, J. M., & Roberts, L. W. (1993). Gender differences in mate selection among law students: Divergence and convergence of criteria. *Journal of Psychology, 29*, 507–528.

Treadwell, H. M., & Young, A. M. (2013). The right US men's health report: High time to adjust priorities and attack disparities. *American Journal of Public Health, 103*, 5–6.

Trivers, R. (1972). Parental investment and sexual selection. In B. Campbell (Ed.), *Sexual selection and the descent of man: 1871–1971* (pp. 136–179). Chicago: Aldine.

UNICEF (United Nations Children's Fund). (2003). *Official summary: The state of the world's children 2002*. New York: Oxford University Press.

United Nations Development Program, Regional Bureau for Europe and the CIS. (1998). *Poverty in transition?* New York: Author.

Weber, A. W., & Vedder, A. (1983). Population dynamics of the Virunga gorillas: 1959–1978. *Biological Conservation, 26*, 341–366.

Wei, C. (2007). Induced abortion and its demographic consequences in China. In Z. Zhao & F. Guo (Eds.), *Transition and challenge: China's population at the beginning of the 21st century*. New York: Oxford University Press.

Weisfeld, G. E. (1999). *Evolutionary principles of human adolescence*. New York: Basic Books.

Wiederman, M. W., & Allgeier, E. R. (1992). Gender differences in mate selection criteria: Sociobiological or socioeconomic explanation? *Ethology and Sociobiology, 13*, 115–124.

Williams, G. C. (1957). Pleiotropy, natural selection, and the evolution of senescence. *Evolution, 11*, 398–411.

Williams, G. C. (1975). *Sex and evolution*. Princeton, NJ: Princeton University Press.

Wilson, M., & Daly, M. (1993). Lethal confrontational violence among young men. In N. J. Bell & R. W. Bell (Eds.), *Adolescent risk taking* (pp. 84–106). Newbury Park, CA: Sage.

Wilson, M., & Daly, M. (1997). Life expectancy, economic inequality, homicide, and reproductive timing in Chicago neighbourhoods. *British Medical Journal, 314*, 1271–1274.

Wilson, M. L., & Wrangham, R. W. (2003). Intergroup relations in chimpanzees. *Annual Review of Anthropology, 32*, 363–392.

Wrangham, R. W. (1993). The evolution of sexuality in chimpanzees and bonobos. *Human Nature, 4*, 47–79.

Zahavi, A. (1975). Mate selection—A selection for a handicap. *Journal of Theoretical Biology, 53*, 205–213.

Zhang, X., Sasaki, S., & Kesteloot, H. (1995). The sex ratio of mortality and its secular trends. *International Journal of Epidemiology, 24*, 720–729.

Zhu, W. X., Lu, L., & Hesketh, T. (2009). China's excess males, sex selective abortion, and one child policy: Analysis of data from 2005 national intercensus survey. *British Medical Journal, 338*, b1211.

Male Production of Humor Produced by Sexually Selected Psychological Adaptations

Gil Greengross

Influenced by Hollywood and the theatrics of a beauty pageant won by her mother, a former Mrs. Los Angeles, a young girl decided she would become an actress when she grew up. Years later, while making her first steps into show business, the aspiring actress, imbued with her mother's sense of style and independence, was about to audition for a role in a new play on Broadway, a big opportunity to launch her acting career. The little known clumsy-looking playwright, who was also the director and the lead actor in the play, was conducting auditions to find the leading female role, his onstage companion. This was only his second play, and he was waiting to make a breakthrough of his own. The actress auditioned successfully for her role as Linda Christie, a performance that earned her a Tony nomination. The play, *Play It Again Sam*, was a big hit and was turned into a film, starring her, Diane Keaton, and Woody Allen, the writer, director, and actor. And just as the two insecure characters on the stage fall in love, the two actors also fell for each other in real life (Keaton, 2012).

What attracted Keaton to Allen, who by most accounts is not considered a physically attractive man? In her autobiography, Keaton, who is 11 years his junior (and 2 in. taller), attributed her enchantment with Allen to his sense of humor.

Upon meeting Allen for the first time, she wrote to her mother: "Woody Allen is cute, and of course very funny" (p. 61), and what really got her was that he was "...looking down in a self-deprecating way while he told jokes like... 'I'd rather be with a beautiful woman than anything else except my stamp collection.'" She was charmed by him, captivated by his jokes, recalling "I was a good audience. I laughed in between the jokes. I think he liked that..." (pp. 86–87).

Keaton's attraction to Allen's sense of humor and personality and Allen's successful endeavors to woo her with his wit are a good example of the importance of humor creativity in mating. The story about Allen, whose self-deprecation and funniness allure Keaton, might be only one anecdote, but nonetheless, it reveals a larger truth about how humor is used to attract mates. As we will see, humor plays an important role in mate choice, a role in which males and females are not equal partakers. Men and women view humor differently, and their motivations, experiences, usage, and consumption of humor are not the same. These differences might be best understood in light of sexual selection theory and by looking at the distinct evolutionary forces that shaped the psychological adaptations of men and women.

What Is Humor?

Before delving into the evolutionary roots of humor, it is important to discuss the notion

G. Greengross (✉)
Department of Anthropology, University of New Mexico, Albuquerque, NM, USA
e-mail: Humorology@gmail.com

V.A. Weekes-Shackelford and T.K. Shackelford (eds.), *Evolutionary Perspectives on Human Sexual Psychology and Behavior*, Evolutionary Psychology, DOI 10.1007/978-1-4939-0314-6_9,
© Springer Science+Business Media New York 2014

of humor. Developing a comprehensive theory of humor poses a challenge because any attempt at framing such a broad topic often results in more questions than answers. Is humor a distinct concept that can be easily recognized and defined? What does it mean to say that someone has a good sense of humor? What is the quality that he or she possesses? Is there even agreement of what constitutes a humorous event and what does not? Philosophers and researchers have been debating the definition of humor for centuries and searching for an ultimate and complete theory of humor, one that explains all humor formations and occurrences and elucidates what makes things funny (Martin, 2007; Morreall, 1987; Schmidt & Williams, 1971). One of the main difficulties in defining humor or finding a comprehensive theory of humor is that humor can be seen as a personality trait, a habitual behavior, a temperament, an ability, or an attitude (Feingold & Mazzella, 1991; Greengross & Miller, 2011; Martin, 2003, 2007; Ruch, 1998, 2004). Humor appears easier to recognize than define, and most people have some intuitive sense of what humor is. But people also use the term to refer to many different experiences and usages and do not always agree about what comprises a humorous episode. It is outside the scope of this chapter to introduce a complete review of humor theories, but I will highlight a few key features pertaining to the understanding of humor, especially as a social phenomenon. These will help illustrate the complexity of the humor experience and assist in evaluation of any theory which tries to explicate humor.

Sense of humor also largely depends on the context in which it is used and the interactions between the participants in the situation. What is funny and what is not largely depend on the individual assessing the humor and the context in which humor is used. The best example is the contagious nature of laughter. Most laughter takes place in spontaneous social situations, usually in response to other people's sayings or actions. The presence of other people, and their audible laughter, increases the amount of laughter produced by an individual (Martin & Kuiper, 1999; Provine, 2000; Provine & Fischer, 1989). This contagious laughter effect is well known to comedy show producers, who use laugh tracks to boost audience laughter (Graziano & Bryant, 1998; Smyth & Fuller, 1972). Different moods also affect our perception of humor and can increase or reduce the amount of laughter produced (Deckers, 1998; Martin & Lefcourt, 1983). These effects underline the notion that to some degree, humor is a subjective experience, depending on external and internal cues. In order to recognize that something is funny, we cannot focus solely on the stimulus itself but must take into account the circumstances around it. We need a person to process and interpret the stimulus and decide whether or not it is funny. By emphasizing the subjective experience of humor, we concede that it is not always possible to understand why someone finds something funny. For example, seeing a person slipping on a banana peel would be viewed by many as a funny event, but others may recoil at the view of a person falling down and would not deem the incident funny. We cannot disconnect the event itself from the cognitive processes of the person viewing the incident.

On the other hand, it is important to recognize that humor is, to some extent, objective, and there is agreement among people about what is funny and what is not. If this were not the case, comedy shows and stand-up comedians could not possibly succeed in appealing to wide audiences. These objective types of humor usually come in the form of jokes and are somewhat easier to analyze than more spontaneous, unscripted humor. Jokes are self-contained units of analysis and usually devoid of social context or external cues that might influence their evaluation for funniness. This is why jokes are frequently used in humor research as stimuli, where researchers can disband the different parts of a joke, to try to understand how the incompatible parts produce humor (Attardo, 1994; Raskin, 1984).

One simple way to characterize humor is by defining it as anything that makes an individual laugh. While still emphasizing the subjective experience of humor, this definition allows for people to respond to the same stimulus differently. One advantage of using such a simple, even simplistic, approach is that it is quite comprehensive in capturing a wide range of humorous events. The rudimentary definition is very intuitive and enables both researchers and laymen to agree on what constitutes a humorous event, without needing to apply a sophisticated definition, one that is more detached from everyday uses of humor.

Nevertheless, defining humor by its relationship with laughter has limitations. Though humor and laughter are strongly intertwined, the relationship between them is more complex, and the two are distinct concepts. While there is much overlap between humor and laughter, not everything that is considered funny makes people laugh, and not every laugh indicates the existence of humor. For example, tickling causes an involuntary laughter but there is nothing funny about the situation, and most people are irritated by it. In other cases, an individual can appreciate a joke but would not laugh out loud in response, for example, when consuming humor alone. A more complicated situation is when we recognize an attempt to tell a joke, but do not find it very funny and, therefore, do not laugh. This attempted humor does not generate laughter, though may count as humor in the view of the joke teller. Other times, people laugh when no obvious funny stimulus is present, as when they are nervous, or in some pathologies, following neurological damage, such as a stroke (Oh, Kim, Kim, Park, & Lee, 2007).

A central part of understanding humor is viewing it as a social phenomenon. Studies show that most accounts of everyday laughter arise in respond to mundane comments during routine conversations, not in response to purposeful attempts to make others laugh. Provine (1993, 2000) documented pre-laugh comments that elicited laughter among listeners in regular, everyday conversations. He found out that only about 10–20 % of the comments were considered remotely funny. Remarks such as "I'll see you guys later" or "It was nice meeting you, too" tended to generate the most laughter. It is unclear though if such comments were perceived as humorous by the appreciators or their laughter was just an indication of social gesture. As argued before, humor is partially subjective, and the fact that for an outsider these comments were not perceived even marginally humorous does not preclude that for the people involved in those conversations, these ordinary statements were meaningful and funny. Nonetheless, it is important to acknowledge that jokes, laughter, and humor are not synonyms to each other but are distinct concepts. This is especially important because many people do perceive these concepts as the same, and most humor research focuses on analysis of jokes, or uses them as stimuli in lab experiments, as a proxy for humor.

Another key feature that helps to construe humor in its social context is the distinction between the joke teller and the appreciator, especially in the context of spontaneous humor. Many people view humor as a unified construct, not separating the producer of humor from the receiver. This dissociation is crucial since there are clear differences between the humor producer and the appreciator. The motivations to initiate humor are often very different from the impetus of those who want to enjoy humor, and being funny is much harder than just appreciating humor. Thus, when discussing humor, one must focus separately on the roles of the humor producer and the humor appreciator and their unique contributions to the existence of the humorous event. This is especially true for understanding the evolutionary roots of humor, since humor evolved within a social context, and even more so when looking at the roles men and women play in that regard.

There is little doubt that sense of humor is a multidimensional construct that includes social, developmental, emotional, cognitive, and biological aspects (Gervais & Wilson, 2005; Mobbs, Hagan, Azim, Menon, & Reiss, 2005; O'Quin & Derks, 1997). The points raised here are not intended to confuse the reader, or take an extreme view that there is no such a thing as humor, but rather to challenge the visceral feeling most people have that humor is ostensibly easy to conceptualize and define. Nonetheless, we should also not lose sight of the larger picture, that is, that no matter how evasive the definition of humor is, it plays a large role in people's lives. As Martin (2007, p. 3) concluded: "being able to enjoy humor and express it through laughter seems to be an essential part of what it means to be human."

Evolutionary Roots of Humor

There is no consensus among researchers regarding the ultimate function of humor, but most evolutionary theories can be explained by the processes of natural selection and sexual selection. Natural selection explanations center on how humor can help individuals to survive. Humor could potentially contribute to one's health, prolong life, or help avoid dangerous situations that could reduce survivorship, either directly or indirectly. Explanations focusing on sexual selection theory emphasize the importance that humor plays in finding a mate and how it can enhance the chances of reproducing successfully.

How Do We Know That Humor Has an Evolutionary Basis?

Humor is a universal phenomenon, enjoyed daily by people of all ages, in both tribal and industrialized societies, though the exact uses and experiences vary (Apte, 1985; Davies, 1998; Martin, 2007; Weisfeld, 1993). Basic mechanisms such as surprise and incongruity in non-serious social interactions are universal in eliciting humor and producing physiological responses of mirth (Gervais & Wilson, 2005). In addition to the universality of humor, smiling and laughter have been documented not only in all human societies but also in other species, especially apes and primates (Gamble, 2001;

Preuschoft & Van-Hooff, 1997). In primates, there are two distinct facial expressions that are presumed to be homologous to human smiles and laughter. The silent bared teeth display is equivalent to the human smile and appears as a sign of submissive appeasement that leads to an inhibition of aggression in the receiver, while the relaxed open mouth display, homologous to human laughter, appears in social play as a sign of enjoyment. While these two displays are quite distinct in apes and emerge only in specific situations, they appear to converge in humans. Humans smile and laugh interchangeably in response to the same stimuli, and the smile or laughter might reflect the magnitude of joy and not the nature of the interaction as with other apes. Research suggests that lauger might have emerged deep in our evolutionary history, even as far back as rats (Panksepp, 2007; Panksepp & Burgdorf, 2003). Rats seek to be tickled by pursuing the tickling stimuli (usually a hand), which suggest they enjoy it, and tickling them produces high-frequency chirping sound, which some view as an antecedent to primitive laughter.

Support for the view that humor is well rooted in our evolutionary history comes from the fact that smile and laughter develop about the same time, early and spontaneously, in every culture in the world (Bergen, 1998; McGhee, 1979). Babies who are just born smile reflexively and start laughing vocally at about 2–4 months of age. As with many other basic facial expressions, smiles and laughs develop before language and have stereotypical expression and sounds (Ekman, 1993; Provine, 2000). People in virtually every culture in the world recognize a genuine smile (the Duchenne smile, named after the French neurologist Duchenne de Boulogne) and laughter presented to them from other cultures and attribute the correct emotion of mirth to them (Keltner & Ekman, 1994). Even babies who are born blind or deaf smile and laugh involuntary, not needing to see or hear others around them, lending support to the notion that smile and laughter are not restricted by culture (Freedman, 1964).

Evolutionary Mechanisms That Could Explain Humor

The various evolutionary theories offered over the years to explain the adaptive function of humor vary in scope and illuminate different aspects of humor and laughter. The first of these theories was proposed by Charles Darwin himself, in his seminal work, *The Expression of the Emotions in Man and Animals* (Darwin, 1872). Darwin contemplates what function humor and laughter may confer, among other emotions and behaviors. Darwin considered humor to be "tickling of the mind," a stimulus in the brain that produces laughter and brings joy or happiness. Laughter, in his view, occurs when an unexpected idea or a surprising event transpires, but only while the mind is in a "pleasurable condition." Because the incongruity needs a resolution, there is a pressure of nervous energy building up in the body that needs to be discharged. Laughter serves as the medium that frees all the superfluous energy from the body. This explanation is a variant of one of the classical theories of humor, the incongruity-resolution theory (Beattie, 1778; Koestler, 1964).

Play and Humor

Researchers noted that much laughter occurs during social play, especially among children (Bergen, 1998). This connection led to the hypothesis that humor evolved from social play (Preuschoft & Van-Hooff, 1997; Van-Hooff & Preuschoft, 2003; Vettin & Todt, 2005). Children all over the world laugh the most during play, and similar to other primates, it largely arises during chase and fleeing games or wrestling with each other (McGhee, 1979). In many primates, rates of affinity among chimpanzees and other primates increase following relaxed open mouth display (the equivalent to human laughter), a display that is observed primarily during such play (Preuschoft & Van-Hooff, 1997).

Play might serve as a safe environment to rehearse and develop the physical and social skills children will need as adults, such as social bonding and cooperation, that will later contribute to their survival. The laughter that accompanies such play signals to the participants that the activity is playful, without serious ramifications (McGhee, 1979). Moreover, humor may serve another function that scuffling has among children and other primates, a ritual or symbolic fighting that has a winner or loser without seriously hurting any of the participants (Pinker, 1997). Children and primates practice play wrestling among themselves, and the tickling and laughter involved indicate that it is "just for fun." As adults, instead of getting involved in a physical fight, people can use humor as a refined tool to undermine superior authorities, a way to gain status or put down others, and a weapon that carries no physical risk for the individual. Laughter, therefore, indicates for both children and adults that the aggression is not real, and by using humor effectively, people can poke fun at others without putting themselves in harm's way.

Social Function

Prima facie, humor does not seem to provide obvious survival benefits. Nonetheless, many evolutionary explanations for humor focus on the possibility that humor can contribute to one's survivorship, either directly or indirectly, especially within the social domain. Humor serves many social functions, such as helping break down interpersonal barriers or as an icebreaker in awkward situations or among strangers (Martin, 2007). As discussed earlier, people are much more likely to laugh when they are surrounded by others, which led researchers to hypothesize that humor evolved to facilitate bonding in social groups, as a way to promote cooperation, mitigate conflicts, or help identify in-group members (Flamson & Barrett, 2008; Gervais & Wilson, 2005). Cooperation is one of the most important features that makes humans so successful as a species. Our hominid ancestors learned that acting alone in harsh environments was too costly and risky, and cooperation among group members became increasingly important for survivorship. To facilitate such cooperation, there must be some social mechanism that could coordinate the actions of everyone involved. Humor and laughter can serve such a function by inducing a playful mind-set that is shared by all members in the group at a given time (Gervais & Wilson, 2005). Laughter is contagious, and when everyone in the group laughs and shares the same feeling, it is easier to work together and reach the group's goals. Additionally, it might confer a benefit to the group as a whole, giving it a competitive advantage over other, less mirthful groups, though this view of group selection is less sustainable and poses serious challenges to standard evolutionary thought (Williams, 1966).

Circuit Breaker

Humor can also aid in easing the tension before a dangerous situation has the potential to deteriorate further. One evolutionary hypothesis posits that humor evolved to serve as a disabling mechanism, operating like a circuit breaker or a safety valve (Chafe, 1987). When people laugh, they are immediately distracted from anything else, and hence, laughter prevents them from doing things that are counterproductive, damaging, or even disastrous. In this view, humor is an adaptive mechanism whose function is diversion, forcing people to stop and think, and consider their actions before they do something that might be dangerous to them. Physiologically, when people laugh, their muscle tension decreases, and they are incapable of doing anything for a short time, thus disabling them from any effective action. Humor then helps to shift the focus from the external situation inward and causes one to evaluate the situation more thoroughly.

False Alarm

The distraction that laughter evokes not only could save people from trouble and from taking things too seriously, but it also sends this message to others. It alerts the surrounding people that what is happening has only trivial consequences, and there is no real threat to them in the current situation. Humor usually involves two ideas that seem incompatible with each other until the end, when the incongruity between them is resolved, and it all makes sense.

This ambiguous situation may lead someone to contemplate a serious action when it might lead to dire consequences. For example, someone might hear a strange noise at night and suspect that there is a burglar inside the house. He/She becomes vigilant and is ready to use a weapon. However, upon further inspection he/she discovers that the house cat is to blame for the noise and starts laughing. Laughter acts as a false alarm indicator that signals that nobody needs to take the situation seriously, nor allocate valuable resources and energy to it, preventing the situation from further escalating (Ramachandran, 1998).

Debugging Mechanism

From a psychological point of view, assessing an ambiguous situation correctly enables the individual to avoid wasting limited cognitive resources that could have been invested elsewhere. The brain is bombarded with information and needs not allocate resources to process insignificant events. It has been suggested that humor acts as a debugging mechanism that assists in removing erroneous ideas or information that somehow crept into one's mind and hinders its function (Hurley, Dennett, & Adams, 2011). Since our brain has limited resources, evolution should favor an efficient mechanism that would facilitate removing unnecessary and mistaken information, before it can cause any damage, and direct the brain resources to more fruitful needs. This is best illustrated with jokes, the basic form of humor. Jokes start with a setup that introduces a certain idea that leads people to believe one thing, and then the punch line alters that perception, forcing them to reinterpret that idea and realize that what they thought was actually wrong. The reward system that motivates people to conduct such debugging is manifested by the emotion of mirth, the good feeling that we get after a laugh. This is a comprehensive and nuanced theory, but most of the evidence supporting it comes from the analyses of jokes, a form of humor that is subjective and does not fully account for all humor expressions, and little other evidence supports it (for a full review of the theory, see Greengross & Mankoff, 2012).

It is important to note that no matter what were the evolutionary forces that help shaped humor, the modern environment overstimulates our desire to consume humor, the same way eating sugary donuts overexcites our basic need for high-calorie and high-fat food that was rare in our ancestral environment (Hurley et al., 2011). This is often referred to as supernormal stimuli, the propensity to overconsume something that we are evolutionarily predisposed to desire; something that was rare when we lived as hunter gatherers, but in the current environment is in abundance (Barrett, 2010). Humor might have evolved to solve a specific adaptive problem, but because the reward system is so strong, we might seek many other unrelated humor stimuli that can satisfy our desire for a good laugh, apart from its original purpose. The entertainment business capitalizes on such supernormal humor stimuli, by creating sitcoms, movies, and comedy shows that can tickle our need for endless laughs.

Sexual Selection Theory and Humor

There is no doubt that the evolutionary theories reviewed here embody some hidden truth about the forces that helped shaped humor and how it is used. However, they also have a few shortcomings. Theories focusing on the social aspect of humor center on specific situations where humor bestows some fitness benefits. For example, humor can be useful to identify in-group members or prevent us from rushing into actions that might harm us. But the circumstances in which these occurrences present themselves in daily life are rather rare. It is not clear how and why such a complex adaptation as humor would have evolved to specifically address these unique and unusual circumstances. It is also not apparent why humor and laughter should be selected as the mechanisms which enable individuals to deal with such problems. Obviously, understanding jokes depends, in part, on recognizing cultural specific knowledge and norms. But this understanding by itself is not

evidence that humor evolved to serve as the means to help identify group members from strangers. Many other social attributes, cultural systems, and forms of communication such as gossip, songs, stories, or religion can achieve the same goal (Dunbar, 1998; Sosis, 2003). Humor is a social activity, but that alone does not suggest that any social use of humor is evolutionary based.

As noted above, situations where humor can help individuals avoid pitfalls, ease tensions, or prevent an ambiguous situation from escalating are quite rare. Moreover, these are usually serious circumstances, with possible dire consequences for the parties involved. But most humor uses are among friends, in a relaxed atmosphere, when our mind, as Darwin put it, is in a "pleasurable condition." Also, people actively seek to laugh wherever they go and do not just wait for the right (and serious) situation to arise. Oftentimes, as the history of comedy from ancient Greek and Shakespearean comedy through vaudeville shows and modern stand-up comedy demonstrates, people are quite willing to pay for a good laugh. So it seems obvious that humor plays a much larger role in the life of people than what some of the social theories suggest.

Many evolutionary theories focusing on the survival benefits of humor overlook the large individual differences in humor use and experiences. Individuals vary largely in their ability to make others laugh, their humor styles, their enjoyment of sexual and aggressive forms of humor, their motivations for using humor, how funny they think they are, and virtually every aspect of humor consumption and appreciation (Greengross & Miller, 2008, 2011; Hay, 2000; Lampert & Ervin-Tripp, 1998; Martin, Puhlik-Doris, Larsen, Gray, & Weir, 2003; Mickes, Walker, Parris, Mankoff, & Christenfeld, 2011; Thomas & Esses, 2004). Most evolutionary theories fail to recognize this diversity of humor uses and incorporate it into their theories or to explain how this variation translates into an adaptive advantage. Humor production is especially variable, as is the ability to discriminate between high- and low-quality humor (Greengross & Miller, 2011).

Theories that focus on the survival benefits of humor, that humor is good for our health, or that humor contributes to social bonding, assume that there is little variability in the ability to create humor or the funniness of the jokes. For these theories, humor itself is the focal analysis and not the individuals who produce and appreciate it. According to these theories, there is something in the quality of humor that benefits the people using it, regardless of who they are. Virtually all people get the same advantages by using humor. But knowing that a joke is funny means that there are also other jokes, which are not particularly funny. People can distinguish between good jokes and bad ones and only laugh at the jokes that they find funny (Miller, 2000a). The ability to differentiate between the two is crucial for the existence of good humor. There is a need for a theory that centers on individual differences, one that will focus on the relationship between the producer of humor and the appreciator. We need to explain why so many people vigorously pursue humor and why people with a great sense of humor are highly desired in social interactions and as mates. What does production of high-quality humor tell us about the person, and what are the benefits of portraying a great sense of humor?

Sexual selection theory offers one of the best explanations for humor's origins, functions, correlates, and social attractiveness (Darwin, 1871; Miller, 2000a). Different evolutionary life histories for males and females helped shape their mate preferences and behaviors and resulted in some disparities in the way they enjoy and use humor today. These differences arise from asymmetry in their reproductive costs and the amount of time and energy devoted to parental investment (Buss, 2003). In humans, as with most other mammals, women bear the heavier costs of reproduction, such as pregnancy and child rearing, while having a shorter reproductive span. This leads women to become choosier in selecting a mate, since the consequences of selecting the wrong partner could be much more costly (e.g., raising a child alone). Thus, women should be more attentive to cues that indicate high mate value, while men would try to signal that they are high-quality mates.

Sometimes, mate quality can be directly observed, as in the cases of masculinity in men, youth in women, and symmetry in the face and the body of both sexes—all direct indicators of reproductive value and health (Buss, 2003; Thornhill & Gangestad, 2008). Other times, assessing mate quality of another individual cannot be attained directly and has to rely on advertisement (Miller, 2000b). Mate quality is advertised by ornaments that are correlated with other traits which contribute directly to fitness. The trait being advertised has to bear some reproductive advantage for the individual; otherwise, it will not be attractive, and the advertisement also must be an honest fitness indicator, or else it will be easy to fake by other individuals. One well-known example is the peacock's tail. Peacocks possess an extraverted tail, a very heavy and colorful ornament, one that requires much energy to develop and support. The bright tail is also very visible and easy to spot by predators. It seems apparent that a shorter and lighter tail would be better for survivorship. However, peacocks with the bigger and more colorful tails, ones that are more symmetrical and costly, are actually more attractive to peahens (Zahavi, 1975; Zahavi & Zahavi, 1997). Why would the peahen select mates that seemingly reduce their survivorship chances? Why would peacocks handicap themselves by wasting valuable resources to grow and maintain a beautiful tail, one that puts them at risk? The answer is that an extravagant and costly tail is a true indicator of fitness, an advertisement for underlying genetic quality (low mutation load), a trait that cannot be observed directly by the peahens. Peacocks that are less fit do not have enough resources to allocate for the growth and maintenance of such a beautiful and burdensome tail and cannot fake such a tail. The high-quality peacocks that can afford to grow an attractive tail are advertising their mate quality by showing off that they have the resources to sustain a large, heavy tail and still survive.

Advertisement of underlying genetic quality is not confined to physical characteristics alone. According to the theory of mental fitness indicators (Miller, 2000a, 2000b, 2007), many human capacities such as language, art, music, sports, altruism, moral virtues, and humor also evolved through mutual mate choice to advertise mate quality. These traits evolved to serve as indirect signals for individual genetic quality because they are honest, hard to fake indicators. One way these traits transfer into fitness is by being true indicators of intelligence, a trait that offers clear fitness benefits and is also highly desired when choosing a mate. Humor is hypothesized to be one such fitness indicator. Because women are choosier than men, we should expect men to use humor more often and more creatively to signal their mate quality and attract women, while women should be more sensitive to men producing high-quality humor when choosing a mate.

In the next parts, I will examine the evidence for humor production ability as a sexually selected trait and other predictions stemming from sexual selection theory and the fitness indicator theory.

Sex Differences in Humor Preferences

Sense of humor is regarded as one of the most socially desired traits. Individuals with a good sense of humor are perceived as friendlier, more interesting, pleasant, emotionally stable, fun to be around, socially adept, intelligent, and creative (Cann & Calhoun, 2001; Kaufman, Kozbelt, Bromley, Geher, & Miller, 2008; Martin, 2014; O'Quin & Derks, 1997). Moreover, a good sense of humor is consistently ranked as one of the most desirable traits in a potential mate, especially for women (Buss, 1988; Daniel, O'Brien, McCabe, & Quinter, 1985; Goodwin, 1990; Hansen, 1977; Sprecher & Regan, 2002; Todosijević, Ljubinković, & Arančić, 2003; Toro-Morn & Sprecher, 2003).

If humor is the product of sexual selection and a mental fitness indicator, it should be a sexually dimorphic trait, with some predicted differences in the way it is used and perceived. Because women are choosier, they should place greater importance on humor when selecting a mate and

be more sensitive to men who portray a great sense of humor. Men, on the other hand, should care less about women's humor ability and should not rank it as high in their mate preferences as women. They should, however, be more attentive to cues showing that women appreciate their sense of humor.

A meta-analysis conducted on seven samples with a total of 4,000 subjects found that women considered humor to be a more important trait in a mate than men (Feingold, 1992). Though effect sizes were relatively small (ranging from 0 to 0.55, unweighted $d = 0.22$, weighted $d = 0.14$) (Cohen, 1988), no single study showed that men emphasize humor more than women in selecting a mate. In a cross-national study, more than 200,000 participants were asked to rank their preferred traits in a desired partner from a list of 23 traits (Lippa, 2007). Humor was ranked first among women, while men placed it third, with a sex difference of $d = 0.22$.

These studies indicate that humor is an important trait when choosing a mate and more so for women. However, it is important to note that in many studies humor is vaguely defined, if at all, which leaves the subjects to interpret humor as they perceive it. For example, Buss (1988) found that among undergraduate students, both males and females reported that displaying a good sense of humor was the most effective act to attract mates. Yet, displaying a good sense of humor can indicate that the person laughs often, or it can mean that the person is telling funny jokes. We cannot tell from the study design and results how the subjects construe the term "display" or if men and women had different definitions in mind. As we saw earlier, though intuitively understood, sense of humor can mean different things to different people. In addition to the ambiguity of the term "humor," the relationship in which subjects are asked to state their humor preferences varies depending on the study, or it is not always stated clearly. Subjects on various studies were asked to state their humor preferences for anything from a date to a long-term relationship. In some cases, subjects were asked about a generic partner or mate, leaving the kind of a relationship open to interpretation. Most sex differences in sexually selected traits are pronounced for short-term mating or during courtship, while for long-term relationships both sexes tend to be equally choosy (Buss, 2003; Buss & Schmitt, 1993; Miller, 2000a). For a long-term relationship, sex differences such as mate preference tend to converge on similar tastes. Thus, not mentioning what kind of a relationship the humor mate preferences refer to may be confounding the overall effects.

A good way to unmask the true sex differences in humor preferences is to look at the actual behaviors of men and women. One common method is by looking at personal ads on dating sites and newspapers. This is a more ecologically valid study since single people state their true preferences for a mate, and they have little incentive to lie. In one study that analyzed more than 500 personal ads from a singles' magazine, Smith, Waldorf, and Trembath (1990) categorized 28 common descriptors of dating preferences found in the ads. The results showed that women sought a humorous mate twice as often as men did. Women desired a guy with a good sense of humor in 41.1 % of the ads (the second most desired trait), while men indicated their preferences for a humorous partner only 20.8 % of the time (seventh overall). While it is not clear from the study what exactly accounted for a humorous preference, or how it was coded, it is quite clear that whatever the definition was, women's preference for a humorous partner was stronger than that of men. In a similar study, Provine (2000) analyzed 3,745 personal ads published on the same day by heterosexual men and women in eight different newspapers. Overall, about one-eighth of the ads included humor-related references such as "funny," "witty," and "humorous," and women were more likely to mention humor-related words, roughly 62 % more than men did.

Studies that have looked at real personal ads lend further support to the notion that humor is a sexually selected trait sought out more by women. However, it is not always easy to interpret what people mean when they say they want a humorous partner. For example, in Provine's study, ads were separated into two groups: people who seek someone with a sense of humor and people who offer humor in their ads. A seeker was defined as someone who looks for a date that loves to laugh or that is "funny," and conversely, an offerer of humor was defined as a person who laughs a lot, appreciates good humor, or has a good sense of humor of his or her own. The problem with these definitions is that humor appreciation and humor production ability are mixed in both categories. In order to test the sexual selection theory, we need to separate the appreciators from the producers.

One study clearly separated people who are seeking humor production and those who are offering their humor production ability (Wilbur & Campbell, 2011). In the study, almost 500 college students were asked to imagine trying to get to know a potential romantic partner and rated the likelihood of using certain humor strategies in attracting this mate. The results showed that men reported a desire to use humor production statements such as "I would make a lot of jokes" or "I would try to make him/her laugh" significantly more than women. In contrast, women were more likely than men to prefer statements where they act as evaluators, such as "I would tell him/her that he/she is funny" and "I would laugh at his/her jokes." In a subsequent study, the same researchers examined real Internet dating ads of 266 people (half men, half women) from a dating site in Canada. They looked at how often people proclaimed to be funny or actually tried to be funny and how often they requested a partner with a good humor production ability. Consistent with sexual selection and mental fitness indicator predictions, men were much more inclined to offer their humor production ability, claiming that they had a great sense of humor and they could make their potential date laugh. Women, on the other hand, were significantly more likely than men to state that they want a mate that offered humor production.

A few other experiments have also looked at sex differences in humor appreciation and production ability and came to the same conclusions. In one study, 210 students of both sexes were presented with a series of photographs of people of the opposite sex, two at a time (Bressler & Balshine, 2006). Each photograph was accompanied by a series of statements, fake depictions of the individual which were either funny or not. Only women viewing pictures of men chose the humorous men as a desirable partner more often than what was expected by chance alone. Men, on the other hand, did not show a preference for a humorous partner. In another study, Bressler, Martin, and Balshine (2006) specifically tested whether women prefer men who display a good sense of humor, and men prefer women who appreciate their humor. Seventy-five women and 55 men from a student sample read fictitious descriptions of two individuals of the opposite sex. One individual produced humor that the subject enjoyed but was not appreciative of the subject's own humor. The second individual was very receptive of the subject's own humor, but the subject did not appreciate his or her humor. Participants then had to choose which individual they would prefer as a partner for various relationship types. The results revealed that although both men and women valued a good sense of humor in their respective partners, women showed a preference for a man with great humor production ability over a man that appreciated their humor production, while men preferred a woman that would appreciate their humor over a woman that would make them laugh. Women showed their preference for a humor producer for all relationship types (dating, one-night stand, short- and long-term relationships, and friendship). Men especially valued women who laughed at their jokes for a date. Only for a friendship did men show a preference for a humor producer over an appreciator. These results support the notion that when men and women talk about wanting a partner with a great sense of humor, they mean vastly different things. Men want a humor appreciator, while women want someone that will make them laugh.

Another study examined the effects of self-deprecating humor and physical attractiveness on opposite sex romantic preferences for various types of relationships (Lundy, Tan, & Cunningham, 1998). Fifty-four males and 58 female students were shown a photograph and a fake interview transcript from a person of the opposite sex. The person was either attractive or not, and his or her answers were either humorous or not. The subjects were then asked to rate their desire to meet this person again for anything from a date to a long-term relationship. Not surprisingly, men showed a stronger preference for dating an attractive woman, but using humor did little to increase their desire to meet her again. In fact, the data suggest that humorous women decreased their desirability as mates, regardless of how attractive they were. For women, the use of humor by an attractive man increased his desirability as a mate, for both short- and long-term relationships, but had no effect on his desirability if he was less attractive.

In sum, the cumulative research that comprises actual and imaginary choices people make when choosing a mate, including analyses of real personal ads, lends support to the hypothesis that humor is used as a mental fitness indicator, and is a sexually dimorphic trait. Men show proclivity to advertise their humor ability, and try to put more effort into producing high-quality humor, while women recognize that humor creativity is important, and seek men who offer it. Evidence from mock ads also showed that men who used humor in their ads were more likely to be successful in finding a date, but it made no difference for women using humor, as men do not particularly care if a woman is funny (though they would like her to laugh at their jokes). The emphasis that both sexes put on the humor production abilities of men, and the reverse role it plays in mate choice, is a recognition of the significance of humor creation in signaling mate quality and the fact women are choosier than men.

Humor Production Ability

In the previous part, I reviewed the literature on sex differences in humor preferences. The amassing evidence supports the view that men try to advertise their humor production abilities while women evaluate it, providing support for humor acting as a mental fitness indicator, a product of sexual selection. In this part, I will review the evidence for sex differences in humor production ability and its effects on mating success, mating strategies, and relationship to intelligence. Women's choosiness fosters competition among men for being selected as mates. If humor is a good indicator of mate quality, women should have a penchant for finding a humorous partner, while the strong intra-sexual selection among men should result in higher humor production abilities.

The topic of sex differences in humor production abilities is often reduced to stereotypical assertions such as "Women are not funny" (e.g., Hitchens, 2007). As we saw earlier, humor is a multidimensional concept, with many definitions and multiple ways of expression. It is impossible to substantiate broad claims about such a complex phenomenon as humor. In fact, in many aspects, men and women share similar experiences in regard to humor (Martin, 2014). Moreover, the differences that we do find are generalizations, based on averages of large samples, and do not necessarily reflect an individual ability. The research presented here will focus on a very specific aspect of humor, and its relationship to mating, and should therefore not be assumed to represent the types and magnitudes of other humor-related sex differences.

Conversational Humor

There are several ways in which humor production ability could be assessed. If a great sense humor is defined as one that makes other people smile or laugh, then by studying conversational laughter, we can compare individuals who initiate humor to those who appreciate it. If humor is a mental fitness indicator, men should be the main initiators, while women are expected to laugh more, and especially in the presence of, or in response to men. Provine (1993) studied conversational laughter by analyzing 1,200 episodes of dyadic interactions from natural conversations in shopping malls, city sidewalks,

and a university campus. Of the four possible interactions between a speaker and audience (male–male, female–female, male–female, and female–male), the male–female interaction, where the man was the speaker, produced the highest audience laughter, about 71 % of the time. When females were the speakers and males were the appreciators, men laughed only 39 % of the time. (The least amount of laughter occurred when two females talked.) In a similar study, researchers observed 212 people of various group sizes, in bars and restaurants, and documented the frequency of smiles and laughter expressed (Mehu & Dunbar, 2008). While the overall rates of smiles and laughter were similar between men and women, women laughed significantly more in mixed group interactions, especially if they were young (and more likely to be single). In contrast, the amount of laughter displayed by men did not vary, and they laughed the same amount in both mixed- and same-sex groups. Age had no effect on the frequency of laughter produced by the men. Other researchers that observed natural dyadic interactions of men and women in restaurants, shopping malls, and university campuses also reached similar results (Adams & Kirkevold, 1978; Chapell et al., 2002; Smoski & Bachorowski, 2003).

Another study that analyzed conversations of mixed-sex groups found that men were more likely than women to tell jokes, and they were also more successful in doing so, as evident by the amount of laughter manifested (Robinson & Smith-Lovin, 2001). Men also reported using more humor than women (Myers, Ropog, & Rodgers, 1997), and when asked to describe someone with an outstanding sense of humor, or to name which sex is funnier, both men and women were much more likely to choose a man (Crawford & Gressley, 1991; Nevo, Nevo, & Yin, 2001). Both men and women are also more likely to attribute humorous punch lines to men, when introduced with a cartoon in which its author's identity is obscured (Mickes et al., 2011). In addition, women believe that men's pickup lines containing humor are much more likely to be successful, compared to men's opinions of women's pickup lines (Cooper,

O'Donnell, Caryl, Morrison, & Bale, 2007). In complement to these results, a meta-analysis of sex differences in smiling that included 162 studies with over a 100,000 subjects found a tendency for women and adolescent girls to smile more than men and adolescent boys, with an average effect size of $d = 0.41$ (LaFrance, Hecht, & Paluck, 2003).

In other studies, Grammer (1990) and Grammer and Eibl-Eibesfeldt (1990) investigated whether conversational laugher indicates physical attraction. The researchers randomly matched pairs of men and women that were strangers to each other and measured the amount of laughter produced in the interaction between them. Consistent with other studies, women laughed more than men, and in addition, the amount of laughter by the woman predicted both her and the man's interests in dating each other. In contrast, men's laughter did not evoke such interest in dating in either of the pair. Li et al. (2009) also found that humor conveyed romantic interest in others. In this study, subjects who watched mock one-on-one dating sessions perceived the man to be more attracted to his date when he initiated humor, compared to when he did not. Also, the woman was perceived as more attracted to the man when she appreciated his humor, than when she did not. Thus, humor production either can enhance the attractiveness of a man or can be seen as an indicator of an already existing attraction, and complementarily, women appreciating humor indicates attraction to the men. Similarly, Penton-Voak and Chang (2008) found that smiling increased the attractiveness of women, but not men, as rated by both sexes.

Another study looked at the effect of a smiling woman on men's courtship behavior (Guéguen, 2008). On 100 different occasions, an average-looking woman made eye contact with a man who was sitting alone at a bar and either smiled at him or did not. The results showed that men who were smiled at were more than five times more likely to approach the woman and start a conversation with her, compared to when the woman did not smile at them (11 vs. 2 times). Even if the men did not approach the woman, the men who got a smile glanced at the woman for an

average of 5 s longer, compared to when she did not smile at them (7 vs. 2 s). Mehu, Little, and Dunbar (2008) also found that a woman's smile increased her attractiveness in the eyes of both men and women, while male smiles had no such effect on either sex.

The data from conservational humor studies support the notion that humor is a sexually dimorphic trait. Men initiate humor more than women, especially when interacting with women. Women, on the other hand, laugh more than men, and particularly in response to male speakers. Men's production of humor increases their attractiveness as mates in women's view, while women's smiles and laughter both signal romantic interest and enhance their attractiveness.

Studying interactions between men and women is important because the focus is on humor's most important product: laughter. However, not all humor production induces laughter in others, and people smile and laugh for various other reasons. For example, Provine (2000) found that most laughter occurs in response to mundane comments, and the speakers themselves laughed more than their audiences. Though the evidence does support the idea that humor production ability and humor appreciation are sexually selected traits, indirect measures of humor production have their shortcomings, and more direct and reliable appraisals of humor creativity are needed.

Humor Creation Ability

Relatively few studies have looked at how men and women differ in their humor creation ability, perhaps because most humor research focuses on humor appreciation, which is easier to study with jokes and cartoons. Studying humor creativity poses a challenge for researchers, but nevertheless, there have been several attempts to study the subject and specifically, sex differences in humor production ability.

One simple way to evaluate humor production is by asking people how funny they think they are. Some evidence suggests there is a modest correlation between self-rated wittiness and other more objective measures of humor ability

(Feingold & Mazzella, 1993), but overall, self-reports are not considered a reliable way to assess humor creativity. One problem with this method is that we are measuring biased perceptions individuals have about their own humor ability rather than true humor production. Most people rate themselves above average in humor ability, a statistical impossibility, and while both sexes tend to think that men are funnier than women, men overestimate their abilities more than women (Crawford & Gressley, 1991; Mickes et al., 2011; Myers et al., 1997). A more reliable alternative is to ask friends, family members, or teachers to evaluate the humor production of an individual (Bergen, 1998). This indirect method has some merit, but is usually more time-consuming and costly and hence, not very practical. Another alternative is to give subjects the beginning of a joke, and ask them to complete the punch line, either from a list of possible punch lines or from their own imaginations (Feingold, 1983). The problem with this approach is that it utilizes "canned" jokes that are not a good representation of spontaneous, everyday humor and are also too restrictive. It also is not a very reliable measure of humor creativity, which makes the whole approach less appealing.

A more objective method to assess spontaneous humor creativity is by presenting subjects with a cartoon that has no caption, and ask them to write witty captions for it, that will later be evaluated by independent judges for funniness (Brodzinsky & Rubien, 1976; Feingold & Mazzella, 1993; Turner, 1980). Several studies have utilized the captionless cartoons approach to study sex differences in humor production. In these studies, researchers either remove captions from existing cartoons or use cartoons and pictures with no captions. (In recent years, researchers have been using cartoons from The New Yorker magazine, which runs a weekly competition that introduces a specially drawn cartoon without a caption and asks readers to send them funny captions.) In one study, 200 men and 200 women from a student sample were asked to write as many funny captions as they could think of for three such cartoons in 10 min (Greengross & Miller, 2011). Later, six independent judges (four women, two men), blind to the sex or any other characteristic of the subjects, rated the funniness of the captions. The judges' sex did not have an effect on the ratings, and the overall ratings yielded high reliability scores. The results showed that on average, the men's captions were rated as funnier than the women's, with medium effect sizes (average $d = 0.40$). Men also produced slightly more captions than the women.

In another similar study, albeit with a smaller sample, 32 students (16 men, 16 women) wrote captions for captionless cartoons, which were rated by 81 independent judges (34 men, 47 women) (Mickes et al., 2011). The results showed that on average, men's scores were higher than women's on the humor production task, regardless of the judge's sex, with an effect size of $d = 0.24$. Another study that asked subjects to write both funny descriptions of people, based on photographs, and funny answers to generic questions such as "What do you think the world will be like in a hundred years?" reached the same conclusions with an average effect size of $d = 0.40$ (Howrigan & MacDonald, 2008). Brodzinsky and Rubien (1976) used cartoons from contemporary books and magazines with their captions removed to evaluate humor production ability. Four of the cartoons were overtly sexual in nature, four were aggressive, and four were neutral. Six independent judges (three men, three women) scored the cartoons for funniness. The results showed that males generated funnier captions than females for sexual and aggressive cartoons, but there were no sex differences for the neutral cartoons. The results might be impacted by women's tendency not to enjoy sexual and aggressive humor, which might impede their ability to produce funny captions for such cartoons (Lampert & Ervin-Tripp, 1998). In another study, Edwards and Martin (2010) reported no significant sex differences in humor production ability, using captionless cartoons as their measure of humor creativity. However, the lack of significant results might be attributed to low statistical power, and calculations of effect size based on their data reveal that men scored higher than women on the task, with $d = 0.24$, which is in accordance with other studies.

In sum, the evidence shows that both men and women believe men to have higher humor production abilities compared to women, and objective judgments of humor creativity affirm that this perception is correct and men are better than women at producing humor. These differences are small to medium, but consistent and robust. It is important to remember that these differences reflect averages, and both men and women vary in their humor production abilities. Indeed, if humor is a mental fitness indicator, we should expect variability in the ability to make others laugh. If all humor attempts were equally successful, humor would not be a good and reliable signal of mate quality.

Moreover, production and appreciation of humor are based on similar mental capacities and mutual mate choice—the result of coevolution between males and females. In order to produce high-quality humor, one must understand how humor works and be capable of anticipating how it will be perceived (Miller, 2000a). Hence, trying to create high-quality humor enables the individual to discriminate between good and bad humor ability, which jokes work and which do not, and what is funny and what falls flat. That expectation, therefore, is the key for both producing and appreciating humor, since without expectations that could be violated, there would be no evolutionary pressure to produce better and funnier humor, and sexual selection would stall. Thus, while we should expect men to produce, on average, higher quality humor than women, the differences should not be too large, and that is precisely what the data show.

Furthermore, it is imperative to remember that though females are the choosier sex, it does not mean they cannot or should not produce high-quality humor. As discussed earlier, most sex differences in sexually selected traits are more prominent in short-term mating, while for long-term relationships, mate preferences and choices tend to be similar for both sexes (Buss, 2003; Buss & Schmitt, 1993; Miller, 2000a). Because of the disparity in parental investment and reproduction costs, men are more motivated to have short-term sexual relationships and thus are more motivated to flaunt their humor ability when interested in a short-term partner or at the early stages of courting when it is still unclear whether there is even the possibility for a long-term relationship.

Production of Humor and Mating Success

So far, we have reviewed research that shows humor to be a sexually dimorphic trait. Humor is preferred more by women, while men try to signal their quality by producing high-quality humor. Men are also the predominant initiators of humor, while women are the main appreciators who tend to smile and laugh more in general, but especially in response to male speakers. But for humor to serve as a mental fitness indicator, it has to translate into mating success. Does humor affect romantic choices? Do women actually choose men with a great sense of humor as dates? Several studies have attempted to answer these questions.

In one study mentioned earlier, researchers created fictitious online dating ads that contained a "one-liner" joke at the start of the ad (Wilbur & Campbell, 2011). One hundred and fourteen college participants (73 women, 41 men) were then asked to evaluate the humor in the ad and to state their romantic interest in that person. The "romantic interest" variable was assessed by computing an average score of the participants' interest in either getting to know the person better, having a long-term relationship with the individual or possibly seeing themselves marrying that person. The results showed that for women's ads, adding humor did little to attract the romantic interest of men. On the other hand, judging a man's ad to be humorous significantly increased the romantic interests of the women evaluating it.

In a more direct test of the influence of humor production on mating success, Greengross and Miller (2011) looked at how good humor production ability translates into mating success. This

study, discussed earlier, evaluated humor creativity using the captionless cartoon task. Mating
success was measured by the Sociosexual Orientation Inventory (Simpson & Gangestad, 1991), a
self-report questionnaire that includes questions
pertaining to actual sexual behaviors, such as age
at first intercourse, lifetime number of sex
partners, and acts of intercourse in the past
month. The results showed that subjects who
scored higher on the humor production task
enjoyed greater mating success (started having
sex earlier, had a higher number of sexual
partners, and had more sex in general), compared
to the less funny individuals. Interestingly, these
results were true for both men and women, but
since their actual humor abilities differ, men's
humor is presumably more effective in attracting
mates. This is because the motivations for men
and women to use humor differ. As discussed
earlier, women know that their ability to make
men laugh does little to attract men, while men
recognize the value of humor in alluring women.
The asymmetry in the benefits of humor production ability that each sex gains could be the
driving force behind men's attempts to make
women laugh. It might also explain why men
think they are funnier than women, regardless
of their true humor ability. Overestimating
one's humor abilities has its advantages for
men. A man is better off thinking he can make
a woman laugh, even if he often fails to do so,
than not to think he is funny and therefore not
make an attempt. The risk of not even trying to
make women laugh may result in losing a mating
opportunity. This type of cognitive bias is often
referred to as a false-positive error, and is quite
common for many evolutionary-based attributes.
For example, men tend to overestimate women's
sexual availability because it is better for men to
be refused than to lose a chance at mating
(Haselton & Buss, 2000).

Another study, in a more valid ecological
setting, tested whether men's sense of humor
helps increase their mating success. On 60 different occasions, three men sat at an outdoor table
near a bar next to a young woman sitting alone.
One of the three men then started telling jokes,
while the two others laughed (Guéguen, 2010).

An observer noted whether the woman listened
to the jokes and laughed. Half of the time, the
two appreciators left, and the joke teller
approached the woman, asking for her phone
number. In another condition, one of the men
that laughed at the jokes, but was not the joke
teller, asked for her phone number after two of
his friends left (in both cases it was the same
confederate). The results showed that women
were three times more likely to give their phone
number to the man who told jokes, compared
to the man who appreciated the jokes
(42.9–15.4 %). The joke teller was also considered more attractive, intelligent, funny, sociable,
and a more desirable mate for a long-term relationship, compared to the appreciator (with
medium to large effect sizes).

One other study set out to test whether humor
was a mental fitness indicator among married
couples (Weisfeld et al., 2011). More than
3,000 couples in five countries answered
questions regarding the importance of humor in
their marriages. The results showed that, overall,
both husbands and wives were happier with a
humorous partner, but spousal humorousness
was more important for the marital satisfaction
of the wives than the husbands in all five cultures,
though only three were statistically significant.
In four countries (USA, UK, China, and Turkey),
both husbands and wives thought that the husband produced more humor. Only in Russia the
results were reversed, though frequency of
humor production was the lowest there, and the
women outnumbered the men, which might indicate a more intense competition for husbands.

In sum, studies confirm that humorous people,
especially men, attract more mates, enjoy better
mating success as measured by actual sexual
behavior, and are more satisfied in their
relationships. Women, on the other hand, seek
mates with great humor production ability, and
high levels of humor creativity enhance their
interest and attraction to men. It is worth noting
that these findings are somewhat at odds with
another evolutionary theory, which posits that
humor evolved to pique our interest in others
(Li et al., 2009). According to the interest indicator theory, any individual interested in a

relationship, regardless of sex, could equally initiate humor, have the same capacity to produce humor, and should reap the benefits of great humor production ability. However, as the data reviewed here shows, humor is sexually dimorphic when it comes to mating. Men produce better humor on average, and women are attracted to men with great humor abilities. In contrast, men have little interest in a woman with high humor ability, and they are more interested in her laughing at their humor. Furthermore, according to the interest indicator model, humor production and humor appreciation are the result of physical attraction, and humor creativity should not enhance the attractiveness of the producer. While it is generally true that being attracted to someone could increase his or her perceived humor ability, research shows that the opposite is also true, independent of the initial attraction the couple might have to each other. Moreover, high-quality humor increases the attractiveness of men, but not of women, producing high-quality humor, thus lending further support to humor being a sexually selected trait.

Extreme Humor Ability

There are large individual differences in the ability to make others laugh. If humor is a sexually selected trait, one might expect not only to find sex differences in humor production ability among ordinary people but also that these differences would be manifested at the highest level of humor creativity with professional humorists. One such group of humorist is professional stand-up comedians. Comedians' great humor ability is evident not only by their occupation but also by independent tests of humor creativity. One study used the captionless cartoon task discussed earlier to assess comedians' humor production ability and compare it to a student sample. The results showed large differences in favor of the comedians, with an average effect size of $d = 1.60$ (Greengross, Martin, & Miller, 2012b). While professional comedians do not necessarily represent everyday uses of humor, studying sex differences at the extreme level of humor ability could shed light on everyday uses of humor, just as the study of

homicide can help illuminate general patterns of violence (Daly & Wilson, 1988).

To estimate which sex is a better producer of humor among professional humorists, we can look at the number of men and women in such professions. If men have better humor production abilities, then they should be overrepresented in those jobs. Though no official registry of comedians exists, all indications are that there are more male stand-up comedians. In one study of professional stand-up comedians, of the 31 comedians in the study, only three were women (Greengross, Martin, & Miller, 2012a; Greengross et al., 2012b; Greengross & Miller, 2009). Also, on the list of the 100 greatest stand-up comedians published by Comedy Central, only nine were women (http://www.listology.com/list/comedy-central-100-greatest-standups-all-time). In another study on professional cartoonists, researchers looked at sex differences in cartoonists' styles (Samson & Huber, 2007). The researchers made a comprehensive effort to include as many female cartoonists as possible, searching magazines, books, journals, special volumes, Internet databases, and personal contacts. In the end, they were able to find a total of 1,519 cartoonists from 61 countries. Of them, only 9 % were women.

The data on comedians and cartoonists suggest that there are far more men at the highest level of humor production than women. While there might be some societal barriers and stereotypes that prevent women from getting into or succeeding in those professions, the overwhelming disproportional representation of men and women suggests that at least some of the differences are due to men's superior humor ability at the extremely high end. Another factor that might influence the scarcity of women in such professions is lower motivation to pursue such careers. Stand-up comedy, for example, is a very demanding job, with little job security and strong competition. Women might be less inclined to desire such high-risk jobs, while men's ambition for high status would drive them to seek what is considered to be a highly sought-after profession. In the view of sexual selection theory, high status is favored by women when choosing a mate, because it gives them access to resources which are valuable for survival, food, and health and can help raise future offspring (Buss, 2003). Thus, men's pursuit of high status and women's desire for such men as mates could motivate more men to look for a career in stand-up comedy, while for women, being a professional comedian may not enhance their mate value by much (Buss, 2003). It is worth noting that humor itself can increase mate desirability just because it is associated with another, sexually dimorphic trait such as status. Funny individuals with higher status are considered more attractive than lower status individuals, especially when using self-deprecating humor that can be seen as a form of handicap, similar to the peacock's tail (Greengross & Miller, 2008).

Humor Production as an Indicator of Intelligence

One possible mechanism in which humor could serve as a sexually selected mental fitness indicator and transfer into mating success is by signaling intelligence (Miller, 2000a). Intelligence itself is highly desirable in a potential mate, and it is correlated with fitness-related traits such as physical health (Deary, 2005), longevity (Gottfredson & Deary, 2004), physical attractiveness (Langlois et al., 2000), body symmetry (an indicator of developmental stability) (Banks, Batchelor, & McDaniel, 2010; Prokosch, Yeo, & Miller, 2005), and even semen quality (Arden, Gottfredson, Miller, & Pierce, 2008)—all associated with fitness.

Studies show a close relationship between humor production ability and intelligence. Greengross and Miller (2009) calculated the correlations between humor production and two intelligence tests, a vocabulary test and an abstract reasoning test, the Raven's Advanced Progressive Matrices (RAPM). Given that the humor production task was to make verbal jokes, it was not surprising that this humor ability yielded a stronger correlation with the verbal test than the abstract reasoning test ($r = 0.39$ and

$r = 0.27$, respectively). Also, the correlation between humor production and the verbal test was stronger for men ($r = 0.42$ compared to $r = 0.30$ for women), suggesting that verbal intelligence more strongly predicts capacity for verbal humor in men than in women. In addition, a mediation model showed that humor ability strongly mediates the positive effect of intelligence on mating success, for both sexes. The results support the view that humor is a manifestation of intelligence and that humor can translate either directly or through intelligence to mating success.

In another study that investigated the relationship between humor and intelligence, Wilbur and Campbell (2011) found that in real personal dating ads and for both sexes, those who offered their humor production abilities and those who sought partners who were funny also offered and requested intelligence, respectively, implying that the two attributes are intertwined. Moreover, when evaluating fake ads that either contained humor or not, women's judgments of men's humor were strongly correlated with how intelligent and warm they perceived the men to be. No such association was found among men evaluating women's ads, suggesting that the connection between humor and intelligence is more important for women's mate choices.

Also, professional stand-up comedians consistently score higher than the average population in verbal intelligence. One study found that the IQ scores of 55 professional male comedians, estimated based on the verbal portion of the Wechsler Adult Intelligence Scale, range between 115 and 160, with an average of 138, well above the average of 100 in the general population (Janus, 1975). In a follow-up study with 14 female comedians, the range of IQ was 112–144 with an average of 126 (Janus, Bess, & Janus, 1978). In a more recent study, vocabulary scores of 31 professional comedians were compared to those of students, and the results showed comedians to have much better verbal intelligence, which is highly correlated with general intelligence (Carless, 2000), with a large effect size of $d = 1.34$ (Greengross et al., 2012b). Though comedians are expected to score high on verbal intelligence, as their profession requires a display of superior verbal skills, the difference from the general population is substantial.

It is interesting to note that despite the apparent correlation between humor production and intelligence, results are somewhat inconsistent. For example, Howrigan and MacDonald (2008) found an overall correlation of $r = 0.29$ between humor creativity and general intelligence as measured by the RAPM, but women's correlation was stronger compared to that of the men ($r = 0.33$ to $r = 0.15$). However, the measured intelligence of abstract reasoning may be less relevant for displaying verbal humor abilities, compared to other types of intelligence such as verbal intelligence.

A few studies have found that perceptions of an individual's intelligence are not always aligned with the perceptions of that person's humor ability. In one study, humorous individuals were rated as less intellectual than the non-humorous individuals (Lundy et al., 1998), and in another study described earlier (Bressler & Balshine, 2006), humorous people were perceived as less intelligent, though women did prefer them as mates, and rated them as more fun, friendly, and popular. The discrepancy between the existence of a correlation between humor and intelligence and the perception that they are not correlated might be attributed to the student samples used in the latter studies. College students tend to equate intelligence with being educated, a concept that is not equivalent to general intelligence as measured by standardized tests. Also, the humor ascribed to the humorous people who were evaluated by the students was immature and not sophisticated in nature. However, the fact that women actually found men more attractive for mating despite using this childish humor lends stronger support to the importance of humor creativity in mate choice.

Heritability of Sense of Humor

Evolution is all about reproduction and passing the genes from one generation to another. In order for humor to be a sexually selected trait, it needs to have a heritable component to it. Humor production ability could be inherited either directly or indirectly through the mediated effect of another desirable trait that is correlated with humor. One such trait could be intelligence. As we saw earlier, there is a correlation between humor production ability and intelligence, and there is growing evidence that general intelligence is heritable (Plomin & Spinath, 2004; Rushton, Bons, Vernon, & Čvorović, 2007).

Only a few studies have looked at the heritability of humor, and each focused on a different aspect of humor. Unfortunately, none of the studies to date have tested whether humor production ability is heritable. Most research on the subject compared monozygous (MZ, identical) twins to dizygous (DZ, fraternal) twins. If humor is indeed inheritable, we should expect MZ twins to be more similar to each other compared to the DZ twins.

In one study, researchers compared how similar appreciation of cartoons was among MZ and DZ twins (Cherkas, Hockberg, MacGregor, Snieder, & Spector, 2000). One hundred and twenty-seven pairs of female British twins (71 MZ and 56 DZ, ages 20–75) were asked to rate the funniness of five "The Far Side" cartoons. The researchers found that shared environment, but not genetic factors, contributed to similarities in humor appreciation. In contrast, several other studies, which used different measures of humor, did find humor to have a genetic component to it. In one study of adults, 300 MZ twins and 156 DZ twins from Canada and the USA completed the Humor Styles Questionnaire, a questionnaire that measures four daily uses of humor (Martin et al., 2003). The results showed that the two positive humor styles, humor that is used to put others at ease through telling jokes and having a humorous outlook of life, had strong genetic contributions to individual differences and are attributed to nonshared environmental factors (Vernon, Martin, Schermer, & Mackie, 2008). On the other hand, the negative humor styles, styles that are used to ridicule others or make oneself the butt of the joke, were largely a product of shared and nonshared environment and not due to genetic factors. Another study of almost 2,000 twins in the UK that used the same questionnaire found that individual differences in all four styles were due to genetic and nonshared environment factors (Vernon, Martin, Schermer, Cherkas, & Spector, 2008). Other studies which examined adolescent twin children, or compared adoptive and nonadaptive children to their parents, also found that genetic factors significantly contributed to individual differences in sense of humor, as measured by a standard humor questionnaire focusing on interpersonal and daily uses of humor (Manke, 1998). In sum, despite the somewhat mixed evidence, the data suggest that at least some aspects of humor are heritable.

Conclusion

Humor and laughter are powerful displays enjoyed daily by people all over the world. There are many mysteries yet to be unlocked regarding the origin and uses of humor, but it is clear that humor has strong evolutionary roots. The data presented here support the view that humor is sexual selected and a fitness indicator. Differences in humor production ability and humor appreciation do not seem to be random, and knowing that someone has a great sense of humor tells us something about that person, far beyond his or her humor ability. Evidence suggests that humor is a sexually dimorphic trait, and humor production is an overt manifestation of intelligence that increases mate value, especially in men. Humor could have evolved as part of mutual, sex-specific selection, where men's and women's humor production, uses, preferences, motivations, perceptions, and influences vary. Women seek mates with a sense of humor and place greater importance on finding a mate with a sense of humor, a trait that is highly attractive for them. Men, on the other hand, try to produce high-quality humor to attract women, while women's humor creativity does little to attract men. Women's laughter signals their romantic interest in a man, while men's laughter does not.

Humor serves many other functions in our daily lives, and while the data does support the view that humor production is a sexually selected trait, it does not necessarily exclude other explanations, evolutionary or not, for humor's origin, function, and uses. Humor offers a strong reward system, and supernormal stimuli tickle our desire for a good laugh all the time. Other complementary explanations could be in place, and future studies will help fill some of the gaps in empirical data on the subject.

References

Adams, R. M., & Kirkevold, B. (1978). Looking, smiling, laughing, and moving in restaurants: Sex and age differences. *Journal of Nonverbal Behavior, 3*(2), 117–127.

Apte, M. L. (1985). *Humor and laughter: An anthropological approach*. Ithaca, NY: Cornell University Press.

Arden, R., Gottfredson, L. S., Miller, G., & Pierce, A. (2008). Intelligence and semen quality are positively correlated. *Intelligence, 37*(3), 277–282.

Attardo, S. (1994). *Linguistic theories of humor*. Berlin: Walter de Gruyter.

Banks, G. C., Batchelor, J. H., & McDaniel, M. A. (2010). Smarter people are (a bit) more symmetrical: A meta-analysis of the relationship between intelligence and fluctuating asymmetry. *Intelligence, 38*(4), 393–401.

Barrett, D. (2010). *Supernormal stimuli: How primal urges overran their evolutionary purpose*. New York: W.W. Norton & Company.

Beattie, J. (1778). On laughter and ludicrous composition. In J. Beattie (Ed.), *Essays*. London: E. & C. Dilly.

Bergen, D. (1998). Development of the sense of humor. In W. Ruch (Ed.), *The sense of humor: Explorations of a personality characteristic* (pp. 329–358). Berlin: Walter de Gruyter.

Bressler, E., & Balshine, S. (2006). The influence of humor on desirability. *Evolution and Human Behavior, 27*(1), 29–39.

Bressler, E., Martin, R. A., & Balshine, S. (2006). Production and appreciation of humor as sexually selected traits. *Evolution and Human Behavior, 27*(2), 121–130.

Brodzinsky, D. M., & Rubien, J. (1976). Humor production as a function of sex of subject, creativity, and cartoon content. *Journal of Consulting and Clinical Psychology, 44*(4), 597–600.

Buss, D. M. (1988). The evolution of human intrasexual competition: Tactics of mate attraction. *Journal of Personality and Social Psychology, 54*(4), 616–628.

Buss, D. M. (2003). *The evolution of desire: Strategies of human mating* (2nd ed.). New York: Basic Books.

Buss, D. M., & Schmitt, D. P. (1993). Sexual strategies theory: An evolutionary perspective on human mating. *Psychological Review, 100*(2), 204–232.

Cann, A., & Calhoun, L. G. (2001). Perceived personality associations with differences in sense of humor: Stereotypes of hypothetical others with high or low senses of humor. *Humor: International Journal of Humor Research, 14*(2), 117–130.

Carless, S. A. (2000). The validity of scores on the Multidimensional Aptitude Battery. *Educational and Psychological Measurement, 60*(4), 592–603.

Chafe, W. (1987). Humor as a disabling mechanism. *American Behavioral Scientist, 30*(1), 16–26.

Chapell, M., Batten, M., Brown, J., Gonzalez, E., Herquet, G., & Massar, C. (2002). Frequency of public laughter in relation to sex, age, ethnicity, and social context. *Perceptual and Motor Skills, 95*(3), 746.

Cherkas, L., Hockberg, F., MacGregor, A. J., Snieder, H., & Spector, T. D. (2000). Happy families: A twin study of humour. *Twin Research, 3*, 17–22.

Cohen, J. (1988). *Statistical power analysis for the behavioral sciences* (2nd ed.). Hillsdale, NJ: Lawrence Erlbaum.

Cooper, M., O'Donnell, D., Caryl, P. G., Morrison, R., & Bale, C. (2007). Chat-up lines as male displays: Effects of content, sex, and personality. *Personality and Individual Differences, 43*(5), 1075–1085.

Crawford, M., & Gressley, D. (1991). Creativity, caring, and context: Women's and men's accounts of humor preferences and practices. *Psychology of Women Quarterly, 15*, 217–231.

Daly, M., & Wilson, M. (1988). *Homicide*. New York: Aldine de Gruyter.

Daniel, H. J., O'Brien, K. F., McCabe, R. B., & Quinter, V. E. (1985). Values in mate selection: A 1984 campus survey. *College Student Journal, 19*(1), 44–50.

Darwin, C. (1871). *The descent of man, and selection in relation to sex*. London: John Murray.

Darwin, C. (1872). *The expression of the emotions in man and animals*. London: John Murray.

Davies, C. (1998). The dog that didn't bark in the night: A new sociological approach to the cross-cultural study of humor. In W. Ruch (Ed.), *The sense of humor: Explorations of a personality characteristic* (pp. 293–306). Berlin: Walter de Gruyter.

Deary, I. J. (2005). Intelligence, health and death. *The Psychologist, 18*(10), 610–613.

Deckers, L. (1998). Influence of mood on humor. In W. Ruch (Ed.), *The sense of humor: Explorations of a personality characteristic* (pp. 309–328). Berlin: Walter de Gruyter.

Dunbar, R. (1998). *Grooming, gossip, and the evolution of language*. Cambridge, MA: Harvard University Press.

Edwards, K. R., & Martin, R. A. (2010). Humor creation ability and mental health: Are funny people more psychologically healthy? *Europe's Journal of Psychology, 6*(3), 196–212.

Ekman, P. (1993). Facial expression and emotion. *American Psychologist, 48*(4), 384.

Feingold, A. (1983). Measuring humor ability: Revision and construct validation of the Humor Perceptiveness Test. *Perceptual and Motor Skills, 56*(1), 159–166.

Feingold, A. (1992). Gender differences in mate selection preferences: A test of the parental investment model. *Psychological Bulletin, 112*(1), 125–139.

Feingold, A., & Mazzella, R. (1991). Psychometric intelligence and verbal humor ability. *Personality & Individual Differences, 12*(5), 427–435.

Feingold, A., & Mazzella, R. (1993). Preliminary validation of a multidimensional model of wittiness. *Journal of Personality, 61*(3), 439–456.

Flamson, T., & Barrett, H. C. (2008). The encryption theory of humor: A knowledge-based mechanism of honest signaling. *Journal of Evolutionary Psychology, 6*(4), 261–281.

Freedman, D. G. (1964). Smiling in blind infants and the issue of innate vs. acquired. *Journal of Child Psychology and Psychiatry, 5*(3–4), 171–184.

Gamble, J. (2001). Humor in apes. *Humor: International Journal of Humor Research, 14*(2), 163–179.

Gervais, M., & Wilson, D. S. (2005). The evolution and functions of laughter and humor: A synthetic approach. *The Quarterly Review of Biology, 80*(4), 395–430.

Goodwin, R. (1990). Sex differences among partner preferences: Are the sexes really very similar? *Sex Roles, 23*(9), 501–513.

Gottfredson, L. S., & Deary, I. J. (2004). Intelligence predicts health and longevity, but why? *Current Directions in Psychological Science, 13*(1), 1–4.

Grammer, K. (1990). Strangers meet: Laughter and nonverbal signs of interest in opposite-sex encounters. *Journal of Nonverbal Behavior, 14*(4), 209–236.

Grammer, K., & Eibl-Eibesfeldt, I. (1990). The ritualisation of laughter. In W. Koch (Ed.), *Natürlichkeit der Sprache und der Kultur: Acta Colloquii* (pp. 192–214). Bochum: Brockmeyer.

Graziano, W. G., & Bryant, W. H. M. (1998). Self-monitoring and the self-attribution of positive emotions. *Journal of Personality and Social Psychology, 74*(1), 250–261.

Greengross, G., & Mankoff, R. (2012). Inside "Inside Jokes": The hidden side of humor. A review of Matthew M. Hurley, Daniel C. Dennett, and Reginald B. Adams Jr., Inside jokes: Using humor to reverse-engineer the mind. *Evolutionary Psychology, 10*(3), 443–456.

Greengross, G., Martin, R. A., & Miller, G. F. (2012a). Childhood experiences of professional comedians: Peer and parent relationships and humor use. *Humor: International Journal of Humor Research, 25*(4), 491–505.

Greengross, G., Martin, R. A., & Miller, G. F. (2012b). Personality traits, intelligence, humor styles, and humor production ability of professional stand-up comedians compared to college students. *Psychology of Aesthetics, Creativity and the Arts, 6*(1), 74–82.

Greengross, G., & Miller, G. F. (2008). Dissing oneself versus dissing rivals: Effects of status, personality, and sex on the short-term and long-term attractiveness of self-deprecating and other-deprecating humor. *Evolutionary Psychology, 6*(3), 393–408.

Greengross, G., & Miller, G. F. (2009). The Big Five personality traits of professional comedians compared to amateur comedians, comedy writers, and college students. *Personality and Individual Differences, 47* (2), 79–83.

Greengross, G., & Miller, G. F. (2011). Humor ability reveals intelligence, predicts mating success, and is higher in males. *Intelligence, 39*(4), 188–192.

Guéguen, N. (2008). The effect of a woman's smile on men's courtship behavior. *Social Behavior and Personality, 36*(9), 1233–1236.

Guéguen, N. (2010). Men's sense of humor and women's responses to courtship solicitations: An experimental field study. *Psychological Reports, 107*(1), 145–156.

Hansen, S. L. (1977). Dating choices of high school students. *Family Coordinator, 26*(2), 133–138.

Haselton, M. G., & Buss, D. M. (2000). Error management theory: A new perspective on biases in cross-sex mind reading. *Journal of Personality and Social Psychology, 78*(1), 81–91.

Hay, J. (2000). Functions of humor in the conversations of men and women. *Journal of Pragmatics, 32*(6), 709–742.

Hitchens, C. (2007). Why women aren't funny. *Vanity Fair, 557*, 54–59.

Howrigan, D. P., & MacDonald, K. B. (2008). Humor as a mental fitness indicator. *Evolutionary Psychology, 6* (4), 652–666.

Hurley, M., Dennett, D., & Adams, R., Jr. (2011). *Inside jokes: Using humor to reverse-engineer the mind* (1st ed.). Cambridge, MA: The MIT Press.

Janus, S. S. (1975). The great comedians: Personality and other factors. *American Journal of Psychoanalysis, 35* (2), 169–174.

Janus, S. S., Bess, B. E., & Janus, B. R. (1978). The great comediennes: Personality and other factors. *The American Journal of Psychoanalysis, 38*(4), 367–372.

Kaufman, S. B., Kozbelt, A., Bromley, M. L., Geher, G., & Miller, G. (2008). The role of creativity and humor in human mate selection. In G. Geher & G. Miller (Eds.), *Mating intelligence: Sex, relationships, and the mind's reproductive system* (pp. 227–262). Mahwah, NJ: Lawrence Erlbaum.

Keaton, D. (2012). *Then again.* New York: Random House.

Keltner, D., & Ekman, P. (1994). Facial expressions of emotion. In V. S. Ramachandran (Ed.), *Encyclopedia of human behavior* (Vol. 2, pp. 361–369). San Diego, CA: Academic.

Koestler, A. (1964). *The act of creation: A study of the conscious and unconscious processes of humor, scientific discovery and art.* London: Hutchison Press.

LaFrance, M., Hecht, M. A., & Paluck, E. L. (2003). The contingent smile: A meta-analysis of sex differences in smiling. *Psychological Bulletin, 129*(2), 305–334.

Lampert, M. D., & Ervin-Tripp, S. M. (1998). Exploring paradigms: The study of gender and sense of humor near the end of the 20th century. In W. Ruch (Ed.), *The sense of humor: Explorations of a personality characteristic* (pp. 231–270). Berlin: Walter de Gruyter.

Langlois, J. H., Kalakanis, L., Rubenstein, A. J., Larson, A., Hallam, M., & Smoot, M. (2000). Maxims or myths of beauty? A meta-analytic and theoretical review. *Psychological Bulletin, 126*(3), 390–423.

Li, N. P., Griskevicius, V., Durante, K. M., Jonason, P. K., Pasisz, D. J., & Aumer, K. (2009). An evolutionary perspective on humor: Sexual selection or interest indication? *Personality and Social Psychology Bulletin, 35*, 923–936.

Lippa, R. A. (2007). The preferred traits of mates in a cross-national study of heterosexual and homosexual men and women: An examination of biological and cultural influences. *Archives of Sexual Behavior, 36* (2), 193–208.

Lundy, D. E., Tan, J., & Cunningham, M. R. (1998). Heterosexual romantic preferences: The importance of humor and physical attractiveness for different types of relationships. *Personal Relationships, 5*(3), 311–325.

Manke, B. (1998). Genetic and environmental contributions to children's interpersonal humor. In W. Ruch (Ed.), *The sense of humor: Explorations of a personality characteristic* (pp. 361–384). Berlin: Walter de Gruyter.

Martin, R. A. (2003). Sense of humor. In S. J. Lopez & C. R. Snyder (Eds.), *Positive psychological assessment: A handbook of models and measures* (pp. 313–326). Washington, DC: American Psychological Association.

Martin, R. A. (2014). Humor and gender: An overview of psychological research. In D. Chiaro & R. Baccolini (Eds.), *Gender and humor: Interdisciplinary and international perspectives.* Berlin: Mouton de Gruyter.

Martin, R. A. (2007). *The psychology of humor: An integrative approach.* London: Elsevier Academic Press.

Martin, R. A. (2013). Humor and gender: An overview of psychological research. In D. Chiaro & R. Baccolini (Eds.), *Humor and gender.* Berlin: Mouton de Gruyter.

Martin, R. A., & Kuiper, N. (1999). Daily occurrence of laughter: Relationships with age, gender, and type a personality. *Humor: International Journal of Humor Research, 12*(4), 355–384.

Martin, R. A., & Lefcourt, H. (1983). Sense of humor as a moderator of the relation between stressors and moods. *Journal of Personality and Social Psychology, 45*, 1313–1324.

Martin, R. A., Puhlik-Doris, P., Larsen, G., Gray, J., & Weir, K. (2003). Individual differences in uses of humor and their relation to psychological well-being: Development of the Humor Styles Questionnaire. *Journal of Research in Personality, 37*, 48–75.

McGhee, P. E. (1979). *Humor: Its origin and development.* San Francisco: W.H. Freeman.

Mehu, M., & Dunbar, R. I. M. (2008). Naturalistic observations of smiling and laughter in human group interactions. *Behaviour, 145*(12), 1747–1780.

Mehu, M., Little, A. C., & Dunbar, R. I. M. (2008). Sex differences in the effect of smiling on social judgments: An evolutionary approach. *Journal of Social, Evolutionary, and Cultural Psychology, 2*(3), 103–121.

Mickes, L., Walker, D., Parris, J., Mankoff, R., & Christenfeld, N. (2011). Who's funny: Gender stereotypes, humor production, and memory bias. *Psychonomic Bulletin & Review, 19*, 108–112.

Miller, G. (2000a). *The mating mind: How sexual selection shaped the evolution of human nature.* New York: Anchor Books.

Miller, G. (2000b). Mental traits as fitness indicators: Expanding evolutionary psychology's adaptationism. In D. LeCroy & P. Moller (Eds.), *Evolutionary perspectives on human reproductive behavior* (pp. 62–74). New York: New York Academy of Sciences.

Miller, G. (2007). Sexual selection for moral virtues. *Quarterly Review of Biology, 82*(2), 97–125.

Mobbs, D., Hagan, C. C., Azim, E., Menon, V., & Reiss, A. L. (2005). Personality predicts activity in reward and emotional regions associated with humor. *Proceedings of the National Academy of Sciences of the United States of America, 102*(45), 16502–16506.

Morreall, J. (Ed.). (1987). *The philosophy of laughter and humor.* Albany, NY: SUNY Press.

Myers, S. A., Ropog, B. L., & Rodgers, R. P. (1997). Sex differences in humor. *Psychological Reports, 81*, 221–222.

Nevo, O., Nevo, B., & Yin, J. L. (2001). Singaporean humor: A cross-cultural, cross-gender comparison. *Journal of General Psychology, 128*(2), 143–156.

Oh, K., Kim, H.-J., Kim, B.-J., Park, K.-W., & Lee, D.-H. (2007). Pathological laughter as an unusual manifestation of acute stroke. *European Neurology, 59*(1–2), 83–84.

O'Quin, K., & Derks, P. (1997). Humor and creativity: A review of the empirical literature. In M. Runco (Ed.), *Creativity research handbook* (Vol. 1, pp. 223–252). Cresskill, NJ: Hampton Press.

Panksepp, J. (2007). Neuroevolutional sources of laughter and social joy: Modeling primal human laughter in laboratory rats. *Behavioural Brain Research, 182*(2), 231–244.

Panksepp, J., & Burgdorf, J. (2003). 'Laughing' rats and the evolutionary antecedents of human joy? *Physiology & Behavior, 79*(3), 533–547.

Penton-Voak, I. S., & Chang, H. Y. (2008). Attractiveness judgements of individuals vary across emotional expression and movement conditions. *Journal of Evolutionary Psychology, 6*(2), 89–100.

Pinker, S. (1997). *How the mind works.* New York: W.W. Norton & Company.

Plomin, R., & Spinath, F. M. (2004). Intelligence: Genetics, genes, and genomics. *Journal of Personality and Social Psychology, 86*(1), 112–129.

Preuschoft, S., & Van-Hooff, J. A. (1997). The social function of 'smile' and 'laughter': Variations across primate species and societies. In U. Segerstrale & P. Molnar (Eds.), *Nonverbal communication: Where nature meets culture* (pp. 171–190). Mahwah, NJ: Lawrence Erlbaum.

Prokosch, M. D., Yeo, R. A., & Miller, G. F. (2005). Intelligence tests with higher g-loadings show higher correlations with body symmetry: Evidence for a general fitness factor mediated by developmental stability. *Intelligence, 33*(2), 203–213.

Provine, R. (1993). Laughter punctuates speech: Linguistic, social and gender contexts of laughter. *Ethology, 95*(4), 291–298.

Provine, R. (2000). *Laughter: A scientific investigation.* New York: Viking.

Provine, R., & Fischer, K. (1989). Laughing, smiling, and talking: Relation to sleeping and social context in humans. *Ethology, 83*(4), 295–305.

Ramachandran, V. S. (1998). The neurology and evolution of humor, laughter, and smiling: The false alarm theory. *Medical Hypotheses, 51*(4), 351–354.

Raskin, V. (1984). *Semantic mechanisms of humor.* Dordrecht: D. Reidel.

Robinson, D. T., & Smith-Lovin, L. (2001). Getting a laugh: Gender, status, and humor in task discussions. *Social Forces, 80*(1), 123–158.

Ruch, W. (Ed.). (1998). *The sense of humor: Explorations of a personality characteristic* (Vol. Humor research-3). Berlin: Walter De Gruyter.

Ruch, W. (2004). Humor. In C. P. Peterson & M. E. P. Seligman (Eds.), *Character strengths and virtues: A handbook of classification* (pp. 583–598). Washington, DC: American Psychological Association.

Rushton, J. P., Bons, T. A., Vernon, P. A., & Čvorović, J. (2007). Genetic and environmental contributions to population group differences on the Raven's Progressive Matrices estimated from twins reared together and apart. *Proceedings of the Royal Society B: Biological Sciences, 274*(1619), 1773–1777.

Samson, A. C., & Huber, O. (2007). The interaction of cartoonist's gender and formal features of cartoons. *Humor: International Journal of Humor Research, 20*(1), 1–25.

Schmidt, N. E., & Williams, D. I. (1971). The evolution of theories of humor. *Journal of Behavioral Science, 1*, 95–106.

Simpson, J. A., & Gangestad, S. W. (1991). Individual differences in sociosexuality: Evidence for convergent and discriminant validity. *Journal of Personality and Social Psychology, 60*(6), 870–883.

Smith, J. E., Waldorf, V. A., & Trembath, D. L. (1990). Single white male looking for thin, very attractive.... *Sex Roles, 23*(11/12), 675–685.

Smoski, M. J., & Bachorowski, J.-A. (2003). Antiphonal laughter between friends and strangers. *Cognition & Emotion, 17*(2), 327–340.

Smyth, M. M., & Fuller, R. G. C. (1972). Effects of group laughter on responses to humorous laughter. *Psychological Reports, 30*, 132–134.

Sosis, R. (2003). Why aren't we all hutterites? Costly signaling theory and religious behavior. *Human Nature, 14*(2), 91–127.

Sprecher, S., & Regan, P. C. (2002). Liking some things (in some people) more than others: Partner preferences in romantic relationships and friendships. *Journal of Social and Personal Relationships, 19*(4), 463–481.

Thomas, C. A., & Esses, V. M. (2004). Individual differences in reaction to sexist humor. *Group Processes and Intergroup Relations, 7*(1), 89–100.

Thornhill, R., & Gangestad, S. W. (2008). *The evolutionary biology of human female sexuality*. New York: Oxford University Press.

Todosijević, B., Ljubinković, S., & Arančić, A. (2003). Mate selection criteria: A trait desirability assessment study of sex differences in Serbia. *Evolutionary Psychology, 1*, 116–126.

Toro-Morn, M., & Sprecher, S. (2003). A cross-cultural comparison of mate preferences among university students: The United States vs. the People's Republic of China (PRC). *Journal of Comparative Family Studies, 34*(2), 151–170.

Turner, R. G. (1980). Self-monitoring and humor production. *Journal of Personality, 48*(2), 163–172.

Van-Hooff, J. A. R. A. M., & Preuschoft, S. (2003). Laughter and smiling: The intertwining of nature and culture. In F. B. M. D. Waal & P. L. Tyack (Eds.), *Animal social complexity* (pp. 260–287). Cambridge, MA: Harvard University Press.

Vernon, P., Martin, R. A., Schermer, J. A., Cherkas, L., & Spector, T. (2008). Genetic and environmental contributions to humor styles: A replication study. *Twin Research and Human Genetics, 11*(1), 44–47.

Vernon, P., Martin, R. A., Schermer, J. A., & Mackie, A. (2008). A behavioral genetic investigation of humor styles and their correlations with the big-5 personality dimensions. *Personality and Individual Differences, 44*(5), 1116–1125.

Vettin, J., & Todt, D. (2005). Human laughter, social play, and play vocalizations of non-human primates: An evolutionary approach. *Behaviour, 142*(2), 217–240.

Weisfeld, G. E. (1993). The adaptive value of humor and laughter. *Ethnology and Social Biology, 14*(2), 141–169.

Weisfeld, G. E., Nowak, N. T., Lucas, T., Weisfeld, C. C., Imamoğlu, E. O., & Butovskaya, M. (2011). Do women seek humorousness in men because it signals intelligence? A cross-cultural test. *Humor: International Journal of Humor Research, 24*(4), 435–462.

Wilbur, C. J., & Campbell, L. (2011). Humor in romantic contexts: Do men participate and women evaluate? *Personality and Social Psychology Bulletin, 37*(7), 918–929.

Williams, G. C. (1966). *Adaptation and natural selection*. Princeton, NJ: Princeton University Press.

Zahavi, A. (1975). Mate selection—A selection for a handicap. *Journal of Theoretical Biology, 53*, 205–214.

Zahavi, A., & Zahavi, A. (1997). *The handicap principle: A missing piece of Darwin's puzzle*. New York: Oxford University Press.

Male Adaptations to Retain a Mate

10

Valerie G. Starratt and Michele N. Alesia

Men expend significant amounts of time, effort, and resource on finding, attracting, and sustaining a relationship with a mate. Those resources may have been used in vain if the relationship in which he invested fails. If a woman defects from the relationship entirely, he has lost all previous investment and must start his reproductive efforts from the beginning. Alternatively, and perhaps even more detrimentally, a woman may engage in only brief defections from the relationship (i.e., engage in sexual infidelity). Under these conditions, a man may continue to invest in the relationship while unwittingly investing his resources in the survival and development of offspring to whom he is not genetically related. This situation, known as cuckoldry, is detrimental because a man is simultaneously promoting the survival of a rival male's genes and losing resources that could otherwise be used to promote the survival of his own genetic children. Whether a woman's defection is permanent or temporary, the resulting potential loss of investment is so disadvantageous that men are hypothesized to have evolved psychological mechanisms devoted to the detection and prevention of such risks of loss.

Types of Mate Retention Behaviors

Although there are a wide variety of behaviors that function as mate retention efforts, several categories of behaviors have been identified. On one level, mate retention behaviors can be categorized as either intersexual manipulations or intrasexual manipulations (Buss, 1988). Intersexual manipulations are directed toward a man's current partner and function by manipulating her interest in the current relationship or perceptions of her ability to find another, better relationship should she defect from the existing relationship. For instance, a man may attempt to maintain his partner's interest in him by attempting to enhance his own appearance, thus making himself appear more physically attractive to his partner. Alternatively, he may attempt to make other men look bad by derogating them or telling his partner negative things about them. If he can convince her that other men are unattractive or have characteristics that would make them bad partners, she may be less interested in them. In each instance, he is making the current relationship appear more appealing by tipping the relative attractiveness scales in his favor.

Another way of manipulating a woman's interest in her current relationship may be to convince her that the current relationship is her only option. To this end, some intersexual mate retention behaviors involve restricting a woman's interactions with people other than her current partner. A man who insists his partner

V.G. Starratt (✉) • M.N. Alesia
Division of Social and Behavioral Sciences, Nova Southeastern University, Fort Lauderdale, FL 33314, USA
e-mail: valerie.starratt@nova.edu; ma1404@nova.edu

V.A. Weekes-Shackelford and T.K. Shackelford (eds.), *Evolutionary Perspectives on Human Sexual Psychology and Behavior*, Evolutionary Psychology, DOI 10.1007/978-1-4939-0314-6_10,
© Springer Science+Business Media New York 2014

spend all of her time with him, and keeps her away from social circumstances involving other men, effectively removes other men from the equation. After all, a woman cannot have sex with a man whom she never meets. However, in the event that a man is unsuccessful in completely removing rival males from his partner's perceived alternatives, he may still attempt to maintain her investment in him by punishing her for expressing any interest in those alternatives. Hitting a woman for talking to another man effectively reduces the likelihood that she will engage in that behavior again. So, whether by self-enhancement or partner-abuse, a man may manipulate his partner's continued commitment by manipulating the alternatives she perceives.

Intrasexual manipulations, on the other hand, function by actually reducing the availability of alternative mating opportunities his partner would have. This is accomplished by directing the manipulative behavior toward a man's potential rivals. In some instances, these behaviors involve demonstrations of possessiveness of the woman. These demonstrations, such as holding his partner's hand when in public, may highlight her status as "taken" and may reduce the likelihood that she will be approached by other men. Other intrasexual manipulations, however, may function by highlighting other, less positive features of a woman in an attempt to reduce her perceived value. So while hand holding may suggest that a woman is taken and is not available to other men, telling other men that she is damaged or diseased may convince them that, even if she were available, they wouldn't want her anyway (Buss, 1988). Though these tactics work in different ways, both share the end result of reducing a woman's available alternatives and consequently decreasing her likelihood of defection.

Mate retention behaviors also can be characterized in terms of the costs they inflict or benefits they provide, rather than to whom they are directed. Men's mate retention behaviors can function either by enticing a woman to stay invested in the current relationship or by discouraging her defection from the relationship. Those behaviors that entice continued

investment are considered benefit provisioning mate retention behaviors. They function by providing benefits to the woman for her continued investment in and fidelity to the existing relationship. This may include behaviors such as buying gifts for a woman or complimenting her appearance, both of which may inflate the woman's perception of the quality of the current relationship and the benefits she receives for being a part of it. Cost inflicting mate retention behaviors, on the other hand, function either by inflicting costs on a woman for failing to demonstrate continued investment in and fidelity to the existing relationship or by reducing a woman's self-perception to the point where she perceives there to be no alternatives to her current relationship. Convincing a woman that there are no other available men, that she is not valuable enough to attract whatever available men there may be, and punishing her expression of interest in potential alternatives are all behaviors that serve the same purpose of promoting a woman's commitment to the existing relationship, albeit potentially to her detriment (Miner, Starratt, & Shackelford, 2009).

In general, though, whether directed toward partners or potential rivals and whether enticing or punishing, evidence suggests that men and women tend to agree on the frequency and type of mate retention behaviors men produce. Data from married couples indicate that men's self-reports of their own behaviors are positively correlated with women's partner-reports of their husbands' behavior. This relationship appears to be particularly robust for overt behaviors that are easily observable. Some behaviors, such as holding a partner's hand in the presence of other men, are obvious to everyone involved. A woman knows her hand is being held, and anyone around the couple can see that behavior occurring. Other behaviors, however, may not be as evident. For instance, reading a partner's private mail, derogating a partner to another man, and snooping through a partner's personal belongings are behaviors that may occur more frequently in the absence of one's partner. After all, if a woman were aware of it, it would hardly be called snooping. So, a woman's report that her husband does not snoop through her personal belongings may be more a function of his clandestine ability than his failure to perform such behaviors (Shackelford, Goetz, & Buss, 2005).

When Men Use Mate Retention Behaviors

Although there is strong theoretical and empirical support for the idea that mate retention behaviors are beneficial for men, we would not anticipate all men using all behaviors in all circumstances. Rather, we would expect certain men to use specific behaviors in particular circumstances, where the benefits of producing such behaviors would outweigh the costs to him.

Partner's Mate Value

First, there is an abundance of evidence suggesting that men are significantly more likely to employ a variety of mate retention tactics when they are mated to women of relatively high mate value. Mate value is a measure of one's worth as a reproductive partner, and is a value associated with a variety of characteristics. For instance, women of high value, compared to women of lower value, tend to score higher on measures of youth, physical attractiveness, fertility, and fidelity (for review, see Buss, 2003). A man mated to a woman who possesses such characteristics may be at a greater loss should he lose that mate compared to a man mated to a woman who does not possess these characteristics. Not only would he lose his current mate, but he may be unlikely to find another partner of equally high value. A man mated to a woman of lower mate value is also at risk of losing her and all of the investment he has made in her should she defect from the relationship, but, unlike the man mated to the woman of higher value, he may be able to replace her more easily with a woman of at least comparable value. Consequently, the man who has more to lose may be more motivated to engage in mate

retention activities to reduce the likelihood of such losses.

Evidence from a variety of sources supports this hypothesis. Men married to younger women and women whom they perceive to be physically attractive report engaging in more mate retention behaviors than men married to older, less physically attractive women (Buss & Shackelford, 1997). As both youth and physical attractiveness are indicators of higher mate value, men mated to young attractive women may have more to lose from the dissolution of a relationship compared to men mated to older, less attractive women. The relationship between a woman's age and her partner's mate retention behaviors persists even after controlling for men's age and the length of the relationship, both of which tend to covary with women's age. This suggests a unique contribution of women's mate value relevant characteristics to men's use of mate retention tactics.

Goetz et al. (2005) reported similar findings. Men mated to women of greater physical and sexual attractiveness engage in a variety of both benefit provisioning and cost inflicting mate retention behaviors. These men also engage in specific copulatory behaviors associated with semen displacement (i.e., removing rival male's semen from the female's reproductive tract), such as producing a greater number of deeper thrusts during longer durations of sexual intercourse. These semen displacement behaviors have been proposed as a category of corrective mate retention tactics. In the event that a woman has engaged in a short-term defection from the relationship, i.e., had sex with a man other than her current partner, she is putting her partner at risk of cuckoldry. A man who detects this risk, though, and engages in mate retention behaviors that function to reduce the number of rival sperm in his partner's reproductive tract and increase the number of his own sperm, may successfully reduce his risk of being cuckolded.

This goal of decreased cuckoldry risk via sperm competition behaviors can also be achieved through the manipulation of other copulatory behaviors, such as in-pair copulation frequency. The frequency with which men initiate intercourse with their partners has been proposed as a mate retention tactic, has been associated with women's physical attractiveness, and is correlated with other measures of mate retention. Increasing the frequency with which a man copulates with his partner subsequently increases the amount of his sperm in her reproductive tract, thus increasing the likelihood that, should she conceive, her offspring will carry his genetic material. Women's physical attractiveness, however, partially mediates the relationship between men's in-pair copulation frequency and men's use of other mate retention tactics. This may suggest that, when mated to higher value women, men may perform more preventative *and* corrective mate retention behaviors (Kaighobadi & Shackelford, 2008).

One of the proposed explanations for the relationship between female mate value and male mate retention is that women's mate value may itself be an indicator of cuckoldry risk. Women who are of higher value may be more likely to be poached (i.e., enticed away) from the existing relationship. This increased risk of poaching produces an increased risk not only of relationship dissolution but also of cuckoldry. This increased risk of relationship defection and cuckoldry may motivate men to engage in mate retention behaviors to reduce that risk. Research using various measures of cuckoldry risk in addition to female physical attractiveness seems to support this explanation.

Risk of Cuckoldry

One objective measure of risk of cuckoldry that has been associated with men's mate retention behaviors is the percent of time a man spends away from his partner since the last time he had sex with her. As most people do not have extra-pair sexual encounters in the presence of their current partners, the likelihood of a woman engaging in sex with someone other than her partner necessarily increases when the percent of time spent apart is greater than zero. To determine the extent to which this objective risk of sexual infidelity and potential cuckoldry is

associated with men's mate retention behaviors, Starratt et al. correlated the percent of time a man had spent apart from his partner since the last time they had sex together with his self-reported mate retention behaviors. Results showed a significant positive correlation between the two. Men at a higher risk of cuckoldry, measured in terms of the portion of time away from his partner since the last time the couple had sex, engage in more mate retention behaviors (Starratt, Shackelford, Goetz, & McKibbin, 2007).

Another objective risk of cuckoldry is ovulatory status. Logistically, any extra-pair sexual encounters a woman engages in around the time of ovulation are physiologically more likely to lead to cuckoldry compared to extra-pair sexual encounters that occur at other times in her cycle. However, women also appear to display behavioral changes around the time of ovulation that may further increase this risk of cuckoldry. For instance, data on the relationship between women's behavior and fertility status suggest that women report being more sexually interested in men other than their primary partners when they are ovulating. This does not appear to reflect a general increased sex drive, though, as women do not display any increased sexual interest in their primary partners during this time. So, it is not just that women are more likely to express heightened sexual interest when they are most fertile, but they are expressing interest in sexual activity that is most likely to be associated with relationship defection and cuckoldry. Not coincidentally, it is also during this time of peak fertility when men who are mated to these women are more likely to engage in mate retention behaviors (Haselton & Gangestad, 2006).

While men are not likely to be privy to women's increased extra-pair fantasies and interests around the time of ovulation, there are other physiological and behavioral correlates of women's fertility that may provide cues to men that increases in mate retention efforts may be warranted. For instance, evidence suggests that women's physical appearance may change during ovulation. Specifically, women's physiologies change in such a way that they appear to be more physically attractive. In general, both men and women judge women in the fertile phase of their cycle to be more attractive than in the non-fertile phase, even when fertility status is not expressly known (Roberts et al., 2004). This increase in perceived physical attractiveness may be partially accounted for by an increase in symmetry.

Facial and body symmetry are indicators of high genetic quality, are perceived to be more attractive than asymmetry, and increase around the time of ovulation (Scutt & Manning, 1996). These indicators of genetic quality also appear to be apparent in body odor, which likewise changes around the time of ovulation and may influence women's perceived attractiveness. Not only can men detect individual differences in body odor, but they seem to prefer the scents of body odor produced by women who are in the fertile phase of their cycle compared to odors produced by women in non-fertile phases (Singh & Bronstad, 2001).

So, although men may not be directly aware of their partners' ovulatory status or their interest in extra-pair sexual opportunities, they still may be indirectly detecting these changes. Detection of these changes may, in turn, affect men's behavior, making them more likely to engage in a variety of mate retention behaviors when their partners are ovulating compared to when they are not ovulating. This relationship between ovulatory status and mate retention, though, may be mediated by a woman's mate value, such that all men do not respond to changes in women's fertility status equally. Specifically, the increase in mate retention behaviors resulting from increases in fertility appears less prominent among men who are mated to women of higher value. Women of higher relative mate value may be more likely to be the targets of steadily high levels of guarding (Haselton & Gangestad, 2006). Lower value women, on the other hand, may be guarded more or less closely depending on ovulatory status. This adjustment in guarding may be a function of the relative increase in perceived attractiveness around time of fertility, such that men are more likely to guard higher value women, and women appear to be of higher value when they are fertile.

In addition to these physiological changes in appearance and perceived attractiveness, evidence suggests women actively alter their appearance in accordance with fertility status. For example, women's clothing choices differ according to fertility status. Women who are ovulating are more likely to choose more ornamental apparel (e.g., articles of clothing that incorporate lace, or additional accessories) and clothing that shows more skin (Haselton, Mortezaie, Pillsworth, Bleske-Rechek, & Frederick, 2007). This may be a reflection of the fact that women who are ovulating perceive themselves to be more attractive than at other times. Or, they may be manifesting an increased interest in extra-pair sexual encounters by engaging in behaviors that are more likely to attract extra-pair sexual opportunities. Whatever the motivation may be, these physiological and behavioral changes associated with fertility may serve as cues to men that they are at an increased risk of cuckoldry. These cues may then motivate men to engage in additional mate retention efforts.

Other, less biologically based and so more subjective measures of cuckoldry risk, such as men's self-reported perceived risk of cuckoldry, also predict men's mate retention behaviors. For instance, men's accusations of their partners' sexual infidelity have been proposed as a measure of their perceived risk of infidelity and are positively related to men's mate retention behaviors. Specifically, men who accuse their partners of being sexually unfaithful—and so may actually believe themselves to be at some risk of female infidelity and cuckoldry—report engaging in more violent and nonviolent mate retention behaviors, compared to men who make no such accusations. However, the relationship between men's accusations of sexual infidelity and men's use of violent mate retention behaviors is mediated by men's use of nonviolent mate retention behaviors. It may be that men who suspect themselves to be at some risk of losing a mate may engage in a variety of mate retention behaviors, perhaps in a hierarchical fashion. Nonviolent mate retention behaviors may be a first line of defense against female defection from the relationship, and more violent retention behaviors may only be employed if a man continues to perceive himself to be at risk. Performing these violent mate retention behaviors carries with them greater potential costs of social exile and retribution by the woman or her family and so may only be used as a last resort (Kaighobadi, Starratt, Shackelford, & Popp, 2008).

Additional experimental evidence supports the hypothesis that perceived risk of cuckoldry influences men's use of mate retention behaviors. In one study, after being presented with a story implying that a fictitious man's equally fictitious girlfriend had engaged in a sexual infidelity, men reported a change in perception of their own partners. Specifically, men reported experiencing greater distress in response to imagining that their partner rejected their sexual advances than they had reported before the manipulation. However, this difference only occurred for men who believed themselves to be at some risk of cuckoldry in their own relationships. Men who perceived no such personal risk were not influenced by the experimental manipulation. Women, who by virtue of biology are never at risk of cuckoldry, also were not influenced by the experimental manipulation (Starratt, McKibbin, & Shackelford, 2013). So, it seems that men's use of mate retention behaviors may be influenced by both objective and subjective risks of female infidelity and cuckoldry.

Although men seem to adjust their mate retention efforts in response to current features of their partners, these efforts may be additionally tempered by perceived characteristics of the circumstances. For example, evidence suggests that men's use of mate retention tactics in the context of marriage decreases with the number of years married (Kaighobadi, Shackelford, & Buss, 2010). This may also be an indirect reflection of the relationship between characteristics associated with female mate value and men's mate retention behaviors. Specifically, women who have been married longer may also be older and may be perceived to be less physically and sexually attractive, and so may not be displaying cues that trigger men's use of mate

retention behaviors. Alternatively, being married longer may be an indication of increases in trust and subsequent decreases in perceived likelihood of a woman's defection from the relationship. Whatever the process, though, the result is the same. Decreases in (at least perceived) risk of cuckoldry and partner defection that are associated with increased years of marriage are associated with decreases in men's use of mate retention behaviors.

Other correlates of marriage, such as the presence of children in the relationship and the relationship of each parent to those children, may affect men's mate retention behaviors. For instance, some evidence suggests that men's cost inflicting mate retention behaviors are related to their preference for self-resemblance in their offspring. Specifically, partnered men who showed a greater preference for depictions of babies that were manipulated to look more like them, compared to depictions of babies that were manipulated to look more like an unknown other male, were more likely to report using cost inflicting mate retention behaviors. This suggests a relationship between men's use of mate retention behaviors and potential cuckoldry. Men who perceive cues to potential cuckoldry risk, which in this instance would be a baby who looks like another man, may be more likely to use certain mate retention behaviors. Alternatively, it may be that men who already perceive themselves to be at some risk of cuckoldry are sensitive to the self-resemblance features of offspring. In either case, however, the relationship between the perception of infant facial features and men's use of mate retention behaviors suggests these behaviors may function to solve the problem of paternity uncertainty (Welling, Burriss, & Puts, 2011).

Additional evidence continues to highlight the relationship between children and men's use of mate retention behaviors with the inclusion of more severe categories of mate retention: severe domestic violence and death. Women who are victims of severe domestic physical abuse are more likely than average to have at least one child in the house who is not biologically related to their current male partner. This increased likelihood is even higher among women who were killed by their intimate partners (Miner, Shackelford, Block, Starratt, & Weekes-Shackelford, 2012). It may be that the presence of genetically unrelated children is a cue to his partner's past or potential future relationship defection, which motivates men's engagement in mate retention behaviors, even to the point of his partner's death. However, it may also be that there is something about the men who find themselves in circumstances where they are faced with nongenetically related children that also makes them more likely to engage in negative mate retention behaviors.

Characteristics of Men Who Use Mate Retention Behaviors

While there is an abundance of evidence suggesting men's mate retention behaviors are related to characteristics of their partners and/or the circumstances of the relationship, additional evidence suggests that it is characteristics of the men producing the mate retention behaviors that may be most relevant. For instance, when directly comparing the predictive utility of women's mate value and men's mate value for men's mate retention behaviors, women's reports indicate that men's value is a better predictor of men's behavior. Specifically, men of higher mate value produce more benefit provisioning and fewer cost inflicting mate retention behaviors compared to lower value men (Miner et al., 2009). Additionally, according to women's reports of their partners' sexual attractiveness, jealousy, and possessiveness, men who were of lower value demonstrated greater use of negative mate retention tactics compared to men of higher value. These increases in their mate retention tactics also became more pronounced around the time of ovulation. So, while men do increase their mate retention efforts in response to women's fertility status, not all men respond equally. It was the men rated by their partners to be least sexually attractive who were showing the greatest increases in retention efforts (Haselton & Gangestad, 2006).

There is some debate, though, as data from men's reports do not mirror those from women's data. According to men's reports, men's mate value does not predict men's use of any mate retention behaviors. Rather, men's reports suggest a relationship between women's mate value and men's use of benefit provisioning mate retention behaviors. However, it has been argued that this may result from a sex difference in the salience of the costs of men's use of mate retention behaviors. Women may be more aware of the relationship between men's value and their behavior because of the potential costs of those behaviors to women. Those behaviors are, of course, also costly to men, but the unreliability of those costs may obscure the relationship. For example, if a man engages in negative mate retention behavior, and that gets noticed by male members of his partner's family, he may be at risk of costs ranging from social exile to retaliatory death. However, if he successfully engages in those same behaviors furtively, he may gain the benefit of retaining his mate with no costs to him whatsoever. The varied potential outcomes render the potential costs uncertain for men. Women, however, share no such uncertainty. The costs of being punished for displaying interest in another man are consistent, regardless of who is aware of it (Starratt & Shackelford, 2012).

Still, when not directly comparing the influence of men's and women's mate value, evidence supports that a variety of men's characteristics influence the use of men's mate retention behaviors. For instance, men's height, an objective measure of genetic quality and overall mate value, is negatively related to cognitive and behavioral measures of jealousy—an emotion associated with motivation to produce a variety of mate retention behaviors (Brewer & Riley, 2009). So, men of shorter stature are more likely to demonstrate emotions and behaviors indicative of mate retention efforts. Other indicators of lower mate value in men demonstrate a similar association. Machiavellianism, narcissism, and psychopathy, all indicators of low mate value, are positively related to men's mate retention behaviors. Men who are high on these traits, both the individual traits and as a collection of traits, report greater use of mate retention behaviors (Jonason, Li, & Buss, 2010).

The relationship between men's mate value and mate retention behaviors is not a simple one, however. Men's mate value interacts with risk of cuckoldry to produce differential employment of men's mate retention behaviors. Specifically, men of different mate values tend to employ different types of mate retention behaviors when faced with an increased risk of cuckoldry. For instance, men who were reported by their partners to be less sexually attractive showed greater increases in their use of mate retention behaviors when their partners were fertile compared to men reported to be more sexually attractive. However, it is not simply that lower value men produce more mate retention behaviors. Men of higher investment value (i.e., demonstrating higher financial status, social status, and intelligence) demonstrated increased positive mate retention behaviors when their partners were most fertile (Pillsworth & Haselton, 2006). It has been suggested that this difference reflects the fact that all men may be motivated to engage in mate retention behaviors, but the particular behaviors they choose may relate to what they can afford. Higher value men may have the physical and psychological resources available to them to be able to afford engaging in benefit provisioning mate retention behaviors. Lower value men may not have such resources, and so may have to rely on cost inflicting mate retention behaviors (Miner et al., 2009).

In addition to determining which mate retention behaviors men choose to employ, it may also be that men's mate value helps determine whether men engage in mate retention behaviors at all. For example, men's use of sexual coercion—a specific category of cost inflicting mate retention behaviors—is positively related to men's perceived risk of cuckoldry, such that men who perceive themselves to be at some risk of cuckoldry are more likely to engage in sexually coercive behaviors toward their partners. However, this relationship is only significant for men who perceive themselves to be

of equal or greater desirability than his partner. Men's perceptions of their risk of cuckoldry are not related to sexual coercion for men who perceive that they are less desirable than their partners (Starratt, Popp, & Shackelford, 2008). This is not to suggest that men who are of lower mate value than their partners are not motivated to engage in mate retention behaviors. Rather, the motivation to engage in mate retention behaviors may be overridden by the motivation to not risk the cost of losing a partner who is of high enough value she could not be easily replaced.

References

Brewer, G., & Riley, C. (2009). Height, relationship satisfaction, jealousy, and mate retention. *Evolutionary Psychology, 7,* 477–489.

Buss, D. M. (1988). From vigilance to violence: Tactics of mate retention in American undergraduates. *Ethology and Sociobiology, 9,* 291–317.

Buss, D. M. (2003). *The evolution of desire* (rev.th ed.). New York: Basic Books.

Buss, D. M., & Shackelford, T. K. (1997). From vigilance to violence: Mate retention tactics in married couples. *Journal of Personality and Social Psychology, 72,* 346–361.

Goetz, A. T., Shackelford, T. K., Weekes-Shackelford, V. A., Euler, H. A., Hoier, S., Schmitt, D. P., et al. (2005). Mate retention, semen displacement, and human sperm competition: A preliminary investigation of tactics to prevent and correct female infidelity. *Personality and Individual Differences, 38,* 749–763.

Haselton, M. G., & Gangestad, S. W. (2006). Conditional expression of women's desires and men's mate guarding across the ovulatory cycle. *Hormones and Behavior, 49,* 509–518.

Haselton, M. G., Mortezaie, M., Pillsworth, E. G., Bleske-Rechek, A., & Frederick, D. A. (2007). Ovulatory shifts in human female ornamentation: Near ovulation, women dress to impress. *Hormones and Behavior, 51,* 40–45.

Jonason, P. K., Li, N. P., & Buss, D. M. (2010). The costs and benefits of the Dark Triad: Implications for mate poaching and mate retention tactics. *Personality and Individual Differences, 48,* 373–378.

Kaighobadi, F., & Shackelford, T. K. (2008). Female attractiveness mediates the relationship between in-pair copulation frequency and men's mate retention behaviors. *Personality and Individual Differences, 45,* 293–295.

Kaighobadi, F., Shackelford, T. K., & Buss, D. M. (2010). Spousal mate retention in the newlywed year and three years later. *Personality and Individual Differences, 48*, 414–418.

Kaighobadi, F., Starratt, V. G., Shackelford, T. K., & Popp, D. (2008). Male mate retention mediates the relationship between female sexual infidelity and female-directed violence. *Personality and Individual Differences, 44*, 1422–1431.

Miner, E. J., Shackelford, T. K., Block, C. R., Starratt, V. G., & Weekes-Shackelford, V. A. (2012). Risk of death or life-threatening injury for women with children not-sired by the abuser. *Human Nature, 23*, 89–97.

Miner, E. J., Starratt, V. G., & Shackelford, T. K. (2009). It's not all about her: Men's mate value and mate retention. *Personality and Individual Differences, 47*, 214–218.

Pillsworth, E. G., & Haselton, M. G. (2006). Male sexual attractiveness predicts differential ovulatory shifts in female extra-pair attraction and male mate retention. *Evolution and Human Behavior, 27*, 247–258.

Roberts, S. C., Havlicek, J., Flegr, J., Hruskova, M., Little, A. C., Jones, B. C., et al. (2004). Female facial attractiveness increases during the fertile phase of the menstrual cycle. *Proceedings: Biological Sciences, 271*, S270–S272.

Scutt, D., & Manning, J. T. (1996). Symmetry and ovulation in women. *Human Reproduction, 11*, 2477–2480.

Shackelford, T. K., Goetz, T. K., & Buss, D. M. (2005). Mate retention in marriage: Further evidence of the reliability of the Mate Retention Inventory. *Personality and Individual Differences, 39*, 415–425.

Singh, D., & Bronstad, P. M. (2001). Female body odour is a potential cue to ovulation. *Proceedings: Biological Sciences, 268*, 797–801.

Starratt, V. G., McKibbin, W. F., & Shackelford, T. K. (2013). Experimental activation of anti-cuckoldry mechanisms responsive to female sexual infidelity. *Personality and Individual Differences, 55*, 59–62.

Starratt, V. G., Popp, D., & Shackelford, T. K. (2008). Not all men are sexually coercive: A preliminary investigation of the moderating effect of mate desirability on the relationship between female infidelity and male sexual coercion. *Personality and Individual Differences, 45*, 10–14.

Starratt, V. G., & Shackelford, T. K. (2012). He said, she said: Men's reports of mate value and mate retention behaviors in intimate relationships. *Personality and Individual Differences, 53*, 459–462.

Starratt, V. G., Shackelford, T. K., Goetz, A. T., & McKibbin, W. F. (2007). Male mate retention behaviors vary with risk of partner infidelity and sperm competition. *Acta Psychologica Sinica, 39*, 523–527.

Welling, L. L. M., Burriss, R. P., & Puts, D. A. (2011). Mate retention behavior modulates men's preference for self-resemblance in infant faces. *Evolution and Human Behavior, 32*, 118–126.

Part III

Sexual Adaptations in Women

Evolutionary Psychology and Rape Avoidance

William F. McKibbin

This chapter reviews the topic of women's rape avoidance from a modern evolutionary psychological perspective (for an overview, see Confer et al., 2010). Evolutionary psychology provides researchers with a powerful heuristic tool that can be used to generate new testable hypotheses across all domains of psychology. Evolutionary psychology rests on a number of key premises (Buss, 2004). The first premise states that natural selection is the only known process capable of producing complex functional systems such as the human brain. The complexity of human behavior can only be understood completely by taking into account human evolutionary history and natural selection.

The second premise of evolutionary psychology is that behavior depends on evolved psychological mechanisms. These are information processing mechanisms housed in the brain that register and process specific information and generate as output specific behaviors, physiological activity, or input relayed to other psychological mechanisms. The third premise is that these evolved psychological mechanisms are functionally specialized to perform a specific task or to solve a specific adaptive problem. Adaptive problems are defined as specific problems that recurrently affected reproductive success over evolutionary history.

This premise is often referred to as domain specificity. Finally, the premise of numerousness states that human brains consist of many specific evolved psychological mechanisms that work together to produce behavior. Together with other theoretical tools and heuristics provided by modern evolutionary theory, these premises are used to generate evolutionary theories of psychology and behavior.

One such heuristic tool that informs evolutionary psychology is parental investment theory (Trivers, 1972). Parental investment theory consists of two important premises. First, in sexually reproducing species, the sex that invests more in offspring (typically the female) will be more discriminating about mating. Second, the sex that invests less in offspring (typically the male) will be more intrasexually competitive for sexual access to the higher-investing sex. These premises have been supported in research with numerous species, including humans. Human females, like the females of most biparental species, invest more in offspring, whereas males invest more in mating effort. These sex differences are greatest in short-term mating contexts (Buss, 1994a, 1994b, 2004).

Misconceptions About Evolutionary Psychology

Some authors claim that evolutionary psychology is somehow conducted in order to justify such reprehensible concepts as racism or sexism, or

W.F. McKibbin (✉)
Department of Psychology, University of Michigan-Flint,
411 MSB, 303 E. Kearsley Street, Flint, MI 48502-1950,
USA
e-mail: wmckibbi@umflint.edu

V.A. Weekes-Shackelford and T.K. Shackelford (eds.), *Evolutionary Perspectives on Human Sexual Psychology and Behavior*, Evolutionary Psychology, DOI 10.1007/978-1-4939-0314-6_11,
© Springer Science+Business Media New York 2014

sexual coercion and rape. For example, Tang-Martinez (1997, p. 116) claims that evolutionary psychology is, "inherently misogynistic and provides a justification for the oppression of women." However, this is a clear example of what is known as the *naturalistic fallacy*: the error of deriving what *ought* to be from what *is*. This error can be demonstrated clearly with an example. Obviously, no sensible person would argue that a scientist researching the causes of cancer is thereby justifying or promoting cancer. Yet, some people continue to argue that investigating rape from an evolutionary perspective justifies or legitimizes rape (e.g., Baron, 1985; Marshall & Barrett, 1990, cited in Thornhill & Palmer, 2000). Relatedly, studying women's rape avoidance behavior is in no way intended to shift the blame to victims. Rather, an understanding of how women vary in their use of rape avoidance behavior provides greater opportunities to understand and reduce the rates of rape.

Related to the naturalistic fallacy is the idea of genetic determinism: the idea if behavior is influenced by evolved adaptations, then it is programmed or otherwise unable to be modified. This argument has been thoroughly debunked on numerous occasions. For example, biologist John Maynard Smith noted that genetic determinism is, "an incorrect idea that is largely irrelevant, because it is not held by anyone, or at least not by any competent evolutionary biologist" (1997, p. 524).

No evolutionary psychologist would argue that because rape is produced by evolved mechanisms, it cannot be prevented or that we should simply accept its occurrence. The goal of evolutionary psychology is simply to better understand a phenomenon of interest. In this case, that phenomenon is rape and, more specifically, women's rape avoidance. Researching rape from an evolutionary psychological perspective does not justify or promote this heinous act, nor does studying rape avoidance shift blame to the victim. Whether evolutionary psychological hypotheses about rape are correct, new perspectives often allow researchers to gain new insights into the targeted phenomenon.

Gaining a greater understanding about why rape occurs and how women avoid it is fundamental to decreasing its occurrence.

Finally, evolutionary psychologists often frame hypotheses in terms of the costs and benefits to an organism of performing a particular behavior. These costs and benefits refer to the effects on reproductive success over evolutionary time, i.e., costs decreased the probability of successful reproduction, whereas benefits increased the probability of successful reproduction. These terms are sometimes misconstrued as referring to a more general idea of perceived costs and benefits to the individual or to society. However, these terms carry no moral or ethical meaning, and are used only in terms of naturally selected biological functioning. For example, one may argue that rape may benefit a male under certain circumstances. This reflects only the likely *genetic* benefits if the rape results in offspring, and is not intended to suggest any other type of benefit in the vernacular sense.

Definitions of rape vary. It is typically defined, and will be defined in this chapter, as the use of force or threat of force to achieve sexual penile–vaginal penetration of a woman without her consent (Kilpatrick, Edmunds, & Seymour, 1992; Thornhill & Palmer, 2000). Rape is a fact of life across cultures (Broude & Greene, 1978; Rozée, 1993; Sanday, 1981). In American samples, estimates of the prevalence of rape are as high as 13 % for women (Kilpatrick et al., 1992; Resnick, Kilpatrick, Dansky, Saunders, & Best, 1993). Rape is likely more common, however, because rapes often go unreported (Kilpatrick et al., 1992). Although other forms of rape occur (e.g., male–male rape), this chapter focuses on how women may behave to avoid being raped by a man.

Rape became a public and academic focus following the publication of Brownmiller's (1975) book, *Against our will*: *Men, women, and rape*. Brownmiller argued that rape is "a conscious process of intimidation by which *all men* keep *all women* in a state of fear" (p. 15, emphasis in original). Since then, feminist theories of rape have dominated the rape research literature. A prominent version of feminist theory contends that rape is the result of social traditions in which men have dominated political, economic, and other sources of power (Ellis, 1989). Feminist theorists inspired by Brownmiller often interpret rape as a method by which men maintain this power and dominance over women. Moreover, feminist theorists have argued explicitly that rape is not about sexual gratification and often seem more focused on making ideological, rather than scientific, statements about human psychology and behavior (Thornhill & Palmer, 2000). Recently, researchers have begun to examine rape and rape avoidance from a comparative and evolutionary psychological perspective.

Comparative Psychology of Sexual Coercion and Rape

Comparative evidence demonstrates that males of many species have evolved strategies to sexually coerce and rape females. Rape in humans must also reflect adaptations that evolved over evolutionary time. While numerous explanations have been offered to explain rape in humans (e.g., learning or enculturation, mental illness, personality differences, drug and alcohol use, and other factors) (Bergen & Bukovec, 2006; Brecklin & Ullman, 2001; Dean & Malamuth, 1997; Lalumiére & Quinsey, 1996), these factors alone cannot explain the existence of such seemingly complex behavior. These factors may mediate the likelihood of rape occurring, but alone cannot explain the complex organized behavior seen in rape. Only two explanations are likely to be true: that rape is the product of specialized psychological adaptation, or that it is a by-product of other adaptations in the male mind (Palmer & Thornhill 2003a, 2003b; Thornhill & Palmer, 2000). What evidence supports the hypothesis that rape is the result of an adaptation?

Sexual coercion occurs in many species, with behaviors ranging from harassment and intimidation to forced copulation (Clutton-Brock & Parker, 1995). Evolutionary theory predicts that

in general, sexual coercion and rape will occur in species in which males are more aggressive, more eager to mate, more sexually assertive, and less discriminating in choosing a mate (Thornhill & Palmer, 2000). Research demonstrates that sexual coercion and rape occur in many species, including (but not limited to) insects (Dunn, Crean, & Gilburn, 2002; Linder & Rice, 2005; Thornhill, 1980, 1981, 1987; Vahed, 2002), amphibians and reptiles (Olsson, 1995; Reyer, Frei, & Som, 1999; Shine, Langkilde, & Mason, 2003; Sztatecsny, Jehle, Burke, & Hödl, 2006), fish (Magurran, 2001; Plath, Parzefall, & Schlupp, 2003), birds (Gowaty & Buschhaus, 1998; McKinney, Derrickson, & Mineau, 1983; Pizzari & Birkhead, 2000), and primates (Robbins, 1999; Smuts & Smuts, 1993; Wrangham & Peterson, 1996), among other species.

Two species in particular provide clear-cut examples of adaptations in males to sexually coerce and rape females. A substantial amount of research demonstrates that male scorpionflies (*Panorpa vulgaris*) have an anatomical adaptation that is designed only to facilitate sexual access to a female in a coercive fashion, i.e., rape. Male scorpionflies possess a notal organ that is used specifically and exclusively for rape (Thornhill, 1980, 1981, 1987; Thornhill & Sauer, 1991).

It should be noted that scorpionfly males do not necessarily always secure copulations through rape. Instead, males display different mating strategies. Males that are able to produce a nuptial gift of food for the female are allowed to mate without coercion. It is only the males that are not able to do so who resort to a conditional rape strategy and use of the notal organ (Thornhill, 1980, 1981, 1987; Thornhill & Palmer, 2000). Thus, male scorpionflies exhibit evidence of specific anatomical adaptations that evolved to facilitate rape. It may also be the case that animals, including humans, possess specific psychological adaptations that facilitate rape. Scorpionflies also exhibit evidence of a conditional strategy of sexual coercion. This illustrates an important point, that rape need not be the sole mechanism through which a male attempts to reproduce. Instead, rape may best be thought of as a conditional strategy used online when other reproductive attempts fail.

Male orangutans (*Pongo pygmaeus*) also use conditional strategies of sexual coercion and rape. Orangutans are unique among apes in that they live solitary lives rather than in groups. Females therefore do not have mates or kin that may deter or prevent rape (Wrangham & Peterson, 1996). This fact alone makes rape a more viable strategy for male orangutans. Forced copulations account for up to half of all copulations (Mitani, 1985; Wrangham & Peterson, 1996). These forced copulations seem to be performed primarily by a subset of males. Wrangham and Peterson (1996) review evidence indicating that male orangutans exist as one of two distinct morphs or behavioral types. The large morphs weigh significantly more, move much slower, and are typically able to find females willing to mate. The small morphs typically are unable to find females willing to mate with them. These small morphs are more likely to chase down and rape females. This represents a conditional strategy. If the smaller males are unable to gain sexual access to females through intrasexual competition and by being attractive to females, they may use the conditional strategy of chasing down and raping a female. These are just a few of the many examples of sexual coercion in nonhuman species.

The preceding theory and research leads to the conclusion that rape is associated with severe costs for females of many species. This suggests that females will evolve counter-adaptations in response to the recurrent adaptive problem of rape. Clutton-Brock and Parker (1995) argue that the consequences of coercion in non-human species are evident in the behavior of many animal species. For example, male harassment leads females to avoid areas where males are abundant, or to associate with males who can provide protection against unwanted advances with other males (Clutton-Brock & Parker, 1995). Females may also enter into coalitions together in order to protect themselves against males (see also Smuts & Smuts, 1993). Finally, Clutton-Brock and Parker (1995) argue that selection may have favored traits in females that would increase their ability to defend against coercion or to reduce costs associated with harassment or forced copulation, e.g., thicker skin in female blue sharks which are regularly bitten during mating. Human females likely possess adaptations for rape avoidance as well.

Women's Defenses Against Rape

Rape is a traumatic event that is likely to have been a recurrent problem for women over evolutionary history (Thornhill & Palmer, 2000). As in other species, rape often leads to severe negative consequences for women. Because of the severe costs associated with experiencing a rape, it is likely that women may possess adaptations in response. In particular, women may have evolved psychological mechanisms designed to motivate rape avoidance behaviors. There are several reasons why rape is traumatic for women. These include disrupting a woman's parental care, causing a woman's partner to abandon her, and causing a woman serious physical injury or death (Thornhill & Palmer, 2000). Women who experience a rape report significantly more negative outcomes in domains including self-esteem, reputation, and self-perceptions of mate value, among others (Perilloux, Duntley, & Buss, 2012). Women are sometimes killed after being raped (Shackelford, 2002a, 2002b). Aside from death, perhaps the greatest cost to women who are raped is the circumvention of their mate choice (Wilson, Daly, & Scheib, 1997). As predicted by parental investment theory (Trivers, 1972) this is because anything that circumvents women's choice in mating can severely jeopardize their reproductive success (Symons, 1979).

Researchers have speculated that a variety of female traits evolved to reduce the risks associated with experiencing a rape. Smuts (1992) argued that women form alliances with groups of men and other women for protection against would-be rapists. Similarly, Wilson and Mesnick (1997) presented the bodyguard hypothesis. This hypothesis posits that women's mate preferences for physically and socially dominant men may reflect anti-rape adaptation. Of course, women may enter into alliances or exhibit preferences for dominant mates for reasons other than to avoid rape. Alliances offer protection from such dangers as assault or predation, and dominant mates may possess higher quality genes, for example.

Finally, Davis and Gallup (2006) proposed the intriguing possibility that preeclampsia and spontaneous abortion may be adaptations that function to terminate pregnancies not in the woman's best reproductive interests, such as those resulting from rape. A growing body of empirical work has been conducted over the past few years in order to identify specific psychological mechanisms that evolved to solve the recurrent problem of rape avoidance.

Thornhill and Thornhill (1990a, 1990b, 1990c, 1991) have demonstrated that the psychological pain that women experience after being raped may be produced by evolved mechanisms designed to focus women's attention on the circumstances of the rape, particularly the social circumstances that resulted in the rape. Thornhill and Thornhill (1990a, 1990b, 1990c, 1991) argue that, like physical pain, psychological pain motivates individuals to attend to the circumstances that led to the pain and to avoid those circumstances in the future. In this case, psychological pain may help victims to avoid the specific circumstances leading to a rape. The researchers predicted that victims of rape who have more to lose in terms of future reproductive success will also experience more psychological pain relative to women with less to lose in terms of future reproductive success (Thornhill & Palmer, 2000; Thornhill & Thornhill, 1983, 1990a). For example, reproductive-aged women were hypothesized to experience more psychological pain due to the greater risk of conception. Thornhill and Thornhill (1990a) demonstrated support for this hypothesis, documenting that reproductive-aged women are more traumatized by rape than are post-reproductive-aged women or pre-reproductive-aged girls. This suggests evolved psychological mechanisms that are responsive to the costs associated with rape,

motivating the greatest fear when the risks are the greatest as well.

The research conducted by Thornhill and Thornhill focuses on the aftereffects of being raped and on the psychological pain that may motivate women to avoid the circumstances leading to the rape. More recently researchers have begun to identify the specific behaviors women may deploy to avoid being raped. Scheppele and Bart (1983) conducted interviews of women who had been raped, or who had been attacked and successfully avoided being raped. Some of these women described "rules of rape avoidance" (p. 64) and how they followed them, e.g., "I would never be alone on the street" and "I would watch what I wear" (p. 65). These qualitative data provide preliminary evidence for rape avoidance adaptations in women.

Petralia and Gallup (2002) examined whether a woman's capacity to resist rape varies across the menstrual cycle. Women in the fertile phase of their menstrual cycle showed an increase in handgrip strength, but only when presented with a sexual coercion scenario. Women not in their fertile phase did not show an increase in handgrip strength. Furthermore, women in all other conditions, including women in the fertile phase who were presented with the neutral control scenario, showed a *decrease* in hand strength posttest. This provides evidence for specialized mechanisms designed to motivate women to behave in ways that cause them to be less likely to be raped. Women who experience increased strength during their fertile phase would be better equipped to defend themselves from would-be rapists. The research by Petralia and Gallup (2002) provides evidence consistent with the hypothesis that women have evolved mechanisms that motivate rape avoidance behaviors.

Chavanne and Gallup (1998) investigated the performance of risky behaviors by women in the fertile phase of their menstrual cycles. A sample of women were asked where they were in their menstrual cycles, and to indicate whether they had performed a range of behaviors in the past 24 h. Behaviors were ranked by women in a previous study according to how likely performing the behaviors might result in a woman being sexually assaulted, with riskier behaviors given higher risk scores. Individuals' risky behavior was estimated by taking the summed composite score of all performed activities. Women in the fertile phase of their menstrual cycle reported performing fewer behaviors representing a greater risk of being raped. There was no difference in the likelihood of performing low-risk behaviors between women in their fertile phase and women outside their fertile phase. This research has some methodological problems that prevent firm conclusions, however. First, the researchers used only one method (i.e., the forward-cycle method) to assess women's menstrual status. Also, Chavanne and Gallup do not specify how the inventory of risky behaviors was developed, noting only that a preliminary sample of women rated the riskiness of the behaviors. In addition, the dependent variable may be confounded by diversity of activity. For example, a woman who performed ten non-risky behaviors (each scored as a one on the riskiness scale) could receive the same score as a woman who performed two high-risk behaviors (each scored as a five on the riskiness scale; see Bröder & Hohmann, 2003, for discussion). Despite these methodological issues, this research documented a significant decrease in performance of risky behaviors by women in the fertile phase of their menstrual cycle. This evidence is consistent with the hypothesized function of rape avoidance mechanisms, particularly when women are fertile.

Chavanne and Gallup's (1998) study was replicated by Bröder and Hohmann (2003) using a within-subjects design. Twenty-six women who did not use oral contraceptives were tested weekly for 4 successive weeks. The results indicated that women in the fertile phase of their cycle selectively inhibit behaviors that would expose them to a higher risk of being raped, despite performing *more* non-risky behaviors. These results provide a conceptual replication of the results reported by Chavanne and Gallup. Women perform fewer risky behaviors when they are fertile, while still demonstrating a higher overall activity level

(Morris & Udry, 1970) and even while engaging in more consensual sex (Morris & Udry, 1982). This selective behavior indicates that women may have evolved specialized psychological mechanisms designed to motivate behaviors that decrease the risk of being raped. Although this study addressed many of the issues in the Chavanne and Gallup research, there is still no indication of how risky behaviors were identified. This study also used the somewhat problematic forward- and reverse-cycle counting methods for identifying the fertile phase of the menstrual cycle, both of which depend on the potentially unreliable self-reports of participants (Bröder & Hohmann, 2003).

A recent study by Garver-Apgar, Gangestad, and Simpson (2007) tested the hypothesis that women are more attuned to signs of a man's potential sexual coerciveness during the fertile phase and are more accurate at detecting sexually coercive men during the fertile phase. A sample of 169 normally ovulating women watched short segments of videotaped interviews of men. The women were then asked to rate the men on several items that were summed to create an overall coerciveness rating. Average coerciveness ratings for each man were computed. Finally, women's menstrual status was estimated using the reverse-cycle counting method. The results indicated that women in the fertile phase of their menstrual cycle rated the men as more sexually coercive. This suggests that women at greater risk of conception may be more attuned to signs of male sexual coerciveness than women at lesser risk of conception. This may represent an evolved cognitive error management bias (see Haselton, Nettle, & Andrews, 2005, for an overview) towards identifying men as sexually coercive, which might serve to protect women from being raped. This research provides more evidence that women may have evolved psychological mechanisms that motivate behaviors that guard against men's sexual coercion and rape. Note, however, that the participants viewed videos of strangers. Studies demonstrate that women have a greater fear of stranger rape than of being raped by someone they know (Thornhill & Thornhill, 1990b), which suggests that stranger rape was the greater adaptive problem. This is despite modern patterns of rape, which indicate that women are more likely to be raped by someone they know (Kilpatrick et al., 1992; Resnick et al., 1993). These results may reflect the greater potential costs associated with stranger rape, such as a decreased likelihood of investment by the genetic father of the resulting offspring. Would similar results be found by testing women's coerciveness ratings of acquaintances or other familiar men? Future research is needed to explore these effects in greater detail. For example, researchers might ask women to rate the coerciveness of familiar faces of classmates or celebrities.

More recent research also suggests that women may have more biased judgments of men when ovulating, particularly men who are members of out-groups. Specifically, when conception risk was increased, women demonstrated greater levels of race bias, as measured through implicit evaluation, implicit stereotyping, mate attraction, and fear of male targets (Navarrete, Fessler, Fleischman, & Geyer, 2009). This relationship was strongest for women who had high levels of perceived vulnerability to sexual coercion. Navarrete and colleagues (2009) argued that race provides a simple and salient cue of out-group membership. Men from out-groups, they argued, may have represented a greater risk of sexual assault relative to in-group men. Subsequent research demonstrates that this bias is indeed not necessarily based on race. Intergroup bias is increased as conception risk increases, even for minimally defined groups (McDonald, Asher, Kerr, & Navarrete, 2011). These studies suggest that evolved psychological mechanisms are attentive to the risks of sexual coercion and the likelihood of conception, as would be expected.

In summary, several studies provide evidence that women may have mechanisms that motivate rape avoidance. Women may have mechanisms that motivate them to assess the risk of being raped (e.g., the riskiness of walking in a dark parking lot alone) or the likelihood that a particular man may be sexually coercive. However, these previous studies of rape avoidance assessed different behaviors that were selected for assessment without an explicit rationale, making it difficult to compare specific results across the studies. There exists a need for a standard instrument to assess women's specific rape avoidance behaviors that has been shown to be broad in scope and empirically sound (McKibbin et al., 2009). After presenting an argument for the need for a reliable, valid measure of rape avoidance, McKibbin et al. (2009) developed just such a measure.

Rape Avoidance Inventory

Beginning with act nomination procedures similar to those developed by Buss and Craik (1983), McKibbin et al. (2009) sought to first identify specific behaviors women may perform to avoid being sexually assaulted or raped. Using the behaviors nominated through women's self-reports, the researchers constructed an inventory to assess these behaviors. The Rape Avoidance Inventory (RAI) assesses performance of 69 behaviors, all specifically nominated by women as behaviors they performed to avoid being raped. Using principal components analysis, behaviors nominated by women were identified as belonging to one of four relatively independent components: Avoid Strange Men, Avoid Appearing Sexually Receptive, Avoid Being Alone, and Awareness of Surroundings/Defensive Preparedness.

The Avoid Strange Men component consists of behaviors which appear to motivate women to avoid unfamiliar men, and behaviors motivating women to avoid men who may represent a greater risk of being sexually coercive (e.g., "Avoid men who make me feel uncomfortable," "Avoid drunk men"). The Avoid Appearing Sexually Receptive component consists of behaviors that may diminish a woman's physical or sexual attractiveness to a potential rapist (e.g., "Avoid wearing sexy clothing," "Avoid making out with a man I have just met"). The Avoid Being Alone component consists of behaviors that appear to motivate a woman to stay around others (e.g., "When I go out, I stay with at least one other person that I know"). Finally, the Awareness of Surroundings/Defensive Preparedness component includes behaviors that appear to motivate a woman to be especially attentive to her surroundings (e.g., "Pay special attention to my surroundings"), as well as behaviors that enhance a woman's ability to thwart a would-be rapist (e.g., "Carry a knife").

Interestingly, these components map closely onto a taxonomy of four "guidelines" for female defense against rape derived independently by Judson (2002, p. 121) following a review of cross-species research addressing primarily nonhumans. These four guidelines are "avoid groups of idle males," "don't attract attention," "don't leave home alone," and "do carry weapons." While Judson (2002) does not provide empirical support for this taxonomy of guidelines, the conceptual confluence of the current four components with those derived by Judson perhaps provides interesting evidence for the construct validity of the RAI.

It could be argued that the RAI consists of a disproportionate number of items which relate to stranger rape rather than acquaintance rape. This is despite the fact that rapes are most often perpetrated by someone known to the victim (Kilpatrick et al., 1992). The items on the RAI were derived from behaviors nominated by women themselves, however. This, the authors suggest, indicates that while indeed less frequently occurring, stranger rape may elicit more fear in women. Items on the RAI may reflect the most relevant adaptive problems experienced by women over human evolutionary history (McKibbin et al., 2009).

Further analyses provided preliminary evidence of both the reliability and validity of the RAI. The full-scale and four-component scales demonstrated high-level internal reliability. Uniformly positive yet moderate correlations among scores on the total and component scales of the RAI provided additional evidence of the utility of the four-component nature of the RAI. These scores demonstrated that the four components were interrelated, yet still relatively distinct from one another. Finally, McKibbin et al. (2009) demonstrated a consistent pattern of

negative correlations between RAI scores and interest in and pursuit of short-term sex (which places women at increased risk of rape). As predicted, items on the RAI (which represent decreased risk of sexual assault or rape) were negatively correlated with a measure consisting of behaviors which represent a greater risk of sexual assault or rape. These findings provided initial evidence for the convergent and discriminative validity of the RAI as an assessment of women's rape avoidance behaviors.

Individual Differences in Rape Avoidance

As the work reviewed previously has demonstrated, women appear to possess evolved psychological mechanisms associated with rape avoidance. This is because ancestral women who responded to increased rape-related risk (such as at time of ovulation) with more rape avoidance behaviors may have been more reproductively successful than women who did not. It may be the case that there are a number of other individual differences in women which lead to differences in the deployment of rape avoidance behaviors. Guided by an evolutionary perspective, McKibbin, Shackelford, Miner, Bates, and Liddle (2011) identified several such variables that may influence women's rape-related risk. Specifically, they predicted that individual differences in women's attractiveness, relationship status, number of family members living nearby, and age would covary with women's rape avoidance behaviors.

Cross-culturally, men more than women report a preference for physical attractiveness in a prospective romantic partner, because attractiveness in women more than in men is an indicator of fertility and expected future reproduction (Buss, 1989; Buss & Schmitt, 1993; Symons, 1979). Research evidence suggests that would-be rapists also may prefer and target more attractive women, in order to maximize the probability of conception (Ghiglieri, 2000; Greenfield, 1997; Kilpatrick et al., 1992; McKibbin, Shackelford, Goetz, &

Starratt, 2008; Thornhill & Palmer, 2000; Thornhill & Thornhill, 1983).

If women's psychology includes mechanisms that motivate rape avoidance behaviors, then more attractive women may be more motivated to perform rape avoidance behaviors, relative to less attractive women. Therefore, McKibbin et al. (2011) predicted that women's attractiveness will correlate positively with women's reports of the frequency with which they perform rape avoidance behaviors.

Mated women, as compared with unmated women, may incur additional costs associated with being raped (Thornhill, 1996; Thornhill & Palmer, 2000). Specifically, if a woman's regular partner interprets the rape as infidelity, a mated woman risks losing her partner's support and resources for herself and her offspring (Thornhill & Palmer, 2000; Thornhill & Thornhill, 1992). Thornhill and Thornhill (1990a, 1990b, 1990c, 1991) documented that mated women report more psychological pain than did unmated women following rape. They suggested that the psychological pain experienced by mated women functions to focus women's attention on the costs or losses they have experienced such that women will find ways to avoid similar costly situations. Unmated women might be expected to experience greater costs associated with being raped, because the rape may produce offspring that would not benefit from the support and investment of a regular partner. Based on the findings of Thornhill and Thornhill, however, McKibbin et al. (2011) generated the following prediction. Because mated women may experience greater losses than unmated women as a result of a rape, women in a relationship will report higher frequencies of rape avoidance behaviors than women not in a relationship.

Over evolutionary history, individuals with psychological mechanisms that motivated reciprocal exchange of resources and support with close family members are likely to have been more successful than individuals without such mechanisms (Hamilton, 1964). Close genetic relatives also may incur costs if a female relative is raped, such as decline in inclusive fitness associated with her injury, inability to contribute to the family, or care for her own offspring. This helping may occur in multiple domains and may include behaviors that decrease the risk of a female genetic relative being raped (e.g., parents discouraging their daughter from wearing revealing clothing or men accompanying their daughters or sisters at night). Indeed, research has demonstrated that family members do act in such ways. Figueredo et al. (2001) found that the presence of adult male kin living nearby decreased the likelihood of a female relative being raped, perhaps because would-be rapists fear retaliation by the rape victim's adult male kin. Individuals also may act in ways that more directly decrease the likelihood of a female relative being raped. Perilloux, Fleischman, and Buss (2008) found that parents exerted more control over their daughters' behavior than their sons' behavior, particularly their mating behavior. Compared to how they interacted with their sons, parents were more likely to express upset in response to a daughter's risky sexual activity, to use curfews to control a daughter's behavior, and to exert control over a daughter's clothing choices, all of which may decrease a daughter's risk of being vulnerable to rape or being targeted for rape. Other close kin, such as siblings, also may act to prevent women from being raped. For example, brothers may accompany a sister outside at night. Because a woman's relatives may guard her directly or attempt to influence her rape-relevant behaviors, it was predicted that the number of women's family members living in close proximity will correlate positively with the frequency with which women perform rape avoidance behaviors (McKibbin et al., 2011).

Women's fertility—risk of conception per copulation—peaks in the early 20s and declines with age (Thornhill & Thornhill, 1983). Men have evolved preferences for fertile mates and, accordingly, men generally express a preference for younger mates (Buss, 1989). Would-be rapists also may target younger women, relative to older women. Indeed, younger women are overrepresented in reported rapes and rapes unreported to authorities (Greenfield, 1997; Kilpatrick et al., 1992; Thornhill & Palmer, 2000; Thornhill & Thornhill, 1983). Because younger women are more likely to be raped, it was predicted that women's age would correlate negatively with the frequency with which women perform rape avoidance behaviors (McKibbin et al., 2011). In general, results generated using women's self-reports of their rape avoidance behaviors supported the predictions such that the frequency with which women reported performing rape avoidance behaviors varied predictably with several individual differences among women.

The results of the correlational analyses provided support for the prediction that women's attractiveness would correlate positively with women's reports of the frequency with which they performed rape avoidance behaviors. A positive correlation was found between women's self-reported attractiveness and total rape avoidance behavior. Because attractive women may be preferentially targeted by rapists (McKibbin et al., 2008; Thornhill & Palmer, 2000), these women appeared to perform more rape avoidance behaviors relative to less attractive women. These findings provide preliminary evidence that more attractive women, relative to less attractive women, avoid situations in which they are alone and vulnerable. They also pay special attention to their surroundings and were more likely to carry defensive weapons such as mace.

There was also as predicted a positive correlation between relationship status and the frequency of women's rape avoidance behaviors. Women who reported being in a long-term committed relationship reported greater frequencies of total rape avoidance behaviors than women who did not report being in a committed, long-term relationship. This may be because mated women must manage the additional risk of losing their partner's investment. Specifically, mated women performed more behaviors in the Avoid Appearing Sexually Receptive and Awareness of Surroundings/ Defensive Preparedness categories of rape avoidance behaviors. Mated women performed more behaviors that downplayed their attractiveness and perceived sexual receptivity. They also paid extra attention to their surroundings and were more likely to carry defensive weapons. Because

mated women bear additional potential costs associated with being raped (Thornhill, 1996; Thornhill & Palmer, 2000; Thornhill & Thornhill 1990a, 1990b, 1990c; Wilson & Mesnick, 1997), they appear to perform more rape avoidance behavior relative to non-mated women.

McKibbin et al. (2011) also predicted that the number of women's family members living in close proximity would correlate positively with the frequency with which women performed rape avoidance behaviors. Women's reports of rape avoidance behaviors were indeed positively correlated with the number of male and female family members living close by. Individuals are able to manage their inclusive fitness interests by protecting genetic female relatives from being raped. This protection may often be indirect, with relatives encouraging women to behave in ways that diminish the risk of being raped. Examining the component scores for women's rape avoidance revealed two components in particular that seemed to drive this effect. Specifically, men and women encouraged behaviors in the Awareness of Surroundings/Defensive Preparedness component. Men also appeared to encourage behaviors from the Avoid Appearing Sexually Receptive component. Examining subsequent multiple regression analyses, McKibbin et al. (2011) demonstrated that the number of female family members living close by did not appear to uniquely predict women's rape avoidance. Rather, in particular, it is the number of male family members living close by that predicted uniquely women's behaviors in the Awareness of Surroundings/Defensive Preparedness component. Although men and women appeared to actively encourage rape avoidance behaviors in their female close relatives, men in particular seemed to encourage their female family members to behave in ways to avoid rape.

McKibbin et al. (2011) did not find support for the prediction that women's age correlated negatively with the frequency with which women performed rape avoidance behaviors. Only one component, Avoid Appearing Sexually Receptive, correlated significantly with age, and this was in the opposite direction than predicted. The researchers noted, however, that the current results were inconsistent with the preponderance of evidence linking rape and the age of the victim (Felson & Krohn, 1990; Greenfield, 1997; Kilpatrick et al., 1992; Perkins & Klaus, 1996; Perkins, Klaus, Bastian, & Cohen, 1996; Thornhill & Thornhill, 1983). They also noted that approximately 80 % of the participants in the study were under 30 years old, arguing that this restricted age range may have made it difficult to find the predicted relationship between rape avoidance behavior and age.

Limitations of RAI Research

The research highlighted above is based exclusively on data self-reported by women. Although the women may not accurately remember how often they performed each rape avoidance behavior, such data cannot be defensibly secured from other data sources. Because the researchers were interested in behaviors that women perform specifically for the purpose of avoiding rape, there is no compelling reason to believe that other parties, such as independent observers or a woman's close friends, would have the information and perspective to provide more accurate reports than the women themselves.

Women in long-term committed relationships scored higher on the RAI. These findings were interpreted to suggest that mated women perform more rape avoidance behaviors to avoid the additional potential costs for mated women associated with being raped. An alternative explanation for the difference between mated and unmated women may be that mated women are less likely to go to parties or clubs, or to perform mate-seeking behaviors such as flirting (McKibbin et al., 2011). Similarly, mated women may be less likely to be alone than are unmated women, simply by spending much of their time in their partner's presence. However, regression analyses indicated that women in long-term committed relationships also reported a greater frequency of behaviors associated with awareness of the environment and preparedness. In addition, women who did not report being in a committed, long-term relationship may

nevertheless be in another type of non-committed or short-term relationship. Their responses may be different than the responses provided by women who were not in any type of relationship. These findings cannot lead to a conclusive argument that mated women perform more rape avoidance behaviors. Subsequent studies should more carefully define relationship status and more carefully examine shifts in women's rape avoidance associated with relationship status, perhaps by examining shifts in frequency of individual behaviors rather than categories of overall rape avoidance behavior.

The samples highlighted in research utilizing the RAI (McKibbin et al., 2009, 2011) were limited to relatively affluent college students attending psychology courses at a single state university in Florida. Future studies should attempt to replicate these findings in other samples, particularly from other countries or cultures when possible, although some of the items in the RAI may not apply to non-Western cultures equally well.

Because of the severe costs associated with rape, it is likely that women have evolved psychological mechanisms that motivate rape avoidance behavior. However, because the risk of rape is not the same for every woman, these mechanisms may be sensitive to individual differences between women that influence their risk of being raped. A growing body of research suggests that this may be the case. Women do appear to possess evolved mechanisms that motivate rape avoidance behavior. Research also suggests that these evolved mechanisms are sensitive to individual differences in women and their environments.

Few researchers have studied women's strategies of rape avoidance, particularly from an evolutionary psychological perspective. Thankfully, this is changing as more researchers begin investigations in this area. With a greater understanding of the underlying psychological processes associated with women's rape avoidance, researchers and other professionals can better help women to avoid being raped. One such way, for example, may be to design rape awareness or prevention programs that are informed by the empirical work presented here and in other studies.

The variables examined in this chapter do not represent an exhaustive list of the variables that may influence rape avoidance behavior. An evolutionary perspective can be used to identify other important variables for future study. For example, there may be a relationship between the number of dependent children a mated woman has and her performance of rape avoidance behaviors. A mated woman who has dependent children may perform more rape avoidance behaviors than a mated woman without dependent children because she risks losing her partner's support for herself as well as her offspring.

Previous studies have identified ovulatory shifts in women's behavior associated with increased risk of rape (Bröder & Hohmann, 2003; Chavanne & Gallup, 1998). Women might exhibit similar shifts on behaviors included in the RAI. If the RAI does in fact represent a valid measure of women's rape avoidance behavior, subsequent research should find that women show clear shifts in the behaviors indexed by the RAI when they are ovulating. Future research is needed to evaluate whether these shifts do in fact occur.

Finally, women's self-reports of their rape avoidance behaviors may differ from the actual frequency with which they perform these behaviors. Or women may perform behaviors without consciously understanding why they do so. Future research might examine whether observer-reported (e.g., as reported by same-sex best friend) frequencies of these behaviors differ from women's self-reports. Furthermore, no research has assessed the effectiveness of these behaviors. Future research should assess whether women who more frequently perform these behaviors (or particular components of these behaviors) in fact are less likely to report being raped.

Evolutionary psychology is a powerful heuristic tool that allows researchers to consider rape in a new light. Researchers have hypothesized that women have evolved mechanisms that motivate behaviors to avoid being raped. A growing body of evidence supports this hypothesis (e.g.,

Bröder & Hohmann, 2003; Chavanne & Gallup, 1998; Petralia & Gallup, 2002). Researchers should continue to investigate the psychological mechanisms associated with women's rape avoidance behavior. Such information will not only inform scientific theory but more importantly can only improve the lives of women around the world.

References

Baron, L. (1985). Does rape contribute to reproductive success? Evaluations of sociobiological views of rape. *International Journal of Women's Studies, 8,* 266–277.

Bergen, R. K., & Bukovec, P. (2006). Men and intimate partner rape: Characteristics of men who sexually abuse their partner. *Journal of Interpersonal Violence, 21,* 1375–1384.

Brecklin, L. R., & Ullman, S. E. (2001). The role of offender alcohol use in rape attacks. *Journal of Interpersonal Violence, 16,* 3–21.

Bröder, A., & Hohmann, N. (2003). Variations in risk-taking behavior over the menstrual cycle: An improved replication. *Evolution and Human Behavior, 24,* 391–398.

Broude, G. J., & Greene, S. J. (1978). Cross-cultural codes on 20 sexual attitudes and practices. *Ethnology, 15,* 409–429.

Brownmiller, S. (1975). *Against our will: Men, women, and rape.* New York: Simon and Schuster.

Buss, D. M. (1989). Sex differences in human mate preferences: Evolutionary hypotheses tested in 37 cultures. *Behavioral and Brain Sciences, 12,* 1–49.

Buss, D. M. (1994a). The strategies of human mating. *American Scientist, 82,* 238–249.

Buss, D. M. (1994b). *The evolution of desire: Strategies of human mating.* New York: Basic Books.

Buss, D. M. (2004). *Evolutionary psychology: The new science of the mind* (4th ed.). Boston: Allyn & Bacon.

Buss, D. M., & Craik, K. H. (1983). The act frequency approach to personality. *Psychological Review, 90,* 105–126.

Buss, D. M., & Schmitt, D. P. (1993). Sexual Strategies Theory: An evolutionary perspective on human mating. *Psychological Review, 100,* 204–232.

Chavanne, T. J., & Gallup, G. G. (1998). Variation in risk taking behavior among female college students as a function of the menstrual cycle. *Evolution and Human Behavior, 19,* 27–32.

Clutton-Brock, T. H., & Parker, G. A. (1995). Sexual coercion in animal societies. *Animal Behaviour, 49,* 1345–1365.

Confer, J. C., Easton, J. A., Fleischman, D. S., Goetz, C. D., Lewis, D. M. G., Perilloux, C., et al. (2010). Evolutionary psychology: Controversies, questions, prospects, and limitations. *American Psychologist, 65,* 110–126.

Davis, J. A., & Gallup, G. G., Jr. (2006). Preeclampsia and other pregnancy complications as an adaptive response to unfamiliar semen. In S. M. Platek & T. K. Shackelford (Eds.), *Female infidelity and paternal uncertainty* (pp. 191–204). New York: Cambridge University Press.

Dean, K. E., & Malamuth, N. M. (1997). Characteristics of men who aggress sexually and men who imagine aggressing: Risk and moderating variables. *Journal of Personality and Social Psychology, 72*, 449–455.

Dunn, D. W., Crean, C. S., & Gilburn, A. S. (2002). The effects of exposure to seaweed on willingness to mate, oviposition, and longevity in seaweed flies. *Ecological Entomology, 27*, 554–564.

Ellis, L. (1989). *Theories of rape: Inquiries into the causes of sexual aggression.* New York: Hemisphere Publishing Corporation.

Felson, R., & Krohn, M. (1990). Motives for rape. *Journal of Research in Crime and Delinquency, 27*, 222–242.

Figueredo, A. J., Corral-Verdugo, V., Frias-Armenta, M., Bachar, K. J., White, J., McNeill, P. L., et al. (2001). Blood, solidarity, status, and honor: The sexual balance of power and spousal abuse in Sonora, Mexico. *Evolution and Human Behavior, 22*, 293–328.

Garver-Apgar, C. E., Gangestad, S. W., & Simpson, J. A. (2007). Women's perceptions of men's sexual coerciveness change across the menstrual cycle. *Acta Psychologica Sinica, 39*, 536–540.

Ghiglieri, M. P. (2000). *The dark side of man.* New York: Perseus Books.

Gowaty, P. A., & Buschhaus, N. (1998). Ultimate causation of aggressive and forced copulation in birds: Female resistance, the CODE hypothesis, and social monogamy. *Integrative and Comparative Biology, 38*, 207–225.

Greenfield, L. (1997). *Sex offenses and offenders.* Washington, DC: Bureau of Justice Statistics, US Department of Justice.

Hamilton, W. D. (1964). The genetical evolution of social behavior. I and II. *Journal of Theoretical Biology, 7*, 1–52.

Haselton, M. G., Nettle, D., & Andrews, P. W. (2005). The evolution of cognitive bias. In D. M. Buss (Ed.), *The handbook of evolutionary psychology* (pp. 724–746). Hoboken, NJ: Wiley.

Judson, O. (2002). *Dr. Tatiana's sex advice to all creation.* New York: Henry Holt & Company.

Kilpatrick, D., Edmunds, C., & Seymour, A. (1992). *Rape in America.* Arlington, VA: National Victim Center.

Lalumiére, M. L., & Quinsey, V. L. (1996). Sexual deviance, antisociality, mating effort, and the use of sexually coercive behaviors. *Personality and Individual Differences, 21*, 33–48.

Linder, J. E., & Rice, W. R. (2005). Natural selection and genetic variation for female resistance to harm from males. *Journal of Evolutionary Biology, 18*, 568–575.

Magurran, A. E. (2001). Sexual conflict and evolution in Trinidadian guppies. *Genetica, 112–113*, 463–474.

Maynard Smith, J. (1997). Commentary. In P. Gowaty (Ed.), *Feminism and evolutionary biology* (p. 522). New York: Chapman & Hall.

McDonald, M. M., Asher, B. D., Kerr, N. L., & Navarrete, C. D. (2011). Fertility and intergroup bias in racial and minimal-group contexts: Evidence for shared architecture. *Psychological Science, 22*, 860–865.

McKibbin, W. F., Shackelford, T. K., Goetz, A. T., & Starratt, V. G. (2008). Why do men rape? An evolutionary psychological perspective. *Review of General Psychology, 12*, 86–97.

McKibbin, W. F., Shackelford, T. K., Goetz, A. T., Bates, V. M., Starratt, V. G., & Miner, E. J. (2009). Development and initial psychometric assessment of the Rape Avoidance Inventory. *Personality and Individual Differences, 39*, 336–340.

McKibbin, W. F., Shackelford, T. K., Miner, E. J., Bates, V. M., & Liddle, J. R. (2011). Individual differences in women's rape avoidance behaviors. *Archives of Sexual Behavior, 40*, 343–349.

McKinney, F., Derrickson, S. R., & Mineau, P. (1983). Forced copulation in waterfowl. *Behavior, 86*, 250–294.

Mitani, J. C. (1985). Mating behavior of male orangutans in the Kutai Reserve. *Animal Behaviour, 33*, 392–402.

Morris, N. M., & Udry, J. R. (1970). Variations in pedometer activity during the menstrual cycle. *Sensory Processing, 2*, 90–98.

Morris, N. M., & Udry, J. R. (1982). Epidemiological patterns of sexual behavior in the menstrual cycle. In R. C. Friedman (Ed.), *Behavior and the menstrual cycle* (pp. 129–153). New York: Marcel Dekker.

Navarrete, C. D., Fessler, D. M. T., Fleischman, D. S., & Geyer, J. (2009). Race bias tracks conception risk across the menstrual cycle. *Psychological Science, 20*, 661–665.

Olsson, M. (1995). Forced copulation and costly female resistance behavior in the lake eyre dragon, *Ctenophorus maculosus. Herpetologica, 51*, 19–24.

Palmer, C. T., & Thornhill, R. (2003a). Straw men and fairy tales: Evaluating reactions to *A natural history of rape. The Journal of Sex Research, 40*, 249–255.

Palmer, C. T., & Thornhill, R. (2003b). A posse of good citizens bring outlaw evolutionists to justice. A response to *Evolution, gender, and rape.* Edited by Cheryl Brown Travis. (2003). Cambridge, MA: MIT Press. *Evolutionary Psychology, 1*, 10–27.

Perilloux, C., Duntley, J. D., & Buss, D. M. (2012). The costs of rape. *Archives of Sexual Behavior, 41*, 1099–1106.

Perilloux, C., Fleischman, D. S., & Buss, D. M. (2008). The daughter-guarding hypothesis: Parental influence on, and emotional reactions to, offspring's mating behavior. *Evolutionary Psychology, 6*, 217–233.

Perkins, C., & Klaus, P. (1996). *Criminal victimization 1994. National crime victimization survey.* Bulletin. Washington, DC: Bureau of Justice Statistics, U.S. Department of Justice.

Perkins, C., Klaus, P., Bastian, L., & Cohen, R. (1996). *Criminal victimization in the United States, 1993. National crime victimization survey report.* Washington, DC: Bureau of Justice Statistics, U.S. Department of Justice.

Petralia, S. M., & Gallup, G. G. (2002). Effects of a sexual assault scenario on handgrip strength across the menstrual cycle. *Evolution and Human Behavior, 23,* 3–10.

Pizzari, T., & Birkhead, T. R. (2000). Female feral fowl eject sperm of subdominant males. *Nature, 405,* 787–789.

Plath, M., Parzefall, J., & Schlupp, I. (2003). The role of sexual harassment in cave and surface dwelling populations of the Atlantic molly, *Poecilia mexicana* (Poeciliidae, Teleostei). *Behavioral Ecology and Sociobiology, 54,* 303–309.

Resnick, H. S., Kilpatrick, D. G., Dansky, B. S., Saunders, B. E., & Best, C. L. (1993). Prevalence of civilian trauma and post-traumatic stress disorder in a representative national sample of women. *Journal of Consulting and Clinical Psychology, 61,* 984–991.

Reyer, H.-U., Frei, G., & Som, C. (1999). Cryptic female choice: frogs reduce clutch size when amplexed by undesired males. *Proceedings of the Royal Society B: Biological Sciences, 266,* 2101.

Robbins, M. M. (1999). Male mating patterns in wild multimale mountain gorilla groups. *Animal Behaviour, 57,* 1013–1020.

Rozée, P. D. (1993). Forbidden or forgiven? Rape in cross-cultural perspective. *Psychology of Women Quarterly, 17,* 499–514.

Sanday, P. R. (1981). The socio-cultural context of rape: A cross-cultural study. *Journal of Social Issues, 37,* 5–27.

Scheppele, K. L., & Bart, P. B. (1983). Through women's eyes: Defining danger in the wake of sexual assault. *Journal of Social Issues, 39,* 63–81.

Shackelford, T. K. (2002a). Are young women the special targets of rape-murder? *Aggressive Behavior, 28,* 224–232.

Shackelford, T. K. (2002b). Risk of multiple-offender rape-murder varies with female age. *Journal of Criminal Justice, 30,* 135–141.

Shine, R., Langkilde, T., & Mason, R. T. (2003). Cryptic forcible insemination: Male snakes exploit female physiology, anatomy, and behavior to obtain coercive matings. *American Naturalist, 162,* 653–667.

Smuts, B. B. (1992). Male aggression against women. *Human Nature, 6,* 1–32.

Smuts, B. B., & Smuts, R. W. (1993). Male aggression and sexual coercion of females in nonhuman primates and other mammals: Evidence and theoretical implications. *Advances in the Study of Behavior, 22,* 1–63.

Symons, D. (1979). *The evolution of human sexuality.* New York: Oxford University Press.

Sztatecsny, M., Jehle, R., Burke, T., & Hödl, W. (2006). Female polyandry under male harassment: The case of the common toad (*Bufo bufo*). *Journal of Zoology, 270,* 517.

Tang-Martinez, Z. (1997). The curious courtship of sociobiology and feminism: A case of irreconcilable differences. In P. Gowaty (Ed.), *Feminism and evolutionary biology* (pp. 116–150). New York: Chapman & Hall.

Thornhill, R. (1980). Rape in *Panorpa* scorpionflies and a general rape hypothesis. *Animal Behavior, 28,* 52–59.

Thornhill, R. (1981). *Panorpa* (Mecoptera: Panorpidae) scorpionflies: Systems for understanding resource-defense polygyny and alternative male reproductive efforts. *Annual Review of Ecology and Systematics, 12,* 355–386.

Thornhill, R. (1987). The relative importance of intra- and interspecific competition in scorpionfly mating systems. *American Naturalist, 130,* 711–729.

Thornhill, N. (1996). Psychological adaptation to sexual coercion in victims and offenders. In D. M. Buss & N. Malamuth (Eds.), *Sex, power, conflict* (pp. 90–104). New York: Oxford University Press.

Thornhill, R., & Palmer, C. P. (2000). *A natural history of rape.* Cambridge, MA: MIT Press.

Thornhill, R., & Sauer, K. (1991). The notal organ of the scorpionfly (*Panorpa vulgaris*): An adaptation to coerce mating duration. *Behavioral Ecology, 2,* 156–164.

Thornhill, R., & Thornhill, N. (1983). Human rape: An evolutionary analysis. *Ethology and Sociobiology, 4,* 137–173.

Thornhill, N., & Thornhill, R. (1990a). Evolutionary analysis of psychological pain of rape victims I: The effects of victim's age and marital status. *Ethology and Sociobiology, 11,* 155–176.

Thornhill, N., & Thornhill, R. (1990b). Evolutionary analysis of psychological pain following rape II: The effects of stranger, friend, and family member offenders. *Ethology and Sociobiology, 11,* 177–193.

Thornhill, N., & Thornhill, R. (1990c). Evolutionary analysis of psychological pain following rape victims III: The effects of force and violence. *Aggressive Behavior, 16,* 297–320.

Thornhill, N., & Thornhill, R. (1991). An evolutionary analysis of psychological pain following rape IV: The effect of the nature of the sexual act. *Journal of Comparative Psychology, 105,* 243–252.

Thornhill, R., & Thornhill, N. (1992). The evolutionary psychology of men's coercive sexuality. *Behavioral and Brain Sciences, 15,* 363–375.

Trivers, R. L. (1972). Parental investment and sexual selection. In B. Campbell (Ed.), *Sexual selection and the descent of man: 1871–1971* (pp. 136–179). Chicago: Aldine.

Vahed, K. (2002). Coercive copulation in the Alpine Bushcricket *Anonconotus alpinus* Yersin (Tettigoniidae: Tettigoniinae: Platycleidini). *Ethology, 108,* 1065–1075.

Wilson, M., Daly, M., & Scheib, J. (1997). Femicide: an evolutionary psychological perspective. In P. A. Gowaty (Ed.), *Feminism and evolutionary biology: Boundaries, intersections, and frontiers* (pp. 431–465). New York: Chapman & Hall.

Wilson, M., & Mesnick, S. L. (1997). An empirical test of the bodyguard hypothesis. In P. A. Gowaty (Ed.), *Feminism and evolutionary biology* (pp. 505–511). New York: Chapman & Hall.

Wrangham, R., & Peterson, D. (1996). *Demonic males.* New York: Houghton Mifflin.

Female Orgasm

12

Lisa L.M. Welling

Introduction

Female orgasm is accompanied by pleasure, relaxation (Hite, 1976), decreased activation of the cerebral cortex, increased activation of dopamine-related systems in the brain (Georgiadis et al., 2006; Georgiadis, Reinders, Paans, Renken, & Kortekaas, 2009), and behavioral responses, such as arching of the back and muscle tension (Komisaruk, Beyer-Flores, & Whipple, 2006). Orgasm is also often associated with vocalizations (Hamilton & Arrowood, 1978), which are especially prevalent during penile-vaginal intercourse and may be under at least partial conscious control, providing women with an opportunity to manipulate male sexual behavior (Brewer & Hendrie, 2011). Women tend to additionally experience involuntary muscle contractions in the vagina and anus and increases in blood pressure, heart rate, and respiration (Komisaruk et al., 2006; Masters & Johnson, 1966) at orgasm.

Sex hormone levels likely play an important role in women's orgasm frequency and individual experience. Oxytocin, a hormone that causes muscle contractions and increases gratification (Blaicher et al., 1999; Carmichael et al., 1987; Carmichael, Warburton, Dixen, & Davidson, 1994), but that is likewise involved in maternal care, pair bonding, and affiliation in female mammals (Campbell, 2008), is released at orgasm. Sexual activity may increase men's (Dabbs & Mohammed, 1992) and women's (van Anders, Hamilton, Schmidt, & Watson, 2007) testosterone levels and may also increase estradiol and decrease cortisol in women (van Anders, Brotto, Farrell, & Yule, 2009). Androgen deficiency is one cause of female sexual dysfunction, and female sexual dysfunction is often treated with testosterone (Apperloo, Van Der Stege, Hoek, & Weijmar Schultz, 2003). Trait testosterone (van Anders et al., 2007) and testosterone levels across the menstrual cycle (Bancroft, Sanders, Davidson, & Warner, 1983) are positively associated with women's orgasm frequency. Women's testosterone levels are positively related to their reports of past sexual excitement (van Anders et al., 2009) and may also increase to a small extent at orgasm (Exton et al., 1999; van Anders et al., 2007). Recently, van Anders and Dunn (2009) found that women's estradiol level was associated with their reported sexual desire and that women's testosterone level was associated with their reports of positive orgasm experience. In men, however, testosterone (not estradiol) level was associated with their reported sexual desire and was not related to their reports of orgasm experience. These findings highlight how male and female orgasmic experience may differ biologically, but they may also differ subjectively.

Women, in contrast to men, report that their orgasms can differ in intensity, location, sensory qualities, and emotional components (Hite, 1976).

L.L.M. Welling (✉)
Department of Psychology, Oakland University, 212
Pryale Hall, Rochester, MI 48309, USA
e-mail: welling@oakland.edu

V.A. Weekes-Shackelford and T.K. Shackelford (eds.), *Evolutionary Perspectives on Human Sexual Psychology and Behavior*, Evolutionary Psychology, DOI 10.1007/978-1-4939-0314-6_12,
© Springer Science+Business Media New York 2014

For example, King, Belsky, Mah, and Binik (2011) recently described four different classes of female orgasm. Women can also achieve orgasm in various ways. While stimulation of the glans of the clitoris is typically the fastest and most reliable way for a woman to orgasm, is not the only way (e.g., Bentler & Peeler, 1979; Schober, Meyer-Bahlburg, & Ransley, 2004), nor is it the only location at which women can experience orgasm. Different neural pathways in the vaginal area that are independent of the clitoral pathway can trigger orgasm, even in some (human and animal) cases where the spinal cord has been completely severed (Komisaruk et al., 1996, 2004; Komisaruk & Sansone, 2003; Komisaruk & Whipple, 2005). Indeed, women with complete spinal cord injury at the tenth thoracic vertebrae (T10) or higher report sensations generated through vaginal-cervical stimulation, seemingly because of a pathway that can convey adequate sensory activity from the cervix to induce orgasm via the vagus nerve (Komisaruk & Whipple, 2005).

Female orgasm does not occur with the same reliability as male orgasm, but not all researchers agree to what extent (e.g., Puts, 2006a; Wallen, 2006). Baker and Bellis (1993) found that nearly 50 % of female orgasms occurred via masturbation, that approximately 35 % of sexual intercourse did not result in orgasm for the woman, and that the woman usually climaxed first when copulatory orgasms did occur. Fisher (1973) reported that 20 % of women claim to never need clitoral stimulation in order to achieve orgasm, although Wallen (2006) later asserted that the number of women who achieve orgasm through penile-vaginal penetration alone might be as low as 6 %. However, Fisher (1973) also found that 35 % of women needed manual stimulation 50 % or more of the time to achieve orgasm, a figure that Puts (2006a) used to state that 65 % of women usually do not require manual clitoral stimulation to achieve copulatory orgasm. In line with this assertion, Tavris and Sadd (1977) found that 63 % of women recount usually having an orgasm with intercourse, and Lloyd (2005) estimated that 55 % of women have orgasm with intercourse more than half the time. Finally, while Dawood, Kirk, Bailey, Andrews, and Martin

(2005) found that 34.7 % of women never (13.7 %) or rarely (21 %) experienced orgasm via sexual intercourse, roughly the same number of women (36.3 %) indicated that they usually (13.1 %), almost always (17.9 %), or always (5.3 %) experience orgasm through sexual intercourse, with 82.8 % of respondents indicating that they are capable of achieving orgasm this way.

Genetic, environmental (Dawood et al., 2005; Dunn, Cherkas, & Spector, 2005), psychosocial (Cohen & Belsky, 2008; Harris, Cherkas, Kato, Heiman, & Spector, 2008), and cultural (Davenport, 1977) factors all appear to contribute to female orgasm frequency and experience, but the quality of the sexual experience undoubtedly plays an important role (Brody & Weiss, 2010; Puppo, 2011; Richters, de Visser, Rissel, & Smith, 2006; Weiss & Brody, 2009). Although some women (Brindley & Gillian, 1982) and men (Rowland et al., 2010) are not capable of experiencing orgasm, reports on the proportion of women who have ever experienced orgasm, at least, may underestimate the amount of women capable of achieving orgasm (see also Puts, 2007; Puts, Dawood, & Welling, 2012). For instance, Marshall (1971) reported that all women on the Polynesian island of Mangaia, a culture that places a high importance on men pleasing their female partners sexually, report achieving orgasm during intercourse. In Western populations, approximately 90–95 % of women have experienced orgasm, with close to 90 % having experienced orgasm during intercourse (Lloyd, 2005). Furthermore, while cross-species comparisons will not be the focus of this chapter, it is important to mention that there is evidence of female orgasm within nonhuman primate species (reviewed in Allen & Lemmon, 1981; Puts, Dawood, et al., 2012). Female gorillas (*Gorilla gorilla*) (Harcourt, Harvey, Larson, & Short, 1981; Nadler, 1976; Schaller, 1963) and chimpanzees (*Pan troglodytes*) (Allen & Lemmon, 1981; Hauser, 1990), among others (Puts, Dawood, et al., 2012; Zumpe & Michael, 1968), also exhibit signs of orgasm, including changes in respiratory patterns, vocalizations, and vaginal contractions. This demonstrates that female orgasm may be more widespread than previously believed.

Women are more likely than men to fake orgasm (Muehlenhard & Shippee, 2010; Thornhill, Gangestad, & Comer, 1995). Roughly half of all women admit to having faked an orgasm at some point (Darling & Davidson, 1986; Hite, 1976; Muehlenhard & Shippee, 2010; Wiederman, 1997), and one study found that women fake orgasm approximately 13 % of the time (Thornhill et al., 1995). Women who began having sexual intercourse at a young age (Darling & Davidson, 1986; Davidson & Darling, 1988), who have more sexual partners (Davidson & Darling, 1988), and who act in less exclusive ways with their partners (Thornhill et al., 1995) tend to fake orgasm more often. Similarly, Wiederman (1997) found that women who have faked orgasm began having sexual intercourse at a younger age, were older, rated themselves as more facially attractive, reported more sexual partners, and scored higher on sexual esteem than women who had not faked orgasm. Just over half of women in one sample report that they fake orgasm because it is important to satisfy their partner (Darling & Davidson, 1986), but other reasons for faking orgasm include meeting a partner's expectations, to boost a partner's ego, and to increase sexual excitement (Muehlenhard & Shippee, 2010). These data underline the complexity of male–female sexual interactions.

Whether or not female orgasm serves an adaptive purpose has become a controversial topic (Alcock, 1980, 1987; Barash, 1977, 2005; Barash & Lipton, 2009; Beach, 1974; Eibl-Eibesfeldt, 1975; Gould, 1987; Hamburg, 1978; Judson, 2005; Morris, 1967; Puts, 2006a, 2006b; Puts & Dawood, 2006; Symons, 1979). Some scholars insist that female orgasm serves no evolutionary function (Lloyd, 2005; Wallen, 2006, 2007), while others believe it may serve one or more adaptive purposes (Baker & Bellis, 1993; Costa & Brody, 2007; Meston, Levin, Sipski, Hull, & Heiman, 2004; Puts, Welling, Burriss, & Dawood, 2012; Shackelford et al., 2000; Singh, Meyer, Zambarano, & Hurlbert, 1998; Smith, 1984; Thornhill et al., 1995; Wildt, Kissler, Licht, & Becker, 1998). Thus, there are two competing explanations for why women can experience orgasm: the adaptation hypothesis and the by-product hypothesis.

Adaptation Versus By-Product

An adaptation is any trait that increases the organism's inclusive fitness. Although environmental circumstances may play a vital role in their development (reviewed in Buss, Haselton, Shackelford, Bleske, & Wakefield, 1998), adaptations are inherited, reliably developing traits that exist as a feature of a species through natural selection because they either directly or indirectly facilitated reproduction (Buss et al., 1998; Tooby & Cosmides, 1992; Williams, 1966). Put another way, "adaptation refers to any functional characteristic whose origin or maintenance must be explained by the process of natural selection" (Buss et al., 1998, p.536). For example, the common fear of spiders in humans would adaptively discourage dangerous behavior (i.e., handling potentially poisonous insects) and thus increase chances of survival. By-products, on the other hand, are characteristics that do not serve a specific function and do not solve adaptive problems. A by-product, also called a *spandrel*, is a trait that is not itself a product of natural selection, but instead arose as an indirect consequence of an adaptation (Buss et al., 1998; Gould & Lewontin, 1979). A commonly used example of a by-product is the color of bones, which are white due to the fact that they contain large amounts of calcium, presumably selected because of properties such as strength and not color (Buss et al., 1998; Shackelford, Goetz, Liddle, & Bush, 2012; Symons, 1992).

Sex-specific adaptations can arise when alleles are expressed in both sexes but are selected for one sex or the other (Rice & Chippindale, 2001). In these cases, selection can disrupt the expression of a sex-specific adaptation in the opposite sex by regulating the associated genes with sex steroids, such as the evolution of wider hips in women, which evolved to more safely accommodate the head width of a fetus at birth (LaVelle, 1995). However, because of the genetic similarity between the sexes, genes that produce an adaptation in one sex can produce a trait that is not adaptive in the other, referred to as a sexually antagonistic by-product (Rice & Chippindale, 2001). A common example in humans is male nipples, which are clearly adaptive in women (used in breastfeeding), but serve no function in men (Fox, 1993; Puts, Dawood, et al., 2012; Symons, 1979; Wallen & Lloyd, 2008). Like other by-products, selection also tends to reduce the expression of sexually antagonistic by-products, as demonstrated by male nipples being smaller than female nipples. Therefore, by-products often appear vestigial and do not appear to serve any relative function.

Female Orgasm as a Functionless By-Product

Fisher (1930) argued that low genetic variation within a population implies strong selection. Following this hypothesis and observations of haplodiploid insects, Crespi and Vanderkist (1997) concluded that relatively high variability in traits indicated a lack of selection for functionality. The large variability in reports of incidence and method of achieving female orgasm (Dawood et al., 2005; Fisher, 1973; Lloyd, 2005; Symons, 1979; Tavris & Sadd, 1977) has led some to claim that female orgasm is reduced in comparison to male orgasm and, therefore, likely a by-product of the male's ability to orgasm (Lloyd, 2005; Symons, 1979; Wallen & Lloyd, 2008). Arguably, the inconsistency of female orgasm, in comparison to male orgasm, may indicate that female orgasm is under significantly less selective pressure (Lloyd, 2005; Symons, 1979), which supports the idea that it was not selectively designed. If female orgasm was adaptively important and subject to strong selection pressure, the percentage of women who never experience orgasm, or who never experience it through intercourse, may be expected to be considerably lower. Eschler (2004) found that

only one third (33.3 %) of women indicated that vaginal stimulation led to orgasm, compared to 77.4 % who indicated that manual clitoral stimulation led to orgasm. Wallen (2006) claims that 5–10 % of women never experience orgasm under any circumstances and that approximately 75 % of women never experience orgasm through penile-vaginal intercourse alone. Wallen (2006) goes on to argue that if female orgasm during intercourse ever conferred a reproductive advantage, orgasm would be more prevalent in modern women.

Gender in humans is determined at conception, but the early gonadal development of humans in utero is identical in both sexes and no physically dimorphic effects of the initial sex determination seem to occur until around 6 weeks (Blecher & Erickson, 2007). At this point in males, under the influence of testosterone, the labioscrotal folds fuse to form the scrotum, the genital tubercle becomes the penis, and, later, the testes descend into the scrotum. In females, the labioscrotal folds do not fuse and form the labia, the genital tubercle forms the clitoris, and the ovaries do not descend (Blecher & Erickson, 2007). Given the homologous nature of male and female anatomical structures involved in orgasm and reproduction, it is evident that the ability of men and women to achieve orgasm is developmentally related. Wallen and Lloyd (2008) consequently looked at the variation in length in male and female genital structures, finding that clitoral length was more variable than penile length. They argued that the marked variability in clitoral size suggests little or no selective pressure on its development and, by extension, on the development of female orgasm. However, Wallen and Lloyd (2008) have received some criticism for aspects of their study design and interpretation. Their argument assumes that clitoral/penile length is important for orgasmic potential, but current evidence suggests that neither penile (Lynch, 2008) nor clitoral length (Masters & Johnson, 1966) affects the ability to orgasm. As pointed out by Puts, Dawood, et al. (2012), the assumption that increased variability in clitoral (versus penile) length is related to orgasm potential is flawed because the penis has the additional function of being necessary for both urination and sperm transfer. The clitoris also differs from the penis in the proportion that is external versus internal, making comparison possibly inappropriate (Lynch, 2008). Using volume instead of length, Lynch (2008) used the same data as Wallen and Lloyd (2008) and found no difference between variation in clitoral and penile volume. Hosken (2008) further highlights how it is unclear from Wallen and Lloyd's (2008) data whether allometric slope or the dispersion of the data drives the differences reported. The increased variance in clitoral versus penile length, therefore, is inadequate evidence to conclude definitively that selection did not favor the female orgasm.

Some have argued that the position of the clitoris is sexually dysfunctional in comparison to the penis because it requires extra stimulation that does not often occur naturally during penile-vaginal intercourse (Eibl-Eibesfeldt, 1989; Lloyd, 2005; Morris, 1985). This might suggest that the clitoris did not evolve to function in coital orgasm, thereby supporting the by-product hypothesis. Then again, this conclusion may be shortsighted because the position of the clitoris, while apparently inconvenient for consistent coital orgasmic stimulation, may reduce the risk of damage from vaginal tearing during childbirth (Potts & Short, 1999). Moreover, because women are far more likely to experience multiple orgasms than men (Darling, Davidson, & Cox, 1991; Masters & Johnson, 1966; Sherfey, 1973), are widely capable of experiencing orgasm (Davenport, 1977; Marshall, 1971), and seem to experience more complex, elaborate, and intense orgasms than men (Mah & Binik, 2001, 2002), some have reasoned that the female orgasm is not reduced compared to the male orgasm (Puts & Dawood, 2006; Puts, Dawood, et al., 2012). Female orgasm may also serve one or more functions (e.g., sperm retention, Baker & Bellis, 1993) and may be facultative, reflecting possible aspects of female choice (Puts, 2007; Thornhill & Gangestad, 1996), potentially explaining the variation in women's orgasm frequency. Finally, if orgasm is maintained by a selection favoring male orgasm, there should be a strong positive correlation in orgasmic sensitivity between male

and female relatives, but Zietsch and Santtila (2011) found no significant correlations in orgasmic function between opposite sex twins or non-twin siblings. This finding contradicts the by-product hypothesis because it suggests that different genetic factors underlie male and female orgasmic function.

In light of the above, the evidence in favor of the by-product hypothesis of female orgasm appears insufficient to declare female orgasm a "happy accident" with full certainty. Other evidence supports the alternative view that female orgasm is its own adaptation, separate from male orgasm.

Female Orgasm as an Adaptation

The most common reasons given by women as to why they would fake an orgasm are to keep their partner interested or excited and to reduce the likelihood of a partner being unfaithful or of a partner defecting from the relationship (Muehlenhard & Shippee, 2010). It may not seem initially obvious why female orgasm would lead to an increase in male sexual satisfaction or decrease the likelihood of male relationship defection, but if female orgasm serves any adaptive function, then men should have a vested interest in their partner's orgasm. Accordingly, McKibbin, Bates, Shackelford, Hafen, and LaMunyon (2010) found that partnered men who report higher relationship satisfaction also report greater interest in, and attentiveness to, their partner's copulatory orgasm than men who report lower relationship satisfaction and that this relationship was strongest among men reporting a higher perceived risk of sperm competition through partner infidelity. Recently, Kaighobadi, Shackelford, and Weekes-Shackelford (2012) tested the relationship between the frequency of faking orgasm and the frequency of reported mate retention tactics (behaviors designed to reduce the likelihood of a partner straying or being poached by a rival, Buss, 1988; Buss, Shackelford, & McKibbin, 2008; Welling, Burriss, & Puts, 2011; Welling, Puts, Roberts, Little, & Burriss, 2012). They found that women who perceived a higher risk of partner infidelity were more likely to report faking orgasm and that women who reported greater probability of faking orgasm also reported performing more mate retention behaviors. Interestingly, there was also a relationship between faking orgasm and the frequency of negative mate retention behaviors, which was mediated by women's perceptions of the risk of partner infidelity. Kaighobadi et al. (2012) interpreted these findings as evidence that faking orgasm may be part of a broader strategy aimed at retaining one's mate, which may be performed by women who perceive a greater risk of their partner straying. If female orgasms are completely inconsequential, these findings become difficult to explain.

Hrdy (1996) suggested that female orgasm in primate females may have been adaptive for prehominid ancestors of *Homo sapiens*, meaning that the benefits were greater than any possible cost to reproductive success, although it may not be adaptive in all contexts. Thornhill and Gangestad (1996) further suggested the possibility that female orgasm may be functional for modern humans but that its original function in prehominid ancestors may have been different than the function it serves now. In this case, the function of human female orgasm may differ from functions that led to it in nonhuman primates. A secondary adaptation, also called an *exaptation*, is an adaptation that originated as a by-product but was then modified over time by selection to serve a new, adaptive function (Gould & Vrba, 1982). One possible example of a secondary adaptation is the ability of most bird species to fly. Some scholars (Ostrom, 1974, 1979; Rayner, 2001) believe that feathers originally evolved for the purposes of insulation but that eventually they also functioned with increasing efficiency in flight for many bird species. Analogously, perhaps female orgasm began as a by-product of male orgasm but may have gradually been shaped as a secondary adaptation.

Adaptive explanations for female orgasm mainly center around four hypotheses: promotion of future copulations, pair bonding, promotion of fertilization, and mate/sire selection. All four propositions posit that female orgasm is an adaptation in its own right and not merely a by-product

resulting from similar ontogeny with men. Unlike the by-product explanation of female orgasm, the different adaptive theories behind female orgasm are not necessarily mutually exclusive.

Promotion of Future Copulations

Hypotheses surrounding the idea that orgasm promotes future copulations infer that the intense pleasure associated with orgasm serves as a reward for engaging in sexual behaviors, thereby promoting future sexual encounters. Because orgasm is accompanied by extreme pleasure, feelings of release, and relaxation (Meston et al., 2004), the psychological rewards may motivate people to continue to engage in sexual activity, which would augment fitness by increasing the likelihood of sexual activity during fertile periods and, thus, possibly increase conception rates. This principle can be applied to male orgasm as well as female orgasm because the physiological aspects of male orgasm that lead to ejaculation need not necessarily be accompanied by pleasurable sensations, which are not necessary for conception. For example, many species of fish fertilize eggs externally by ejaculating into the water without stimulation (Stockley, Gage, Parker, & Moller, 1996). This introduces the possibility that the pleasurable sensations associated with orgasm in humans may function to increase both interest and likelihood of engaging in sexual behaviors. Psychological and affective rewards could also explain why women feel the urge to copulate outside the fertile window, when sexual intercourse carries no reproductive reward. Therefore, it is important to contemplate the psychological factors, as well as the biological ones, when considering the adaptive significance of orgasm.

Orgasmic sensations are greatly important to the majority of women. Eschler (2004) found that 75.8 % of women rated having an orgasm with a partner as either somewhat or very important, while only 6 % rated having an orgasm with a partner as somewhat unimportant or very unimportant. Additionally, 29.4 % of women said it was very unlikely that they would enjoy sex without an orgasm, compared to only 9.1 %

who said it was very likely that they would still enjoy sex even if they did not have an orgasm. The feelings of release described by women who experience orgasm (Hite, 1976) could reward feelings of sexual desire by reducing sexual tension and increasing relaxation. Certainly, orgasm activates the dopamine-related ventral midbrain and right caudate nucleus, known to be involved in reward-driven learning and motivation (Georgiadis et al., 2006, 2009). Altogether, this research emphasizes the importance of women's subjective experience and pleasure in wanting to continue engaging in sexual activities and provides support for the assumption that orgasm acts as a reward for sexual behavior. Similarly, orgasm may motivate women to continue copulating until they achieve orgasm, thus increasing the likelihood that the man will have ejaculated, or it may encourage women to copulate again with men that have brought them to orgasm. This latter explanation could function to encourage women to remain with their current partners, thereby promoting pair bonding for the purposes of later raising offspring.

Pair Bonding

Pair bonding theories suggest that the female orgasm evolved to strengthen the connection between mates, leading to greater biparental care of offspring and, by extension, enhanced fitness (Eibl-Eibesfeldt, 1989; Morris, 1967). Sexual arousal and orgasm deactivate a region in the human frontal cortex that overlaps the deactivated region observed in romantic love (Zeki, 2007). Thornhill and Gangestad (1996) suggested that copulatory orgasm may reduce the number of partners that women pursue by creating strong feelings of intimacy with one or only a few mates but that a lack of copulatory orgasms may increase female infidelity. This hypothesis seems plausible given the importance of orgasm to women's sexual satisfaction (Eschler, 2004) and that sexual dissatisfaction is related to infidelity (Buss & Shackelford, 1997). Moreover, Gebhard (1966) found that women in longer marriages tended to experience more

orgasms (see also Kinsey, Pomeroy, Martin, & Gebhard, 1953), which suggests that women may be more likely to orgasm with men they are comfortable and familiar with, or that long-term partners may be more likely to induce orgasm.

Across cultures (Symons, 1979), women are less likely than men to seek uncommitted sex (Clark & Hatfield, 1989; Oliver & Hyde, 1993), possibly in part because uncommitted sexual encounters (one-night stands) are unlikely to result in orgasm for the woman (Eschler, 2004) and may function to bond women to their investing partner, thus acting in selection of a long-term mate (Barash, 1977; Beach, 1974; Hamburg, 1978; Morris, 1967). It should be noted that the term investing is here used to refer to investment in the relationship via partner emotional and/or physical support and help with childrearing, but not necessarily financial support since, as Hrdy (1997) pointed out, the presumed innate universal of women's preferences for wealthy mates may be facultative accommodations by women to constraints brought about by patriarchal monopolization of resources needed by women and their offspring to survive and reproduce. Indeed, the number of sex partners a woman has is increased in social settings in which each man has limited resources to provide in exchange for sexual access (Buss, 1994), suggesting that monopolization of resources can influence female reproductive strategy, possibly out of necessity, in ways that may not be directly comparable to social systems in ancestral times (O'Connell, Hawkes, & Blurton Jones, 1999).

Other evidence indicates that women have more satisfying sex lives with long-term partners. Women believe that sexual encounters within a long-term relationship are more likely to result in orgasm (Eschler, 2004), premarital orgasms are more likely for women in stable relationships, and women's coital orgasm frequency is predicted by their active participation in sexual encounters and the duration of foreplay (Tavris & Sadd, 1977). Higher reported marital happiness is positively related to a higher percentage of penile-vaginal sexual intercourse that resulted in orgasm for the wife (Gebhard, 1966), and women in long-term relationships report greater emotional and physical satisfaction with their sex lives than women in comparatively shorter relationships (Laumann, Gagnon, Michael, & Michaels, 1994). In a sample of Portuguese women, both the frequency of penile-vaginal intercourse and the frequency of orgasm from penile-vaginal intercourse were positively associated with several aspects of relationship quality, and penile-vaginal orgasm frequency was negatively related to masturbation frequency (Costa & Brody, 2007). Coital orgasms are also more sexually satisfying to women than noncoital (i.e., clitoral) orgasms (Davidson & Darling, 1989). On the other hand, noncoital sexual behaviors with a partner were not correlated with any measured dimensions of mate quality, although masturbation frequency was negatively related to reported love (Costa & Brody, 2007).

Still, other findings contradict the supposed relationship between female orgasm frequency and long-term relationship satisfaction. Despite initial reports that male income, a possible indicator of male investment potential, predicted female partner orgasm frequency (Pollet & Nettle, 2009), later work (Herberich, Hothorn, Nettle, & Pollet, 2010; Pollet & Nettle, 2010) revealed that the association between partner wealth and female self-reported orgasm frequency was confounded by women with higher-income partners being healthier, happier, younger, and better educated than women with lower-income partners. Thornhill et al. (1995) found no association between women's orgasm frequency and either relationship duration of their professed love for their partner, nor did they find relationships between female orgasm frequency and male ratings of indicators of investment, such as reported commitment, nurturance, relationship duration, and reported love. Finally, Laumann et al. (1994) found a negative relationship between female orgasm frequency and relationship duration. These contradictory results suggest that relationship between pair bonding and orgasm may be more complex.

Some researchers have nominated the hormone oxytocin as responsible for, or encouraging of, pair bond formation in couples (Campbell,

2010; Fisher, Aron, & Brown, 2006; Skuse & Gallagher, 2009), opening the possibility that sexual intercourse and orgasm may influence pair bonding via associated hormonal release (Puts, Dawood, et al., 2012; Young & Wang, 2004). Oxytocin is released at orgasm in both sexes (Carmichael et al., 1987; Murphy, Seckl, Burton, Checkley, & Lightman, 1987) and in response to vaginocervical stimulation, lactation, and childbirth in women (reviewed in Komisaruk & Whipple, 2005). Oxytocin is also released during stress (Jezova, Skultetyova, Tokarev, Bakos, & Vigas, 1995), may be involved in reducing anxiety (Heinrichs, von Dawans, & Domes, 2009; McCarthy & Altemus, 1997), and reduces activation of the amygdala (Kirsch et al., 2005), which is involved in the expression of fear and anxiety (Davis, 1992). Oxytocin also improves the ability to infer the mental state of others from social cues (Domes, Heinrichs, Michel, Berger, & Herpertz, 2007), increases prosocial behavior (Campbell, 2010; Heinrichs & Domes, 2008; Zak, Stanton, & Ahmadi, 2007), and is higher in people reporting greater partner support (Grewen, Girdler, Amico, & Light, 2005; Sanchez, Parkin, Chen, & Gray, 2009). Prenatal and postpartum oxytocin levels enhance the formation of maternal-infant bonds and reduce maternal stress reactivity, and the experience of being trusted and reciprocating trust seems to raise oxytocin levels (reviewed in Campbell, 2010). Similarly, oxytocin appears to be involved in the formation of pair bonds, sexual and affiliative behavior, and parenting behavior (Campbell, 2010; Carter et al., 1997; Carter, Williams, Witt, & Insel, 1992; Curley & Keverne, 2005) in nonhuman animals. However, oxytocin levels have also been associated with greater interpersonal distress (Turner, Altemus, Enos, Cooper, & McGuinness, 1999) and, in postmenopausal women, are negatively correlated with marriage quality, physically affectionate partner contact, and reports of partner relations (Taylor et al., 2006). Nonetheless, if oxytocin is involved in human pair bonding, orgasm may play an important role and may additionally function in promoting fertility via uterine contractions (Wildt et al., 1998).

Promotion of Fertilization

Promotion of fertilization theories hypothesize that female orgasm leads to physiological processes that enhance the likelihood of conception via easier transport of sperm towards the unfertilized egg (Baker & Bellis, 1993; Fox, Wolff, & Baker, 1970; Levin, 2002; Meston et al., 2004; Singh et al., 1998; Wildt et al., 1998). According to Lloyd (2005), the fact that the low number of women who reliably achieve orgasm through penile-vaginal intercourse reproduce as well as the women who rarely or never experience orgasm brings the adaptive nature of the female orgasm into question, at least with reference to conception (see also Wallen, 2006). However, there is evidence that women are more likely to experience orgasm when they are fertile (Matteo & Rissman, 1984; Udry & Morris, 1968), likely because of changes in hormone levels across the menstrual cycle (van Anders & Dunn, 2009). Female orgasm activates the paraventricular nucleus (Komisaruk et al., 2004), which is involved with oxytocin release (Fliers, Swaab, Pool, & Verwer, 1985; Powell & Rorie, 1967), and activates the cingulate cortex and medial amygdala (Komisaruk et al., 2004), which may cause uterine contractions (Beyer, Anguiano, & Mena, 1961; Setekleiv, 1964). Moreover, women's desires to become pregnant are associated with their likelihood of achieving orgasm shortly after their partner (Singh et al., 1998) when sperm would already be present in the reproductive tract. Indeed, Baker and Bellis (1993) found that female orgasms that climaxed between 1 min before the male ejaculated and 45 min after led to the retention of more sperm, while either no orgasm or one occurring more than 1 min before the male ejaculated led to comparatively low sperm retention.

Both orgasm (Fox et al., 1970) and oxytocin (Wildt et al., 1998) released at orgasm (Blaicher et al., 1999) cause uterine contractions and change uterine pressure from outward to inward, creating an "upsuck" of seminal fluids into the uterus (Fox et al., 1970; Wildt et al., 1998) that may reduce the amount of sperm that flows back out of the vagina (i. e., "flowback"). The oxytocin-induced contractions in the uterus and oviducts also seem to act directly in transporting sperm, turning the uterus and fallopian tubes into a sort of functional peristaltic pump (Wildt et al., 1998; Zervomanolakis et al., 2007, 2009). Mimicking oxytocin release at orgasm by administering hormones to women induces uterine contractions and transports seminal-like particles up into the uterus during both the luteal (infertile) and follicular (fertile) phases of the menstrual cycle, but that transport is directed into the specific fallopian tube that would be releasing an egg during the fertile phase of the cycle only (Wildt et al., 1998; Zervomanolakis et al., 2007, 2009). The biological significance of this finding is demonstrated by the observation that the pregnancy rate was higher in women who demonstrated transport of fluid into the appropriate fallopian tube than in those women who failed to exhibit lateralization (Wildt et al., 1998; Zervomanolakis et al., 2007). Although two studies failed to find movement of semen-like substances through the cervix following orgasm (Grafenberg, 1950; Masters & Johnson, 1966), the significance of these null findings has since been contested (see also Puts & Dawood, 2006; Puts, Dawood, et al., 2012) because both studies placed a cap over the cervix, which may have prevented the flow of fluids (Fox et al., 1970). Finally, while oxytocin may be released during sexual stimulation without orgasm (Lloyd, 2005), uterine contractions (Komisaruk et al., 2006), uterine suction (Fox et al., 1970), and oxytocin release (Carmichael et al., 1994) have been found to increase following orgasm. Therefore, peristaltic contractions, like those experienced at orgasm, should increase the chance of fertilization by way of decreasing the distance sperm need to travel to reach the dominant follicle.

During sexual arousal, a physiological change known as "vaginal tenting" occurs in which the inner third of the anterior wall of the vagina becomes elevated away from the posterior wall along with the uterus and cervix, thereby removing it from the pool of semen (Levin, 2002; Masters & Johnson, 1966). This may function to create a space for the ejaculate to pool, thus reducing flowback losses (Baker & Bellis, 1995; Levin, 2002), and to provide time for the ejaculate to decoagulate (Levin, 2002). Human sperm cannot fertilize an ovum immediately, but requires time within the female reproductive tract to acquire the ability to fertilize, a process called *capacitation* (Eisenbach, 1995; Levin, 2002). Female orgasm may allow earlier entry of sperm into the cervix by resolving the vaginal tenting that accompanies sexual arousal (Puts, Dawood, et al., 2012), which would remove sperm from the vagina into the cervix, help decrease the flowback of sperm, and bring sperm closer to the fallopian tubes (Fox & Fox, 1971). Additionally, Meston et al. (2004) suggested that vaginal contractions may excite male ejaculation, possibly increasing the odds that the woman will be fertilized by her chosen partner, and the secretion of prolactin at orgasm may increase sperm capacitation (see also Reyes, Parra, Chavarria, Goicoechea, & Rosado, 1979). These findings compliment previous findings on the uptake of sperm into the cervix and oviducts via uterine contractions associated with orgasm and point out the probable importance of the role of female mate choice for procreation.

Mate Selection: Sire and Mate Choice

Theories surrounding mate/sire selection purport that female orgasm functions to encourage repeated sex with either high quality or investing males or that high quality or investing males are better able to induce orgasm, which serves to increase the fitness of resulting offspring through genetic and/or other benefits associated with the high quality or investing father (Alcock, 1980; Alexander, 1979; Puts, Welling, et al., 2012; Shackelford et al., 2000; Thornhill et al., 1995). Women stand to lose more than men through an inefficient allocation of mating effort due to their higher investment in childrearing via gestation and lactation, leading women to be choosier than men regarding mate choice (Clark & Hatfield, 1989; Daly & Wilson, 1983; Schmitt, 2005; Trivers, 1972). Angier (1999) suggested that the clitoral orgasm's function may reflect this choosiness, with the clitoris responding only when the male partner has expended sufficient effort as to demonstrate his willingness to invest in his partner. Female orgasm acting as a mate/ sire choice mechanism supposes that orgasm

should be more difficult for women to achieve because they are choosier about mate choice than men (Allen & Lemmon, 1981; Hosken, 2008; Puts, Dawood, et al., 2012) and that this choosiness should be most applicable to penile-vaginal intercourse that may result in conception (Puts, 2007).

Unlike other adaptive explanations of the female orgasm, the mate/sire choice hypothesis hinges on orgasm also functioning in either a pair bonding capacity (if orgasm functions in mate choice and women use orgasm to choose investing males) or a promotion of fertilization capacity (if orgasm functions in sire choice and women orgasm more with genetically fit men). If female orgasm reflects male investment, women should be less likely to orgasm with males who are not interested in a long-term relationship. In fact, women are less likely to seek uncommitted sex (Clark & Hatfield, 1989; Oliver & Hyde, 1993; Symons, 1979) and are less likely to orgasm during short-term sexual encounters than men (Eschler, 2004), indicating that orgasm in women may function in part to seek out a long-term, investing partner. This argument differs from the pair bonding hypothesis in a subtle way: while the pair bond hypothesis stipulates that orgasm functions to bond a woman to a man or vice versa, the mate choice hypothesis stipulates that orgasm is more likely to happen when a man is already showing long-term invest-ment potential. This would explain the strong associations between relationship length, aspects of relationship quality in a long-term partner, and orgasm frequency (Costa & Brody, 2007; Gebhard, 1966; Laumann et al., 1994). Alterna-tively, orgasm could function in the selection of a high quality mate, rather than an investing mate, per se. Under this view, orgasm likelihood would depend less on male investment and more on cues to underlying quality and by extension would be more relevant to sire choice than long-term mate choice.

Indirect evidence suggests that women may be more likely to copulate with, and possibly experience orgasm with, high quality men at ovulation. Women report being less committed to their partners (Jones et al., 2005) and may be more likely to seek extra-pair copulations (Bellis & Baker, 1990; Gangestad, Thornhill, & Garver, 2002; Gangestad, Thornhill, & Garver-Apgar, 2005) (but see Pillsworth, Haselton, & Buss, 2004) at peak fertility. Women are also more likely to experience orgasm near peak fertility (Matteo & Rissman, 1984; Udry & Morris, 1968) and demonstrate increased preference for cues to male mate quality at peak fertility, including cues to male symmetry (Little, Apicella, & Marlowe, 2007; Little & Jones, 2011; Little, Jones, & Burriss, 2007; Little, Jones, Burt, & Perrett, 2007) (but see Koehler, Rhodes, & Simmons, 2002; Koehler, Rhodes, Simmons, & Zebrowitz, 2006), masculinity (Feinberg et al., 2006; Frost, 1994; Johnston, Hagel, Franklin, Fink, & Grammer, 2001; Jones et al., 2005; Little, Apicella, et al., 2007; Little, Jones, & Burriss, 2007; Little, Jones, Burt, et al., 2007; Little, Jones, & DeBruine, 2008; Penton-Voak et al., 1999; Penton-Voak & Perrett, 2000; Puts, 2005; Welling et al., 2007), and dominance (Gangestad, Simpson, Cousins, Garver-Apgar, & Christensen, 2004). If women are more likely to orgasm with high quality men (Garver-Apgar, Gangestad, Thornhill, Miller, & Olp, 2006; Puts, Welling, et al., 2012; Shackelford et al., 2000; Thornhill et al., 1995), are more attracted to cues to high male quality at peak fertility, and are more likely to seek extra-pair sex at peak fertility, this could support the premise that female orgasm functions in sire choice. Furthermore, it could provide additional evidence of a dual mating system, whereby women seek good genes for potential offspring while fertile through extra-pair sex but seek longer-term mating opportunities with investing males at other points in the cycle (reviewed in Gangestad & Thornhill, 2008).

One putative cue to underlying quality is symmetry, as any deviation from bilateral symmetry implies developmental instability on the part of the organism (Møller, 1997; Møller & Pomiankowski, 1993; Parsons, 1990, 1992). Fluctuating asymmetry is negatively related to male mating success in humans (Bogaert & Fisher, 1995; Thornhill & Gangestad, 1994) and symmetry is considered attractive by women

(Gangestad, Thornhill, & Yeo, 1994; Grammer & Thornhill, 1994; Little, Apicella, et al., 2007; Little, Jones, & Burriss, 2007; Little, Jones, Burt, et al., 2007; Thornhill & Gangestad, 1994). Women's extra-pair sexual partners tend to have low fluctuating asymmetry (Gangestad & Thornhill, 1997), and women may be more likely to orgasm with extra-pair, versus in-pair, males (Baker & Bellis, 1993) (but see Eschler, 2004), alluding to the conclusion that women may have more orgasms with symmetrical companions. Indeed, Thornhill et al. (1995) found that women coupled with men lower in fluctuating asymmetry reported more orgasms than women coupled with relatively asymmetric men. Physical attractiveness is another putative measure of underlying genetic quality (Fink & Penton-Voak, 2002; Grammer, Fink, Moller, & Thornhill, 2003; Rhodes, 2006; Scheib, Gangestad, & Thornhill, 1999; Shackelford & Larsen, 1999; Thornhill & Gangestad, 1999), which may be related to semen quality (Soler et al., 2003) (but see Peters, Rhodes, & Simmons, 2008). Shackelford et al. (2000) found that women were more likely to have experienced orgasm at last copulation if they rated their partner as more attractive (see also Thornhill et al., 1995), even after controlling for relationship satisfaction, relationship duration, and age. More recently, Puts, Welling, et al. (2012) found that women with more attractive partners reported more frequent orgasms during or after male ejaculation, which is within the optimum window for sperm retention described by Baker and Bellis (1993). In addition, a principal component composed of several measures of masculinity (another presumed marker of men's genetic quality, Fink & Penton-Voak, 2002; Gangestad & Simpson, 2000; Rhodes, Chan, Zebrowitz, & Simmons, 2003) and dominance was related to more frequent and earlier-timed orgasms in women. That men's attractiveness and masculinity predicted their female partners' orgasm frequency was taken as evidence by Puts and colleagues that male sire quality increases incidences of female orgasm. Assuming that female orgasm increases the probability of conception, selective orgasms with suitors of higher genetic quality, rather than indiscriminant orgasms, could increase the probability of impregnation by genetically fit men, thereby augmenting offspring viability through the associated genetic benefits.

Past work, however, has provided little information about the differences in subjective sexual experience between women mated to attractive versus unattractive men and those mated to masculine versus more feminine men. For example, possible differences in penis size between subgroups of men may be a factor in female sexual satisfaction or male sexual confidence (Brody & Weiss, 2010; Costa, Miller, & Brody, 2012; Lever, Frederick, & Peplau, 2006). For instance, Costa et al. (2012) found that a longer penis was related to greater vaginal orgasm frequency, but not to the frequency of clitoral orgasms. Also, more attractive and more masculine/dominant men tend to have more sexual experience (Keller, Elliott, & Gunberg, 1982; Puts, Gaulin, & Verdolini, 2006; Rhodes, Simmons, & Peters, 2005), and this greater experience could lead to better sexual techniques or duration. Finally, that women with masculine partners are more likely to climax before their partners (Puts, Welling, et al., 2012) may be better explained by sexual excitability than an adaptation to acquire good sire genes for offspring. Earlier-timed orgasms are associated with greater sexual arousal and more physiological and psychological sexual satisfaction (Darling et al., 1991), but orgasm more than 1 min prior to male ejaculation may not increase chances of conception (Baker & Bellis, 1993). When taken with the findings that masculine men are considered sexually attractive by women (Little, Jones, Penton-Voak, Burt, & Perrett, 2002), the earlier timing of female orgasms with masculine partners (Puts, Welling, et al., 2012) may not necessarily be related to conceiving with masculine men. More research on the circumstances leading to, and timing of, female orgasm, and its relationship with conception, is clearly needed.

Perhaps the best evidence for the hypothesis that female orgasm functions in selecting a father with good genes comes from a study by Garver-Apgar et al. (2006) on major histocompatibility complex (MHC) genes. Genetic complementarity at the MHC (also called human leukocyte antigen, or HLA) may be beneficial for offspring. MHC molecules mediate interactions between white blood cells (cells of the immune system that are involved in defending the body against infections, diseases, and foreign materials) and other cells. Selection of an MHC-dissimilar (i.e., compatible) mate increases the heterozygosity of offspring at the MHC, thereby decreasing the chances that the offspring will have a weak immune system or suffer genetic consequences of inbreeding (Havlíček & Roberts, 2009). Garver-Apgar et al. (2006) found that women mated with an MHC-compatible partner experienced more orgasms, but only during the fertile phase of the ovulatory cycle. If orgasm and conception are related, then these findings are evidence that orgasm may function in selecting good genes for offspring. This is, however, a speculative argument in need of further investigation.

Conclusions

Because there is evidence in favor of more than one of the above hypothesized functions of the female orgasm, it is again important to stress that more than one function could be correct and that seemingly different functions could be related. For example, it is possible that orgasm in women functions to encourage sexual behavior more generally (i.e., as a reward for, and reinforcement to continue, sexual behavior that may result in conception) but that it also promotes fertilization with chosen sires, potentially of higher genetic quality (Garver-Apgar et al., 2006; Puts, Welling, et al., 2012; Shackelford et al., 2000; Thornhill et al., 1995), during peak fertility when orgasm is more easily induced (Matteo & Rissman, 1984; Udry & Morris, 1968) and attraction to men of high genetic quality highest (e.g., Gangestad & Thornhill, 2008). Female orgasm may simultaneously foster pair bonds with chosen long-term partners at nonfertile points in the cycle, potentially via oxytocin release (Campbell, 2010; Fisher et al., 2006; Skuse & Gallagher, 2009), when orgasm induction may take relatively more specialized partner attention. Otherwise, perhaps female orgasm was originally a by-product that has been shaped as a secondary adaption over time or, alternatively but perchance unlikely, that it no longer functions in the capacity for which it was designed.

Although the available evidence is not wholly conclusive, there is strong evidence to suggest that a by-product explanation of female orgasm alone may be insufficient. Certainly, more research is needed. For example, if inducing orgasm (or even uterine contractions) increases the likelihood of pregnancy relative to no orgasm, as some work suggests (Wildt et al., 1998), this would be compelling evidence that orgasm promotes conception. Relatedly, whether the timing of female orgasm relative to male orgasm influences conception (Baker & Bellis, 1993) could be tested, as could whether variation in the level of oxytocin released during coital orgasm correlates with a woman's feelings towards her partner. These and other research hypotheses surrounding the utility of female orgasm should be investigated cross-culturally and across different mammal and primate species. Such comparative work will improve our understanding of the physiology and purpose of the female orgasm and enable a better insight into our species' evolved sexual responses. Indeed, it is clear from current work that female orgasm is a complex, unique experience worthy of the continued attention from investigators.

References

Alcock, J. (1980). Beyond the sociobiology of sexuality: Predictive hypotheses. *Behavioral and Brain Sciences, 3*, 181–182.

Alcock, J. (1987). Ardent adaptationism. *Natural History, 96*, 4.

Alexander, R. D. (1979). Sexuality and sociality in humans and other primates. In A. Katchadourian (Ed.), *Human sexuality: A comparative and developmental perspective* (pp. 81–97). Berkeley, CA: University of California Press.

Allen, M. L., & Lemmon, W. B. (1981). Orgasm in female primates. *American Journal of Primatology, 1*, 15–34.

Angier, N. (1999). *Woman: An intimate geography.* New York, NY: Houghton Mifflin Company.

Apperloo, M. J. A., Van Der Stege, J. G., Hoek, A., & Weijmar Schultz, W. C. M. (2003). In the mood for sex: The value of androgens. *Journal of Sex and Marital Therapy, 29*, 87–102.

Baker, R. R., & Bellis, M. A. (1993). Human sperm competition: Ejaculate manipulation by females and a function for the female orgasm. *Animal Behaviour, 46*, 887–909.

Baker, R. R., & Bellis, M. A. (1995). *Human sperm competition: Copulation, masturbation and infidelity.* London: Chapman and Hall.

Bancroft, J., Sanders, D., Davidson, D., & Warner, P. (1983). Mood, sexuality, hormones, and the menstrual cycle. III. Sexuality and the role of androgens. *Psychosomatic Medicine, 45*, 509–516.

Barash, D. (1977). *Sociobiology and behavior.* New York, NY: Elsevier North-Holland, Inc.

Barash, D. (2005). Let a thousand orgasms bloom! *Evolutionary Psychology, 3*, 347–354.

Barash, D. P., & Lipton, J. E. (2009). *How women got their curves and other just-so stories: Evolutionary enigmas.* New York, NY: Columbia University Press.

Beach, F. A. (1974). Human sexuality and evolution. In W. Montagna & W. A. Sadler (Eds.), *Reproductive behavior* (pp. 333–365). New York, NY: Plenum.

Bellis, M. A., & Baker, R. R. (1990). Do females promote sperm competition? Data for humans. *Animal Behaviour, 40*, 997–999.

Bentler, P. M., & Peeler, W. H. (1979). Models of female orgasm. *Archives of Sexual Behavior, 8*, 405–423.

Beyer, C., Anguiano, G., & Mena, F. (1961). Oxytocin release by stimulation of the cingulate gyrus. *American Journal of Physiology, 200*, 625–627.

Blaicher, W., Gruber, D., Biegelmayer, C., Blaicher, A. M., Knogler, W., & Huber, J. C. (1999). The role of oxytocin in relation to female sexual arousal. *Gynecologic and Obstetric Investigation, 47*, 125–126.

Blecher, S. R., & Erickson, R. P. (2007). Genetics of sexual development: A new paradigm. *American Journal of Medical Genetics Part A, 143A*, 3054–3068.

Bogaert, A. F., & Fisher, W. A. (1995). Predictors of university men's number of sexual partners. *Journal of Sex Research, 32*, 119–130.

Brewer, G., & Hendrie, C. (2011). Evidence to suggest that copulatory vocalizations in women are not a reflexive consequence of orgasm. *Archives of Sexual Behavior, 40*, 559–564.

Brindley, G. S., & Gillian, P. (1982). Men and women who do not have orgasms. *British Journal of Psychiatry, 140*, 351–356.

Brody, S., & Weiss, P. (2010). Vaginal orgasm is associated with vaginal (not clitoral) sex education, focusing mental attention on vaginal sensations, intercourse duration, and a preference for a longer penis. *The Journal of Sexual Medicine, 7*, 2774–2781.

Buss, D. M. (1988). From vigilance to violence: Tactics of mate retention in American undergraduates. *Ethology and Sociobiology, 9*, 291–317.

Buss, D. M. (1994). *The evolution of desire: Strategies of human mating.* New York: Basic Books.

Buss, D. M., Haselton, M. G., Shackelford, T. K., Bleske, A. L., & Wakefield, J. C. (1998). Adaptations, exaptations, and spandrels. *American Psychologist, 53*, 533–548.

Buss, D. M., & Shackelford, T. K. (1997). Susceptibility to Infidelity in the first year of marriage. *Journal of Research in Personality, 31*, 193–221.

Buss, D. M., Shackelford, T. K., & McKibbin, W. F. (2008). The mate retention inventory-short form (MRI-SF). *Personality and Individual Differences, 44*, 322–334.

Campbell, A. (2008). Attachment, aggression and affiliation: The role of oxytocin in female social behavior. *Biological Psychology, 77*, 1–10.

Campbell, A. (2010). Oxytocin and human social behavior. *Personality and Social Psychology Review, 14*, 281–295.

Carmichael, M. S., Humbert, R., Dixen, J., Palmisano, G., Greenleaf, W., & Davidson, J. M. (1987). Plasma oxytocin increases in the human sexual response. *Journal of Clinical Endocrinology and Metabolism, 64*, 27–31.

Carmichael, M. S., Warburton, V. L., Dixen, J., & Davidson, J. M. (1994). Relationships among cardiovascular, muscular, and oxytocin responses during human sexual activity. *Archives of Sexual Behavior, 23*, 59–79.

Carter, C. S., DeVries, A. C., Taymans, S. E., Roberts, R. L., Williams, J. R., & Getz, L. L. (1997). Peptides, steroids, and pair bonding. *Annals of the New York Academy of Sciences, 807*, 260–272.

Carter, C. S., Williams, J. R., Witt, D. M., & Insel, T. R. (1992). Oxytocin and social bonding. *Annals of the New York Academy of Sciences, 652*, 204–211.

Clark, R., & Hatfield, E. (1989). Gender differences in receptivity to sexual offers. *Journal of Psychology and Human Sexuality, 2*, 39–55.

Cohen, D. L., & Belsky, J. (2008). Avoidant romantic attachment and female orgasm: Testing an emotion-regulation hypothesis. *Attachment and Human Development, 10*, 1–10.

Costa, R. M., & Brody, S. (2007). Women's relationship quality is associated with specifically penile-vaginal intercourse orgasm and frequency. *Journal of Sex and Marital Therapy, 33*, 319–327.

Costa, R. M., Miller, G. F., & Brody, S. (2012). Women who prefer longer penises are more likely to have vaginal orgasms (but not clitoral orgasms): Implications for an evolutionary theory of vaginal orgasm. *The Journal of Sexual Medicine, 9*(12), 3079–3088.

Crespi, B. J., & Vanderkist, B. A. (1997). Fluctuating asymmetry in vestigial and functional traits of a haplodiploid insect. *Heredity, 79*, 624–630.

Curley, J. P., & Keverne, E. B. (2005). Genes, brains and mammalian social bonds. *Trends in Ecology and Evolution, 20*, 561–567.

Dabbs, J. M., Jr., & Mohammed, S. (1992). Male and female salivary testosterone concentrations before and after sexual activity. *Physiology and Behavior, 52*, 195–197.

Daly, M., & Wilson, M. (1983). *Sex, evolution and behavior* (2nd ed.). Boston: PWS.

Darling, C. A., & Davidson, J. K. (1986). Enhancing relationships: Understanding the feminine mystique of pretending orgasm. *Journal of Sex and Marital Therapy, 12*, 182–196.

Darling, C. A., Davidson, J. K., & Cox, R. P. (1991). Female sexual response and the timing of partner orgasm. *Journal of Sex and Marital Therapy, 17*, 3–21.

Davenport, W. H. (1977). Sex in cross-cultural perspective. In F. A. Beach (Ed.), *Human sexuality* (pp. 115–163). Baltimore: The John Hopkins University Press.

Davidson, J. K., & Darling, C. A. (1988). The sexually experienced woman: Multiple sex partners and sexual satisfaction. *Journal of Sex Research, 24*, 141–154.

Davidson, J. K., & Darling, C. A. (1989). Self-perceived differences in the female orgasmic response. *Family Practice Research Journal, 8*, 75–84.

Davis, M. (1992). The role of the amygdala in fear and anxiety. *Annual Review of Neuroscience, 15*, 353–375.

Dawood, K., Kirk, K. M., Bailey, J. M., Andrews, P. W., & Martin, N. G. (2005). Genetic and environmental influences on the frequency of orgasm in women. *Twin Research and Human Genetics, 8*, 27–33.

Domes, G., Heinrichs, M., Michel, A., Berger, C., & Herpertz, S. C. (2007). Oxytocin improves "mind-reading" in humans. *Biological Psychiatry, 61*, 731–733.

Dunn, K. M., Cherkas, L. F., & Spector, T. D. (2005). Genetic influences on variation in female orgasmic function: A twin study. *Biology Letters, 1*, 260–263.

Eibl-Eibesfeldt, I. (1975). *Ethology: The biology of behavior.* New York, NY: Holt, Rinehart, and Winston.

Eibl-Eibesfeldt, I. (1989). *Human ethology.* New York: Aldine de Gruyter.

Eisenbach, M. (1995). Sperm changes enabling fertilization in mammals. *Current Opinion in Endocrinology, Diabetes, and Obesity, 2*, 468–475.

Eschler, L. (2004). The physiology of the female orgasm as a proximate mechanism. *Sexualities, Evolution and Gender, 6*, 171–194.

Exton, M. S., Bindert, A., Krüger, T., Scheller, F., Hartmann, U., & Schedlowski, M. (1999). Cardiovascular and endocrine alterations after masturbation-induced orgasm in women. *Psychosomatic Medicine, 61*, 280–289.

Feinberg, D. R., Jones, B. C., Law Smith, M. J., Moore, F. R., DeBruine, L. M., Cornwell, R. E., et al. (2006). Menstrual cycle, trait estrogen level, and masculinity preferences in the human voice. *Hormones and Behavior, 49*, 215–222.

Fink, B., & Penton-Voak, I. (2002). Evolutionary psychology of facial attractiveness. *Current Directions in Psychological Science, 11*, 154–158.

Fisher, R. A. (1930). *The genetical theory of natural selection.* Oxford: Clarendon.

Fisher, S. (1973). *The female orgasm: Psychology, physiology, fantasy.* New York: Basic Books.

Fisher, H. E., Aron, A., & Brown, L. L. (2006). Romantic love: A mammalian brain system for mate choice. *Philosophical Transactions of the Royal Society, B: Biological Sciences, 361,* 2173–2186.

Fliers, E., Swaab, D. F. W., Pool, C., & Verwer, R. W. H. (1985). The vasopressin and oxytocin neurons in the human supraoptic and paraventricular nucleus; changes with aging and in senile dementia. *Brain Research, 342,* 45–53.

Fox, R. (1993). Male masturbation and female orgasm. *Society, 30,* 21–25.

Fox, C. A., & Fox, B. (1971). A comparative study of coital physiology, with special reference to the sexual climax. *Journal of Reproduction and Fertility, 24,* 319–336.

Fox, C. A., Wolff, H. S., & Baker, J. A. (1970). Measurement of intra-vaginal and intra-uterine pressures during human coitus by radio-telemetry. *Journal of Reproduction and Fertility, 22,* 243–251.

Frost, P. (1994). Preference for darker faces in photographs at different phases of the menstrual cycle: Preliminary assessment of evidence for a hormonal relationship. *Perceptual and Motor Skills, 79,* 507–514.

Gangestad, S. W., & Simpson, J. A. (2000). The evolution of human mating: Trade-offs and strategic pluralism. *Behavioural and Brain Sciences, 23,* 573–644.

Gangestad, S. W., Simpson, J. A., Cousins, A. J., Garver-Apgar, C. E., & Christensen, P. N. (2004). Women's preferences for male behavioral displays change across the menstrual cycle. *Psychological Science, 15,* 203–207.

Gangestad, S. W., & Thornhill, R. (1997). The evolutionary psychology of extrapair sex: The role of fluctuating asymmetry. *Evolution and Human Behavior, 18,* 69–88.

Gangestad, S. W., & Thornhill, R. (2008). Human oestrus. *Proceedings of the Royal Society B-Biological Sciences, 275,* 991–1000.

Gangestad, S. W., Thornhill, R., & Garver, C. E. (2002). Changes in women's sexual interests and their partners' mate-retention tactics across the menstrual cycle: Evidence for shifting conflicts of interest. *Proceedings of the Royal Society B-Biological Sciences, 269,* 975–982.

Gangestad, S. W., Thornhill, R., & Garver-Apgar, C. E. (2005). Women's sexual interests across the ovulatory cycle depend on primary partner developmental instability. *Proceedings of the Royal Society B-Biological Sciences, 272,* 2023–2027.

Gangestad, S. W., Thornhill, R., & Yeo, R. A. (1994). Facial attractiveness, developmental stability, and fluctuating asymmetry. *Ethology and Sociobiology, 15,* 73–85.

Garver-Apgar, C. E., Gangestad, S. W., Thornhill, R., Miller, R. D., & Olp, J. (2006). Major histocompatibility complex alleles, sexual responsivity, and unfaithfulness in romantic couples. *Psychological Science, 17,* 830–835.

Gebhard, P. H. (1966). Factors in marital orgasm. *Journal of Social Issues, 22,* 88–95.

Georgiadis, J. R., Kortekaas, R., Kuipers, R., Nieuwenburg, A., Pruim, J., Reinders, A. A. T. S., et al. (2006). Regional cerebral blood flow changes associated with clitorally induced orgasm in healthy women. *European Journal of Neuroscience, 24,* 3305–3316.

Georgiadis, J. R., Reinders, A. A. T. S., Paans, A. M. J., Renken, R., & Kortekaas, R. (2009). Men versus women on sexual brain function: Prominent differences during tactile genital stimulation, but not during orgasm. *Human Brain Mapping, 30,* 3089–3101.

Gould, S. J. (1987). Freudian slip. *Natural History, 87,* 14–21.

Gould, S. J., & Lewontin, R. C. (1979). The spandrels of San Marco and the Panglossian paradigm: A critique of the adaptationist programme. *Proceedings of the Royal Society of London B, 205,* 581–598.

Gould, S. J., & Vrba, E. S. (1982). Exaptation: A missing term in the science of form. *Paleobiology, 8,* 4–15.

Grafenberg, E. (1950). The role of the urethra in female orgasm. *The International Journal of Sexology, 3,* 145–148.

Grammer, K., Fink, B., Moller, A. P., & Thornhill, R. (2003). Darwinian aesthetics: Sexual selection and the biology of beauty. *Biological Reviews, 78,* 385–407.

Grammer, K., & Thornhill, R. (1994). Human (*Homo sapiens*) facial attractiveness and sexual selection: The role of symmetry and averageness. *Journal of Comparative Psychology, 108,* 233–242.

Grewen, K. M., Girdler, S. S., Amico, J., & Light, K. C. (2005). Effects of partner support on resting oxytocin, cortisol, norepinephrine, and blood pressure before and after warm partner contact. *Psychosomatic Medicine, 67,* 531–538.

Hamburg, B. A. (1978). The biosocial basis of sex differences. In W. S. L. & E. R. McCrown (Eds.), *Human evolution: Biosocial perspectives* (pp. 155–213). Menlo Park, CA: Benjamin/Cummings.

Hamilton, W. J., III, & Arrowood, P. C. (1978). Copulatory vocalizations of chacma baboons (*Papio ursinus*), gibbons (*Hylobates hoolock*), and humans. *Science, 200,* 1405–1409.

Harcourt, A. H., Harvey, P. H., Larson, S. G., & Short, R. V. (1981). Testis weight, body weight and breeding system in primates. *Nature, 293,* 55–57.

Harris, J. M., Cherkas, L. F., Kato, B. S., Heiman, J. R., & Spector, T. D. (2008). Normal variations in personality are associated with coital orgasmic infrequency in heterosexual women: A population-based study. *The Journal of Sexual Medicine, 5,* 1177–1183.

Hauser, M. D. (1990). Do chimpanzee copulatory calls incite male-male competition? *Animal Behavior, 39,* 596–597.

Havlíček, J., & Roberts, S. C. (2009). MHC-correlated mate choice in humans: A review. *Psychoneuroendocrinology, 34,* 497–512.

Heinrichs, M., & Domes, G. (2008). Neuropeptides and social behaviour: Effects of oxytocin and vasopressin in humans. In D. N. Inga & L. Rainer (Eds.), *Progress in brain research* (Vol. 170, pp. 337–350). New York: Elsevier.

Heinrichs, M., von Dawans, B., & Domes, G. (2009). Oxytocin, vasopressin, and human social behavior. *Frontiers in Neuroendocrinology, 30*, 548–557.

Herberich, E., Hothorn, T., Nettle, D., & Pollet, T. V. (2010). A re-evaluation of the statistical model in Pollet and Nettle 2009. *Evolution and Human Behavior, 31*, 150–151.

Hite, S. (1976). *The Hite Report: A nationwide survey of female sexuality*. London: Bloomsbury.

Hosken, D. J. (2008). Clitoral variation says nothing about female orgasm. *Evolution and Development, 10*, 393–395.

Hrdy, S. B. (1996). The evolution of female orgasms: Logic please but no atavism. *Animal Behavior, 52*, 851–852.

Hrdy, S. B. (1997). Raising Darwin's consciousness: Female sexuality and the prehominid origins of patriarchy. *Human Nature, 8*, 1–49.

Jezova, D., Skultetyova, I., Tokarev, D. I., Bakos, P., & Vigas, M. (1995). Vasopressin and oxytocin in stress. *Annals of the New York Academy of Sciences, 771*, 192–203.

Johnston, V. S., Hagel, R., Franklin, M., Fink, B., & Grammer, K. (2001). Male facial attractiveness: Evidence for hormone-mediated adaptive design. *Evolution and Human Behavior, 21*, 251–267.

Jones, B. C., Little, A. C., Boothroyd, L., DeBruine, L. M., Feinberg, D. R., Smith, M. J. L., et al. (2005). Commitment to relationships and preferences for femininity and apparent health in faces are strongest on days of the menstrual cycle when progesterone level is high. *Hormones and Behavior, 48*, 283–290.

Judson, O. P. (2005). Anticlimax. *Nature, 436*, 916–917.

Kaighobadi, F., Shackelford, T. K., & Weekes-Shackelford, V. A. (2012). Do women pretend orgasm to retain a mate? *Archives of Sexual Behavior, 41*, 1121–1125.

Keller, J. F., Elliott, S. S., & Gunberg, E. (1982). Premarital sexual intercourse among single college students: A discriminant analysis. *Sex Roles, 8*, 21–32.

King, R., Belsky, J., Mah, K., & Binik, Y. (2011). Are there different types of female orgasm? *Archives of Sexual Behavior, 40*, 865–875.

Kinsey, A. C., Pomeroy, W. B., Martin, C. E., & Gebhard, P. H. (1953). *Sexual behavior in the human female*. Philadelphia: W. B. Saunders.

Kirsch, P., Esslinger, C., Chen, Q., Mier, D., Lis, S., Siddhanti, S., et al. (2005). Oxytocin modulates neural circuitry for social cognition and fear in humans. *The Journal of Neuroscience, 25*, 11489–11493.

Koehler, N., Rhodes, G., & Simmons, L. W. (2002). Are human female preferences for symmetrical male faces enhanced when conception is likely? *Animal Behaviour, 64*, 233–238.

Koehler, N., Rhodes, G., Simmons, L. W., & Zebrowitz, L. A. (2006). Do cyclic changes in women's face preferences target cues to long-term health? *Social Cognition, 24*, 641–656.

Komisaruk, B. R., Beyer-Flores, C., & Whipple, B. (2006). *The science of orgasm*. Baltimore, MD: Johns Hopkins University Press.

Komisaruk, B. R., Bianca, R., Sansone, G., Gómez, L. E., Cueva-Rolón, R., Beyer, C., et al. (1996). Brain-mediated responses to vaginocervical stimulation in spinal cord-transected rats: Role of the vagus nerves. *Brain Research, 708*, 128–134.

Komisaruk, B. R., & Sansone, G. (2003). Neural pathways mediating vaginal function: The vagus nerves and spinal cord oxytocin. *Scandinavian Journal of Psychology, 44*, 241–250.

Komisaruk, B. R., & Whipple, B. (2005). Functional MRI of the brain during orgasm in women. *Annual Review of Sex Research, 16*, 62–86.

Komisaruk, B. R., Whipple, B., Crawford, A., Liu, W. C., Kalnin, A., & Mosier, K. (2004). Brain activation during vaginocervical self-stimulation and orgasm in women with complete spinal cord injury: fMRI evidence of mediation by the vagus nerves. *Brain Research, 1024*, 77–88.

Laumann, E. O., Gagnon, J. H., Michael, R. T., & Michaels, S. (1994). *The social organization of sexuality: Sexual practices in the United States*. Chicago: University of Chicago Press.

LaVelle, M. (1995). Natural selection and developmental sexual variation in the human pelvis. *American Journal of Physical Anthropology, 98*, 59–72.

Lever, J., Frederick, D. A., & Peplau, L. A. (2006). Does size matter? Men's and women's views on penis size across the lifespan. *Psychology of Men and Masculinity, 7*, 129–143.

Levin, R. J. (2002). The physiology of sexual arousal in the human female: A recreational and procreational synthesis. *Archives of Sexual Behavior, 31*, 405–411.

Little, A. C., Apicella, C. L., & Marlowe, F. W. (2007). Preferences for symmetry in human faces in two cultures: Data from the UK and the Hadza, an isolated group of hunter-gatherers. *Proceedings of the Royal Society B-Biological Sciences, 274*, 3113–3117.

Little, A. C., & Jones, B. C. (2011). Variation in facial masculinity and symmetry preferences across the menstrual cycle is moderated by relationship context. *Psychoneuroendocrinology, 37*, 999–1008.

Little, A. C., Jones, B. C., & Burriss, R. P. (2007). Preferences for masculinity in male bodies change across the menstrual cycle. *Hormones and Behavior, 51*, 633–639.

Little, A. C., Jones, B. C., Burt, D. M., & Perrett, D. I. (2007). Preferences for symmetry in faces change across the menstrual cycle. *Biological Psychology, 76*, 209–216.

Little, A. C., Jones, B. C., & DeBruine, L. M. (2008). Preferences for variation in masculinity in real male faces change across the menstrual cycle: Women prefer more masculine faces when they are more fertile. *Personality and Individual Differences, 45,* 478–482.

Little, A. C., Jones, B. C., Penton-Voak, I. S., Burt, D. M., & Perrett, D. I. (2002). Partnership status and the temporal context of relationships influence human female preferences for sexual dimorphism in male face shape. *Proceedings of the Royal Society B-Biological Sciences, 269,* 1095–1100.

Lloyd, E. A. (2005). *The case of female orgasm: Bias in the science of evolution.* Cambridge, MA: Harvard University Press.

Lynch, V. J. (2008). Clitoral and penile size variability are not significantly different: Lack of evidence for the byproduct theory of the female orgasm. *Evolution and Development, 10,* 396–397.

Mah, K., & Binik, Y. M. (2001). The nature of human orgasm: A critical review of major trends. *Clinical Psychology Review, 21,* 823–856.

Mah, K., & Binik, Y. M. (2002). Do all orgasms feel alike? Evaluating a two-dimensional model of the orgasm experience across gender and sexual context. *Journal of Sex Research, 39,* 104–113.

Marshall, D. S. (1971). Sexual behavior on Mangaia. In D. S. Marshall & R. C. Suggs (Eds.), *Human sexual behavior* (pp. 103–162). New York, NY: Basic Books.

Masters, W. H., & Johnson, V. E. (1966). *Human sexual response.* Boston: Little, Brown.

Matteo, S., & Rissman, E. F. (1984). Increased sexual activity during the midcycle portion of the human menstrual cycle. *Hormones and Behavior, 18,* 249–255.

McCarthy, M. M., & Altemus, M. (1997). Central nervous system actions of oxytocin and modulation of behavior in humans. *Molecular Medicine Today, 3,* 269–275.

McKibbin, W. F., Bates, V. M., Shackelford, T. K., Hafen, C. A., & LaMunyon, C. W. (2010). Risk of sperm competition moderates the relationship between men's satisfaction with their partner and men's interest in their partner's copulatory orgasm. *Personality and Individual Differences, 49,* 961–966.

Meston, C. M., Levin, R. J., Sipski, M. L., Hull, E. M., & Heiman, J. R. (2004). Women's orgasm. *Annual Review of Sex Research, 15,* 173–257.

Møller, A. P. (1997). Developmental stability and fitness: A review. *American Naturalist, 149,* 916–942.

Møller, A. P., & Pomiankowski, A. (1993). Fluctuating asymmetry and sexual selection. *Genetica, 89,* 267–279.

Morris, D. (1967). *The naked ape.* New York, NY: Dell Publishing Co.

Morris, D. (1985). *Bodywatching: A field guide to the human species.* New York, NY: Crown Books.

Muehlenhard, C. L., & Shippee, S. K. (2010). Men's and women's reports of pretending orgasm. *Journal of Sex Research, 47,* 552–567.

Murphy, M. E., Seckl, J. R., Burton, S., Checkley, S. A., & Lightman, S. L. (1987). Changes in oxytocin and vasopressin secretion during sexual activity in men. *Journal of Clinical Endocrinology and Metabolism, 65,* 738–741.

Nadler, R. D. (1976). Sexual behavior of captive lowland gorillas. *Archives of Sexual Behavior, 5,* 487–502.

O'Connell, J. F., Hawkes, K., & Blurton Jones, N. G. (1999). Grandmothering and the evolution of *Homo erectus. Journal of Human Evolution, 36,* 461–485.

Oliver, M. B., & Hyde, J. S. (1993). Gender differences in sexuality: A meta-analysis. *Psychological Bulletin, 114,* 29–51.

Ostrom, J. H. (1974). *Archaeopteryx* and the origin of flight. *The Quarterly Review of Biology, 49,* 27–47.

Ostrom, J. H. (1979). Bird flight: How did it begin? *American Scientist, 67,* 46–56.

Parsons, P. A. (1990). Fluctuating asymmetry: An epigenetic measure of stress. *Biological Review, 65,* 131–145.

Parsons, P. A. (1992). Fluctuating asymmetry: A biological monitor of environmental and genomic stress. *Heredity, 68,* 361–364.

Penton-Voak, I. S., & Perrett, D. I. (2000). Female preference for male faces changes cyclically—Further evidence. *Evolution and Human Behavior, 21,* 39–48.

Penton-Voak, I. S., Perrett, D. I., Castles, D. L., Kobayashi, T., Burt, D. M., Murray, L. K., et al. (1999). Menstrual cycle alters face preference. *Nature, 399,* 741–742.

Peters, M., Rhodes, G., & Simmons, L. W. (2008). Does attractiveness in men provide clues to semen quality? *Journal of Evolutionary Biology, 21,* 572–579.

Pillsworth, E. G., Haselton, M. G., & Buss, D. M. (2004). Ovulatory shifts in female sexual desire. *Journal of Sex Research, 41,* 55–65.

Pollet, T. V., & Nettle, D. (2009). Partner wealth predicts self-reported orgasm frequency in a sample of Chinese women. *Evolution and Human Behavior, 30,* 146–151.

Pollet, T. V., & Nettle, D. (2010). Correction to Pollet and Nettle (2009): "Partner wealth predicts self-reported orgasm frequency in a sample of Chinese women". *Evolution and Human Behavior, 31,* 149.

Potts, M., & Short, R. (1999). *Ever since Adam and Eve.* Cambridge, MA: Cambridge University Press.

Powell, E. W., & Rorie, D. K. (1967). Septal projections to nuclei functioning in oxytocin release. *American Journal of Anatomy, 120,* 605–610.

Puppo, V. (2011). Embryology and anatomy of the vulva: The female orgasm and women's sexual health. *European Journal of Obstetrics and Gynecology and Reproductive Biology, 154,* 3–8.

Puts, D. A. (2005). Mating context and menstrual phase affect women's preferences for male voice pitch. *Evolution and Human Behavior, 26,* 388–397.

Puts, D. A. (2006a). And hast thou slain the Jabberwock? Response to Wallen. *Archives of Sexual Behavior, 35,* 637–639.

Puts, D. A. (2006b). Review of "The Case of Female Orgasm: Bias in the Science of Evolution," by Elizabeth Lloyd. *Archives of Sexual Behavior, 35,* 103–108.

Puts, D. A. (2007). Of bugs and boojums: Female orgasm as a facultative adaptation. *Archives of Sexual Behavior, 36*, 337–339.

Puts, D. A., & Dawood, K. (2006). The evolution of female orgasm: Adaptation or byproduct? *Twin Research and Human Genetics, 9*, 467–472.

Puts, D. A., Dawood, K., & Welling, L. L. M. (2012). Why women have orgasms: An evolutionary analysis. *Archives of Sexual Behavior, 41*, 1127–1143.

Puts, D. A., Gaulin, S. J. C., & Verdolini, K. (2006). Dominance and the evolution of sexual dimorphism in human voice pitch. *Evolution and Human Behavior, 27*, 283–296.

Puts, D. A., Welling, L. L. M., Burriss, R. P., & Dawood, K. (2012). Men's masculinity and attractiveness predict their female partners' reported orgasm frequency and timing. *Evolution and Human Behavior, 33*, 1–9.

Rayner, J. (2001). On the origin and evolution of flapping flight aerodynamics in birds. In J. Gauthier & L. F. Gall (Eds.), *New perspectives on the origin and early evolution of birds: Proceedings of the International Symposium in Honor of John H. Ostrom* (pp. 363–381). New Haven, CT: Peabody Museum of Natural History.

Reyes, A., Parra, A., Chavarria, M. E., Goicoechea, B., & Rosado, A. (1979). Effect of prolactin on the calcium binding and/or transport of ejaculated and epididymal human spermatozoa. *Fertility and Sterility, 31*, 669–672.

Rhodes, G. (2006). The evolutionary psychology of facial beauty. *Annual Review of Psychology, 57*, 199–226.

Rhodes, G., Chan, J., Zebrowitz, L. A., & Simmons, L. W. (2003). Does sexual dimorphism in human faces signal health? *Proceedings of the Royal Society B-Biological Sciences, 270*, S93–S95.

Rhodes, G., Simmons, L. W., & Peters, M. (2005). Attractiveness and sexual behavior: Does attractiveness enhance mating success? *Evolution and Human Behavior, 26*, 186–201.

Rice, W. R., & Chippindale, A. K. (2001). Intersexual ontogenetic conflict. *Journal of Evolutionary Biology, 14*, 685–693.

Richters, J., de Visser, R., Rissel, C., & Smith, A. (2006). Sexual practices at last heterosexual encounter and occurrence of orgasm in a national survey. *Journal of Sex Research, 43*, 217–226.

Rowland, D., McMahon, C. G., Abdo, C., Chen, J. Y., Jannini, E., Waldinger, M. D., et al. (2010). Disorders of orgasm and ejaculation in men. *The Journal of Sexual Medicine, 7*, 1668–1686.

Sanchez, R., Parkin, J. C., Chen, J. Y., & Gray, P. B. (2009). Oxytocin, vasopressin, and human social behavior. In P. T. Ellison & P. B. Gray (Eds.), *Endocrinology of social relationships* (pp. 319–339). Cambridge, MA: Harvard University Press.

Schaller, G. B. (1963). *The mountain gorilla: Ecology and behavior*. Chicago: University of Chicago Press.

Scheib, J. E., Gangestad, S. W., & Thornhill, R. (1999). Facial attractiveness, symmetry and cues to good genes. *Proceedings of the Royal Society B-Biological Sciences, 266*, 1913–1917.

Schmitt, D. P. (2005). Sociosexuality from Argentina to Zimbabwe: A 48-nation study of sex, culture, and strategies of human mating. *Behavioral and Brain Sciences, 28*, 247–275.

Schober, J. M., Meyer-Bahlburg, H. F. L., & Ransley, P. G. (2004). Self-assessment of genital anatomy, sexual sensitivity and function in women: Implications for genitoplasty. *BJU International, 94*, 589–594.

Setekleiv, J. (1964). Uterine motility of the estrogenized rabbit. *Acta Physiologica Scandinavica, 62*, 79–93.

Shackelford, T. K., Goetz, A. T., Liddle, J. R., & Bush, L. S. (2012). Sexual conflict in humans. In T. K. Shackelford & A. T. Goetz (Eds.), *Oxford handbook of sexual conflict in humans* (pp. 3–14). New York, NY: Oxford University Press.

Shackelford, T. K., & Larsen, R. J. (1999). Facial attractiveness and physical health. *Evolution and Human Behavior, 21*, 71–76.

Shackelford, T. K., Weekes-Shackelford, V. A., LeBlanc, G. J., Bleske, A. L., Euler, H. A., & Hoier, S. (2000). Female coital orgasm and male attractiveness. *Human Nature, 11*, 299–306.

Sherfey, M. J. (1973). *The nature and evolution of female sexuality*. New York, NY: Vintage Books.

Singh, D., Meyer, W., Zambarano, R. J., & Hurlbert, D. F. (1998). Frequency and timing of coital orgasm in women desirous of becoming pregnant. *Archives of Sexual Behavior, 27*, 15–29.

Skuse, D. H., & Gallagher, L. (2009). Dopaminergic-neuropeptide interactions in the social brain. *Trends in Cognitive Sciences, 13*, 27–35.

Smith, R. L. (1984). Human sperm competition. In R. L. Smith (Ed.), *Sperm competition and the evolution of animal mating systems* (pp. 601–660). London: Academic.

Soler, C., Núñez, M., Gutiérrez, R., Núñez, J., Medina, P., Sancho, M., et al. (2003). Facial attractiveness in men provides clues to semen quality. *Evolution and Human Behavior, 24*, 199–207.

Stockley, P., Gage, M. J. G., Parker, G. A., & Moller, A. P. (1996). Female reproductive biology and the coevolution of ejaculate characteristics in fish. *Proceedings of the Royal Society B: Biological Sciences, 263*, 451–458.

Symons, D. (1979). *The evolution of human sexuality*. Oxford: Oxford University Press.

Symons, D. (1992). On the use and misuse of Darwinism in the study of human behavior. In J. Barkow, L. Cosmides, & J. Tooby (Eds.), *The adapted mind: Evolutionary psychology and the generation of culture* (pp. 137–159). New York, NY: Oxford University Press.

Tavris, C., & Sadd, S. (1977). *The Redbook report on female sexuality*. New York: Delacorte Press.

Taylor, S. E., Gonzaga, G. C., Klein, L. C., Hu, P., Greendale, G. A., & Seeman, T. E. (2006). Relation of oxytocin to psychological stress responses and hypothalamic-pituitary-adrenocortical axis activity in older women. *Psychosomatic Medicine, 68*, 238–245.

Thornhill, R., & Gangestad, S. W. (1994). Human fluctuating asymmetry and sexual behaviour. *Psychological Science, 5*, 297–302.

Thornhill, R., & Gangestad, S. W. (1996). Human female copulatory orgasm—A human adaptation or phylogenetic holdover. *Animal Behaviour, 52*, 853–855.

Thornhill, R., & Gangestad, S. W. (1999). Facial attractiveness. *Trends in Cognitive Science, 3*, 452–460.

Thornhill, R., Gangestad, S. W., & Comer, R. (1995). Human female orgasm and mate fluctuating asymmetry. *Animal Behaviour, 50*, 1601–1615.

Tooby, J., & Cosmides, L. (1992). The psychological foundations of culture. In J. H. Barkow, L. Cosmides, & J. Tooby (Eds.), *The adapted mind* (pp. 19–136). New York, NY: Oxford University Press.

Trivers, R. L. (1972). Parental investment and sexual selection. In B. Campbell (Ed.), *Sexual selection and the descent of man, 1871–1971* (pp. 136–179). Chicago: Aldine.

Turner, R. A., Altemus, M., Enos, T., Cooper, B., & McGuinness, T. (1999). Preliminary research on plasma oxytocin in normal cycling women: Investigating emotion and interpersonal distress. *Psychiatry: Interpersonal and Biological Processes, 62*, 97–113.

Udry, J. R., & Morris, N. (1968). Distribution of coitus in the menstrual cycle. *Nature, 200*, 593–596.

van Anders, S. M., Brotto, L., Farrell, J., & Yule, M. (2009). Associations between physiological and subjective sexual response, sexual desire, and salivary steroid hormones in healthy premenopausal women. *Journal of Sexual Medicine, 6*, 739–751.

van Anders, S. M., & Dunn, E. J. (2009). Are gonadal steroids linked with orgasm perceptions and sexual assertiveness in women and men? *Hormones and Behavior, 56*, 206–213.

van Anders, S. M., Hamilton, L. D., Schmidt, N., & Watson, N. V. (2007). Associations between testosterone secretion and sexual activity in women. *Hormones and Behavior, 51*, 477–482.

Wallen, K. (2006). Commentary on Puts' (2006) review of *The case of the female orgasm: Bias in the science of evolution. Archives of Sexual Behavior, 35*, 633–636.

Wallen, K. (2007). Be careful that your snark is not a boojum. *Archives of Sexual Behavior, 36*, 335–336.

Wallen, K., & Lloyd, E. A. (2008). Clitoral variability compared with penile variability supports nonadaptation of female orgasm. *Evolution and Development, 10*, 1–2.

Weiss, P., & Brody, S. (2009). Women's partnered orgasm consistency is associated with greater duration of penile–vaginal intercourse but not of foreplay. *The Journal of Sexual Medicine, 6*, 135–141.

Welling, L. L. M., Burriss, R. P., & Puts, D. A. (2011). Mate retention behavior modulates men's preferences for self-resemblance in infant faces. *Evolution and Human Behavior, 32*, 118–126.

Welling, L. L. M., Jones, B. C., DeBruine, L. M., Conway, C. A., Law Smith, M. J., Little, A. C., et al. (2007). Raised salivary testosterone in women is associated with increased attraction to masculine faces. *Hormones and Behavior, 52*, 156–161.

Welling, L. L. M., Puts, D. A., Roberts, S. C., Little, A. C., & Burriss, R. P. (2012). Hormonal contraceptive use and mate retention behavior in women and their male partners. *Hormones and Behavior, 61*, 114–120.

Wiederman, M. W. (1997). Pretending orgasm during sexual intercourse: Correlates in a sample of young adult women. *Journal of Sex and Marital Therapy, 23*, 131–139.

Wildt, L., Kissler, S., Licht, P., & Becker, W. (1998). Sperm transport in the human female genital tract and its modulation by oxytocin as assessed by hysterosalpingoscintigraphy, hysterotonography, electrohysterography and Doppler sonography. *Human Reproduction Update, 4*, 655–666.

Williams, G. C. (1966). *Adaptation and natural selection: A critique of some current evolutionary thought.* Princeton, NJ: Princeton University Press.

Young, L. J., & Wang, Z. (2004). The neurobiology of pair bonding. *Nature Neuroscience, 7*, 1048–1054.

Zak, P. J., Stanton, A. A., & Ahmadi, S. (2007). Oxytocin increases generosity in humans. *PLoS One, 2*, e1128.

Zeki, S. (2007). The neurobiology of love. *FEBS Letters, 581*(14), 2575–2579.

Zervomanolakis, I., Ott, H. W., Hadziomerovic, D., Mattle, V., Seeber, B. E., Virgolini, I., et al. (2007). Physiology of upward transport in the human female genital tract. *Annals of the New York Academy of Sciences, 1101*, 1–20.

Zervomanolakis, I., Ott, H. W., Müller, J., Seeber, B. E., Friess, S. C., Mattle, V., et al. (2009). Uterine mechanisms of ipsilateral directed spermatozoa transport: Evidence for a contribution of the utero-ovarian countercurrent system. *European Journal of Obstetrics and Gynecology and Reproductive Biology, 144*, S45–S49.

Zietsch, B. P., & Santtila, P. (2011). Genetic analysis of orgasmic function in twins and siblings does not support the by-product theory of female orgasm. *Animal Behaviour, 82*, 1097–1101.

Zumpe, D., & Michael, R. P. (1968). The clutching reaction and orgasm in the female rhesus monkey (*macaca mulatta*). *Journal of Endocrinology, 40*, 117–123.

Lisa L.M. Welling and David A. Puts

Introduction

Cues to ovulation status in nonhuman primates are varied and numerous, including exaggerated sexual swellings (Nunn, 1999), changes in proceptive and receptive behavior (Baum, Everitt, Herbert, & Keverne, 1977), and changes in body odor (Clarke, Barrett, & Henzi, 2009). Anthropoid primates (those comprising apes, Old World monkeys, and New World monkeys) differ from the general mammalian pattern of a precise estrous period (Heistermann et al., 2001; Hrdy & Whitten, 1987). Catarrhines (apes and Old World monkeys), in particular, demonstrate ovarian cycles characterized by long follicular phases and extended periods of mating, resulting in alterations or an end to the usual harmonization between ovulation and sexual activity (Heistermann et al., 2001; Hrdy & Whitten, 1987; Nunn, 1999; van Schaik, Hodges, & Nunn, 2000). Certainly, humans are not the only primate species where the female is sexually receptive throughout her cycle. For example, both chimpanzees (*Pan troglodytes*) and bonobos (*Pan paniscus*) practice nonconceptive sexual behavior (sexual activity that cannot result in conception), but female bonobos are especially known for mating with multiple males throughout the cycle (reviewed in Wrangham, 1993).

Some female primates, such as vervet monkeys (Andelman, 1987) and Hanuman langurs (Heistermann et al., 2001), have apparently evolved the capacity to conceal ovulation from males. This may function to confuse paternity among males, possibly leading to a reduction in infanticide (Heistermann et al., 2001; Hrdy, 1979; Hrdy & Whitten, 1987; van Schaik et al., 2000). Infanticide by males is common among primates when a new male takes over breeding in a single-male group or rises to breeding status in a multi-male group. Although this behavior benefits the infanticidal male by returning nursing females to estrus, it represents a substantial reproductive loss for the females (reviewed in van Schaik et al., 2000), who invest heavily in their offspring. Therefore, an extended period of sexual activity coupled with a polyandrous mating strategy would make assessing paternity difficult (van Schaik et al., 2000, van Schaik, van Noordwijk, & Nunn, 1999), which may affect males' propensity to commit infanticide (Borries, Launhardt, Epplen, Epplen, & Winkler, 1999; Heistermann et al., 2001; Hrdy, 1979; Robbins, 1995; Soltis, Thomsen, Matsubayashi, & Takenaka, 2000; van Schaik et al., 1999). Concealing ovulation not only would thus confuse paternity but could also potentially allow more room for female choice by preventing dominant males from knowing when to monopolize fertile females.

L.L.M. Welling (✉)
Department of Psychology, Oakland University, 212 Pryale Hall, Rochester, MI 48309, USA
e-mail: welling@oakland.edu

V.A. Weekes-Shackelford and T.K. Shackelford (eds.), *Evolutionary Perspectives on Human Sexual Psychology and Behavior*, Evolutionary Psychology, DOI 10.1007/978-1-4939-0314-6_13,
© Springer Science+Business Media New York 2014

Concealed Ovulation in Humans

Several scholars have suggested that human females lack estrus, a sharp increase in sexual interest and activity that typically occurs at or near ovulation, and have also evolved to conceal ovulation from males (Benshoof & Thornhill, 1979; Burley, 1979; Daniels, 1983; Manson, 1986; Marlowe, 2004; Pawłowski, 1999; Sillen-Tullberg & Møller, 1993; Strassmann, 1981; Turke, 1984). Certainly, women are continuously receptive to sexual advances throughout their menstrual cycles, and ovulation is not generally consciously perceived by men or even by the ovulating women themselves (Burley, 1979). Menstruation is the only overt sign of a woman's ovulatory cycle, although there may be other, more subtle cues to a woman's fertility status (discussed later). In fact, scientists did not determine the timing of ovulation until 1930 (Burley, 1979; Campbell, 1966), prior to which some believed a woman could conceive throughout her cycle (Latz, 1939) or were most fertile near or during menstruation (Campbell, 1960). That the timing of peak fertility was unknown by medical professionals and scholars for so long demonstrates how well ovulation is concealed from both men and women. Moreover, while the Hadza, a hunter-gatherer society in Tanzania, know that sex causes conception, most wrongly believe that conception occurs immediately after menstruation ends (Marlowe, 2004). That the timing of conception is unknown in traditional societies similar to those in which humans evolved reinforces the idea that ovulation is not consciously perceived.

Because ovulation appears to be concealed from the women experiencing it, as well as the men around them (Alexander & Noonan, 1979; Burley, 1979; Daniels, 1983; Marlowe, 2004), it may be concealed for more than one purpose. Concealed ovulation may enable women to better deceive their mates (Alexander & Noonan, 1979; Daniels, 1983) and may have evolved as a way of preventing women from avoiding conception through abstinence from intercourse near ovulation (Burley, 1979). If women had

knowledge of ovulation, they would be able to exercise considerable control over their reproductive status, perhaps having fewer children or possibly none at all. Clearly, these practices are nonadaptive as they limit reproductive potential; thus physiological changes that lessened female awareness of ovulation may have been selected because women who were less aware of ovulation would have left more descendants (Burley, 1979). However, it is plausible that human females evolved the capacity to conceal ovulation and human males lost the ability to detect ovulation for several other related reasons. Like scholars have suggested for other primates (van Schaik et al., 1999, 2000), our extended periods of mating would make assessing paternity difficult if mating were polyandrous. Confusing paternity may have the added benefits of improving male behavior toward potential offspring (Sillen-Tullberg & Møller, 1993) and reducing rates of males committing infanticide (Borries et al., 1999; Heistermann et al., 2001; Hrdy, 1979; Robbins, 1995; Soltis et al., 2000; van Schaik et al., 1999), as they may be less likely to deduce nonpaternity. Indeed, men favor children who resemble them (Burch & Gallup, 2000; DeBruine, 2004; Platek et al., 2003, Platek, Burch, Panyavin, Wasserman, & Gallup, 2002; Volk & Quinsey, 2002; Welling, Burriss, & Puts, 2011) and are more likely to abuse stepchildren or adopted children than biological children (Daly & Wilson, 1984, 1985; Wilson & Daly, 1987, 2002), indicating that doubts surrounding paternity may increase risks to an infant and that these risks may be abated if the timing of peak fertility is unknown.

In line with the above reasoning, Alexander and Noonan (1979) argued that the lack of cues to ovulation evolved to increase paternal certainty and force males into pair bonds. In other words, they suggest that women have evolved the capacity to conceal ovulation to, in essence, trick men into long-term relationships because men will not know when or how often to copulate to ensure conception and will therefore be less tempted to leave the female to look for others to impregnate (see also Strassmann, 1981; Turke, 1984). Extended receptivity, ovulatory asynchrony across women, and concealed ovulation would thus pressure men to engage in extended courtships and behave increasingly paternally (Alexander & Noonan, 1979; Turke, 1984). Furthermore, men mated to women who do not advertise their fertility status would be less victimized by mate-poaching rivals. This would increase paternity certainty and, by extension, male investment in offspring (Alexander & Noonan, 1979; Symons, 1979; Turke, 1984), which would benefit the woman. Burley (1979), however, pointed out that these arguments (Alexander & Noonan, 1979; Symons, 1979; Turke, 1984) are somewhat flawed because they imply that women obtained mates ancestrally by getting pregnant and that men's explicit purpose in seeking out females is to get them pregnant. First, because women invest more in offspring care (e.g., via gestation and lactation), it would make more sense for women to be relatively certain of male investment prior to becoming pregnant because conceiving before attaining male investment would likely promote, rather than discourage, male abandonment. Burley asserted that "[the] establishment of a pair bond prior to having offspring is a norm found in many, if not most, human cultures, and is certainly found throughout the animal kingdom when biparental care is present" (Burley, 1979, p.839). Also, because of the extended period of offspring dependency in humans, males may also benefit from forming pair bonds as the increased paternal investment likely increased offspring survival (Alexander & Noonan, 1979; Burley, 1979; Sillen-Tullberg & Møller, 1993; Strassmann, 1981), particularly in the mobile hunter-gatherer groups that predominated the ancestral past of humans (Lee & DeVore, 1968). It therefore seems unlikely that concealed ovulation evolved for the purposes of female deception used to force males into pair bonds.

However, Burley's (1979) assertion that concealed ovulation functions to prevent women from avoiding pregnancy is likely incorrect because it assumes that women's receptivity and initiation of sexual activity is not increased as a function of ovulation, which may not be the case. Indeed, women may initiate more sexual

activity during the fertile period of their menstrual cycles than at other times (Adams, Burt, & Gold, 1978; Matteo & Rissman, 1984; but see Brewis & Meyer, 2005). Others have supposed that concealed ovulation allows women greater flexibility in choosing a mate (Benshoof & Thornhill, 1979; Strassmann, 1981; Symons, 1979). Concealing ovulation could facilitate cuckoldry by limiting males' perceived need to guard their partners during peak fertility and could allow women to choose genetically superior men to sire their offspring (Benshoof & Thornhill, 1979). In other words, concealed ovulation might facilitate successful deception by women seeking extra-pair copulations. Also, concealing ovulation may limit indiscriminate attention from males, thereby reducing potentially dangerous attention from unwanted suitors (Provost, Quinsey, & Troje, 2008). Strassmann (1981) suggests that low status males, in particular, would benefit from monogamy and investment (rather than lots of mating effort) if only they could be confident in their paternity. Concealing ovulation from males could offer this confidence by reducing the perceived risk of cuckoldry. As discussed by Marlowe (2004), ovulation would be easy to detect by men if it were in the interest of women for men to be able to detect it.

Relatively recently, evidence that cues to fertility status have not been totally lost has been accumulating (Gangestad & Thornhill, 2008). Women lack the overt cues (e.g., exaggerated sexual swellings) to fertility status that are demonstrated by many fertile nonhuman primate females (Wallen & Zehr, 2004). However, selection pressures favoring complete concealment of ovulation by women, combined with mechanisms to detect fertility status by men, may have resulted in partial concealment of ovulation. Similarly, perhaps complete concealment of ovulation would be maladaptive because women would not be better able to attract high-quality men around ovulation, when conception is more likely, than during infertile phases of the menstrual cycle. Regardless of the possible reasons, it seems that, in contrast to earlier assertions, women may demonstrate semi-concealed ovulation.

Cues to Ovulation in Human Females

Increasing research on physical and behavioral cues to women's fertility status has surfaced over the last decade (Gangestad & Thornhill, 2008). For example, women decrease their food consumption and increase their motor activity around ovulation (Fessler, 2003a; Gong, Garrel, & Calloway, 1989), possibly to focus on other important behaviors, such as mating effort (Fessler, 2003a). Among women with premenstrual syndrome, the preovulatory increase in estradiol is associated with an increase in positive mood (Bäckström et al., 1983). Women also experience improved creativity during the preovulatory phase relative to the mid-luteal phase and menses (Krug, Finn, Pietrowsky, Fehm, & Born, 1996, Krug, Stamm, Pietrowsky, Fehm, & Born, 1994) and improvement in some cognitive tasks around ovulation (Becker, Creutzfeldt, Schwibbe, & Wuttke, 1982; Broverman et al., 1981). Overall, these studies underline the possibility that hormonal variation across the ovulatory cycle may alter female behavior. Such variations could have implications for women's reproductive status if they influence female or male mating behavior or perceptions of female attractiveness.

The variety and volume of studies investigating human sexual behavior as a function of cycle status are substantial and indicate that the fertile period of the menstrual cycle may be accompanied by an increase in physical attractiveness (e.g., Roberts et al., 2004), sexual motivation (e.g., Grammer, Jutte, & Fischmann, 1997), and sexual activity (e.g., Adams et al., 1978; Wilcox et al., 2004; but see Brewis & Meyer, 2005). Ovulatory cues may even be perceived by men to some extent (Haselton & Gildersleeve, 2011) and may be accompanied by other adaptive behaviors, such as shifts in preferences toward cues to genetic fitness when conception is most likely (Gangestad & Thornhill, 2008; Jones et al., 2008). These subtle

physical and behavioral signs of conception risk indicate that the previously accepted conclusion that women have evolved to conceal ovulation does not fully represent reality.

Changes in Attractiveness

The long-held assumptions that physical cues to human female fertility status and changes in female attractiveness as a function of fertility status have disappeared over time have been challenged by recent findings. Women are rated as more attractive in terms of facial appearance (Puts et al., 2013; Roberts et al., 2004), vocal characteristics (Bryant & Haselton, 2009; Pipitone & Gallup, 2008; Puts et al., 2013), and body fat distribution (i.e., have a more attractive waist-to-hip ratio, Kirchengast & Gartner, 2002) around ovulation than at other nonfertile times in their menstrual cycles. Peak fertility is associated with greater breast symmetry (Manning, Scutt, Whitehouse, Leinster, & Walton, 1996; Scutt & Manning, 1996), with symmetric breasts possibly signaling underlying phenotypic quality and fertility in women (Manning, Scutt, Whitehouse, & Leinster, 1997). Finally, one study found that naturally cycling (i.e., not using hormonal contraceptives) exotic dancers receive more tips during peak fertility versus other points in the menstrual cycle (Miller, Tybur, & Jordan, 2007). While it remains unclear whether changes in physical or behavioral characteristics (or both) in women at ovulation are driving this change in male spending patterns, it is nonetheless striking.

Women, similar to females of several other primate species (e.g., Cerda-Molina et al., 2006; Crawford, Boulet, & Drea, 2011; Smith & Abbott, 1998), appear to have a more appealing body odor around peak fertility (Doty, Ford, Preti, & Huggins, 1975; Gildersleeve, Haselton, Larson, & Pillsworth, 2012; Havlíček, Dvořáková, Bartoš, & Flegr, 2006; Kuukasjärvi et al., 2004; Miller & Maner, 2010; Singh & Bronstad, 2001; Thornhill et al., 2003). Doty et al. (1975) found that male judges rated the scent of vaginal secretions sampled at high fertility as more pleasant than vaginal secretion samples taken from the same women at low fertility. Sampling body odor using cotton pads worn in the armpit for 24 h in 3 different menstrual cycle phases, Havlíček et al. (2006) found that men rated the odor of women in the fertile follicular phase of their menstrual cycles as more attractive than the odor of women in the menstrual or luteal phases. Together with the evidence of increased physical and vocal attractiveness at ovulation, these studies suggest that a woman's attractiveness and, by extension, her ability to attract a mate are highest on the fertile days of her cycle, which would not be expected if ovulation was truly no longer detectable in women. Thus, it appears that men are maximally attracted to ovulating women.

Women also use strategies to augment their physical attractiveness around ovulation, with several studies finding that women modulate their appearance and clothing to enhance their attractiveness when they are most fertile (Durante, Li, & Haselton, 2008; Haselton, Mortezaie, Pillsworth, Bleske-Rechek, & Frederick, 2007; Hill & Durante, 2009; Röder, Brewer, & Fink, 2009; Schwarz & Hassebrauck, 2008), possibly as a reaction to a periovulatory decrease in self-esteem (Hill & Durante, 2009). Using diary data from 40 naturally cycling women and male ratings of photographs, Schwarz and Hassebrauck (2008) found that women dressed more provocatively and were rated as more attractive during high-fertility days compared to low-fertility days (Durante et al., 2008; Haselton et al., 2007). Women also report feeling more attractive and desirable (Röder et al., 2009; but see Schwarz & Hassebrauck, 2008) and draw more revealing, sexier clothing when asked to illustrate an outfit they would wear to a social function (Durante et al., 2008) near ovulation. Lastly, Hill and Durante (2009) found that women's self-esteem decreases near ovulation, when they are most attractive to men, which may function to increase motivation to enhance attractiveness. Collectively, these studies suggest an increase in women's sexual motivation and desire to attract a mate while fertile.

Sexual Behavior and Motivation

Peak fertility is accompanied by an increase in motor (Morris & Udry, 1970) and sexual activities (Morris & Udry, 1982), with some evidence indicating that sexual encounters increase (Wilcox et al., 2004; but see Brewis & Meyer, 2005) and are more likely to be female-initiated around ovulation (Adams et al., 1978; Matteo & Rissman, 1984). Ovulation is also associated with an increase in sexual desire (Stanislaw & Rice, 1988) and fantasy (Regan, 1996), attention to attractive men (Anderson et al., 2010), sexual self-stimulation (Harvey, 1987), and arousal in response to sexually explicit material (Slob, Bax, Hop, Rowland, & van der Werff ten Bosch, 1996; Zillmann, Schweitzer, & Mundorf, 1994). Furthermore, women describe an increased desire for orgasm at peak fertility compared to other points in the menstrual cycle (Regan, 1996), which may have important implications if, as some research suggests (Baker & Bellis, 1993; Wildt, Kissler, Licht, & Becker, 1998; Zervomanolakis et al., 2009), orgasm increases the likelihood of conception. Therefore, contrary to the idea that women have evolved the capacity to conceal ovulation from themselves and others, the signs of peak fertility may simply be less overt than they are in some other primates. Additionally, attitudes toward risk-taking, which are correlated with the probability of victimization (Fetchenhauer & Rohde, 2002), may decrease at ovulation (Bröder & Hohmann, 2003; Chavanne & Gallup, 1998), which suggests that women alter their behavior to avoid rape and possible impregnation by unwanted males, although one study has found that rape is no less frequent during the ovulatory phase of the menstrual cycle (Fessler, 2003b). Similarly, ratings of disgust toward incest increase around mid-cycle (Fessler & Navarrete, 2003). Taken together, these findings intimate an increase in sexual motivation associated with peak fertility that is accompanied by a decrease in behaviors that may lead to a detrimental pairing.

The apparent changes in female sexual psychology associated with conception risk appear to elevate competition with same-sex competitors over potential mates. Women derogate same-sex competitors by downplaying their physical attractiveness (Fisher, 2004; Jones, Vukovic, Little, Roberts, & DeBruine, 2011; Vukovic et al., 2009; Welling et al., 2007), which causes men to lower their attractiveness ratings of the derogated rivals (Fisher & Cox, 2009). Fisher (2004) found that competition and derogation, meaning any act intended to decrease the perceived value of a rival, increased during periods of the menstrual cycle characterized by high estrogen, such as ovulation. While presumed estrogen level was negatively related to women's ratings of the facial attractiveness of other women, there was no relationship between estrogen and women's ratings of the attractiveness of male faces (Fisher, 2004). Correspondingly, Vukovic et al. (2009) found that postmenopausal women rated photographs of feminine-faced (i.e., attractive, O'Toole et al., 1998) women as more attractive than premenopausal women, but there was no difference in ratings of male faces (see also Jones et al., 2011). This effect was independent of possible effects of participant age and suggests that dislike of attractive same-sex competitors decreases as fertility decreases (Jones et al., 2011; Vukovic et al., 2009). Women also feel more attractive (Röder et al., 2009; Schwarz & Hassebrauck, 2008) and are more willing to spend money on sexy, rather than functional, clothing (Hill & Durante, 2009) around ovulation than at other times, though they do not spend money at an increased rate more generally at ovulation (Röder et al., 2009).

There is some evidence, as indicated by pupil dilation, that women have a greater interest in their primary partners during the fertile phase of the menstrual cycle, but this pattern is also observed in response to attractive opposite-sex celebrities (Laeng & Falkenberg, 2007), suggesting a general response not directed specifically at long-term partners. Additionally, although Brewis and Meyer's (2005) large-scale cross-cultural study on sexual intercourse over the menstrual cycle found no increase in sexual intercourse around ovulation, this study only looked at coitus rates among married couples. It is possible that ovulation-related changes in sexual behavior would be more evident in short-term mating contexts and/or extra-pair copulations (see Gangestad & Simpson, 2000). Certainly, a significant amount of research suggests that women increase their interest in extra-pair, versus in-pair, men surrounding ovulation. Women are less motivated toward sex for the purposes of intimacy (Sheldon, Cooper, Geary, Hoard, & DeSoto, 2006) and are more sexually opportunistic (Gangestad et al., 2010) near ovulation than at other times. They demonstrate a greater interest in attending social gatherings (Haselton & Gangestad, 2006), visiting singles nightclubs without their romantic partner (Grammer et al., 1997), extra-pair men (Gangestad, Thornhill, & Garver, 2002), extra-pair sexual activity (Baker & Bellis, 1995; Bellis & Baker, 1990), and extra-pair sexual fantasies (Gangestad et al., 2002) around ovulation. Women also report less commitment to, and relationship satisfaction with, their current primary partner, and feel and are perceived by others to be more desirable and physically attractive around ovulation, possibly because of increases in estradiol levels (Durante & Li, 2009). Certainly, high estradiol, which first peaks around ovulation in humans (Baird & Fraser, 1974), appears to play a role in female receptivity to copulatory solicitation across several species (Beach, 1948; Kendrick & Dixson, 1985).

That ovulation is associated with increased attractiveness (Bryant & Haselton, 2009; Havlíček et al., 2006; Kirchengast & Gartner, 2002; Kuukasjärvi et al., 2004; Miller et al., 2007; Pipitone & Gallup, 2008; Puts et al., 2013; Roberts et al., 2004; Singh & Bronstad, 2001) and increases in possible sexually motivated behavior (Durante et al., 2008; Grammer et al., 1997; Haselton et al., 2007; Hill & Durante, 2009; Röder et al., 2009; Schwarz & Hassebrauck, 2008) contradicts the supposition that humans have lost estrus. However, it is worth underlining that cues to human fertility over the menstrual cycle are very subtle, indicating that obvious fertility signals that would attract indiscriminate attention, potentially cause dominant males to monopolize fertile women, and constrain or eliminate female choice would be detrimental. Nonetheless, ovulation is associated with several within-subject changes, including a greater interest in extra-pair men among women with partners who carry less complementary MHC alleles (Garver-Apgar, Gangestad, Thornhill, Miller, & Olp, 2006), among women with less attractive partners (Haselton & Gangestad, 2006; Pillsworth & Haselton, 2006), and among women with less symmetrical partners (Gangestad, Thornhill, & Garver-Apgar, 2005). These latter findings may reflect a tendency to seek out men of better genetic quality when conception is likely. Therefore, it is possible that women engage in a dual-mating strategy, whereby they seek out men of high genetic quality when conception is likely in order to secure good genes for potential offspring and seek out caring, investing mates during other times (Gangestad & Simpson, 2000).

Cyclic Variation in Preferences for Male Traits

According to the ovulatory shift hypothesis, systematic changes in female mating-related behavior and preferences should be expected over the course of the menstrual cycle (Gangestad & Thornhill, 1998; Grammer, 1993; Thornhill & Gangestad, 1999). Women who procreate with genetically fit men may reap reproductive benefits if those genes are passed on to offspring because it could increase the likelihood that the offspring will survive and eventually reproduce themselves. Using this reasoning, preferences should not necessarily remain constant because men who possess good genes may not offer other benefits to the mother and child, such as caring or investing behaviors (Perrett et al., 1998). However, preferences for good genes should be maximal at peak conception (Gangestad & Thornhill, 1998). In fact, there is evidence that men who possess good genes invest less in their mates and offspring (Penton-Voak & Perrett, 2001; Perrett et al., 1998), explaining why

preference shifts for putative cues to good genes are most pronounced when women judge men's attractiveness for a short-term (i.e., sexual) relationship versus a long-term (i.e., committed) one (Gangestad, Simpson, Cousins, Garver-Apgar, & Christensen, 2004; Little, Cohen, Jones, & Belsky, 2007, Little & Jones, 2011; Little, Jones, Penton-Voak, Burt, & Perrett, 2002; Penton-Voak et al., 1999; Puts, 2005).

Several researchers have hypothesized that attractiveness judgments reflect evolved preferences that identify aspects of underlying mate quality and heritable immunity to multiple forms of genetic and environmental stress (e.g., DeBruine, Jones, Crawford, Welling, & Little, 2010, DeBruine, Jones, Little, Crawford, & Welling, 2011; Fink & Penton-Voak, 2002; Langlois, Roggman, & Musselman, 1994; Miller & Todd, 1998; Møller & Thornhill, 1998; Thornhill & Gangestad, 1993). Consistent with this view, male facial attractiveness has been found to be positively related to a genetic profile associated with immunity to infectious diseases (Lie, Rhodes, & Simmons, 2008; Roberts et al., 2005), good semen quality (Soler et al., 2003; but see Peters, Rhodes, & Simmons, 2008), reproductive success (Jokela, 2009), and longevity (Henderson & Anglin, 2003). More specifically, traits such as symmetry and masculinity affect male attractiveness and are thought to signal genetic quality (reviewed in Gangestad & Thornhill, 2008), with symmetric (Miller & Todd, 1998; Thornhill & Møller, 1997; Waynforth, 1998) and masculine (Apicella, Feinberg, & Marlowe, 2007; Rhodes, Chan, Zebrowitz, & Simmons, 2003, Rhodes, Simmons, & Peters, 2005; Thornhill & Gangestad, 2006) traits positively related to long-term health and reproductive success in men.

In line with the ovulatory shift hypothesis, several studies report increases in women's preferences for putative cues to male mate quality, including preferences for the odor of men who are more dominant, symmetrical, and heterozygous at the MHC (Gangestad & Thornhill, 1998; Havlíček, Roberts, & Flegr, 2005; Rikowski & Grammer, 1999; Thornhill et al., 2003; Thornhill

& Gangestad, 1999). Women also demonstrate a stronger preference for male facial symmetry (Little, Jones, Burt, & Perrett, 2007; but see Cárdenas & Harris, 2007; Koehler, Rhodes, Simmons, & Zebrowitz, 2006), the faces of men with symmetrical bodies (Thornhill & Gangestad, 2003), masculine male faces (Johnston, Hagel, Franklin, Fink, & Grammer, 2001; Jones, Little, et al., 2005; Little, Jones, & DeBruine, 2008; Penton-Voak et al., 1999; Penton-Voak & Perrett, 2000; Welling et al., 2007), masculine male body shape (Little, Jones, & Burriss, 2007), masculine vocal characteristics in men's voices (Feinberg et al., 2006; Puts, 2005), and height (Pawlowski & Jasienska, 2005) around ovulation than at other times in the menstrual cycle. These shifts in preferences are likely driven by hormonal variation across the menstrual cycle, although debate still surrounds whether menstrual cycle preference shifts are driven by estradiol (Feinberg et al., 2006; Garver-Apgar, Gangestad, & Thornhill, 2008; Roney & Simmons, 2008; Rosen & López, 2009; Rupp et al., 2009), progesterone (Garver-Apgar et al., 2008; Jones, Little, et al., 2005; Puts, 2006; Rupp et al., 2009), prolactin (Puts, 2006), testosterone (Welling et al., 2007), cortisol (López, Hay, & Conklin, 2009), or some hormonal combination (Frost, 1994; Garver-Apgar et al., 2008; Lukaszewski & Roney, 2009; Puts, 2006; Welling et al., 2007). Furthermore, women's accuracy at classifying faces as male is greatest at peak fertility (Macrae, Alnwick, Milne, & Schloerscheidt, 2002), particularly when those faces are more sex typical (i.e., masculine, Johnston, Miles, & Macrae, 2008). Notably, lesbian women categorize female, not male, faces more accurately around ovulation (Brinsmead-Stockham, Johnston, Miles, & Macrae, 2008), which suggests that these findings are dependent on the mate choice relevance of the target faces.

In line with the above findings for physical traits, preferences for nonphysical traits, such as male-dominant and competitive behavioral displays (Gangestad et al., 2004; Gangestad, Garver-Apgar, Simpson, & Cousins, 2007; Lukaszewski & Roney, 2009) and courtship language (Rosen & López, 2009), are also highest around ovulation in women. Using video clips of men competing for a lunch date, Gangestad et al.

(2004) found that women rated men who displayed social presence and direct intrasexual competitiveness as more attractive on high-fertility days of the menstrual cycle than on low-fertility days, although this association was only evident when judging men's attractiveness for a short-term (versus long-term) relationship. More recently, Guéguen (2009a, 2009b) found that women are more likely to agree to a man's request to exchange phone numbers or dance if they are in the late-follicular phase of the menstrual cycle (the fertile phase immediately preceding ovulation) compared to the luteal phase of the menstrual cycle (the nonfertile phase following ovulation), indicating that women may be most receptive to courtship at peak fertility. Therefore, changes in women's preferences for male traits generalize to behavioral ones and are not limited to physical characteristics.

Male Detection of Ovulation

In addition to assuming that ovulation is concealed from women's conscious detection (e.g., Burley, 1979; Daniels, 1983), those who argue that ovulation is concealed also stipulate that it is imperceptible to men (e.g., Marlowe, 2004; Pawłowski, 1999; Strassmann, 1981). That women are rated as more attractive near ovulation (Bryant & Haselton, 2009; Doty et al., 1975; Havlíček et al., 2006; Kirchengast & Gartner, 2002; Kuukasjärvi et al., 2004; Miller & Maner, 2010; Pipitone & Gallup, 2008; Puts et al., 2013; Roberts et al., 2004; Singh & Bronstad, 2001; Thornhill et al., 2003) suggests that physical cues to ovulation can be perceived by others. Moreover, as mentioned earlier, Miller et al. (2007) found that naturally cycling lap dancers earn significantly more money in tips at high fertility ($335 per shift) than at low fertility ($260 per shift) across the menstrual cycle. This result effectively demonstrates that women are not only more attractive at ovulation but that this change in attractiveness can also have a direct impact on male behavior.

Attractive women have particularly high mating standards (Buss & Shackelford, 2008), receive more male attention (Buss & Barnes, 1986), and are more likely to be poached by a rival (Schmitt & Buss, 2001). Given that women appear to be more attractive and sexually motivated around mid-cycle and also show more interest in extra-pair copulations, increased attention from long-term partners would be expected in order for men to decrease the likelihood that their partner will stray or be poached by a rival. In fact, three studies have shown a relationship between female conception risk and female perceptions of attentive, jealous, and proprietary behaviors from their male partners (Gangestad et al., 2002; Haselton & Gangestad, 2006; Pillsworth & Haselton, 2006). Jealousy and other mate guarding behaviors are hypothesized to function to reduce the likelihood of a partner straying or being poached (e.g., Buss, 1988; Daly, Wilson, & Weghorst, 1982; Shackelford, Besser, & Goetz, 2008; Shackelford, Goetz, Buss, Euler, & Hoier, 2005; Welling et al., 2011), which, given that the potential reproductive costs of infidelity would be highest around ovulation, would make an increase in these behaviors at peak fertility a potentially adaptive tactic. Gangestad et al. (2002) asked women about their sexual interests and the behavior of their partners twice: once within 5 days before a luteinizing hormone surge (i.e., at high fertility) and once during the luteal phase (i.e., at low fertility). They found that women reported greater interest in, and fantasy about, extra-pair men during the high-fertility test session compared to the low-fertility test session. There was no effect of fertility status on women's interest in or fantasy about their primary partners. Interestingly, women also reported that their primary partners were more attentive and proprietary toward them near ovulation than during the luteal phase, suggesting that men engage in more mate retention tactics when their partners are more likely to get pregnant (Gangestad et al., 2002).

Haselton and Gangestad (2006) expanded on the above work, finding that partnered women reported more extra-pair flirtations and an increase in mate guarding tactics by their partners near ovulation. The increase in mate retention tactics was modulated by female attractiveness, whereby the mid-cycle shift in mate guarding behaviors by primary partners was higher for less attractive women versus attractive women (who experience relatively high levels of mate guarding throughout the cycle). Also, this male increase in proprietary behaviors during their partner's fertile phase is strongest in men with partners demonstrating a stronger desire to engage in extra-pair mating (Gangestad et al., 2002; Haselton & Gangestad, 2006), suggesting either that women's attention to extra-pair men may drive this increased attention or that men are sensitive to other fertility-associated cues and become more responsive to the threat of extra-pair men as a result. Men do indeed increase their ratings of the dominance of other men when their partners are fertile (Burriss & Little, 2006), which supports the notion that men are able to detect the increased risk of cuckoldry, at least to some extent. Importantly, these findings demonstrate that partner ovulation-dependent shifts in male behavior may be sensitive to possible fitness rewards (Haselton & Gangestad, 2006). Similarly, women with less sexually attractive partners report receiving more love and attention from their male partners around ovulation than women who rated their partners as more sexually attractive (Pillsworth & Haselton, 2006). While these reported increases in mate retention tactics may be reactionary to women's increased attractiveness (e.g., Miller et al., 2007) and interest in extra-pair males (e.g., Gangestad et al., 2002), these findings contrast with the concept that ovulation is fully concealed. However, converging evidence from the male partners themselves is needed because, at present, it is not clear whether these female perceptions reflect an actual increase in male behavior or whether women simply notice these behaviors more when their interest in extra-pair men is highest.

A recent double-blind study provides additional evidence that men both perceive subtle cues to ovulation and that those cues affect their mating behaviors. Miller and Maner (2010) investigated how the scents of women at peak fertility influence male endocrinological responses by having men smell T-shirts worn by women near ovulation or T-shirts worn by the same women during the luteal (nonfertile) phase of the menstrual cycle. Prior to smelling the T-shirt randomly assigned to them, men provided a baseline saliva sample that was used to measure testosterone level. Next, participants smelled the T-shirt three times over a 15-min interval and then provided another saliva sample. They found that, when controlling for baseline testosterone levels, testosterone was substantially higher in men exposed to the odor of a woman close to ovulation than in men exposed to the odor of a woman in the luteal phase of her cycle (Miller & Maner, 2010; but see Roney & Simmons, 2012). This is the first research to provide direct evidence that olfactory cues to female fertility across the menstrual cycle can influence male hormonal responses. Testosterone levels in men are associated with competitiveness and dominance (Mazur & Booth, 1998; Zitzmann & Nieschlag, 2001), which are behavioral cues that women find particularly attractive at ovulation (Gangestad et al., 2004). Significantly, some evidence suggests that men's testosterone levels respond to mating-relevant cues, such as interacting with a woman (Ronay & von Hippel, 2010; Roney, Lukaszewski, & Simmons, 2007; Roney, Mahler, & Maestripieri, 2003) or viewing erotic films (Hellhammer, Hubert, & Schürmeyer, 1985; Rubin, Henson, Falvo, & High, 1979), suggesting that testosterone may be related to an increase in men's mating motivation. In line with this hypothesis, male exposure to the scent of a woman near ovulation leads to increased implicit accessibility of sexual concepts and heightened perceptions of women's sexual arousal (Miller & Maner, 2011). Men are also more likely to mimic a woman (a behavior that reflects attraction between people) and make risky decisions (a decision-making strategy men use to display desirable traits to women) when face-to-face with a fertile-phase female confederate than when interacting with a confederate during other nonfertile menstrual cycle phases (Miller & Maner, 2011). These findings thus imply that men not only perceive cues to female

conception risk but also that these cues may have a direct influence on their behavior.

Hormonal Contraceptives

It is highly probable that the various changes that occur over the ovulatory cycle are driven by natural changes in hormone levels (e.g., Garver-Apgar et al., 2008; Jones et al., 2008; Jones, Little, et al., 2005; Little et al., 2008, Little, Burriss, Tufte, & Jones, 2006; Puts, 2006; Puts et al., 2013; Welling et al., 2007). Given this relationship, it is perhaps predictable that these hormone-mediated changes in women's appearance, behavior, and preferences are largely absent in women using hormonal contraceptives (e.g., Gangestad et al., 2007; Guéguen, 2009b; Jones, Perrett, et al., 2005; Krug et al., 1994; Laeng & Falkenberg, 2007; Little, Jones, & Burriss, 2007; Pawlowski & Jasienska, 2005; Penton-Voak et al., 1999; Puts, 2005, 2006; Rosen & López, 2009). For example, changes in gross electrical activity in the brain over the menstrual cycle, and the corresponding increase in scores on certain performance tasks during the periovulatory period, are not present in women using hormonal contraceptives (Becker et al., 1982). Also, the rise in female-initiated sexual activity around peak fertility is eliminated in hormonal contraceptive users (Adams et al., 1978).

Hormonal contraceptives may interfere with the cyclic nature of women's attractiveness. As mentioned, women are rated as more attractive around ovulation compared to other points in the cycle (e.g., Bryant & Haselton, 2009; Miller et al., 2007; Pipitone & Gallup, 2008; Puts et al., 2013; Roberts et al., 2004), but studies have found no such variation in attractiveness in women using contraceptives (Kuukasjärvi et al., 2004; Miller et al., 2007; Pipitone & Gallup, 2008). In contrast to naturally cycling women, hormonally contracepting lap dancers showed no earnings peak associated with cycle phase (Miller et al., 2007). Pill users also show no peak in odor (Kuukasjärvi et al., 2004) or vocal (Pipitone & Gallup, 2008) attractiveness. This may limit women's overall ability to attract a high-quality mate. Additionally, women's potentially adaptive shifts in preferences over the menstrual cycle, such as increases in preferences for masculinity (Penton-Voak et al., 1999; Puts, 2006) and male scent (Thornhill & Gangestad, 2003), and shifts in attention toward courtship language (Rosen & López, 2009) are not present in hormonal contraceptive users. These findings have led some researchers to speculate that the hormonal contraceptive pill may detrimentally influence mate preferences and mate choice (Alvergne & Lummaa, 2009; Havlíček & Roberts, 2009; Roberts, Gosling, Carter, & Petrie, 2008; Wedekind & Füri, 1997; Welling, 2013). Regardless, the absence of menstrual cycle shifts in attractiveness, behavior, and preferences in hormonal contraceptive users emphasizes the importance of underlying hormonal mechanisms on human mating behavior and psychology.

Conclusions

Previously, it has been argued that women would not benefit from advertising their fertility status for several reasons, such as the possibility that advertising high conception risk may lead to unwanted male attention that could constrain female choice (Gangestad & Thornhill, 2008; Thornhill & Gangestad, 2008). However, because women are more attractive, appear more sexually motivated, and increase their preferences for putative cues to male genetic quality around ovulation and because men appear capable of detecting these subtle cues to ovulation, it is evident that ovulation is not entirely concealed. This has led some to speculate that women have evolved to conceal cues to ovulation but that men have simultaneously evolved to detect ovulation (Gangestad & Thornhill, 2008; Haselton & Gildersleeve, 2011; Thornhill & Gangestad, 2008). This view stipulates that the existing signs of approaching ovulation are not shaped by selection but leak out despite female selection to conceal them. Alternatively, it is possible that selection favored cues that are subtle enough to allow women to avoid unwanted male attention but

that also allow them to attract attention from desired mates at opportune times. Behavioral cues could be especially easily directed toward desired mates. This would provide women with clear reproductive advantages and may also benefit male partners, who may be more likely than other men to detect these fertility-related changes in their partners (Haselton & Gildersleeve, 2011) and may engage in tactics designed to reduce the risk of cuckoldry (Gangestad et al., 2002; Haselton & Gangestad, 2006; Pillsworth & Haselton, 2006).

As mentioned, the specific endocrine mechanisms behind women's changes in attractiveness, behavior, and preferences are still under debate. In many species, including nonhuman primates (Wallen & Zehr, 2004), estrogen seems to facilitate estrus behaviors (Giraldi et al., 2004). In human females, although some researchers have found associations with estradiol and periovulatory changes (Feinberg et al., 2006; Garver-Apgar et al., 2008; Roney & Simmons, 2008; Rosen & López, 2009; Rupp et al., 2009), other work has found independent effects of progesterone (Jones, Little, et al., 2005), prolactin (Puts, 2006), testosterone (Welling et al., 2007), cortisol (López et al., 2009), or a combination of various hormones (Frost, 1994; Garver-Apgar et al., 2008; Lukaszewski & Roney, 2009; Puts, 2006; Welling et al., 2007). For instance, Puts et al. (2013) found that progesterone and its interaction with estradiol negatively predicted vocal attractiveness and overall (facial plus vocal) attractiveness to men across the cycle but that progesterone alone negatively predicts ratings of facial attractiveness. Therefore, it is possible that the causes of estrus-like behaviors in women are less straightforward than similar behaviors in other primates, indicating that more work on the hormonal mechanisms underpinning women's cyclic shifts is clearly needed.

Contrary to earlier assertions, current research suggests that women's ovulatory status is not entirely hidden. Although overt signals that indicate impending ovulation, like those present in some other primates (Baum et al., 1977; Clarke et al., 2009; Nunn, 1999), are absent or reduced in human females, subtle indicators of peak fertility remain. Indeed, observable cues to ovulation and associated shifts in behavior and preferences are becoming increasingly well documented. Continued investigation of these cyclic shifts promises to further illuminate important design features of human mating psychology and elucidate the mating dynamics of ancestral human populations.

References

Adams, D., Burt, A., & Gold, A. R. (1978). Rise in female-initiated sexual activity at ovulation and its suppression by oral contraception. *New England Journal of Medicine, 299,* 1145–1150.

Alexander, R. D., & Noonan, K. M. (1979). Concealment of ovulation, parental care and human social evolution. In N. Chagnon & W. Irons (Eds.), *Evolutionary biology and human social behavior.* North Scituate, MA: Duxbury Press.

Alvergne, A., & Lummaa, V. (2009). Does the contraceptive pill alter mate choice in humans? *Trends in Ecology and Evolution, 25,* 171–179.

Andelman, S. J. (1987). Evolution of concealed ovulation in vervet monkeys (*Cercopithecus aethiops*). *The American Naturalist, 129,* 785–799.

Anderson, U. S., Perea, E. F., Vaughn Becker, D., Ackerman, J. M., Shapiro, J. R., Neuberg, S. L., et al. (2010). I only have eyes for you: Ovulation redirects attention (but not memory) to attractive men. *Journal of Experimental Social Psychology, 46,* 804–808.

Apicella, C. L., Feinberg, D. R., & Marlowe, F. W. (2007). Voice pitch predicts reproductive success in male hunter-gatherers. *Biology Letters, 3,* 682–684.

Bäckström, T., Sanders, D., Leask, R., Davidson, D., Warner, P., & Bancroft, J. (1983). Mood, sexuality, hormones, and the menstrual cycle. II. Hormone levels and their relationship to the premenstrual syndrome. *Psychosomatic Medicine, 45,* 503–507.

Baird, D. T., & Fraser, I. S. (1974). Blood production and ovarian secretion rates of estradiol-17β and estrone in women throughout the menstrual cycle. *The Journal of Clinical Endocrinology and Metabolism, 38,* 1009–1017.

Baker, R. R., & Bellis, M. A. (1993). Human sperm competition: Ejaculate manipulation by females and a function for the female orgasm. *Animal Behaviour, 46,* 887–909.

Baker, R. R., & Bellis, M. A. (1995). *Human sperm competition: Copulation, masturbation and infidelity.* London: Chapman and Hall.

Baum, M. J., Everitt, B. J., Herbert, J., & Keverne, E. B. (1977). Hormonal basis of proceptivity and receptivity in female primates. *Archives of Sexual Behavior, 6,* 173–192.

Beach, F. A. (1948). *Hormones and behavior: A survey of interrelationships between endocrine secretions and patterns of overt response.* Oxford, England: Hoeber.

Becker, D., Creutzfeldt, O. D., Schwibbe, M., & Wuttke, W. (1982). Changes in physiological, EEG and psychological parameters in women during the spontaneous menstrual cycle and following oral contraceptives. *Psychoneuroendocrinology, 7,* 75–90.

Bellis, M. A., & Baker, R. R. (1990). Do females promote sperm competition? Data for humans. *Animal Behaviour, 40,* 997–999.

Benshoof, L., & Thornhill, R. (1979). The evolution of monogamy and the loss of estrous in humans. *Journal of Social and Biological Structures, 2,* 95–106.

Borries, C., Launhardt, K., Epplen, C., Epplen, J. T., & Winkler, P. (1999). Males as infant protectors in Hanuman langurs (*Presbytis entellus*) living in multimale groups—Defence pattern, paternity and sexual behaviour. *Behavioural Ecology and Sociobiology, 46,* 350–356.

Brewis, A., & Meyer, M. (2005). Demographic evidence that human ovulation is undetectable (at least in pair bonds). *Current Anthropology, 46,* 465–471.

Brinsmead-Stockham, K., Johnston, L., Miles, L., & Macrae, C. N. (2008). Female sexual orientation and menstrual influences on person perception. *Journal of Experimental Social Psychology, 44,* 729–734.

Bröder, A., & Hohmann, N. (2003). Variations in risk taking behavior over the menstrual cycle: An improved replication. *Evolution and Human Behavior, 24,* 397–398.

Broverman, D. M., Vogel, W., Klaiber, E. L., Majcher, D., Shea, D., & Paul, V. (1981). Changes in cognitive task performance across the menstrual cycle. *Journal of Comparative and Physiological Psychology, 95,* 646–654.

Bryant, G. A., & Haselton, M. G. (2009). Vocal cues of ovulation in human females. *Biology Letters, 5,* 12–15.

Burch, R. L., & Gallup, G. G. (2000). Perceptions of paternal resemblance predict family violence. *Evolution and Human Behavior, 21,* 429–435.

Burley, N. (1979). The evolution of concealed ovulation. *American Naturalist, 114,* 835–858.

Burriss, R. P., & Little, A. C. (2006). Effects of partner conception risk phase on male perception of dominance in faces. *Evolution and Human Behavior, 27,* 297–305.

Buss, D. M. (1988). From vigilance to violence: Tactics of mate retention in American undergraduates. *Ethology and Sociobiology, 9,* 291–317.

Buss, D. M., & Barnes, M. (1986). Preferences in human mate selection. *Journal of Personality and Social Psychology, 50,* 559–570.

Buss, D. M., & Shackelford, T. K. (2008). Attractive women want it all: Good genes, economic investment, parenting proclivities, and emotional commitment. *Evolutionary Psychology, 6,* 134–146.

Campbell, F. (1960). Birth control and the Christian churches. *Population Studies, 14*, 131–147.

Campbell, B. G. (1966). *Human evolution.* Chicago, IL: Aldine.

Cárdenas, R. A., & Harris, L. J. (2007). Do women's preferences for symmetry change across the menstrual cycle? *Evolution and Human Behavior, 28*, 96–105.

Cerda-Molina, A. L., Hernández-López, L., Chavira, R., Cárdenas, M., Paez-Ponce, D., Cervantes-De la Luz, H., et al. (2006). Endocrine changes in male stumptailed macaques (*Macaca arctoides*) as a response to odor stimulation with vaginal secretions. *Hormones and Behavior, 49*, 81–87.

Chavanne, T. J., & Gallup, G. G. (1998). Variation in risk taking behavior among female college students as a function of the menstrual cycle. *Evolution and Human Behavior, 19*, 27–32.

Clarke, P. M. R., Barrett, L., & Henzi, S. P. (2009). What role do olfactory cues play in chacma baboon mating? *American Journal of Primatology, 71*, 493–502.

Crawford, J. C., Boulet, M., & Drea, C. M. (2011). Smelling wrong: Hormonal contraception in lemurs alters critical female odour cues. *Proceedings of the Royal Society B: Biological Sciences, 278*, 122–130.

Daly, M., & Wilson, M. (1984). A sociobiological analysis of human infanticide. In G. Hausfater & S. Hrdy (Eds.), *Infanticide: Comparative and evolutionary perspectives* (pp. 487–502). New York: Aldine Press.

Daly, M., & Wilson, M. (1985). Child abuse and other risks of not living with both parents. *Ethology and Sociobiology, 6*, 197–210.

Daly, M., Wilson, M., & Weghorst, S. J. (1982). Male sexual jealousy. *Ethology and Sociobiology, 3*, 11–27.

Daniels, D. (1983). The evolution of concealed ovulation and self-deception. *Ethology and Sociobiology, 4*, 69–87.

DeBruine, L. M. (2004). Resemblance to self increases the appeal of child faces to both men and women. *Evolution and Human Behavior, 25*, 142–154.

DeBruine, L. M., Jones, B. C., Crawford, J. R., Welling, L. L. M., & Little, A. C. (2010). The health of a nation predicts their mate preferences: Cross-cultural variation in women's preferences for masculinized male faces. *Proceedings of the Royal Society B: Biological Sciences, 277*, 2405–2410.

DeBruine, L. M., Jones, B. C., Little, A. C., Crawford, J. R., & Welling, L. L. M. (2011). Further evidence for regional variation in women's masculinity preferences. *Proceedings of the Royal Society B: Biological Sciences, 278*, 813–814.

Doty, R. L., Ford, M. E., Preti, G., & Huggins, G. R. (1975). Changes in the intensity and pleasantness of human vaginal odors during the menstrual cycle. *Science, 190*, 1316–1318.

Durante, K. M., & Li, N. P. (2009). Oestradiol level and opportunistic mating in women. *Biology Letters, 5*, 179–182.

Durante, K. M., Li, N. P., & Haselton, M. G. (2008). Changes in women's choice of dress across the ovulatory cycle: Naturalistic and laboratory task-based evidence. *Personality and Social Psychology Bulletin, 34*, 1451–1460.

Feinberg, D. R., Jones, B. C., Law Smith, M. J., Moore, F. R., DeBruine, L. M., Cornwell, R. E., et al. (2006). Menstrual cycle, trait estrogen level, and masculinity preferences in the human voice. *Hormones and Behavior, 49*, 215–222.

Fessler, D. M. T. (2003a). No time to eat: An adaptationist account of periovulatory behavioral changes. *The Quarterly Review of Biology, 78*, 3–21.

Fessler, D. M. T. (2003b). Rape is not less frequent during the ovulatory phase of the menstrual cycle. *Sexualities, Evolution and Gender, 5*, 127–147.

Fessler, D. M. T., & Navarrete, C. D. (2003). Domain-specific variation in disgust sensitivity across the menstrual cycle. *Evolution and Human Behavior, 24*, 406–417.

Fetchenhauer, D., & Rohde, P. A. (2002). Evolutionary personality psychology and victimology: Sex differences in risk attitudes and short-term orientation and their relation to sex differences in victimizations. *Evolution and Human Behavior, 23*, 233–244.

Fink, B., & Penton-Voak, I. (2002). Evolutionary psychology of facial attractiveness. *Current Directions in Psychological Science, 11*, 154–158.

Fisher, M. L. (2004). Female intrasexual competition decreases female facial attractiveness. *Proceedings of the Royal Society of London B, 271*, S283–S285.

Fisher, M. L., & Cox, A. (2009). The influence of female attractiveness on competitor derogation. *Journal of Evolutionary Psychology, 7*, 141–155.

Frost, P. (1994). Preference for darker faces in photographs at different phases of the menstrual cycle: Preliminary assessment of evidence for a hormonal relationship. *Perceptual and Motor Skills, 79*, 507–514.

Gangestad, S. W., Garver-Apgar, C. E., Simpson, J. A., & Cousins, A. J. (2007). Changes in women's mate preferences across the cycle. *Journal of Personality and Social Psychology, 92*, 151–163.

Gangestad, S. W., & Simpson, J. A. (2000). The evolution of human mating: Trade-offs and strategic pluralism. *Behavioural and Brain Sciences, 23*, 573–644.

Gangestad, S. W., Simpson, J. A., Cousins, A. J., Garver-Apgar, C. E., & Christensen, P. N. (2004). Women's preferences for male behavioral displays change across the menstrual cycle. *Psychological Science, 15*, 203–207.

Gangestad, S. W., & Thornhill, R. (1998). Menstrual cycle variation in women's preferences for the scent of symmetrical men. *Proceedings of the Royal Society B: Biological Sciences, 265*, 927–933.

Gangestad, S. W., & Thornhill, R. (2008). Human oestrus. *Proceedings of the Royal Society B: Biological Sciences, 275*, 991–1000.

Gangestad, S. W., Thornhill, R., & Garver, C. E. (2002). Changes in women's sexual interests and their partners' mate-retention tactics across the menstrual cycle: Evidence for shifting conflicts of interest. *Proceedings of the Royal Society B: Biological Sciences, 269*, 975–982.

Gangestad, S. W., Thornhill, R., & Garver-Apgar, C. E. (2005). Women's sexual interests across the ovulatory cycle depend on primary partner developmental instability. *Proceedings of the Royal Society B: Biological Sciences, 272*, 2023–2027.

Gangestad, S. W., Thornhill, R., & Garver-Apgar, C. E. (2010). Men's facial masculinity predicts changes in their female partners' sexual interests across the cycle, whereas men's intelligence does not. *Evolution and Human Behavior, 31*, 412–424.

Garver-Apgar, C. E., Gangestad, S. W., & Thornhill, R. (2008). Hormonal correlates of women's mid-cycle preference for the scent of symmetry. *Evolution and Human Behavior, 29*, 223–232.

Garver-Apgar, C. E., Gangestad, S. W., Thornhill, R., Miller, R. D., & Olp, J. (2006). Major histocompatibility complex alleles, sexual responsivity, and unfaithfulness in romantic couples. *Psychological Science, 17*, 830–835.

Gildersleeve, K. A., Haselton, M. G., Larson, C. M., & Pillsworth, E. G. (2012). Body odor attractiveness as a cue of impending ovulation in women: Evidence from a study using hormone-confirmed ovulation. *Hormones and Behavior, 61*, 157–166.

Giraldi, A., Marson, L., Nappi, R., Pfaus, J., Traish, A. M., Vardi, Y., et al. (2004). Physiology of female sexual function: Animal models. *The Journal of Sexual Medicine, 1*, 237–253.

Gong, E. J., Garrel, D., & Calloway, D. H. (1989). Menstrual cycle and voluntary food intake. *The American Journal of Clinical Nutrition, 49*, 252–258.

Grammer, K. (1993). 5-α-androst-16en-3α-on: A male pheromone? A brief report. *Ethology and Sociobiology, 14*, 201–208.

Grammer, K., Jutte, A., & Fischmann, B. (1997). Der kampf der geschlechter und der krieg der signale. In B. Karnitschneider (Ed.), *Liebe, Lust, und Leidenschaft. Sexualitat im Spiegal der Wissenschaft*. Stuttgart: Hirzel.

Guéguen, N. (2009a). Menstrual cycle phases and female receptivity to a courtship solicitation: An evaluation in a nightclub. *Evolution and Human Behavior, 30*, 351–355.

Guéguen, N. (2009b). The receptivity of women to courtship solicitation across the menstrual cycle: A field experiment. *Biological Psychology, 80*, 321–324.

Harvey, S. M. (1987). Female sexual behavior: Fluctuations during the menstrual cycle. *Journal of Psychosomatic Research, 31*, 101–110.

Haselton, M. G., & Gangestad, S. W. (2006). Conditional expression of women's desires and men's mate guarding across the ovulatory cycle. *Hormones and Behavior, 49*, 509–518.

Haselton, M. G., & Gildersleeve, K. A. (2011). Can men detect ovulation? *Current Directions in Psychological Science, 20*, 87–92.

Haselton, M. G., Mortezaie, M., Pillsworth, E. G., Bleske-Rechek, A. L., & Frederick, D. A. (2007). Ovulatory

shifts in human female ornamentation: Near ovulation, women dress to impress. *Hormones and Behavior, 51*, 40–45.

Havlíček, J., Dvořáková, R., Bartoš, L., & Flegr, J. (2006). Non-advertized does not mean concealed: Body odour changes across the human menstrual cycle. *Ethology, 112*, 81–90.

Havlíček, J., & Roberts, S. C. (2009). MHC-correlated mate choice in humans: A review. *Psychoneuroendocrinology, 34*, 497–512.

Havlíček, J., Roberts, S. C., & Flegr, J. (2005). Women's preference for dominant male odour: Effects of menstrual cycle and relationship status. *Biology Letters, 1*, 256–259.

Heistermann, M., Ziegler, T., van Schaik, C. P., Launhardt, K., Winkler, P., & Hodges, J. K. (2001). Loss of oestrus, concealed ovulation and paternity confusion in free-ranging Hanuman langurs. *Proceedings of the Royal Society of London. Series B: Biological Sciences, 268*, 2445–2451.

Hellhammer, D. H., Hubert, W., & Schürmeyer, T. (1985). Changes in saliva testosterone after psychological stimulation in men. *Psychoneuroendocrinology, 10*, 77–81.

Henderson, J. J. A., & Anglin, J. M. (2003). Facial attractiveness predicts longevity. *Evolution and Human Behavior, 24*, 351–356.

Hill, S. E., & Durante, K. M. (2009). Do women feel worse to look their best? Testing the relationship between self-esteem and fertility status across the menstrual cycle. *Personality and Social Psychology Bulletin, 35*, 1592–1601.

Hrdy, S. B. (1979). Infanticide among mammals: A review, classification, and examination of the implications for the reproductive strategies of females. *Ethology and Sociobiology, 1*, 13–40.

Hrdy, S. B., & Whitten, P. L. (1987). Patterning of sexual activity. In B. S. Smuts, D. L. Cheney, R. M. Seyfarth, R. W. Wrangham, & T. T. Struhsaker (Eds.), *Primate societies* (pp. 370–384). Chicago, IL: University of Chicago Press.

Johnston, V. S., Hagel, R., Franklin, M., Fink, B., & Grammer, K. (2001). Male facial attractiveness: Evidence for hormone-mediated adaptive design. *Evolution and Human Behavior, 21*, 251–267.

Johnston, L., Miles, L., & Macrae, C. N. (2008). Was that a man? Sex identification as a function of menstrual cycle and masculinity. *Applied Cognitive Psychology, 22*, 1185–1194.

Jokela, M. (2009). Physical attractiveness and reproductive success in humans: Evidence from the late 20th century United States. *Evolution and Human Behavior, 30*, 342–350.

Jones, B. C., DeBruine, L. M., Perrett, D. I., Little, A. C., Feinberg, D. R., & Law Smith, M. J. (2008). Effects of menstrual cycle phase on face preferences. *Archives of Sexual Behavior, 37*, 78–84.

Jones, B. C., Little, A. C., Boothroyd, L., DeBruine, L. M., Feinberg, D. R., Law Smith, M. J., et al. (2005). Commitment to relationships and preferences for femininity and apparent health in faces are strongest on days of the menstrual cycle when progesterone level is high. *Hormones and Behavior, 48*, 283–290.

Jones, B. C., Perrett, D. I., Little, A. C., Boothroyd, L., Cornwell, R. E., Feinberg, D. R., et al. (2005). Menstrual cycle, pregnancy and oral contraceptive use alter attraction to apparent health in faces. *Proceedings of the Royal Society B: Biological Sciences, 272*, 347–354.

Jones, B. C., Vukovic, J., Little, A. C., Roberts, S. C., & DeBruine, L. M. (2011). Circum-menopausal changes in women's preferences for sexually dimorphic shape cues in peer-aged faces. *Biological Psychology, 87*, 453–455.

Kendrick, K. M., & Dixson, A. F. (1985). Effects of oestradiol 17β, progesterone and testosterone upon proceptivity and receptivity in ovariectomized common marmosets (*Callithrix jacchus*). *Physiology and Behavior, 34*, 123–128.

Kirchengast, S., & Gartner, M. (2002). Changes in fat distribution (WHR) and body weight across the menstrual cycle. *Collegium Antropologicum, 26*, 47–57.

Koehler, N., Rhodes, G., Simmons, L. W., & Zebrowitz, L. A. (2006). Do cyclic changes in women's face preferences target cues to long-term health? *Social Cognition, 24*, 641–656.

Krug, R., Finn, M., Pietrowsky, R., Fehm, H. L., & Born, J. (1996). Jealousy, general creativity, and coping with social frustration during the menstrual cycle. *Archives of Sexual Behavior, 25*, 181–199.

Krug, R., Stamm, U., Pietrowsky, R., Fehm, H. L., & Born, J. (1994). Effects of menstrual cycle on creativity. *Psychoneuroendocrinology, 19*, 21–31.

Kuukasjärvi, S., Eriksson, C. J. P., Koskela, E., Mappes, T., Nissinen, K., & Rantala, M. J. (2004). Attractiveness of women's body odors over the menstrual cycle: The role of oral contraceptives and receiver sex. *Behavioral Ecology, 15*, 579–584.

Laeng, B., & Falkenberg, L. (2007). Women's pupillary responses to sexually significant others during the hormonal cycle. *Hormones and Behavior, 52*, 520–530.

Langlois, J. H., Roggman, L. A., & Musselman, L. (1994). What is average and what is not average about attractive faces. *Psychological Science, 5*, 214–219.

Latz, L. J. (1939). *The rhythm of sterility and fertility in women*. Chicago, IL: Latz Foundation.

Lee, R. B., & DeVore, I. (1968). *Man the hunter*. Oxford, England: Aldine.

Lie, H. C., Rhodes, G., & Simmons, L. W. (2008). Genetic diversity revealed in human faces. *Evolution, 62*, 2473–2486.

Little, A. C., Burriss, R. P., Tufte, A. D., & Jones, B. C. (2006). Hormone mediated preferences for bodies and faces. *Journal of Reproductive and Infant Psychology, 24*, 270.

Little, A. C., Cohen, D. L., Jones, B. C., & Belsky, J. (2007). Human preferences for facial masculinity change with relationship type and environmental harshness. *Behavioral Ecology and Sociobiology, 61*, 967–973.

Little, A. C., & Jones, B. C. (2011). Variation in facial masculinity and symmetry preferences across the menstrual cycle is moderated by relationship context. *Psychoneuroendocrinology, 37*, 999–1008.

Little, A. C., Jones, B. C., & Burriss, R. P. (2007). Preferences for masculinity in male bodies change across the menstrual cycle. *Hormones and Behavior, 51*, 633–639.

Little, A. C., Jones, B. C., Burt, D. M., & Perrett, D. I. (2007). Preferences for symmetry in faces change across the menstrual cycle. *Biological Psychology, 76*, 209–216.

Little, A. C., Jones, B. C., & DeBruine, L. M. (2008). Preferences for variation in masculinity in real male faces change across the menstrual cycle: Women prefer more masculine faces when they are more fertile. *Personality and Individual Differences, 45*, 478–482.

Little, A. C., Jones, B. C., Penton-Voak, I. S., Burt, D. M., & Perrett, D. I. (2002). Partnership status and the temporal context of relationships influence human female preferences for sexual dimorphism in male face shape. *Proceedings of the Royal Society B: Biological Sciences, 269*, 1095–1100.

López, H. H., Hay, A. C., & Conklin, P. H. (2009). Attractive men induce testosterone and cortisol release in women. *Hormones and Behavior, 56*, 84–92.

Lukaszewski, A. W., & Roney, J. R. (2009). Estimated hormones predict women's mate preferences for dominant personality traits. *Personality and Individual Differences, 47*, 191–196.

Macrae, C. N., Alnwick, K. A., Milne, A. B., & Schloerscheidt, A. M. (2002). Person perception across the menstrual cycle: Hormonal influences of social-cognitive functioning. *Psychological Science, 13*, 532–536.

Manning, J. T., Scutt, D., Whitehouse, G. H., & Leinster, S. J. (1997). Breast asymmetry and phenotypic quality in women. *Evolution and Human Behavior, 18*, 223–236.

Manning, J. T., Scutt, D., Whitehouse, G. H., Leinster, S. J., & Walton, J. M. (1996). Asymmetry and the menstrual cycle in women. *Ethology and Sociobiology, 17*, 129–143.

Manson, W. C. (1986). Sexual cyclicity and concealed ovulation. *Journal of Human Evolution, 15*, 21–30.

Marlowe, F. W. (2004). Is human ovulation concealed? Evidence from conception beliefs in a hunter-gatherer society. *Archives of Sexual Behavior, 33*, 427–432.

Matteo, S., & Rissman, E. F. (1984). Increased sexual activity during the midcycle portion of the human menstrual cycle. *Hormones and Behavior, 18*, 249–255.

Mazur, A., & Booth, A. (1998). Testosterone and dominance in men. *Behavioral and Brain Sciences, 21*, 353–397.

Miller, S. L., & Maner, J. K. (2010). Scent of a woman: Men's testosterone responses to olfactory ovulation cues. *Psychological Science, 21*, 276–283.

Miller, S. L., & Maner, J. K. (2011). Ovulation as a male mating prime: Subtle signs of women's fertility influence men's mating cognition and behavior. *Journal of Personality and Social Psychology, 100*, 295–308.

Miller, G. F., & Todd, P. M. (1998). Mate choice turns cognitive. *Trends in Cognitive Science, 2*, 190–198.

Miller, G., Tybur, J. M., & Jordan, B. D. (2007). Ovulatory cycle effects on tip earnings by lap dancers: Economic evidence for human estrus? *Evolution and Human Behavior, 28*, 375–381.

Møller, A. P., & Thornhill, R. (1998). Bilateral symmetry and sexual selection: A meta-analysis. *American Naturalist, 151*, 174–192.

Morris, N. M., & Udry, J. R. (1970). Variations in pedometer activity during the menstrual cycle. *Obstetrics and Gynecology, 35*, 199–201.

Morris, N. M., & Udry, J. R. (1982). Epidemiological patterns of sexual behavior in the menstrual cycle. In R. C. Friedman (Ed.), *Behavior and the menstrual cycle* (pp. 129–154). New York: Marcel Dekker.

Nunn, C. L. (1999). The evolution of exaggerated sexual swellings in primates and the graded-signal hypothesis. *Animal Behavior, 58*, 229–246.

O'Toole, A. J., Deffenbacher, K. A., Valentin, D., McKee, K., Huff, D., & Abdi, H. (1998). The perception of face gender: The role of stimulus structure in recognition and classification. *Memory and Cognition, 26*, 146–160.

Pawłowski, B. (1999). Loss of oestrus and concealed ovulation in human evolution: The case against the sexual selection hypothesis. *Current Anthropology, 40*, 257–276.

Pawlowski, B., & Jasienska, G. (2005). Women's preferences for sexual dimorphism in height depend on menstrual cycle phase and expected duration of relationship. *Biological Psychology, 70*, 38–43.

Penton-Voak, I. S., & Perrett, D. I. (2000). Female preference for male faces changes cyclically—Further evidence. *Evolution and Human Behavior, 21*, 39–48.

Penton-Voak, I. S., & Perrett, D. I. (2001). Male facial attractiveness: Perceived personality and shifting female preferences for male traits across the menstrual cycle. *Advances in the Study of Behavior, 30*, 219–259.

Penton-Voak, I. S., Perrett, D. I., Castles, D. L., Kobayashi, T., Burt, D. M., Murray, L. K., et al. (1999). Menstrual cycle alters face preference. *Nature, 399*, 741–742.

Perrett, D. I., Lee, K. J., Penton-Voak, I. S., Rowland, D. R., Yoshikawa, S., Burt, D. M., et al. (1998). Effects of sexual dimorphism on facial attractiveness. *Nature, 394*, 884–887.

Peters, M., Rhodes, G., & Simmons, L. W. (2008). Does attractiveness in men provide clues to semen quality? *Journal of Evolutionary Biology, 21*, 572–579.

Pillsworth, E. G., & Haselton, M. G. (2006). Male sexual attractiveness predicts differential ovulatory shifts in female extra-pair attraction and male mate retention. *Evolution and Human Behavior, 27*, 247–258.

Pipitone, R. N., & Gallup, G. G. (2008). Women's voice attractiveness varies across the menstrual cycle. *Evolution and Human Behavior, 29*, 268–274.

Platek, S. M., Burch, R. L., Panyavin, I. S., Wasserman, B. H., & Gallup, G. G. (2002). Reactions to children's faces—Resemblance affects males more than females. *Evolution and Human Behavior, 23*, 159–166.

Platek, S. M., Critton, S. R., Burch, R. L., Frederick, D. A., Myers, T. E., & Gallup, G. G. (2003). How much paternal resemblance is enough? Sex differences in hypothetical investment decisions but not in the detection of resemblance. *Evolution and Human Behavior, 24*, 81–87.

Provost, M. P., Quinsey, V. L., & Troje, N. F. (2008). Differences in gait across the menstrual cycle and their attractiveness to men. *Archives of Sexual Behavior, 37*, 598–604.

Puts, D. A. (2005). Mating context and menstrual phase affect women's preferences for male voice pitch. *Evolution and Human Behavior, 26*, 388–397.

Puts, D. A. (2006). Cyclic variation in women's preferences for masculine traits: Potential hormonal causes. *Human Nature, 17*, 114–127.

Puts, D. A., Bailey, D. H., Cárdenas, R. A., Burriss, R. P., Welling, L. L. M., Wheatley, J. R., et al. (2013). Women's attractiveness changes with estradiol and progesterone across the ovulatory cycle. *Hormones and Behavior, 63*(1), 13–19. http://dx.doi.org/10.1016/j.yhbeh.2012.11.007

Regan, P. C. (1996). Rhythms of desire: The association between menstrual cycle phases and female sexual desire. *The Canadian Journal of Human Sexuality, 5*, 145–156.

Rhodes, G., Chan, J., Zebrowitz, L. A., & Simmons, L. W. (2003). Does sexual dimorphism in human faces signal health? *Proceedings of the Royal Society B: Biological Sciences, 270*, S93–S95.

Rhodes, G., Simmons, L. W., & Peters, M. (2005). Attractiveness and sexual behavior: Does attractiveness enhance mating success? *Evolution and Human Behavior, 26*, 186–201.

Rikowski, A., & Grammer, K. (1999). Human body odour, symmetry and attractiveness. *Proceedings of the Royal Society B: Biological Sciences, 266*, 869–874.

Robbins, M. M. (1995). A demographic analysis of male life history and social structure of mountain gorillas. *Behaviour, 132*, 21–47.

Roberts, S. C., Gosling, L. M., Carter, V., & Petrie, M. (2008). MHC-correlated odour preferences in humans and the use of oral contraceptives. *Proceedings of the Royal Society B: Biological Sciences, 275*, 2715–2722.

Roberts, S. C., Havlicek, J., Flegr, J., Hruskova, M., Little, A. C., Jones, B. C., et al. (2004). Female facial attractiveness increases during the fertile phase of the menstrual cycle. *Proceedings of the Royal Society B: Biological Sciences, 271*, S270–S272.

Roberts, S. C., Little, A. C., Gosling, L. M., Perrett, D. I., Carter, V., Jones, B. C., et al. (2005). MHC-heterozygosity and human facial attractiveness. *Evolution and Human Behavior, 26*, 213–226.

Röder, S., Brewer, G., & Fink, B. (2009). Menstrual cycle shifts in women's self-perception and motivation: A daily report method. *Personality and Individual Differences, 47*, 616–619.

Ronay, R., & von Hippel, W. (2010). The presence of an attractive woman elevates testosterone and physical risk taking in young men. *Social Psychological and Personality Science, 1*, 57–64.

Roney, J. R., Lukaszewski, A. W., & Simmons, Z. L. (2007). Rapid endocrine responses of young men to social interactions with young women. *Hormones and Behavior, 52*, 326–333.

Roney, J. R., Mahler, S. V., & Maestripieri, D. (2003). Behavioral and hormonal responses of men to brief interactions with women. *Evolution and Human Behavior, 24*, 365–375.

Roney, J. R., & Simmons, Z. L. (2008). Women's estradiol predicts preference for facial cues of men's testosterone. *Hormones and Behavior, 53*, 14–19.

Roney, J. R., & Simmons, Z. L. (2012). Men smelling women: Null effects of exposure to ovulatory sweat on men's testosterone. *Evolutionary Psychology, 10*, 703–713.

Rosen, M. L., & López, H. H. (2009). Menstrual cycle shifts in attentional bias for courtship language. *Evolution and Human Behavior, 30*, 131–140.

Rubin, H. B., Henson, D. E., Falvo, R. E., & High, R. W. (1979). The relationship between men's endogenous levels of testosterone and their penile responses to erotic stimuli. *Behaviour Research and Therapy, 17*, 305–312.

Rupp, H. A., James, T. W., Ketterson, E. D., Sengelaub, D. R., Janssen, E., & Heiman, J. R. (2009). Neural activation in women in response to masculinized male faces: Mediation by hormones and psychosexual factors. *Evolution and Human Behavior, 30*, 1–10.

Schmitt, D. P., & Buss, D. M. (2001). Human mate poaching: Tactics and temptations for infiltrating existing mateships. *Interpersonal Relations and Group Processes, 80*, 894–917.

Schwarz, S., & Hassebrauck, M. (2008). Self-perceived and observed variations in women's attractiveness throughout the menstrual cycle—A diary study. *Evolution and Human Behavior, 29*, 282–288.

Scutt, D., & Manning, J. T. (1996). Symmetry and ovulation in women. *Human Reproduction, 11*, 2477–2480.

Shackelford, T. K., Besser, A., & Goetz, A. T. (2008). Personality, marital satisfaction, and probability of marital infidelity. *Individual Differences Research, 6*, 13–25.

Shackelford, T. K., Goetz, A. T., Buss, D. M., Euler, H. A., & Hoier, S. (2005). When we hurt the ones we love: Predicting violence against women from men's mate retention. *Personal Relationships, 12*, 447–463.

Sheldon, M. S., Cooper, M. L., Geary, D. C., Hoard, M., & DeSoto, M. C. (2006). Fertility cycle patterns in motives for sexual behavior. *Personality and Social Psychology Bulletin, 32*, 1659–1673.

Sillen-Tullberg, B., & Møller, A. P. (1993). The relationship between concealed ovulation and mating systems in anthropoid primates: A phylogenetic analysis. *American Naturalist, 141*, 1–25.

Singh, D., & Bronstad, P. M. (2001). Female body odour is a potential cue to ovulation. *Proceedings of the Royal Society B: Biological Sciences, 268*, 797–801.

Slob, A. K., Bax, C. M., Hop, W. C. J., Rowland, D. L., & van der Werff ten Bosch, J. J. (1996). Sexual arousability and the menstrual cycle. *Psychoneuroendocrinology, 21*, 545–558.

Smith, T. E., & Abbott, D. H. (1998). Behavioral discrimination between circumgenital odor from peri-ovulatory dominant and anovulatory female common marmosets (*Callithrix jacchus*). *American Journal of Primatology, 46*, 265–284.

Soler, C., Núñez, M., Gutiérrez, R., Núñez, J., Medina, P., Sancho, M., et al. (2003). Facial attractiveness in men provides clues to semen quality. *Evolution and Human Behavior, 24*, 199–207.

Soltis, J., Thomsen, R., Matsubayashi, K., & Takenaka, O. (2000). Infanticide by resident males and female counter-strategies in wild Japanese macaques (*Macaca fuscata*). *Behavioral Ecology and Sociobiology, 48*, 195–202.

Stanislaw, H., & Rice, F. J. (1988). Correlation between sexual desire and menstrual cycle characteristics. *Archives of Sexual Behavior, 17*, 499–508.

Strassmann, B. I. (1981). Sexual selection, paternal care, and concealed ovulation in humans. *Ethology and Sociobiology, 2*, 31–40.

Symons, D. (1979). *The evolution of human sexuality.* Oxford: Oxford University Press.

Thornhill, R., & Gangestad, S. W. (1993). Human facial beauty: Averageness, symmetry, and parasite resistance. *Human Nature, 4*, 237–269.

Thornhill, R., & Gangestad, S. W. (1999). The scent of symmetry: A human sex pheromone that signals fitness? *Evolution and Human Behavior, 20*, 175–201.

Thornhill, R., & Gangestad, S. W. (2003). Do women have evolved adaptation for extra-pair copulation? In E. Voland & K. Grammer (Eds.), *Evolutionary aesthetics* (pp. 341–368). Heidelberg: Springer.

Thornhill, R., & Gangestad, S. W. (2006). Facial sexual dimorphism, developmental stability, and susceptibility to disease in men and women. *Evolution and Human Behavior, 27*, 131–144.

Thornhill, R., & Gangestad, S. W. (2008). *The evolutionary biology of human female sexuality.* New York: Oxford University Press.

Thornhill, R., Gangestad, S. W., Miller, R., Scheyd, G., McCollough, J. K., & Franklin, M. (2003). Major histocompatibility complex genes, symmetry, and body scent attractiveness in men and women (*Homo sapiens*). *Behavioral Ecology, 14*, 668–678.

Thornhill, R., & Møller, A. P. (1997). Developmental stability, disease and medicine. *Biological Reviews, 72*, 497–548.

Turke, P. W. (1984). Effects of ovulatory concealment and synchrony on protohominid mating systems and parental roles. *Ethology and Sociobiology, 5*, 33–44.

van Schaik, C. P., Hodges, J. K., & Nunn, C. L. (2000). Paternity confusion and the ovarian cycles of female primates. In C. P. van Schaik & C. H. Janson (Eds.), *Infanticide by males and its implications* (pp. 361–387). Cambridge, MA: Cambridge University Press.

van Schaik, C. P., van Noordwijk, M. A., & Nunn, C. L. (1999). Sex and social evolution in primates. In P. C. Lee (Ed.), *Primate socioecology* (pp. 204–240). Cambridge: Cambridge University Press.

Volk, A., & Quinsey, V. L. (2002). The influence of infant facial cues on adoption preferences. *Human Nature, 13*, 437–455.

Vukovic, J., Jones, B. C., DeBruine, L. M., Little, A. C., Feinberg, D. R., & Welling, L. L. M. (2009). Circummenopausal effects on women's judgements of facial attractiveness. *Biology Letters, 5*, 62–64.

Wallen, K., & Zehr, J. L. (2004). Hormones and history: The evolution and development of primate female sexuality. *Journal of Sex Research, 41*, 101–112.

Waynforth, D. (1998). Fluctuating asymmetry and human male life-history traits in rural Belize. *Proceedings of the Royal Society B: Biological Sciences, 265*, 1497–1501.

Wedekind, C., & Füri, S. (1997). Body odour preferences in men and women: Do they aim for specific MHC combinations or simply heterozygosity? *Proceedings of the Royal Society B: Biological Sciences, 264*, 1471–1479.

Welling, L. L. M. (2013). Psychobehavioral effects of hormonal contraceptive use. *Evolutionary Psychology, 11*(3), 718–742.

Welling, L. L. M., Burriss, R. P., & Puts, D. A. (2011). Mate retention behavior modulates men's preferences for self-resemblance in infant faces. *Evolution and Human Behavior, 32*, 118–126.

Welling, L. L. M., Jones, B. C., DeBruine, L. M., Conway, C. A., Law Smith, M. J., Little, A. C., et al. (2007). Raised salivary testosterone in women is associated with increased attraction to masculine faces. *Hormones and Behavior, 52*, 156–161.

Wilcox, A. J., Baird, D. D., Dunson, D. B., McConnaughey, D. R., Kesner, J. S., & Weinberg, C. R. (2004). On the frequency of intercourse around ovulation: Evidence for biological influences. *Human Reproduction, 19*, 1539–1543.

Wildt, L., Kissler, S., Licht, P., & Becker, W. (1998). Sperm transport in the human female genital tract and its modulation by oxytocin as assessed by hysterosalpingoscintigraphy, hysterotonography, electrohysterography and Doppler sonography. *Human Reproduction Update, 4*, 655–666.

Wilson, M., & Daly, M. (1987). Risk of maltreatment of children living with stepparents. In R. J. Gelles & J. B. Lancaster (Eds.), *Child abuse and neglect: Biosocial dimensions* (pp. 215–232). Hawthorne, New York: Aldine de Gruyter.

Wilson, M., & Daly, M. (2002). Infanticide. In M. Pagel (Ed.), *Encyclopedia of evolution*. Oxford: Oxford University Press.

Wrangham, R. (1993). The evolution of sexuality in chimpanzees and bonobos. *Human Nature, 4*, 47–79.

Zervomanolakis, I., Ott, H. W., Müller, J., Seeber, B. E., Friess, S. C., Mattle, V., et al. (2009). Uterine mechanisms of ipsilateral directed spermatozoa transport: Evidence for a contribution of the utero-ovarian countercurrent system. *European Journal of Obstetrics and Gynecology and Reproductive Biology, 144*, S45–S49.

Zillmann, D., Schweitzer, K. J., & Mundorf, N. (1994). Menstrual cycle variation of women's interest in erotica. *Archives of Sexual Behavior, 23*, 579–597.

Zitzmann, M., & Nieschlag, E. (2001). Testosterone levels in healthy men and the relation to behavioural and physical characteristics: Facts and constructs. *European Journal of Endocrinology, 144*, 183–197.

Women's Preferences for Male Facial Features

14

Lisa M. DeBruine

Human Face Preferences

Humans face perception is highly specialized and a focus of much research in diverse areas (Little, Jones, & DeBruine, 2011a). One area of particular interest is whether and how face perception functions in mate choice. Opposite-sex face preferences are proposed to function, at least in part, to identify appropriate mates (Little, Jones, & DeBruine, 2011b; Thornhill & Gangestad, 1999). Because an ideal mate for both men and women is one who is healthy, fertile, and investing, one might predict few sex differences in preferences for traits that signal these attributes. Indeed, both men and women show preferences for traits that have been linked to health, such as symmetry and averageness (reviewed in Little et al., 2011b; Rhodes, 2006). The same prediction might be made for preferences for enhanced sex-typical characteristics (i.e., male masculinity and female femininity), but research shows that men tend to have strong, consistent preferences for feminine female faces, while women do not have strong, consistent preferences for masculine male faces (Perrett et al., 1998).

In this chapter, I will briefly review the evidence for similarity between women's and men's face preferences before focusing on women's preferences for male masculinity. First, I will review the evidence for a sex difference in preferences for exaggerated sex-typical characteristics in opposite-sex faces. Next, I will outline the trade-off theory (Gangestad & Simpson, 2000) and evidence supporting this explanation for systematic variation in women's preferences for male masculinity. Finally, I will describe some of the controversy surrounding certain aspects of this theory.

Sex Similarity in Face Preferences

Symmetry

Symmetry is proposed to be a useful proxy for health and quality because levels of fluctuating asymmetry (i.e., nondirectional deviations from perfect symmetry) increase when organisms are subject to a wide range of stressors during development, such as pathogens or genetic diseases (Thornhill & Møller, 1997). While some have proposed that preferences for symmetry are simply an artifact of human visual perception (Enquist & Arak, 1994; Enquist & Johnstone, 1997), both men and women prefer symmetry in upright, but not inverted, opposite-sex faces (Little & Jones, 2003). Indeed, the correlation between measured asymmetry and attractiveness judgments is same for male and female faces (Jones et al., 2001). Additionally, while ecological factors and individual differences affect the extent of preferences for symmetry, both men

14

L.M. DeBruine (✉)
Institute of Neuroscience and Psychology, University of Glasgow, Scotland G12 8QB, UK
e-mail: lisa.debruine@glasgow.ac.uk

and women in the UK and in the Hadza tribe of Tanzania prefer symmetry in opposite-sex faces to the same extent (Little, Apicella, & Marlowe, 2007). These findings suggest that symmetry preferences function similarly for men and women.

Averageness

Averageness (i.e., similarity to the majority of faces in a population) is proposed to be a proxy for genetic diversity, which is linked to increased resistance to pathogens and a lower risk of deleterious allele combination from inbreeding (Thornhill & Gangestad, 1993). Indeed, facial averageness is associated with both heterozygosity of the major histocompatibility complex (Lie, Rhodes, & Simmons, 2008) and good medical health (Rhodes et al., 2001). The effect of facial averageness on both men's and women's perceptions of male and female facial attractiveness is so profound that early researchers suggested that facial attractiveness *is* simply averageness (Langlois & Roggman, 1990). While subsequent research has identified components of attractiveness that are not explained by averageness (DeBruine, Jones, Unger, Little, & Feinberg, 2007; Perrett, May, & Yoshikawa, 1994), averageness remains a powerful contributor to perceptions of attractiveness, even after controlling for the increased symmetry and skin smoothness that characterize average faces (Jones, DeBruine, & Little, 2007).

Facial Adiposity

Body weight is strongly linked to health (reviewed in Coetzee, Perrett, & Stephen, 2009). While most research on preferences for cues to weight focuses on perceptions of bodies (Tovée & Cornelissen, 2001; Tovée, Reinhaardt, Emery, & Cornelissen, 1998), facial adiposity also has significant effects on perceptions of facial attractiveness. Both men and women judge both men and women with intermediate facial adiposity to be more attractive than those

with very low or high facial adiposity (Coetzee et al., 2009). Men's facial adiposity has been linked with both immune response and women's judgments of men's facial attractiveness (Rantala, Coetzee, et al., 2012).

Sex Differences in Face Preferences

Female Femininity Versus Male Masculinity

Early research on the effects of increasing sexual dimorphism on facial attractiveness (Perrett et al., 1998) proposed that exaggerated sex-typical face shape should be preferred by both men and women because female femininity signals fertility and health (Barber, 1995), while male masculinity signals immunocompetence and dominance (Thornhill & Gangestad, 1996). However, the first empirical evidence showed that both female and male faces with feminized shape were preferred to the same faces with masculinized shape (Perrett et al., 1998; Rhodes, Hickford, & Jeffery, 2000).

Subsequent research using a wide variety of methods confirms the strong male preferences for feminized female faces (reviewed in Little et al., 2011b; Rhodes, 2006). However, subsequent research on women's preferences for male masculinity has shown considerable variation. While this variation is sometimes attributed to differences in methodology (Rennels, Bronstad, & Langlois, 2008; Rhodes, 2006), even studies using the same computer-graphic methods have variously observed general preferences for masculinity (DeBruine et al., 2006; Feinberg, DeBruine, Jones, & Little, 2008; Johnston, Hagel, Franklin, Fink, & Grammer, 2001; Little, Cohen, Jones, & Belsky, 2007; Little, Jones, DeBruine, & Feinberg, 2008), general preferences for femininity (Little, Burt, Penton-Voak, & Perrett, 2001; Little, Jones, Penton-Voak, Burt, & Perrett, 2002; Penton-Voak et al., 1999, 2003; Perrett et al., 1998; Rhodes et al., 2000; Welling et al., 2007; Welling, Jones, & DeBruine, 2008, Study 1), and no significant preference for masculinity or femininity

(Cornwell et al., 2004; Swaddle & Riersen, 2002; Welling et al., 2008, Study 2).

Further research has shown systematic variation between populations (e.g., DeBruine, Jones, Crawford, Welling, & Little, 2010; Penton-Voak, Jacobson, & Trivers, 2004), between individuals (e.g., DeBruine, Jones, Tybur, Lieberman, & Griskevicius, 2010; Little et al., 2001, Little et al., 2002; Smith et al., 2009), and even within individuals (e.g., Little, DeBruine, & Jones, 2011; Little & Mannion, 2006; Penton-Voak et al., 1999). This variation is consistent with and has been predicted by trade-off theory (Gangestad & Simpson, 2000).

Trade-Off Theory

Trade-off theory (Gangestad & Simpson, 2000) is the dominant explanation for variation in women's preferences for male masculinity. This theory posits that women's masculinity preferences are a function of factors that influence how they weigh the various costs and benefits signaled by male masculinity (for comprehensive reviews, see Fink & Penton-Voak, 2002; Gangestad & Simpson, 2000; Jones et al., 2008; Little et al., 2011b).

Heritable (i.e., genetic) health is a major benefit posited to be signaled by male masculinity. Male facial masculinity is associated with reduced biomarkers of oxidative stress (Gangestad, Merriman, & Emery Thompson, 2010), increased health scores based on medical records (Rhodes, Chan, Zebrowitz, & Simmons, 2003), decreased incidence and duration of respiratory illness (Thornhill & Gangestad, 2006), and increased vaccine antibody response (Rantala, Coetzee, et al., 2012). Male masculinity is also correlated with other putative signals of heritable health, such as symmetry (Gangestad & Thornhill, 2003; Little, Jones, Waitt, et al., 2008).

While male masculinity may signal the benefit of heritable health, it also signals the potential cost of personality characteristics that are detrimental to committed relationships. Masculine male faces are ascribed traits such as low warmth, low emotionality, poor quality as a parent, low

cooperativeness, and dishonesty (Boothroyd, Jones, Burt, & Perrett, 2007; Perrett et al., 1998). Masculine men are both perceived to have (Kruger, 2006) and report having (Rhodes, Simmons, & Peters, 2005) a greater interest in short-term relationships than their more feminine-faced peers. Although testosterone has a complicated relationship to facial masculinity (Pound, Penton-Voak, & Surridge, 2009), testosterone is also related to family-oriented behavior, such as increased rates of divorce and marital problems (Booth & Dabbs, 1993) and decreased emotional responses to infant distress (Fleming, Corter, Stallings, & Steiner, 2002).

Given these potential benefits and costs associated with masculine male traits, a strong prediction of trade-off theory is that factors affecting the relative importance of heritable health and relationship investment will correspondingly influence women's preferences for male masculinity. The next part will briefly review some of the substantial body of evidence for this proposal.

Systematic Variation in Women's Masculinity Preferences

Hormone-Mediated Preferences

One of the primary predictions of trade-off theory follows from the fact that women are only able to translate a male partner's heritable health into health offspring when they are fertile. Therefore, women may have enhanced preferences for masculine men when they are fertile versus nonfertile. This predictions have been tested in three main ways: fertility changes across the menstrual cycle (reviewed in Jones et al., 2008), fertility changes associated with oral contraceptives (reviewed in Alvergne & Lummaa, 2010), and fertility changes across women's lifespan (Little et al., 2010).

Despite some failures to observe changes in women's mate preferences across the menstrual cycle (e.g., Harris, 2011), such changes are well established (reviewed in DeBruine, Jones, Frederick, et al., 2010; Gangestad & Thornhill, 2008; Jones et al., 2008). Early research determined that women's masculinity preferences were higher on days of the menstrual cycle where the probability of pregnancy was high (e.g., the late follicular phase) versus days of the menstrual cycle where the probability of pregnancy was low (e.g., the mid-luteal phase; Johnston et al., 2001; Penton-Voak & Perrett, 2000; Penton-Voak et al., 1999). Later research focused on establishing the hormonal mechanisms responsible for this difference (Jones et al., 2005; Roney, Simmons, & Gray, 2011; Welling et al., 2007) and determining the neurobiological correlates (Rupp et al., 2009). The predictions from trade-off theory have been refined as evidence suggests that cyclic shifts in masculinity preference are more pronounced in partnered women and when women judge men for short-term relationships (Penton-Voak et al., 1999).

In addition to a large body of evidence showing cyclic shifts in preferences for male facial masculinity, corroborating evidence from judgments of male vocal (Feinberg et al., 2006; Puts, 2005), body (Little, Jones, & Burriss, 2007), olfactory (Grammer, 1993), personality (Lukaszewski & Roney, 2009), and behavioral (Gangestad, Garver-Apgar, Simpson, & Cousins, 2007; Gangestad, Simpson, Cousins, Garver-Apgar, & Christensen, 2004) masculinity also support this prediction from trade-off theory.

The oral contraceptive pill reduces fertility and many of the hormonal changes across the menstrual cycle. Therefore, oral contraceptive use is likely to also be associated with changes in either general preferences for masculinity or changes to the pattern of cyclic shifts in masculinity preferences. Such effects have been observed (Feinberg et al., 2008; Little et al., 2002), although whether these effects are due to the pill itself or other factors confounded with pill use is far from certain (reviewed in Alvergne & Lummaa, 2010).

Puberty and menopause mark major changes in women's fertility status; trade-off theory would predict that women's masculinity preferences would be weaker before puberty and after menopause. In line with this prediction, male facial masculinity preferences are higher in reproductive-aged women than in prepubescent girls or postmenopausal women (Little et al., 2010). Another study assessing circummenopausal women's preferences for peer-aged male faces found that, controlling for age, premenopausal women showed stronger preferences for male facial masculinity than did postmenopausal women (Jones, Vukovic, Little, Roberts, & DeBruine, 2011).

Although an exhaustive review of the research on hormone-mediated preferences for male masculinity is outside the score of this chapter, several excellent reviews (Alvergne & Lummaa, 2010; Gangestad & Thornhill, 2008; Jones et al., 2008) and a comprehensive meta-analysis (Gildersleeve, Haselton, & Fales, 2014) give overviews of this area and provide evidence supporting strong predictions from trade-off theory (but see Wood, Kressel, Joshi, & Louie, 2014).

Condition Dependence

A related prediction of trade-off theory is that, if male masculinity signals both high health and low relationship commitment, then attractive, high-quality women may show stronger preferences for masculine men because they can either obtain more investment from masculine men than can lower-quality women or they can more easily replace a deserting mate. Supporting this prediction, several studies have found that women who judge themselves as attractive (Little et al., 2001) or have attractive body shapes (Penton-Voak et al., 2003; Smith et al., 2009) have stronger male facial masculinity preferences than their relatively less attractive peers. Experimental evidence also supports this prediction; women who are shown pictures of very attractive women report both lower self-rated attractiveness and lower male facial masculinity preferences than women who are shown pictures of relatively unattractive women (Little & Mannion, 2006).

Sexual Strategy

A straightforward prediction of trade-off theory is that women should prefer masculine men more in the context of short-term relationships than long-term relationships (Gangestad & Simpson,

2000). This is because the potential costs signaled by masculinity, namely, low relationship commitment, are a much less serious threat to short-term or extra-pair relationship than they are to long-term, committed relationships. The evidence supporting this prediction is very robust.

Research using computer-graphic manipulations of male facial masculinity has shown that women prefer more masculine faces when judging men in the context of a short-term relationship than in the context of a long-term relationship (Little et al., 2002; Penton-Voak et al., 2003), and this result has been replicated in a rural Malaysian population (Scott, Swami, Josephson, & Penton-Voak, 2008). Other research using the technique of q-sorting confirmed that, in a naturally varying set of faces, masculine male characteristics were preferred more for potential short-term mates than for potential long-term mates (Burt et al., 2007). This study also demonstrated that individual differences in sociosexual strategies also predicted face preferences; women with a greater preference for short-term relationships also showed a greater general preference for masculine male faces (Burt et al., 2007). In addition, research using facialmetric measurements of masculinity (i. e., increased jaw size and eyebrow ridge development) found that, although women did not show a general preference for masculine facial measurements, women with greater preferences for short-term relationships showed greater preferences for male faces with masculine measurements (Waynforth, Delwadia, & Camm, 2005).

In sum, the empirical evidence suggests that a major determinant of the degree to which women prefer masculine or feminine male facial characteristics is whether they are considering men for long-term or short-term relationships. This evidence is consistent with trade-off theory, as the putative costs signaled by masculine male faces are only important in long-term, committed relationships.

Pathogen-Linked Preferences

A final prediction of trade-off theory is that factors that increase the importance women place on offspring health will also cause women to increase their preferences for masculine men.

The threat of infectious disease may have been important for the evolution of many social behaviors, including mate preferences (Tybur & Gangestad, 2011) and group-related behaviors (Fincher & Thornhill, 2012). Evidence for a role of infectious disease in shaping women's masculinity preferences comes from three streams of research: individual differences in women's pathogen sensitivity, regional variation in pathogen prevalence, and experimental manipulation of pathogen concerns.

A first link between pathogens and masculinity preferences came from a study of the three domains of disgust: moral, sexual, and pathogen (Tybur, Lieberman, & Griskevicius, 2009). If male masculinity signals health to women, then women with greater concern about pathogens should show greater preferences for masculine men. Pathogen disgust, but not moral or sexual disgust, was positively correlated with women's masculinity preferences (DeBruine, Jones, Tybur, et al., 2010). This result was replicated in two separate studies, one using computer-graphic manipulations of masculinity and the other using naturally varying male masculinity. Subsequent studies have replicated and extended this finding for women's preferences for masculine faces, voices, and bodies (Jones et al., 2013). This study also found that women's pathogen disgust was positively correlated with their ratings of their current and ideal partner's masculinity.

While the previous studies implicated individual differences in concern about pathogens in individual variation in women's masculinity preference, regional differences in pathogen prevalence have also been implicated in population-level variation in women's masculinity preferences. A study of 30 Western, industrialized nations showed that women's average preferences for masculine male face shapes were correlated with a proxy measure for pathogen stress: a composite measure derived from World Health Organization statistics for mortality and life expectancy (DeBruine, Jones, Crawford, et al., 2010). Although initial reanalysis of these data suggested that regional variation in intrasexual competition might explain women's masculinity preferences better than regional variation in pathogen prevalence

(Brooks et al., 2011), further analyses controlling for regional variation in wealth, mating strategies, and homicide rates continued to show a significant relationship between health and women's masculinity preferences (DeBruine, Jones, Little, Crawford, & Welling, 2011). A new sample of women's masculinity preferences in 50 US states also replicated the relationship between health and women's masculinity preferences (DeBruine et al., 2011). Both the cross-national and cross-state data were later reanalyzed using published parasite stress measures (Fincher & Thornhill, 2012); parasite stress was positively and significantly correlated with masculinity preferences in both samples (DeBruine, Little, & Jones, 2012).

The final category of evidence for the predicted relationship between parasite stress and women's masculinity preferences comes from a study of experimental manipulation of pathogen concern (Little, DeBruine, et al., 2011). In this study, women were exposed to a slideshow of either pathogen-related stimuli, such as a moldy sandwich or an ill-looking person, or matched control stimuli, such as a non-moldy sandwich or a healthy-looking person (Curtis, Aunger, & Rabie, 2004). Women who viewed the pathogen-related stimuli subsequently showed stronger preferences for male facial masculinity than did women who saw the control stimuli. Interestingly, women's preferences for femininity in female faces were not affected by the pathogen-related stimuli, suggesting that priming pathogen concerns results in a change in face perception that functions for mate choice, rather than general social preference. A subsequent study showed that women reported stronger preferences for masculine male faces after being primed with pathogen concerns than after they were primed with resource concerns (Watkins, DeBruine, Little, Feinberg, & Jones, 2012), further supporting predictions from trade-off theory.

Controversy

While the evidence presented above for systematic variation in women's masculinity preferences is well-explained by and predicted from trade-off theory, the interpretation of these studies is not without controversy. Below, I will outline some of the main controversies: the validity of the immunocompetence handicap hypothesis, the link between testosterone and male facial masculinity, the link between male masculinity and attractiveness, and methods for measuring masculinity preferences. I will also describe corroborating evidence for masculinity preferences in other domains and links between mate preferences and actual mate choice.

The Immunocompetence Handicap Hypothesis

One potential mechanism for the link between masculinity and health is the immunocompetence handicap hypothesis (Folstad & Karter, 1992), which states that the immunosuppressant effects of testosterone (see (Roberts, 2004) for a meta-analytic review) act as a Zahavian handicap, honestly signaling a healthy immune system. The immunocompetence handicap hypothesis has attracted strong criticism on the basis that evidence for links between human male testosterone and immune function is weak (Boothroyd, Burt, & Lawson, 2009; Klein, 2000; Scott, Clark, Boothroyd, & Penton-Voak, 2013).

More recent research directly assessing links between men's testosterone levels and biomarkers of immune function have found a strong positive relationship between testosterone and immune response to a hepatitis B vaccine (Rantala, Moore, et al., 2012). However, this response was modulated by cortisol levels, such that men with lower levels of this stress hormone showed a stronger relationship between testosterone and immune response. This evidence supports an alternative formulation of the immunocompetence handicap hypothesis, the stress-linked immunocompetence handicap hypothesis (Evans, Goldsmith, & Norris, 2000; Møller, 1995). Further evidence for the stress-linked immunocompetence handicap hypothesis comes from studies showing that women's preferences for markers of testosterone in men's faces are strongest in men with low cortisol levels (Moore et al., 2011).

However, the (stress-linked) immunocompetence handicap hypothesis is only one possible mechanism for the links between masculine male traits and health or parental investment that are essential for trade-off theory. Regardless of the mechanisms, several lines of evidence do point to a link between masculinity and measures of potentially heritable health (Gangestad et al., 2010; Rantala, Coetzee, et al., 2012; Rhodes et al., 2003; Thornhill & Gangestad, 2006). Additionally, testosterone is thought to mediate the trade-off between men's mating effort and parental investment. Consistent with this idea, men with high testosterone have been shown to have increased mating success (Peters, Simmons, & Rhodes, 2008), decreased relationship success (Booth & Dabbs, 1993), and decreased emotional responses to infant distress (Fleming et al., 2002).

Testosterone and Masculinity

Another controversy surrounding women's masculinity preferences and trade-off theory is that masculinity and testosterone are not related in a straightforward way. The immunocompetence handicap hypothesis (and the stress-linked version) requires some link between facial masculinity and testosterone. While the evidence that testosterone plays a role in the development of masculine facial features at puberty is strong (Verdonck, 1999), the evidence for a link between male facial masculinity and adult circulating levels of testosterone is weak, at best. While some studies have found significant (Penton-Voak & Chen, 2004) or marginally significant (Rantala, Coetzee, et al., 2012) correlations between measured testosterone and rated facial masculinity, others have found no significant correlation (Neave, Laing, Fink, & Manning, 2003; Peters et al., 2008; Roney, Hanson, Durante, & Maestripieri, 2006).

However, there is some indication that measures of prenatal or reactive testosterone may be more closely linked to male facial masculinity. Research on men's responses to a competitive task showed that facial masculinity was positively associated with the extent to which winning a rigged competition increased men's testosterone, but was not related to the same men's baseline testosterone levels (Pound et al.,

2009). Second-to-fourth digit ratios indicating higher levels of prenatal testosterone are also associated with higher masculinity ratings of male faces (Neave et al., 2003).

Masculinity and Attractiveness

Some researchers have cited the lack of stable, general masculinity preferences across a population of women as evidence that male masculinity is not important n women's mate choice (Scott, Pound, Stephen, Clark, & Penton-Voak, 2010; Stephen et al., 2012). For example, a shape-based measure of facial masculinity was not correlated with women's ratings of the attractiveness of unmanipulated male faces, although human masculinity ratings of these same faces were positively correlated with attractiveness ratings (Scott et al., 2010). While the authors concluded that the geometric morphometric shape-based measure of masculinity was more objective than human ratings, the relationship between this new "objective" measure and human perception has not yet been investigated.

Many of the studies that question the role of masculinity in women's mate preferences have cited evidence that other characteristics, such as skin color (Stephen et al., 2012) or facial adiposity (Rantala, Coetzee, et al., 2012), are more closely linked to women's attractiveness judgments than masculinity is. However, these results are unsurprising, given that theory and evidence both suggest that women's preferences for masculinity are much more variable than their preferences for other traits that show a consistent directional preference (reviewed in Little et al., 2011b; Rhodes, 2006). The lack of a general, directional preference for male masculinity is certainly not indicative that masculinity plays no role in women's preferences. Indeed, the large body of evidence about systematic variation in women's masculinity preferences reviewed in the previous part suggests that this is exactly what one would expect.

Measuring Masculinity Preferences

Methodological issues are frequently cited as possible sources of variable general masculinity

Fig. 14.1 Example of a masculinized (*left*), unmanipulated (*center*), and feminized (*right*) version of the same individual

Fig. 14.2 An average of 50 male faces (*center*) and averages of the 15 men rated as most masculine (*left*) and least masculine (*right*)

preferences (Rennels et al., 2008; Rhodes, 2006; Scott et al., 2013). However, several lines of evidence suggest that methodological differences between studies contribute little to reports of systematic variation in women's masculinity preferences.

For example, in an influential meta-analytic review, Rhodes suggested that the use of composite faces artificially increases preferences for male femininity, as masculine face shape would be incompatible with the smoother, more feminine skin texture of composite faces (Rhodes, 2006). However, experimental investigation of this claim showed that composite faces actually elicit stronger, not weaker, preferences for masculinity than individual faces (Scott & Penton-Voak, 2011). While methodological issues did affect the level of general masculinity preferences, they did so in a way that could not explain away the somewhat surprising finding from many studies that women, on average, prefer more feminine than average male face shapes (e.g., Penton-Voak et al., 1999; Perrett et al., 1998; Rhodes et al., 2000).

Another example of methodological critique is a study comparing manipulated and perceived masculinity (Rennels et al., 2008). In this study, preferences for an average male face that had manipulated along a vector representing the two-dimensional shape differences between an average male face and an average female face (similar to those in Fig. 14.1) were compared with preferences for composite faces of men who had been rated as high or low in masculinity (similar to those in Fig. 14.2). General preferences for femininity were observed for the manipulated masculinity stimuli, while general preferences for masculinity were observed for the perceived masculinity stimuli (Rennels et al., 2008). However, the stimuli differed not only in facial appearance but also in apparent hairstyle. A replication of this study using both hair-masked and unmasked versions of the original stimuli replicated these results for the unmasked stimuli but showed consistent general femininity preferences for both types of hair-masked stimuli (DeBruine, Jones, Smith, & Little, 2010). These results are consistent with previous research showing correlated masculinity preferences using three different types of masculinity manipulations, including methods similar to the two explained above (DeBruine et al., 2006).

In addition, many studies using computer-graphic manipulations of masculinity have been replicated using alternative methods such as rated masculinity of unmanipulated faces. For example, the same link between women's masculinity preferences and pathogen disgust, but not moral or sexual disgust, was found using both manipulated and rated masculinity (DeBruine, Jones, Tybur, et al., 2010). Additionally, cyclic shifts in women's masculinity preferences have been replicated using masculinity ratings of unmanipulated men's face images (Little, Jones, & DeBruine, 2008).

While methodological difference between studies are clearly a potential source of differences in average, general preferences for masculinity, these differences are generally unimportant when assessing systematic differences (i.e., between-individual differences) in women's masculinity preferences. Unless a method produces masculinity preferences that are so strong or so weak that ceiling or floor effects may limit individual variation, all available evidence suggests that the various techniques for measuring women's masculinity preferences produce results that are consistent with one another and that strongly support predictions from trade-off theory (Little et al., 2011b).

Corroborating Evidence

In addition to studies directly exploring the effects of methodological differences between studies, several additional lines of evidence support the findings of studies of women's systematic variation in masculinity preferences.

While studies of facial masculinity have been criticized for methodological issues, as described above, corroborating evidence from studies of masculinity in other domains support many of these findings. For example, cyclic shifts in women's masculinity preferences are found, not only for faces, but also for masculine characteristics in men's voices (Feinberg et al., 2006; Puts, 2005,

2006), body shapes (Little, Jones, et al., 2007) (Feinberg et al., 2008; Gangestad et al., 2004; Provost, Kormos, Kosakoski, & Quinsey, 2006), odor (Grammer, 1993), personality (Lukaszewski & Roney, 2009), and behavior (Gangestad et al., 2004, 2007).

Indeed, many of the findings for systematic variation in women's facial masculinity preferences described in part "Facial Adiposity" of this chapter have been replicated in the vocal domain (reviewed in Puts, Jones, & DeBruine, 2012). In addition to consistent cyclic shifts in vocal masculinity preferences (Feinberg et al., 2006; Puts, 2005, 2006), consistent condition-dependent vocal masculinity preferences have also been observed (Feinberg et al., 2011; Vukovic et al., 2008). Vocal masculinity preferences are also related to pathogen concerns in the same way as facial masculinity preferences (Jones et al., 2013).

Masculinity Preferences and Partner Choice

A final, potential critique of trade-off theory is that mate preferences that are not translated into mate choice cannot influence the evolution of preferences via sexual selection. The extent to which experimentally measured mate preferences in the laboratory predict actual mate choices in the real world is a critical research question with far-reaching implications for theories of both the function and evolution of human mate choice. Indeed, some researchers have suggested that different cognitive processes underlie mate preferences and mate choices (Eastwick, Eagly, Finkel, & Johnson, 2011; Todd, Penke, Fasolo, & Lenton, 2007), leading to the idea that (at least some) mate preferences reflect psychological processes that are unrelated to mate choice and, therefore, cannot have evolved through sexual selection.

However, initial attempts to answer this question have found links between mate preferences and mate choice. Women's rating of both their actual partner and ideal partner is positively correlated with their masculinity preferences as measures by various computer-graphic manipulation techniques (DeBruine et al., 2006).

Additionally, women's pathogen disgust is not only positively correlated with their masculinity preferences but also with their ratings of their current and ideal partner's masculinity (Jones et al., 2013).

Further research on actual romantic couples suggests that men's self-rated masculinity predicts their female partner's preferences for computer-graphic-manipulated masculinity (Burriss, Welling, & Puts, 2011). A recent study using perceptual rating of the masculinity of color-standardized versions of couples' faces (so that only shape masculinity/femininity could be assessed) showed that both men's and women's preferences for masculinity/femininity in opposite-sex faces were correlated with the masculinity or femininity of their romantic partner (DeBruine, Fincher, Watkins, Little, & Jones, 2012).

While these findings are only preliminary evidences, these findings begin to answer these questions by demonstrating direct links between actual mate choices and experimentally measured face preferences, providing critical evidence to support theories of both the function and evolution of human mate choice.

Conclusions

Due to human biparental care, we might expect few differences in the characteristics that men and women find attractive in opposite-sex faces. Indeed, evidence shows that both men and women prefer opposite-sex faces with characteristics that are likely to signal current or long-term health, such as symmetry, averageness, and a healthy weight. However, while men have strong preferences for feminine female faces, women do not show the strong, consistent preferences for male masculinity that were initially predicted. Trade-off theory suggests that this may be due to male masculinity signaling both positive traits (e.g., health) and negative traits (e.g., low investment). In this chapter, I reviewed the substantial evidence for the predictions of trade-off theory and outlined some of the more controversial aspects of this theory. Despite disagreement among researchers about the exact mechanisms involved, trade-off theory has shown great utility in predicting the circumstances under which women prefer masculine male traits more or less.

Acknowledgement LMD's research on human mate preferences is supported by a grant from the UK Economic and Social Research Council (ES/I031022/1).

References

Alvergne, A., & Lummaa, V. (2010). Does the contraceptive pill alter mate choice in humans? *Trends in Ecology and Evolution, 25*(3), 171–179. doi:10.1016/j.tree.2009.08.003.

Barber, N. (1995). The evolutionary psychology of physical attractiveness: Sexual selection and human morphology. *Ethology and Sociobiology, 16*, 395–424.

Booth, A., & Dabbs, J. M. J. (1993). Testosterone and men's marriages. *Social Forces, 72*, 463–477.

Boothroyd, L. G., Burt, D. M., & Lawson, J. F. (2009). Testing immunocompetence explanations of male facial masculinity. *Journal of Evolutionary Psychology, 7*(1), 65–81. doi:10.1556/JEP.7.2009.1.7.

Boothroyd, L. G., Jones, B. C., Burt, D. M., & Perrett, D. I. (2007). Partner characteristics associated with masculinity, health and maturity in male faces. *Personality and Individual Differences, 43*, 1161–1173. doi:10.1016/j.paid.2007.03.008.

Brooks, R., Scott, I. M. L., Maklakov, A. A., Kasumovic, M. M., Clark, A. P., & Penton-Voak, I. S. (2011). National income inequality predicts women's preferences for masculinized faces better than health does. *Proceedings of the Royal Society of London B, 278*(1707), 810–814. doi:10.1098/rspb.2010.0964.

Burriss, R. P., Welling, L. L. M., & Puts, D. A. (2011). Mate-preference drives mate-choice: Men's self-rated masculinity predicts their female partner's preference for masculinity. *Personality and Individual Differences, 51*(8), 1023–1027. doi:10.1016/j.paid.2011.08.018.

Burt, D. M., Kentridge, R. W., Good, J. M. M., Perrett, D. I., Tiddeman, B. P., & Boothroyd, L. G. (2007). Q-cgi: New techniques to assess variation in perception applied to facial attractiveness. *Proceedings of the Royal Society of London B, 274*, 2779–2784.

Coetzee, V., Perrett, D. I., & Stephen, I. D. (2009). Facial adiposity: A cue to health? *Perception, 38*(11), 1700–1711. doi:10.1068/p6423.

Cornwell, R. E., Boothroyd, L. G., Burt, D. M., Feinberg, D. R., Jones, B. C., Little, A. C., et al. (2004). Concordant preferences for opposite-sex signals? Human pheromones and facial characteristics. *Proceedings of the Royal Society of London B, 271*, 635–640.

Curtis, V., Aunger, R., & Rabie, T. (2004). Evidence that disgust evolved to protect from risk of disease.

Proceedings of the Royal Society of London B, 271 (Suppl), S131–S133. doi:10.1098/rsbl.2003.0144.

DeBruine, L. M., Fincher, C. L., Watkins, C. D., Little, A. C., & Jones, B. C. (2012). Preference versus Choice: Do face preferences predict actual partner choice? In *Human Behavior and Evolution Society Conference in Albuquerque*. New Mexico.

DeBruine, L. M., Jones, B. C., Crawford, J. R., Welling, L. L. M., & Little, A. C. (2010). The health of a nation predicts their mate preferences: Cross-cultural variation in women's preferences for masculinized male faces. *Proceedings of the Royal Society of London B.* doi:10.1098/rspb.2009.2184.

DeBruine, L. M., Jones, B. C., Frederick, D. A., Haselton, M. G., Penton-voak, I. S., & Perrett, D. I. (2010). Evidence for menstrual cycle shifts in women's preferences for masculinity: A response to Harris (in press) "Menstrual Cycle and Facial Preferences Reconsidered". *Evolutionary Psychology, 8*(4), 768–775.

DeBruine, L. M., Jones, B. C., Little, A. C., Boothroyd, L. G., Perrett, D. I., Penton-Voak, I. S., et al. (2006). Correlated preferences for facial masculinity and ideal or actual partner's masculinity. *Proceedings of the Royal Society of London B, 273*, 1355–1360. doi:10.1098/rspb.2005.3445.

DeBruine, L. M., Jones, B. C., Little, A. C., Crawford, J. R., & Welling, L. L. M. (2011). Further evidence for regional variation in women's masculinity preferences. *Proceedings of the Royal Society B: Biological Sciences, 278*(1707), 813–814. doi:10.1098/rspb.2010.2200.

DeBruine, L. M., Jones, B. C., Smith, F. G., & Little, A. C. (2010). Are attractive men's faces masculine or feminine? The importance of controlling confounds in face stimuli. *Journal of Experimental Psychology: Human Perception and Performance, 36*(3), 751–758. doi:10.1037/a0016457.

DeBruine, L. M., Jones, B. C., Tybur, J. M., Lieberman, D., & Griskevicius, V. (2010). Women's preferences for masculinity in male faces are predicted by pathogen disgust, but not by moral or sexual disgust. *Evolution and Human Behavior, 31*(1), 69–74. doi:10.1016/j.evolhumbehav.2009.09.003.

DeBruine, L. M., Jones, B. C., Unger, L., Little, A. C., & Feinberg, D. R. (2007). Dissociating averageness and attractiveness: Attractive faces are not always average. *Journal of Experimental Psychology: Human Perception and Performance, 33*, 1420–1430.

DeBruine, L. M., Little, A. C., & Jones, B. C. (2012). Extending parasite-stress theory to variation in human mate preferences. *The Behavioral and Brain Sciences, 35*(2), 86–87. doi:10.1017/S0140525X11000987.

Eastwick, P. W., Eagly, A. H., Finkel, E. J., & Johnson, S. E. (2011). Implicit and explicit preferences for physical attractiveness in a romantic partner: A double dissociation in predictive validity. *Journal of Personality and Social Psychology, 101*(5), 993–1011. doi:10.1037/a0024061.

Enquist, M., & Arak, A. (1994). Symmetry, beauty and evolution. *Nature, 372*, 169–172.

Enquist, M., & Johnstone, R. A. (1997). Generalization and the evolution of symmetry preferences. *Proceedings of the Royal Society B: Biological Sciences, 264*(1386), 1345–1348. doi:10.1098/rspb.1997.0186.

Evans, M. R., Goldsmith, A. R., & Norris, S. R. A. (2000). The effects of testosterone on antibody production and plumage coloration in male house sparrows (Passer domesticus). *Behavioral Ecology and Sociobiology, 47*(3), 156–163. doi:10.1007/s002650050006.

Feinberg, D. R., DeBruine, L. M., Jones, B. C., & Little, A. C. (2008). Correlated preferences for men's facial and vocal masculinity. *Evolution and Human Behavior, 29*(4), 233–241.

Feinberg, D. R., Debruine, L. M., Jones, B. C., Little, A. C., O'Connor, J. J. M., & Tigue, C. C. (2011). Women's self-perceived health and attractiveness predict their male vocal masculinity preferences in different directions across short- and long-term relationship contexts. *Behavioral Ecology and Sociobiology, 66* (3), 413–418. doi:10.1007/s00265-011-1287-y.

Feinberg, D. R., Jones, B. C., Law Smith, M. J., Moore, F. R., DeBruine, L. M., Cornwell, R. E., et al. (2006). Menstrual cycle, trait estrogen level and masculinity preferences in the human voice. *Hormones and Behavior, 49*(2), 215–222. doi:10.1016/j.yhbeh.2005.07.004.

Fincher, C. L., & Thornhill, R. (2012). Parasite-stress promotes in-group assortative sociality: The cases of strong family ties and heightened religiosity. *The Behavioral and Brain Sciences, 35*(2), 61–79. doi:10.1017/S0140525X11000021.

Fink, B., & Penton-Voak, I. S. (2002). Evolutionary psychology of facial attractiveness. *Current Directions in Psychological Science, 11*, 154–158.

Fleming, A. S., Corter, C., Stallings, J., & Steiner, M. (2002). Testosterone and prolactin are associated with emotional responses to infant cries in new fathers. *Hormones and Behavior, 42*, 399–413. doi:10.1006/hbeh.2002.1840.

Folstad, I., & Karter, A. J. (1992). Parasites, bright males, and the immunocompetence handicap. *The American Naturalist, 139*(3), 603–622. doi:10.1086/281919.

Gangestad, S. W., Garver-Apgar, C. E., Simpson, J. A., & Cousins, A. J. (2007). Changes in women's mate preferences across the ovulatory cycle. *Journal of Personality and Social Psychology, 92*(1), 151–163. doi:10.1037/0022-3514.92.1.151.

Gangestad, S. W., Merriman, L. A., & Emery Thompson, M. (2010). Men's oxidative stress, fluctuating asymmetry and physical attractiveness. *Animal Behaviour, 80*(6), 1005–1013. doi:10.1016/j.anbehav.2010.09.003.

Gangestad, S. W., & Simpson, J. A. (2000). The evolution of human mating: Trade-offs and strategic pluralism. *Behavioral and Brain Sciences, 23*, 573–644.

Gangestad, S. W., Simpson, J. A., Cousins, A. J., Garver-Apgar, C. E., & Christensen, P. N. (2004). Women's preferences for male behavioral displays change across the menstrual cycle. *Psychological Science, 15*, 203–207.

Gangestad, S. W., & Thornhill, R. (2003). Facial masculinity and fluctuating asymmetry. *Evolution and Human Behavior, 24*, 231–241.

Gangestad, S. W., & Thornhill, R. (2008). Human oestrus. *Proceedings of the Royal Society of London B, 275*, 991–1000.

Gildersleeve, K., Haselton, M. G., & Fales, M. R. (2014). Do women's mate preferences change across the ovulatory cycle? A meta-analytic review. *Psychological Bulletin, in press.*

Grammer, K. (1993). 5-α-androst-16en-3α-on: A male pheromone? A brief report. *Ethology and Sociobiology, 14*, 201–208.

Harris, C. R. (2011). Menstrual cycle and facial preferences reconsidered. *Sex Roles, 64*(9–10), 669–681. doi:10.1007/s11199-010-9772-8.

Johnston, V. S., Hagel, R., Franklin, M., Fink, B., & Grammer, K. (2001). Male facial attractiveness: Evidence for a hormone-mediated adaptive design. *Evolution and Human Behavior, 22*, 251–267.

Jones, B. C., DeBruine, L. M., & Little, A. C. (2007). The role of symmetry in attraction to average faces. *Perception and Psychophysics, 69*, 1273–1277.

Jones, B. C., DeBruine, L. M., Perrett, D. I., Little, A. C., Feinberg, D. R., & Law Smith, M. J. (2008). Effects of menstrual cycle on face preferences. *Archives of Sexual Behavior, 37*, 78–84. doi:10.1007/s10508-007-9268-y.

Jones, B. C., Feinberg, D. R., Watkins, C. D., Fincher, C. L., Little, A. C., & DeBruine, L. M. (2013). Pathogen disgust predicts women's preferences for masculinity in men's voices, faces, and bodies. *Behavioral Ecology, 24*, 373–379. doi:10.1093/beheco/ars173.

Jones, B. C., Little, A. C., Boothroyd, L. G., DeBruine, L. M., Feinberg, D. R., Law Smith, M. J., et al. (2005). Commitment to relationships and preferences for femininity and apparent health in faces are strongest on days of the menstrual cycle when progesterone level is high. *Hormones and Behavior, 48*, 283–290. doi:10.1016/j.yhbeh.2005.03.010.

Jones, B. C., Little, A. C., Penton-Voak, I. S., Tiddeman, B. P., Burt, D. M., & Perrett, D. I. (2001). Facial symmetry and judgements of apparent health: Support for a "good genes" explanation of the attractiveness-symmetry relationship. *Evolution and Human Behavior, 22*, 417–429.

Jones, B. C., Vukovic, J., Little, A. C., Roberts, S. C., & DeBruine, L. M. (2011). Circum-menopausal changes in women's preferences for sexually dimorphic shape cues in peer-aged faces. *Biological Psychology, 87*(3), 453–455. doi:10.1016/j.biopsycho.2011.04.004.

Klein, S. L. (2000). The effects of hormones on sex differences in infection: From genes to behavior. *Neuroscience and Biobehavioral Reviews, 24*(6), 627–638.

Kruger, D. J. (2006). Male facial masculinity influences attributions of personality and reproductive strategy. *Personal Relationships, 13*, 451–463.

Langlois, J. H., & Roggman, L. A. (1990). Attractive faces are only average. *Psychological Science, 1*, 115–121.

Lie, H. C., Rhodes, G., & Simmons, L. W. (2008). Genetic diversity revealed in human faces. *Evolution, 2.* doi:10.1111/j.1558-5646.2008.00478.x.

Little, A. C., Apicella, C. L., & Marlowe, F. W. (2007). Preferences for symmetry in human faces in two cultures: Data from the UK and the Hadza, an isolated group of hunter-gatherers. *Proceedings of the Royal Society of London B, 274*(1629), 3113–3117. doi:10.1098/rspb.2007.0895.

Little, A. C., Burt, D. M., Penton-Voak, I. S., & Perrett, D. I. (2001). Self-perceived attractiveness influences human female preferences for sexual dimorphism and symmetry in male faces. *Proceedings of the Royal Society of London B, 268*, 39–44.

Little, A. C., Cohen, D. L., Jones, B. C., & Belsky, J. (2007). Human preferences for facial masculinity change with relationship type and environmental harshness. *Behavioral Ecology and Sociobiology, 61*, 967–973.

Little, A. C., DeBruine, L. M., & Jones, B. C. (2011). Exposure to visual cues of pathogen contagion changes preferences for masculinity and symmetry in opposite-sex faces. *Proceedings of the Royal Society of London B, 278*, 2032–2039. doi:10.1098/rspb.2010.1925.

Little, A. C., & Jones, B. C. (2003). Evidence against perceptual bias views for symmetry preferences in human faces. *Proceedings of the Royal Society of London B, 279*, 1759–1763.

Little, A. C., Jones, B. C., & Burriss, R. P. (2007). Preferences for masculinity in male bodies change across the menstrual cycle. *Hormones and Behavior, 52*, 633–639.

Little, A. C., Jones, B. C., & DeBruine, L. M. (2008). Preferences for variation in masculinity in real male faces change across the menstrual cycle. *Personality and Individual Differences, 45*, 478–482.

Little, A. C., Jones, B. C., & DeBruine, L. M. (2011a). The many faces of research on face perception. *Philosophical Transactions of the Royal Society, B: Biological Sciences, 366*(1571), 1634–1637. doi:10.1098/rstb.2010.0386.

Little, A. C., Jones, B. C., & DeBruine, L. M. (2011b). Facial attractiveness: Evolutionary based research. *Philosophical Transactions of the Royal Society, B: Biological Sciences, 366*(1571), 1638–1659. doi:10.1098/rstb.2010.0404.

Little, A. C., Jones, B. C., DeBruine, L. M., & Feinberg, D. R. (2008). Symmetry and sexual-dimorphism in human faces: Interrelated preferences suggest both signal quality. *Behavioral Ecology, 19*, 902–908.

Little, A. C., Jones, B. C., Penton-Voak, I. S., Burt, D. M., & Perrett, D. I. (2002). Partnership status and the temporal context of relationships influence human female preferences for sexual dimorphism in male face shape. *Proceedings of the Royal Society of London B, 269*, 1095–1103. doi:10.1098/rspb.2002.1984.

Little, A. C., Jones, B. C., Waitt, C., Tiddeman, B. P., Feinberg, D. R., Perrett, D. I., et al. (2008). Symmetry is related to sexual dimorphism in faces: Data across culture and species. *PLoS ONE, 3*(5).

Little, A. C., & Mannion, H. (2006). Viewing attractive or unattractive same-sex individuals changes self-rated attractiveness and face preferences in women. *Animal Behaviour, 72*, 981–987.

Little, A. C., Saxton, T. K., Roberts, S. C., Jones, B. C., DeBruine, L. M., Vukovic, J., et al. (2010). Women's preferences for masculinity in male faces are highest during reproductive age range and lower around puberty and post-menopause. *Psychoneuroendocrinology, 35*(6), 912–920. doi:10.1016/j.psyneuen. 2009.12.006.

Lukaszewski, A. W., & Roney, J. R. (2009). Estimated hormones predict women's mate preferences for dominant personality traits. *Personality and Individual Differences, 47*(3), 191–196. doi:10.1016/j.paid. 2009.02.019.

Møller, A. P. (1995). Hormones, handicaps and bright birds. *Trends in Ecology & Evolution, 10*(3), 121. doi:10.1016/S0169-5347(00)89008-4.

Moore, F. R., Cornwell, R. E., Smith, M. J. L., Al Dujaili, E. A. S., Sharp, M., & Perrett, D. I. (2011). Evidence for the stress-linked immunocompetence handicap hypothesis in human male faces. *Proceedings. Biological Sciences/The Royal Society, 278*(1706), 774–780. doi:10.1098/rspb.2010.1678.

Neave, N., Laing, S., Fink, B., & Manning, J. T. (2003). Second to fourth digit ratio, testosterone, and perceived male dominance. *Proceedings of the Royal Society of London B, 270*, 2167–2172.

Penton-Voak, I. S., & Chen, J. Y. (2004). High salivary testosterone is linked to masculine male facial appearance in humans. *Evolution and Human Behavior, 25*, 229–241.

Penton-Voak, I. S., Jacobson, A., & Trivers, R. L. (2004). Populational differences in attractiveness judgements of male and female faces: Comparing British and Jamaican samples. *Evolution and Human Behavior, 25*, 355–370. doi:10.1016/j.evolhumbehav.2004.06.002.

Penton-Voak, I. S., Little, A. C., Jones, B. C., Burt, D. M., Tiddeman, B. P., & Perrett, D. I. (2003). Female condition influences preferences for sexual dimorphism in faces of male humans (Homo sapiens). *Journal of Comparative Psychology, 117*, 264–271.

Penton-Voak, I. S., & Perrett, D. I. (2000). Female preference for male faces changes cyclically: Further evidence. *Evolution and Human Behavior, 21*, 39–48.

Penton-Voak, I. S., Perrett, D. I., Castles, D. L., Kobayashi, T., Burt, D. M., Murray, L. K., et al. (1999). Menstrual cycle alters face preference. *Nature, 399*(6738), 741–742. doi:10.1038/21557.

Perrett, D. I., Lee, K., Penton-Voak, I. S., Rowland, D. A., Yoshikawa, S., Burt, D. M., et al. (1998). Effects of sexual dimorphism on facial attractiveness. *Nature, 394*, 884–887.

Perrett, D. I., May, K. A., & Yoshikawa, S. (1994). Facial Shape and Judgments of female attractiveness. *Nature, 368*, 239–242.

Peters, M., Simmons, L. W., & Rhodes, G. (2008). Testosterone is associated with mating success but not attractiveness or masculinity in human males. *Animal Behaviour, 76*(2), 297–303. doi:10.1016/j.anbehav. 2008.02.008.

Pound, N., Penton-Voak, I. S., & Surridge, A. K. (2009). Testosterone responses to competition in men are related to facial masculinity. *Proceedings of the Royal Society of London B, 276*(1654), 153–159. doi:10.1098/rspb.2008.0990.

Provost, M. P., Kormos, C., Kosakoski, G., & Quinsey, V. L. (2006). Sociosexuality in women and preference for facial masculinization and somatotype in men. *Archives of Sexual Behavior, 35*(3), 305–312. doi:10. 1007/s10508-006-9029-3.

Puts, D. A. (2005). Mating context and menstrual phase affect women's preferences for male voice pitch. *Evolution and Human Behavior, 26*, 388–397.

Puts, D. A. (2006). Cyclic variation in women's preferences for masculine traits—Potential hormonal causes. *Human Nature, 17*(1), 114–127. doi:10.1007/ s12110-006-1023-x.

Puts, D. A., Jones, B. C., & DeBruine, L. M. (2012). Sexual selection on human faces and voices. *Journal of Sex Research, 49*(2–3), 227–243. doi:10.1080/ 00224499.2012.658924.

Rantala, M. J., Coetzee, V., Moore, F. R., Skrinda, I., Kecko, S., Krama, T., et al. (2012). Adiposity, compared with masculinity, serves as a more valid cue to immunocompetence in human mate choice. *Proceedings of the Royal Society B: Biological Sciences, 280*(1751), 20122495. doi:10.1098/rspb. 2012.2495.

Rantala, M. J., Moore, F. R., Skrinda, I., Krama, T., Kivlieniece, I., Kecko, S., et al. (2012). Evidence for the stress-linked immunocompetence handicap hypothesis in humans. *Nature Communications, 3*, 694. doi:10.1038/ncomms1696.

Rennels, J. L., Bronstad, P. M., & Langlois, J. H. (2008). Are attractive men's faces masculine or feminine? The importance of type of facial stimuli. *Journal of Experimental Psychology: Human Perception and Performance, 34*, 884–893.

Rhodes, G. (2006). The evolutionary psychology of facial beauty. *Annual Review of Psychology, 57*, 199–226. doi:10.1146/annurev.psych.57.102904.190208.

Rhodes, G., Chan, J., Zebrowitz, L. A., & Simmons, L. W. (2003). Does sexual dimorphism in human faces signal health? *Proceedings of the Royal Society of London B, 270*, S93–S95. doi:10.1098/rsbl. 2003. 0023.

Rhodes, G., Hickford, C., & Jeffery, L. (2000). Sextypicality and attractiveness: Are supermale and superfemale faces super-attractive? *British Journal of Psychology, 91*, 125–140.

Rhodes, G., Simmons, L. W., & Peters, M. (2005). Attractiveness and sexual behaviour: Does attractiveness enhance mating success? *Evolution and Human Behavior, 26*, 186–201.

Rhodes, G., Zebrowitz, L. A., Clark, A., Kalick, S. M., Hightower, A., & McKay, R. (2001). Do facial averageness and symmetry signal health? *Evolution and Human Behavior, 22,* 31–46.

Roberts, M. (2004). Testing the immunocompetence handicap hypothesis: A review of the evidence. *Animal Behaviour, 68*(2), 227–239. doi:10.1016/j.anbehav.2004.05.001.

Roney, J. R., Hanson, K. N., Durante, K. M., & Maestripieri, D. (2006). Reading men's faces: Women's mate attractiveness judgments track men's testosterone and interest in infants. *Proceedings of the Royal Society of London B, 273,* 2169–2175.

Roney, J. R., Simmons, Z. L., & Gray, P. B. (2011). Changes in estradiol predict within-women shifts in attraction to facial cues of men's testosterone. *Psychoneuroendocrinology, 36*(5), 742–749. doi:10.1016/j.psyneuen.2010.10.010.

Rupp, H. A., James, T. W., Ketterson, E. D., Sengelaub, D. R., Janssen, E., & Heiman, J. R. (2009). Neural activation in women in response to masculinized male faces: Mediation by hormones and psychosexual factors. *Evolution and Human Behavior, 30,* 1–10. doi:10.1016/j.evolhumbehav.2008.08.006.

Scott, I. M. L., Clark, A. P., Boothroyd, L. G., & Penton-Voak, I. S. (2013). Do men's faces really signal heritable immunocompetence? *Behavioral Ecology, 24,* 579–589. doi:10.1093/beheco/ars092.

Scott, I. M. L., & Penton-Voak, I. S. (2011). The validity of composite photographs for assessing masculinity preferences. *Perception, 40*(3), 323–331. doi:10.1068/p6723.

Scott, I. M. L., Pound, N., Stephen, I. D., Clark, A. P., & Penton-Voak, I. S. (2010). Does masculinity matter? The contribution of masculine face shape to male attractiveness in humans. (V. J. Vitzthum, Ed.). *PLoS ONE, 5*(10), e13585. doi:10.1371/journal.pone.0013585.

Scott, I. M. L., Swami, V., Josephson, S. C., & Penton-Voak, I. S. (2008). Context-dependent preferences for facial dimorphism in a rural Malaysian population. *Evolution and Human Behavior, 29,* 289–296.

Smith, F. G., Jones, B. C., Welling, L. L. M., Little, A. C., Vukovic, J., Main, J. C., et al. (2009). Waist–hip ratio predicts women's preferences for masculine male faces, but not perceptions of men's trustworthiness. *Personality and Individual Differences, 47*(5), 476–480. doi:10.1016/j.paid.2009.04.022.

Stephen, I. D., Scott, I. M. L., Coetzee, V., Pound, N., Perrett, D. I., & Penton-Voak, I. S. (2012). Cross-cultural effects of color, but not morphological masculinity, on perceived attractiveness of men's faces. *Evolution and Human Behavior.* doi:10.1016/j.evolhumbehav.2011.10.003.

Swaddle, J. P., & Riersen, G. W. (2002). Testosterone increases perceived dominance but not attractiveness in human males. *Proceedings of the Royal Society of London B, 269,* 2285–2289.

Thornhill, R., & Gangestad, S. W. (1993). Human facial beauty: Averageness, symmetry, and parasite resistance. *Human Nature, 4,* 237–269.

Thornhill, R., & Gangestad, S. W. (1996). The evolution of human sexuality. *Trends in Ecology and Evolution, 11,* 98–102.

Thornhill, R., & Gangestad, S. W. (1999). Facial attractiveness. *Trends in Cognitive Sciences, 3,* 452–460.

Thornhill, R., & Gangestad, S. W. (2006). Facial sexual dimorphism, developmental stability, and susceptibility to disease in men and women. *Evolution and Human Behavior, 27,* 131–144.

Thornhill, R., & Møller, A. P. (1997). Developmental stability, disease and medicine. *Biological Review, 72,* 497–548.

Todd, P. M., Penke, L., Fasolo, B., & Lenton, A. P. (2007). Different cognitive processes underlie human mate choices and mate preferences. *Proceedings of the National Academy of Sciences of the United States of America, 104*(38), 15011–15016. doi:10.1073/pnas.0705290104.

Tovée, M. J., & Cornelissen, P. L. (2001). Female and male perceptions of female physical attractiveness in front-view and profile. *British Journal of Psychology, 92 Part 2,* 391–402.

Tovée, M. J., Reinhaardt, S., Emery, J. L., & Cornelissen, P. L. (1998). Optimum body-mass index and maximum sexual attractiveness. *The Lancet, 352,* 548.

Tybur, J. M., & Gangestad, S. W. (2011). Mate preferences and infectious disease: Theoretical considerations and evidence in humans. *Philosophical Transactions of the Royal Society, B: Biological Sciences, 366*(1583), 3375–3388. doi:10.1098/rstb.2011.0136.

Tybur, J. M., Lieberman, D., & Griskevicius, V. (2009). Microbes, mating, and morality: Individual differences in three functional domains of disgust. *Journal of Personality and Social Psychology, 97*(1), 103–122. doi:10.1037/a0015474.

Verdonck, A. (1999). Effect of low-dose testosterone treatment on craniofacial growth in boys with delayed puberty. *The European Journal of Orthodontics, 21*(2), 137–143. doi:10.1093/ejo/21.2.137.

Vukovic, J., Feinberg, D. R., Jones, B. C., DeBruine, L. M., Welling, L. L. M., Little, A. C., et al. (2008). Self-rated attractiveness predicts individual differences in women's preferences for masculine men's voices. *Personality and Individual Differences, 45,* 451–456.

Watkins, C. D., DeBruine, L. M., Little, A. C., Feinberg, D. R., & Jones, B. C. (2012). Priming concerns about pathogen threat versus resource scarcity: Dissociable effects on women's perceptions of men's attractiveness and dominance. *Behavioral Ecology and Sociobiology, 66*(12), 1549–1556. doi:10.1007/s00265-012-1408-2.

Waynforth, D., Delwadia, S., & Camm, M. (2005). The influence of women's mating strategies on preference for masculine facial architecture. *Evolution and Human Behavior, 26*, 409–416.

Welling, L. L. M., Jones, B. C., & DeBruine, L. M. (2008). Sex drive is positively associated with women's preferences for sexual dimorphism in men's and women's faces. *Personality and Individual Differences, 44*, 161–170.

Welling, L. L. M., Jones, B. C., DeBruine, L. M., Conway, C. A., Law Smith, M. J., Little, A. C., et al. (2007). Raised salivary testosterone in women is associated with increased attraction to masculine faces. *Hormones and Behavior, 52*, 156–161.

Wood, W., Kressel, L., Joshi, P., & Louie, B. (2014). Meta-analysis of menstrual cycle effects on women's mate preferences. *Emotion Review, in press*.

Women's Disgust Adaptations

15

Diana Santos Fleischman

Consider for a moment a few things that you find disgusting. You may find that these disgust elicitors have a few things in common such as the ability to make you sick or poison you, or, perhaps, you will have a more diverse set of ideas on mind. In many ways disgust is one of the more straightforward emotional motivational states given that it distances individuals from cues of contamination or disease, and yet it is evoked in diverse contexts. You may be disgusted by thinking of eating meat with maggots in it, feeling a stranger sneeze all over your arm, considering someone who steals from the disabled, or imagining having sex with a relative or unattractive person. Like many aspects of evolved psychology considered in this volume, disgust is one emotional domain in which men and women have faced somewhat different selection pressures, in this case the costs and benefits related to disease avoidance.

Why Disgust?

Pathogens are a central adaptive problem almost all organisms face; even the pathogens themselves sometimes have pathogens! Pathogens, like parasitic bacteria, helminths, viruses, and protozoa, derive nutrients and shelter and breed grounds from hosts who are then often disadvantaged in terms of both survival and reproductive success. Pathogens like bacteria and viruses have advantages over complex multicellular organisms like humans. Their arsenal, mutations and short generational times along with gene swapping and recombination, can enable them to adapt quickly to exploit host environments and overcome defenses. In response to this constant threat, immune systems of incredible complexity and adaptability have been developed. Humans come preequipped to build billions of antibodies and antigen receptors, molecules that bind to parasitic elements and by-products. However, mounting a defense against pathogens is costly. It is estimated in humans that metabolic demands go up by 16 % after a vaccine and 30 % during sepsis (Lochmiller & Deerenberg, 2000). Moreover, immune activation doesn't come without collateral damage. Immune products and inflammation that fight infection can have harmful effects that last long after the infection is cleared; macrophages that consume bacteria leak digestive enzymes, damaging surrounding tissues (Clark, 2007, p. 16). In the case of diseases such as tuberculosis and hepatitis B, it is the immune system that destroys the lungs and liver, respectively, not the pathogen itself (Clark, 2007).

Given these high costs, prevention is indeed the best medicine; if and when recurrent and reliable cues to disease exist, one should expect that organisms will adapt to identify and avoid

D.S. Fleischman (✉)
Department of Psychology, University of Portsmouth,
Portsmouth PO1 2DY, UK
e-mail: dianafleischman@gmail.com

V.A. Weekes-Shackelford and T.K. Shackelford (eds.), *Evolutionary Perspectives on Human Sexual Psychology and Behavior*, Evolutionary Psychology, DOI 10.1007/978-1-4939-0314-6_15,
© Springer Science+Business Media New York 2014

them. There are many examples of disease avoidance analogous to disgust in nonhuman animals. Sheep, horses, and cows avoid grazing in areas heavily contaminated with fecal matter (Hart, 1990). Eating conspecifics offers a nearly optimal nutrient balance; however, many omnivores and carnivores display a "cannibalism taboo" because, even in this case, the cost of contracting illness exceeds the nutritional benefits (Hart, 1990). Acquired taste aversions, that is, avoiding foods that taste like ones that previously caused illness, are well documented, especially in animals like rats that cannot vomit (Hart, 1990). Many nonhuman animals also avoid mating with kin or sick conspecifics (Hart, 1990). However, while disgust may be a disease avoidance system, not all disease avoidance systems are disgust.

What Is Disgust?

Although nonhuman animals engage in some very complex disease avoidance strategies, disgust, when defined as an emotion, is distinctively human. But what is disgust? It seems difficult to define disgust without referencing the very things we find disgusting. Darwin defined disgust as referring to "something revolting, primarily in relation to the sense of taste, as actually perceived or vividly imagined; and secondarily to anything which causes a similar feeling, through the sense of smell, touch and even of eyesight" (Darwin, 1872, p. 253). Many definitions tend to be similarly circuitous and appealing to intuitive understanding; disgusting stuff is, well, disgusting. More enlightening is to consider disgust within the framework of computational theory of mind as a motivational system with inputs and outputs including the adaptive salience of the cue and the condition of the organism.

Disgust can be called an "affect program," an emotional response that is automatically triggered, coordinated, and often elicited by adaptively relevant stimuli (Kelly, 2011, p. 15). Disgust is associated with a number of defined physiological correlates including activation of the parasympathetic nervous system, reduced heart rate, heightened galvanic skin response

(Rohrmann & Hopp, 2008), and increased salivation (saliva prevents damage to tooth enamel during vomiting) (Angyal, 1941). The facial expression associated with disgust is similarly specific and considered one of the five basic universal emotional expressions (Ekman & Friesen, 1971). Moreover, disgust shows consistent neural localization in the anterior insular cortex which responds preferentially to images of contamination and facial expressions of disgust (Stark et al., 2003, 2007; Wright, He, Shapira, Goodman, & Liu, 2004) including heightened activation in those with elevated disgust sensitivity or obsessive–compulsive disorder (OCD) (Calder et al., 2007; Shapira et al., 2003).

Although the function of disgust may seem straightforward, coming up with an explanation that encompasses not just obvious cues of pathogen presence but also myriad other disgust elicitors has been the focus of some debate. One of the dominant paradigms has been the model of Rozin, Haidt, McCauley, and colleagues (Rozin & Fallon, 1987; Rozin, Haidt, & McCauley, 2008). Rozin et al. (2008) state that disgust begins its evolutionary trajectory as a distaste response focused on the mouth. Certainly there is evidence for this in the emotion-specific expression of disgust (Ekman & Friesen, 1971) (e.g., dropping the corners of the mouth) which plausibly imitate the facial movements of retching. This explains the so-called "core disgust," but for many other common disgust elicitors, Rozin and colleagues developed "animal reminder disgust," a domain that spans everything from corpses and wounds to sexual behavior (Rozin et al., 2008). Because (a) nonhuman animals do not have disgust or awareness of their own mortality and (b) humans have mortality in common with animals, Rozin and colleagues hypothesized that animal reminder disgust serves to manage the existential fear of one's own mortality ("Terror Management"). Terror management as an explanation for disgust sensitivity has been heavily critiqued from an adaptationist perspective (e.g., Fessler & Navarrete, 2005). Moreover, most things animals do are not disgusting: "nonhuman animals can be readily observed running and jumping like humans, breathing like humans, sleeping like humans, and caring for their offspring like humans, yet none of these behaviors elicit disgust" (Tybur, Lieberman, Kurzban, & DeScioli, 2012, p. 2).

There is a now good deal of consensus that a central adaptive function of disgust is to reduce the risk of infection by distancing one from cues of the presence of pathogens (Curtis, Aunger, & Rabie, 2004; Fessler, Eng, & Navarrete, 2005; Laland & Brown, 2011; Oaten, Stevenson, & Case, 2009; Schaller & Duncan, 2007; Tybur et al., 2012), but disgust is obviously elicited by many other kinds of stimuli. Even if sensitivities to all domains of disgust are related, an adaptationist perspective suggests sex differences in specific domains.

Measures of Disgust Sensitivity

In order to understand how disgust has been studied and how different domains are defined, what follows is a short introduction on the common measures of disgust sensitivity.

Disgust Sensitivity Scale and Disgust Sensitivity Scale Revised

The Disgust Sensitivity (DS) scale was one of the first measures of disgust sensitivity widely used. It contains 32 items and specifies seven domains of disgust: food, animals, body products, sex, envelope violations, death, and hygiene. The DS was criticized and subsequently revised (Olatunji, Haidt, McKay, & David, 2008) creating the disgust scale revised (DS-R) which has fewer items and three factors, core disgust, animal reminder disgust, and contamination-based disgust, showing good validity and reliability (Van Overveld, De Jong, Peters, & Schouten, 2011). The DS scale is an outgrowth of the idea that disgust began as a response against oral incorporation and serves in part to distance oneself from reminders of mortality and animal nature.

Three Domains of Disgust Scale

A more recent scale developed divides disgust into three domains (Tybur, Lieberman, & Griskevicius, 2009) using a 21-item questionnaire. The three domains are pathogen disgust (regarding cues or contexts of disease that aren't sexual (e.g., stepping on dog poop)), sexual disgust (which motivates away from cues or context that could jeopardize reproductive success (e.g., hearing two strangers have sex)), and moral disgust (which facilitates coordinating judgment against norm violations (e.g., deceiving a friend)) (Tybur et al., 2012).

Image-Based Rating Systems

The disgust scales above require the respondent to read and imagine various disgusting scenarios. A potentially more ecologically valid way to measure disgust is through images or behavioral measures. One of the better-known image sets used to measure disgust was used by Curtis et al. (2004) and contains 19 images of varying disease salience (e.g., a bowl of blue viscous liquid compared to a bowl of yellow viscous liquid with red flecks). Images from the International Affective Picture System (Lang, Bradley, & Cuthbert, 1999) are also used to both elicit disgust and measure disgust sensitivity. Behavioral measures used to measure disgust sensitivity (e.g., (Borg & De Jong, 2012; Rozin, Haidt, McCauley, Dunlop, & Ashmore, 1999)) will be discussed more in detail below.

Measures of Disgust Facial Expression

Disgust has very specific muscular activity associated with it including gaping, retracting the upper lip, wrinkling the nose, and dropping the corners of the mouth (Ekman & Friesen, 1971). Disgust studies have used coders to rate the degree of disgust expressed facially (De Jong, Peters, & Vanderhallen, 2002); the most rigorous is the Facial Action Coding System (Ekman, Friesen, & Hager, 2002). Other studies use facial electromyography (fEMG) where electrodes sense movements in the face in response to stimuli (e.g., Borg, De Jong, & Schultz, 2010; De Jong et al., 2002).

Sex Differences in Disgust

One of the most consistent findings in the disgust literature is that women are more disgust-sensitive than men. Women score significantly higher in total on the DS-R (Olatunji et al., 2008, 2009) with the largest effects in core disgust (Olatunji, personal communication). Studies using the original DS found that women were more disgust-sensitive overall (Quigley, Sherman, & Sherman, 1997) and across all domains (Haidt, McCauley, & Rozin, 1994; Schienle, Stark, Walter, & Vaitl, 2003). Using the DS with seven domains, Haidt et al. (1994) found the largest sex differences in animal disgust (e.g., it would bother me to see a rat run across my path) and magic (e.g., a friend offers you a piece of chocolate shaped like dog-doo) and the smallest sex difference in the sex domain (e.g., I think homosexual activities are immoral). In contrast, the Three Domains of Disgust scale (TDD) has found that the largest and most consistent sex difference between men and women is in the sexual domain d (475), 1.44, as compared to pathogen d (475), 0.32, and moral domains d (475), 0.23 (Tybur, Bryan, Lieberman, Caldwell Hooper, & Merriman, 2011). Women are also more disgusted by pornography than men (Koukounas & McCabe, 1997). Relatedly, women are more disgusted by a thought experiment involving transplanting organs including genital transplant (Fessler & Haley, 2006).

The sex difference in pathogen disgust holds when using images and behavioral measures as well. Using 19 images and nearly 40,000 participants, Curtis et al. (2004) found women showed higher disgust scores on the seven specifically disease-salient images (e.g., oozing wound). Rozin et al. (1999) found that women were significantly less likely than men to engage fully with 26 tasks designed to elicit disgust (e.g., eating a piece of fudge in the shape of feces).

The contamination obsessions and washing compulsions that are commonly seen in OCD may be an overexpression of motivations and behaviors that have adaptively reduced the probability of infection. In nonclinical samples, women score higher than men on measures of OCD-related contamination fear (Mancini, Gragnani, & D'Olimpio, 2001; Mancini, Gragnani, Orazi, & Grazia Pietrangeli, 1999; Van Oppen, 1992). Estimates suggest that women tend to be more at risk for developing OCD (Weissman, Bland, Canino, & Greenwald, 1994). Specifically, OCD-related cleaning compulsions are more likely to develop in females (Zohar, 1999; Zohar & Bruno, 2006).

These sex differences in disgust sensitivity do not seem to manifest until puberty or young adulthood. One of the only studies investigating disgust sensitivity in children did not find significant gender differences. Using both parental reports of children's (mean age 7 years old) disgust reactions and behavioral tasks intended to elicit disgust in children, gender did not come out as a significant predictor (Stevenson, Oaten, Case, Repacholi, & Wagland, 2010). This implies that sex difference in disgust sensitivity takes some time to socialize or that these differences are related functionally and physiologically to reproduction and mating.

Why Are Women More Disgust-Sensitive Than Men?

For a variety of functional reasons, both for the protection of self and offspring, women may have had unique selection pressure for increased disgust sensitivity, especially with regard to sexually transmitted diseases, pathogen cues, and suboptimal mate choice.

Functional Reasons for Heightened Disgust in Women

With regard to danger to self and future reproductive success, women have a great deal more at stake when engaging in sexual behavior than men. The problem of avoiding sexually transmitted infections (STIs) is complicated in that these pathogens rely on their hosts to be chosen as mates. Therefore, sexually transmitted pathogens are under unique selection pressure to cryptically infect hosts, that is, to show few signs of infection that would cause them to be detectable (Tybur & Gangestad, 2011). Women have a greater area of mucous membranes and experience more tissue damage during intercourse than heterosexual men, making them more prone to STIs such as human immunodeficiency virus, human papilloma virus, and human herpesvirus (Madkan, Giancola, Sra, & Tyring, 2006). Women are more than three times as likely to contract chlamydia (Madkan et al., 2006). It is perhaps one explanation for why women high in sexual disgust as measured by the TDD are more avoidant of sex generally (Kurzban, Dukes, & Weeden, 2010).

When women contract STIs they suffer a much greater disease burden than men because of pelvic inflammatory disease (PID), an infection of the upper genital tract affecting the ovaries, uterus, and fallopian tubes. PID is uniquely possible because human female anatomy is such that pathogens can travel through the vagina and into the peritoneal cavity (Madkan et al., 2006). Of women with untreated chlamydia, 40 % will develop (PID) (Madkan et al., 2006). Of women with a single episode of PID, 8 % are rendered infertile; more rarely acute PID develops into a systemic infection (Madkan et al., 2006). STIs can also cause other long-term and systemic diseases; for instance previous gonorrhea infection can cause dermatitis and arthritis (Bleich, Sheffield, Wendel, Sigman, & Cunningham, 2012).

Women, compared to men, are unique in that they can pass disease on to their gestating or nursing offspring, having serious consequences including loss of considerable maternal investment. Babies born to mothers with chlamydia are at risk for pneumonia and eye infections which can result to blindness, and mothers can pass HIV on to offspring during childbirth or while nursing (Madkan et al., 2006). Due to women exclusively breastfeeding and a gender-based division of labor, in traditional hunter-gatherer societies, mothers and other female kin are those most involved in caring for infants and small children. Heightened female disgust sensitivity could also function to protect human infants and children who are highly altricial and vulnerable to disease (Curtis et al., 2004). Many of the diseases used as examples here may be quite recent in our evolutionary history (Diamond, 1999); however, the factors that contribute to greater vulnerability and more serious adaptive consequences in women compared to men have been selection pressures for millions of years.

Women have greater obligate parental investment than men (Trivers, 1996) making it possible for them to have, at most, two offspring in a year. Females are choosier with regard to mates than males (e.g., Clark & Hatfield, 1989). In addition to the more immediate costs of sex including infection, disease burden, and contagion to offspring, female strategy should guide women away from using one of their comparatively few reproductive opportunities on a genetically inferior male. It's unclear whether direct benefits (e.g., not contracting infections either sexually or being in close proximity to someone with an infection) or indirect benefits (i.e., choosing a mate who would produce offspring with less disease susceptibility) are responsible for women's preference for male traits. A treatment of female mate choice for markers of health and immunocompetence in males is beyond the scope of this chapter; however, an adaptationist perspective predicts disgust will augment female choosiness in mate selection. Baseline disgust sensitivity and pathogen priming have been shown to influence aspects of mate choice.

Pathogen disgust but not sexual disgust or moral disgust predicts women's preferences for masculinity in male faces, a putative marker of immunocompetence (DeBruine, Jones, Tybur, Lieberman, & Griskevicius, 2010). Debruine, Jones, Crawford, Welling, and Little (2010) found that a nation's health indicators predict women's preference for facial masculinity. Jones et al. (2008) conclude that preference for health in male faces is more pronounced during the luteal phase when immunocompetence is compromised, while preference for facial masculinity is highest during the ovulatory phase with the highest fertility (more on that later in the chapter). However, Little, DeBruine, and Jones (2011) found that after priming participants with pathogen cues, women showed greater preference for symmetry (another putative indicator of health) and facial masculinity.

Another reason women might show higher disgust sensitivity is because men may have experienced selection pressures to display a *lack* of disgust to cues of contamination. Secondary sexual characteristics such as facial masculinity, low voice pitch, and facial hair advertise high androgen levels, which may have immunosuppressive effects (Moore et al., 2011; Thornhill & Gangestad, 2006). It is hypothesized that these characteristics thus act as a costly signal; a male displaying both health and high androgen features signals to possible mates that he has a robust immune system. Because disgust acts to distance humans from cues of disease, males may also display their robust immunity by showing indifference toward common disgust elicitors or even make a show of their disgust insensitivity (e.g., fraternity induction involving eating vomit (Lohse, 2012)). Males may also display less disgust sensitivity as a by-product; men's greater propensity for risk taking in other domains may also manifest in the domain of disease avoidance (Fessler, Pillsworth, & Flamson, 2004).

The Original Omnivore's Dilemma

Other than sexual disgust there is also reason to believe that women should be more sensitive at the potential evolutionary origin of disgust, food selection. Humans, like other species that are nutrition generalists, face an "omnivore's dilemma"; there are a large number of foods that can be eaten but they differ in their nutritional quality and in the probability that they will contain dangerous pathogens:

> During the evolutionary transition in which our ancestors' brains expanded greatly, so did their production of tools and weapons, and so did their consumption of meat (Leakey, 1994)...But when early humans went for meat, including scavenging

the carcasses left by other predators, they exposed themselves to a galaxy of new microbes and parasites, most of which are contagious- they spread by contact. (Haidt, 2006)

Meat, a principal source of foodborne illness, is also a source of potential teratogens, say agents that cause abnormal infant development like *Toxoplasma gondii*; meat is the subject of most food taboos and women may be predisposed to be disgusted by it (for a review see Fessler & Navarrete, 2003a). Four times as many women are vegetarians than men (Neumark-Sztainer, Story, Resnick, & Blum, 1997), and disgust sensitivity is higher in moral vegetarians than meat eaters (Fessler, Arguello, Mekdara, & Macias, 2003).

Women may also have higher disgust sensitivity overall because they go through periods of heightened sensitivity to disease both luteally (during the menstrual cycle) and during pregnancy.

Reproductive Cycle Effects on Disgust Modulation in Women

The Compensatory Behavioral Prophylaxis Hypothesis

Disgust has many possible adaptive effects. However, avoiding cues of contamination isn't always equally advantageous especially when sensing and identifying these cues can be cognitively taxing and ambiguous. Disease avoidant behavior motivated by disgust entails the costs of increased time and energy removed from other adaptive behaviors such as foraging and engaging socially. Hypervigilance in the disgust domain can be debilitating, as OCD aptly shows. Throughout deep time, women have experienced fluctuating vulnerability to infection as a consequence of specific hormonal shifts. The Compensatory Behavioral Prophylaxis Hypothesis or CBPH (Fessler et al., 2005) predicts that reactions to circumstances associated with the risk of pathogen transmission are predicted to vary in an adaptive manner, enhancing prophylactic behavior during times of elevated susceptibility.

Upregulated disgust sensitivity and attention to cues of possible disease in the face of immune vulnerability have been demonstrated in a handful of studies on both men and women. One way such vulnerability has been measured is with the Perceived Vulnerability to Disease scale (PVD) which has two main factors: "perceived infectability" (e.g., if an illness is "going around," I will get it) and germ aversion (Duncan, Schaller, & Park, 2009). Both factors correlate significantly with all three DS-R factors (Olatunji et al., 2008) with germ aversion correlating more highly than perceived infectability (Duncan et al., 2009).

Disease avoidance doesn't just manifest as disgust sensitivity toward pathogen cues but also spills into other domains of social processing. The smoke alarm principle (Nesse, 2005) or error management theory (Haselton & Buss, 2000) posits that given errors with different adaptive consequences, the more costly error will be minimized by skewing response toward the less costly error, in this case reacting with disgust at elements that do not connote contagious disease. Just as the immune system sometimes reacts against elements that are not pathogenic (e.g., dust allergy), so too can psychological mechanisms designed to avoid disease interpret benign cues as disgusting. In many contexts the psychology of disease avoidance seems calibrated in a sensitive way to minimize the number of false negatives and to overinterpret the likelihood of disease presence. For example, birthmarks and other facial irregularities which are not contagious elicit as much avoidance and disgust facial expression as influenza (Ryan, Oaten, Stevenson, & Case, 2012). Those who trigger disease avoidance and disgust may be rejected and stigmatized, and this might be especially likely when (a) there are other cues of disease presence or (b) when one is especially susceptible to infection. Miller and Maner (2011) found that those who had recently been ill and therefore were more susceptible to disease showed heightened attention and avoidance of disfigured individuals. Age and obesity, conditions that alter human morphology, may superficially mimic cues of disease. Stigma against the elderly and obese is associated

positively with PVD (Miller & Maner, 2012; Schaller & Park, 2011).

Another aspect of psychology that is associated with disease avoidance and disgust is ethnocentrism and xenophobia. The full reasoning for this connection is beyond the scope of this chapter but some surmise that (a) it is because foreign and unfamiliar people have carried novel and thus potentially fatal diseases and engaged in practices (e.g., cooking, hygiene) that may not be as optimal for disease avoidance as those adopted by the local culture (Diamond, 1999; Schaller, Park, & Faulkner, 2003) and/or (b) foreigners and other out-group members are linguistically and culturally connected to disease (e.g., Jewish vermin) and thus cognitively associated with disease avoidance psychology (Faulkner, Schaller, Park, & Duncan, 2004; Navarette, Fessler, & Eng, 2007). Both disgust and PVD have been shown to positively associate with ethnocentrism (Navarrete & Fessler, 2006), and PVD as well as disease priming has been shown to increase measures of xenophobia (Schaller & Park, 2011).

Pregnancy Is a Dangerous Time Both for the Embryo and for the Mother

Women experience significant immunomodulation during the first trimester as well as fostering a developmentally sensitive embryo. Because the immune system is designed to recognize self from nonself, there is a danger that the maternal immune system will destroy the embryo that is made up of half-paternal genetic material. High progesterone levels stimulate progesterone-induced blocking factor (PIBF). PIBF stimulates the immune system to shift toward more anti-inflammatory immune components to tolerate the conceptus. At the same time a woman's immune functioning is compromised, the embryo is undergoing organogenesis and is most vulnerable to environmental insults: teratogens and infections (for a review see Fessler, 2002). As mentioned previously, food, especially meat, is a major vector for diseases including those with teratogenic effects. During the first trimester in particular, pregnant

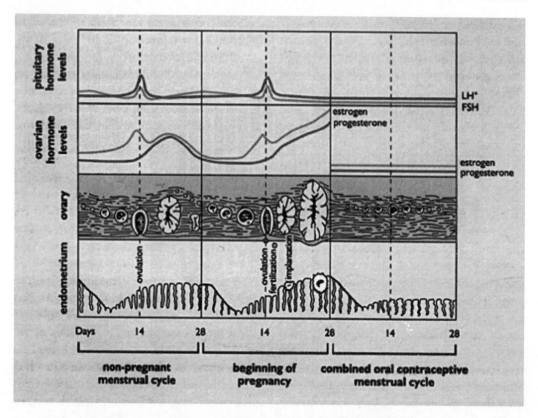

Fig. 15.1 Follicle-stimulating hormone, luteinizing hormone, estrogen, and progesterone in women in normally cycling women, pregnant women, and women on hormonal contraceptives. Taken from Drife (1996) The Benefits and Risks of Oral Contraceptives Today (1st ed.). Informa HealthCare

women often experience nausea and vomiting; these symptoms which may be elicited by smelling or eating specific foods are thought to compensate for vulnerability to infection and the sensitivity of the conceptus (Fessler, 2002; Flaxman & Sherman, 2000). Fessler et al. (2005) found elevated disgust sensitivity, primarily in the food domain of the DS (Haidt et al., 1994) in the first relative to second and third trimesters of pregnancy, a period of heightened vulnerability to infection. Navarette et al. (2007) found the same pattern with regard to hostility toward out-group members.

Progesterone, the Menstrual Cycle and Immunomodulation

The menstrual cycle consists of functionally distinct phases marked by characteristic variations in hormonal levels. Progesterone is also elevated in anticipation of pregnancy during the latter portion of the menstrual cycle. The highest levels of progesterone outside of pregnancy occur during the luteal phase, the period after the rupture of the ovarian follicle in which the corpus luteum secretes progesterone (Hatcher & Namnoum, 2004) (see Fig. 15.1). The body prepares for conception and implantation during the luteal phase by downregulating inflammatory responses. Inflammatory immunity is the first line of defense against foreign agents in the body and thus is less discerning and more likely to destroy an ambiguous entity (Clark, 2007). Luteal phase immunomodulation is hypothesized to be an adaptation much like the immunomodulation in early pregnancy that prevents the maternal immune system from attacking the conceptus, making it possible for implantation and development to occur. Heightened proneness to infection is the cost of this immune tolerance (Fessler, 2001).

The shift in inflammatory immune response during the luteal phase is evident in a variety of ways. Studies have shown that levels of proinflammatory cytokines decline, and natural killer cells are downregulated (Bouman, Moes, Heineman, De Leij, & Faas, 2001; Faas et al., 2000; Trzonkowski et al., 2001). It also appears that TH2 or anti-inflammatory immune response increases relative to the TH1 or inflammatory immune response during the luteal phase (Faas et al., 2000). Autoimmune diseases characterized by proinflammatory activity such as rheumatoid arthritis diminish luteally, while the opposite occurs with disorders such as lupus erythematosus associated with excess anti-inflammatory activity (Kozlowski et al., 2002). Consistent with the important defensive functions of inflammation, chronic infections worsen (Wilder, 2006) and response to vaccination is diminished (Kozlowski et al., 2002). Thus, the menstrual cycle offers a natural experiment for fluctuations in immune susceptibility.

Testing Disgust and the Psychology of Disease Avoidance in the Luteal Phase

Studies have tested how immunomodulation in the luteal phase effects the psychology of disease avoidance with a variety of measures including dietary intake, disgust sensitivity, preference for healthy faces, and hygiene concerns.

As mentioned previously, meat is a principal source of foodborne illness and frequently avoided during pregnancy (Fessler, 2002; Flaxman & Sherman, 2000). However, Fleischman and Fessler (2007) did not find a reduction in meat consumption in a repeated sample using daily food diaries. In a follow-up cross-sectional design study using progesterone salivary assays, Fleischman and Fessler (2009) also did not find that progesterone or luteal phase was associated with disgust at photographs of raw or cooked meat. It may be that evolved mechanisms are calibrated to express disgust at unfamiliar foods or foods that have previously

been associated with illness rather than meat. Another possibility is that there has been no selection pressure to avoid meat during the (comparatively short) luteal phase given that incubation period of meat-borne illnesses can be days or weeks long (Bloom, 2002). Finally, cues like smell and taste may be better indicators of disease risk than visual cues in a food context.

Disgust sensitivity has been measured across the menstrual cycle. Using the DS (Haidt et al., 1994), Fessler and Navarrete (2003b) failed to find increases in disgust during the luteal phase. However, as discussed previously, the original DS had some shortcomings in terms of factor structure and may not have been a sensitive or ecologically valid enough instrument to detect effects. In contrast, using the disgust images from Curtis et al. (2004), two studies found an increase in disgust ratings. Fleischman and Fessler (2009) found an effect of cycle phase such that those women in the luteal phase showed significantly higher disgust reactivity than women in the follicular phase. Fleischman and Fessler (2011) found that progesterone is significantly correlated with disgust image ratings (Fig. 15.2).

Disgust facial expressions and facial quality may also be important cues in the psychology of disease avoidance. Looking at facial expressions, the direction of gaze may be important in perceiving these cues such that an averted gaze indicates a looming threat in the environment whereas a direct gaze may imply that *you* are the source of the facial expression. Conway et al. (2007) found that during the luteal phase, women experience others' facial expressions of both fear and disgust as more intense when they display averted as opposed to direct gaze. Although sensitivity to disgust facial expressions is predicted by the CBPH, sensitivity to fear expressions is not. However, it's possible that the same underlying psychological and physiological changes that make increased disgust sensitivity during the luteal phase possible also predispose women to be more sensitive to other negative emotions like fear. Disgust or aversion toward disease cues is one avenue toward disease avoidance, but preferences for cues of health

Fig. 15.2 Relationship between log-transformed salivary progesterone and self-reported disgust to photographic stimuli, $n = 97$. Adapted from Fleischman and Fessler (2011)

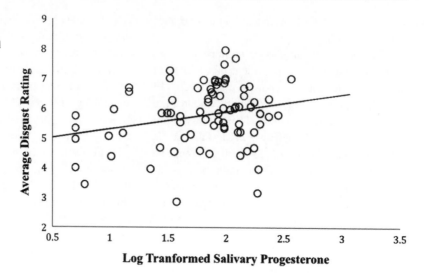

may also change as a function of immunomodulation. In six studies Jones et al. (2005) found increased preference for healthy over unhealthy faces in women who are in the high progesterone period (either estimated or measured directly).

As discussed above, the contamination obsessions and washing compulsions in OCD can be considered an overexpression of disease avoidance behaviors that are adaptive, and this domain of OCD is more frequently expressed in women (Bogetto, Venturello, Albert, Maina, & Ravizza, 1999). In women, OCD onset is also likely to follow significant reproductive milestones like menarche and pregnancy (Labad et al., 2005). Studies of clinical samples have shown that OCD symptoms are heightened during the luteal phase when progesterone is highest (Vulink, Denys, Bus, & Westenberg, 2006; Williams & Koran, 1997), and one study of a nonclinical samples has shown that women engage in more cleaning behavior during the luteal phase (Dillon & Brooks, 1992).

OCD symptomology also encompasses other obsessions and compulsions regarding checking and ritualistic behavior. However, the CBPH only predicts that those behaviors related to disease avoidance will be exacerbated by luteal immunomodulation. Modifying a self-report OCD symptomology scale (Burns, Keortge, Formea, & Sternberger, 1996) and administering to a nonclinical sample, Fleischman and Fessler (2011) tested the CBPH with contamination-related symptomology (e.g., "In the last 24 hours I've felt my hands were dirty when I touched money" and "In the last 24 hours if I touched something I thought was 'contaminated', I immediately had to wash or clean myself") and non-contamination-related symptomology (e.g., "In the last 24 hours before going to sleep, I've had to do certain things in a certain order" and "In the last 24 hours when I heard about a disaster, I've thought it was somehow my fault"). The study found that contamination-related OCD symptomology was significantly correlated with progesterone (Fig. 15.3) but non-contamination-related OCD symptomology was not significantly correlated with progesterone (Fessler & Fleischman, 2011). However, Fleischman and Fessler (2009) found that both aspects of OCD symptomology increased significantly during the luteal phase.

Evidence from Fleischman and Fessler (2011) and Conway et al. (2007) point to the luteal phase's association with not only disgust but also heightened sensitivity to fear and ruminations unrelated to contamination. Perhaps the cognitive readiness needed for sensitivity to disease cues is entangled with other types of fear and anxiety. The area of the brain that responds preferentially to disgust, the anterior insular cortex, is also stimulated by fear-inducing images (Stark et al., 2003). If disgust and fear share a common neurological system that would

Fig. 15.3 Relationship between log-transformed salivary progesterone and self-reported contamination-related and non-contamination-related OCD symptomology. The dashed line represents the trend line for non-contamination-related OCD symptomology

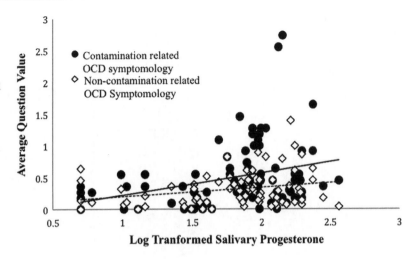

constrain the adaptive expression of one without the other.

Related to disease avoidance, in public restrooms, modern women encounter cues of contamination, and this context poses a problem both in terms of contamination fear and obsessive hand washing for those with OCD (Abramowitz, Braddock, & Moore, 2008). Fleischman and Fessler (2011) found that salivary progesterone in women was correlated with disease avoidance behaviors in public restrooms (e.g., "In the last 24 h, have you used a paper towel or anything else to open a bathroom door rather than touching it with your hands?" and "In the last 24 h, have you washed your hands two or more times in the bathroom?") in a nonclinical sample.

Another facet of disease avoidance that humans have in common with nonhuman animals is grooming and ectoparasite removal. When they feed on blood, organisms like ticks, lice, and flies bypass the skin barrier and transmit disease. Just as OCD may be an overexpression of adaptive disease avoidance, trichotillomania may be an overexpression of the prophylactic behavior of grooming, removing parasites, and preventing them from penetrating the body envelope wherein they can cause infection. Women with trichotillomania exhibit increased symptoms during the early stages of pregnancy and the luteal phase (Keuthen et al., 1997). Fleischman and Fessler (2011) found that self-grooming behavior (e.g., "In the last 24 h, have

you picked at a scab?" and "In the last 24 h, have you picked at or around your eyes?") was correlated with salivary progesterone. This area of disease avoidance and behavior generally has hardly been explored in the literature.

Immunomodulation, Progesterone, and Exogenous Progestins

Combined hormonal contraceptives, so-called because they contain both synthetic estradiol and progesterone, inhibit the natural production of these hormones, essentially flatlining any menstrual cycle variability. The rise in progesterone that occurs after ovulation is mainly produced in the empty ovarian follicle (Hatcher & Namnoum, 2004), and because women on hormonal contraceptives don't ovulate, this rise in progesterone does not occur in pill-taking women. Studies have shown that the progesterone and estradiol of nonsmoking women is lower in pill-using women (Arnold, Tóth, & Faredin, 1980; Thorneycroft & Stone, 1972). However, there is some evidence that exogenous progestins, like their natural counterparts, lower inflammatory immune responses. The progestins found in commonly prescribed oral contraceptives have been shown to lessen the severity of the autoimmune disease, lupus (Buyon, 1996), and reduce natural killer cell numbers and cytotoxicity (Scanlan, Werner, Legg, & Laudenslager, 1995). Women on the pill report more gastrointestinal distress

Fig. 15.4 Differences in disgust sensitivity between women in the follicular phase, women in the luteal phase, and women on hormonal contraceptives in response to images. Follicular $n = 25$, luteal $n = 40$, and hormonal contraceptive $n = 41$

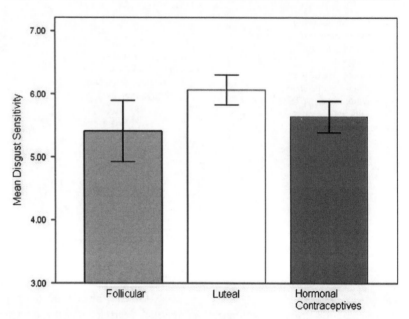

and respiratory illness than nonusers (Auerbach, Hafner, Huber, & Panzer, 2002).

Previous research has shown that women using the pill offer a quasi-control group for research on hormonal and menstrual cycle effects on behavior, showing a lower frequency of hormonally mediated behaviors (Chavanne & Gallup, 1998; Miller, Tybur, & Jordan, 2007; Wedekind, Seebeck, Bettens, & Paepke, 1995). Fleischman and Fessler (2009) found that pill-using women showed significantly lower salivary progesterone than women in the luteal phase and that women on hormonal contraceptives showed no heightened disgust sensitivity or other disease avoidance behaviors relative to nonusers in the follicular or the luteal phase. The reason for this is unclear. Perhaps only endogenously produced progesterone acts as a proximate indicator of disease susceptibility, or the level of progesterone relative to estrogen may be the relevant proximate cue. Another possibility is that ovulation and heightened progesterone must occur in proximity with one another to cause the relevant increase in disgust sensitivity (Fig. 15.4).

Sexual Disgust and Ovulation

If one accepts that sexual disgust is a means toward the functional goal of avoiding contexts that jeopardize reproductive success, we should also see that the salience of sexual disgust elicitors varies across the menstrual cycle as a function of conception risk. One mating behavior significantly associated with disgust sensitivity is incest avoidance as inbreeding depression increases the likelihood of recessive alleles in offspring ultimately making it more likely that reproduction will be unsuccessful (e.g., miscarriage) or result in reduced fitness in resultant offspring. There have been no studies of disgust toward incest across the menstrual cycle; however, one study has shown that women are less likely to interact with their fathers around ovulation (Lieberman, Pillsworth, & Haselton, 2011). Fessler and Navarrete (2003a, 2003b) found that women were more likely to exhibit disgust in the sexual domain when fertile. Of the women's disgust adaptations thus far, this area is one in most need of further research especially in combination with biomarkers of high fertility (e.g., estrogen, luteinizing hormone).

Disgust and Sexual Arousal

Although humans generally avoid being in close proximity with disease cues; such avoidance is fundamentally incompatible with engaging in sexual behavior. Reproductive success is the currency of fitness, yet sex involves extensive exposure to stimuli that indicate disease risk. Sexual behavior entails increased contact with disease cues but also increased vulnerability to disease. The direct exchange of body fluids and exposure of mucous membranes—along with abrasion associated with the friction of intercourse—present an entry possibility for pathogenic microorganisms. Moreover, close proximity and fast breathing increase the risk of contracting airborne pathogens from a sexual partner or surrounding environment. In line with the possible disease risk of sexual behavior, one study in men has shown an increase in lymphocytes in sexually aroused men (Haake et al., 2004).

Secretions and odors frequently encountered in sexual contexts are strong disgust elicitors (Rozin & Fallon, 1987). However, intuitively it seems that disgust is not an integral part of normal sexual activity. If stimuli are found disgusting outside of a sexual context but not in one, does sexual arousal have the evolved function of dispelling the emotion of disgust?

How Sexual Arousal Influences Disgust Reactions

Two studies with male samples have looked at how sexual arousal influences disgust. Ariely and Loewenstein (2006) found that men who were exposed to photos of naked women compared to those men who viewed photos of clothed women were significantly more likely to state they would engage in a variety of potentially disgusting sexual acts such as having sexual contact with an animal, having anal sex, or watching a woman urinating. Stevenson, Case, and Oaten (2011) investigated the hypothesis that sexual arousal would specifically influence disgust at sexually relevant disgust cues. Stevenson et al. (2011) used three modalities (aural, visual, and tactile) of disgust stimuli with one sex-related stimulus (e.g., feeling lubricated condoms in a bowl, looking at a picture of a woman's torso with a large scar) and one non-sex-related stimulus presented in each modality (e.g., feeling cold ham and pea soup, looking at a picture of a polluted landscape). Men who had viewed sexually arousing images versus other images (e.g., positive arousal such as images of skydiving) showed reduced disgust reactions in the sexual domain, but arousal had no effect on disgust reactions to nonsexual stimuli (Stevenson et al., 2011).

The ultimate adaptive function of sexual arousal, achieving reproductive success, is the same for men as it is for women and similarly for women can only happen in contexts with intimate contact with pathogen cues. On the other hand, as explained above, women are uniquely vulnerable to infection during coitus, and thus, sexual arousal may not have the same dampening effect on disgust sensitivity in women as in men. Two studies have looked at how women respond to disgust when sexually aroused. Borg and De Jong (2012) split women into one of three mood induction groups: positive arousal, negative arousal, and sexual arousal. Women watched a mood induction video and intermittently "completed" disgust tasks (rather than doing the task participants could choose to imagine how disgusted they would be to engage with the task). They found that there was a significant main effect of group on approach and completion of the tasks such that the sexual arousal group conducted significantly more tasks than either the positive arousal or the neutral control groups. Women in the sexual arousal condition compared to women in the positive arousal and negative arousal conditions reported less disgust at the sexually disgusting tasks (e.g., lubricating a vibrator, handling a pair of stained underwear). Borg and De Jong (2012) also found those in the sexual arousal group compared to the neutral group found nonsexual disgust tasks (e.g., inserting a pin into a cow eyeball) less disgusting.

Fleischman, Hamilton, Fessler, and Meston (2014) investigated the effect of sexual arousal on disgust sensitivity by dividing women into four groups: neutral film → erotic film → rate disgust images; neutral film → rate disgust images → erotic film; neutral film → rate fear images → erotic film; neutral film → erotic film → rate fear images. None of the disgust or fear images were sexual in nature. All women were between day 5 and 10 of the menstrual cycle in order to homogenize any menstrual cycle effects. Genital arousal in response to the erotic films was measured using a vaginal photoplethysmograph (Sintchak & Geer, 1975) which measures vaginal engorgement controlling for heartbeat, producing a measurement, vaginal pulse amplitude (VPA). The relevant dependent variable in Fleischman et al. (n.d.) is percent change, that is, the percentage change in VPA from the neutral film to the erotic film.

At the time when this chapter was written data were still being collected. Fleischman et al. (n.d.) did not find that women in the sexual arousal condition (neutral film → erotic film → rate disgust images) showed lower disgust reactivity than women in the other conditions or that the intensity of sexual arousal had any direct effect on disgust reactivity. However, Fleischman et al. (n.d.) did find that the interaction of sexual arousal and a baseline measure of disgust *sensitivity* taken before the experimental protocol began (a subset of the paper and pencil pathogen sensitivity factor from (Tybur et al., 2009)) was the significant predictor of disgust ratings. In this study, women high in disgust sensitivity show a positive association between sexual arousal and disgust reactivity such that increase in sexual arousal causes an increase in disgust ratings, while women who are low in disgust sensitivity show a more similar pattern to studies of sexual arousal's effect on disgust in male participants (e.g., Ariely & Loewenstein, 2006; Stevenson et al., 2011), that is, reduced disgust ratings in response to heightened sexual arousal. In other words, disgust-sensitive women become more disgusted when aroused and less disgust-sensitive women become less disgusted when aroused. There was no effect of self-reported sexual arousal on any measures.

This result is intriguing in light of compensatory behavioral prophylaxis. If low baseline disgust sensitivity is indicative of robust immunity, perhaps the system is calibrated such that those who can afford exposure to disease cues during sexual arousal show decreased disgust reactivity and those that cannot show the opposite effect. The stimuli used in Fleischman et al. (2014) were also very rich in pathogen cues (images included corpses, people vomiting, and feces) indicating that individual differences can fundamentally change the way disease-salient disgust stimuli is processed in the presence of competing motivational states. Further research must disentangle sex differences in sexual disgust. Stevenson et al. (2011) did not find decreased disgust sensitivity in aroused male participants to one image without pathogen salience (the stimuli was of a river covered in garbage). Further research should determine whether men, who tend to have lower disgust sensitivity, show the same reduction in disgust reactivity to pathogen cues overall as those women with low disgust sensitivity.

How Disgust Influences Sexual Arousal

The presence of disgust elicitors or the emotion of disgust may indicate that an unpropitious mating is more likely thus reducing the motivation, through sexual arousal, to mate. Clinically, disgust has been shown to have important effects on women's sexual functioning. Women diagnosed with vaginismus (a condition in which vaginal spasms make intercourse difficult or impossible) were found to have greater overall disgust sensitivity as measured by the DS (Haidt et al., 1994) than women with dyspareunia (genital pain related to intercourse) and women without sexual complaints (De Jong, Van Overveld, Weijmar Schultz, Peters, & Buwalda, 2009). Unexpectedly, this study showed no differences between groups on ratings from the Sexual Disgust Questionnaire (e.g., "To what extent are you willing to lie beneath bedclothes in a hotel that look unwashed, and below which previous guests may have had sexual intercourse?") (De Jong et al., 2009). However, a follow-up study found both women with vaginismus and dyspareunia showed greater implicit disgust associations to sexual stimuli, and that women with vaginismus showed greater facial muscle activation reflecting disgust when viewing an erotic film (Borg et al., 2010).

Although the clinical implications of heightened disgust sensitivity have been explored, how disgust influences sexual arousal has not been tested extensively. Some previous studies have explored how disgust within a sexual context influences reported arousal. Women who report more disgust at erotica also report less sexual arousal (Koukounas & McCabe, 1997). Malamuth and Check (1980) found that males who read vignettes of sexual encounters found those in which the woman was described as disgusted as less sexually arousing. Vonderheide and Mosher (1988) found the more disgust women reported when imagining inserting a contraceptive diaphragm, the less arousal they report at imagining a subsequent sexual interaction, but have evidence this reflects underlying negative attitudes about sexuality. One study is unique in that it tested participants' sexual decision-making after disgust was elicited. Participants exposed to the smell of feces reported greater propensity to wear a condom than controls (Tybur, Bryan, Magnan, & Hooper, 2011).

In the same study described more in detail above, Fleischman et al. (n.d.) induced disgust by having participants rate 18 disgusting images before viewing an erotic video. The study found that those in the disgust before erotic condition showed lower sexual arousal (as gauged with VPA) than women in the other conditions. Moreover, disgust had a linear effect on sexual arousal. There was a strong direct correlation between the strength of disgust ratings and the decrease in subsequent sexual arousal. Disgust, here elicited by extreme cues of pathogen presence, seems well designed to dampen sexual arousal and prevent the motivation to engage in a dangerous or unpropitious mating.

Disgust has been implicated in asexuality (Carrigan, 2011), sexual aversion (Carnes, 1998), and hypoactive sexual desire (Brauer et al., 2012) as well as vaginismus and dyspareunia (Borg et al., 2010; De Jong et al., 2009). Although Fleischman et al. (n.d.) cannot speak to how long the effects of disgust on dampened sexual arousal will last, it is clinically relevant to consider the greater risks of mating for women over evolutionary time when considering female sexual disorders. From an evolutionary perspective, aversion toward sexual contact, especially in the face of cues and contexts of possible disease presence, would no doubt have been adaptive. Moreover, the adaptive payoff of sexual activity is likely part of the information processing. The previous study only involved women between day 5 and 10 of the menstrual cycle; however, hormonal effects on the reciprocal interaction of disgust and sexual arousal in women would be a fruitful new avenue for research.

Conclusions and Future Directions

The study of disgust is still in its infancy in many ways. One of the most intriguing ideas to come out of the disgust literature recently is the idea that the immune system and the disgust system are proximately integrated in some way. As mentioned previously, recently ill participants show enhanced attention to disease cues (S. Miller & Maner, 2011). Schaller, Miller, Gervais, Yager, and Chen (2010) found that mere exposure to pathogen cues increased cytokine circulation in the blood. Men and women have experienced different selection pressures with regard to pathogens and the costs and benefits of disease avoidance. Further work should be conducted using immune markers to investigate men and women's different response to disease cues. Finally, pathogens may alter sexual disgust. Dawkins (2006) speculated that sexually transmitted diseases might increase the libido of their hosts. Certainly it could also be in sexually transmitted pathogens' best interest to decrease the sexual disgust of their hosts.

References

Abramowitz, J. S., Braddock, A. E., & Moore, E. L. (2008). Psychological treatment of obsessive-compulsive disorder. In M. M. Antony & M. B. Stein (Eds.), *Oxford handbook of anxiety and related disorders: Oxford library of psychology* (pp. 391–404). New York: Oxford University Press. Retrieved from http://books.google.co.uk/books?hl=en&lr=&id=DKD DqOw6Y7wC&oi=fnd&pg=PA391&dq=abramowitz+ oxford+handbook+of+anxiety+moore&ots=oRvJSWntb 1&sig=5FLIdu7DCdgIeTjz6woHUHty2eE#v=onepage &q=abramowitz%20oxford%20handbook%20of%20 anxiety%20moore&f=false

Angyal, A. (1941). Disgust and related aversions. *The Journal of Abnormal and Social Psychology, 36* (3), 393.

Ariely, D., & Loewenstein, G. (2006). The heat of the moment: The effect of sexual arousal on sexual decision making. *Journal of Behavioral Decision Making, 19*(2), 87–98.

Arnold, M., Tóth, I., & Faredin, I. (1980). Radioimmunological study of the effect of hormonal contraceptives upon the progesterone level of saliva (author's transl). *Zahn-, Mund-, und Kieferheilkunde mit Zentralblatt, 68*(7), 713.

Auerbach, L., Hafner, T., Huber, J. C., & Panzer, S. (2002). Influence of low-dose oral contraception on peripheral blood lymphocyte subsets at particular phases of the hormonal cycle. *Fertility and Sterility, 78*(1), 83–89.

Bleich, A. T., Sheffield, J. S., Wendel, G. D., Sigman, A., & Cunningham, F. G. (2012). Disseminated gonococcal infection in women. *Obstetrics & Gynecology, 119* (3), 597–602. doi:10.1097/AOG.0b013e318244eda9.

Bloom, S. (2002). *Practical gastroenterology: A comprehensive guide.* London: Martin Dunitz.

Bogetto, F., Venturello, S., Albert, U., Maina, G., & Ravizza, L. (1999). Gender-related clinical differences in obsessive-compulsive disorder. *European Psychiatry, 14*(8), 434–441.

Borg, C., & De Jong, P. J. (2012). Feelings of disgust and disgust-induced avoidance weaken following induced sexual arousal in women. *PLoS One, 7*(9), e44111.

Borg, C., De Jong, P. J., & Schultz, W. W. (2010). Vaginismus and dyspareunia: Automatic vs. deliberate disgust responsivity. *The Journal of Sexual Medicine, 7*(6), 2149–2157. doi:10.1111/j.1743-6109.2010.01800.x.

Bouman, A., Moes, H., Heineman, M. J., De Leij, L., & Faas, M. (2001). The immune response during the luteal phase of the ovarian cycle: Increasing sensitivity of human monocytes to endotoxin. *Fertility and Sterility, 76*(3), 555–559.

Brauer, M., van Leeuwen, M., Janssen, E., Newhouse, S. K., Heiman, J. R., & Laan, E. (2012). Attentional and affective processing of sexual stimuli in women with hypoactive sexual desire disorder. *Archives of Sexual*

Behavior, 41(4), 891–905. doi:10.1007/s10508-011-9820-7.

Burns, G. L., Keortge, S. G., Formea, G. M., & Sternberger, L. G. (1996). Revision of the Padua Inventory of obsessive compulsive disorder symptoms: Distinctions between worry, obsessions, and compulsions. *Behaviour Research and Therapy, 34*(2), 163–173.

Buyon, J. P. (1996). Oral contraceptives in women with systemic lupus erythematosus. In *Annales De Médecine Interne* (Vol. 147, pp. 259–264). Retrieved from http:// cat.inist.fr/?aModele=afficheN&cpsidt=3233753

Calder, A. J., Beaver, J. D., Davis, M. H., Van Ditzhuijzen, J., Keane, J., & Lawrence, A. D. (2007). Disgust sensitivity predicts the insula and pallidal response to pictures of disgusting foods. *European Journal of Neuroscience, 25*(11), 3422–3428. doi:10. 1111/j.1460-9568.2007.05604.x.

Carnes, P. J. (1998). The case for sexual anorexia: An interim report on 144 patients with sexual disorders. *Sexual Addiction & Compulsivity, 5*(4), 293–309. doi:10.1080/10720169808402338.

Carrigan, M. (2011). There's more to life than sex? Difference and commonality within the asexual community. *Sexualities, 14*(4), 462–478. doi:10.1177/ 1363460711406462.

Chavanne, T. J., & Gallup, G. G. J. (1998). Variations in risk taking behavior among female college students as a function of the menstrual cycle. *Evolution and Human Behavior, 19*(1), 27–32. doi:10.1016/S1090-5138(98)00016-6.

Clark, W. R. (2007). *In defense of self: How the immune system really works in managing health and disease.* Oxford, USA: Oxford University Press.

Clark, R. D., & Hatfield, E. (1989). Gender differences in receptivity to sexual offers. *Journal of Psychology & Human Sexuality, 2*(1), 39–55.

Conway, C. A., Jones, B. C., DeBruine, L. M., Welling, L. L. M., Law Smith, M. J., Perrett, D. I., et al. (2007). Salience of emotional displays of danger and contagion in faces is enhanced when progesterone levels are raised. *Hormones and Behavior, 51*(2), 202–206.

Curtis, V., Aunger, R., & Rabie, T. (2004). Evidence that disgust evolved to protect from risk of disease. *Proceedings: Biological Sciences, 271*, 131–133.

Darwin, C. (1872/1965). *The expression of the emotions in man and animals.* London, UK: John Murray.

Dawkins, R. (2006). *The selfish gene.* New York: Oxford University Press.

De Jong, P. J., Peters, M., & Vanderhallen, I. (2002). Disgust and disgust sensitivity in spider phobia: Facial EMG in response to spider and oral disgust imagery. *Journal of Anxiety Disorders, 16*(5), 477–493. doi:10. 1016/S0887-6185(02)00167-6.

De Jong, P. J., Van Overveld, M., Weijmar Schultz, W., Peters, M. L., & Buwalda, F. M. (2009). Disgust and contamination sensitivity in vaginismus and dyspareunia. *Archives of Sexual Behavior, 38*(2), 244–252.

DeBruine, L. M., Jones, B. C., Tybur, J. M., Lieberman, D., & Griskevicius, V. (2010). Women's preferences for masculinity in male faces are predicted by pathogen disgust, but not by moral or sexual disgust. *Evolution and Human Behavior, 31*(1), 69–74.

DeBruine, L. M., Jones, B. C., Crawford, J. R., Welling, L. L. M., & Little, A. C. (2010). The health of a nation predicts their mate preferences: cross-cultural variation in women's preferences for masculinized male faces. *Proceedings of the Royal Society B: Biological Sciences, 277*(1692), 2405–2410. doi:10.1098/rspb.2009.2184.

Diamond, J. (1999). *Guns, steel and germs: The fate of human societies*. New York: WW Norton.

Dillon, K. M., & Brooks, D. (1992). Unusual cleaning behavior in the luteal phase. *Psychological Reports, 70*(1), 35.

Drife, J. O. (1996). *The benefits and risks of oral contraceptives today* (1st ed.). London: Informa HealthCare.

Duncan, L. A., Schaller, M., & Park, J. H. (2009). Perceived vulnerability to disease: Development and validation of a 15-item self-report instrument. *Personality and Individual Differences, 47*(6), 541–546.

Ekman, P., & Friesen, W. V. (1971). Constants across cultures in the face and emotion. *Journal of Personality and Social Psychology, 17*(2), 124.

Ekman, P., Friesen, W. V., & Hager, J. C. (2002). Facial action coding system. *A Human Face*. Retrieved from http://library.wur.nl/WebQuery/clc/1810828

Faas, M., Bouman, A., Moesa, H., Heineman, M. J., De Leij, L., & Schuiling, G. (2000). The immune response during the luteal phase of the ovarian cycle: A Th2-type response? *Fertility and Sterility, 74*(5), 1008–1013.

Faulkner, J., Schaller, M., Park, J. H., & Duncan, L. A. (2004). Evolved disease-avoidance mechanisms and contemporary xenophobic attitudes. *Group Processes & Intergroup Relations, 7*(4), 333–353. doi:10.1177/1368430204046142.

Fessler, D. M. (2001). Luteal phase immunosuppression and meat eating. *Rivista di Biologia Biology Forum, 94*(3), 403–426.

Fessler, D. M. T. (2002). Reproductive immunosuppression and diet. An evolutionary perspective on pregnancy sickness and meat consumption. *Current Anthropology, 43*(1), 19–61.

Fessler, D. M. T., Arguello, A. P., Mekdara, J. M., & Macias, R. (2003). Disgust sensitivity and meat consumption: A test of an emotivist account of moral vegetarianism. *Appetite, 41*(1), 31–41.

Fessler, D. M. T., Eng, S. J., & Navarrete, C. D. (2005). Elevated disgust sensitivity in the first trimester of pregnancy: Evidence supporting the compensatory prophylaxis hypothesis. *Evolution and Human Behavior, 26*(4), 344–351.

Fessler, D. M. T., & Fleischman, D. S. (2011). Progesterone's effects on the psychology of disease avoidance: Support for the compensatory behavioral prophylaxis hypothesis. *Hormones and Behavior, 59* (2), 271–275.

Fessler, D. M. T., & Haley, K. (2006). Guarding the perimeter: The outside-inside dichotomy in disgust and bodily experience. *Cognition & Emotion, 20*(1), 3–19. doi:10.1080/02699930500215181.

Fessler, D. M. T., & Navarrete, C. D. (2003a). Meat is good to taboo: Dietary proscriptions as a product of the interaction of psychological mechanisms and social processes. *Journal of Cognition and Culture, 3* (1), 1–40. doi:10.1163/156853703321598563.

Fessler, D. M. T., & Navarrete, C. D. (2003b). Domain-specific variation in disgust sensitivity across the menstrual cycle. *Evolution and Human Behavior, 24*(6), 406–417. doi:10.1016/S1090-5138(03)00054-0.

Fessler, D. M. T., & Navarrete, C. D. (2005). The effect of age on death disgust: Challenges to terror management perspectives. *Evolutionary Psychology*. Retrieved from http://psycnet.apa.org/psycinfo/2006-23138-019

Fessler, D. M. T., Pillsworth, E. G., & Flamson, T. J. (2004). Angry men and disgusted women: An evolutionary approach to the influence of emotions on risk taking. *Organizational Behavior and Human Decision Processes, 95*(1), 107–123.

Flaxman, S. M., & Sherman, P. W. (2000). Morning sickness: A mechanism for protecting mother and embryo. *Quarterly Review of Biology, 75*(2), 113–148.

Fleischman, D. S., & Fessler, D. M. T. (2007). Differences in dietary intake as a function of sexual activity and hormonal contraception. *Evolutionary Psychology, 5*(1), 642–652.

Fleischman, D. S., & Fessler, D. M. T. (2009). *Progesterone effects on women's psychology: Support for the compensatory prophylaxis hypothesis*. Paper presented at the 21st Annual Human Behavior and Evolution Society Conference, Fullerton, CA.

Fleischman, D. S., Hamilton, L. D., Fessler, D. M. T., & Meston, C. (2014). *Disgust versus lust: Exploring the reciprocal interaction of disgust and fear on sexual arousal in women*. Manuscript submitted for publication.

Haake, P., Krueger, T. H. C., Goebel, M. U., Heberling, K. M., Hartmann, U., & Schedlowski, M. (2004). Effects of sexual arousal on lymphocyte subset circulation and cytokine production in man. *Neuroimmunomodulation, 11*(5), 293–298.

Haidt, J. (2006). *The happiness hypothesis*. New York: Basic Books.

Haidt, J., McCauley, C., & Rozin, P. (1994). Individual differences in sensitivity to disgust: A scale sampling seven domains of disgust elicitors. *Personality and Individual Differences, 16*(5), 701–713.

Hart, B. L. (1990). Behavioral adaptations to pathogens and parasites: Five strategies. *Neuroscience & Biobehavioral Reviews, 14*(3), 273–294.

Haselton, M. G., & Buss, D. M. (2000). Error management theory: A new perspective on biases in cross-sex mind reading. *Journal of Personality and Social Psychology, 78*(1), 81.

Hatcher, R. A., & Namnoum, A. B. (2004). The menstrual cycle. *Contraceptive Technology, 18*, 63–72.

Jones, B. C., DeBruine, L. M., Perrett, D. I., Little, A. C., Feinberg, D. R., & Law Smith, M. J. (2008). Effects of menstrual cycle phase on face preferences. *Archives of Sexual Behavior, 37*(1), 78–84.

Jones, B. C., Perrett, D. I., Little, A. C., Boothroyd, L., Cornwell, R. E., Feinberg, D. R., et al. (2005). Menstrual cycle, pregnancy and oral contraceptive use alter attraction to apparent health in faces. *Proceedings of the Royal Society B: Biological Sciences, 272*(1561), 347.

Kelly, D. (2011). *Yuck!: The nature and moral significance of disgust.* MIT Press. Retrieved from http://books.google.co.uk/books?hl=en&lr=&id=j-VGSQPE40oC&oi=fnd&pg=PP1&dq=yuck+kelly&ots=WdzpPXPAKr&sig=S-z80IvvuMRnrgOnijDb0BD9vKM

Keuthen, N. J., O'Sullivan, R. L., Hayday, C. F., Peets, K. E., Jenike, M. A., & Baer, L. (1997). The relationship of menstrual cycle and pregnancy to compulsive hairpulling. *Psychotherapy and Psychosomatics, 66*(1), 33–37.

Koukounas, E., & McCabe, M. (1997). Sexual and emotional variables influencing sexual response to erotica. *Behaviour Research and Therapy.* Retrieved from http://psycnet.apa.org/psycinfo/1997-08057-005

Kozlowski, P. A., Williams, S. B., Lynch, R. M., Flanigan, T. P., Patterson, R. R., Cu-Uvin, S., et al. (2002). Differential induction of mucosal and systemic antibody responses in women after nasal, rectal, or vaginal immunization: Influence of the menstrual cycle. *Journal of Immunology (Baltimore, Md.: 1950), 169*(1), 566–574.

Kurzban, R., Dukes, A., & Weeden, J. (2010). Sex, drugs and moral goals: Reproductive strategies and views about recreational drugs. *Proceedings of the Royal Society B: Biological Sciences, 277*(1699), 3501–3508.

Labad, J., Menchon, J. M., Alonso, P., Segalas, C., Jimenez, S., & Vallejo, J. (2005). Female reproductive cycle and obsessive-compulsive disorder. *The Journal of Clinical Psychiatry, 66*(4), 428.

Laland, K. N., & Brown, G. R. (2011). *Sense and nonsense: Evolutionary perspectives on human behaviour.* Oxford: Oxford University Press.

Lang, P. J., Bradley, M. M., & Cuthbert, B. N. (1999). *International affective picture system (IAPS): Instruction manual and affective ratings.* Gainesville, FL: The Center for Research in Psychophysiology, University of Florida.

Leakey, R. (1994). *The origin of humankind.* London: Weidenfeld and Nicolson.

Lieberman, D., Pillsworth, E. G., & Haselton, M. G. (2011). Kin affiliation across the ovulatory cycle: females avoid fathers when fertile. *Psychological Science, 22*(1), 13–18.

Little, A. C., DeBruine, L. M., & Jones, B. C. (2011). Exposure to visual cues of pathogen contagion changes preferences for masculinity and symmetry in opposite-sex faces. *Proceedings of the Royal Society B: Biological Sciences, 278*(1714), 2032–2039.

Lochmiller, R. L., & Deerenberg, C. (2000). Trade-offs in evolutionary immunology: Just what is the cost of immunity? *Oikos, 88*(1), 87–98.

Lohse, A. (2012, January 25). Lohse: Telling the truth. *The Dartmouth.* Retrieved from http://thedartmouth.com/2012/01/25/opinion/lohse

Madkan, V. K., Giancola, A. A., Sra, K. K., & Tyring, S. K. (2006). Sex differences in the transmission, prevention, and disease manifestations of sexually transmitted diseases. *Archives of Dermatology, 142*(3), 365.

Malamuth, N. M., & Check, J. V. (1980). Sexual arousal to rape and consenting depictions: The importance of the woman's arousal. *Journal of Abnormal Psychology, 89*(6), 763.

Mancini, F., Gragnani, A., & D'Olimpio, F. (2001). The connection between disgust and obsessions and compulsions in a non-clinical sample. *Personality and Individual Differences, 31*(7), 1173–1180.

Mancini, F., Gragnani, A., Orazi, F., & Grazia Pietrangeli, M. (1999). Obsessions and compulsions: Normative data on the Padua Inventory from an Italian non-clinical adolescent sample. *Behaviour Research and Therapy, 37*(10), 919–925.

Miller, S. L., & Maner, J. K. (2011). Sick body, vigilant mind the biological immune system activates the behavioral immune system. *Psychological Science, 22*(12), 1467–1471.

Miller, S. L., & Maner, J. K. (2012). Overperceiving disease cues: The basic cognition of the behavioral immune system. *Journal of Personality and Social Psychology, 102*(6), 1198.

Miller, G., Tybur, J. M., & Jordan, B. D. (2007). Ovulatory cycle effects on tip earnings by lap dancers: Economic evidence for human estrus? *Evolution and Human Behavior, 28*(6), 375–381.

Moore, F. R., Cornwell, R. E., Smith, M. J. L., Al Dujaili, E. A. S., Sharp, M., & Perrett, D. I. (2011). Evidence for the stress-linked immunocompetence handicap hypothesis in human male faces. *Proceedings of the Royal Society B: Biological Sciences, 278*(1706), 774–780.

Navarette, C. D., Fessler, D. M. T., & Eng, S. J. (2007). Elevated ethnocentrism in the first trimester of pregnancy. *Evolution and Human Behavior, 28*(1), 60–65. doi:10.1016/j.evolhumbehav.2006.06.002.

Navarrete, C. D., & Fessler, D. M. T. (2006). Disease avoidance and ethnocentrism: The effects of disease vulnerability and disgust sensitivity on intergroup attitudes. *Evolution and Human Behavior, 27*(4), 270–282. doi:10.1016/j.evolhumbehav.2005.12.001.

Nesse, R. M. (2005). Natural selection and the regulation of defenses: A signal detection analysis of the smoke detector principle. *Evolution and Human Behavior, 26* (1), 88–105.

Neumark-Sztainer, D., Story, M., Resnick, M. D., & Blum, R. W. (1997). Adolescent vegetarians: A behavioral profile of a school-based population in Minnesota. *Archives of Pediatrics and Adolescent Medicine, 151*(8), 833.

Oaten, M., Stevenson, R. J., & Case, T. I. (2009). Disgust as a disease-avoidance mechanism. *Psychological Bulletin, 135*(2), 303.

Olatunji, B. O., Haidt, J., McKay, D., & David, B. (2008). Core, animal reminder, and contamination disgust: Three kinds of disgust with distinct personality, behavioral, physiological, and clinical correlates. *Journal of Research in Personality, 42*(5), 1243–1259.

Olatunji, B. O., Moretz, M. W., McKay, D., Bjorklund, F., De Jong, P. J., Haidt, J., et al. (2009). Confirming the three-factor structure of the Disgust Scale—Revised in eight countries. *Journal of Cross-Cultural Psychology, 40*(2), 234–255.

Quigley, J. F., Sherman, M. F., & Sherman, N. C. (1997). Personality disorder symptoms, gender, and age as predictors of adolescent disgust sensitivity. *Personality and Individual Differences, 22*(5), 661–667. doi:10.1016/S0191-8869(96)00255-3.

Rohrmann, S., & Hopp, H. (2008). Cardiovascular indicators of disgust. *International Journal of Psychophysiology.* Retrieved from http://psycnet.apa.org/psycinfo/2008-05424-006

Rozin, P., & Fallon, A. E. (1987). A perspective on disgust. *Psychological Review, 94*(1), 23–41.

Rozin, P., Haidt, J., & McCauley, C. R. (2008). *Disgust.* Retrieved from http://doi.apa.org/?uid=2008-07784-047

Rozin, P., Haidt, J., McCauley, C., Dunlop, L., & Ashmore, M. (1999). Individual differences in disgust sensitivity: Comparisons and evaluations of paper-and-pencil versus behavioral measures. *Journal of Research in Personality, 33*(3), 330–351.

Ryan, S., Oaten, M., Stevenson, R. J., & Case, T. I. (2012). Facial disfigurement is treated like an infectious disease. *Evolution and Human Behavior, 33*(6), 639–646. doi:10.1016/j.evolhumbehav.2012.04.001.

Scanlan, J. M., Werner, J. J., Legg, R. L., & Laudenslager, M. L. (1995). Natural killer cell activity is reduced in association with oral contraceptive use. *Psychoneuroendocrinology, 20*(3), 281–287. doi:10.1016/0306-4530(94)00059-J.

Schaller, M., & Duncan, L. A. (2007). The behavioral immune system: Its evolution and social psychological implications. In J. P. Forgas, M. G. Haselton, & W. von Hippel (Eds.), *Evolution and the social mind* (pp. 293–307). New York: Psychology Press.

Schaller, M., Miller, G. E., Gervais, W. M., Yager, S., & Chen, E. (2010). Mere visual perception of other people's disease symptoms facilitates a more aggressive immune response. *Psychological Science, 21*(5), 649.

Schaller, M., & Park, J. H. (2011). The behavioral immune system (and why it matters). *Current Directions in Psychological Science, 20*(2), 99–103.

Schaller, M., Park, J., & Faulkner, J. (2003). Prehistoric dangers and contemporary prejudices. *European Review of Social Psychology, 14*(1), 105–137.

Schienle, A., Stark, R., Walter, B., & Vaitl, D. (2003). The connection between disgust sensitivity and blood related fears, faintness symptoms, and obsessive compulsiveness in a non clinical sample. *Anxiety, Stress & Coping, 16*(2), 185–193. doi:10.1080/10615806.2003.10382972.

Shapira, N. A., Liu, Y., He, A. G., Bradley, M. M., Lessig, M. C., James, G. A., et al. (2003). Brain activation by disgust-inducing pictures in obsessive-compulsive disorder. *Biological Psychiatry, 54*(7), 751–756.

Sintchak, G., & Geer, J. H. (1975). A vaginal plethysmograph system. *Psychophysiology, 12*(1), 113–115.

Stark, R., Schienle, A., Walter, B., Kirsch, P., Sammer, G., Ott, U., et al. (2003). Hemodynamic responses to fear and disgust-inducing pictures: an fMRI study. *International Journal of Psychophysiology, 50*(3), 225–234.

Stark, R., Zimmermann, M., Kagerer, S., Schienle, A., Walter, B., Weygandt, M., et al. (2007). Hemodynamic brain correlates of disgust and fear ratings. *NeuroImage, 37*(2), 663–673. doi:10.1016/j.neuroimage.2007.05.005.

Stevenson, R. J., Case, T. I., & Oaten, M. J. (2011). Effect of self-reported sexual arousal on responses to sex-related and non-sex-related disgust cues. *Archives of Sexual Behavior, 40*(1), 79–85.

Stevenson, R. J., Oaten, M. J., Case, T. I., Repacholi, B. M., & Wagland, P. (2010). Children's response to adult disgust elicitors: Development and acquisition. *Developmental Psychology, 46*(1), 165.

Thorneycroft, I. H., & Stone, S. C. (1972). Radioimmunoassay of serum progesterone in women receiving oral contraceptive steroids. *Contraception, 5*(2), 129–146.

Thornhill, R., & Gangestad, S. W. (2006). Facial sexual dimorphism, developmental stability, and susceptibility to disease in men and women. *Evolution and Human Behavior, 27*(2), 131–144.

Trivers, R. L. (1996). Parental investment and sexual selection. In L. D. Houck & L.C. Drickamer (Eds.), *Foundations of animal behavior: Classic papers with commentaries* (pp. 795–838). Chicago, USA: University of Chicago Press.

Trzonkowski, P., Myśliwska, J., Tukaszuk, K., Szmit, E., Bryl, E., & Myśliwski, A. (2001). Luteal phase of the menstrual cycle in young healthy women is associated with decline in interleukin 2 levels. *Hormone and Metabolic Research, 33*(6), 348–353. doi:10.1055/s-2001-15420.

Tybur, J. M., Bryan, A. D., Lieberman, D., Caldwell Hooper, A. E., & Merriman, L. A. (2011). Sex differences and sex similarities in disgust sensitivity. *Personality and Individual Differences, 51*(3), 343–348.

Tybur, J. M., & Gangestad, S. W. (2011). Mate preferences and infectious disease: Theoretical considerations and evidence in humans. *Philosophical*

Transactions of the Royal Society, B: Biological Sciences, 366(1583), 3375–3388.

Tybur, J. M., Lieberman, D., & Griskevicius, V. (2009). Microbes, mating, and morality: Individual differences in three functional domains of disgust. *Journal of Personality and Social Psychology, 97*(1), 103–122.

Tybur, J. M., Bryan, A. D., Magnan, R. E., & Hooper, A. E. C. (2011). Smells like safe sex olfactory pathogen primes increase intentions to use condoms. *Psychological Science, 22*(4), 478–480.

Tybur, J. M., Lieberman, D., Kurzban, R., & DeScioli, P. (2012). Disgust: Evolved function and structure. *Psychological Review.* doi:10.1037/a0030778.

Van Oppen, P. (1992). Obsessions and compulsions: Dimensional structure, reliability, convergent and divergent validity of the Padua Inventory. *Behaviour Research and Therapy, 30*(6), 631–637.

Van Overveld, M., De Jong, P. J., Peters, M. L., & Schouten, E. (2011). The Disgust Scale-R: A valid and reliable index to investigate separate disgust domains? *Personality and Individual Differences, 51*(3), 325–330.

Vonderheide, S. G., & Mosher, D. L. (1988). Should I put in my diaphragm? *Journal of Psychology & Human Sexuality, 1*(1), 97–111.

Vulink, N. C., Denys, D., Bus, L., & Westenberg, H. G. (2006). Female hormones affect symptom severity in obsessive-compulsive disorder. *International Clinical Psychopharmacology, 21*(3), 171.

Wedekind, C., Seebeck, T., Bettens, F., & Paepke, A. J. (1995). MHC-dependent mate preferences in humans.

Proceedings: Biological Sciences, 260(1359), 245–249.

Weissman, M. M., Bland, R. C., Canino, G. J., & Greenwald, S. (1994). The cross national epidemiology of obsessive compulsive disorder: The Cross National Collaborative Group. *Journal of Clinical Psychiatry.* Retrieved from http://psycnet.apa.org/psycinfo/1994-37618-001

Wilder, R. L. (2006). Hormones, pregnancy, and autoimmune diseases. *Annals of the New York Academy of Sciences, 840*(Neuroimmunomodulation: Molecular aspects, integrative systems, and clinical advances), 45–50.

Williams, K. E., & Koran, L. M. (1997). Obsessive-compulsive disorder in pregnancy, the puerperium, and the premenstruum. *The Journal of Clinical Psychiatry, 58*(7), 330.

Wright, P., He, G., Shapira, N. A., Goodman, W. K., & Liu, Y. (2004). Disgust and the insula: fMRI responses to pictures of mutilation and contamination. *Neuroreport, 15*(15), 2347.

Zohar, A. H. (1999). The epidemiology of obsessive-compulsive disorder in children and adolescents. *Child and Adolescent Psychiatric Clinics of North America.* Retrieved from http://psycnet.apa.org/psycinfo/1999-03673-001

Zohar, A. H., & Bruno, R. (2006). Normative and pathological obsessive-compulsive behavior and ideation in childhood: A question of timing. *Journal of Child Psychology and Psychiatry, 38*(8), 993–999.

Female Perceptions of Male Body Movements

16

Bernhard Fink, Bettina Weege, Nick Neave, Bettina Ried, and Olival Cardoso Do Lago

Introduction

The morphology of both the human face and body affects people's social perception of others, and this has consequences for human mate preferences (for review, see Fink & Penton-Voak, 2002; Gangestad & Scheyd, 2005; Rhodes, 2006). Evolutionary psychologists argue that the sensitivity towards variation in facial and body morphology is neither arbitrarily nor culturally bound, but reflects evolved cognitive mechanisms which facilitate mate selection and reproductive success (for review see Grammer, Fink, Møller, & Thornhill, 2003; Little, Jones, & DeBruine, 2011). Following this logic, it is thought that attractiveness decisions in particular characterize people's preference for an individual's facial and/or body morphology, as they convey aspects of mate quality. This quality includes physical and personality characteristics, both of which affect the way we perceive the attractiveness of others (Buss, 1985; Buss & Barnes, 1986; Buss & Schmitt, 1993).

While the evidence in support of the evolutionary psychology perspective on human social perception seems to be strong, most of the studies investigating the relationships between certain physical features and attractiveness perception have concentrated on static representations of faces and bodies. These studies have typically utilized two-dimensional (2D) stimuli in the form of face and/or body photographs (for review see Grammer, Fink, et al., 2003; Grammer, Keki, Striebel, Atzmüller, & Fink, 2003). Such experiments are useful for testing people's sensitivity and evaluations of static representations of the face and body, but they can only explain some proportion of the variation in everyday social perception, as there is an inherent limitation with these stimuli in terms of ecological validity. As such, there is comparably little insight into the significance of quality cues that may be derived from dynamic representations of human faces and bodies and how they could affect mate preferences.

In a meta-analysis, Langlois et al. (2000) reported that studies in attractiveness research used different types of stimulus presentation modes (photographic images, video clips, and in situ encounters) and that these different types convey different information, which subsequently leads to different attractiveness judgments. With regard to face perception, Roark, Barrett, Spence, Abdi, and O'Toole (2003) showed that the implicit social signals provided by a moving face (such as gaze cues, expression, and facial speech) mediate the effects of facial motion on recognition. As with

B. Fink (✉)
Department of Psychology, University of Göttingen, Goßlerstraße 14, 37073 Göttingen, Germany

Courant Research Centre Evolution of Social Behavior, Kellnerweg 6, 37077 Göttingen, Germany
e-mail: bernhard.fink@ieee.org; bfink@gwdg.de

V.A. Weekes-Shackelford and T.K. Shackelford (eds.), *Evolutionary Perspectives on Human Sexual Psychology and Behavior*, Evolutionary Psychology, DOI 10.1007/978-1-4939-0314-6_16, © Springer Science+Business Media New York 2014

faces, viewpoint-dependent perceptions are also known for the body. Doyle (2009) reported a peak shift effect in male attractiveness perception of female bodies when they were moving, suggesting that while walking, the movement of the waist and hip results in continuously alternate representations of left and right side waist-to-hip ratios (WHR; for review see Singh, 2002). This result seems to sit comfortably with the findings of Johnson and Tassinary (2005) who varied both body morphology (in terms of WHR) and motion (male exaggerated vs. female exaggerated movements) of animated human walkers, showing that when making social judgments, participants devoted particular visual attention to the waist and hip region.

These and related studies have stimulated scholars to investigate the role of movement cues within the evolutionary psychology framework. They have thus studied whether certain physical and personality characteristics, which are known to influence the perception of static representations of human faces and bodies, can also be derived from their dynamic displays (for review see Hugill, Fink, & Neave, 2010). In this chapter we do not address facial motion, which is an emerging topic that deserves attention in its own right, but instead concentrate on female perception of male body movements and review studies in support of the hypothesis that they affect female mate preferences.

Before we discuss the details of these studies, we consider it essential to give a brief review of the history of human movement research as such knowledge will facilitate the understanding and assessment of more recent approaches. We then deal with studies on key characteristics that can be derived from motion, such as age, gender, and emotional status, and discuss implications for social perception. In considering the most recent research on female perception of male body movements, we present evidence on female perceptions of physical and personality characteristics from male dance movements. Finally, we support our statements by reporting preliminary data on cross-cultural assessments of male dance movements and data on associations of female perception of different types of body movements (i.e., dancing, running, and walking).

A Brief History of Movement Research

The first scientific investigation on human body movement dates back around 150 years, when Charles Darwin performed systematic observations on how individuals communicate nonverbally with each other using direct or indirect "body language," and how this could be understood and interpreted. In *The Expression of the Emotions in Man and Animals*, Darwin (1872) stated that the "language of emotions" is evolved, adaptive, and universal to human culture and serves as a communicator in-between individuals.

At that time, the study of locomotion in living creatures was promoted by the discovery and invention of photographic techniques, as this allowed detailed movement analysis independent of the perceptual limitations of the human visual apparatus. In 1894, Etienne-Jules Marey developed a "methode graphique" in order to study the human body and the physiology of animals; later he invented a high-speed photographic technique called "chronophotography." In 1882 he used this method to capture multiple consecutive images of a variety of animals in motion on a single photographic glass plate, which he later replaced with transparent celluloid film stripes (Braun, 1992; Marey, 1894). At this time, the American businessman and racehorse owner Leland Stanford hired the English photographer Eadweard James Muybridge to analyze his horses' movements. To settle a wager and investigate whether the four hooves of a galloping horse do all leave the ground, Muybridge positioned a set of cameras in a row, activated by trip wires, and captured single shots of the passing horse within less than half a second. He proved that all four hooves lift off the ground, and this was only the beginning of a series of hundreds of thousands of images Muybridge took of animals

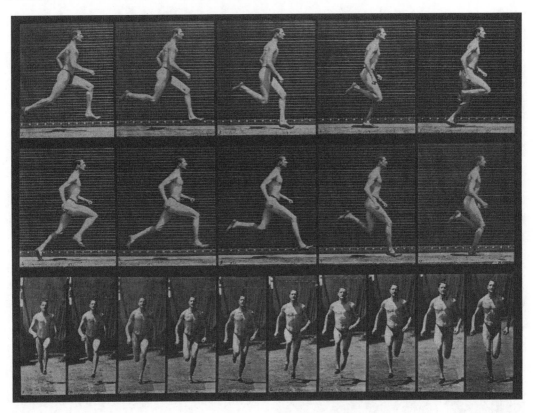

Fig. 16.1 Photographic sequence of a nude running male by Eadweard Muybridge, ca. 1887 (Muybridge Animal Locomotion, plate 60; University of Pennsylvania Digital Archives, with permission)

and humans using his motion sequence photography technique (Braun, 1992). Most famous in his time were Muybridge's studies on human bodies in motion, showing naked males and females performing everyday activities such as walking, dancing, sweeping, or dressing (see Fig. 16.1).

The work of both Marey and Muybridge marked a breakthrough in the representation of human body movement and provided the basis for the later development of cinematography, i.e., the creation of motion picture images. It took several decades before in the 1970s the Swedish psychophysicist Gunnar Johansson started his pioneering work on the scientific understanding of "biological motion," which is the depiction of movement patterns using point-light (P-L) displays. The idea behind this technique was to remove the pictographic shape information of a moving animal or human from the motion pattern itself. Johansson positioned light bulbs onto the head and major joints of a moving participant and filmed them while they walked and danced in a dark room. The resulting video clips of moving light dots were presented to observers, who were able to perceive vivid motion. In the following years Johansson refined this technique and showed that within a fraction of a second, observers were able to perceive human form from motion and identify certain actions from viewing only short clips of P-L displays (Johansson, 1973, 1976; Johansson, von Hofsten, & Jansson, 1980; see Fig. 16.2).

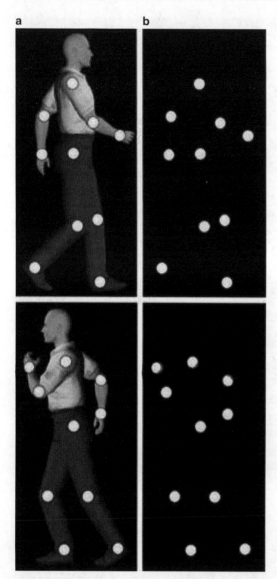

Fig. 16.2 Illustration of the point-light (P-L) displays approach to the study of biological motion as devised by Johansson (1973). Light bulbs were attached to major joints of an actor (**a**), who performed different types of movements. Participants were able to perceive the animations as "human" and identified the character's action from videos, but not from still images (frames) of P-L displays (**b**) (Figure taken from Giese & Poggio, 2003, with permission)

Once the P-L methodology was established, researchers began to use the technique to see if observers could identify specific aspects of information about the moving figure.

What Can Be Perceived from Body Movements?

Recognition of Self and Others

It is vital for humans, a highly social species, to be able to recognize their conspecifics and respond appropriately based upon previous social interactions and/or current knowledge. Relevant information about an individual is provided via several modalities (e.g., appearance, clothing, posture, smell, voice) and in a typical social setting the observer considers and integrates these multiple signals (Grammer, Fink, Juette, Ronzal, & Thornhill, 2001). While researchers were able to isolate some of the key static social cues and investigate their influence upon person perception (e.g., facial attractiveness), it was not until the development of Johansson's P-L technique that researchers could begin to focus their attention onto possible cues provided by motion.

In an initial study using the P-L technique, Cutting and Kozlowski (1977) filmed six close friends as they walked along a straight line. Two months later the same individuals were shown the videos presented from a sagittal viewpoint and asked to identify each walker and provide information as to how they had reached their decision. While the initial performance was not so good (accuracy of 38 % compared to 16.7 % expected by chance), it improved on subsequent trials to 59 %. The observers stated that they were using cues provided by body movement, such as speed, rhythm, amount of arm swing, and stride length, to make their judgments. Interestingly self-recognition was at 46 %, and at first this seems surprisingly good as we hardly view ourselves from a third-person perspective, but perhaps the observers were simply picking the stimulus that they hadn't recognized as being one of their friends?

Stevenage, Nixon, and Vince (1999) expanded this research by investigating how easy it would be to train individuals to recognize gait in unknown individuals under different lighting conditions. They had six volunteers walk in a straight line under daylight, dusk, and

P-L conditions. Observers viewed each walker and were told their "names" and then had to see if they could recognize the same individuals in subsequent clips. It was found that observers could easily learn to recognize the walkers, and this was not influenced by lighting condition or gender of the observer, but female walkers were easier to subsequently identify than males.

In an attempt to uncover the mechanisms that individuals use to recognize someone by their gait, Troje, Westhoff, and Lavrov (2005) presented male and female observers with P-L stimuli from different viewpoint angles. The stimuli were systematically altered such that observers would see the normal unaltered walk, walks in which all stimuli had been normalized with respect to body size or body shape, and two conditions in which walking frequency was altered. After an initial presentation in which observers saw the stimuli and were told the names of the walkers, they then received a series of training sessions. Recognition performance reached a ceiling of 90 % correct recognition after five training sessions, with frontal views providing greater accuracy. The most important cues for recognition were hip rotation, lateral body sway, ratio between hip and shoulder width, and elbow position. Observers were able to accurately identify an individual when their stimuli had been normalized for body shape and walking frequency, leading the researchers to conclude that structural information plays a secondary role to gait kinematics for personal identification. Jokisch, Daum, and Troje (2006) confirmed that recognition of friends was better from a frontal viewpoint, but viewing angle did not influence recognition of self. Clearly then, observers can readily recognize conspecifics just from their body movement patterns, but as mate selection forms an integral part of our sociocultural world, we would expect that the ability to determine the sex of another individual would be not only possible but vital.

Sex and Gender Identification

Using the P-L technique, Kozlowski and Cutting (1977) presented male and female walkers in sagittal view to 30 observers, who were asked to indicate the sex of the walker. Accuracy was significantly above chance and was most accurate when the whole body was presented for viewing. Interestingly, when participants were asked which parts of the movement they thought indicated the person's sex, 76 % of the sample stated that "maleness" was being indicated by shoulder sway, while the entire sample identified hip movements as indicating a female gait. A subsequent meta-analysis of relevant studies confirmed that sex identification accuracy is approximately 66 % from side views and around 71 % from frontal views (Pollick, Kay, Heim, & Stringer, 2005).

Runeson and Frykholm (1983) investigated whether a person could actively deceive an observer into believing they were viewing a member of the opposite sex. Volunteers were asked to perform a range of actions as normal, in an exaggerated gender-typical manner, and in a way that they thought the opposite sex would perform the action. Sex identification accuracy of the P-L stimuli was high in the natural and exaggerated conditions, while accuracy was only slightly lower for the deception condition. This suggests that dynamic displays (even if the person is attempting to fake them) can provide a strong clue as to the sex of a person.

Barclay, Cutting, and Kozlowski (1978) noted that P-L stimuli duration influenced recognition accuracy. In their study males and females were recorded walking and observers viewed four gait samples differing in duration (0.4, 0.8, 1.6, and 4.4 s) and had to judge whether the walker was male or female. Not surprisingly, accuracy was highest at the longest duration, falling to below chance at the two shortest intervals. Thus, viewing at least two complete gait cycles appears to be crucial for sex recognition. In a subsequent experiment the authors reported that sex recognition was severely impaired if the presentation rate was slowed down, a feature that they explained by the observation that in real life we do not see males and females walking in such a manner, and so there are no adequate reference points for comparison.

A key factor in judging the sex of a P-L walker could be the difference in the structural sway of the shoulders and hips (males have broader shoulders and females have a wider pelvis). Cutting (1978a, 1978b) provided support for this by creating artificial walkers differing only in these attributes. Movements of the shoulders or the hips provided in isolation did indeed provide diagnostic cues as to the sex of the walker. Mather and Murdoch (1994) held these anatomical differences constant and established that recognition was still significantly above chance and could be determined by lateral body sway. Here the dynamic cues clearly outweighed the structural cues.

Using a more advanced three-dimensional (3D) motion capture camera system, Troje (2002) recorded males and females walking on a treadmill and created P-L animations that comprised the original walker or were manipulated to display exaggerated male or female movement patterns. Sex recognition accuracy was optimized when the animation was seen in the frontal view and gradually declined as the viewing angle changed. When the viewer was deprived of structural information, performance was barely affected, but when deprived of dynamic information, performance was severely impaired. In order to confirm exactly what observers are looking at when asked to make a sex discrimination decision, Saunders, Williamson, and Troje (2010) presented clips of P-L animations derived from real male and female walkers where their gender could be exaggerated by the technique developed by Troje (2002). Observers viewed an original walk, which had been gender "exaggerated" and was rotated from a front-facing view by up to 90°; viewer gaze patterns were recorded via eye-tracking equipment. When asked to determine the sex of the animation, eye-tracking analysis revealed that observers focused their attention primarily on the shoulders and the hips. Changing the viewing angle and the degree of "maleness"/"femaleness" significantly affected recognition performance, though this did not seem to affect viewing fixations.

The research described thus far appears to suggest that body movement in addition to form is crucial for accurate sex identification. However, other researchers have questioned this with

regard to the P-L methodology. Male and female bodies are morphologically distinctive, a key difference being the size of the waist, which is known to affect judgments of both sex and gender (Lippa, 1983; Singh, 2002). P-L animations provide little information about body shape neither in general nor of the waist specifically, and while researchers have been able to manipulate the shoulder-to-waist ratio (e.g., Mather & Murdoch, 1994), it is impossible to manipulate the WHR using the P-L technique. Johnson and Tassinary (2005) used animated stimuli that depicted a human form of ambiguous sex, which varied both in WHR (ranging from a ratio of 0.5 to 0.9) and in gait (extreme shoulder swagger to extreme hip sway). Observers were shown the figures and asked to judge the sex of the walker and their gender (i.e., how masculine or feminine they were). Judgments of the sex and gender of the walker were more strongly influenced by morphology than by the motion.

In a similar study, McDonnell, Jorg, Hodgins, Newell, and O'Sullivan (2007) created four different animated figures (virtual characters or "avatars")—a realistic male, a realistic female, an androgynous character, and a P-L walker. Motion-captured walks from males and females and walks specifically created to be gender neutral were then applied to the figures, and observers were asked to state whether the figure was male or female. Not surprisingly female walks applied to the female figure and male walks applied to the male figure were perceived as being gender congruent. Neutral walks applied to the male and female figures were also rated as being gender congruent showing that body morphology takes precedence over motion. However, when neutral walks were applied to an androgynous character, motion then became more important in making gender judgments. So, studies have clearly shown that the sex of an individual can easily be determined via the P-L and other motion capture techniques. Humans thus appear to be primed to derive important sociosexual information from an individual's body movements.

Sexual Orientation

As morphology and motion both contribute to assessments of sex and gender, it raises an interesting question as to whether observers can accurately discern the sexual orientation of a walker. Folk wisdom dictates that homosexual males and females possess "gaydar"—the ability to discern homosexuality in others, and there is a cultural stereotype that homosexual males walk in a more feminine manner, while lesbians walk with a more masculine style. Johnson, Gill, Reichman, and Tassinary (2007) set out to specifically assess perceptions of sexual orientation by presenting animated figures that varied morphologically (five levels of WHR) and dynamically (five levels of motion ranging from extreme shoulder swagger to extreme hip sway). Judgments of sexual orientation of walkers perceived to be male were strongly affected by motion but not morphology, while perceptions of sexual orientation of walkers perceived to be female were influenced by both motion and morphology. In a subsequent experiment, males and females categorized themselves as heterosexual or homosexual and were recorded walking on a treadmill. Males and females transformed the movies into figural outlines that were then rated. Accuracy of judgments of sexual orientation was significantly above chance, though accuracy was higher for male than female targets. The adaptive benefit of being able to correctly identify someone's sexual orientation is obvious, and research suggests that such identification may be possible from observing movement patterns. However, support at present is limited; clearly, additional research addressing this question is necessary.

Emotion Perception

Numerous expressive statements underpinned by nonverbal communication govern everyday social interactions. While a significant amount of research has focused on the perception and understanding of emotions from facial expressions, relatively little work had focused on emotions expressed via body movements. An initial attempt by Walk and Homan (1984) assessed viewers' ability to identify different types of dancing and emotions displayed by female actors presented as P-Ls. Mimed emotional sequences (anger, disgust/contempt, fear, happiness, sadness, and surprise) were found to be difficult to interpret on an initial presentation, but following the second presentation, accuracy improved markedly. Interestingly females averaged higher accuracy compared to males, reflecting a consistent finding that females are better at interpreting nonverbal cues than males (Hall, 1978).

In a study also using dancers, Brownlow, Dixon, Egbert, and Radcliffe (1997) asked observers to judge happy from sad in P-L presentations. Sad movements were characterized as non-energetic, slow, sweeping movements, while happy movements were energetic and exaggerated. Dittrich, Troscianko, Lea, and Morgan (1996) also had two experienced dancers (one male, one female) portraying a series of emotions (anger, disgust, fear, grief, joy, and surprise) using both P-L and standard recording techniques. Emotion recognition accuracy was 88 % in the standard video recording condition and 63 % in the P-L animated condition (still significantly above chance).

Atkinson, Dittrich, Gemmell, and Young (2004) asked ten actors to portray anger, disgust, fear, happiness, and sadness in typical, exaggerated, and extremely exaggerated forms. Observers then rated the different versions of the stimuli (P-L dynamic, P-L still, full video dynamic, full video still). Not surprisingly performance was best in the full video dynamic conditions, followed closely by P-L dynamic stimuli. Exaggerating body movements led to a significant increase in accuracy (and higher ratings for "emotional intensity") with the exception of sadness. Focusing just on walking, Roether, Omlor, Christensen, and Giese (2009) asked male and female volunteers to walk in a straight line employing a neutral gait and then with emotionally expressive gaits (anger, fear, happiness, and sadness). Analysis revealed emotion-specific postural and kinematic features of gait; greater head inclination (denoting sadness) and greater elbow flexion (revealing anger and fear) indicated specific emotional states. In addition, walking speed and increases/decreases in the size of particular movements were associated with specific emotions.

It thus appears that observers can detect emotions expressed in movements with a fair degree of accuracy, but what about individuals who have deficits in the processing of social cues? Hubert et al. (2007) assessed emotion recognition in individuals with autism and Asperger's syndrome, and in a group of matched controls. Observers saw 5 s clips of P-L displays comprising actors performing a range of actions (e.g., climbing, jumping) and emotional states and were simply asked to describe what they saw. The autistic participants performed at the same level of the controls in describing the actions, but significantly worse when asked to identify and describe the emotions being portrayed. Once more, the available evidence suggests that humans are primed to perceive key information about another individual (in this case their emotional state) via their body movements.

Social Significance of Body Movement Perception

The evidence we have presented so far demonstrates that humans have a deep-seated ability to perceive critical aspects of person identification from their body movements. Individuals are able to extract information about conspecifics from their gait that could be used to make relevant social decisions; this even extends to making inferential decisions about individuals. Thus, observers can also accurately estimate the weight of an item being raised by an actor from the lifting motion depicted via the P-L technique (Bingham, 1993) and the elasticity of a surface by observing a P-L figure moving across it (Stoffregen & Flynn, 1994). Such decisions are made very rapidly, despite attempts to mask the information (Cutting, Moore, & Morrison, 1988; Johansson,

1976). An advantage of dynamic cues is that they are visible over much greater distances than are say facial expressions, thus providing advance warning of another's possible intentions. It is logical to conclude that the ability to decode information about other people appears to have an innate evolutionary basis; if that is the case, then we should be able to identify the neurological underpinnings of such abilities.

Evidence from Neurobiology/Brain Imaging Studies

Converging lines of evidence point to specific regions of the cortex being involved in the processing of biological motion. Single-cell recordings in macaques have revealed that neurons in the posterior superior temporal sulcus (STS) of both hemispheres were selectively responsive to both form and motion (Perrett et al., 1985). In humans, research using positron emission tomography (PET) and functional magnetic resonance imaging (fMRI) has shown that an analogous region is preferentially activated when observers view P-L figures (Bonda, Petrides, Ostry, & Evans, 1996; Grossman et al., 2000). Further confirmation is provided from studies of individuals with brain injuries localized to this region; damage to the STS causes a specific deficit in biological motion recognition, but spares other aspects of motion perception (Schenk & Zihl, 1997a, 1997b). In an extension of such research, Heberlein, Adolphs, Tranel, and Damasio (2004) asked participants with and without brain damage to view P-L animations and make judgments about their emotional state and personality. Individuals with damage to the right somatosensory cortices were impaired in judging emotions, while impairments in judging personality were associated with damage to the left frontal operculum. This dissociation implies that we possess distinct neural systems for perceiving emotions and personality.

In individuals without brain damage, temporary neurological disruption can be created via transcranial magnetic stimulation (TMS). When

TMS was applied to the scalp overlying the STS, observers experienced difficulties in recognizing P-L sequences presented with "noise" (Grossman, Battelli, & Pascual-Leone, 2005). Thus, both "bottom-up" and "top-down" studies indicate that the STS is specialized for the processing of biological movement. The STS shares reciprocal connections with the amygdala and orbitofrontal cortex, both of which play an important role in social perception and cognition (Adolphs, 1999). There is thus a complex subcortical/cortical system involved in social perception and cognition that begins with the initial processing of movement as "biological" and which then infers the actions, intentions, and emotions of another individual (Allison, Puce, & McCarthy, 2000).

Universality of Body Movement Perception

The fact that the human ability to decode information from P-L animations is done rapidly and accurately and is subserved by dedicated neurological components suggests that the detection and interpretation of biological motion is a fundamental evolutionary mechanism. If this is so, then one might expect to find early developmental abilities in the perception of biological motion. In support, Bertenthal, Proffitt, and Cutting (1984) demonstrated that by 4 months of age, human infants could distinguish between P-L animations presented normally or inverted. In a similar study Simion, Regolin, and Bulf (2008) showed that 2-day-old infants could differentiate between biological motion and random motion P-L displays and prefer to look at human motion than nonhuman motion. Further research has revealed that human infants can also extract meaning from displays of biological motion. For example, Yoon and Johnson (2009) showed that by a year old, infants could track the "gaze" of a P-L actor, despite the absence of socially informative features (face and eyes), indicating that biological motion perception and social cognitive abilities are closely integrated early in development. Children with developmental disorders associated with profound deficits in social

processing (i.e., autism) also experience difficulties in the processing of biological motion in the form of P-L animations (Blake, Turner, Smoski, Pozdol, & Stone, 2003; Moore, Hobson, & Lee, 1997).

If the perception of biological motion is a hardwired adaptation, then one might also expect to find substantial cross-cultural agreement in the perception of certain attributes. While the study of facial expressions of emotion has revealed cultural universals in presentation and perception (Ekman & Friesen, 1971; Ekman et al., 1987), surprisingly little research has focused on cross-cultural perceptions of body movement. Gestures, postures, and spatial orientation vary greatly between and within cultures, though some appear to be universal; for example, greeting behaviors (head nod, eyebrow flash, smiling, mutual gaze) share common components (Argyle, 1988). More recently, Pica, Jackson, Blake, and Troje (2011) presented P-L stimuli of walking cats, pigeons, and humans to the Mundurucu people in the Amazonian territories in Brazil and found that they could readily perceive the global shape that was depicted in the walking characters. Considering this finding, it is likely that the variation in human body movements is perceived in a similar fashion across countries and societies. In pursuing this line of research, we report preliminary data of a study that tested possible similarities of Brazilian and German females' attractiveness perceptions of male dance movements.

Study 1: Brazilian and German Females' Perceptions of British Males' Dances
We had two samples, one of Brazilian and one of German females. Both judged the virtual characters (avatars) of 80 British male dancers (all nonprofessional dancers, whose movements were captured using 3D optical motion capture technology; aged 18–42 years, $M = 21.6$, $SD = 4.0$) on perceived attractiveness. Brazilian females were recruited from the student population at the Escola Superior de Educação Física de Jundiaí, a college near São Paulo (Brazil). Of all 111 participating females, aged 17–42 years, we selected only those who identified themselves as

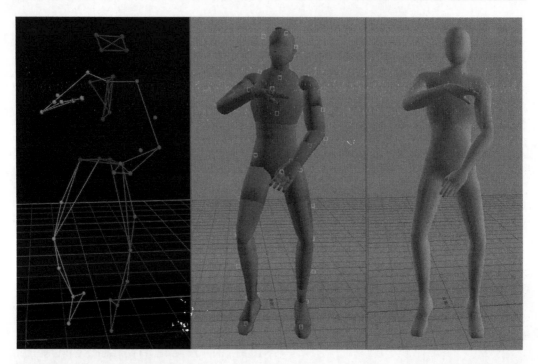

Fig. 16.3 Snapshots of the creation process of a virtual dance character. The initial stick figure with captured markers (*left*), application of the motion data to the actor (*middle*), and the final avatar for presentation (*right*) (Figure taken from Fink et al., 2012, with permission)

having "Latin American" descent. Thus, 48 females remained ($M = 22.4$, SD $= 6.0$) for the statistical analysis. Female judges in Germany were recruited from the local student population at the University of Göttingen (Germany). Of 139 females, aged 17–36 years, six participants did not identify themselves as being of European descent; thus, our sample for the analysis was 133 females ($M = 23.6$, SD $= 2.7$).

These participants were recruited in the course of a large-scale project on body movements in relation to anthropometric and personality characteristics at Northumbria University (UK), in which male dance movements were captured with a 12-camera optical motion capture system (Vicon, Oxford) at a constant rate of 100 Hz. Thirty-nine retroreflective markers were attached to each participant in accordance with the Vicon Plug-In-Gait marker set to capture all major body structures. After performing one static calibration capture ("T-pose"), participants were instructed to dance for 30 s to a basic drum beat rhythm. The resulting motion

capture data of each participant were applied to a gender-neutral, shape- and texture-standardized virtual character using Autodesk MotionBuilder (Autodesk, Inc., San Rafael, CA, USA) (see also Fink et al., 2012; Neave et al., 2011; Fig. 16.3).

Brazilian females provided dance attractiveness ratings using Qualtrics web-based software (www.qualtrics.com). Of the entire set of 80 male dance characters, a subset of ten dancers was randomly chosen for each female rater and presented on $21''$ computer screens. The length of each dance clip was trimmed down to a sequence of 10 s (chosen from the middle of each dance recording; see also Weege, Lange, & Fink, 2012). Participants could view the videos as long as they wished (and replay them). Ratings were made on a 5-point Likert-type scale (1 $=$ very unattractive to 5 $=$ very attractive), which was presented below each clip in the form of radio buttons. German females provided attractiveness ratings of dance characters using the same setup, but they were presented with a random selection of 20 dances of the entire set of stimuli.

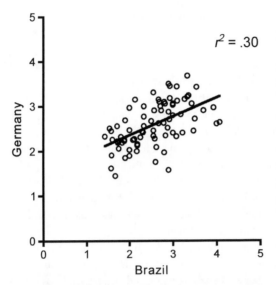

$r^2 = .30$

Fig. 16.4 Scatterplot of the association between Brazilian and German females' attractiveness judgments of gender-neutral dance characters with the body movements of British male dancers applied (see Fig. 16.3)

Brazilian females' attractiveness judgments ranged from 1.42 to 4.07 ($M = 2.56$, SD $= 0.65$) and those of the German sample from 1.45 to 3.68 ($M = 2.59$, SD $= 0.49$) with no significant differences between the two samples ($t = -0.55$, $p = 0.59$). Zero-order correlation statistics (Pearson r) revealed a significant positive association of Brazilian and German females' assessments of (British) males' dance attractiveness ($r = 0.55$, $p < 0.001$; see Fig. 16.4).

A more detailed inspection of possible differences between Brazilian and German females' judgments of male body movement attractiveness considered personality of male dancers (as assessed via the NEO-FFI inventory; Costa & McCrae, 1992) as covariates. There was a significant difference between Brazilian and German females' ratings of male dance movements ($F = 4.42$, $p < 0.05$) as well as significant interaction effects of country * neuroticism ($F = 5.51$, $p < 0.05$) and country * conscientiousness ($F = 8.06$, $p < 0.01$). Extraversion ($p = 0.34$), openness ($p = 0.73$), and social agreeableness ($p = 0.74$) did not show significant interaction effects with country as factor.

Although these data should be considered as preliminary, they suggest both cross-cultural similarities and differences of Brazilian and German females' assessment of male dance movements, as there was a significant correlation between females' attractiveness ratings of both countries, but also differences between them when considering dancer's personality as a covariate. As such these data suggest that there is cross-cultural consensus in females' perceptions of male dance movements, which is moderated by the dancer's personality, possibly because Brazilian and German females put different emphases on certain (personality) aspects they derive from dance movements when evaluating them.

The previous sections have demonstrated that the processing of biological motion is of fundamental importance to human social perception. The fact that such processing shows cross-cultural similarities and has a neurological basis attests to its adaptive significance. In considering the ultimate question on whether and how females assess male dance movements, and if they are indeed able to derive certain aspects of male quality from body movement, the following section deals with studies that have been conducted in the attempt of identifying quality cues, which are known to play a role in the assessment of static representations of male facial and body morphology, such as symmetry, physical strength, and personality. We review studies that show the significance of movement in mate selection in both animals and humans and suggest that the human body provides a single condition-dependent ornament of quality. We discuss evidence from studies showing links between dancing and symmetry and strength and personality. We conclude by describing some cutting-edge research, which employs stimuli in the form of controlled virtual characters (avatars) combined with detailed biomechanical assessments in order to assess the possibility that male dance moves are providing cues to their reproductive quality.

Body Movement Within the Evolutionary Psychology Framework

Animals of various species show a variety of dynamic displays, primarily in the context of courtship as part of ritualized patterns in order to attract potential mating partners. An inspection of the literature shows that such displays can be found at various taxonomic levels, and it is most often the males that employ them. Female fruit flies, for example, choose (male) mating partners based on "dance" movement as compared to "scissoring," which is observed in isolated males (Maynard-Smith, 1956). In arthropods, it has been reported that in some species of spiders, males attract mating partners via abdominal sway, and those who sway their abdomen with a higher frequency have higher reproductive success (Clark & Morjan, 2001; Singer et al., 2000).

Such "courtship dances" are particularly well studied in male birds, which use head and beak movements, plumage erection, and flight performances as part of their arsenal (in addition to singing) to attract female mating partners (Patricelli, Uy, & Borgia, 2003; Williams, 2001). In fish, female sticklebacks prefer males with high swimming speed (Rowland, 1995). Finally, there is related behavioral observation in nonhuman primates, as our closest relatives in evolutionary genealogy, with male chimpanzees displaying typical dynamic displays such as the "bipedal swagger" as part of their courtship behavior (Goodall, 1968). Considering such comparative studies on the significance of male movements as feature that should attract female conspecifics, it is probably not surprising that researchers have also begun to identify similar behavioral patterns in human male courtship.

Dance as Male Motor Behavior

It was in fact Darwin (1871) himself, who suggested that human dance is a sexually selected courtship signal that relates to an individual's quality. However, as it was the case with other seminal suggestions of Darwin, it took science almost a hundred years to catch up on this insight and apply a systematic approach to the study of human dance. There are anthropological and ethnographic reports on the role of human dance suggesting that dance is an activity displayed in rituals as a form of social communication and in courtship context (for reviews see Kaeppler, 1978; Kurath, 1960). These studies have predominantly focused on behavioral observation and were not concerned with identifying links between male quality, dancing ability, and female choice.

Meanwhile it is known from the comparative biological study of male motor performance that features such as vigor and strength are conveyed via body movements (Byers, Hebets, & Podos, 2010). Furthermore, there is corroborating evidence for the hypothesis that as in animals, human dance may be an adaptive behavioral display in sexual selection, which communicates health, strength, and thus sexual attractiveness (Hanna, 1987, 2010; Hugill et al., 2010). Dance is a universal form of human expression and is strongly associated with physical virtuosity. Dancers at the peak of their abilities exhibit limb coordination, strength, flexibility, and aesthetic qualities far in advance of the average person. They are able to learn complex sequences of movements, and synchronize their actions to changing musical speed and rhythm (Bläsing et al., 2012). Thus, dancing expertise reflects the interplay between physical, cognitive, and aesthetic qualities and as such is a likely candidate for an "honest" signal.

Features that have been studied in relation to female perceptions of males' dances primarily relate to physical and personality characteristics, which are known to affect female perceptions of static representations of male morphology (i.e., faces and bodies). From that research it is known that certain male physical and personality characteristics affect female partner preferences. In brief, it has been reported that females prefer male masculine features, particularly around the time of ovulation, and this has been shown to be the case for faces (Johnston, Hagel, Franklin, Fink, & Grammer, 2001; Penton-Voak et al., 1999) and bodies (Little, Jones, & Burriss, 2007). In addition, cross-cultural research states that females have a preference for certain male personality characteristics that indicate male status (Schmitt, 2005; Schmitt et al., 2003). Recent research suggests that these features are—to some extent—also conveyed via male body movements (dance in particular) as they reflect aspects of male mate quality. Taken together, this research expands the study of the role of male facial and body morphology in female mate preference by suggesting that male quality is signaled not only via (static) physical features but also via dynamic displays. The general assumption of these studies is that if dance, for example, is a sexually selected trait, it should reflect the genetic or phenotypic quality of the dancer.

The Case of Dance and Symmetry

One of the most frequently used epigenetic measures of developmental homeostasis (as proxy to genetic and phenotypic quality) has been fluctuating asymmetry (FA), which is characterized by small and random deviations from symmetry of bilaterally symmetrical structures (Ludwig, 1932). Such minor physical anomalies occur in response to genetic and environmental stress, including disease, parasitism, or elevated levels of sex steroids, and manifest themselves in the form of right minus left differences in physical structures (Livshits & Kobyliansky, 1991). The relationships of human facial and body FA with behavioral, cognitive, and health measures have been studied quite extensively in the past 15 years (for reviews see, Grammer, Fink, et al., 2003; Thornhill & Møller, 1997), although the predictive value of FA for attractiveness has been questioned, particularly in human males (Weeden & Sabini, 2005; for a comment see Grammer, Fink, Møller, & Manning, 2005).

Probably inspired by this line of research, Brown et al. (2005) set out to investigate associations between body FA and dance

perception in a sample of Jamaican males and females.[1] They hypothesized that symmetrical individuals would be perceived as being better dancers and that this should be particularly the case for males, as females are considered to be more selective in choosing their partners, while males invest more in courtship display (Trivers, 1972). Clearly, the correlations of symmetry and dance quality assessments should be stronger in males than in females. In addition, they tested whether FA of male and female evaluators had an effect on their judgments of opposite-sex dancing ability (assuming that judges who themselves have high FA would adjust their preferences accordingly and express weaker preferences for low FA dancers). Using 3D optical motion capture technology, Brown et al. collected dances of 183 young males and females, who danced for 1 min to the same song while their body movements were tracked. FA of each dancer was measured from nine morphological features (i.e., ankles, ears, elbows, fingers, and wrists) following the protocol of Trivers, Manning, Thornhill, Singh, and McGuire (1999) and summarized into a composite FA score corrected for trait size. Based on these scores, the authors selected 20 symmetrical (ten males, ten females) and 20 asymmetrical dancers (ten males, ten females) and presented their dance movements in the form of 3D skeleton animations to a sample of 155 young male and female Jamaican judges, who scored them on a visual analogue scale for perceived dancing ability.

Brown et al. reported a significant main effect for both symmetry and sex, as well as an interaction effect between them, these being independent of age and body mass index (BMI). In other words, the dance animations of both symmetrical males and females were perceived as significantly better than those of asymmetrical males and females, though the effect was stronger with male than with female dancers. In addition, it was reported that female evaluators had a stronger preferences for symmetrical male dancers

---

[1] The Brown et al., (2005) paper was retracted on December 19, 2013.

than male evaluators and that male evaluators gave higher ratings to female dancers than did female assessors. Finally, it was found that FA of male evaluators was negatively related to their preferences for symmetry in female dancers, which would argue for a condition-dependent adjustment of preferences in males. These results seemed to be in accord with the hypotheses, and the authors admitted in fairness that they did not know what actually caused these reported associations. Systemic health, neuromuscular coordination capability, parasite resistance, and energetic expenditure were identified as possible mediators that should be addressed in future studies.

There is certainly much to like about this study. It used 3D motion capturing, which allowed the presentation of dance movement independent from body morphology and texture features; still it comprised a set of anthropometric measurements that facilitated the authors to control for possible covariates (such as age and BMI). Moreover, it followed standard protocols in assessing FA by creating a composite measure of symmetry rather than relying on the study of associations of single traits' FA with perception. In 2005 it was the first systematic assessment of male and female dance quality within the evolutionary psychology framework and as such groundbreaking.

However, there has been controversy about the actual value of this study, as a later reanalysis of the data by Trivers, Palestis, and Zataari (2009) could not confirm many of the original results reported by Brown et al. (2005). Using recalculated (average) dance ratings, Trivers et al. obtained a significant overall model, as reported in Brown et al. (2005). However, unlike in the 2005 publication, none of the independent variables or covariates turned out to be significant predictors of dancing ability. That is, the reanalysis could not confirm the significant main effect of symmetry and sex (as well as their interaction) on dance perception and did not detect a significant effect of age and BMI, although it is noted that with one exception (sex * FA interaction, $p = 0.15$), all p values were smaller than 0.10. An omnibus pairwise

comparison of ratings of symmetrical/asymmetrical male and female dancers based on the recalculated dance scores revealed a significant difference only for symmetrical/asymmetrical male dancers ($p = 0.03$). In terms of the variation in dance ratings explained by the difference between symmetrical/asymmetrical males and females, Trivers et al. arrive at lower numbers than reported by Brown et al. (males, 22.3 % vs. 48 %; females, 12.8 % vs. 23 %). Finally, with regard to the hypothesized effect of evaluator FA on dance ability ratings, Trivers et al. (2009) could not replicate the significant association reported for male evaluators judging female dancers. At this point, we omit from presenting additional data of the reanalysis that were in 2005 presented as (online) supplementary data. However, one result reported by Trivers et al. is possibly noteworthy, and that is the one of a significant relationship between facial attractiveness and dance ability ($p = 0.03$). The authors state that different from that in the Brown et al. report, this finding is based on attractiveness ratings by Jamaican peers only, but they also acknowledge that ratings are missing for many dancers.

The discrepancies between the Brown et al. (2005) report and the reanalysis by Trivers et al. (2009) raise the questions whether there is in fact a relationship between FA and dancing ability and, if so, whether it is especially present in young males. In an attempt to answer this question, Trivers et al. had 162 dances evaluated by two (Rutgers) dance students. There was no significant association between symmetry (mean FA measured in 1996 and 2002) and dancing ability either with or without age and BMI as covariates. In considering the 2002 data only, the authors found a significant but weak relationship between symmetry and dance ability in males ($p = 0.04$) and an almost significant association in females ($p = 0.05$), which disappears when entering age and BMI as covariates into the model.

In conclusion, it seems that the hypotheses of the Brown et al. (2005) paper cannot be fully supported after the reanalysis by Trivers et al. (2009). However, using recalculated data, it still seems that there is some effect in support of the assertion of associations between FA and dancing ability, albeit a smaller effect than originally stated. We still feel that it is worth investigating this relationship, particularly from the perspective that females should be more sensitive to the variation in male dance movements than vice versa. The present evidence, however, suggests that even if such an effect were true, it may explain only a relatively small proportion of the variance in female perceptions of male dance movements. Thus, we consider it worthwhile to include additional measures of biological "quality" such as physical strength and personality, both of which are known to affect female preferences of static representations of male face/bodies, also in the investigation of what characterizes a "good" male dancer.

Perception of Strength from Dance Movements

It has been reported that females are able to perceive male physical strength from static representations of male faces and bodies and that they are quite accurate in making these assessments (Fink, Neave, & Seydel, 2007; Sell et al., 2009). More recently, Windhager, Schaefer, and Fink (2011) showed that male facial configurations associated with measures of physical strength (i.e., handgrip strength) are characterized by an overall robust facial morphology, which does not necessarily resemble that of an attractive face. However, the reported associations of female perception of male facial masculinity and dominance with physical strength seem to be robust. Evolutionary psychologists have argued that this link may be caused by female adaptive preferences for male physical fitness, athletic abilities, and thus competitiveness, all of which are on the proximate level moderated by testosterone (T), and thus, T may shape male faces accordingly. But can females also derive these qualities from male dance movements?

In the attempt to investigate the association of female perceptions of male dance movements and physical strength, Hugill, Fink, Neave, and Seydel (2009) recoded dance movements of 40 heterosexual male students at a German University, all nonprofessional dancers, and recorded 30 s of their dance movements using a digital video camera. Male dancers provided a measure of handgrip strength in addition to physical assessments of height and weight. Video clips were converted into grey-scale and blurred by using a Gaussian filter in order to degrade information about face/body morphology and texture. Fifty female judges rated 10 s of these video clips on perceived attractiveness and assertiveness. It was found that handgrip strength of male dancers correlated significantly positively with female assessments of attractiveness ($r = 0.35$) and assertiveness ($r = 0.31$), this result being independent of the dancers' weight. To clarify this, females perceived dances of males who were physically stronger as more attractive and assertive (with these two attributes being highly intercorrelated, $r = 0.72$). Thus, Hugill et al. concluded that male physical strength is signaled not only via static representations of male morphology but also via their dance movements.

Hugill et al. speculated that the association between physical strength and dancing ability in males could be moderated by an effect of T on both measures. There is indeed evidence for a dose-dependent effect of T on athletic abilities and physical strength in males (Di Luigi, Romanelli, & Lenzi, 2005) as T improves muscular volume and thus physical performance (Cardinale & Stone, 2006). Studies on static representations of male faces/bodies report that females are quite accurate in assessing physical strength from male morphology (Fink, Neave, et al., 2007; Sell et al., 2009), thus arguing that women may have developed cognitive adaptations to assess male physical strength as it correlates with competitiveness. Studies on women's perceptions of male faces reported a preference for male faces associated with high levels of circulating T (Penton-Voak & Chen, 2004). Similar studies on the relationship of male dancing ability and circulating T do not exist, at least not within the evolutionary psychology framework.

However, there is preliminary evidence that digit ratio (2D:4D), a proxy of prenatal T, correlates with female perceptions of dominance, masculinity, and attractiveness of male dances. Here, Fink, Seydel, Manning, and Kappeler (2007) recorded dances of 52 heterosexual Caucasian male students (using the same protocol as in Hugill et al., 2009) in addition to digit ratio and other anthropometric measures (e.g., height, weight). The dances of six males with the lowest (high prenatal T) and six males with the highest (low prenatal T) 2D:4D ratios were presented to a panel of 104 women. Dances of males with low 2D:4D ratios were judged significantly higher on assertiveness, attractiveness, and dominance, while measures of physical morphology did not differ significantly between low and high 2D:4D dancers. The study concluded that prenatal levels of T might serve to organize not only male facial characteristics but also male dance movements. Furthermore, Fink, Seydel, et al. (2007) suggested that the female preference for male dancers with low 2D:4D might reflect the preference for males who are supposedly more successful in competition, thereby signaling higher status. Other studies on the relationship of 2D:4D and male competitiveness and strength seem to support this. For example, Manning and Taylor (2001) showed that male professional soccer players had lower 2D:4D ratios than controls, concluding that prenatal T promotes male development and the maintenance of traits which are useful in sports and, more generally, male competition. In addition, Fink, Thanzami, Seydel, and Manning (2006) reported physical strength (as measured via handgrip strength) as higher in males of two ethnic groups (Germany and Mizos males), thus concluding that prenatal T may have an early organizing effect on strength in males.

Whether or not male dancing ability and female perceptions of it are indeed systematically related needs to be confirmed in future studies. However, the present evidence suggests that T has an effect on male physical features that females are able to derive from their dancing ability. Studies of associations of T with facial and body morphology and female preferences for certain configurations of them indicate that females have a preference for "masculine" features, particularly at times of high fertility (Johnston et al., 2001), and that T is crucial in developing them. As it is known from the study of male facial masculinity, females tend to associate negative personality attributes with extreme forms of male masculinity. For example, Johnston et al. (2001) reported that while females preferred masculine-looking male faces at times of peak fertility, they considered these faces as aggressive, manipulating, and selfish. More feminized versions of male faces were rated at times outside of the fertile window and were also judged more positively in terms of their personality. We are about to examine whether the "dual sexual strategy hypothesis" (Thornhill & Gangestad, 2008) that has been reported for male physical features also applies to female perceptions of male body movements. However, independent from possible influences of the ovulatory cycle, there is evidence that females derive certain personality characteristics from male dance movements.

Perception of Personality from Body Movements

People readily ascribe emotions, intentions, and personality to animated figures that may not even have biological forms. For example, Koppensteiner (2011) asked male and female observers to view animations consisting of a ball, whose trajectory varied in terms of its amplitude and speed. In an initial session volunteers had been asked to alter the animation using these parameters so that different personality types reflecting the "Big Five" (high and low values of extraversion, emotional stability, conscientiousness, agreeableness, and openness) could be represented. Averaged values were then used to create prototype stimuli that were shown to raters; they had to state which personality was being displayed. Significant differences between low and high values of each personality factor were found, with extraversion being identified with the highest levels of agreement.

In terms of human dancing, it should be expected that the personality of the dancer would be reflected in their dance moves. Luck, Saarikallio, and Toiviainen (2009) recorded male and female dance movements and converted them into P-L stimuli. The dancers also completed an assessment of the Big Five. Correlations were found between certain personality traits and specific movement parameters, but they failed to reach significance. Their only significant findings were in relation to neuroticism and openness. Neuroticism was positively correlated with acceleration of the feet and jerky movements of the feet, while openness was negatively correlated with jerky movements of the central body. In a more comprehensive study, Luck, Saarikallio, Burger, Thompson, and Toiviainen (2010) asked over 900 volunteers to complete the Big Five Inventory (Costa & McCrae, 1992; Digman, 1990; McCrae & Costa, 1997), and a sample of 60 extreme scorers were asked to dance to different musical clips from six genres. The different personality dimensions were associated with different movement patterns, with extraversion and neuroticism eliciting the clearest characteristics. Extraverts produced higher movement speeds of the head, hands, and central body; neuroticism was associated with jerky and accelerated movements, especially of the head, hands, and feet. This work demonstrates that personality traits may be reflected by specific movement patterns when dancing, and so the interesting question relates to how might such information be used in female judgments of male mate quality.

Fink et al. (2012) sought to test whether female perception of male dance quality also shows systematic associations with global descriptors of the dancer's personality, i.e., the Big Five. Using a set of 48 humanoid dance characters (as described above; see Fig. 16.3) that were presented to a sample of 53 female judges, the authors hypothesized that male dance quality perception should show positive correlations with extraversion, openness, conscientiousness, and agreeableness scores and a negative association with neuroticism. There was some support for these hypotheses, as male dancing ability was correlated significantly positively with conscientiousness and social agreeableness. Male extraversion showed a positive correlation with female dance quality perception, but this was not significant. Neuroticism and openness were negatively correlated with dance quality judgments, but again these relationships failed to reach statistical significance. Thus, as with face perception (Penton-Voak, Pound, Little, & Perrett, 2006), there seems to be some kernel of truth behind the assumption that male dancing ability signals certain aspects of their personality to females. Fink et al. argue that their finding provides evidence for the assertion that, in addition to aspects of health and fitness, male dance quality may also convey aspects of personality and is thus in line with earlier studies suggesting that movement signals information about an individual's psychological propensities and intentions (Cutting & Proffitt, 1981). Although these data should be considered as preliminary, we may speculate that if an association between male personality and female perception of their dance movements turns out to be true, this would suggest that male dance movements play a significant role in female mate preferences.

The relationship between female perceptions of male body movements need not be restricted to dance. Koppensteiner and Grammer (2010) presented stick-figure animations of public speeches from German Houses of Parliament members (20 males and 20 females) to a sample of male and female judges who rated them on the Big Five. Certain movement parameters were associated with specific judgments of personality; for example, figures which displayed high overall activity with amplitude in horizontal and vertical arm movements were regarded as being more extraverted; figures displaying a greater amplitude in their head movements were rated as being less conscientious and less emotionally stable. This demonstrated that viewers extract meaning from certain body parts and from movement patterns, which are partly independent of the specific body parts used.

In a subsequent study using the same stimuli, Koppensteiner and Grammer (2011) found that judges attributed different personalities to male and female body movements, such that animations of male speakers received higher ratings on "extraversion" and "emotional stability" than female speakers, while "agreeableness" was perceived to be "typically female." Thus, the authors concluded that gender-related differences in even global descriptors of personality are communicated via body movement. However, the authors admitted that they were unable to disentangle personality perceptions that might be due to actual sex differences from those that are due to gender stereotypes. This issue is perhaps reflected in the work of Thoresen, Vuong, and Atkinson (2012). They assessed personality traits in 14 females and 12 males and recorded them as they walked in a straight line. Observers showed strong reliability of their personality judgments, but little validity, as their judgments did not match with the actual personality of the walker. Observers thus agree with one another that a person appears to be extraverted in how they walk, but this is not in accord with how the walkers rate themselves! In a subsequent study these authors demonstrated that the perception of emotion, masculinity, and attractiveness might act as mediating factors for the attribution of personality traits.

So, global aspects of personality appear to be conveyed by certain movements, but what about specific aspects of personality? We have already explained that females seem to assess male physical strength from their dance movements, and recent research suggests that this relationship is moderated by T (Fink, Seydel, et al., 2007; Hugill et al., 2009). It has been reported that both prenatal and circulating T is one of the major endocrinological substrates that moderate sex differences and sex-dependent behavior (Collaer & Hines, 1995; Manning, 2002). One of the most robust sex differences in human personality characteristics is that of risk-taking behavior with males being more willing to engage in risky situations than females (Zuckerman, 1991; Zuckerman, Eysenck, & Eysenck, 1978), possibly due to a stronger exposure to T. Evolutionary psychologists have argued that this difference may reflect evolved aspects of male masculinity resulting from sexual selection, as males advertise their quality (to both males and females) through the display of risky behavior (Wilke, Hutchinson, Todd, & Kruger, 2006; Wilson & Daly, 1985). There is indeed evidence that females are particularly attracted to males who engage in high-risk activities, particularly in the context of short-term relationships (Bogaert & Fisher, 1995; Farthing, 2005).

Recent research reports that male risk taking is associated with physical strength by concluding that this relationship is possibly driven by an effect of T on both measures (Fink, Täschner, Neave, Hugill, & Dane, 2010). Thus, in considering the associations of female perceptions of male dances and strength and (prenatal) T and the evidence of the effect of T on risk-taking behavior in males, Hugill, Fink, Neave, Besson, and Bunse (2011) hypothesized that females might derive male risk-taking behavior also from their dance movements. They recorded dances of 50 males and had them judged by 60 females on perceived attractiveness and risk taking following the protocol of Hugill et al. (2009). It was found that females rated dance movements of males who scored high on the SSS-V (Sensation Seeking Scale Form V; Zuckerman, 2007; Zuckerman et al., 1978) higher on attractiveness and risk-taking behavior. In particular, thrill and adventure seeking, disinhibition, and boredom susceptibility showed significant positive correlations with perceptions of dance attractiveness. The authors concluded that females are able to perceive male sensation seeking propensity from dance movements and that this may have consequences on female assessments of potential male partners. In addition, Hugill et al. suggested that the female sensitivity towards risk-taking propensity (as derived from dance movements) might indicate that male body movement signals aspects of personality and emotion, which has consequences on interpersonal behavior, including that of mate preference and selection.

Risk taking is a costly behavioral trait, and there may be differences with regard to female preferences for males who score high on risk taking depending on the temporal context of relationship, i.e., short or long term. Hugill et al. did not differentiate between attractiveness as a short-term or long-term partner when asking females to assess male dance movements, so this is clearly an issue that needs to be addressed in future studies. However, one may speculate that there will be differences in female assessments, because for long-term relationships the negative consequences of risk-taking behavior may lower male mate value by reducing the chance of survival and thus parenting (Sylwester & Pawlowski, 2011).

Biomechanics of Dance Movements

Within the evolutionary psychology framework, most of the current evidence on female perceptions of male body movements concerns studies that assessed female evaluations of male body movement in relation to anthropometric measures (e.g., symmetry, digit ratio, physical strength) or personality characteristics (e.g., risk taking, Big Five). While such studies provide information on impression formation and preferences, it does not tell us which movement characteristics actually cause the variation in females' response. It would certainly be crucial to know how the objective assessment of variation in male body movement relates to that of female perception and evaluation. Studies on human kinetics are typically conducted in health and sports sciences (e.g., Koutedakis, Owolabi, & Apostolos, 2008), but have rarely been applied to evolutionary psychology investigations. Neave et al. (2011) reported preliminary data on biomechanical characteristics of male dance movements in relation to female judgments of dance quality. Using 3D optical motion capture technology, they collected dance movements of 19 British males and applied them to featureless virtual characters (see Fig. 16.3). Video clips (15 s) of each avatar were then presented to a total of 37 females, who rated them on dance quality (1 = extremely bad dancer to 7 = extremely good

dancer). In addition, biomechanical features of the dancer's movements, especially those of three main body regions, i.e., legs (ankle, hip, and knee), arms (shoulder, elbow, and wrist), and the central body (head and trunk), were extracted and correlated with dance quality judgments. It was found that "good" dancers differ from "bad" dancers in the amplitude and variability of body movements, particularly in the head/neck and trunk region and the speed of the right knee.

This study thus provided the first evidence relating female perceptions of male dance quality to certain biomechanical characteristics. As these characteristics (movement amplitude, variability, and speed) could relate to vigor, a quality clearly established as being important in nonhuman male mating displays (Byers et al., 2010), it is tempting to conclude that human male dancing provides an honest indication of male vigor to females. However, the Neave et al. (2011) study did not specifically address this issue and so this remains to be confirmed. More recently, Weege et al. (2012) tracked the eye gaze of 46 women while they viewed pairs of male dancers (one good and one bad). Women fixated more on good dancers and their visual attention was positively correlated with the perceived attractiveness of the dancer. Clearly then women are sensitive to variation in male dance quality though to what extent such perceptions are related to his actual physical qualities (i.e., his health, physical fitness) remains to be confirmed. However, as research has already established clear links between male physical strength and his dance quality (Hugill et al., 2009), it is expected that such associations will be revealed.

If male movements form honest cues to their reproductive quality, then one would assume that the same information should be conveyed in different modalities. While male animals tend to perform a stereotypical courtship "dance," human males can potentially reveal their physical qualities in different modalities, i.e., walking, running, and dancing. It would be expected that perceived dance quality might be positively associated with perceived walking and running quality as well.

Study 2: A Comparison of Females' Perceptions of Male Dance, Gait, and Running

In this study we sought to determine possible relationships between female perceptions of male dance, gait, and running. Our initial stimuli were body movement recordings as described in Study 1 of this chapter, i.e., 3D optical motion capture data of male participants, whose dance, running, and walking movements were recorded and subsequently applied to virtual humanoid characters for presentation to female judges. Motion capture data of all movement types were available from 70 British males aged 18–42 years ($M = 21.6$, SD $= 4.1$). We had 120 female judges aged 15–46 years ($M = 23.8$, SD $= 4.3$) who were mainly recruited from the local student population at the University of Göttingen, Germany. Independent samples of 40 females each judged short video clips of males dancing, running, and walking on 15.4″ laptop computers, using MediaLab software (Empirisoft Inc., NY, USA), on perceived attractiveness on a 7-point Likert-type scale (1 = very unattractive to 7 = very attractive). The presentation order of stimuli for each experiment was randomized between participants. The calculated means of female perceptions (for each of the three movement types) were used for the statistical analyses.

Female perceptions of male dances ranged from 1.85 to 4.75 ($M = 3.28$, SD $= 0.66$), for running from 1.63 to 4.90 ($M = 3.42$, SD $= 0.76$), and for walking from 1.25 to 5.75 ($M = 3.23$, SD $= 0.90$) with no significant difference between the three movement conditions ($F = 2.06$, $p = 0.13$). The correlational analysis revealed that attractiveness of dance and running perceptions were significantly positively correlated ($r = 0.37$, $p < 0.001$) (Fig. 16.5a). Female perceptions of male dance attractiveness and walking attractiveness were also correlated positively, but failed to reach statistical significance ($r = 0.16$, $p = 0.19$) (Fig. 16.5b). Attractiveness perception of male running and walking movements correlated significantly positively with one another ($r = 0.54$, $p < 0.001$). Finally,

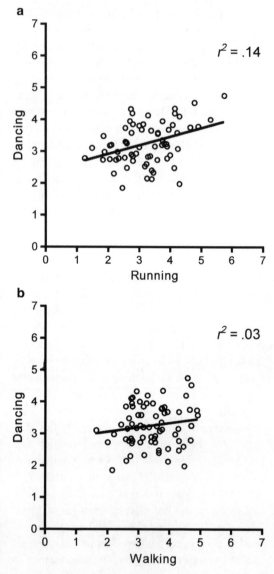

Fig. 16.5 Scatterplots of the associations between females' attractiveness judgments of male dancing and running (**a**) and walking (**b**)

there was no significant correlation of body height and weight with either of the three movement types. An additional regression analysis of dance attractiveness perception as dependent variable and running and walking attractiveness as independent variables revealed an overall significant model ($F = 5.59$, $p < 0.01$) with running, but not walking attractiveness being a significant predictor (running: $\beta = 0.41$, $p < 0.01$; walking: $\beta = -0.06$, $p = 0.64$). These results did not change substantially when adding male body height and weight as predictors of female perception of dance attractiveness.

Although we consider these data as preliminary, they show that there is considerable agreement in female perceptions of male body movements across different types of movements, with dancing being more strongly associated with running than with walking. This is perhaps not surprising as both movement styles reflect higher energy expenditure and might be more useful to females when trying to gain an impression of male physical quality. We suggest that future studies should particularly employ measures of energy expenditure in their protocols when assessing relationships between subjective perceptions of male body movements and objective measures of male quality.

Conclusion

Finding a "perfect" mate is arguably one of the most important but also difficult tasks an individual has to master during its reproductive life. Evolutionary psychologists theorize that via appropriate choice, an individual can ensure that its genes are passed on to offspring. Based on some 20 years of research, there is strong evidence that the human face and body (in static representation) provide a number of (mate) "quality" cues. Studies have shown that people are remarkably sensitive to even subtle variations of facial and/or body characteristics and react correspondingly in terms of age, attractiveness, and health assessments. Comparably little is known on the role of facial and body dynamics in this context, although it seems obvious that considering biological motion in evolutionary psychology, studies on physical appearance would bring additional ecological validity to the study of human mate preferences and choice.

In this present chapter we have reviewed evidence on the social significance of body movement with a focus on female perceptions of male body movements. The available studies suggest that females derive certain "quality" cues from male body movements and that these cues are more or less the same as those derived from static representations of male faces and bodies. In summary, the evidence is as follows:

- Females perceive dance movements of symmetrical males higher on attractiveness than those of unsymmetrical males (although this result remains to be confirmed).
- Females judge dance movements of physically stronger males higher on attractiveness, dominance, and masculinity than those of physically weaker males.
- Females perceive dances of higher risk-taking males as more attractive and assertive than dances of males who score lower on risk-taking propensity.
- Females are visually sensitive (in terms of attention) to male dance movements such that they focus more attention on "good" than "bad" dancers; and they judge better dancers to be more attractive.
- Females' perceptions of "good" male dancers are characterized by variability in males' body movements, particularly those of the upper body (head/neck and trunk region).
- Females of different societies/cultures are broadly comparable in their judgments of male dance movement attractiveness (though this evidence needs to be expanded to further populations), although there seems to be local variation in regard to the influence of personality of the dancer that drives these assessments.
- Females share judgments of different types of male body movements, such as dancing, running, and walking.

Clearly there is much that remains to be understood in relation to perceptions of human movements from an evolutionary psychology perspective. A key issue is certainly that of cross-cultural evidence. We know that human dance is strongly determined by the sociocultural background, and even within cultures, certain dance moves and actions reflect different trends and youth cultures. It is thus likely that there may be cross-cultural differences in perceptions of dance quality, though if we are correct in assuming that dance serves to accurately reflect the individual qualities of the dancer, then perhaps cross-cultural differences may be minimal. Indeed, our preliminary data on Brazilian and German females' perceptions of male dance movements suggest that in both societies, females perceive the quality of (British) male dancers similarly, although there seem to be local differences with regard to the moderating role of personality cues they derive from dance movements.

In addition, while we speculate that dance serves to convey information about the physical and psychological qualities of the dancer, it has not yet been confirmed that physical qualities such as age, health, and physical fitness, for example, are accurately signaled via dance movements. With reference to our preliminary data on the relationships between female perceptions of male dancing, running, and walking, it may be that further studies on energy expenditure of different types of body movements will reveal insight into the key cues females derive from them.

Most of the studies on female perceptions of male body movements were concerned with dance movements in which they did not explicitly test for the ability of an individual to adjust the moves to a certain beat. Neither did female judges get an idea on this (male) ability as movements were commonly presented without audio information. Just from an everyday observation, it may well be that the male ability to adjust dance movements to the beat also provides a reliable cue that women can base their assessments of dance quality and attractiveness on. In regard to the ecological validity of studies investigating male dance movement perceptions, this is an issue that needs to be urgently addressed.

Along this line, it remains to be shown how strong the cues individuals derive from body movements actually are. While it is probably obvious that body movements form an initial signal when perceiving people from distance, it is yet unknown how strong these signals are in comparison to those of facial characteristics. In other words, can the initial impression formation based on body movement be outperformed by facial and body morphology? Future research is needed to determine some feature hierarchy in people's social perception of others by adding dynamic aspects of human physical appearance. The present evidence on female perceptions of male body movements seems to suggest that static and dynamic representations of the male physique signal similar aspects of male quality. For example, females are attracted to male facial features that indicate physical strength (Fink, Neave, et al., 2007), and they seem to derive these qualities also from male body movements (Hugill et al., 2009). This suggests that not only male faces and body form a condition-dependent ornament of quality but also that movement is condition dependent. What comprises (male) condition may be manifold, although features such as symmetry, T-dependent traits, and certain personality characteristics (e.g., risk taking) are likely candidates that could explain part of the variance in attraction to females.

Finally, the available studies on male body movements reflect human intersexual selection, thus concerning the cause for female preferences of male movements. In addition to establishing the significance of body movement in this context, it will be interesting to see to what extent they also convey information to potential male rivals. In following Puts (2010), we speculate that like static physical features, male body movement is both a cue to male quality that females employ in assessing potential mates and also a feature that other males may use to assess potential competitors.

References

Adolphs, R. (1999). Social cognition and the human brain. *Trends in Cognitive Sciences, 3*, 469–479.

Allison, T., Puce, A., & McCarthy, G. (2000). Social perception from visual cues: Role of the STS region. *Trends in Cognitive Sciences, 4,* 267–278.

Argyle, M. (1988). *Bodily communication* (2nd ed.). London: Routledge.

Atkinson, A. P., Dittrich, W. H., Gemmell, A. J., & Young, A. W. (2004). Emotion perception from dynamic and static body expressions in point-light and full-light displays. *Perception, 33,* 717–746.

Barclay, C. D., Cutting, J. E., & Kozlowski, L. T. (1978). Temporal and spatial factors in gait perception that influence gender recognition. *Perception & Psychophysics, 23,* 145–152.

Bertenthal, B. I., Proffitt, D. R., & Cutting, G. E. (1984). Infant sensitivity to figural coherence in biomechanical motions. *Journal of Experimental Child Psychology, 37,* 213–230.

Bingham, G. P. (1993). Scaling judgments of lifted weight: Lifter size and the role of the standard. *Ecological Psychology, 5,* 31–64.

Blake, R., Turner, L. M., Smoski, M. J., Pozdol, S. L., & Stone, W. L. (2003). Visual recognition of biological motion is impaired in children with autism. *Psychological Science, 14,* 151–157.

Bläsing, B., Calvo-Merino, B., Cross, E. S., Jola, C., Honisch, J., & Stevens, C. J. (2012). Neurocognitive control in dance perception and performance. *Acta Psychologica, 139,* 300–308.

Bogaert, A. F., & Fisher, W. A. (1995). Predictors of university men's number of sexual partners. *Journal of Sex Research, 32,* 119–130.

Bonda, E., Petrides, M., Ostry, D., & Evans, A. (1996). Specific involvement of human parietal systems and the amygdala in the perception of biological motion. *Journal of Neuroscience, 16,* 3737–3744.

Braun, M. (1992). *Picturing time: The work of Étienne-Jules Marey (1830–1904).* Chicago: University of Chicago Press.

Brown, W. M., Cronk, L., Grochow, K., Jacobson, A., Liu, C. K., Popovic, Z., et al. (2005). Dance reveals symmetry especially in young men. *Nature, 438,* 1148–1150.

Brownlow, S., Dixon, A. R., Egbert, C. A., & Radcliffe, R. D. (1997). Perception of movement and dancer characteristics from point-light displays of dance. *The Psychological Record, 47,* 411–421.

Buss, D. M. (1985). Human mate selection. *American Scientist, 73,* 47–51.

Buss, D. M., & Barnes, M. L. (1986). Preferences in human mate selection. *Journal of Personality and Social Psychology, 50,* 559–570.

Buss, D. M., & Schmitt, D. P. (1993). Sexual strategies theory: An evolutionary perspective on human mating. *Psychological Review, 100,* 204–232.

Byers, J., Hebets, E., & Podos, J. (2010). Female mate choice based upon male motor performance. *Animal Behaviour, 79,* 771–778.

Cardinale, M., & Stone, M. H. (2006). Is testosterone influencing explosive performance? *Journal of Strength and Conditioning Research, 20,* 103–107.

Clark, D. L., & Morjan, C. L. (2001). Attracting female attention: The evolution of dimorphic courtship displays in the jumping spider *Maevia inclemens* (Araneae: Salticidae). *Proceedings of the Royal Society of London, Series B, 268,* 2461–2465.

Collaer, M. L., & Hines, M. (1995). Human behavioral sex differences: A role for gonadal hormones during early development? *Psychological Bulletin, 118,* 55–107.

Costa, P. T., & McCrae, R. R. (1992). *Revised NEO Personality Inventory (NEO-PI-R) and the NEO Five-Factor Inventory (NEO-FFI): Professional manual.* Odessa, FL: Psychological Assessment Resources.

Cutting, J. E. (1978a). A biomechanical invariant of gait perception. *Journal of Experimental Psychology: Human Perception and Performance, 4,* 357–372.

Cutting, J. E. (1978b). Generation of synthetic male and female walkers through manipulation of a biomechanical invariant. *Perception, 7,* 393–405.

Cutting, J. E., & Kozlowski, L. T. (1977). Recognizing friends by their walk: Gait perception without familiarity cues. *Bulletin of the Psychonomic Society, 9,* 353–356.

Cutting, G. E., Moore, C., & Morrison, R. (1988). Masking the motions of human gait. *Perception & Psychophysics, 44,* 339–347.

Cutting, J. E., & Proffitt, D. R. (1981). Gait perception as an example of how we may perceive events. In R. D. Walk & H. L. Pick (Eds.), *Intersensory perception and sensory integration* (pp. 249–273). New York: Plenum Press.

Darwin, C. (1871). *The descent of men, and selection in relation to sex.* Princeton, NJ: Princeton University Press.

Darwin, C. (1872). *The expression of emotions in man and animals.* London: Harper Collins.

Di Luigi, L., Romanelli, F., & Lenzi, A. (2005). Androgenic-anabolic steroids abuse in males. *Journal of Endocrinological Investigation, 28,* 81–84.

Digman, J. M. (1990). Personality structure: Emergence of the five-factor model. *Annual Review of Psychology, 41,* 417–440.

Dittrich, W. H., Troscianko, T., Lea, S. E. G., & Morgan, D. (1996). Perception of emotion from dynamic point-light displays represented in dance. *Perception, 25,* 727–738.

Doyle, J. F. (2009). A woman's walk: Attractiveness in motion. *Journal of Social, Evolutionary, and Cultural Psychology, 3,* 81–92.

Ekman, P., & Friesen, W. V. (1971). Constants across cultures in the face and emotion. *Journal of Personality and Social Psychology, 17,* 124–129.

Ekman, P., Friesen, W. V., O'Sullivan, M., Chan, A., Diacoyanni-Tarlatzis, I., Heider, K., et al. (1987). Universals and cultural differences in the judgments of facial expressions of emotion. *Journal of Personality and Social Psychology, 53,* 712–717.

Farthing, G. W. (2005). Attitudes towards heroic and non heroic risk takers as mates and friends. *Evolution and Human Behavior, 26,* 171–185.

Fink, B., Neave, N., & Seydel, H. (2007). Male facial appearance signals physical strength to women. *American Journal of Human Biology, 19*, 82–87.

Fink, B., & Penton-Voak, I. S. (2002). Evolutionary psychology of facial attractiveness. *Current Directions in Psychological Science, 11*, 154–158.

Fink, B., Seydel, H., Manning, J. T., & Kappeler, P. M. (2007). A preliminary investigation of the association between digit ratio and women's perception of men's dance. *Personality and Individual Differences, 42*, 381–390.

Fink, B., Täschner, K., Neave, N., Hugill, N., & Dane, L. (2010). Male faces and bodies: Evidence of a condition-dependent ornament of quality. *Personality and Individual Differences, 49*, 436–440.

Fink, B., Thanzami, V., Seydel, H., & Manning, J. T. (2006). Digit ratio and hand-grip strength, in German and Mizos men: Cross-cultural evidence for an organizing effect of prenatal testosterone on strength. *American Journal of Human Biology, 18*, 776–782.

Fink, B., Weege, B., Flügge, J., Röder, S., Neave, N., & McCarty, K. (2012). Men's personality and women's perception of their dance quality. *Personality and Individual Differences, 52*, 232–235.

Gangestad, S. W., & Scheyd, G. J. (2005). The evolution of human physical attractiveness. *Annual Review of Anthropology, 34*, 523–548.

Giese, M., & Poggio, T. (2003). Neural mechanisms for the recognition of biological movements. *Nature Reviews Neuroscience, 4*, 179–192.

Goodall, J. (1968). A preliminary report on expressive movement and communication in the Gombe Stream chimpanzees. In P. C. Jay (Ed.), *Primates: Studies in adaptation and variability* (pp. 313–374). New York: Holt, Rinehart and Winston.

Grammer, K., Fink, B., Juette, A., Ronzal, G., & Thornhill, R. (2001). Female faces and bodies: n-dimensional feature space and attractiveness. In G. Rhodes & L. Zebrobwitz (Eds.), *Advances in visual cognition. Volume I: Facial attractiveness* (pp. 97–125). Westport, CT: Alex.

Grammer, K., Fink, B., Møller, A. P., & Manning, J. T. (2005). Physical attractiveness and health: Comment on Weeden and Sabini (2005). *Psychological Bulletin, 131*, 658–661.

Grammer, K., Fink, B., Møller, A. P., & Thornhill, R. (2003). Darwinian aesthetics: Sexual selection and the biology of beauty. *Biological Reviews, 78*, 385–407.

Grammer, K., Keki, V., Striebel, B., Atzmüller, M., & Fink, B. (2003). Bodies in motion: A window to the soul. In E. Voland & K. Grammer (Eds.), *Evolutionary aesthetics* (pp. 295–323). Berlin: Springer.

Grossman, E. D., Battelli, L., & Pascual-Leone, A. (2005). Repetitive TMS over STSp disrupts perception of biological motion. *Vision Research, 45*, 2847–2853.

Grossman, E., Donnelly, M., Price, R., Pickens, D., Morgan, V., Neighbour, G., et al. (2000). Brain areas involved in perception of biological motion. *Journal of Cognitive Neuroscience, 12*, 711–720.

Hall, J. A. (1978). Gender effects in decoding nonverbal cues. *Psychological Bulletin, 85*, 845–857.

Hanna, J. L. (1987). *Dance, sex and gender: Signs of identity, dominance, defiance, and desire.* Chicago: University of Chicago Press.

Hanna, J. L. (2010). Dance and sexuality: Many moves. *Journal of Sex Research, 47*, 212–241.

Heberlein, A. S., Adolphs, R., Tranel, D., & Damasio, H. (2004). Cortical regions for judgments of emotions and personality traits from point-light walkers. *Journal of Cognitive Neuroscience, 16*, 1143–1158.

Hubert, B., Wicker, B., Moore, D. G., Monfardini, E., Duverger, H., Da Fonséca, D., et al. (2007). Recognition of emotional and non-emotional biological motion in individuals with autistic spectrum disorders. *Journal of Autism and Developmental Disorders, 37*, 1386–1392.

Hugill, N., Fink, B., & Neave, N. (2010). The role of human body movements in mate selection. *Evolutionary Psychology, 8*, 66–89.

Hugill, N., Fink, B., Neave, N., Besson, A., & Bunse, L. (2011). Women's perception of men's sensation seeking propensity from their dance movements. *Personality and Individual Differences, 51*, 483–487.

Hugill, N., Fink, B., Neave, N., & Seydel, H. (2009). Men's physical strength is associated with women's perceptions of their dancing ability. *Personality and Individual Differences, 47*, 527–530.

Johansson, G. (1973). Visual perception of biological motion and a model for its analysis. *Perception & Psychophysics, 14*, 201–211.

Johansson, G. (1976). Spatio-temporal differentiation and integration in visual motion perception. *Psychological Research, 38*, 379–393.

Johansson, G., von Hofsten, C., & Jansson, G. (1980). Event perception. *Annual Review of Psychology, 31*, 27–63.

Johnson, K. L., Gill, S., Reichman, V., & Tassinary, L. G. (2007). Swagger, sway, and sexuality: Judging sexual orientation from body motion and morphology. *Journal of Personality and Social Psychology, 93*, 321–334.

Johnson, K. L., & Tassinary, L. G. (2005). Perceiving sex directly and indirectly. Meaning in motion and morphology. *Psychological Science, 16*, 890–897.

Johnston, V. S., Hagel, R., Franklin, M., Fink, B., & Grammer, K. (2001). Male facial attractiveness: Evidence for hormone mediated adaptive design. *Evolution and Human Behavior, 22*, 251–267.

Jokisch, D., Daum, I., & Troje, N. F. (2006). Self recognition versus recognition of others by biological motion: Viewpoint-dependent effects. *Perception, 35*, 911–920.

Kaeppler, A. L. (1978). Dance in anthropological perspective. *Annual Review of Anthropology, 7*, 31–49.

Koppensteiner, M. (2011). Perceiving personality in simple motion cues. *Journal of Research in Personality, 45*, 358–363.

Koppensteiner, M., & Grammer, K. (2010). Motion patterns in political speech and their influence on personality ratings. *Journal of Research in Personality, 44*, 374–379.

Koppensteiner, M., & Grammer, K. (2011). Body movements of male and female speakers and their influence on personality ratings. *Personality and Individual Differences, 51*, 743–747.

Koutedakis, Y., Owolabi, E. O., & Apostolos, M. (2008). Dance biomechanics: A tool for controlling health, fitness, and training. *Journal of Dance Medicine and Science, 12*, 83–90.

Kozlowski, L. T., & Cutting, J. E. (1977). Recognizing the sex of a walker from a dynamic point-light display. *Perception & Psychophysics, 21*, 575–580.

Kurath, G. P. (1960). Panorama of dance ethnology. *Current Anthropology, 1*, 233–254.

Langlois, J. H., Kalakanis, L., Rubenstein, A. J., Larson, A., Hallam, M., & Smoot, M. (2000). Maxims or myths of beauty? A meta-analytic and theoretical review. *Psychological Bulletin, 126*, 390–423.

Lippa, R. (1983). Sex typing and the perception of body outlines. *Journal of Personality, 51*, 667–682.

Little, A. C., Jones, B. C., & Burriss, R. P. (2007). Preferences for masculinity in male bodies change across the menstrual cycle. *Hormones & Behaviour, 51*, 633–639.

Little, A. C., Jones, B. C., & DeBruine, L. (2011). Facial attractiveness: Evolutionary based research. *Philosophical Transactions of the Royal Society, B: Biological Sciences, 66*, 1638–1659.

Livshits, G., & Kobyliansky, E. (1991). Fluctuating asymmetry as a possible measure of developmental homeostasis in humans: A review. *Human Biology, 63*, 441–466.

Luck, G., Saarikallio, S., Burger, B., Thompson, M. R., & Toiviainen, P. (2010). Effects of the Big Five and musical genre on music-induced movement. *Journal of Research in Personality, 44*, 714–720.

Luck, G., Saarikallio, S., & Toiviainen, P. (2009). Personality traits correlate with characteristics of music-induced movement. In: *Proceedings of the 7th triennial conference of European Society for the Cognitive Sciences of Music (ESCOM)* (pp. 276–279).

Ludwig, W. (1932). *Das Rechts-Links Problem im Tierreich und beim Menschen*. Berlin: Springer.

Manning, J. T. (2002). *Digit ratio: A pointer to fertility, behavior, and health*. New Brunswick, NJ: Rutgers University Press.

Manning, J. T., & Taylor, R. P. (2001). Second to fourth digit ratio and male ability in sport: Implications for sexual selection in humans. *Evolution and Human Behavior, 22*, 61–69.

Marey, É. J. (1894). *Le Mouvement*. Paris: G. Masson.

Mather, G., & Murdoch, L. (1994). Gender discrimination in biological motion displays based on dynamic cues. *Proceedings of the Royal Society of London, Series B, 258*, 273–279.

Maynard-Smith, J. (1956). Fertility, mating behaviour and sexual selection in Drosophila subobscura. *Journal of Genetics, 54*, 261–279.

McCrae, R. R., & Costa, P. T., Jr. (1997). Personality trait structure as a human universal. *American Psychologist, 52*, 509–516.

McDonnell, R., Jorg, S., Hodgins, J. K., Newell, F., & O'Sullivan, C. (2007). Virtual shapers & movers: Form and motion affect sex perception. *Proceedings of the 4th symposium on applied perception in graphics and visualization* (pp. 7–10).

Moore, D. G., Hobson, R. P., & Lee, A. (1997). Components of person perception: An investigation with autistic, non-autistic retarded and typically developing children and adolescents. *British Journal of Developmental Psychology, 15*, 401–423.

Neave, N., McCarty, K., Freynik, J., Caplan, N., Hönekopp, J., & Fink, B. (2011). Male dance moves that catch a woman's eye. *Biology Letters, 7*, 221–224.

Patricelli, G. L., Uy, A. C., & Borgia, G. (2003). Multiple male traits interact: Attractive bower decorations facilitate attractive behavioural displays in satin bowerbirds. *Proceedings of the Royal Society of London, Series B, 270*, 2389–2395.

Penton-Voak, I. S., & Chen, J. Y. (2004). High salivary testosterone is linked to masculine male facial appearance in humans. *Evolution and Human Behavior, 25*, 229–241.

Penton-Voak, I. S., Perrett, D. I., Castles, D. L., Kobayashi, T., Burt, D. M., Murray, L. K., et al. (1999). Menstrual cycle alters face preference. *Nature, 399*, 741–742.

Penton-Voak, I. S., Pound, N., Little, A. C., & Perrett, D. I. (2006). Personality judgments from natural and composite facial images: More evidence for a 'kernel of truth' in social perception. *Social Cognition, 24*, 490–524.

Perrett, D. I., Smith, P., Mistlin, A., Chitty, A. J., Heads, A. S., Potter, D. D., et al. (1985). Visual analysis of body movements by neurons in the temporal cortex of the macaque monkey. *Behavioral Brain Research, 16*, 153–170.

Pica, P., Jackson, S., Blake, R., & Troje, N. (2011). Comparing biological motion perception of two distinct human societies. *PLoS One, 6*, e28391.

Pollick, F. E., Kay, J. W., Heim, K., & Stringer, R. (2005). Gender recognition from point-light walkers. *Journal of Experimental Psychology: Human Perception and Performance, 31*, 1247–1265.

Puts, D. A. (2010). Beauty and the beast: Mechanisms of sexual selection in humans. *Evolution and Human Behavior, 31*, 157–175.

Rhodes, G. (2006). The evolutionary psychology of facial beauty. *Annual Review of Psychology, 57*, 199–226.

Roark, D. A., Barrett, S. E., Spence, M. J., Abdi, H., & O'Toole, A. J. (2003). Psychological and neural perspectives on the role of motion in face recognition. *Behavioral and Cognitive Neuroscience Reviews, 2*, 15–46.

Roether, C. L., Omlor, L., Christensen, A., & Giese, M. A. (2009). Critical features for the perception of emotion from gait. *Journal of Vision, 9*, 1–32.

Rowland, W. J. (1995). Do female stickleback care about male courtship vigour? Manipulation of display tempo using video playback. *Behaviour, 132*, 951–961.

Runeson, S., & Frykholm, G. (1983). Kinematic specification of dynamics as an informational basis for person-and-action perception: Expectation, gender recognition, and deceptive intention. *Journal of Experimental Psychology: General, 112*, 585–615.

Saunders, D. R., Williamson, D. K., & Troje, N. F. (2010). Gaze patterns during perception of direction and gender from biological motion. *Journal of Vision, 10*, 1–10.

Schenk, T., & Zihl, J. (1997a). Visual motion perception after brain damage: I. Deficits in global motion perception. *Neuropsychologia, 35*, 1289–1297.

Schenk, T., & Zihl, J. (1997b). Visual motion perception after brain damage: II. Deficits in form from motion perception. *Neuropsychologia, 35*, 1299–1310.

Schmitt, D. P. (2005). Sociosexuality from Argentina to Zimbabwe: A 48-nation study of sex, culture, and strategies of human mating. *Behavioral and Brain Sciences, 28*, 247–275.

Schmitt, D. P., Alcalay, L., Allik, J., Ault, L., Austers, I., Bennett, K. L., et al. (2003). Universal sex differences in the desire for sexual variety: Tests from 52 nations, 6 continents, and 13 islands. *Journal of Personality and Social Psychology, 85*, 85–104.

Sell, A., Cosmides, L., Tooby, J., Sznycer, D., von Rueden, C., & Gurven, M. (2009). Human adaptations for the visual assessment of strength and fighting ability from the body and face. *Proceedings of the Royal Society of London, Series B, 276*, 575–584.

Simion, F., Regolin, L., & Bulf, H. (2008). A predisposition for biological motion in the newborn baby. *Proceedings of the National Academy of Science, 105*, 809–813.

Singer, F., Riechert, S. E., Xu, H., Morris, A. W., Becker, E., Hale, J. A., et al. (2000). Analysis of courtship success in the funnel-web spider *Agelenopsis aperta*. *Behaviour, 137*, 93–117.

Singh, D. (2002). Female mate value at a glance: Relationship of waist-to-hip ratio to health, fecundity and attractiveness. *Neuroendocrinology Letters, 23*, 81–91.

Stevenage, S. V., Nixon, M. S., & Vince, K. (1999). Visual analysis of gait as a cue to identity. *Applied Cognitive Psychology, 13*, 513–526.

Stoffregen, T. A., & Flynn, S. B. (1994). Visual perception of support-surface deformability from human body kinematics. *Ecological Psychology, 6*, 33–64.

Sylwester, K., & Pawlowski, B. (2011). Daring to be darling: Attractiveness of risk takers as partners in long- and short-term sexual relationships. *Sex Roles, 64*, 695–706.

Thoresen, J. C., Vuong, Q. C., & Atkinson, A. P. (2012). First impressions: Gait cues drive reliable trait judgments. *Cognition, 124*, 261–271.

Thornhill, R., & Gangestad, S. W. (2008). *The evolutionary biology of human female sexuality*. New York: Oxford University Press.

Thornhill, R., & Møller, A. P. (1997). Developmental stability, disease and medicine. *Biological Reviews, 72*, 497–548.

Trivers, R. (1972). Parental investment and sexual selection. In B. Campbell (Ed.), *Sexual selection and the descent of man, 1871–1971* (pp. 136–179). Chicago: Aldine.

Trivers, R., Manning, J. T., Thornhill, R., Singh, D., & McGuire, D. (1999). Jamaican symmetry project: Long term study of fluctuating symmetry in rural Jamaican children. *Human Biology, 71*, 417–430.

Trivers, R., Palestis, B., & Zataari, D. (2009). *The anatomy of a fraud: Symmetry and dance*. Antioch, CA: TPZ Publishers.

Troje, N. F. (2002). Decomposing biological motion: A framework for analysis and synthesis of human gait patterns. *Journal of Vision, 2*, 371–387.

Troje, N. F., Westhoff, C., & Lavrov, M. (2005). Person identification from biological motion: Effects of structural and kinematic cues. *Perception & Psychophysics, 67*, 667–675.

Walk, R. D., & Homan, C. P. (1984). Emotion and dance in dynamic point-light displays. *Bulletin of the Psychonomic Society, 22*, 437–440.

Weeden, J., & Sabini, J. (2005). Physical attractiveness and health in Western societies: A review. *Psychological Bulletin, 131*, 635–653.

Weege, B., Lange, B. P., & Fink, B. (2012). Women's visual attention to variation in men's dance quality. *Personality and Individual Differences, 53*, 236–240.

Wilke, A., Hutchinson, J. M. C., Todd, P. M., & Kruger, D. J. (2006). Is risk taking used as a cue in mate choice? *Evolutionary Psychology, 4*, 367–393.

Williams, H. (2001). Choreography of song, dance and beak movements in the zebra finch (Taeniopygia guttata). *Journal of Experimental Biology, 204*, 3497–3506.

Wilson, M., & Daly, M. (1985). Competitiveness, risk taking, and violence: The young male syndrome. *Ethology and Sociobiology, 6*, 59–73.

Windhager, S., Schaefer, K., & Fink, B. (2011). Geometric morphometrics of male facial shape in relation to physical strength and perceived attractiveness, dominance and masculinity. *American Journal of Human Biology, 23*, 805–814.

Yoon, J. M. D., & Johnson, S. C. (2009). Biological motion displays elicit social behavior in 12-month-olds. *Child Development, 80*, 1069–1075.

Zuckerman, M. (1991). *Psychobiology of personality*. Cambridge, UK: Cambridge University Press.

Zuckerman, M. (2007). The Sensation Seeking Scale V (SSS-V): Still reliable and valid. *Personality and Individual Differences, 43*, 1303–1305.

Zuckerman, M., Eysenck, S., & Eysenck, H. J. (1978). Sensation seeking in England and America: Cross-cultural, age, and sex comparisons. *Journal of Consulting and Clinical Psychology, 46*, 139–149.

Intrasexual Competition and Other Theories of Eating Restriction

17

Norman P. Li, April R. Smith, Jose C. Yong, and Tiffany A. Brown

Over 24 million people in the United States and as many as 70 million worldwide are afflicted with an eating disorder, and many more are undiagnosed (Renfrew Center Foundation for Eating Disorders, 2003). Indeed, 80 % of women report being dissatisfied with their body shape (Smolak, 1996), and half of teenage girls skip meals, vomit, or engage in other extreme weight control practices (Neumark-Sztainer, 2005). In this chapter, we describe the etiology and epidemiology of disordered eating and review both traditional, non-evolutionary perspectives and evolutionary perspectives, with particular attention given to the intrasexual competition hypothesis. We then close the chapter by considering unanswered questions and future directions for research on disordered eating.

Disordered Eating

Three major categories of eating disorders exist in the Diagnostic and Statistical Manual of Mental Disorders, Fifth Edition (DSM-5; American Psychiatric Association, 2000): anorexia nervosa (AN), bulimia nervosa (BN), and binge eating disorder (BED). Individuals with a clinically significant disorder of eating that does not meet the criteria for AN, BN, or BED, are diagnosed with an other specified feeding or eating disorder (OSFED). Subsumed within OSFED are atypical AN, subthreshold BN, subthreshold BED, purging disorder (PD), and night eating syndrome (NES).

DSM-5 AN is primarily characterized by the restriction of food intake leading to significantly low body weight (i.e., less than minimally normal for age, sex, developmental trajectory, and physical health). Additional criteria for AN include an intense fear of gaining weight or becoming fat or persistent behavior that interferes with weight gain, and body image disturbance. AN also includes two subtypes, to denote the presence or absence of binge eating/purging during the current episode. The restricting subtype specifies presentations with weight loss occurring as a result of dieting, fasting, and/or excessive exercise. The binge eating/purging subtype includes individuals who have regularly engaged in binge eating or purging (self-induced vomiting, laxatives, diuretics) or both. AN affects disproportionately more women than men, with lifetime prevalence rates approximating 0.9 % in women and 0.3 % in men (Hudson, Hiripi, Pope, & Kessler, 2007).

BN is primarily characterized by recurrent episodes of binge eating and inappropriate compensatory behaviors to prevent weight gain. Binge eating episodes are typified by both eating an amount of food that is definitely larger than what most people would consume within a 2-h period *and* experiencing a sense of

N.P. Li (✉)
Singapore Management University, School of Social Sciences, 90 Stamford Road, Level 4, Singapore 178903, Singapore
e-mail: normanli@smu.edu.sg

V.A. Weekes-Shackelford and T.K. Shackelford (eds.), *Evolutionary Perspectives on Human Sexual Psychology and Behavior*, Evolutionary Psychology, DOI 10.1007/978-1-4939-0314-6_17, © Springer Science+Business Media New York 2014

loss of control over the eating episode. Inappropriate compensatory behaviors can either include purging (self-induced vomiting, laxative use, or diuretics) or non-purging behaviors (fasting or excessive exercise), to influence weight or shape. To meet full criteria for BN, these binge eating and compensatory behaviors must occur, on average, once per week for 3 months. Additionally, BN is characterized by an undue influence of weight and shape on self-evaluation and cannot be diagnosed concurrently with AN. As with AN, BN affects a greater proportion of females, with lifetime prevalence estimates approximating 1.5 % of women and 0.5 % of men (Hudson et al., 2007).

BED is characterized by recurrent binge eating episodes in the absence of any recurrent compensatory behaviors. To meet criteria for BED, three of several cognitive and behavioral features must also be associated with the binge episodes, including: eating more rapidly, eating until uncomfortably full, eating when depressed, eating in the absence of hunger, eating alone due to embarrassment over food consumption, or feeling disgusted or guilty after eating. To meet full criteria for BED, binge eating episodes must occur on average at least once per week for three months. BED affects more females than males, with lifetime prevalence estimates at 3.5 % and 2.0 %, respectively; however, the gender ratio is far less skewed than in AN and BN (Hudson et al., 2007). As a residual category, OSFED includes any clinically significant disorder of eating that does not meet criteria for AN, BN, or BED, including subthreshold and atypical forms of AN, BN, and BED, along with alternative symptom configurations. These alternative symptom configurations include PD and NES. PD is characterized by recurrent episodes of purging (vomiting, laxative, or diuretic use) to control weight or shape in the absence of binge eating episodes among normal weight individuals. NES is primarily characterized by recurrent episodes of night eating (either eating after awakening from sleep or by excessive food consumption after the evening meal). NES must be associated with clinical distress/impairment and cannot be better explained by another eating,

mental, or medical disorder. Given that the DSM-5 has just recently been published, there is not enough information to determine the prevalence of OSFED. The lifetime prevalence estimate of DSM-IV eating disorder not otherwise specified (EDNOS) was approximately 4.62 %, which was greater than those observed for both AN and BN (Le Grange, Swanson, Crow, & Merikangas, 2012); however, given that the changes made to DSM-5 AN, BN, and BED were meant to reduce the preponderance of the residual EDNOS category, the estimates of OSFED are likely to be somewhat lower than those for EDNOS.

Regarding course and outcome, AN has typically been associated with a more chronic course and poorer prognosis compared to BN and EDNOS (Keel, Brown, Holland, & Bodell, 2012; Steinhausen, 2002). Indeed, AN is associated with lower remission rates compared to BN over the course of 10 or more years of follow-up (approximately 50 % for AN and 75 % for BN; Keel & Brown, 2010). Relapse affects a substantial minority of individuals who achieve remission, with one study finding that relapse occurred in 26.0 % of patients with AN compared to 17.7 % of patients with BN (Castellini et al., 2011). These remission rates support the relatively more chronic course of AN. Consistent with this, the longitudinal stability of AN is more common than diagnostic crossover; however, approximately 18 % of individuals initially diagnosed with AN crossover to a diagnosis of BN at some point (Keel et al., 2012). Further supporting the severity of the disorder, AN has been consistently associated with increased mortality (Herzog et al., 2000; Sullivan, 1995) and suicidality (Preti, Rocchi, Sisti, Camboni, & Miotto, 2011). Indeed, risk for death by suicide among individuals with AN was found to be approximately 28-fold that of the general population (Preti et al., 2011).

Research has supported a slightly more favorable prognosis for BN as compared to AN. BN appears to have lower remission rates compared to bulimic-type EDNOS and BED at shorter-term follow-up (Agras, Crow, Mitchell, Halmi, & Bryson, 2009; Milos, Spindler,

Schnyder, & Fairburn, 2005); however, rates between diagnoses appear more comparable at longer-term follow-up (Fichter & Quadflieg, 2007; Grilo et al., 2007; Keel, Gravener, Joiner, & Haedt, 2010). Similar to AN, BN is more likely to remain stable over time than to crossover to another eating disorder. Among those who do change diagnoses, the most common crossover patterns are from BN to AN (7 %) and from BN to BED (2 %; Keel et al., 2012). Notably, the crossover rate from BN to AN is lower than that of AN to BN, supporting the greater severity of AN. Evidence supports elevated mortality rates among individuals with BN (Franko & Keel, 2006; Nielsen, 2003); however, these rates have typically been lower than those observed in AN. Individuals with BN are also at increased risk for suicide (Crow et al., 2009; Preti et al., 2011; Smith et al., 2013), with an approximately 14-fold higher risk of suicide compared to that of the general population (Preti et al., 2011).

BED appears to have a more favorable course and outcome compared to both AN and BN. Remission rates are generally higher for individuals with BED (up to 82 %) and individuals with BED appear to achieve remission in a shorter amount of time than either those with AN or BN (Agras et al., 2009). Remission among 11.4 % of patients with BED (Castellini et al., 2011). Unlike the diagnostic stability observed across AN and BN, BED is actually more likely to crossover to BN than to remain stable (Fichter & Quadflieg, 2007; Keel et al., 2012). Also unlike AN and BN, there does not appear to be an increased risk of death by suicide in BED (Keel et al., 2012). Given the new designation of named syndromes (i.e. atypical AN, PD) and heterogeneity within the category of OSFED, relatively few studies have examined course and outcome in this group, which limits definitive conclusions regarding prognosis for specific types of OSFED. Studies examining DSM-IV EDNOS have supported more encouraging outcomes as compared to AN and BN in the short term (Keel & Brown, 2010). While higher remission rates for

EDNOS compared to AN persist over longer-term follow-up, differences between EDNOS and BN tend to diminish over time (Keel & Brown, 2010). Among those who do achieve remission, relapse rates are comparatively lower to those observed in AN, supporting a more favorable outcome across EDNOS diagnoses. Indeed, Castellini and colleagues (2011) found that among EDNOS diagnoses, relapse occurred in 4.4 % of those with subthreshold AN, 15.6 % of those with subthreshold BN, and 12.1 % of those with subthreshold BED. Although few studies have examined the stability of PD, one short-term study provides evidence for greater stability of diagnosis than crossover, with crossover to BN being relatively low (4 %; Keel, Haedt, & Edler, 2005). Studies have also provided evidence for an elevated rate of death among EDNOS, somewhat comparable to BN, but lower than that for AN (Button, Chadalavada, & Palmer, 2010; Crow et al., 2009). EDNOS also appears to have increased risk for suicide, similar to rates observed for BN (Crow et al., 2009).

Traditional (Non-evolutionary) Perspectives on Disordered Eating

Since the description of AN in 1873 by Sir William Gull, thousands of articles and books have been written on the possible causes of eating disorders (bulimia was not described until 1979; thus, earlier perspectives on eating disorder etiology focused on AN). Early models tended to highlight specific factors, like puberty or family, to be at the root of the development of eating disorders. However, most current researchers agree that the etiology of eating disorders is complex and multiply determined, and modern researchers discuss the development of disordered eating in the context of an integrated biopsychosocial model. Despite this, various etiological perspectives differ by the relative importance they accord for the role of factors such as family, peers, culture, emotion regulation, interpersonal strategies, cognitive processes, and biology. Below, we briefly review each of these perspectives.

The Onset of Puberty

One of the early influential writers on AN was Hilde Bruch, who focused on puberty as a pivotal trigger for the development of AN. Puberty is a time when young women's bodies go through a variety of changes, including increased fat accumulation. Further, puberty is also associated with greater challenges in terms of role expectations and peer relationships. A large proportion of eating disorders onset around puberty; thus, Bruch suggested that AN results in those adolescent girls who experience puberty as overwhelming. She speculated that these adolescent girls desired to revert to a prepubertal stage, one before the overwhelming demands of puberty were placed on them (1978). Similarly, writing some 20 years later, Crisp (1997) speculated that young women were motivated to engage in self-starvation as a way to revert to an earlier pubertal stage. In fact, Crisp hypothesized that women with AN had such a pronounced phobic avoidance of their adult body that they engaged in severe dietary restriction in order to avoid developing an adult physique.

Although these theories hold some intuitive appeal, they are largely untested. Further, they fail to account for various aspects of disordered eating. For instance, they do not address the development of disordered eating in boys and men, despite the fact that men account for approximately 10–25 % of individuals diagnosed with an eating disorder (Carlat, Camargo, & Herzog, 1997; Weltzin et al., 2005). Additionally, these explanations do not take into account the development of eating disorders in prepubertal or postpubertal women, though these two groups are noted to make up a proportion of eating disorder cases (e.g., Keel et al., 2010; WCEDCA, 2007). Moreover, these accounts fail to explain the development of eating disorders in individuals who do not express maturity fears.

Psychosomatic Families

Around the same time as Bruch, Minuchin and colleagues (1975, 1978) developed a theory of AN that laid the etiological blame on the family, coining the term "psychosomatic family" to describe families of girls with AN. According to Minuchin et al. (1978), these families were characterized by high conflict avoidance, high enmeshment, and great emphasis on bodily functions. Minuchin stated that the child with AN used her illness as a way to gain control in the context of an overcontrolled family. According to Minuchin, "for the sick child, the experience of being able to protect the family by using the symptoms may be a major reinforcement for the illness" (p. 31). However, although family therapy is a successful form of treatment for adolescents with AN (e.g., Lock, 2011), the role of the psychosomatic family in the development of AN has not been empirically supported (e.g., Eisler, 2005). Thus, although families are important in the treatment process, current theories do not suggest that controlling families "cause" eating disorders.

Western Culture, Media, and the Thin Ideal

More recent researchers have speculated that eating disorders are a product of modern Western culture. Support for this comes from the fact that eating disorders are most common in Western societies, and there appears to be some evidence that the incidence of bulimia is increasing along with Westernization (Keel & Klump, 2003). More specifically, some researchers have suggested that the internalization of the Western beauty ideal, which has become thinner over the past 60 years (Seifert, 2005), is a major contributor to the development of eating disorders (e.g., Striegel-Moore, Silberstein, & Rodin, 1986; Sypeck, Gray, & Ahrens, 2004).

Thin-ideal internalization results when individuals internalize attitudes that are revered by sources such as peers, media, and family. It is hypothesized that failure to live up to the thin ideal creates body dissatisfaction (Thompson & Stice, 2001). Body dissatisfaction is a well-established risk factor for disordered eating (Stice & Shaw, 2002); thus, it is believed that thin-ideal internalization leads to body dissatisfaction, which in turn leads to disordered eating. Other researchers have emphasized the role of social comparison processes (Festinger, 1954) in the development of body dissatisfaction. According to the appearance comparison perspective, exposure to a host of idealized, thin images forces individuals to make upward comparisons between themselves and the idealized images; the result of these upward comparisons is believed to be the dissatisfaction in one's appearance (Thompson, Heinberg, Altabe, & Tantleff-Dunn, 1999). These upward comparisons are thought to be particularly pernicious for individuals who internalize the thin ideal (Thompson, van den Berg, Roehrig, Guarda, & Heinberg, 2004).

There is a large body of research that supports positive relationships between media consumption, body dissatisfaction, and disordered eating (cf. Grabe, Ward, & Hyde, 2008). Additionally, studies have found cross-cultural support for the association between Western media and problematic eating behaviors. For example, Becker, Burwell, Herzog, Hamburg, and Gilman (2002) examined eating behaviors among adolescent Fijian girls before and after the arrival of Western TV. After 3 years of Western TV exposure, the authors reported self-induced vomiting went from being nonexistent in the population to being endorsed by 11.3 % of the population. Further, there was a reported 16.5 % increase in clinical levels of disordered eating attitudes (as measured by a score of 20 or above on the Eating Attitudes Tests; Becker et al., 2002).

Experimental studies have also supported this relationship. In a typical design, participants are randomly assigned to view either thin images or normal weight images; researchers have continuously found that participants report greater body dissatisfaction after being exposed to images exhibiting the thin ideal as compared to the participants who do not view this ideal

(e.g., Birkeland, Thompson, & Herbozo, 2005; Dittmar & Howard, 2004). These findings are supported by a recent meta-analysis of experimental and correlational studies, which found small to moderate effects for the impact of thin-ideal media exposure on body image concerns among women (Grabe et al., 2008).

Although current evidence suggests that culture may play a role in the development of eating disorders, culture is clearly not the whole story, as not everyone who is exposed to and internalizes the thin ideal develops an eating disorder. In addition, although there is evidence that the incidence of bulimia has been increasing since its introduction into the DSM in 1983, the incidence of AN does not appear to be increasing (Keel & Klump, 2003). Further, there are numerous accounts of AN that predate the rise of thin ideal in Western culture, including saints like Catherine of Sienna, who engaged in severe dietary restriction and sometimes fasted to the point of death (Keel, 2005).

Peer Influence

Some researchers place more emphasis on the role of peer influence over societal influence in the development of eating disorders. Peer influence models build off of learning theory and suggest that peers inculcate certain behaviors (e.g., laxative use) and beliefs (e.g., the importance of a slim body) in other peers (Levine, Smolak, & Hayden, 1994). In a study involving friendship groups, Paxton, Schutz, Wertheim, and Muir (1999) found that cliques were similar with respect to their body image concerns, use of compensatory behaviors, and dietary restraint. Further, these authors found that a clique's use of compensatory behaviors accounted for unique variance in the prediction of an individual clique member's engagement in compensatory behaviors, over and above a host of well-known contributors to disordered eating, like BMI, depression, and self-esteem. As with sociocultural models, limitations of peer influence models include a lack of specificity. In other words, peer influence is so broad that if it was a necessary contributor to eating disorders, then we would expect much higher rates of eating disorders.

Interpersonal Formulation

Building off of a peer influence model, the interpersonal formulation model of eating disorders (Rieger et al., 2010) proposes that in response to negatively valenced social interactions, individuals may engage in disordered eating in an attempt to repair self-esteem and regain their sense of self. Supporting evidence for this model comes from multiple studies which have found that difficult interpersonal situations trigger binge-like behavior (e.g., Baumeister, DeWall, Ciarocco, & Twenge, 2005; Tanofsky-Kraff, Wilfley, & Spurrell, 2000). For instance, study participants who were told that they had been rejected by their peers ate a significantly larger amount of cookies as compared to non-rejected participants (Baumeister et al., 2005).

The interpersonal formulation model (Rieger et al., 2010) further stipulates maintenance factors. Engagement in disordered eating behaviors is believed to increase interpersonal problems; in turn, these interpersonal problems exacerbate eating disorder symptoms. Support for the escalation of disordered eating in response to interpersonal difficulties comes from a longitudinal study which examined the effect of negative feedback seeking on eating disorder-related variables (Joiner, 1999). Over the course of 5 weeks, this study found that among college-aged women, interest in negative feedback led to body dissatisfaction and, in turn, increased bulimic symptoms. Additionally, Rieger and colleagues (2010) hypothesize that indirect sources of evaluative information, such as social comparisons, lead to increased body dissatisfaction and disordered eating. In support of this claim, an experimental study found that female participants exposed to a thin confederate reported worse body dissatisfaction as compared to female participants exposed to a normal weight confederate (Krones, Stice, Batres, & Orjada, 2005).

Cognitive Biases

Leading cognitive theories of AN and BN hold that extreme overvaluation of shape and weight is central to the disorders (e.g., Fairburn, Shafran, & Cooper, 1998). Disordered cognitions and cognitive biases are believed to play a major role in the development and maintenance of eating disorders (e.g., Cooper, 1997, 2005; Shafran, Lee, Cooper, Palmer, & Fairburn, 2007). Specifically, cognitive theories posit that people with eating disorders hold dysfunctional beliefs about their eating habits, shape, and weight. These core beliefs perpetuate negative automatic thoughts and attentional biases in the processing of information (e.g., attending only to information regarding one's body size). Thus, behaviors that reduce these negative thoughts, such as restricting food intake, are highly reinforcing and contribute to the chronicity of the disorder.

Recent work by Guardia and his colleagues (2012) suggests that individuals with eating disorders not only think they are bigger than they actually are, but they perceive themselves that way as well. In their study, individuals with AN exhibited marked distortions regarding the size of their bodies as compared to controls. Specifically, when asked to indicate whether or not they would be able to pass through a door opening that was definitely large enough for them to pass through, the participants with AN were more likely to indicate that they could not as compared to the controls. Further, this perceptual disturbance was found to be specific to their own bodies; individuals with AN could correctly judge whether someone else could or could not fit through a door opening.

Experiments that have used implicit tasks have found support for attentional biases to shape- and weight-related cues among individuals with disordered eating. For example, Ferraro, Andres, Stromberg, and Kristjanson (2003) found that individuals who were at risk for developing an eating disorder were faster at responding to fat-related words (e.g., heavy, plump, cellulite) than words unrelated to fat, whereas control subjects were faster at recognizing "nonfat" words than "fat" words. Additionally, Ahern, Bennett, and Hetherington (2008) found that participants who had positive implicit attitudes toward images of underweight women had higher drive-for-thinness scores on the Eating Disorder Inventory-2 and chose lower ideal body sizes than did participants who had more positive implicit attitudes toward normal weight models.

Emotion Regulation

Although cognitive processes figure prominently in many models of eating disorder development, emotion regulation is considered by some to be particularly important in the development of eating disorders that involve binge eating (i.e., BN, BED). The affect regulation model makes two primary predictions about the relationship between emotion and binge eating: (1) increases in negative affect trigger binge eating and (2) binge eating has a palliative effect and thus reduces negative affect (Hawkins & Clement, 1984). In their meta-analysis of 36 studies using ecological momentary assessment (EMA) methodologies, Haedt-Matt and Keel (2011) examined the validity of both of the hypotheses of the affect regulation model. Their findings indicated that negative affect preceded binge eating; however, the meta-analysis also found that negative affect *increased* following a binge, in opposition to the second hypothesis of the affect regulation model.

Escape

The escape model of binge eating (Heatherton & Baumeister, 1991) is related to the affect regulation model in that it gives affect a primary role; however, it holds that individuals engage in binge eating as a way to *escape* from negative emotional states (as opposed to an attempt at *decreasing* negative emotional states). This theory suggests that in the face of negative affect, individuals turn to binge eating as a way to narrow cognitive processes and reduce

aversive self-awareness. Due to methodological considerations, it has been difficult to design studies that can measure affective states during a binge episode, thus making it difficult to garner concrete support for the escape model of binge eating. However, with the development of psychophysiological ambulatory monitoring, which allows for the measurement of psychophysiological correlates of emotion, such as heart rate variability, respiratory sinus arrhythmia, and skin conductance (Blascovich, Mendes, Vanman, & Dickerson, 2011), it may be possible for future studies to use these types of methods to more accurately assess affective responses during a binge episode.

Biology

With the advent of other new technologies like the functional magnetic resonance imaging (fMRI) and methodologies like genome-wide association studies (GWAS), biological perspectives on the etiology of eating disorders have come to prominence. Beginning in the 1980s, family and twin studies have repeatedly shown evidence of familial aggregation of eating disorders (Bulik et al., 2006; Strober, Freeman, Lampert, Diamond, & Kaye, 2000). Using findings from twin studies, researchers have estimated the heritability of AN to be 33–84 % and bulimia to be 28–83 % (Zerwas & Bulik, 2011). Thus far there has been only one twin adoption study that has been published (Klump, Suisman, Burt, McGue, & Iacono, 2009). Participants for this study were 123 adopted and 56 biological female siblings. This study found that the majority of variance (59–82 %) in eating disorder symptoms was accounted for by genetic factors, while the remainder was accounted for by non-shared environmental factors. Interestingly, shared environmental factors, which include the family environment, did not account for a significant proportion of the variance.

Two primary approaches have been used in order to uncover potential candidate genes that may play a role in the development of eating disorders: association studies and GWAS. Thus far, findings from various association studies suggest that likely gene candidates are those that are involved in the serotonergic and dopaminergic systems and in weight regulation (Hebebrand & Remschmidt, 1995). Currently, only one GWAS study has been published; this study included over a thousand individuals with AN and close to 4000 control subjects (Wang et al., 2010). The authors reported several suggestive single nucleotide polymorphisms (SNPs), which are involved in the transmission and regulation of neurotransmitters; however, none were significant at the genome-wide threshold. The lack of significant findings is likely due to the small sample size for this type of study. Generally speaking, studies are only able to detect SNPs with at least five times as many ill participants as in the Wang et al. (2010) study (Kim, Zerwas, Trace, & Sullivan, 2011). Thus, the results of these types of studies are promising, but very preliminary, and ultimately, the field needs more studies with greater power in order to detect effects. Fortunately, a GWAS with a target sample size of 3000 subjects with AN is underway (Bulik, Collier, & Sullivan, 2011).

Recent work also suggests that hormones likely play an important role in the development of eating disorders (e.g., Klump et al., 2012; Quinton, Smith, & Joiner, 2011; Smith, Hawkeswood, & Joiner, 2010). Specifically, several studies have found that prenatal testosterone levels were higher among controls as compared to women with bulimic symptoms, and thus, prenatal testosterone may protect against bulimic disorders through its organizational effects on the brain (Culbert, Breedlove, Burt, & Klump, 2008; Klump et al., 2006; Smith et al., 2010). Further, Klump and colleagues (2012) have posited that ovarian hormones released at puberty play a role in the development of disordered eating and help explain both the sex difference in eating disorders and the timing of onset, which is often during puberty. Specifically, they speculate that puberty and the attendant effects of ovarian hormones may activate genetic risk in girls (Klump et al., 2012).

These findings mesh with the observations of earlier writers, such as Bruch and Crisp, who suggested that puberty is a trigger for eating disorders; however, these findings suggest a more central role for biological factors that onset at puberty as opposed to environmental factors, though likely both are important.

Further, there appear to be important neurobiological weaknesses in individuals with eating disorders. For instance, individuals with AN have been noted to have altered reward processing, poor set-shifting, and loose central coherence (e.g., Lopez, Tchanturia, Stahl, & Treasure, 2009; Roberts, Tchanturia, & Treasure, 2010). In a recent study by Danner et al. (2012), three groups of participants (women with current AN, recovered women, and healthy control women) completed a battery of neuropsychological instruments (e.g., Berg's Card Sorting Task, Rey-Osterrieth Complex Figure Test, Iowa Gambling Task). This study found that both ill and recovered women with AN demonstrated set-shifting problems; further, individuals with impaired set-shifting also displayed central coherence weaknesses. These findings suggest that a rigid and inflexible thinking style may be associated with the development and maintenance of AN. However, currently there is not strong evidence that these weaknesses play a role in the development of eating disorders due to a lack of prospective studies examining potential neuropsychological impairments in eating disorders. Thus, it is unclear if these impairments predate the onset of the disorder or are a consequence of the disorder.

The above summary of leading etiological perspectives is far from exhaustive; due to space limitations, we did not discuss more general factors, such as depression and low self-esteem, or highly intrapersonal factors, like personality or the experience of traumatic events, like sexual abuse, though all of these other factors have been found to be associated with disordered eating.

All in all, there is a multitude of psychological perspectives through which eating disorders have been examined. Together, the extensive research suggests that many proximate causes may be involved in the onset and maintenance of disordered eating. In addition, biological research, including the results of various behavioral genetics studies, indicates a significant genetic component. Looking for broader, more ultimate explanations, some theorists have proposed how eating restriction and disordered eating might reflect underlying psychological mechanisms that have evolved to provide adaptive benefits. We now examine each of these evolutionary perspectives.

Evolutionary Perspectives on Disordered Eating

Evolutionary psychology provides ultimate explanations for various human thoughts, feelings, and behaviors (Buss, 1995). Although starving oneself can be quite detrimental to one's health or even fatal, there are reasons to believe that adaptive mechanisms may underlie eating restriction and the prevalence of disordered eating. In this part, we consider various evolutionary hypotheses that propose how negative eating attitudes and practices may represent adaptations.

Biological Functions of Fat

In order to understand how an evolutionary perspective can account for eating disorders in women, consideration should be given to the biological functions of adipose tissue (i.e., fat) in mammals and, more specifically, mammalian females. Adipose tissue has been viewed as having two main survival functions for mammals. First, it primarily serves as storage for calories through a reserve of lipids, which are metabolized to meet the energy needs of the body (Cahill, 1982; Norgan, 1997; Pond, 1978). Second, adipose tissue may have evolved as an adaptation for thermal insulation, accumulating in subcutaneous tissue and providing protection from heat and cold (Gesta, Tseng, & Kahn, 2007), although this latter point has been more controversial (cf. Pond, 1998). (For a more thorough review of the biological functions of human adipose tissue, see Wells, 2012.)

In addition to these functions, fat has also been implicated for female mammals in the onset and maintenance of ovulation (Frisch, 1990), working through the organism's endocrine function (Fishman et al., 1975; Frisch et al., 1981; Nimrod & Ryan, 1975). Furthermore, fat is important as a source of calories for the success of pregnancy and lactation (Brown & Konner, 1987). Sex differences in the distribution and abundance of adipose tissue in humans (e.g., Enzi et al., 1986) additionally indicate that natural selection has played a critical role in shaping the anatomy and development of fat, lending further credence to the view that fat serves important survival and reproductive functions. Thus, if attitudes toward fatness in women, perceived either in others or oneself, have any evolutionary importance, that importance ultimately depends on some biological function of adipose tissue. Evolutionary hypotheses about standards of physical appearance and beauty are hence, at some level, attempts to explain how observed patterns in attitudes toward female fatness and in eating behavior could have, at least in ancestral conditions, improved the fitness of individuals relative to other possible patterns.

Reproductive Suppression Hypothesis

One of the most prominent evolutionary theories for eating disorders is the reproductive suppression hypothesis (Condit, 1990; Salmon, Crawford, Dane, & Zuberbier, 2008; Surbey, 1987; Voland & Voland, 1989). This hypothesis suggests that natural selection may have shaped a mechanism in women that alters their proportion of body fat in order to adjust their reproduction in accord with socioecological conditions. This hypothesis was borne out of two well-known biological concepts that were derived from the observation that fat affects the onset and maintenance of ovulation.

The first concept, adaptive reproductive suppression, argues that as reproduction is a highly risky and energetically demanding endeavor for female mammals (Williams, 1966), a female may increase her lifetime reproductive success by timing her reproductive attempts to occur during desirable conditions and, correspondingly, curtailing her reproductive activity at other less favorable times. Natural selection may therefore select for individuals who undergo reproductive suppression under suboptimal reproductive conditions (Wasser & Barash, 1983).

The second concept, known as the critical fat hypothesis (Frisch, 1985, 1990), points out that there is a positive relationship between body fat and the likelihood of ovulation and menstruation. On average, adipose tissue must make up at least 22 % of a woman's body weight to maintain ovulation. Because a female's body fat contains considerable quantities of estrogen and converts androgens to estrogen, changes in the rate of weight gain among adolescent girls or in the weight of lean adult women can influence whether ovulation occurs (Rippon, Nash, Myburgh, & Noakes, 1988). Indeed, for female athletes who are bordering on this threshold, menstruation can be activated or deactivated by the gain or loss of only a few pounds (Frisch et al., 1981). As such, in response to cues relating to reproductive conditions, weight control could have been an effective mechanism for ancestral females to adjust reproductive effort (Becker, Breedlove, & Crews, 1993; Frisch, 1990). Such socioecological cues might include stressful sexual attention from undesirable males and elevated levels of social competition between females.

In modern urban cultures, socioecological cues, which would have signaled the need for temporary postponement of reproduction in ancestral environments, may now be experienced at unprecedented levels of intensity and duration. For some women, the heightened and prolonged body image fears and anti-fat attitudes that abound in today's society may result in reproductive suppression mechanisms being engaged continuously from preadolescence to adulthood and, thus, in the onset and maintenance of disordered eating attitudes and behaviors during that time (Salmon et al., 2008).

Although quite plausible, the reproductive suppression hypothesis nevertheless has some limitations. For instance, it does not directly explain the function of distorted body image; why some more direct and less costly means to stop menstruation did not evolve; why women in modern urban cultures, who are economically well off and have easy access to food, would face poor reproductive prospects; and why men are afflicted. Importantly, as noted earlier, amenorrhea is no longer considered to be a useful indictor of AN and has been deleted as a criterion for AN in DSM-5 (American Psychiatric Association, 2000).

Model of Parental Manipulation

Voland and Voland's (1989) model of parental manipulation provides an interesting account for why eating disorders tend to occur more among wealthier, higher class individuals. This model draws on kin selection theory (Hamilton, 1964) and asserts that AN may be adaptive insofar as it increases the helping behavior of an individual with AN toward her own kin and aids their survival and reproduction while suppressing her own reproductive activity. Such a kin selection-based "helper at the nest" mechanism would have been particularly beneficial in large family units, which were prevalent in human history until recently.

The parental manipulation model suggests that anorexia is instigated by parental dominance—influential parents who are highly involved in the control of resources, offspring livelihood, and family outcomes. Particularly for wealthy large families, males may have relatively better reproductive potential than females, as an abundance of resources contributes to male mate value more than female mate value (Trivers, 1972; Trivers & Willard, 1973). Thus, if affluent parents favor and bestow their resources onto sons and spur the restriction of reproduction of one or a few daughters (via induced anorexia), better inclusive fitness outcomes may be achieved, as those daughters can divert resources that would otherwise have gone to their own offspring toward a male kin.

Consistent with this model, correlational studies have shown that anorexic individuals tend to worry constantly about the well-being of their families, and members of anorexic families possess mutually overprotective attitudes (Minuchin et al., 1975). Specifically, the likelihood of AN development is significantly correlated with having dominant and overprotective mothers (Steiger, Bruce, & Israël, 2003) as well as overly controlling parents (Bruch, 1988). When a daughter is overprotected and dominated by her mother, her ability to find a mate may be reduced, further decreasing her likelihood of producing offspring while increasing the relative benefits of helping her male kin. The parental manipulation model, however, does not account for desires for thinness or anorexic behaviors that derive from sources external to the family.

Adapted-to-Flee-Famine Hypothesis

The curious case of anorexic symptoms leading to a decline in individual fitness by decreasing the carrier's fertility and increasing the risk of death by starvation, while at the same time increasing the carrier's hyperactivity levels, led Guisinger (2003) to propose that anorexia nervosa could exist in its modern form because humans are adapted to flee famine. Like other primates and most mammals, humans cannot store many extra calories as fat; yet, they consistently faced periodic waves of famine. As such, in nomadic tribes, anorexia nervosa might have been a way to help humans overcome food shortages during periods of famine or while traversing vast distances, by facilitating the migration from depleted environments to greener pastures.

Findings from nonhuman populations provide preliminary evidence supporting this view. Food-restricted rats with access to a running wheel and lean-bred pigs with wasting pig syndrome have been found to reject food (Epling & Pierce, 1988; Treasure & Owen, 1997). More generally, Mrosovsky and Sherry (1980) documented the cessation of eating and weight loss of a number of nonhuman species during their seasonal migrations. Animals also increase activity in times of food shortage. When starved in the

laboratory, a number of mammal species ignore their food and exercise excessively (Epling & Pierce, 1992). Lastly, when individuals starve, neurochemical signals of hunger normally are raised, and signals for satiety and activity are typically lowered. In anorexics, however, neuro-modulators and hormones regulating appetite and activity have been found to go against this usual trend and appear instead to facilitate movement and activity (e.g., Leibowitz, 1992; Prentice et al., 1992). Taken together, these findings are consistent with the possibility that there are adaptations to deactivate desires for eating and activate traveling and suggest that AN as an adaptive mechanism might have benefited our ancestors who were faced with food shortages to overcome the pain of hunger and energize them to migrate to more food-abundant locations.

Although the evidence is encouraging, the adapted-to-flee-famine hypothesis does have its own set of limitations. It does not address why individuals with AN resist eating food when food is readily available and why AN is more prevalent in women than men. Furthermore, some studies have shown that not all individuals with AN are hyperactive throughout the entire phase of anorexia.

Restricted Eating as Response to Threat

Gatward (2007) proposed that response to threat may be a reason why individuals get trapped in an anorexic cycle. Because humans are social animals whose survival depends on group inclusion, there will inevitably be competition for status within the group (Baumeister & Leary, 1995). Within-group competition leads to the threat of being expelled from the safety of one's social group, which, in the ancestral past fraught with myriad dangers, would have likely meant certain death. Demonstrating status is thus of paramount importance, as status is an indicator of one's worth to remain in the group. Until recently, fatness was a sign of good resources, as only the wealthy could afford to be overweight. In many cultures today food is relatively abundant and cheap, and resistance to food has become a modern sign of status and self-control (Stevens & Price, 2000). Eating restriction could thus have emerged in order to signal high status as a response to the threat of social exclusion.

Gatward borrows from the adapted-to-flee-famine hypothesis and the adaptive suppression hypothesis to explain the onset and maintenance of AN. Perceived threat of exclusion may activate dietary restriction, which in turn may trigger the adaptive response of decreased appetite and increased hyperactivity to a newly perceived threat of famine (caused by the dietary restriction), and thus cause the individual to experience the symptoms of AN. As these multiple threats of social exclusion and famine, real or imagined, suggest undesirable socio-ecological conditions, females are also likely to undergo suppressed reproductive behavior. Because severe weight loss removes people from competition for status, subsequent weight gain could also be felt as threatening because it could signify reentering within-group competition and risking attack by others and further exclusion. These multiple perceived sources of threat thus maintain restricted eating behaviors in individuals, particularly females. A limitation of this model is that it is difficult to evaluate; furthermore, it does not effectively rule out alternative hypotheses.

Perceived Vulnerability to Disease and Anti-fat Attitudes

Another perspective argues that eating disorders arise out of the association between fat and character undesirability. Specifically, when being fat implies negative traits such as laziness, irresponsibility, lack of self-control, and other qualities pertaining to character and lifestyle flaws (e.g., Björvell, Edman, Rössner, & Schalling, 1985; Fassino et al., 2002), anti-fat attitudes emerge which in turn may result in restricted eating in order to avoid gaining weight and, as a consequence, being associated with those aversive, negative traits.

While such a perspective has tended to reside within the grounds of proximate, social, and non-evolutionary factors, Park, Schaller, and Crandall (2007) explored the possibility that humans have evolved to view obesity as a heuristic cue connoting pathogen transmission. As signal detection of pathogens is often imperfect, humans may have evolved to associate a wide range of superficial cues, such as facial birthmarks and physical disabilities, with pathogens. Humans' behavioral immune system, in the form of aversion, can be triggered by the perception of substantial morphological deviations; thus, perceived obesity may trigger a behavioral immune system of aversion because gross obesity represents one such deviation from species-typical morphological norms. Relatedly, overweight people are commonly stereotyped as unattractive, unclean, and unhealthy, and images of overweight people arouse visceral emotions such as disgust (Harvey, Troop, Treasure, & Murphy, 2002). Antipathy toward overweight people could thus be more fundamentally the result of a pathogen-avoidance mechanism.

Pathogen-avoidance mechanisms typically involve hypervigilance and risk aversion, and avoidant responses to individuals marked by disease-connoting cues are particularly strong when perceivers feel especially vulnerable to disease transmission (Schaller, Park, & Faulkner, 2003). These features allow for an adaptive rejection of individuals afflicted with actual contagious diseases.

Consistent with their hypotheses, the authors found that perceived vulnerability to disease significantly predicted antipathy toward overweight people independently from other variables, such as self-determination ideologies (Schaller et al., 2003). In addition, participants who were primed with images depicting contagious diseases and disease-causing agents were more likely to associate overweight people (as opposed to thin people) with disease using the implicit association test compared to when they were exposed to either accident primes (which eliminate the possibility of negatively valenced primes as a factor), or primes pertaining to work ethics (which eliminate the likelihood that self-determination attitudes accounted for the pattern of results).

The perceived vulnerability to disease and anti-fat attitudes model focuses on antipathy toward overweight individuals other than oneself. Nevertheless, evolved disease- and pathogen-avoidance mechanisms may play a role in shaping attitudes toward one's own weight status and, thus, in the development of restricted eating. This may be especially true for individuals who perceive a lack of social standing in their groups.

In the next part, we consider an additional evolutionary explanation that is perhaps most consistent with all the other theories and is also guided by a fundamental evolutionary theory: intrasexual selection (Darwin, 1871).

Intrasexual Selection Hypothesis

Intrasexual selection involves members of one sex competing among themselves, usually for access to mates or resources. Heritable behaviors or features that provide an advantage in this competition tend to be selected and passed down over the generations. Intrasexual selection is traditionally associated with male–male competition, as in massive male elephant seals battling viciously for a large territory on a beach before female seals arrive for the mating season (e.g., Gould & Gould, 1989). However, recent evidence suggests that females of many species also engage in various forms of intense intrasexual competition (e.g., Clutton-Brock, 2007; Rosvall, 2011).

In humans, intrasexual competition tactics employed by one sex tend to reflect the mate preferences of the other sex (Buss, 1988; Walters & Crawford, 1994). For instance, women's fertility tends to peak at a relatively early age and decreases rapidly after 30. Thus, when considering potential mates, men may have evolved to especially value appearance-related cues that indicate sexual maturity and youth. Such preferences allowed ancestral men to choose mates with greater fertility and reproductive value and, thus, to outreproduce men who did not have such preferences. In contrast to women's

fertility, men's fertility declines significantly slower over the lifespan; thus, there may have been less selective pressure for women to strongly prefer similar cues in their mates. However, because ancestral men varied in their ability to provide key resources essential for offspring survival and eventual reproduction (e.g., Geary, 2009), women may have evolved to prefer men with status and resources (Symons, 1979).

Indeed, numerous studies have found that men value physical attractiveness in their mates more than women do, and women value status and resources more than men do (e.g., Buss, 1989; Li, Bailey, Kenrick, & Linsenmeier, 2002; Li, Valentine, & Patel, 2011; Shackelford, Schmitt, & Buss, 2005). These sex-specific preferences appear to be ingrained in people's self-concepts: when considering themselves as potential long-term mates, men prioritize having status and resources, whereas women prioritize having physical attractiveness (Li, 2007). In line with these differences, women, more than men, express greater usage of intrasexual competition tactics related to physical appearance, including dieting to improve one's figure. Such tactics are also judged to be more effective for female versus male intrasexual competition (Buss, 1988). Furthermore, men are more distressed when a rival surpasses them on financial prospects, job prospects, and physical strength, whereas women are more distressed when a rival surpasses them on facial and bodily attractiveness (Buss, Shackelford, Choe, Buunk, & Dijkstra, 2000).

The intrasexual competition model. Drawing on principles of sexual selection, Abed (1998) proposed an intrasexual competition hypothesis for disordered eating, laying out the following logic. In the ancestral past, the hourglass shape [i.e., waist-to-hip ratio (WHR), Singh, 1993] was a reliable indicator of a female reproductive condition and capacity. As such, men evolved to strongly prefer females with low WHRs as mates because such females had high reproductive capacity and were also not currently pregnant or lactating. As women age, they not only lose the hourglass shape but also tend to gain body mass. This is especially the case when women's bodies are subjected to cycles of pregnancy, childbirth, and nursing, as they would have been from a relatively early age in the ancestral past. Thus, in addition to the hourglass shape, bodily thinness may also have been reliably associated with nubility—a state of fertility with no reproductive history. Whereas WHRs are largely influenced by estrogen levels (Cashdan, 2008; Singh, 1993), thinness may not only be influenced by hormones but may also be controllable through dieting. As such, women may have evolved to be sensitive to perceptions of premature obesity and to strive for being as thin as or thinner than other young nulipara. Such an adaptation may have given ancestral women a competitive edge in attracting long-term mates.

In modern, industrial environments, however, several factors may lead to a destabilization of long-term relationships and, consequently, to a "runaway" intrasexual competition process in which an eating restriction strategy is triggered and maintained to the point of ill health or fatality. With the formation of modern, industrial societies, the size and unity of extended families—which tended to be patrilocally organized (centered around men's genetic relatives) in the ancestral past (e.g., Wrangham, 1999)—greatly decreased. Accordingly, the role of kin as well as the power of men in influencing mating markets and women's sexual behavior greatly diminished, leaving women to promote themselves in the mating markets and with greater autonomy in selecting mates. According to Abed (1998), such forces likely decreased men's paternity confidence and, thus, their paternal investment, which in turn led to a destabilization of marriage and, at the same time, an increase among women in pursuing short-term relationships. Thus, in modern societies, there are more individuals available for a longer time on the mating market and more women competing with each other for mates for many more years than in the ancestral past.

Additionally, children in modern societies are no longer needed to tend to family farms or trades and instead, represent net economic losses. Accordingly, reproduction in modern societies—

in particular, urban environments—is curtailed and delayed, and the birth spacing interval is greater, thereby allowing women to retain a nubile shape for much longer than would be the case in an ancestral or traditional society. Moreover, the population density in modern environments can reach several millions per city—an extremely large-scale increase over the lightly populated ancestral village where 150 might be a maximum total population (Dunbar, 1992). Thus, in modern environments, women are exposed to an unnaturally high number of potential competitors who may appear nubile and trigger intrasexual competition on thinness (Salmon et al., 2008).

Furthermore, in modern environments, the person's perceived intrasexual competitors are not limited to actual competitors. Various lines of research have demonstrated that people (their evolved mechanisms) cannot distinguish between real individuals encountered in the flesh and those seen on television, magazines, Internet, and other forms of media (e.g., Kanazawa, 2002). For example, many people evaluate their social lives more positively after having watched television (Kanazawa, 2002). After being exposed to pictures of physically attractive women, women evaluate themselves more negatively as potential mates and men express reduced commitment to their long-term romantic partners (Kenrick, Neuberg, Zierk, & Krones, 1994). The multibillion dollar pornography industry attests to the ability of psychological mechanisms to be triggered by two-dimensional images (Kenrick, Gutierres, & Goldberg, 1989). These days, people consume electronic media and can expose themselves to more individuals in 1 day than our ancestors encountered in a lifetime. The effects of such exposure are now coming into light. For instance, a recent study indicated that many healthy men in their 20s who regularly consume Internet pornography cannot maintain erections with their actual partners, who likely compare unfavorably to images of naked women on the Internet (Italian men suffer 'sexual anorexia' after Internet porn use, 2011).

All in all, individuals, including women, face an inordinate number of real and virtual same-sex competitors in the modern world. One result of all this competition is that for some women, intrasexual competition mechanisms via dietary control may be excessively triggered, thereby leading to unhealthy dieting practices and, in some instances, disordered eating. We note here that although in this part we refer to disordered eating in general, Abed (1998) makes a distinction between the two main forms. That is, AN is viewed as a manifestation of intrasexual competition with a relatively early onset in which standards for thinness are set extremely low, whereas BN involves a reactivation of intrasexual competition mechanisms for thinness with a somewhat later onset.

Compatibility with other perspectives and research. The intrasexual competition model is compatible with many of the findings on disordered eating reviewed earlier. For instance, various researchers have noted of the high incidence of eating disorders in adolescent females (e.g., Bruch, 1978; Crisp, 1997). Indeed, although both young girls and older women can evidence disordered eating, the average age of onset for anorexia nervosa is 17, and rates tend to drop off after 25 (Substance Abuse and Mental Health Services Administration, 2003). As mentioned earlier, Bruch (1978) suggested that AN might be especially likely to occur in female adolescents who experience puberty as overwhelming. From an intrasexual competition perspective, puberty may be particularly overwhelming and a time when eating disorders are likely to occur because this is precisely when competition for mates has not only set in but is especially intense. Similarly, attempts to repair self-esteem as proposed by the interpersonal formulation model (Rieger et al., 2010) may center around efforts to regain mate value or social status, which, for women, tends to revolve around physical attractiveness and youth. Consistent with this line of reasoning, one study found that women with anorexia were less likely to be married than aged-matched controls (45 % vs. 16 %; Sullivan, Bulik, Fear, & Pickering, 1998).

From the intrasexual competition perspective, the prevalent thin ideal (e.g., Thompson & Stice, 2001) that is thought to be a product of Western culture may represent women's mental composites (Symons, 1979) of the youngest and most fertile-looking potential competitors for mates. Although adaptive for setting comparison standards in a small village setting, this composite in the modern world includes an unnaturally high number of thin, nubile-looking competitors, both real and virtual, thereby leading to perpetual shortcomings between one's self-evaluation and one's ideal, desired state. As described above, such gaps are associated with body dissatisfaction and attempts to eliminate the gaps via various forms of unhealthy caloric restriction and weight reduction practices.

Similarly, the intrasexual competition perspective also offers insights into the numerous studies showing links between women's exposure to thin images and body dissatisfaction, unhealthy eating attitudes, and various eating disorders. That is, the ultimate reason why people—in particular, young women—are susceptible to comparisons of thinness in the first place is because of psychological mechanisms that evolved to promote successful intrasexual competition for mates. Such mechanisms may also be responsible for various cognitive distortions and biases relating to one's own size and shape (e.g., Cooper, 1997), which, alongside body dissatisfaction, serve to motivate eating restriction and weight loss.

From an intrasexual competition perspective, women's interest in consuming fashion-based media and the featured thin models may be stemming from innate, adaptive mechanisms to socially compare and learn from same-sex individuals of higher mate value. Along these lines, one study examined the eye movements of women presented with various target faces. Women with relatively high bulimotypic symptomatology tended to fixate on physically attractive female faces versus average female faces or male faces (Maner et al., 2006).

Empirical investigations of the intrasexual competition model. Various studies have provided direct support for the intrasexual competition hypothesis. For instance, a correlational study found, through structural equation modeling, that female intrasexual competitiveness for mates was the underlying factor behind competition for status, perfectionism, body dissatisfaction, drive for thinness, and both BN and AN (Faer, Hendriks, Abed, & Figueredo, 2005).

Another study examined the relationships between life history strategy, intrasexual competition, and eating disorders (Abed et al., 2012). Life history strategy was developed by evolutionary biologists to explain how organisms (including humans) adaptively allocate energy, time, and resources across their lifetime toward different activities (e.g., Charnov, 1993; Daan & Tinbergen, 1997). Whereas a slow life history strategy is associated with greater somatic effort (development of body, mind, skills, etc.) and parental investment, a fast life history strategy is associated with greater mating and reproductive effort. A structural equation model indicated that intrasexual competitiveness was related to disordered eating behaviors; moreover, a slow life history strategy had negative effects on disordered eating behavior both directly and through its negative effect on intrasexual competitiveness. A subsequent study found evidence that the protective effects of a slow life history strategy may be due to its association with greater behavioral regulation, which is negatively associated with intrasexual competitiveness and disordered eating behaviors (Salmon, Figueredo, & Woodburn, 2009).

Strong evidence for the intrasexual competition model also comes from two recent investigations using an experimental paradigm. First, Li, Smith, Griskevicius, Cason, and Bryan (2010) conducted two studies in which participants were exposed to a series of ten personal profiles allegedly written by same-sex target individuals, describing their interests, school and community activities, and job. The profiles conveyed either a competitive and status-seeking orientation (e.g., playing to win, taking leadership positions, aiming for success) or a noncompetitive and non-status-seeking orientation (e.g., playing for fun, joining but not leading organizations, and being content to get by). Each profile was accompanied by a facial photograph of an individual of average physical attractiveness and normal weight.

In the first study, people saw these profiles and then completed the Eating Attitudes Test (Garner & Garfinkel, 1979), which measures thoughts and feelings related to disordered eating, including restriction (e.g., "I avoid eating when hungry"), purging (e.g., "I have the impulse to vomit after meals"), and a strong desire for thinness (e.g., "I am preoccupied with a desire to be thinner"). Women who were exposed to the competitive target profiles indicated having significantly more negative eating attitudes (some were at clinical levels) than women exposed to the noncompetitive profiles. No effects were found for men, who tended to have low negative eating attitudes in both conditions. Thus, this study indicated that even in the absence of attractiveness and thinness-related cues, instrasexual status competition motives are capable of triggering negative/restrictive eating attitudes.

A unique strength of the intrasexual competition hypothesis is that it addresses eating disorders in men. Although eating disorders predominantly occur in women, they do affect some men, and they are disproportionately represented in gay men (e.g., Herzog, Norman, Gordon, & Pepose, 1984) but not lesbian women (Striegel-Moore, Tucker, & Hsu, 1990). To examine this phenomenon, in their second study, Li et al. (2010) also investigated the effects of sexual orientation in their second study. Similar to heterosexual men, gay men also place great value on youth and physical attractiveness in their mates (Bailey, Gaulin, Agyei, & Gladue, 1994; Kenrick, Keefe, Bryan, Barr, & Brown, 1995). Thus, like heterosexual women, gay men compete intrasexually on appearance and may develop similar issues of body image and eating restriction due to such competition. Indeed, heterosexual women, but not heterosexual men, responded to the competitive target profiles by reporting more negative eating attitudes and worse body image. On the other hand, gay men, but not lesbian women, reported more negative attitudes and worse body image after viewing the competitive profiles. This specific pattern of results reflected the differing values that individuals' mates place on physical attractiveness according to their sex and sexual orientation and lent further support to the intrasexual competition model.

If intrasexual competition underlies the prevalence of eating disorders in modern societies, then competitive individuals who are especially oriented toward the attainment of social status would be expected to be particularly at risk. To investigate this possibility, Smith, Li, and Joiner (2011) measured women's status aspiration with the status aspiration subscale of the Achievement Motivation Scale (Cassidy & Lynn, 1989; e.g., "I would like an important job where people look up to me"). Participants were then exposed to a series of ten same-sex individuals who were either thin or heavy in their photographs and came across as either successful or unsuccessful in their alleged self-descriptions. After being exposed to thin, successful targets, women who were high on status aspiration reported significantly worse body satisfaction and greater ineffectiveness (i.e., a lack of control over their lives) than women who were low on status aspiration. Together with perfectionism, body dissatisfaction and ineffectiveness have been implicated in the development of bulimic symptoms (Bardone-Cone, Abramson, Vohs, Heatherton, & Joiner, 2006) and the maintenance and exacerbation of bulimic symptoms (Joiner, Heatherton, Rudd, & Schmidt, 1997). Thus, together with the other findings, these results suggest that intrasexual competitiveness is a significant factor that underlies the development of modern-day eating disorders.

In summary, an intrasexual competition model provides a promising evolutionary account for the development of disordered eating behaviors. It addresses several of the shortcomings of the other evolutionary hypotheses and is largely consistent with the demographic profile of affected individuals and much of the other research on eating disorders, including the well-established links between media consumption and women's body image and eating attitudes. The model has also been supported by various investigations that have both correlationally and experimentally demonstrated the link between intrasexual competition and body dissatisfaction and disordered eating attitudes. Furthermore, because intrasexual competition is a key evolutionary process for both sexes, the intrasexual competition model addresses why eating disorders occur in some men. Finally, the model is consistent with separate lines of research indicating that various modern-day ills may be due to a mismatch between current living conditions and the ancestral environment in which human psychological mechanisms evolved to function (e.g., Buss, 2000; Kennair, 2002; Nesse & Williams, 1995).

Future Directions and Treatment Implications

As noted in this chapter, numerous theories, including those that embrace an evolutionary perspective, have been offered as explanations for the prevalence of eating disorders. Each of the available theories has various limitations and/or is unable to explain certain aspects of eating disorders. The intrasexual competition model appears to offer a comprehensive account of eating disorder etiology and maintenance; however, more empirical investigations of the intrasexual competition model are needed to substantiate this theoretical framework and to further demonstrate its precision and predictive power compared to existing frameworks.

It will also be important for future work on the intrasexual competition model to incorporate biological factors. Given recent findings, which have found associations with disordered eating and hormonal factors both prenatally (e.g., Quinton, Smith, & Joiner, 2011; Smith et al., 2010) and at puberty (Klump et al., 2012), it will be informative for future work to investigate the ovulatory cycle. Because women are more likely to accentuate their physical appearance during ovulation (Durante, Li, & Haselton, 2008; Haselton, Mortezaie, Pillsworth, Bleske-Recheck, & Frederick, 2007), it may be that women are especially likely to indicate restrictive eating attitudes in response to cues of status competition around the time of ovulation.

It will also be important for future work to continue to investigate potential moderators, like achievement motivation, and situational factors, like power, that may activate intrasexual competition motives. For instance, as women continue to enter the global economy in record numbers (Aguirre, Sabbagh, Rupp, & Hoteit, 2012), power may be a particularly salient factor to examine with respect to disordered eating, as power has been found to activate goal pursuits (e.g., Galinsky, Gruenfeld, & Magee, 2003; Kunstman & Maner, 2011). Thus, success in the workforce could have potentially negative downstream consequences among women whose goals include dieting and weight loss.

The current review also provides suggestions for eating disorder treatment and prevention efforts. Given that the abundance of idealized media images is believed to over-activate intrasexual competition motives, and given that individuals are likely to continue to be increasingly bombarded by such images, interventions, such as media literacy programs, may be particularly indicated for the prevention of eating disorders. These programs are designed to teach participants to be informed consumers of media and typically include psychoeducational components and the viewing of presentations on the treatment of media images (e.g., utilizing techniques such as air brushing and Photoshopping to make images look more "perfect"). Media literacy programs are based on inoculation theory; specifically, they operate under the assumption that by providing participants with facts about advertising and media images, participants will be less susceptible to thin ideal internalization and the pressure to be thin (Wilksch, Durbridge, & Wade, 2008). Further, it is hypothesized that reducing susceptibility to internalization of the thin ideal will improve body image and decrease behaviors that are associated with the development of eating disorders, such as dieting (Yager & O'Dea, 2008).

Recent studies provide support for the effectiveness of media literacy programs in reducing eating disorder-related cognitions. For instance, Watson and Vaughn (2006) found that the female college students who took part in a 4-week intervention group, which consisted of watching a movie about the realities of female images in the media and participating in exercises and discussions to increase media literacy, evidenced less awareness of the thin ideal and greater body satisfaction as compared to the control group. Further, the effects of media literacy programs have been found to persist long term. Specifically, Wilksch and Wade (2009) found that after participating in an eight-session media literacy program, adolescent girls had significantly lower shape and weight concerns, dieting concerns, body dissatisfaction, feelings of ineffectiveness, and depression at post-intervention and at a 30-month follow-up.

Dissonance-based approaches, which are based on Festinger's cognitive dissonance theory (1957), ask participants to take a counter-attitudinal stance against the thin ideal and have also been found to be highly effective at reducing eating disorder-related cognitions and behaviors (Becker, Smith, & Ciao, 2006; Stice, Chase, Stormer, & Appel, 2001; Yager & O'Dea, 2008). For example, Stice, Shaw, Burton, and Wade (2006) found that individuals in the dissonance-based program had lower thin-ideal internalization, dieting, and eating pathology symptoms at a 1-year follow-up compared to assessment only controls. Thus, interventions that combine media literacy and dissonance approaches may be particularly effective in the prevention of disordered eating.

Conclusion

In conclusion, eating restriction is a highly nuanced phenomenon that has been viewed from many perspectives and linked to many different factors. The intrasexual competition model has been especially promising, and further examination is needed on the intrasexual competition processes among people afflicted with disordered eating. Such information would prove useful for the development of prevention and intervention programs that utilize an understanding of both the ancient, adaptive mechanisms that underlie eating restriction and the proximate factors that are likely to trigger these mechanisms in modern environments.

References

Abed, R. T. (1998). The sexual competition hypothesis for eating disorders. *British Journal of Medical Psychology, 71*, 525–547.

Abed, R., Mehta, S., Figueredo, A. J., Aldridge, S., Balson, H., Meyer, C., et al. (2012). Eating disorders and intrasexual competition: Testing an evolutionary hypothesis among young women. *Scientific World Journal, 2012*(290813), 1–8.

Agras, W. S., Crow, S., Mitchell, J. E., Halmi, K. A., & Bryson, S. (2009). A 4-year prospective study of eating disorder NOS compared with full eating disorder syndromes. *International Journal of Eating Disorders, 42*, 565–570.

Aguirre, D., Sabbagh, K., Rupp, C., & Hoteit, L. (2012). *Empowering the third billion: Women and the world of work in 2012.* Retrieved from http://www.booz.com/global/home/what_we_think/third_billion

Ahern, A. L., Bennett, K. M., & Hetherington, M. M. (2008). Internalization of the ultra-thin ideal: Positive implicit associations with underweight fashion models are associated with drive for thinness in young women. *Eating Disorders, 16*, 294–307.

American Psychiatric Association. (2000). *Diagnostic and statistical manual of mental disorders* (5th ed.). Washington, DC: Author.

Bailey, J. M., Gaulin, S., Agyei, Y., & Gladue, B. A. (1994). Effects of gender and sexual orientation on evolutionary relevant aspects of human mating psychology. *Journal of Personality and Social Psychology, 66*, 1081–1093.

Bardone-Cone, A. M., Abramson, L. Y., Vohs, K. D., Heatherton, T. F., & Joiner, T. E., Jr. (2006). Predicting bulimic symptoms: An interactive model of self-efficacy, perfectionism, and perceived weight status. *Behaviour Research and Therapy, 44*, 27–42.

Baumeister, R. F., DeWall, C. N., Ciarocco, N. J., & Twenge, J. M. (2005). Social exclusion impairs self-regulation. *Journal of Personality and Social Psychology, 88*(4), 589.

Baumeister, R. F., & Leary, M. R. (1995). The need to belong: Desire for interpersonal attachments as a fundamental human motivation. *Psychological Bulletin, 117*, 497–529.

Becker, J. B., Breedlove, S. M., & Crews, D. (1993). *Behavioral endocrinology.* Cambridge, MA: MIT Press.

Becker, A. E., Burwell, R. A., Herzog, D. B., Hamburg, P., & Gilman, S. E. (2002). Eating behaviours and attitudes following prolonged exposure to television among ethnic Fijian adolescent girls. *The British Journal of Psychiatry, 180*, 509–514.

Becker, C. B., Smith, L. M., & Ciao, A. C. (2006). Peer-facilitated eating disorder prevention: A randomized effectiveness trial of cognitive dissonance and media

advocacy. *Journal of Counseling Psychology, 53*, 550–555.

Birkeland, R., Thompson, J., & Herbozo, S. (2005). Media exposure, mood, and body image dissatisfaction: An experimental test of person versus product priming. *Body Image, 2*, 53–61.

Björvell, H., Edman, G., Rössner, S., & Schalling, D. (1985). Personality traits in a group of severely obese patients: A study of patients in two self-chosen weight reducing programs. *International Journal of Obesity, 9*, 257–266.

Blascovich, J., Mendes, W. B., Vanman, E., & Dickerson, S. (2011). *Social psychophysiology for social and personality psychology.* London: Sage.

Brown, P. J., & Konner, M. (1987). An anthropological perspective on obesity. *Annals of the New York Academy of Sciences, 499*, 29–46.

Bruch, H. (1978). *The golden cage: The enigma of anorexia nervosa.* Cambridge, MA: Harvard University Press.

Bruch, H. (1988). *Conversations with anorexics.* Northvale, NJ: Aronson.

Bulik, C. M., Collier, D., & Sullivan, P. (2011). WTCCC3 and GCAN: A genomewide scan for anorexia nervosa. *International Conference on Eating Disorders*, Miami, FL.

Bulik, C. M., Sullivan, P. F., Tozzi, F., Furberg, H., Lichtenstein, P., & Pedersen, N. L. (2006). Prevalence, heritability, and prospective risk factors for anorexia nervosa. *Archives of General Psychiatry, 63*, 305–312.

Buss, D. M. (1988). The evolution of human intrasexual competition: Tactics of mate attraction. *Journal of Personality and Social Psychology, 54*, 616–628.

Buss, D. M. (1989). Sex differences in human mate preferences: Evolutionary hypotheses tested in 37 cultures. *Behavioral and Brain Sciences, 12*, 1–49.

Buss, D. M. (1995). Evolutionary psychology: A new paradigm for psychological science. *Psychological Inquiry, 6*, 1–30.

Buss, D. M. (2000). The evolution of happiness. *American Psychologist, 55*, 15–23.

Buss, D. M., Shackelford, T. K., Choe, J., Buunk, B. P., & Dijkstra, P. (2000). Distress about mating rivals. *Personal Relationships, 7*, 235–243.

Button, E. J., Chadalavada, B., & Palmer, R. L. (2010). Mortality and predictors of death in a cohort of patients presenting to an eating disorders service. *International Journal of Eating Disorders, 43*, 387–392.

Cahill, G. C., Jr. (1982). Starvation. *Transactions of the American Clinical and Climatological Association, 94*, 1–21.

Carlat, D. J., Camargo, C. A., & Herzog, D. B. (1997). Eating disorders in males: A report on 135 patients. *American Journal of Psychiatry, 154*, 1127–1132.

Cashdan, E. (2008). Waist-to-hip ratio across cultures: Trade-offs between androgen- and estrogen-dependent traits. *Current Anthropology, 49*, 1099–1107.

Cassidy, T., & Lynn, R. (1989). A multidimensional approach to achievement motivation: The development of a comprehensive measure. *Journal of Occupational Psychology, 62*, 301–312.

Castellini, G., Lo Sauro, C., Mannucci, E., Ravaldi, C., Rotella, C. M., Faravelli, C., et al. (2011). Diagnostic crossover and outcome predictors in eating disorders according to DSM-IV and DSM-V proposed criteria: A 6-year follow-up study. *Psychosomatic Medicine, 73*, 270–279.

Charnov, E. L. (1993). *Life history invariants*. Oxford: Oxford University Press.

Clutton-Brock, T. (2007). Sexual selection in males and females. *Science, 318*, 1882–1885.

Condit, V. K. (1990). Anorexia nervosa: Levels of causation. *Human Nature, 1*, 391–413.

Cooper, M. J. (1997). Cognitive theory of anorexia nervosa and bulimia nervosa: A review. *Behavioural and Cognitive Psychotherapy, 25*, 113–145.

Cooper, M. J. (2005). Cognitive theory in anorexia nervosa and bulimia nervosa: Progress, development and future directions. *Clinical Psychology Review, 25*, 511–531.

Crisp, A. H. (1997). Anorexia nervosa as a flight from growth: Assessment and treatment based on the model. In D. M. Garner & P. E. Garfinkel (Eds.), *Handbook of treatment for eating disorders* (2nd ed., pp. 248–277). New York: Guilford Press.

Crow, S. J., Peterson, C. B., Swanson, S. A., Raymond, N. C., Specker, S., Eckert, E. D., et al. (2009). Increased mortality in bulimia nervosa and other eating disorders. *American Journal of Psychiatry, 166*, 1342–1346.

Culbert, K. M., Breedlove, S. M., Burt, S. A., & Klump, K. L. (2008). Prenatal hormone exposure and risk for eating disorders: A comparison of opposite-sex and same-sex twins. *Archives of General Psychiatry, 65*, 329.

Daan, S., & Tinbergen, J. M. (1997). Adaptation of life histories. In J. R. Krebs & N. B. Davies (Eds.), *Behavioural ecology: An evolutionary approach* (pp. 311–333). Oxford: Blackwell Science.

Danner, U. N., Sanders, N., Smeets, P. A., van Meer, F., Adan, R. A., Hoek, H. W., et al. (2012). Neuropsychological weaknesses in anorexia nervosa: Set-shifting, central coherence, and decision making in currently ill and recovered women. *International Journal of Eating Disorders, 45*, 685–694.

Darwin, C. (1871). *The descent of man and selection in relation to sex*. London: Murray.

Dittmar, H., & Howard, S. (2004). Thin-ideal internalization and social comparison tendency as moderators of media models' impact on women's body-focused anxiety. *Journal of Social and Clinical Psychology, 23*, 768–791.

Dunbar, R. I. M. (1992). Neocortex size as a constraint on group size in primates. *Journal of Human Evolution, 22*, 469–493.

Durante, K. M., Li, N. P., & Haselton, M. G. (2008). Changes in women's choice of dress across the ovulatory cycle: Naturalistic and experimental evidence.

Personality and Social Psychology Bulletin, 34, 1451–1460.

Eisler, I. (2005). The empirical and theoretical base of family therapy and multiple family day therapy for adolescent anorexia nervosa. *Journal of Family Therapy, 27*, 104–131.

Enzi, G., Gasparo, M., Biondetti, P. R., Fiore, D., Semisa, M., & Zurlo, F. (1986). Subcutaneous and visceral fat distribution according to sex, age and overweight, evaluated by computed tomography. *Journal of Clinical Nutrition, 44*, 739–746.

Epling, W. F., & Pierce, W. D. (1988). Activity-based anorexia: A biobehavioral perspective. *International Journal of Eating Disorders, 5*, 475–485.

Epling, W. F., & Pierce, W. D. (1992). *Solving the anorexia puzzle*. Toronto, Ontario, Canada: Hogrefe & Huber.

Faer, L. M., Hendriks, A., Abed, R. T., & Figueredo, A. J. (2005). The evolutionary psychology of eating disorders: Female competition for mates or for status? *Psychology and Psychotherapy: Theory, Research and Practice, 78*, 397–417.

Fairburn, C. G., Shafran, R., & Cooper, Z. (1998). A cognitive behavioral theory of anorexia nervosa. *Behavior Research and Therapy, 37*, 1–13.

Fassino, S., Leombruni, P., Pierò, A., Daga, G. A., Amianto, F., Rovera, G., et al. (2002). Temperament and character in obese women with and without binge eating disorder. *Comprehensive Psychiatry, 43*, 431–437.

Ferraro, F. R., Andres, M., Stromberg, L., & Kristjanson, J. (2003). Processing fat-related information in individuals at risk for developing an eating disorder. *The Journal of Psychology, 137*, 467–475.

Festinger, L. (1954). A theory of social comparison processes. *Human Relations, 7*, 117–140.

Festinger, L. (1957). *A theory of cognitive dissonance*. Stanford, CA: Stanford University Press.

Fichter, M. M., & Quadflieg, N. (2007). Long-term stability of eating disorder diagnoses. *International Journal of Eating Disorders, 40*, S61–S66.

Fishman, J., Fishman, J. H., Nisselbaum, J. S., Menendez-Botet, C., Schwartz, M. K., Martucci, C., et al. (1975). Measurement of the estradiol receptor in human breast tissue by the immobilized antibody method. *Journal of Clinical Endocrinology and Metabolism, 40*, 724–727.

Franko, D. L., & Keel, P. K. (2006). Suicidality in eating disorders: Occurrence, correlates, and clinical implications. *Clinical Psychology Review, 26*, 769–782.

Frisch, R. E. (1985). Fatness, menarche, and female fertility. *Perspectives in Biology and Medicine, 28*, 611–633.

Frisch, R. E. (1990). Body fat, menarche, fitness, and fertility. In R. E. Frisch (Ed.), *Adipose tissue and reproduction* (pp. 1–26). Basel, Switzerland: Karger.

Frisch, R. E., von Gotz-Welbergen, A., McArthur, S., Albright, T., Witschi, J., Bullen, B., et al. (1981). Delayed menarche and amenorrhea of college athletes in relation to age of onset of training. *Journal of the American Medical Association, 246*, 1559–1563.

Galinsky, A. D., Gruenfeld, D. H., & Magee, J. C. (2003). From power to action. *Journal of Personality and Social Psychology, 85*, 453–466.

Garner, D. M., & Garfinkel, P. E. (1979). The Eating Attitudes Test: An index of the symptoms of anorexia nervosa. *Psychological Medicine, 9*, 273–279.

Gatward, N. (2007). Anorexia nervosa: An evolutionary puzzle. *European Eating Disorders Review, 15*, 1–12.

Geary, D. C. (2009). *Male, female: The evolution of human sex differences*. Washington, DC: APA.

Gesta, S., Tseng, Y.-H., & Kahn, C. R. (2007). Developmental origin of fat: Tracking obesity to its source. *Cell, 131*, 242–256.

Gould, J. L., & Gould, G. C. (1989). *Sexual selection* (2nd ed.). New York: Scientific American Library.

Grabe, S., Ward, L. M., & Hyde, J. S. (2008). The role of the media in body image concerns among women: A meta-analysis of experimental and correlational studies. *Psychological Bulletin, 134*(3), 460–476.

Grilo, C. M., Pagano, M. E., Skodol, A. E., Sanislow, C. A., McGlashan, T. H., Gunderson, J. G., et al. (2007). Natural course of bulimia nervosa and of eating disorder not otherwise specified: 5-Year prospective study of remissions, relapses, and the effects of personality disorder psychopathology. *Journal of Clinical Psychiatry, 68*, 738–746.

Guardia, D., Conversy, L., Jardir, R., Lafargue, G., Thomas, P., Dodin, V., et al. (2012). Imagining one's own and someone else's body actions: Dissociation in anorexia nervosa. *PLoS One, 7*, e43241.

Guisinger, S. (2003). Adapted to flee famine: Adding an evolutionary perspective on anorexia nervosa. *Psychological Review, 110*, 745–761.

Haedt-Matt, A. A., & Keel, P. K. (2011). Revisiting the affect regulation model of binge eating: A meta-analysis of studies using ecological momentary assessment. *Psychological Bulletin, 137*, 660–681.

Hamilton, W. D. (1964). The genetical evolution of social behaviour. I and II. *Journal of Theoretical Biology, 7*, 1–52.

Harvey, T., Troop, N. A., Treasure, J. L., & Murphy, T. (2002). Fear, disgust, and abnormal eating attitudes: A preliminary study. *International Journal of Eating Disorders, 32*, 213–218.

Haselton, M. G., Mortezaie, M., Pillsworth, E. G., Bleske-Recheck, A. E., & Frederick, D. A. (2007). Ovulation and human female ornamentation: Near ovulation, women dress to impress. *Hormones and Behavior, 51*, 40–45.

Hawkins, R. C., & Clement, P. F. (1984). Binge eating: Measurement problems and a conceptual model. In R. C. Hawkins, W. J. Fremouw, & P. F. Clement (Eds.), *The binge purge syndrome: Diagnosis, treatment, and research* (pp. 229–251). New York: Springer.

Heatherton, T. F., & Baumeister, R. F. (1991). Binge eating as escape from self-awareness. *Psychological Bulletin, 110*, 86–108.

Hebebrand, J., & Remschmidt, H. (1995). Anorexia nervosa viewed as an extreme weight condition: Genetic implications. *Human Genetics, 95*, 1–11.

Herzog, D. B., Greenwood, D. N., Dorer, D. J., Flores, A. T., Ekeblad, E. R., Richards, A., et al. (2000). Mortality in eating disorders: A descriptive study. *International Journal of Eating Disorders, 28*(1), 20–26.

Herzog, D. B., Norman, D. K., Gordon, C., & Pepose, M. (1984). Sexual conflict and eating disorders in 27 males. *American Journal of Psychiatry, 141*, 989–990.

Hudson, J. I., Hiripi, E., Pope, H. G., Jr., & Kessler, R. C. (2007). The prevalence and correlates of eating disorders in the National Comorbidity Survey Replication. *Biological Psychiatry, 61*, 348–358.

Italian men suffer 'sexual anorexia' after internet porn use. (2011). Retrieved December 29, 2012, from http://www.ansa.it/web/notizie/rubriche/english/2011/02/24/visualizza_new.html_1583160579.html

Joiner, T. E., Jr. (1999). Self-verification and bulimic symptoms: Do bulimic women play a role in perpetuating their own dissatisfaction and symptoms? *International Journal of Eating Disorders, 26*, 145–151.

Joiner, T. E., Jr., Heatherton, T. F., Rudd, M. D., & Schmidt, N. B. (1997). Perfectionism, perceived weight status, and bulimic symptoms: Two studies testing a diathesis-stress model. *Journal of Abnormal Psychology, 106*, 145.

Kanazawa, S. (2002). Bowling with our imaginary friends. *Evolution and Human Behavior, 23*, 167–171.

Keel, P. K. (2005). *Eating disorders*. Upper Saddle River, NJ: Pearson Education.

Keel, P. K., & Brown, T. A. (2010). Update on course and outcome in eating disorders. *International Journal of Eating Disorders, 43*, 195–204.

Keel, P. K., Brown, T. A., Holland, L. A., & Bodell, L. P. (2012). Empirical classification of eating disorders. *Annual Review of Clinical Psychology, 8*, 381–404.

Keel, P. K., Gravener, J. A., Joiner, T. E., Jr., & Haedt, A. A. (2010). Twenty-year follow-up of bulimia nervosa and related eating disorders not otherwise specified. *International Journal of Eating Disorders, 43*, 492–497.

Keel, P. K., Haedt, A., & Edler, C. (2005). Purging disorder: An ominous variant of bulimia nervosa? *International Journal of Eating Disorders, 38*, 191–199.

Keel, P. K., & Klump, K. L. (2003). Are eating disorders culture-bound syndromes? Implications for conceptualizing their etiology. *Psychological Bulletin, 129*, 747–769.

Kennair, L. E. O. (2002). Evolutionary psychology: An emerging integrative perspective within the science and practice of psychology. *Human Nature Review, 2*, 17–61.

Kenrick, D. T., Gutierres, S. E., & Goldberg, L. L. (1989). Influence of popular erotica on judgments of strangers and mates. *Journal of Experimental Social Psychology, 25*, 159–167.

Kenrick, D. T., Keefe, R. C., Bryan, A., Barr, A., & Brown, S. (1995). Age preferences and mate choice among homosexuals and heterosexuals: A case for modular psychological mechanisms. *Journal of Personality and Social Psychology, 69*, 1166–1172.

Kenrick, D. T., Neuberg, S. L., Zierk, K. L., & Krones, J. M. (1994). Evolution and social cognition: Contrast effects as a function of sex, dominance, and physical attractiveness. *Personality and Social Psychology Bulletin, 20*, 210–217.

Kim, Y., Zerwas, S., Trace, S. E., & Sullivan, P. F. (2011). Schizophrenia genetics: Where next? *Schizophrenia Bulletin, 37*(3), 456–463.

Klump, K. L., Culbert, K. M., Slane, J. D., Burt, S. A., Sisk, C. L., & Nigg, J. T. (2012). The effects of puberty on genetic risk for disordered eating: Evidence for a sex difference. *Psychological Medicine, 42*, 627–637.

Klump, K. L., Gobrogge, K. L., Perkins, P. S., Thorne, D., Sisk, C. L., & Breedlove, S. (2006). Preliminary evidence that gonadal hormones organize and activate disordered eating. *Psychological Medicine, 36*, 539–546.

Klump, K. L., Suisman, J. L., Burt, S. A., McGue, M., & Iacono, W. G. (2009). Genetic and environmental influences on disordered eating: An adoption study. *Journal of Abnormal Psychology, 118*, 797.

Krones, P. G., Stice, E., Batres, C., & Orjada, K. (2005). In vivo social comparison to a thin-ideal peer promotes body dissatisfaction: A randomized experiment. *International Journal of Eating Disorders, 38*, 134–142.

Kunstman, J. W., & Maner, J. K. (2011). Sexual overperception: Power, mating motives, and biases in social judgment. *Journal of Personality and Social Psychology, 100*, 282–294.

Le Grange, D., Swanson, S. A., Crow, S. J., & Merikangas, K. R. (2012). Eating disorder not otherwise specified presentation in the US population. *International Journal of Eating Disorders, 45*, 711–718.

Leibowitz, S. (1992). Neurochemical-neuroendocrine systems in the brain control macronutrient intake and metabolism. *Trends in Neuroscience, 15*, 491–497.

Levine, M. P., Smolak, L., & Hayden, H. (1994). The relation of sociocultural factors to eating attitudes and behaviors among middle school girls. *Journal of Early Adolescence, 14*, 471–490.

Li, N. P. (2007). Mate preference necessities in long- and short-term mating: People prioritize in themselves what their mates prioritize in them. *Acta Psychologica Sinica, 39*, 528–535.

Li, N. P., Bailey, J. M., Kenrick, D. T., & Linsenmeier, J. A. W. (2002). The necessities and luxuries of mate preferences: Testing the tradeoffs. *Journal of Personality and Social Psychology, 82*, 947–955.

Li, N. P., Smith, A. R., Griskevicius, V., Cason, M. J., & Bryan, A. (2010). Intrasexual competition and eating restriction in heterosexual and homosexual individuals. *Evolution and Human Behavior, 31*, 365–372.

Li, N. P., Valentine, K. A., & Patel, L. (2011). Mate preferences in the U.S. and Singapore: A cross-cultural test of the mate preference priority model. *Personality and Individual Differences, 50*, 291–294.

Lock, J. (2011). Evaluation of family treatment models for eating disorders. *Current Opinion in Psychiatry, 24*, 274–279.

Lopez, C., Tchanturia, K., Stahl, D., & Treasure, J. (2009). Weak central coherence in eating disorders: A step towards looking for an endophenotype of eating disorders. *Journal of Clinical and Experimental Neuropsychology, 31*, 117–125.

Maner, J. K., Denoma, J. M., Van Orden, K. A., Gailliot, M. T., Gordon, K. H., & Joiner, T. E. (2006). Evidence of attentional bias in women exhibiting bulimotypic symptoms. *International Journal of Eating Disorders, 39*, 55–61.

Milos, G., Spindler, A., Schnyder, U., & Fairburn, C. G. (2005). Instability of eating disorder diagnoses: Prospective study. *British Journal of Psychiatry, 187*, 573–578.

Minuchin, S., Baker, L., Rosman, B. L., Liebman, R., Milman, L., & Todd, T. C. (1975). A conceptual model of psychosomatic illness in children. *Archives of General Psychiatry, 32*, 1031–1038.

Minuchin, S., Rosman, B. L., & Baker, L. (1978). *Psychosomatic families: Anorexia nervosa in context.* Cambridge, MA: Harvard University Press.

Mrosovsky, N., & Sherry, D. F. (1980). Animal anorexias. *Science, 207*, 837–842.

Nesse, R. M., & Williams, G. C. (1995). *Evolution and healing: The new science of Darwinian medicine.* London: Weidenfeld and Nicolson.

Neumark-Sztainer, D. (2005). *I'm, like, SO fat!* New York: Guilford Press.

Nielsen, S. (2003). Standardized mortality ratio in bulimia nervosa. *Archives of General Psychiatry, 60*, 851.

Nimrod, A., & Ryan, K. J. (1975). Aromatization of androgens by human abdominal and breast fat tissue. *Journal of Clinical Endocrinology and Metabolism, 40*, 367–372.

Norgan, N. (1997). The beneficial effects of body fat and adipose tissue in humans. *International Journal of Obesity, 21*, 738–754.

Park, J. H., Schaller, M., & Crandall, C. S. (2007). Pathogen-avoidance mechanisms and the stigmatization of obese people. *Evolution and Human Behavior, 28*, 410–414.

Paxton, S. J., Schutz, H. K., Wertheim, E. H., & Muir, S. L. (1999). Friendship clique and peer influences on body image concerns, dietary restraint, extreme weight-loss behaviors, and binge eating in adolescent girls. *Journal of Abnormal Psychology, 108*, 255–266.

Pond, C. M. (1978). Morphological aspects and the ecological and mechanical consequences of fat deposition in wild vertebrates. *Annual Review of Ecology and Systematics, 9*, 519–570.

Pond, C. M. (1998). *The fats of life.* Cambridge: Cambridge University Press.

Prentice, A. M., Diaz, E., Goldberg, G. R., Jebb, S. A., Coward, W. A., & Whitehead, R. G. (1992). Famine and refeeding: Adaptations in energy metabolism. In G. H. Anderson & S. H. Kennedy (Eds.), *The biology of feast and famine: Relevance to eating disorders* (pp. 22–46). San Diego, CA: Academic Press.

Preti, A., Rocchi, M. B., Sisti, D., Camboni, M. V., & Miotto, P. (2011). A comprehensive meta-analysis of the risk of suicide in eating disorders. *Acta Psychiatrica Scandinavica, 124,* 6–17.

Quinton, S. J., Smith, A. R., & Joiner, T. E. (2011). The 2nd to 4th digit ratio (2D:4D) and eating disorder diagnosis in women. *Personality and Individual Differences, 51,* 402–405.

Renfrew Center Foundation for Eating Disorders. (2003). *Eating disorders 101 guide: A summary of issues, statistics and resources.* Retrieved June 4, 2012, from http://www.renfrew.org

Rieger, E., Van Buren, D. J., Bishop, M., Tanofsky-Kraff, M., Welch, R., & Wilfley, D. E. (2010). An eating disorder-specific model of interpersonal psychotherapy (IPT-ED): Causal pathways and treatment implications. *Clinical Psychology Review, 30,* 400–410.

Rippon, C., Nash, J., Myburgh, K. H., & Noakes, T. D. (1988). Abnormal eating attitude test scores predict menstrual dysfunction in lean females. *International Journal of Eating Disorders, 7,* 617–624.

Roberto, C., Steinglass, J., Mayer, L., Attia, E., & Walsh, B. T. (2008). The clinical significance of amenorrhea as a diagnostic criterion for anorexia nervosa. *International Journal of Eating Disorders, 41,* 559–563.

Roberts, M., Tchanturia, K., & Treasure, J. (2010). Exploring the neurocognitive signature of poor set-shifting in anorexia and bulimia nervosa. *Journal of Psychiatric Research, 44,* 964–970.

Rosvall, K. A. (2011). Cost of female intrasexual aggression in terms of offspring quality: A cross-fostering study. *Ethology, 117,* 1–13.

Salmon, C., Crawford, C., Dane, L., & Zuberbier, O. (2008). Ancestral mechanisms in modern environments: Impact of competition and stressors on body image and dieting behavior. *Human Nature, 19,* 103–117.

Salmon, C., Figueredo, A. J., & Woodburn, L. (2009). Life history strategy and disordered eating behavior. *Evolutionary Psychology, 7,* 585–600.

Schaller, M., Park, J. H., & Faulkner, J. (2003). Prehistoric dangers and contemporary prejudices. *European Review of Social Psychology, 14,* 105–137.

Seifert, T. (2005). Anthropomorphic characteristics of centerfold models: Trends towards slender figures over time. *International Journal of Eating Disorders, 37,* 271–274.

Shackelford, T. K., Schmitt, D. P., & Buss, D. M. (2005). Universal dimensions of human mate preferences. *Personality and Individual Differences, 39,* 447–458.

Shafran, R., Lee, M., Cooper, Z., Palmer, R. L., & Fairburn, C. G. (2007). Attentional bias in eating disorders. *International Journal of Eating Disorders, 40,* 369–380.

Singh, D. (1993). Adaptive significance of female physical attractiveness: Role of waist-to-hip ratio. *Journal of Personality and Social Psychology, 65,* 293–307.

Smith, A. R., Fink, E. L., Anestis, M. D., Ribeiro, J., Gordon, K. H., Davis, H., et al. (2013). Exercise caution: Over-exercise is associated with suicidality in bulimia nervosa. *Psychiatry Research, 206*(2–3), 246–255.

Smith, A. R., Hawkeswood, S. E., & Joiner, T. E. (2010). The measure of a man: Associations between digit ratio and disordered eating in males. *International Journal of Eating Disorders, 43,* 543–548.

Smith, A. R., Li, N. P., & Joiner, T. (2011). The pursuit of success: Can status aspirations negatively affect body satisfaction? *Journal of Social and Clinical Psychology, 30,* 531–547.

Smolak, L. (1996). *National Eating Disorders Association/next door neighbors puppet guide book.* Seattle, WA: National Eating Disorders Association.

Steiger, H., Bruce, K., & Israël, M. (2003). Eating disorders. In G. Stricker, T. A. Widiger, & I. B. Weiner (Eds.), *Handbook of psychology* (Vol. 8, pp. 173–194). New York: Wiley.

Steinhausen, H. C. (2002). The outcome of anorexia nervosa in the 20th century. *American Journal of Psychiatry, 159,* 1284–1293.

Stevens, A., & Price, J. (2000). *Evolutionary psychiatry: A new beginning* (2nd ed.). London: Routledge.

Stice, E., Chase, A., Stormer, S., & Appel, A. (2001). A randomized trial of a dissonance-based eating disorder prevention program. *International Journal of Eating Disorders, 29,* 247–262.

Stice, E., & Shaw, H. E. (2002). Role of body dissatisfaction in the onset and maintenance of eating pathology. *Journal of Psychosomatic Research, 53,* 985–993.

Stice, E., Shaw, H. E., Burton, E., & Wade, E. (2006). Dissonance and healthy weight eating disorder prevention programs: A randomized efficacy trial. *Journal of Consulting and Clinical Psychology, 74,* 263–275.

Striegel-Moore, R. H., Silberstein, L. R., & Rodin, J. (1986). Toward an understanding of risk factors for bulimia. *American Psychologist, 41,* 246–263.

Striegel-Moore, R. H., Tucker, N., & Hsu, J. (1990). Body image dissatisfaction and disordered eating in lesbian college students. *International Journal of Eating Disorders, 9,* 493–500.

Strober, M., Freeman, R., Lampert, C., Diamond, J., & Kaye, W. (2000). Controlled family study of anorexia nervosa and bulimia nervosa: Evidence of shared liability and transmission of partial syndromes. *American Journal of Psychiatry, 63,* 305–312.

Substance Abuse and Mental Health Services Administration. (2003). *Handout-eating disorder.* Retrieved June 4, 2013, from http://mentalhealth.samhsa.gov/publications/allpubs/ken98-0047/default.asp

Sullivan, P. F. (1995). Mortality in anorexia nervosa. *American Journal of Psychiatry, 152,* 1073–1074.

Sullivan, P. F., Bulik, C. M., Fear, J. L., & Pickering, A. (1998). Outcome of anorexia nervosa: A case–control study. *American Journal of Psychiatry, 155,* 939–946.

Surbey, M. K. (1987). Anorexia nervosa, amenorrhea, and adaptation. *Ethology and Sociobiology, 8,* 47–61.

Symons, D. (1979). *The evolution of human sexuality.* New York: Oxford University Press.

Sypeck, M. F., Gray, J. J., & Ahrens, A. H. (2004). No longer just a pretty face: Fashion magazines' depictions of ideal female beauty from 1959 to 1999. *International Journal of Eating Disorders, 36,* 342–347.

Tanofsky-Kraff, M., Wilfley, D. E., & Spurrell, E. (2000). Impact of interpersonal and ego-related stress on restrained eaters. *International Journal of Eating Disorders, 27,* 411–418.

Thompson, J. K., Heinberg, L. J., Altabe, M., & Tantleff-Dunn, S. (1999). *Exacting beauty: Theory, assessment, and treatment of body image disturbance.* Washington, DC: American Psychological Association.

Thompson, J. K., & Stice, E. (2001). Thin-ideal internalization: Mounting evidence for a new risk factor for body-image disturbance and eating pathology. *Current Directions in Psychological Science, 10,* 181–183.

Thompson, J. K., van den Berg, P., Roehrig, M., Guarda, A. S., & Heinberg, L. J. (2004). The Sociocultural Attitudes Towards Appearance Scale-3 (SATAQ-3): Development and validation. *International Journal of Eating Disorders, 35,* 293–304.

Treasure, J. L., & Owen, J. B. (1997). Intriguing links between animal behavior and anorexia nervosa. *International Journal of Eating Disorders, 21,* 307–312.

Trivers, R. L. (1972). Parental investment and sexual selection. In B. Campbell (Ed.), *Sexual selection and the descent of man* (pp. 136–179). Chicago: Aldine.

Trivers, R. L., & Willard, D. E. (1973). Natural selection of parental ability to vary the sex ratio of offspring. *Science, 179,* 90–92.

Voland, E., & Voland, R. (1989). Evolutionary biology and psychiatry: The case of anorexia nervosa. *Ethology and Sociobiology, 10,* 223–240.

Walters, S., & Crawford, C. B. (1994). The importance of mate attraction for intrasexual competition in men and women. *Ethology and Sociobiology, 15,* 5–30.

Wang, K., Zhang, H., Bloss, C. S., Duvvuri, V., Kaye, W., Schork, N. J., et al. (2010). A genome-wide association study on common SNPs and rare CNVs in anorexia nervosa. *Molecular Psychiatry, 16,* 949–959.

Wasser, S. K., & Barash, D. P. (1983). Reproductive suppression among female mammals: Implications for biomedicine and sexual selection theory. *Quarterly Review of Biology, 58,* 513–538.

Watson, R., & Vaughn, L. M. (2006). Limiting the effects of the media on body image: Does the length of the intervention make a difference? *Eating Disorders: The Journal of Treatment and Prevention, 14,* 385–400.

Wells, J. C. K. (2012). The evolution of human adiposity and obesity: Where did it all go wrong? *Disease Models and Mechanisms, 5,* 595–607.

Weltzin, T. E., Weisensel, N., Franczyk, D., Burnett, K., Klitz, C., & Bean, P. (2005). Eating disorders in men: Update. *The Journal of Men's Health & Gender, 2,* 186–193.

Wilksch, S. M., Durbridge, M. R., & Wade, T. D. (2008). A preliminary controlled comparison of programs designed to reduce risk of eating disorders targeting perfectionism and media literacy. *Journal of the American Academy of Child and Adolescent Psychiatry, 47,* 939–947.

Wilksch, S. M., & Wade, T. D. (2009). Reduction of shape and weight concern in young adolescents: A 30-month controlled evaluation of a media literacy program. *Journal of the American Academy of Child and Adolescent Psychiatry, 48,* 652–661.

Williams, C. G. (1966). Natural selection, the costs of reproduction, and a refinement of Lack's principle. *American Naturalist, 100,* 687–690.

Workgroup for Classification of Eating Disorders in Children and Adolescents (WCEDCA). (2007). Classification of child and adolescent eating disturbances. *International Journal of Eating Disorders, 40,* S117–S122.

Wrangham, R. W. (1999). Evolution of coalitionary killing. *Yearbook of Physical Anthropology, 42,* 1–30.

Yager, Z., & O'Dea, J. A. (2008). Prevention programs for body image and eating disorders on University campuses: A review of large, controlled interventions. *Health Promotion International, 23,* 173–189.

Zerwas, S., & Bulik, C. M. (2011). Genetics and epigenetics of eating disorders. *Psychiatric Annals, 41,* 532–538.

Attractiveness and Rivalry in Women's Same-Sex Friendships

18

April Bleske-Rechek, Carolyn M. Kolb, and Katherine Quigley

Introduction

The tendency to affiliate with similar others appears in humans as early as infancy and childhood (Mahajan & Wynn, 2012), exists across human cultures (Brewer, 1979), and has even been documented in other species (de Waal & Luttrell, 1986; Weinstein & Capitanio, 2012). The literature on the human tendency to assort, in particular, is vast (for a review, see McPherson, Smith-Lovin, & Cook, 2001). Research on romantic couples and same-sex friends has shown similarity in education level and intelligence, religiosity, social and political attitudes, interests and activity preferences, and (to a lesser degree) personality traits (Luo & Klohnen, 2005; Tolson & Urberg, 1993; Vandenberg, 1972). Romantic partners are even similar in rated attractiveness (Alvarez & Jaffe, 2004; Bleske-Rechek, Remiker, & Baker, 2009; Feingold, 1988) and in symmetry, which is tied to attractiveness (Burriss, Roberts, Welling, Puts, & Little, 2011). Moreover, studies suggest that observed similarities among friends and mates are due to selection rather than convergence over time. For example, cross-sectional studies show that dating couples are as similar to one another as are newlyweds and couples who have

been married for 20 years (Bleske-Rechek et al., 2009; Luo & Klohnen, 2005); longitudinal studies suggest that adolescents gravitate toward peers who are similar to them (Billy, Rodgers, & Udry, 1984; Cohen, 1977; Fisher & Bauman, 1988; Kandel, 1978; Urberg, Degirmencioglu, & Tolson, 1998); and experimental studies show that adults are attracted to those who share their values and attitudes (Huston & Levinger, 1978).

It is likely that humans' attraction to similar others is an evolved product of selection pressures operating over deep time. The preference for similarity may have evolved because individuals who allied themselves with similar others avoided the dangers posed by out-group individuals and simultaneously obtained the benefits provided by in-group individuals. Over time, those who avoided dissimilar others would have been more likely, on average, to avoid foreign pathogens and aggressive behaviors from out-group individuals (Schaller & Neuberg, 2008). Likewise, those who affiliated with similar others may have accrued a variety of benefits. First, following the logic of kin selection, individuals may have increased their odds of investing in those who share common genes and thus increased the odds of funneling those genes into the next generation (Rushton, Russell, & Wells, 1984). Indeed, humans favor immediate kin over extended kin (Madsen et al., 2007; Webster, 2003, 2004; Webster, Bryan, Crawford, McCarthy, & Cohen, 2008); and even outside the kin group, the variables on which mates and

A. Bleske-Rechek (✉)
Psychology Department, University of Wisconsin-Eau Claire, 255 Hibbard Hall, Eau Claire, WI 54702, USA
e-mail: bleskeal@uwec.edu

V.A. Weekes-Shackelford and T.K. Shackelford (eds.), *Evolutionary Perspectives on Human Sexual Psychology and Behavior*, Evolutionary Psychology, DOI 10.1007/978-1-4939-0314-6_18, © Springer Science+Business Media New York 2014

friends assort are under genetic influence (Rushton, 1989; Rushton & Bons, 2005). Second, affiliating with similar others may have provided strategic confluence. Individuals may have been more likely to achieve their goals when allied with someone also pursuing that goal. For example, individuals in pursuit of ascending the status hierarchy would encounter more experiences and opportunities toward fulfilling that goal in the company of another person who was also pursuing that goal (just as students oriented toward succeeding in college are more apt to be successful when they have friendships with others who are also oriented toward success and thus accompany them to the library rather than draw them out to the bars).

Similarity between interaction partners also provides proximate benefits. Similar others are familiar, which enhances attraction (Reis, Maniaci, Caprariello, Eastwick, & Finkel, 2011). Similar others are easier to predict and easier to get along with. Thus, college roommates with similar hobbies and interests are more likely to become friends (Berg, 1984); dating couples with similar social and religious attitudes are more likely to stay together over time (Bleske-Rechek et al., 2009); married couples with more similar personalities report more satisfaction in their marriage (Luo & Klohnen, 2005); friends who are similar to each other are more likely to stay friends (Ledbetter, Griffin, & Sparks, 2007); and even rhesus monkeys of similar temperaments are likely to become friends and maintain a stable bond (Weinstein & Capitanio, 2012). The fact that similarity promotes stable and satisfying relationships is important because stable, satisfying relationships are linked with psychological and physical well-being. Research on our primate cousins, for example, suggests that females of similar age and dominance rank form strong social bonds, and females with strong social bonds experience less stress and a lower infant mortality rate (Seyfarth & Cheney, 2012; Silk, Alberts, & Altmann, 2003). In humans, long-lasting, close bonds are associated with psychological and physical well-being. Literature on women, in particular, emphasizes

companionship, intimacy, and support from female friends as important across the life course for health and psychological well-being (O'Connor, 1992). Indeed, women experience the most positive emotion when they are with their friends (Larson & Richards, 1994).

At the same time that literature emphasizes the importance of strong female bonds for women's well-being, other literature points out that girls' and women's friendships are fragile and trying, especially in comparison to males' friendships. For example, girls' closest same-sex friendships are less enduring than boys' are, and girls are more likely than boys to report that a close same-sex friend has done something to harm their friendship (Benenson & Christakos, 2003). A number of theorists have tied the fragility of female friendships to feelings of envy and competition. Qualitative research on young adult female friends has found that envy is very common and at times interferes with women's friendships (Gail-Alfonso, 2006). Clinicians and feminist scholars, as well, argue that envy and feelings of competition between close female friends are common (Apter & Josselson, 1998; Eichenbaum & Orbach, 1987; Yager, 2002). For example, in their treatise on women's friendships, Eichenbaum and Orbach (1987) wrote (p. 32), "Feelings... of envy and competition are rampant. No woman today escapes them, but every woman feels conflicted by them."

How do we reconcile research suggesting that young women strongly value their close female friendships and derive tremendous satisfaction from them, with research suggesting that women commonly experience envy and competition in their friendships with women? Intrasexual competition between women in general is a key piece of the apparent contradiction. Across cultures, women compete intensely, particularly on the dimension of physical attractiveness, to attract and maintain the attention of desirable males (Buss, 1988; Buss & Dedden, 1990; Buss, Shackelford, Choe, Buunk, & Dijkstra, 2000; Cashdan, 1998; Dijkstra & Buunk, 2002; Durante, Griskevicius, Hill, Perilloux, & Li, 2011; Hill & Durante, 2011; Maner, Gailliot, & DeWall, 2007; Tooke & Camire, 1991). Indeed, when asked to rank various contexts for how much envy they would produce, women choose "a peer being more physically attractive" as the most prominent envy-provoking context (DelPriore, Hill, & Buss, 2012).

Intrasexual competition may actually be heightened among female *friends*, who are likely to assort on attractiveness and physical features tied to attractiveness. In addition to the previously discussed functions of preferring similar others (e.g., genetic similarity, attitude compatibility), women should ally with similarly *attractive* women because such assortment would facilitate mate attraction. That is, a much more attractive friend might steal all the attention of desirable males or make one feel quite undesirable in comparison (e.g., Gutierres, Kenrick, & Partch, 1999), and a much *less* attractive friend might inhibit desirable males from approaching (Kernis & Wheeler, 1981). In short, women should prefer friends who are attractive enough to attract the males they desire, yet not so attractive that they capture all the attention from those males. Indeed, Vigil (2007) established that young women want female friends who are comparable to them in level of physical attractiveness.

Being similarly attractive, however, does not imply identical levels of attractiveness. Humans are exceptionally good at detecting differences among people, and in any given friendship, there is likely to be one friend who is more attractive than the other. To the extent that women of similar attractiveness would have also ended up competing for limited resources (desirable males with willingness to invest), any discrepancies in those attractiveness levels would produce envy and mating rivalry. Thus, although friendship should be a defense *against* rivalry between women (Eichenbaum & Orbach, 1987), we propose that rivalry is instead endemic to women's friendships because women assort on attractiveness—a primary attribute on which they compete for access to the limited resource of desirable mates (Campbell, 1995, 1999). Indeed, the qualitative research alluded to earlier highlighted physical attractiveness and relationship status as the primary foci of women's feelings of envy toward their friends (Gail-Alfonso, 2006).

The Current Research

In this chapter, we describe research from our lab on attractiveness and rivalry in women's friendships with women. On the basis of previous work showing assortment between relationship partners on many dimensions, our first hypothesis is that female friends assort on physical attractiveness. Under the assumption that women's feelings of envy and rivalry are rooted in competition over attractiveness, our second hypothesis is that women who perceive themselves as less physically attractive than their friend also experience more mating rivalry in their friendship. Because individuals evaluate themselves and others in ways that enable them to maintain positive views of themselves (Tesser & Campbell, 1982) and because women's self-concepts are closely tied to their physical attractiveness (Campbell & Wilbur, 2009), we also hypothesize that women engage in self-evaluation maintenance in the domain of physical attractiveness. That is, we hypothesize that women perceive their own attractiveness and their friend's attractiveness in ways that enable them to maintain positive perceptions of their own attractiveness.

In 2010, our lab published initial support for the first hypothesis that female friends are similar in attractiveness (Bleske-Rechek & Lighthall, 2010). In that research, 46 pairs of female friends came into the lab to complete questionnaires and were photographed from the neck up. Friends' perceptions of their own attractiveness (relative to other women) were positively correlated, as were outsiders' judgments of the friends' overall attractiveness. However, the photos were only headshots. In the current research, we obtained full-body shots of women. Given that both face and body serve as independent predictors of full-body attractiveness (Peters, Rhodes, & Simmons, 2007), we reasoned that female friends may be similar in body attractiveness and full-body attractiveness as well as face attractiveness. In addition, the women in Bleske-Rechek and Lighthall's (2010) study were photographed in their street clothes, and they were allowed to smile; thus, similarity in ratings of friends' attractiveness may have been a function of similarity between them in hairstyle, makeup, or personality traits that were revealed in their clothing choices or facial expressions. To address these concerns in the current research, we asked women to remove their makeup, pull back their hair, and don the same clothing. We also asked women to not smile when we took their picture. In addition to ratings of attractiveness, we also aimed to determine if female friends would be similar in body characteristics that men attend to when evaluating women's attractiveness (Dixson, Grimshaw, Linklater, & Dixson, 2011; Gangestad & Scheyd, 2005; Perilloux, Webster, & Gaulin, 2010; Zelazniewicz & Pawlowski, 2011). Thus, in the current research we measured women's breasts and waist-to-hip ratio.

Bleske-Rechek and Lighthall (2010) also provided initial evidence that discrepancies in female friends' attractiveness levels are tied to feelings of mating rivalry. In their sample, women who perceived themselves as less attractive than their friend reported stronger feelings of mating rivalry. For example, women who perceived themselves as less attractive than their friend were more likely to report feeling in competition with their friend to get attention from the opposite sex. In the current studies, we aimed to replicate this effect and extend it by showing that it is unique to the domain of attractiveness. If competition over physical attractiveness is at the root of female friends' feelings of rivalry, then perceived discrepancies in attractiveness should be tied to rivalry; perceived discrepancies in attributes such as ambition and intelligence, which are less closely tied to young women's mate value, should *not* be tied to rivalry.

In this chapter we describe two studies designed to further test our hypotheses about how female friends' attractiveness levels are tied to feelings of rivalry and competition. In each study, we brought female friendship pairs into the lab; took pictures of them; measured their chest, waist, and hip circumference; and surveyed them about themselves and their friend. In the first study, women were photographed in their street clothes and then again in scrubs with their hair pulled back and makeup removed; in

the second study, women were photographed in a two-piece swimsuit.

Method

Participants

We recruited participants through lower-level and upper-level psychology courses at a public university. We advertised our research as an investigation of female friendship dynamics. Each woman was instructed to bring a casual or close same-sex friend (but not someone who was merely a class acquaintance) with them to the study. Study 1 friends ($N = 43$ pairs) were recruited during the fall of 2010. The typical pair had been friends for over 3 years ($M = 39$ mos, SD = 41.01, range 1–180 mos). Only one pair had been friends for less than 3 months, and only five pairs for less than 6 months. When we asked women the degree to which their friendship was a true friendship (*not at all* to *very much*), 51 % said their friendship was "very much" a true friendship. Study 2 ($N = 37$ pairs) was conducted during the fall of 2011. The typical pair had been friends for 2.5 years ($M = 30$ mos, SD = 23.93, range 5–108 mos). Only one pair had been friends for less than 6 months. Sixty-five percent of the women in Study 2 said their friendship was "very much" a true friendship.

Instruments and Procedure

Female dyads came into the lab knowing only that we were interested in studying female friendship dynamics. When we recruited participants, we intentionally did not tell them that they and their friend would have their picture taken (Study 1 in street clothes and then scrubs; Study 2 in swimsuits) so that women would not (a) select into the studies or select a friend into the study based on her willingness to be photographed or (b) engage in extra self-preparation in anticipation of a photo shoot. Upon their arrival to the lab, we told friends that we were interested in photographing them for research purposes only and that we wanted to know each person's views on friendship. At that point, we asked the two friends to state to us and to each other that they would not discuss the procedure or the questionnaire at any point during the study or thereafter. We wanted friends to answer our questions as honestly as possible, and we used the face-to-face agreement so that friends would see each other comply. One pair in Study 1 did not consent to having their pictures taken; all other friends consented to photographs; and all friends complied with the request to not discuss the study with each other.

In Study 1, each woman was photographed in her original street clothes and then again in scrubs, with her hair pulled back and makeup removed. In Study 2, each woman was photographed wearing a two-piece, royal blue swimsuit with her hair pulled back (see Fig. 18.1). We purchased multiple suits in multiple sizes and sanitized them after each use. In all photographs, women were instructed to not smile. In both studies, researchers took participants' height and weight, followed by measurements of their chest, hip, and waist circumference. After these anthropometric measurements, friends were led to different rooms. As part of a larger questionnaire that included various personal demographics (e.g., age, sexual history, and bra cup size), friendship demographics (e.g., friendship duration), and filler scales, women reported on 52 sources of content and contention in their friendship. Embedded in this latter part were seven items specific to mating rivalry: *I feel undesirable when she's around*; *It is harder to meet men when she's around*; *I feel unattractive in comparison to her*; *I feel in competition with her for attention from men*; *I feel envious of her*; *She has been romantically interested in the same men that I have been interested in*; *She flirts with men I am interested in*. Women provided their responses on a seven-point scale ranging from *Strongly Disagree* to *Strongly Agree*. These seven items were scattered among others of varied valence, such as the following: *She is genuinely happy when things go right for me*,

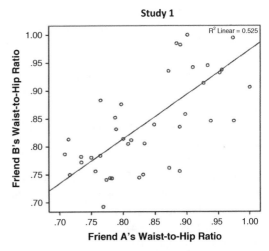

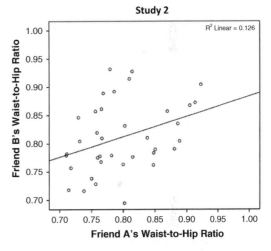

Fig. 18.1 Similarity in Study 1 friends' WHRs (*upper panel*) and Study 2 friends' WHRs (*lower panel*)

She gets upset when we don't do what she wants to do, *She takes the time to listen when I need to talk*, and *I can't always trust her with my secrets*.

In various parts of the questionnaire, women also provided perceptions of themselves, their friend, and their friendship. Specifically, they evaluated their friend, relative to other women, on a variety of attributes: physical attractiveness, intelligence, athleticism, and ambition. On these items, responses were given on a nine-point scale with higher scores in the dataset favoring the friend (e.g., 1 = *She is much less physically attractive than other women*, 5 = *She is the same as other women*, 9 = *She is much more physically attractive than other women).* In a separate part women evaluated themselves, relative to other women, on each of those attributes. On these items, higher scores favored the self (e. g., 1 = *I am much less physically attractive than other women,* 5 = *I am the same as other women,* 9 = *I am much more physically attractive than other women).* In yet another part of the questionnaire, women again evaluated themselves, but this time relative to their *friend,* on those same attributes. For example, women responded to the item, "How do you and your friend compare in physical attractiveness?" On these items, higher scores favored the friend (e. g., 1 = *She is much <u>less</u> physically attractive than I am,* 5 = *We are the same,* 9 = *She is much <u>more</u> physically attractive than I am).*

Photo Preparation and Judging

As displayed in Table 18.1, each woman's photograph was cropped into face and body shots. In Study 1, researchers constructed six separate slideshows of all the women (full body in original clothes, face only in original clothes, body only in original clothes, full body in scrubs, face only in scrubs, body only in scrubs). Women were placed into the slideshow in a random, unpaired order that was the same for each slideshow. Then, students at another university served as attractiveness judges. A different set of judges viewed each slideshow. That is, we gathered six independent sets of 26–30 raters (see Table 18.1). Raters did not know they were looking at pairs of friends. They sat in silence in a classroom setting and viewed the pictures via a PowerPoint slideshow. Participants viewed each picture for 3 s and for each woman they responded to the question, "Compared to other women her age, how physically attractive is this woman (this woman's face, this woman's body)?" Students recorded their responses on paper sheets using a nine-point scale ranging from *Much less attractive* to *The same* to *Much more attractive.* In Study 2, researchers constructed three separate slideshows of the women (full body in swimsuit, face only in

swimsuit, and body only in swimsuit). Researchers generated a new random order and placed the women, unpaired, into each slideshow. Each slideshow was then rated by a distinct set of raters at a different university, this time for physical attractiveness and sexiness (rater sets included 31–40 raters), again using nine-point scales. Sexiness and attractiveness judgments were redundant ($rs > 0.90$), so below we report results for attractiveness judgments only. As in Study 1, judges did not know they were looking at pairs of friends. In both studies, the results were consistent by sex of judge, so below we report the findings from male and female judges combined.

Results

Hypothesis 1: Similarity Between Friends

Our first hypothesis stated that female friends are similar in attractiveness. To test this hypothesis, we first looked at objective measures of body shape, which are tied to attractiveness. Then, we probed judges' ratings of women's full-body, face-only, and body-only attractiveness.

Similarity in Body Shape

Friends' similarity coefficients for continuous body measurements are displayed in Table 18.2. In Study 1, friends were similar in anthropometric measures relevant to mate value. That is, friends' waist-to-hip ratios were strongly correlated, $r(43) = 0.72$, $p < 0.001$, as shown in Fig. 18.1 (upper panel), and their bra cup sizes were moderately correlated, $\chi^2(4, N = 41) = 9.31$, $V = 0.34$, $p = 0.054$, as shown in Fig. 18.2 (upper panel). Moreover, friends' similarity was specific to body shape, not body stature and size, as indicated by height, weight, chest cavity. WHR and BMI themselves were correlated, $r(86) = 0.44$, $p < 0.001$, but friends were similar in WHR, not in BMI.

We found a similar pattern of associations in Study 2. Friends were similar in measures

Table 18.1 Preparation of women's photos

Study 1 slideshows in original clothes	Full body	Face only	Body only

Study 1 slideshows in scrubs	Full body	Face only	Body only

Study 2 slideshows in swimsuits	Full body	Face only	Body only

relevant to mate value, such as waist-to-hip ratio, $r(37) = 0.36$, $p = 0.031$ (Fig. 18.1, lower panel), and bra cup size, $\chi^2(4, N = 36) = 13.47$, $V = 0.43$, $p = 0.009$ (Fig. 18.2, lower panel). Again, friends' similarity was specific to body shape, not size and stature. Women's WHR and BMI were again correlated, $r(74) = 0.48$, $p < 0.001$, but friends were similar in WHR, not in BMI.

In summary, Hypothesis 1 was supported in both studies by the anthropometric data: Female friends were similar in WHR and bra cup size

Table 18.2 Similarity between friends in continuous measures of body size and body shape

| | Study 1 | | Study 2 | |
	r	p	r	p
Weight	0.06	0.686	0.07	0.885
Height	−0.25	0.103	0.06	0.745
BMI	0.08	0.623	0.15	0.364
Chest cavity (circumference)	0.10	0.540	0.04	0.819
Waist circumference	0.15	0.346	0.27	0.111
Hip circumference	0.30	0.051	0.11	0.527
Waist-to-hip ratio	0.72	0.000	0.36	0.031

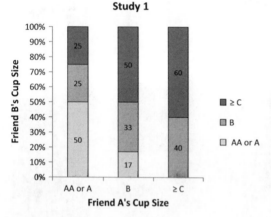

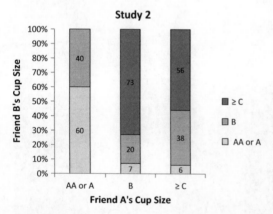

Fig. 18.2 Similarity between friends in cup size in Study 1 (*upper panel*) and in Study 2 (*lower panel*). Note that this display has taken one friend's perspective, as in the percent of Friend A's friends who had a given cup size. The pattern would look slightly different if we displayed the percent of Friend B's friends who had a given cup size

and not in body stature. Similarity in friends' WHRs is important because women's WHR predicted their attractiveness ratings in both studies, regardless of whether judges were viewing

their full body, body, or face [in Study 1, original clothes (full body $r(84) = -0.36$, $p < 0.001$; face only $r(84) = -0.29$, $p = 0.008$; body only $r(84) = -0.27$, $p = 0.014$); in Study 1, scrubs (full body $r(84) = -0.31, p = 0.005$; face only $r(84) = -0.30$, $p = 0.006$; body only $r(84) = -0.41, p < 0.001$); in Study 2, swimsuits (full body $r(72) = -0.51, p < 0.001$; face oniy $r(71) = -0.27$, $p = 0.023$; body only $r(72) = -0.58$, $p < 0.001$)]. Women's bra cup size was not associated with women's attractiveness ratings in either study ($ps > 0.73$).

Similarity in Judged Attractiveness

Table 18.3 displays the results for judges' ratings of female friends' physical attractiveness. In Study 1, friends received similar full-body attractiveness ratings and similar face attractiveness ratings, regardless of whether they were in their original street clothes or scrubs. Randomly constructed friendship pairs did not receive similar attractiveness ratings (mean r from 20 samples of randomly constructed pairs = −0.02). The same pattern was revealed for Study 2: Friends received similar attractiveness ratings from judges who viewed their full-body shots in the two-piece swimsuit, and they tended to receive similar attractiveness ratings from judges who viewed their faces only. The similarity coefficients were strong ($r = 0.52$ and 0.58) for female friends' full-body shots dressed in their original clothes and for the second sample of female friends wearing swimsuits. Figure 18.3 displays assortment between friends on full-body and facial attractiveness.

In neither study did friends receive similar ratings of *body* attractiveness. This lack of

Table 18.3 Tests of similarity between friends' attractiveness ratings

		Number of raters	Rater reliability (α)	Friend similarity coefficient (r)	p
Study 1	Full body in original clothes*	28	0.95	0.52	0.000
	Face only in original clothes*	30	0.97	0.39	0.013
	Body only in original clothes	29	0.97	0.14	0.395
	Full body in scrubs*	28	0.93	0.33	0.038
	Face only in scrubs*	26	0.95	0.35	0.024
	Body only in scrubs	29	0.94	0.10	0.528
Study 2	Full body in swimsuits*	31	0.96	0.58	0.000
	Face only in swimsuits*	34	0.97	0.32	0.061
	Body only in swimsuits	40	0.98	0.20	0.251

*Significant and marginally significant associations. Each correlation coefficient is from a unique set of raters. In Study 1, $N = 41$–42 pairs of friends; in Study 2, $N = 35$–36 pairs of friends

similarity in body attractiveness ratings is difficult to explain because the friends were similar in WHR, which was a strong predictor of body attractiveness (as noted above), and because body-only ratings predicted full-body ratings, on which the friends were similar.

In summary, Hypothesis 1 was supported by the majority of our analyses. Friends' full bodies were rated as similarly attractive, as were their faces. Friends' bodies were not judged as similarly attractive; however, friends' bodies were similar in bra cup size and in WHR, which itself predicted judges' ratings of women's attractiveness.

Hypothesis 2: Discrepant Attractiveness and Rivalry

Our second hypothesis was that women who are less attractive than their friend, as assessed by either self-report or outside judges' ratings, would report more mating rivalry in their friendship. To test this hypothesis, we first averaged each woman's response to the seven questionnaire items that pertain to feelings of mating rivalry (Study 1 $\alpha = 0.70$, Study 2 $\alpha = 0.80$). Across the two samples, rivalry scores were relatively low at a mean of 2.5 on the 1–7 scale.

Support for Hypothesis 2 is displayed in Fig. 18.4 and Table 18.4. Women who perceived

their friend as more attractive than themselves also reported experiencing more rivalry in their friendship. The effect was moderate in magnitude in Study 1 ($r = 0.32$) and strong in Study 2 ($r = 0.50$). And, in discriminant support of our hypothesis, women's perceptions of their friend as more intelligent, athletic, or ambitious were *not* significantly associated with feelings of mating rivalry.

We also looked within dyads to determine if the women who received lower physical attractiveness ratings from outside judges (relative to their friends) were also the women to report more mating rivalry. Study 1 confirmed this prediction: The more one friend was rated as less physically attractive than her friend (full body in original clothes), the more rivalry she felt in comparison to her friend, $r(41) = -0.33$, $p = 0.033$. However, this pattern did not replicate in Study 2, where discrepancies in attractiveness were not significantly related to discrepant perceptions of mating rivalry, $r(35) = -0.11$, $p = 0.525$.

Hypothesis 3: Self-Protective Evaluations of Attractiveness

Hypothesis 3 was that women engage in self-protective evaluations of their own attractiveness relative to their friend's attractiveness. Recall

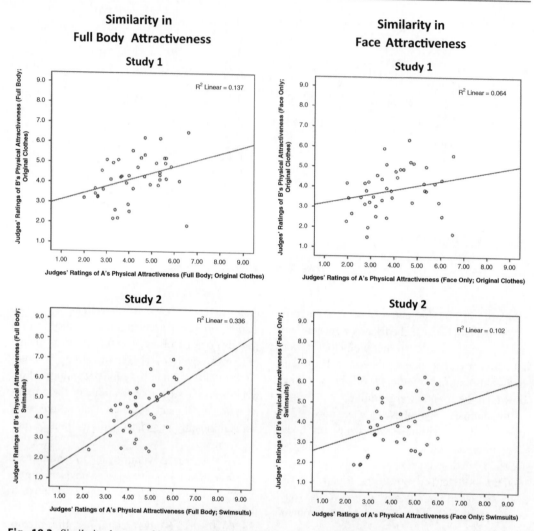

Fig. 18.3 Similarity between friends in full-body and face-only attractiveness (*upper panels* = Study 1, *lower panels* = Study 2)

that in both studies, women evaluated their friend, relative to other women, on physical attractiveness, intelligence, athleticism, and ambition. Women gave responses on a nine-point scale with higher scores favoring the friend. In a separate part they evaluated themselves, relative to other women, on each of those attributes; higher scores favored the self. In another part of the questionnaire, women again evaluated themselves but this time in comparison to their *friend*, on those same attributes of physical attractiveness, intelligence, athleticism, and ambition; on these items, higher scores favored the friend.

Figure 18.5 shows women's mean perception of their friend's attractiveness relative to other women, their own attractiveness relative to other women, and their own attractiveness relative to their friend's. The pattern of effects was consistent in the two studies. In Study 1, women rated their friend as more attractive ($M = 6.40$, $SD = 1.36$) than other women (one-sample t against mean of 5), $t(85) = 9.54$, $p < 0.001$. They rated themselves ($M = 5.46$, $SD = 1.28$) as slightly more attractive than other women, one-sample $t(85) = 3.30, p = 0.001$. The difference between these two means was significant and robust, $t(82) = -4.60$, $p < 0.001$,

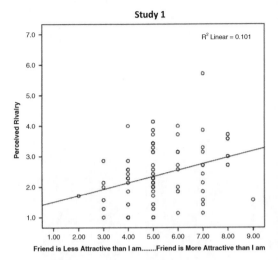

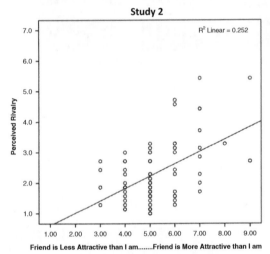

Fig. 18.4 Women's reports of rivalry in their friendship as a function of perceived physical attractiveness in comparison to their friend. Higher scores represent perception of friend as more attractive than self (*upper panel* = Study 1, *lower panel* = Study 2)

$d = -0.50$: Women's ratings of their friend were substantially higher than their ratings of themselves. However, when women compared themselves directly with their friend, their friend received only a marginally significant higher rating (where 5 = *We are the same*, one-sample $t(85) = 1.97, p = 0.052, d = 0.21$).

In Study 2, women rated their friend as more attractive ($M = 6.38$, SD $= 1.07$) than other women (one-sample t against mean of 5), $t(73) = 11.09, p < 0.001$. They rated themselves ($M = 5.31$, SD $= 1.30$) as slightly more attractive than other women, one-sample $t(73) = 2.05$, $p = 0.044$. The difference between these two means was significant, $t(73) = -5.62$, $p < 0.001$, $d = -0.65$: Women's ratings of their friend were much higher than their ratings of themselves. However, when women compared themselves directly with their friend, their friend no longer received a significantly higher rating (where 5 = *We are the same*, one-sample t $(72) = 1.75, p = 0.084, d = 0.21$). In summary, Hypothesis 3 was supported. When women were asked to compare themselves directly against their friend, women's evaluations of attractiveness did not favor their friend.

We conducted further analyses to determine whether this self-protective effect was more robust for attractiveness than for the other characteristics. It was. Although we found some evidence of self-protective evaluations for intelligence, the bias was not as strong and it manifested in Study 1 but not in Study 2. In Study 1, women rated their friend as more intelligent ($M = 6.55$, SD $= 1.36$) than other women (one-sample t against mean of 5), $t(85) = 10.54$,

Table 18.4 Associations between rivalry and evaluations of friend in comparison to self

	Study 1		Study 2	
	r	*p*	*r*	*p*
Association between rivalry and perception of friend as				
More physically attractive	0.32	0.003	0.50	0.000
More intelligent	0.06	0.561	−0.02	0.874
More athletic	0.18	0.110	0.03	0.788
More ambitious	0.07	0.519	0.23	0.052

Note: Study 1 $N = 85$ women, Study 2 $N = 72$ women

Fig. 18.5 Women's self-
protective evaluations of
their own attractiveness
relative to their friend's
attractiveness. *Dashed line*
indicates the midpoint on
each scale: "The same"

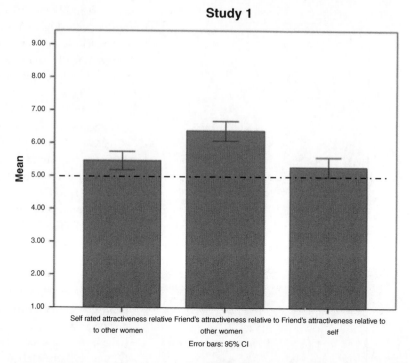

$p < 0.001$. They also rated themselves ($M = 6.12$, SD $= 1.32$) as more intelligent than other women, one-sample $t(82) = 7.74$, $p < 0.001$. The difference between these two means was significant, such that women tended to rate their friend as more intelligent (relative to other women) than they rated themselves (relative to other women), paired-samples $t(82) = -2.37$, $p = 0.020$, $d = -0.26$. When women compared themselves directly with their friend, however, their friend no longer received a significantly higher intelligence rating, one-sample $t(85) = 1.25, p = 0.215, d = 0.13$.

In Study 2, women rated their friend as more intelligent ($M = 6.96$, SD $= 1.30$) than other women (one-sample t against mean of 5), $t(73) = 12.99, p < 0.001$. They also rated themselves ($M = 6.43$, SD $= 1.19$) as more intelligent than other women, one-sample t $(73) = 10.32$, $p < 0.001$. The difference between these two means was significant, such that women rated their friend as more intelligent (relative to other women) than they rated themselves (relative to other women), paired-samples $t(73) = -2.76$, $p = 0.007$, $d = -0.32$. When women compared themselves directly with their friend, women continued to judge their friend as more intelligent than themselves and thus did not show a self-protective response, one-sample t $(72) = 2.66, p = 0.010, d = 0.31$.

We did not find evidence of self-protective responding on ambition or athleticism, as women rated themselves and their friends similarly in comparison to other women (the indirect comparison). Specifically, women perceived their friend and themselves as similarly more ambitious compared to other women, and women perceived their friend and themselves as similarly average on athleticism compared to other women (all $ps < 0.24$).

In summary, self-protective evaluations of physical attractiveness occurred in both studies and did not occur consistently for the other traits, thus offering some support for our general proposal that competition over attractiveness is a key underpinning of feelings of rivalry and threat in women's friendships with women.

Discussion

The human preference for those who are similar to themselves manifests itself across the lifespan and across relationships. Allying with similar others can facilitate goal pursuit, but it can also result in competition when the goal in sight is a limited resource. Thus, in the context of women competing to attract and retain desirable mates,

similarity between female friends in physical attractiveness may be a double-edged sword. We conducted two studies to investigate this possibility. We surveyed young adult female friends, measured their bodies, photographed them, and then asked outside samples of young adults to rate their attractiveness. We found support for our proposal that similar (but not identical) levels of physical attractiveness are tied to rivalry in women's friendships with women. First, female friends were similar in their body shape and rated attractiveness. Second, women who perceived themselves as less attractive than their friends felt more rivalry toward their friend. Third, women's evaluations of their friend's attractiveness surpassed their evaluations of their own attractiveness when in comparison to other women, but not when pitted directly against each other. Below, we discuss our findings in the context of past research on attractiveness, competition, and evolutionary models of females' social development. We also discuss avenues for future research.

Friend Similarity in Body Attributes That Men Attend to

In two samples of young adult female friends, we documented similarity in waist-to-hip ratio and bra cup size. Further, female friends were *not* similar in body mass or stature, which suggests that women select friends who are similar to them in attributes that are relevant specifically to mate search. We did note a somewhat smaller association between friends' waist-to-hip ratios in Study 2 relative to that in Study 1, which was likely due to a restricted range of waist-to-hip ratios in the second sample. Friend similarity in waist-to-hip ratio is a key finding, given waist-to-hip ratio's prominence in men's evaluations of women's attractiveness. In both studies, women with low waist-to-hip ratios did receive higher body and full-body attractiveness ratings; they even received higher *face* attractiveness ratings. This finding replicates Penton-Voak and colleagues' finding of a moderate negative association between women's WHR and face attractiveness (Penton-Voak et al., 2003) and suggests that the neurodevelopmental resources signaled through body shape measures (Lassek & Gaulin, 2008) may be manifested in the face to some degree.

Although female friends were similar in their breast size, as indexed by their bra cup size, breast size was not predictive of how attractive judges perceived the women to be. This pattern of findings coincides with eye-tracking research by Dixson et al. (2011), which showed that men attend to the breast area when evaluating women's attractiveness but that differences in breast size do not systematically predict their ratings of women's attractiveness. We suspect that men attend to breast size but that it may not be an evolved signal of underlying traits such as women's fertility or health.

Friend Similarity in Judged Attractiveness

The two studies here provide consistent evidence that young adult women befriend those who are similar to them in level of attractiveness. Friends' faces were rated as similarly attractive, even when the women were instructed not to smile, their makeup was removed, and their hair was pulled back to mask hairstyle. When friends donned scrubs (Study 1) to remove confounds of dress or clothing style, their faces and full-body shots were still rated as similarly attractive. When friends wore a two-piece swimsuit (Study 2) to remove confounds of clothing style and *reveal* their body shape, female friends received very similar ratings of full-body attractiveness.

Our results did not fully support Hypothesis 1, however. Female friends' bodies were not rated as similarly attractive, even when women wore swimsuits. As noted earlier, this lack of similarity in body attractiveness ratings is difficult to explain. When dressed in swimsuits, friends' *full bodies* were rated as similarly attractive, and women's body-only ratings were strong predictors of those full-body ratings. In trying

to reconcile these patterns, it is notable that men attend more to women's body when evaluating women as short-term partners than when evaluating them as long-term relationship partners (Confer, Perilloux, & Buss, 2010; Currie & Little, 2009). We asked our judges to assess women's physical attractiveness, but we did not ask judges to evaluate women's attractiveness as a potential *short-term* sex partner. Given that both men and women are more long-term oriented than short-term oriented (Jackson & Kirkpatrick, 2007), our judges may have been evaluating women as potential long-term partners by default. Perhaps ratings of female friends' bodies would be rated as similarly attractive if judges had been asked to consider them in the context of short-term mating, especially given that female friends are similar in their willingness to engage in short-term sexual opportunities (Preder, Fasteland, & Bleske-Rechek, 2006). In our second sample, for example, female friends were similar in their number of lifetime sex partners and one-time sex partners, $rs = 0.39$ and 0.44, but not their number of long-term romantic relationship partners (unfortunately, we did not ask friends about their sexual history in Study 1).

Rivalry and Perceived Discrepancies in Friends' Attractiveness

Our second hypothesis that discrepant levels of attractiveness are tied to feelings of rivalry between friends was supported. Women who perceived themselves as less physically attractive than their friend also reported more feelings of rivalry toward their friend. Notably, this association held despite that most women reported low levels of rivalry toward their friend and despite that the women in our samples were relatively unlikely to feel that they were less attractive than their friend. Indeed, only 24 % of women in Study 1 and 26 % of women in Study 2 reported that they were the less attractive friend. Despite that, those who did feel less attractive than their friend felt more rivalry than did those who felt similar to or more attractive than their friend. Moreover, in neither study were women's feelings of rivalry tied to perceiving their friend as more ambitious, athletic, or intelligent.[1] We did not include male friends in the two studies described here, but we speculate that if male friends also compete for attention from desirable women, then feelings of rivalry among male friends should be tied to those attributes more closely tied to *men's* mate value: ambition, intelligence, and athleticism (i.e., physical prowess).

One direction for future research might be to examine the distinct consequences of being the "more attractive" friend as opposed to the "less attractive" friend. Having a more attractive friend may evoke negative emotions like envy, but it is also possible that being the more attractive friend might put one at risk of being the recipient of others' envy and, perhaps even worse, *schadenfreude* or social alienation in general. In an initial attempt to look at this issue, we ran subsequent analyses to determine whether women who perceive themselves as *more* attractive than their friend also perceive more envy *from* their friend. We had one item on the sources of content and contention part that stated, "She is envious of me." We found a pattern in Study 1 that, although it did not replicate in Study 2, supported a unique link between attractiveness and envy. Specifically, women who felt more attractive than their friend were also more likely to agree that their friend was envious of them, r $(85) = -0.39$, $p < 0.001$; and women who perceived themselves as more intelligent, athletic, or ambitious than their friend did *not* report that their friend was envious of them (all $ps > 0.09$).

The link that we established here, between feelings of mating competition and perceptions of one's friend as more attractive than oneself, is potentially exacerbated by links between women's attractiveness and sexual promiscuity. The typical woman is strongly long-term oriented and responds negatively to women (including potential friends) who are sexually promiscuous or who act sexually available (Bleske & Shackelford, 2001; Coutinho, Hartnett, & Sagarin, 2007; Vaillancourt & Sharma, 2011). Such women receive attention from men and tempt their short-term mating desires. Such negativity toward women who act sexually promiscuous is relevant because it is possible that men perceive attractive women as sexually available *because* they are attractive; such a perception, even if in error, would propel men to pursue those women for sexual opportunities. In fact, limited research suggests that women who are rated by others as more attractive score higher on sexual unrestrictedness (Boothroyd, Jones, Burt, DeBruine, & Perrett, 2008). Supplementary analyses of our data coincide with this possibility, as well. In our second study, in which we collected the information on participants' sexual history, the women who were judged as more attractive also reported more one-time sex partners, lifetime sex partners, and long-term relationship partners ($rs > 0.32$, $ps < 0.005$). Perhaps attractive women are pursued more often as both short-term and long-term relationship partners. If so, women who are the "less attractive" friend may feel brushed to the side or under pressure to engage in various efforts to enhance their attractiveness. If intrasexual competition over attractiveness is heightened rather than minimized between female friends, as we suggested earlier, some female friends may get caught up in behaviors that enhance their appearance yet are dangerous to their health (e.g., Hill & Durante, 2011). Competition between friends to possess and display the attributes that men desire might be one explanation for shared body image and eating disorder symptomology between female friends (Hutchinson & Rapee, 2007).

---

[1] One might raise the argument that we found links between rivalry and attractiveness because the items comprising the mating rivalry composite are specific to attractiveness. However, only one of the seven rivalry items actually mentioned attractiveness ("I feel unattractive in comparison to her"), and our findings on attractiveness and rivalry were unchanged when we ran analyses without that item.

Self-Evaluation Maintenance on Attractiveness

According to Tesser's theory of self-evaluation maintenance, individuals are threatened by a close other outperforming them on a trait they highly value (Tesser & Campbell, 1982). Women value attractiveness; indeed, their self-concept hinges on their perceptions of their attractiveness (Campbell & Wilbur, 2009). Hence, we hypothesized that women evaluate their own and their friend's attractiveness in ways that enable them to protect that self-concept. We found support for this hypothesis in both studies. Women evaluated their friend more favorably than themselves when pitted against other women, but not when pitted directly against themselves. In thinking about women's friendships over the lifespan, we speculate that self-evaluation maintenance behavior might be especially prominent in certain contexts that have historically been linked to women's fitness. For example, we predict that women might be especially prone to perceiving their female friends' children as quite bright, attractive, and talented relative to *other* women's children, but not relative to their own.

Evolutionary History and the Intimate Ties of Female Friendship

We began this chapter by noting the simultaneous existence of rivalry and intimacy in women's friendships with women. Perhaps this is a product of both an evolved human adaptation for allying with similar others as well as unique female friendship adaptations that evolved in response to the developmental social challenges that females faced over evolutionary history. In various primate species and human societies, females leave their natal group at sexual maturity and join groups of males who are genetically related; thus, females join groups of individuals to whom they are not related genetically. It is likely that our hominid history was dominated by such patterns. As discussed by others (Baumeister, 2010;

Geary, 2010; Geary & Flinn, 2001; Vigil, 2007), this social context of male philopatry over human ancestral history may have selected for females' tendency to form and value close dyadic relationships with other females. An inability to rely on support of genetically related kin during the prime years of reproduction and offspring care would have selected for adaptations that led women to develop relationships with other women in which the two were mutually irreplaceable (Tooby & Cosmides, 1996; Vigil, 2007). In other words, young females must have been able to form deep, meaningful ties with other females quickly, so that those females invested in her well-being and that of her offspring. Indeed, close female friendships are unique in that they are not, by definition, between *sisters*, yet one of the strongest compliments a female friend can give to one another is to say that they are *like* a sister. In short, females who chose similar others as their allies would have been more likely to benefit from those alliances in both the proximate sense (e.g., strategic confluence) and ultimate sense (e.g., higher probability of investment in shared genes); but, to the extent that those females were unrelated to each other, they would also have ended up competing for access to the same limited resources: men willing and able to invest in them.

Conclusion

Every relationship has both benefits and costs, and women's friendships are no different. Friendships between women tend to be highly valued for both emotional support and companionship; at the same time, they are infamous for being emotionally draining sources of envy and rivalry. In this chapter we have suggested that similarity between female friends, particularly on the attributes that men most desire, is one source of rivalry in women's friendships with women. A number of questions remain. How does rivalry between female friends change over the lifespan? For example, it might continue to reflect discrepancies in women's own attractiveness and mate retention capacity, or it might move to reflect discrepancies in the likelihood that their *children* will obtain desirable mates and other limited resources. Additionally, what contexts predict experiences of rivalry between *male* friends? Given differences in male and female sexual strategies and sociodevelopmental contexts (i.e., male philopatry), we speculate that rivalry over attracting mates might not be viewed as negatively for male friends as for female friends. Yet another question pertains to the contexts in which rivalry between women can enhance women's well-being and when it does not. For some young women, having an attractive friend might promote admiration and even motivate self-improvement; yet having an attractive friend can also promote feelings of resentment. What personality traits and aspects of the friendship itself might buffer women against the negative effects of rivalry? We propose that friends' personality traits and their perceptions of one another as mutually irreplaceable will be key pieces of the puzzle. Our venture into full understanding of female friendship dynamics has only just begun.

References

Alvarez, L., & Jaffe, K. (2004). Narcissism guides mate selection: Humans mate assortatively, as revealed by facial resemblance, following an algorithm of 'self seeking like'. *Evolutionary Psychology, 2*, 177–194.

Apter, T., & Josselson, R. (1998). *Best friends: The pleasures and perils of girls' and women's friendships.* New York: Three Rivers Press.

Baumeister, R. F. (2010). *Is there anything good about men?: How cultures flourish by exploiting men.* Oxford: Oxford University Press.

Benenson, J. F., & Christakos, A. (2003). The greater fragility of females' versus males' closest same-sex friendships. *Child Development, 74*, 1123–1129. doi:10.1111/1467-8624.00596.

Berg, J. H. (1984). Development of friendship between roommates. *Journal of Personality and Social Psychology, 46*, 346–356. doi:10.1037/0022-3514.46.2.346.

Billy, J. O., Rodgers, J. L., & Udry, J. (1984). Adolescent sexual behavior and friendship choice. *Social Forces, 62*, 653–678. doi:10.2307/2578705.

Bleske, A. L., & Shackelford, T. K. (2001). Poaching, promiscuity, and deceit: Combating mating rivalry in same-sex friendships. *Personal Relationships, 8*, 407–424.

Bleske-Rechek, A., & Lighthall, M. (2010). Attractiveness and rivalry in women's friendships with women. *Human Nature, 21*, 82–97. doi:10.1007/s12110-010-9081-5.

Bleske-Rechek, A., Remiker, M. W., & Baker, J. P. (2009). Similar from the start: Assortment in young adult dating couples and its link to relationship stability over time. *Individual Differences Research, 7*, 142–158.

Boothroyd, L. G., Jones, B. C., Burt, D. M., DeBruine, L. M., & Perrett, D. I. (2008). Facial correlates of sociosexuality. *Evolution and Human Behavior, 29*, 211–218.

Brewer, M. B. (1979). In-group bias in the minimal intergroup situation: A cognitive-motivational analysis. *Psychological Bulletin, 86*, 307–324. doi:10.1037/0033-2909.86.2.307.

Burriss, R. P., Roberts, S., Welling, L. M., Puts, D. A., & Little, A. C. (2011). Heterosexual romantic couples mate assortatively for facial symmetry, but not masculinity. *Personality and Social Psychology Bulletin, 37*, 601–613. doi:10.1177/0146167211399584.

Buss, D. M. (1988). The evolution of human intrasexual competition: Tactics of mate attraction. *Journal of Personality and Social Psychology, 54*, 616–628. doi:10.1037/0022-3514.54.4.616.

Buss, D. M., & Dedden, L. A. (1990). Derogation of competitors. *Journal of Social and Personal Relationships, 7*, 395–422. doi:10.1177/0265407590073006.

Buss, D. M., Shackelford, T. K., Choe, J., Buunk, B. P., & Dijkstra, P. (2000). Distress about mating rivals. *Personal Relationships, 7*, 235–243. doi:10.1111/j.1475-6811.2000.tb00014.x.

Campbell, A. (1995). A few good men: Evolutionary psychology and female adolescent aggression. *Ethology & Sociobiology, 16*, 99–123. doi:10.1016/0162-3095(94)00072-F.

Campbell, A. (1999). Staying alive: Evolution, culture, and women's intrasexual aggression. *Behavioral and Brain Sciences, 22*, 203–252. doi:10.1017/S0140525X99001818.

Campbell, L., & Wilbur, C. J. (2009). Are the traits we prefer in potential mates the traits they value in themselves? An analysis of sex differences in the self-concept. *Self and Identity, 8*, 418–446. doi:10.1080/15298860802505434.

Cashdan, E. (1998). Are men more competitive than women? *British Journal of Social Psychology, 37*, 213–229. doi:10.1111/j.2044-8309.1998.tb01166.x.

Cohen, J. M. (1977). Sources of peer group homogeneity. *Sociology of Education, 50*, 227–241. doi:10.2307/2112497.

Confer, J. C., Perilloux, C., & Buss, D. M. (2010). More than just a pretty face: Men's priority shifts toward bodily attractiveness in short-term versus long-term mating contexts. *Evolution and Human Behavior, 31*, 348–353.

Coutinho, S. A., Hartnett, J. L., & Sagarin, B. J. (2007). Understanding promiscuity in strategic friend selection from an evolutionary perspective. *North American Journal of Psychology, 9*, 257–274.

Currie, T. E., & Little, A. C. (2009). The relative importance of the face and body in judgments of human physical attractiveness. *Evolution and Human Behavior, 30*, 409–416. doi:10.1016/j.evolhumbehav.2009.06.005.

de Waal, F. B., & Luttrell, L. M. (1986). The similarity principle underlying social bonding among female rhesus monkeys. *Folia Primatologica, 46*, 215–234. doi:10.1159/000156255.

DelPriore, D. J., Hill, S. E., & Buss, D. M. (2012). Envy: Functional specificity and sex-differentiated design features. *Personality and Individual Differences, 53*, 317–322.

Dijkstra, P., & Buunk, B. P. (2002). Sex differences in the jealousy-evoking effect of rival characteristics. *European Journal of Social Psychology, 32*, 829–852. doi:10.1002/ejsp.125.

Dixson, B. J., Grimshaw, G. M., Linklater, W. L., & Dixson, A. F. (2011). Eye-tracking of men's preferences for waist-to-hip ratio and breast size of women. *Archives of Sexual Behavior, 40*, 43–50. doi:10.1007/s10508-009-9523-5.

Durante, K. M., Griskevicius, V., Hill, S. E., Perilloux, C., & Li, N. P. (2011). Ovulation, female competition, and product choice: Hormonal influences on consumer behavior. *Journal of Consumer Research, 37*, 921–934. doi:10.1086/656575.

Eichenbaum, L., & Orbach, S. (1987). *Between women: Love, envy, and competition in women's friendships.* New York: Penguin Books.

Feingold, A. (1988). Matching for attractiveness in romantic partners and same-sex friends: A meta-analysis and theoretical critique. *Psychological Bulletin, 104*, 226–235. doi:10.1037/0033-2909.104.2.226.

Fisher, L. A., & Bauman, K. E. (1988). Influence and selection in the friend–adolescent relationship: Findings from studies of adolescent smoking and drinking. *Journal of Applied Social Psychology, 18*, 289–314. doi:10.1111/j.1559-1816.1988.tb00018.x.

Gail-Alfonso, N. (2006). *The experience of envy between young women and their female friends: A psychological perspective.* Newton, MA: Dissertation Abstracts International, Massachusetts School of Professional Psychology.

Gangestad, S. W., & Scheyd, G. J. (2005). The evolution of human physical attractiveness. *Annual Review of Anthropology, 34*, 523–548. doi:10.1146/annurev.anthro.33.070203.143733.

Geary, D. C. (2010). *Male, female: The evolution of human sex differences* (2nd ed.). Washington, DC: American Psychological Association.

Geary, D. C., & Flinn, M. V. (2001). Evolution of human parental behavior and the human family. *Parenting: Science and Practice, 1*, 5–61.

Gutierres, S. E., Kenrick, D. T., & Partch, J. J. (1999). Beauty, dominance, and the mating game: Contrast effects in self-assessment reflect gender differences in mate selection. *Personality and Social Psychology Bulletin, 25*, 1126–1134. doi:10.1177/01461672992512006.

Hill, S. E., & Durante, K. M. (2011). Courtship, competition, and the pursuit of attractiveness: Mating goals facilitate health-related risk taking and strategic risk suppression in women. *Personality and Social Psychology Bulletin, 37*, 383–394.

Huston, T. L., & Levinger, G. (1978). Interpersonal attraction and relationships. *Annual Review of Psychology, 29*, 115–156. doi:10.1146/annurev.ps.29.020178.000555.

Hutchinson, D. M., & Rapee, R. M. (2007). Do friends share similar body image and eating problems? The role of social networks and peer influences in early adolescence. *Behaviour Research and Therapy, 45*, 1557–1577. doi:10.1016/j.brat.2006.11.007.

Jackson, J. J., & Kirkpatrick, L. A. (2007). The structure and measurement of human mating strategies: Toward a multidimensional model of sociosexuality. *Evolution and Human Behavior, 28*, 382–391.

Kandel, D. B. (1978). Similarity in real-life adolescent friendship pairs. *Journal of Personality and Social Psychology, 36*, 306–312. doi:10.1037/0022-3514.36.3.306.

Kernis, M. H., & Wheeler, L. (1981). Beautiful friends and ugly strangers: Radiation and contrast effects in perceptions of same-sex pairs. *Personality and Social Psychology Bulletin, 7*, 617–620. doi:10.1177/014616728174017.

Larson, R., & Richards, M. H. (1994). *Divergent realities: The emotional loves of mothers, fathers, and adolescents.* New York: Basic Books.

Lassek, W. D., & Gaulin, S. J. (2008). Waist-hip ratio and cognitive ability: Is gluteofemoral fat a privileged store of neurodevelopmental resources? *Evolution and Human Behavior, 29*, 26–34.

Ledbetter, A. M., Griffin, E., & Sparks, G. G. (2007). Forecasting 'friends forever': A longitudinal investigation of sustained closeness between best friends. *Personal Relationships, 14*, 343–350. doi:10.1111/j.1475-6811.2007.00158.x.

Luo, S., & Klohnen, E. C. (2005). Assortative mating and marital quality in newlyweds: A couple-centered approach. *Journal of Personality and Social Psychology, 88*, 304–326. doi:10.1037/0022-3514.88.2.304.

Madsen, E. A., Tunney, R. J., Fieldman, G., Plotkin, H. C., Dunbar, R. M., Richardson, J., et al. (2007). Kinship and altruism: A cross-cultural experimental study. *British Journal of Psychology, 98*, 339–359. doi:10.1348/000712606X129213.

Mahajan, N., & Wynn, K. (2012). Origins of 'us' versus 'them': Prelinguistic infants prefer similar others. *Cognition, 124*, 227–233. doi:10.1016/j.cognition.2012.05.003.

Maner, J. K., Gailliot, M. T., & DeWall, C. (2007). Adaptive attentional attunement: Evidence for mating-related perceptual bias. *Evolution and Human Behavior, 28*, 28–36. doi:10.1016/j.evolhumbehav.2006.05.006.

McPherson, M., Smith-Lovin, L., & Cook, J. M. (2001). Birds of a feather: Homophily in social networks. *Annual Review of Sociology, 27*, 415–444. doi:10.1146/annurev.soc.27.1.415.

O'Connor, P. (1992). *Friendships between women: A critical review*. New York: Guilford Press.

Penton-Voak, I. S., Little, A. C., Jones, B. C., Burt, D. M., Tiddeman, B. P., & Perrett, D. I. (2003). Female condition influences preferences for sexual dimorphism in faces of male humans (Homo sapiens). *Journal of Comparative Psychology, 117*, 264–271. doi:10.1037/0735-7036.117.3.264.

Perilloux, H. K., Webster, G. D., & Gaulin, S. J. C. (2010). Signals of genetic quality and maternal investment capacity: The dynamic effects of fluctuating asymmetry and waist-to-hip ratio on men's ratings of women's attractiveness. *Social Psychological and Personality Science, 1*, 34–42.

Peters, M., Rhodes, G., & Simmons, L. W. (2007). Contributions of the face and body to overall attractiveness. *Animal Behaviour, 73*, 937–942. doi:10.1016/j.anbehav.2006.07.012.

Preder, S. M., Fasteland, K. A., & Bleske-Rechek, A. (2006, June). *Agreement and assortment in same-sex friendship: Why sexual strategy matters*. Poster presented at the annual conference of the Human Behavior and Evolution Society, Philadelphia, PA.

Reis, H. T., Maniaci, M. R., Caprariello, P. A., Eastwick, P. W., & Finkel, E. J. (2011). Familiarity does indeed promote attraction in live interaction. *Journal of Personality and Social Psychology, 101*, 557–570. doi:10.1037/a0022885.

Rushton, J. (1989). Genetic similarity, human altruism, and group selection. *Behavioral and Brain Sciences, 12*, 503–559. doi:10.1017/S0140525X00057320.

Rushton, J., & Bons, T. (2005). Mate choice and friendship in twins: Evidence for genetic similarity. *Psychological Science, 16*, 555–559. doi:10.1111/j.0956-7976.2005.01574.x.

Rushton, J., Russell, R. J., & Wells, P. A. (1984). Genetic similarity theory: Beyond kin selection. *Behavior Genetics, 14*, 179–193. doi:10.1007/BF01065540.

Schaller, M., & Neuberg, S. L. (2008). Intergroup prejudices and intergroup conflicts. In C. Crawford & D. Krebs (Eds.), *Foundations of evolutionary psychology* (pp. 401–414). New York: Taylor & Francis Group/Lawrence Erlbaum Associates.

Seyfarth, R. M., & Cheney, D. L. (2012). The evolutionary origins of friendship. *Annual Review of Psychology, 63*, 153–177. doi:10.1146/annurev-psych-120710-100337.

Silk, J. B., Alberts, S. C., & Altmann, J. (2003). Social bonds of female baboons enhance infant survival. *Science, 302*, 1231–1234. doi:10.1126/science.1088580.

Tesser, A., & Campbell, J. L. (1982). Self-evaluation maintenance and the perception of friends and strangers. *Journal of Personality, 50*, 261–279. doi:10.1111/j.1467-6494.1982.tb00750.x.

Tolson, J. M., & Urberg, K. A. (1993). Similarity between adolescent best friends. *Journal of Adolescent Research, 8*, 274–288. doi:10.1177/074355489383003.

Tooby, J., & Cosmides, L. (1996). Friendship and the Banker's Paradox: Other pathways to the evolution of adaptations for altruism. In W. G. Runciman, J. Maynard Smith, & R. I. M. Dunbar (Eds.), *Evolution of social behaviour patterns in primates and man* (Proceedings of the British Academy, Vol. 88, pp. 119–143). Oxford: Oxford University Press.

Tooke, W., & Camire, L. (1991). Patterns of deception in intersexual and intrasexual mating strategies. *Ethology & Sociobiology, 12*, 345–364. doi:10.1016/0162-3095(91)90030-T.

Urberg, K. A., Degirmencioglu, S. M., & Tolson, J. M. (1998). Adolescent friendship selection and termination: The role of similarity. *Journal of Social and Personal Relationships, 15*, 703–710. doi:10.1177/0265407598155008.

Vaillancourt, T., & Sharma, A. (2011). Intolerance of sexy peers: Intrasexual competition among women. *Aggressive Behavior, 37*, 569–577. doi:10.1002/ab.20413.

Vandenberg, S. G. (1972). Assortative mating, or who marries whom? *Behavior Genetics, 2*, 127–157. doi:10.1007/BF01065686.

Vigil, J. M. (2007). Asymmetries in the friendship preferences and social styles of men and women. *Human Nature, 18*, 143–161. doi:10.1007/s12110-007-9003-3.

Webster, G. D. (2003). Prosocial behavior in families: Moderators of resource sharing. *Journal of Experimental Social Psychology, 39*, 644–652. doi:10.1016/S0022-1031(03)00055-6.

Webster, G. D. (2004). Human kin investment as a function of genetic relatedness and lineage. *Evolutionary Psychology, 2*, 129–141.

Webster, G. D., Bryan, A., Crawford, C. B., McCarthy, L., & Cohen, B. H. (2008). Lineage, sex, and wealth as moderators of kin investment: Evidence from inheritances. *Human Nature, 19*, 189–210. doi:10.1007/s12110-008-9038-0.

Weinstein, T. R., & Capitanio, J. P. (2012). Longitudinal stability of friendships in rhesus monkeys (*Macaca mulatta*): Individual- and relationship-level effects. *Journal of Comparative Psychology, 126*, 97–108. doi:10.1037/a0025607.

Yager, J. (2002). *When friendship hurts: How to deal with friends who betray, abandon, or wound you*. New York: Simon & Schuster.

Zelazniewicz, A. M., & Pawlowski, B. (2011). Female breast size attractiveness for men as a function of sociosexual orientation (restricted vs. unrestricted). *Archives of Sexual Behavior, 40*, 1129–1135. doi:10.1007/s10508-011-9850-1.

Part IV

Conclusions and Future Directions for Evolutionary Perspectives on Human Sexual Psychology and Behavior

Evolutionary Perspectives on Male Androphilia in Humans

19

Paul L. Vasey and Doug P. VanderLaan

Introduction

Androphilia refers to predominant sexual attraction and arousal to adult males, whereas *gynephilia* refers to predominant sexual attraction and arousal to adult females. Research on the evolution of same-sex sexuality in humans has focused on explaining the origin of exclusive male androphilia and its persistence over time. The evolution of female gynephilia in humans remains under-theorized and researched (but see Diamond, 2006; Zietsch, Morley, Shekar, Verweij, Keller, Macgregor et al., 2008), although a much more substantial body of evolutionary research on female–female sexual behavior exists for non-human primates such as bonobos (Fruth & Hohmann, 2006) and Japanese macaques (Vasey, 2006; Vasey & VanderLaan, 2012).

Until very recently, it would not have been possible to write a book chapter, like this one, which examines the evolution of male androphilia from an evidence-based, quantitative perspective. There simply was not enough information available to justify a review of the literature. In 2004, Andrea Camperio Ciani and his colleagues published what was arguably the first study to gain any traction in relation to understanding the evolutionary paradox

that is male androphilia (Camperio-Ciani, Corna, & Capiluppi, 2004). Prior to that, there existed only a single quantitative study on this topic and it reported nonsignificant findings (Bobrow & Bailey, 2001). Apart from that, the literature on the evolution of male androphilia could aptly be characterized up to that point in time as overwhelmingly theoretical and speculative, with no grounding in any quantitative data whatsoever.

Since the publication of the Camperio-Ciani et al. (2004) study, however, significant advances have been made in understanding how a trait like male androphilia, which lowers reproductive success, might persist over evolutionary time. For example, a number of hypotheses that attempt to account for the evolution of male androphilia have been quantitatively examined in different populations including, importantly, nonindustrialized and non-Western ones. Moreover, data relevant to the testing of evolutionary hypotheses has been collected on different cultural forms of male androphilia, thereby extending our knowledge beyond Western "gays." In what follows, we provide a framework for thinking about how to study the evolution of male androphilia and a review of the pertinent literature.

The Expression of Male Androphilia Varies Cross-Culturally

The manner in which male androphilia is publically expressed varies across cultures (Murray, 2000).

P.L. Vasey (✉)
Department of Psychology, University of Lethbridge,
4401 University Drive, Lethbridge, AB, Canada
T1K 3M4
e-mail: paul.vasey@uleth.ca

V.A. Weekes-Shackelford and T.K. Shackelford (eds.), *Evolutionary Perspectives on Human Sexual Psychology and Behavior*, Evolutionary Psychology, DOI 10.1007/978-1-4939-0314-6_19,
© Springer Science+Business Media New York 2014

This expression typically takes one of two forms, which are related to gender role enactment. These two forms are *sex-gender congruent* and *transgendered* male androphilia. Sex-gender congruent male androphiles occupy the gender role typical of their sex, behave in a relatively masculine manner, and identify as "men." In contrast, transgendered androphilic males typically behave in an effeminate manner and identify as neither "men" nor "women," but rather as members of some "third" gender category. In some cultures, transgendered male androphilia is linked to particular institutionalized labor practices, which often involve specialized religious activities. For example, on the Indian subcontinent, transgendered male androphiles known as *hijra* bestow blessings from Hindu gods and goddesses for luck and fertility at weddings and at the birth of male babies (Nanda, 1999). Some authors refer to such transgendered male androphilia as "role-structured homosexuality" (Herdt, 1997). Both sex-gender congruent and transgendered male androphilia may occur within a given culture, but typically one or the other tends to predominate (Whitam, 1983). For example, the sex-gender congruent form is more common in many Western cultures, whereas the transgendered form appears to be more common in a number of non-Western cultures (Murray, 2000).

Other authors have referred to sex-gender congruent male androphilia as "egalitarian male homosexuality" (Murray, 2000) and "homophilic homosexuality" (Gorer, 1966). However, the term "sex-gender congruent" androphilia highlights the critical role of gender role enactment in distinguishing the two forms of male androphilia under consideration here. There are several reasons why "androphilia" is the preferential term when undertaking cross-cultural comparisons of male same-sex sexuality. First, the usage and meaning of the term "homosexuality" vary cross-culturally, rendering it a poor construct for the type of cross-cultural research reviewed here. Second, "androphilia" pertains to sexual attraction and arousal, not sexual behavior, which may be constrained by cultural circumstances (e.g., taboos against same-sex sexual behavior) or enacted for ritual purposes.

As such, the term "androphilia" makes no assumptions about whether sexual behavior has been expressed. Third, this terminology makes no assumptions about the sexual orientation or the gender role enactment of the *sexual partners* of male androphiles. As such, although transgendered male androphiles routinely engage in sexual activity with masculine males who identify as "men" (Murray, 2000), these men may or may not be androphilic themselves. This may seem perplexing from a Western cultural perspective in which sex-gender congruent male androphiles routinely seek out other sex-gender congruent male androphiles for sexual interactions. However, it is important to note that gynephilic males' willingness to engage in sexual interactions with their less preferred sex varies tremendously across cultures (Whitam & Mathy, 1986). In cultures where transgendered male androphilia predominates, male gynephiles may, for example, experience relatively less sexual aversion to the idea of engaging in certain types of same-sex sexual interactions because, to some extent, transgendered male androphiles represent facsimiles resemble their preferred sex partners (i.e., adult females). The possibility that gynephilic males are cross-culturally invariant in terms of their preference for female sexual partners when given a choice but cross-culturally variable in terms of their aversion to accepting (feminine) male sex partners when they cannot obtain their preferred sex is one that deserves much more research attention.

In addition to these two forms of male androphilia, a third form—transgenerational homosexuality—has also been reported in the literature. Transgenerational homosexuality involves sexual interactions between a sexually immature or younger male and a sexually mature or older male (Murray, 2000). Comparative research on non-human primates suggests that transgenerational homosexuality has a different evolutionary origin than sex-gender congruent and transgendered male androphilia (Dixson, 2010). Furthermore, it is not clear that transgenerational homosexuality is motivated by androphilia on the part of either the older or younger partner. For example, in some instances these same-sex interactions might be enacted for primarily alistic purposes. Moreover, depending on the individual, the older partners in these interactions might be best characterized as either pedophilic (i.e., sexually attracted/aroused to prepubescent individuals), hebephilic (i.e., sexually attracted/aroused to peripubescent individuals), or gynephilic, not androphilic. Similarly, the younger partners might be (pre)gynephilic, not (pre)androphilic. Given these reasons, we do not consider transgenerational homosexuality here. For a discussion of unique properties of transgenerational homosexuality from an ethnological perspective, see Crapo (1995).

Cross-Culturally Invariant Correlates of Male Androphilia

Attempts to draw comparisons between sex-gender congruent and transgendered male androphilic males have been characterized as misguided because, critics argue, these unique patterns cannot be understood outside of the specific cultural contexts in which they exist (Johnson, Jackson, & Herdt, 2000). As such, the overall impression one gleans from this literature is that a panoply of male "androphilias" exists. Not surprisingly, there has been debate in the literature concerning whether distinct or common underlying causal processes characterize male androphilia in different cultures. If it were possible to establish that androphilic males from different cultural backgrounds shared associated features that are indicators, at least in theory, of underlying causal processes, then this would give support to the possibility of common biological bases. Indeed, quantitative research indicates that the sex-gender congruent and transgendered forms of male androphilia share numerous developmental and biodemographic correlates that are cross-culturally invariant.

In terms of biodemographic correlates that exist across cultures, sex-gender congruent and transgendered male androphiles tend to be later born among their siblings (e.g., Blanchard, 2004; VanderLaan & Vasey, 2011; Vasey & VanderLaan, 2007), have greater numbers of older biological brothers

("fraternal birth order effect,"[1] e.g., Bogaert & Skorska, 2011; VanderLaan & Vasey, 2011; Vasey & VanderLaan, 2007), exhibit larger family sizes (Blanchard & Lippa, 2007; Camperio-Ciani et al., 2004; Iemmola & Camperio Ciani, 2009; King, Green, Osborn, Arkell, Heatherton, & Pereira, 2005; Rahman, Collins, Morrison, Orrells, Cadinouche, Greenfield et al., 2008; Schwartz, Kim, Kolundziji, Rieger, & Sanders, 2010; VanderLaan, Forrester, Petterson, & Vasey, 2012; VanderLaan & Vasey, 2011; Vasey & VanderLaan, 2007), cluster within families (e.g., Schwartz et al., 2010; VanderLaan, Forrester, Petterson, & Vasey, 2013a; VanderLaan, Vokey, & Vasey, 2013b), occur at similar prevalence rates across different populations (e.g., Smith, Rissel, Richters, Grulich, & de Visser, 2003; VanderLaan et al., 2013a; Whitam, 1983), and exhibit little or no reproductive success (e.g., King et al., 2005; Schwartz et al., 2010; Vasey, Parker, & VanderLaan, 2014). In addition, the odds ratios associated with the fraternal brother effect in various populations of sex-gender congruent and transgendered male androphiles are remarkably consistent, suggesting that the manner in which older brothers influence the development of male androphilia is constant across diverse populations (e.g., Cantor, Blanchard, Paterson, & Bogaert, 2002; VanderLaan & Vasey, 2011).

Prospective and retrospective cross-cultural research on early psychosocial development among transgendered and sex-gender congruent male androphiles has shown that the childhood behavior of such males is characterized by greater levels of female-typical behavior (e.g., nurturing play with dolls) and lower levels of male-typical behavior (e.g., rough-and-tumble play; Bailey & Zucker, 1995; Bartlett & Vasey, 2006; Cardoso, 2005, 2009; Whitam, 1983). In addition, both types of male androphiles express elevated cross-sex beliefs and wishes in childhood (e.g., "I think I really am a girl") (Bailey & Zucker, 1995; Vasey &

---

[1] The *fraternal birth order effect* refers to the well-established finding that the number of older biological brothers increases the odds of androphilia in later born males (Blanchard, 2004; Bogaert & Skorska, 2011).

Bartlett, 2007; Whitam, 1983). Furthermore, both sex-gender congruent and transgendered male androphiles also experience elevated traits of childhood separation anxiety (i.e., anxiety related to separation from major attachment figures such as parents; VanderLaan, Gothreau, Bartlett, & Vasey, 2011a; Vasey, VanderLaan, Gothreau, & Bartlett, 2011; Zucker, Bradley, & Sullivan, 1996), which tend to be more common among girls compared to boys (e.g., Shear, Jin, Ruscio, Walters, & Kessler, 2006; VanderLaan et al., 2011a). In adulthood, male androphiles from a range of cultures exhibit preferences for a variety of female-typical occupations and hobbies (e.g., interior design) (Lippa, 2005; Whitam, 1983).

Even though sex-gender congruent androphilic males are relatively feminine as boys compared to their gynephilic counterparts (Bailey & Zucker, 1995), they behaviorally defeminize to varying degrees as they develop. It has been suggested that this behavioral defeminization probably occurs in response to culturally specific gender role expectations, which hold that male-bodied individuals should behave in a masculine manner (Bailey, 2003; Berling, 2001; Rieger & Savin-Williams, 2012). In contrast, in cultures where transgendered male androphilia is the norm, feminine boys develop into feminine adult males. Consequently, adult sex-gender congruent male androphiles are relatively masculine when compared to transgendered adult male androphiles (Murray, 2000). Conversely, they are, on average, relatively feminine when compared to adult male gynephiles (Bailey, 2003; Lippa, 2005). Thus, regardless of how it is manifested, male androphilia is associated with gender atypicality in childhood and adulthood. However, the strength of this association varies depending on the manner in which male androphilia is publically expressed.

Taken together, these numerous, cross-culturally invariant biodemograpphic and developmental correlates of male androphilia indicate that sex-gender congruent and transgendered male androphilia share a common etiological basis despite being superficially different in appearance.

Male Androphilia Is an Evolutionary Paradox

The biodemographic and developmental evidence outlined above suggests that sex-gender congruent and transgendered male androphilia are cultural variants of what is essentially the same phenomenon with a common biological basis. The existence of diverse forms of male androphilia across cultures, which nonetheless appear to share similar a etiology, is an evolutionary paradox. There appears to be some genetic influence on male androphilia (e.g., Bailey, Dunne, & Martin, 2000; Kendler, Thornton, Gilman, & Kessler, 2000; Långström, Rahman, Carlström, & Lichtenstein, 2010), yet androphilic men reproduce at significantly lower rates than gynephilic men (e.g., King et al., 2005; Schwartz et al., 2010; Vasey et al., 2014). Consequently, one would have expected genes for male androphilia to become extinct given the relative reproductive costs associated with this trait and the reproductive benefits associated with male gynephilia.

Nevertheless, prehistoric rock art and pottery suggest that male–male sexual activity has existed for millennia (e.g., Larco Hoyle, 1998; Nash, 2001; Yates, 1993). Further, graves containing male skeletal remains and female-typical artifacts are indicative of transgendered males in the distant past (e.g., Hollimon, 1997; Knüsel & Ripley, 2000). Prine (2000) argued that certain architecturally unusual dwellings, inhabited by the Hidatsa[2] people between 1400 and 1800 AD, were the homes of transgendered males known locally as *miati*. Given what we know about the exclusive androphilic orientation of most transgendered males from comparable populations (e.g., Harrington, 1942; Murray, 2000; Nanda, 1999), archaeological indicators of such individual are suggestive of the presence of male androphilia in human antiquity.

---

[2] The Hidatsa are a native North American people that lived in palisaded villages along the Missouri River in North Dakota from 1400 to 1800 AD.

In sum, male androphilia has a genetic component and appears to have existed for millennia; yet male androphiles reproduce at a fraction of the rate that gynephilic males do, if they reproduce at all. For these reasons, male androphilia is widely considered one of the outstanding paradoxes of evolutionary psychology. A trait that lowers direct reproduction and persists over evolutionary time requires explanation when viewed within the context of natural selection, a process that favors the evolution of reproductively viable traits.

Male Androphilia in the Ancestral Environment

Given that the manner in which male androphilia is publically expressed varies cross-culturally, the question arises as to which form, sex-gender congruent or transgendered, was the ancestral form. Identifying the ancestral form of male androphilia is critical if we seek to test hypotheses pertaining to the evolution of this trait in an accurate manner. More derived forms of this trait might reflect historically recent, cultural influences.

With this concern in mind, VanderLaan, Ren, and Vasey (2013) attempted to identify the ancestral form of male androphilia. They did so by examining whether societies in which transgendered male androphilia predominates exhibit more of the sociocultural features that are believed to have characterized the human ancestral past relative to a comparison group of societies in which transgendered male androphilia did not predominate. Numerous researchers have presented evidence indicating that the ancestral human sociocultural environment was likely characterized by hunter-gatherers living in small groups with relatively egalitarian sociopolitical structures and animistic religious belief systems (e.g., Binford, 2001; Hill, Walker, Bozicevic, Eder, Headland, Hewlett et al., 2011; Marlowe, 2005; McBrearty & Brooks, 2000; Sanderson & Roberts, 2008; Smith, 1999; Winkelman, 2010; Woodburn, 1982). If these conditions are more often associated with societies in which transgendered

male androphilia predominates, then this would bolster the argument that male androphilia was predominantly expressed in the transgendered form under ancestral conditions.

Using information derived from the Standard Cross-Cultural Sample (SCCS), VanderLaan Ren et al. (2013c) compared 46 transgendered societies with 146 non-transgendered societies. Their goal was to ascertain whether the former were more likely to be characterized by human ancestral sociocultural conditions (i.e., smaller group size, hunting and gathering, egalitarian political structure, and animistic religious beliefs) compared to the latter. The SCCS provides data related to a subset of the world's nonindustrial societies and circumvents Galton's problem (i.e., common cultural derivation and cultural diffusion) when conducting cross-cultural comparisons. Compared to non-transgendered societies, transgendered societies were characterized by a significantly greater presence of ancestral sociocultural conditions. Given the association between transgendered male androphilia and ancestral human sociocultural conditions, it seems parsimonious to conclude that the ancestral form of male androphilia was the transgendered form. Consistent with this conclusion is the fact that sex-gender congruent male androphilia appears to be a historically recent phenomenon with little precedent outside of a Western cultural context until very recently (Murray, 2000). Accordingly, caution needs to be exercised in utilizing sex-gender congruent male androphiles such as "gay" men as models to test hypotheses pertaining to the evolution of male androphilia.

Kin Selection and the Evolution of Male Androphilia

The Kin Selection Hypothesis holds that genes for male androphilia could be maintained in a population if enhancing one's indirect fitness offset the cost of not reproducing directly (Wilson, 1975). Indirect fitness is a measure of an individual's impact on the fitness of kin (who share some identical genes by virtue of descent), weighted by the degree of relatedness (Hamilton, 1963). Theoretically speaking, androphilic males can increase their indirect fitness by directing altruistic behavior toward kin, which, in principle, allows kin to increase their reproductive success. In particular, androphilic men should allocate altruistic behavior toward close kin because they share more genes in common with such individuals.

In formulating this theory, Wilson (1975) stated that "Freed from the special obligations of parental duties, they [androphilic males] could have operated with special efficiency in assisting close relatives" (p. 555). Similarly, Ruse (1982) commented that "...the effect is that in being homosexual, offspring become altruistic toward close relatives in order thereby to increase their own overall inclusive fitness" (p. 20). Given that what is at issue here is a theory that can account for the origin of same-sex sexual attraction, it seems reasonable to interpret these statements as indicating that same-sex sexual attraction, itself, is a prerequisite for the expression of elevated kin-directed altruism, *not* childlessness. If so, then male androphiles should exhibit elevated kin-directed altruism, whereas male gynephiles (childless or otherwise) should not. Such a pattern would be consistent with the notion that male androphilia is a specially designed adaptation for promoting kin-directed altruism. To date, the most detailed tests of the Kin Selection Hypothesis for male androphilia have been conducted by our own research group. Our cross-cultural tests of this hypothesis have been conducted in Samoa, Canada, and Japan on both transgendered and sex-gender congruent male androphiles.

Test of the Kin Selection Hypothesis in Samoan Transgendered Male Androphiles

Research conducted on transgendered male androphiles in Samoa has repeated furnished support for the Kin Selection Hypothesis. In Samoa, transgendered androphilic males are known locally as *fa'afafine*. Translated literally, *fa'afafine* means "in the manner of a woman." Within Samoan society, *fa'afafine* are not recognized as "men" or "women" and, as such,

have been described as a type of "third" gender. From a Western cultural perspective, most *fa'afafine* would be considered transgendered or, at the very least, highly effeminate. Most *fa'afafine* do not experience dysphoria with respect to their genitals and, as such, could not be accurately characterized as transsexual (Vasey & Bartlett, 2007). With respect to sexual orientation, *fa'afafine* are, almost without exception, exclusively androphilic. Not surprisingly, then, they do not have children of their own (Vasey et al., 2014). *Fa'afafine* enjoy a high level of social acceptance that, while not absolute, is in striking contrast to the situation experienced by Western transgendered male androphiles (Namaste, 2000; Seil, 1996).

Research demonstrates that the avuncular (uncle-like) tendencies of *fa'afafine* are significantly elevated compared to those of Samoan gynephilic males (VanderLaan & Vasey, 2012; Vasey, Pocock, & VanderLaan, 2007; Vasey & VanderLaan, 2010a). *Fa'afafine* also exhibited significantly elevated avuncular tendencies compared to the materteral (aunt-like) tendencies of Samoan women (Vasey & VanderLaan, 2009). Elevated avuncular tendencies among *fa'afafine* were also documented when comparing them to control groups of childless women and gynephilic men (Vasey & VanderLaan, 2009, 2010a). These latter comparisons indicated that the *fa'afafine's* elevated avuncular tendencies cannot be characterized as a simple by-product that is due to a lack of parental care responsibilities, and thus, greater availability of resources for avuncular investment. If this were true, then the avuncular tendencies of *fa'afafine* would be similar to those of childless men and women, but this was not the case. Moreover, these same findings indicate that the elevated avuncular tendencies of *fa'afafine* could not be characterized as a simple by-product that is due to the male members of this "third" gender group adopting feminine gender roles, which included expectations for elevated childcare. If this were true, then the materteral tendencies of Samoan mothers and childless women would be similar to the avuncular tendencies of *fa'afafine*, but again this was not the case.

We have also demonstrated that *fa'afafine's* avuncular tendencies are significantly higher than their altruistic interest in non-kin children (Vasey & VanderLaan, 2010b). As such, *fa'afafine's* elevated avuncular tendencies are not a by-product of general altruistic interested in all children. If this were true, the *fa'afafine's* avuncular tendencies toward nieces and nephews and their altruistic tendencies toward non-kin children would be similar, but this was not the case.

Additional research indicates that *fa'afafine* exhibit similar levels of sexual/romantic relationship involvement compared to Samoan women and gynephilic men (VanderLaan & Vasey, 2012). As such, the *fa'afafine's* relatively elevated avuncular tendencies cannot be characterized as a simple by-product of their failure to form, and invest in, intimate sexual/romantic relationships, which, in turn, leaves them with more time and resources. If that were true, *fa'afafine* should exhibit reduced levels of sexual/romantic relationship involvement compared to men and women, but once again this was not the case.

It should be clear from the research described above that much of our work has focused on falsifying the Kin Selection Hypothesis for male androphilia by examining alternative explanations that might account for the *fa'afafine's* elevated avuncularity. It should be equally clear that none of the alternative explanations we have tested, to date, have been supported. Taken together, this body of work is consistent with the conclusion that elevated avuncularity by androphilic males is an adaptation that evolved via kin selection. That being said, establishing that a given trait is an adaptation involves repeatedly satisfying adaptive design criteria empirically while simultaneously ruling out alternatives (Buss, Haselton, Shackelford, Bleske, & Wakefield, 1998). Adaptive design implies complexity, economy, efficiency, reliability, precision, and functionality (Williams, 1966).

We have conducted several studies that indicate that compared to Samoan women and gynephilic men, the avuncular cognition of *fa'afafine* appears to be more adaptively designed. First, the avuncular tendencies of the *fa'afafine* are more dissociated from (i.e., covary less with) their altruistic interest in non-kin children, compared to Samoan women and gynephilic men (Vasey & VanderLaan, 2010b). Such a dissociation would allow *fa'afafine* to channel resources toward nieces and nephews in a more optimal manner, while minimizing (i.e., economical, efficient, reliable, and precise), while minimizing resources directed toward non-kin children. Second, whereas Samoan men and women show a tendency to decrease their willingness to invest in nieces and nephews when they have sexual/romantic relationship partners, the cognition of *fa'afafine* appears to protect against this tendency by maintaining a high level of willingness to invest in nieces and nephews regardless of relationship status (VanderLaan & Vasey, 2012). Third, due to the mechanics of human reproduction, individuals can always be certain that their sisters' offspring are their genetic relatives. Yet, due to the possibility of cuckoldry, individuals are necessarily less certain in the case of brothers' offspring. The elevated avuncular tendencies of *fa'afafine* are contingent on the presence of sisters, not brothers, which suggests that the avuncular cognition of *fa'afafine* is sensitive to the relative fitness benefits of investing in sisters' versus brothers' offspring (VanderLaan & Vasey, 2013).

Elevated avuncular tendencies must translate into real-world avuncular behavior if they are to have any impact on the fitness of nieces and nephews and the uncles themselves. Vasey and VanderLaan (2010c) used money given to, and received from, oldest and youngest siblings' sons and daughters as a behavioral assay of expressed kin-directed altruism. In line with the predictions of the Kin Selection Hypothesis, compared to women and gynephilic men, *fa'afafine* gave significantly more money to their youngest siblings' daughters. No other group differences were observed for money given to, or received from, nieces and/or nephews. Moreover, among women and gyephilic men, there were no correlations between the number of children parented and monetary exchanges with the niece and nephew categories examined, suggesting that childlessness cannot account for why *fa'afafine* give more money to their youngest siblings' daughters.

Test of the Kin Selection Hypothesis in Western Populations of Sex-Gender Congruent Male Androphiles

Almost no evidence in support of the Kin Selection Hypothesis has been garnered from studies conducted on sex-gender congruent ("gay") males from Western cultures. For example, Bobrow and Bailey (2001) found that sex-gender congruent androphilic males in the USA did not differ significantly from gynephilic males in terms of general familial affinity, generosity, neediness, avuncular tendencies, money received from kin, or money given to parents. Moreover, contrary to the predictions of the Kin Selection Hypothesis, they found that androphilic males gave significantly less money to their siblings, compared to gynephilic males. Likewise, using a UK sample, Rahman and Hull (2005) found no significant differences between gynephilic and sex-gender congruent androphilic men in terms of family affinity, generosity, avuncular tendencies, money received from the family, or money and gifts given to the family.

It has been suggested that the social environments that characterize Western cultures may not be representative of the context in which male androphilia evolved (Bobrow & Bailey, 2001; Vasey et al., 2007), and the relevant ethnological research indicates that this concern is valid (VanderLaan et al., 2013c). Consequently, if an altruistic androphilic male phenotype exists, such social environments may not be conducive to its development. In the absence of a social context that approximates the adaptively relevant environment (ARE) for genetic factors underlying male

androphilia, the theorized functional behavioral expression of such genetic factors is simply not manifested (for a more general discussion of this point, see Irons, 1998; see also Tooby & Cosmides, 2005).

The question thus becomes what features of Western environments might constrain the expression of elevated avuncularity in androphilic males? It has been suggested that sex-gender congruent androphilic males living in Western cultures experience greater than average familial estrangement due to homophobia (D'Augelli, Hershberger, & Pilkington, 1998) and this constrains their ability to exhibit elevated kin-directed altruism (Bobrow & Bailey, 2001). Forrester, VanderLaan, Parker, and Vasey (2011) investigated whether androphilic men would exhibit relatively higher avuncular tendencies in Canada—a relatively non-homophobic culture. Despite Canada's cultural similarity to the USA and the UK, previous authors have cautioned against characterizing all Western populations on the basis of only a few and have encouraged systematic research on differences and similarities among Western nations (Henrich, Heine, & Norenzayan, 2010). In contrast to the USA and the UK, Canadian social and political attitudes are markedly more tolerant and accepting toward homosexuality (Anderson & Fetner, 2008; Widmer, Treas, & Newcombe, 1998). Since 1981, Canada has experienced a dramatic decrease in the stigmatization of homosexuality (Anderson & Fetner, 2008), and conversely, there has been a dramatic increase in support for gay men and lesbians. For example, a 1994 poll found that 46 % of Canadians felt that homosexuality was "not wrong at all," compared to 19 % of the US citizens and 26 % of the UK citizens (Widmer et al., 1998). In 2005, Canada became the fourth nation in the world to legalize same-sex marriage. Part of this process involved the amendment of 68 federal statutes to recognize same-sex couples (e.g., old age pension, income tax, bankruptcy protection). Taken together, this information suggests that gays and lesbians in Canada enjoy more legal rights and social acceptance than almost any other nation. Hence, if the development of elevated avuncular tendencies in androphilic males is contingent on a cultural environment that is less homophobic, then Canadian androphilic men should be more likely to exhibit such tendencies. Consistent with previous studies, however, Forrester et al. (2011) found that gynephilic men and sex-gender congruent androphilic men in Canada did not differ from each other in terms of their willingness to help nieces and nephews.

Interestingly, however, Forrester et al. (2011) did find that the avuncular tendencies of Canadian androphilic men were significantly more dissociated (i.e., covaried less) from their altruistic interest in non-kin children, compared to gynephilic men and androphilic women. As discussed above, similar findings have been reported for Samoan androphilic males, and it was argued that such a cognitive dissociation would allow for allocation of resources to nieces and nephews in a more economical, efficient, reliable, and precise (i.e., adaptive) manner (Vasey & VanderLaan, 2010b). As such, although Canadian androphilic males do not express elevated avuncular tendencies (possibly because their social environment is not conducive to the development of this trait), Forrester et al.'s (2011) results are consistent with the conclusion that the avuncular cognition of Canadian androphilic males has undergone selection for enhancing indirect fitness, as posited by the Kin Selection Hypothesis.

It has also been suggested that sex-gender congruent androphilic males living in Western cultures may be less geographically connected to their kin compared to their non-Western counterparts, thus mitigating their ability to exhibit elevated kin-directed altruism (Bobrow & Bailey, 2001). Indeed, research indicates that sex-gender congruent androphilic men routinely move away from their families to live in urban environments where they can more easily achieve personal goals (Bagley & Tremblay, 1998;

Knopp, 1990). If geographic disconnect from kin constrains the expression of avuncularity by sex-gender congruent androphilic males, then releasing this constrain should, in theory, potentiate the expression of elevated avuncularity. To examine this possibility, Abild, VanderLaan, and Vasey (2014) examined whether Canadian androphilic males expressed elevated willingness to engage in altruistic activities toward nieces and nephews, compared to gynephilic men and androphilic women, when the activities in question could be executed from a distance (e.g., willingness to answer questions about dating, willingness to keep in touch via the Internet). Contrary to their prediction, when comparing groups for willingness to engage in avuncular/materteral activities that could be performed from a distance, they did not find that Canadian androphilic men exhibited significantly higher avuncular tendencies. Thus, even when Canadian androphilic males are able to execute avuncular activities from a distance, they do not express increased willingness to do so. This suggests that geographic disconnect from kin cannot, in and of itself, account for the absence of elevated avuncularity in sex-gender congruent males from Western cultures.

At the same time, however, Abild et al.'s (2014) Canadian participants expressed significantly greater willingness to engage in avuncular/materteral activities that required proximity to kin as opposed to those that could be performed from a distance. Thus, it appears that proximity to kin *is* an important facilitator of kin-directed altruism in Canada. In contrast to Canada, Samoan extended family members often live together or in closely situated dwellings (Mageo, 1998). Furthermore, given Samoa's small landmass (2,934 km^2; Lal & Fortune, 2000), kin members are likely to be less geographically dispersed from each other than in much larger Western nations such as Canada (Bagley & Tremblay, 1998; Knopp, 1990). Thus, differences in spatial proximity among kin members may be one factor contributing, at least in part, to the documented cross-cultural differences in avuncularity by Samoan and Canadian androphilic males.

Given that, in Western cultures, sex-gender congruent androphilic males often move away from their kin to live in urban environments (Bagley & Tremblay, 1998; Knopp, 1990), VanderLaan, Gothreau, Bartlett, and Vasey (2011b) suggested that the avuncular tendencies of these individuals might be expressed in a non-functional manner, namely, by directing altruism toward more accessible recipients like the children of close friends. In other words, androphilic males may interact with "social kin" (i.e., friends) as the closest possible facsimile of family who are then the recipients of avuncular-like acts rather than genetically related, but geographically distant, kin. Indeed, a number of studies have demonstrated that friends are treated like kin in some more industrialized societies (Silk, 2003; Stewart-Williams, 2007). Korchmaros and Kenny (2006) noted that proximate factors such as one's sense of emotional closeness and obligation toward another individual, rather than genetic relatedness per se, likely influence the expression of altruism. With this logic in mind, Abild, VanderLaan, and Vasey (2013) examined whether sex-gender congruent androphilic males in a Canadian sample exhibited elevated altruistic tendencies toward their friends' children compared to gynephilic men and androphilic women. Contrary to their predictions, they found that sex-gender congruent androphilic males did not exhibit elevated altruistic tendencies toward friends' children when compared to the other two groups. They did, however, find that Canadian women were more likely to treat friends' children like kin, in keeping with previous findings reported in the literature (Ackerman, Kenrick, & Schaller, 2007).

Test of the Kin Selection Hypothesis in Japanese Sex-Gender Congruent Male Androphiles

Vasey et al. (2007) suggested differences in *individualism* versus *collectivism* might account for why androphilic males in Samoa exhibit elevated avuncularity, but those in Western countries such

as the USA, the UK, and Canada do not. Individualistic cultures emphasize that people are independent of their groups and contain relatively more *idiocentric* individuals whose psychology and behavior are influenced primarily by their own beliefs and emotions rather than by input from other people. Consequently, the members of individualistic cultures tend to exhibit greater hedonism and, relatively speaking, they are more emotionally distant from the groups to which they belong. In contrast, collectivistic cultures emphasize interdependence and a merging of the self into the group. They contain more *allocentric* individuals who value input from other members of the groups to which they belong. Consequently, the members of collectivistic cultures tend to follow social norms and sacrifice personal goals for the good of the group. In addition, they exhibit high family integrity and close emotional ties with the groups to which they belong. Research demonstrates that patterns of resource distribution are influenced by whether individuals live in collectivistic or individualistic cultures (Leung, 1997; Mills & Clark, 1982). For example, in collectivistic societies, some individuals show a generosity rule with in-group members even when their contributions are clearly higher than the contribution of other members (Triandis, 2001).

The important influences that the individualistic or collectivistic dimensions of culture can have on individual psychology have been well documented (Triandis, 2001). For example, Samoans, who come from a relatively collectivistic culture, are more willing to deceive others if it involves protecting group or family concerns. In contrast, Americans, who come from a relatively individualistic culture, are more willing to deceive others if it involves protecting their personal privacy (Aune & Waters, 1994). Similarly, the more collectivistic Samoans are more likely to favor food products when they are advertised as being for consumption "when the family is at home," whereas the more individualistic New Zealanders favor those that are advertised as being for when "you are on the move" (Jaeger, 2000).

Vasey et al. (2007) hypothesized that the development of elevated avuncularity in androphilic males may be contingent on a relatively collectivistic cultural context. To test this possibility, Vasey and VanderLaan (2012) conducted research in Japan—a relatively collectivistic culture whose members tend to be allocentric (e.g., Kitayama, Markus, Matsumoto, & Norasakkunkit, 1997; Yamaguchi, 1994). Sex-gender congruent male androphilia predominates in Japan, but the idea of a "gay identity" is a relatively new concept compared to the West (McLelland, 2000). Vasey and VanderLaan (2012) found that gynephilic and sex-gender congruent androphilic Japanese men did not differ from each other in terms of their avuncular tendencies. In this regard, research on the avuncular tendencies of sex-gender congruent androphilic males in Japan who do not necessarily identify as "gay" is consistent with similar research on Western sex-gender congruent androphilic males who do identify as "gay."

Triandis (1995) proposed that collectivism could be characterized as *vertical* or *horizontal*. Vertical collectivistic cultures emphasize hierarchical organization of members, whereas horizontal collectivistic cultures emphasize equality of members. Samoa, with its *matai* (chief) system, can be characterized in terms of vertical collectivism (Duranti, 1994; Ochs, 1988; Ritchie & Ritchie, 1989; Shore, 1981). Similarly, Triandis (1995) argued that vertical collectivism is very prevalent in Japan, where citizens have a strong sense of hierarchy, which is reflected in required language forms for each type of status relationship. As such, differences in the expression of avuncularity by androphilic and gynephilic males across these two cultures appear to be unrelated to this aspect of collectivism.

Given Vasey and VanderLaan's (2012) findings from Japan, it appears that if the Kin Selection Hypothesis for male androphilia is correct, and the development of an adaptively designed avuncular male androphilic phenotype is contingent on a particular social environment, then a collectivistic cultural context is insufficient, in and of itself, for the development and expression of such a phenotype. That being said, a collectivistic cultural context might be one important facet of a suite of social factors that promote elevated avuncularity in androphilic males. The simultaneous absence of key social factors (e.g., geographic proximity) or the presence of others (e.g., trans-/homophobia) could theoretically mitigate the trait's expression even when factors thought to promote its development (i.e., collectivism) are present.

In contrast to findings from Samoa (Vasey & VanderLaan, 2010b) and Canada (Forrester et al., 2011). Vasey and VanderLaan (2012) found no evidence that Japanese androphilic males' avuncular tendencies were significantly dissociated (i.e., covaried less) from their altruistic interest in non-kin children, compared to Japanese women and gynephilic men. It is unclear why the findings from Japan differ from those obtained in Samoa and Canada. Null findings, like those observed in Japan, can be difficult to interpret and raise the question of whether these differences in findings are owing to differences in some aspects of the methodologies employed (e.g., sampling method, cultural differences in questionnaire response patterns). Alternatively, these conflicting findings might be reflective of true cultural differences. If this latter scenario is the case, then potentially relevant factors include those that systematically differ between Samoa and Canada versus Japan and also bear relevance to the development of kin-directed altruism (e.g., societal acceptance of androphilic males; Halman, Inglehart, Díez-Medrano, Luijkx, Moreno and Basáñez, 2008; Inglehart, 1990; Widmer et al., 1998).

Kin Selection and the Evolution of Male Androphilia: Concluding Remarks

Tests of the Kin Selection Hypothesis for male androphilia clearly indicate that the avuncular tendencies and behavior of androphilic males vary cross-culturally. Research has demonstrated repeatedly that transgendered male androphiles from Samoa exhibit elevated avuncular tendencies compared to women and gynephilic males (VanderLaan & Vasey, 2012; Vasey et al., 2007;

Vasey & VanderLaan, 2009, 2010a, 2010b, 2010c). In contrast, sex-gender congruent androphilic males from the USA, the UK, Canada, and Japan do not exhibit elevated avuncular tendencies (Abild et al., 2014; Bobrow & Bailey, 2001; Forrester et al., 2011; Rahman & Hull, 2005; Vasey & VanderLaan, 2012). As such, one possible factor influencing the observed cross-cultural differences relates to the manner in which male androphilia is publically expressed. Namely, elevated avuncularity by androphilic males may be contingent on whether they exhibit the transgendered form of male androphilia. To examine whether this is indeed the case, future tests of the Kin Selection Hypothesis for male androphilia will be need in other populations where transgendered male androphiles predominate.

As mentioned previously, research by VanderLaan et al. (2013c) indicates that the ancestral form of male androphilia is likely the transgendered form. Additional analyses by these authors revealed key aspects of the adaptively relevant environment (ARE) of transgendered androphilic males that likely facilitated elevated kin-directed altruism. AREs consist of those features of the environment that must be present in order for an adaptation to be functionally expressed (Irons, 1998). VanderLaan et al. (2013c) found that societies in which transgendered male androphilia predominates were more likely to show social characteristics that facilitate investment in kin, compared to non-transgendered societies. For example, relative to non-transgendered societies, transgendered societies were more likely to exhibit bilateral[3] and double descent[4] systems than patrilineal, matrilineal, and ambilineal[5]

descent systems. In addition, correlational analysis showed that as the presence of ancestral sociocultural conditions increased, so too did the presence of bilateral (and double) descent systems. Ethnologists have argued that bilateral decent systems and bilocal patterns of residence following marriage are maximally inclusive of kin because they do not bias individuals to interact with only one subset of relatives (Alvard, 2002; Ember, 1975; Kramer & Greaves, 2011). Humans have evolved, via kin selection, to preferentially allocate altruism toward close relatives (Daly, Salmon, & Wilson, 1997). Consequently, it is reasonable to deduce that these patterns of bilateral and double descent and bilocal postmarital residence would allow for more altruistic interactions with a full range of genetically related kin. Taken together, these analyses are consistent with the conclusion that bilateral descent characterized ancestral humans and that such patterns were features of ancestral societies in which male androphilia was expressed in the transgendered form.

VanderLaan et al. (2013c) also examined the acceptance of homosexuality in 27 transgendered societies for which information could be obtained. The significant majority of these societies expressed no negative reactions to same-sex sexual behavior. Overall then, the same-sex sexual orientation of transgendered males in transgendered societies appears to be socially tolerated. Such tolerance, particularly on the part of the kin of transgendered androphilic males, might be considered essential for kin selection to be deemed as a plausible contributing factor toward the persistence of male androphilia over evolutionary time. Unless transgendered androphilic males are accepted by their families, their opportunity to invest in kin is likely mitigated.

In sum, transgendered male androphilia is likely the ancestral form of male androphilia, key aspects of the transgendered androphilic male ARE (i.e., bilateral and double descent system, social tolerance of same-sex sexuality) would have facilitate elevated kin-directed altruism, and data from contemporary transgendered males indicates that they exhibit elevated avuncularity. Given all this, it seems reasonable to suggest that kin selection played some role in the evolution of male

---

[3] In bilateral descent systems, ego's mother's and father's lineages are equally important for emotional, social, spiritual, and political support, as well as for transfer of property or wealth.

[4] In double descent systems of descent, individuals receive some rights and obligations from the father's side of the family and others from the mother's side.

[5] Some sources treat ambilineal and bilateral descent systems as synonymous, but ambilineal descent systems are defined as existing when individuals have the option of choosing one of their lineages for membership.

androphilia. As such, the increased kin-directed altruism documented in Samoan *fa'afafine* is more likely to be characteristic of ancestral androphilic males, compared to the lack thereof documented in sex-gender congruent androphilic men from industrialized cultures.

The Sexually Antagonistic Gene Hypothesis and the Evolution of Male Androphilia

Sexually antagonistic selection is a form of balancing selection that occurs when genetic factors that produce fitness costs in one sex result in fitness benefits in the other sex. The Sexually Antagonistic Gene Hypothesis for male androphilia posits that genes associated with the development of androphilia result in decreased reproductive output in male carriers, but the same genes result in increased reproductive output in female carriers. For this reason, this hypothesis is routinely referred to as the Female Fecundity Hypothesis for male androphilia. Given that kin share a disproportionate number of genes in common, the female kin of male androphiles should experience, on average, greater increased reproductive output than females with no androphilic male relatives. In theory, the fitness benefits that accrue to the female relatives of male androphiles balance out the fitness costs associated with male androphilia. Consequently, sexually antagonistic selection occurs for the genes in question owing to their fitness-enhancing properties in female carriers. A by-product of this sexually antagonistic selection is that male androphilia persists in populations over evolutionary time, despite its fitness-reducing consequences. Given all this, the basic prediction that flows from the Sexual Antagonistic Gene Hypothesis is that the female relatives of androphilic males should tend to produce more offspring than those of gynephilic males.

Tests of the Sexually Antagonistic Gene Hypothesis in Western Populations of Sex-Gender Congruent Male Androphiles

To date, several studies carried out in Western populations have compared the reproductive output of the female relatives of male androphiles versus those of male gynephiles. A series of such studies has been conducted by Andrea Camperio Ciani's research group at the University of Padova in Padua, Italy. In three Western European samples (i.e., Italian, Spanish, and French), elevated reproduction was reported in the matrilineal, but not the patrilineal, aunts of male androphiles (Camperio-Ciani et al., 2004; Camperio Ciani & Pellizzari, 2012; Iemmola & Camperio Ciani, 2009). In addition, two of these studies tested for, and found, increased reproduction in the mothers of male androphiles (Camperio-Ciani et al., 2004; Iemmola & Camperio Ciani, 2009). None of the studies by Camperio Ciani's research group has documented significantly elevated offspring production in the grandmothers of androphilic men compared to those of gynephilic men.

Increases in the reproductive output of an androphilic male's mother could, theoretically, occur as a result of the fraternal birth order effect (Blanchard, 2012; Iemmola & Camperio Ciani, 2009) and not because of some true female fecundity effect that influences the production of other sibling categories (i.e., younger brothers, older and younger sisters). As such, it is important to discern whether the observed patterns of offspring production in the mothers of androphilic males reflect fraternal birth order effects, fecundity effects, or both. By comparing the offspring production of mothers with firstborn androphilic sons, to mother's with firstborn gynephilic sons, Iemmola and Camperio Ciani (2009) found that a maternal fecundity effect exists in the absence of any fraternal birth order effect for their Western European sample. However, in a large Western sample of 40,197 firstborn heterosexual men and 4,784 firstborn homosexual men, a contradictory pattern was found. The mothers of firstborn heterosexual men had significantly more offspring than those of firstborn homosexual men (Blanchard, 2012).

In a British sample of Caucasian men, elevated reproduction was also documented among the maternal, but not the patrilineal, aunts of androphilic men (Rahman et al., 2008). Other categories of female kin were examined (i.e., mothers, grandparents), but no significant group differences were observed. In diametric opposition to the predictions of the Sexually Antagonistic Gene Hypothesis, the mothers, paternal aunts, and possibly the maternal and paternal grandmothers of non-Caucasian gynephilic men exhibited significantly higher offspring production than those of non-Caucasian androphilic men. Data pertaining to grandmothers and grandfathers was lumped together in this study as the category "grandparents" and, as such, it is not possible to speak definitively about the unique reproductive output of grandmothers versus grandfathers. Offspring production by maternal aunts did not differ between the groups. In an attempt to account for these unusual results, LeVay (2010) has suggested that Rahman et al.'s (2008) non-Caucasian sample might have been primarily composed of British immigrants who belong to larger families, whose definition of "family" is more inclusive, and who are less accepting and open about homosexuality. All of these factors would have contributed to a less than ideal sample, thereby biasing Rahman et al.'s (2008) results and contributing to the observed racial differences.

Given that this particular group of studies has documented elevated reproduction in maternal-line female relatives, but not in paternal-line ones, Camperio Ciani and his colleagues have argued that the genetic factors influencing the development of male androphilia are located on the X chromosome (Camperio-Ciani et al., 2004; Camperio Ciani & Pellizzari, 2012; Iemmola & Camperio Ciani, 2009). However, similar matrilineal effects have not been found with other samples drawn from Western populations. For example, in one British study of male sexual orientation and family size, androphilic males were shown to have significantly more aunts, uncles, and cousins in the paternal, but not maternal, line (King et al., 2005). This suggests that elevated offspring production characterizes the paternal grandmothers and possibly the paternal aunts of androphilic males, but not their maternal counterparts. Unfortunately, data pertaining to offspring of paternal aunts and paternal uncles ("paternal cousins") was lumped together in this study and, as such, the results cannot be used to speak definitively about the unique reproductive output of aunts versus uncles.

In a study conducted in the USA, elevated reproduction was documented among mothers and paternal grandmothers of androphilic males, compared to those of gynephilic males (Schwartz et al., 2010). The same study documented no group differences in the reproductive output of maternal grandmothers. Further, androphilic and gynephilic males did not differ for number of maternal or paternal cousins, which suggests no group differences in the reproductive output of maternal and paternal aunts. Unfortunately, once again, data pertaining to aunts and uncles was lumped together in this study and, as such, it is not possible to speak definitively about the unique reproductive output of aunts versus uncles on their own.

One important limitation of this literature is its focus on samples drawn from Western European and North American populations. Such populations exhibit relatively low fertility (Central Intelligence Agency, 2012), which is often due to "stopping rules" associated with reproduction. Stopping rules refer to the cessation of reproduction once a certain number of children are produced or once at least one child of each sex is produced. Sampling from low fertility populations that employ stopping rules can obscure natural (i.e., evolved) reproductive output (Blanchard & Lippa, 2007; Zucker, Blanchard, Kim, Pae, & Lee, 2007). The susceptibility of low fertility populations to producing anomalous reproductive patterns raises the possibility that some subset, or possibly all, of the aforementioned tests of the Sexually Antagonistic Gene Hypothesis in Western populations do not provide clear indications of the precise categories of female kin that exhibit elevated reproductive output. Hence, examining the reproductive output of androphilic and gynephilic males' kin in a high fertility population in which women are more likely to be reproducing closer to their maximum capacities could provide valuable insight.

Tests of the Sexually Antagonistic Gene Hypothesis in Samoan Transgendered Male Androphiles

To date, tests of the Sexually Antagonistic Gene Hypothesis have been conducted in one nonindustrialized, non-Western nation: Samoa. Samoa represents a more optimal location in which to test the Sexually Antagonistic Gene Hypothesis because the population is characterized by higher fertility compared to Western European and North American populations (Central Intelligence Agency, 2012). In addition, as outlined above, the purported ancestral form of male androphilia—the transgendered form—predominates in Samoa (VanderLaan et al., 2013c).

Three studies have been conducted in Samoa by our research group that furnish data pertaining to the Sexually Antagonistic Gene Hypothesis. Vasey and VanderLaan (2007) demonstrated that the mothers of *fa'afafine* produce more offspring than those of gynephilic men. This finding was replicated by VanderLaan and Vasey (2011). More recently, VanderLaan et al. (2012) demonstrated that *fa'afafine's* maternal and paternal grandmothers exhibit elevated offspring production, but their maternal or paternal aunts do not.

The main strength of these Samoan studies is that they examine reproductive output among the female relatives of androphilic and gynephilic males in a population that has higher fertility compared to the Western samples that have been examined to date. Consequently, anomalous reproductive patterns should be less likely to occur in the Samoan population. If the Samoan population is relatively free of susceptibility to anomalous reproductive patterns compared to Western populations, then the study by VanderLaan et al. (2012) indicates that male androphilia is actually associated with elevated reproductive output by female kin in both the maternal and paternal lines. Moreover, the study by VanderLaan and Vasey (2011) demonstrated that a true maternal fecundity effect exists independent of any coexisting fraternal birth order effect.

The Sexually Antagonistic Gene Hypothesis and the Evolution of Male Androphilia: Concluding Remarks

The studies reviewed above are largely consistent with the basic prediction of the Sexually Antagonistic Gene Hypothesis. Namely, the female kin of male androphiles exhibited elevated offspring production compared to the female kin of male gynephiles. However, the exact categories of female kin that demonstrate elevated offspring production remain unclear. Identifying the precise categories of female kin that exhibit elevated offspring production is necessary for proper tests of the Sexually Antagonistic Gene Hypothesis. Elevated reproduction by the mothers and the maternal and paternal grandmothers of androphilic males does not provide definitive support for the Sexually Antagonistic Gene Hypothesis because reproduction by these categories of female kin is naturally confounded with that of fathers and grandfathers, all of whom share genes with androphilic and gynephilic male probands.

Elevated reproductive output by androphilic males' maternal aunts, paternal aunts, or both would provide the clearest support for the Sexually Antagonistic Gene Hypothesis because androphilic and gynephilic male probands do not share genes with their aunts' male reproductive partners. All this being said, the existing research reviewed above indicates that the only categories of androphilic male relatives to show elevated reproduction were those comprised partially (i.e., reproduction of aunts and uncles combined) or entirely of female kin. The cumulative weight of this evidence suggests that the Sexual Antagonistic Gene Hypothesis is still a tenable explanation for the evolution of male androphilia.

Identifying whether elevated female reproduction is most likely inherent to both the maternal and paternal lines of androphilic males has important implications regarding the proximate mechanism(s) underlying this pattern. As outlined above, Camperio Ciani's research group have argued on the basis of data derived from various Western European samples that elevated reproductive output is unique to maternal-line female relatives and that such a pattern is indicative of sexually antagonistic genes located on the X-chromosome (Camperio-Ciani et al., 2004; Camperio Ciani & Pellizzari, 2012; Iemmola & Camperio Ciani, 2009; Rahman et al., 2008). However, as our Samoan research and other studies have shown, elevated reproduction has been documented among the patrilineal female kin of androphilic males as well (King et al., 2005; Schwartz et al., 2010; VanderLaan et al., 2012).

Based on these findings, it seems reasonable to argue that X-linked sexual antagonism might not be the form of selection responsible for the evolution of male androphilia. One might instead argue that sexually antagonistic genetic factors are present on the autosomal chromosomes because androphilic males share genetic factors on these chromosomes with both paternal and maternal relatives. Indeed, autosomal linkage of sexually antagonistic genetic factors favoring the evolution of male androphilia is plausible given previously reported mathematical models (Gavrilets & Rice, 2006).

The Balanced Polymorphism Hypothesis and the Evolution of Male Androphilia

The Balanced Polymorphism Hypothesis for male androphilia has been most fully articulated by Miller (2000).[6] This hypothesis takes as its

starting point the assumption that male androphilia is not an isolated trait, but rather is part of a larger package of gender-atypical traits. Ample empirical evidence exists to support this assumption (Bailey & Zucker, 1995; Bartlett & Vasey, 2006; Cardoso, 2005, 2009; Lippa, 2005; VanderLaan et al., 2011a; Vasey & Bartlett, 2007; Whitam, 1983; Zucker et al., 1996). Miller (2000) proposed that multiple genes influence the development of male androphilia and these genes shift male brain development in a female-typical direction. Males who inherit a critical number of these genes become androphilic. Below this critical threshold, males who inherit some of these genes are gynephilic, but are feminized in terms of certain personality traits, which render then more sensitive, empathetic, tender, and kind. These personality traits, in turn, are thought to render gynephilic males more attractive as mates. Indeed, ample empirical evidence exists to support this assumption (e.g., Barclay, 2010; Buss et al., 1990; Buss & Shakelford, 2008; Phillips, Barnard, Ferguson, & Reader, 2008; Tessman, 1995). Owing to their increased attractiveness, Miller (2000) argues that these males obtain more female sexual partners and father more children compared to gynephilic males who have no androphilic male relatives. These males are also hypothesized to be better fathers compared to fathers with no androphilic male relatives. The increased reproductive success experienced by the heterosexual male relatives of androphilic males favors selection for the feminizing genes in question. As such, positive selection for these genes occurs despite the reproductive costs associated with male androphilia itself.

A number of predictions flow from the Balanced Polymorphism Hypothesis. First, androphilic men are more likely to be feminine than masculine. Second, gynephilic males should be more feminine if they have androphilic male relatives, compared to those who do not. Third, gynephilic males should be more attractive if they have androphilic male relatives, compared to those who do not. Fourth, gynephilic males should obtain more female sexual partners if they have androphilic male relatives, compared to those who do not. Fifth, gynephilic males should father more children

---

[6] This hypothesis is sometimes referred to as the "Overdominance Hypothesis" for male androphilia.

if they have androphilic male relatives, compared to those who do not. Sixth, gynephilic males should be better fathers if they have androphilic male relatives, compared to those that do not.

Tests of the Balanced Polymorphism Hypothesis

To date, two studies have been conducted with the explicit goal of testing the Balanced Polymorphism Hypothesis and these have utilized samples of sex-gender congruent males from Western populations. Using a community-based sample of Australian twins, Zietsch et al. (2008) examined whether gynephilic males with an androphilic male co-twin had more opposite sex sexual partners, compared to gynephilic males with no androphilic male co-twin. Contrary to the fourth prediction of the Balanced Polymorphism Hypothesis as stated above, no significant group differences were found.

Using a Finnish sample, Santilla, Högbacka, Jern, Johansson, Varjonen, Witting et al. (2009) compared three groups: (1) gynephilic males with gynephilic brothers, (2) gynephilic males with androphilic monozygotic co-twins ($r_g = 1.00$), and (3) gynephilic males with androphilic brothers ($r_g = 0.50$; e.g., dizygotic twins, sibling-sibling pairs). Based on the second prediction of the Balanced Polymorphism Hypothesis as stated above, one would predict that gynephilic males with androphilic brothers would score lower on measures of psychopathic traits (i.e., sensation seeking, tendency toward ignoring social norms and laws) and sexual aggression/coercion, compared to gynephilic males with no androphilic brothers. However, Santilla et al. (2009) found no such group differences. Likewise, contrary to the fourth prediction of the Balanced Polymorphism Hypothesis as stated above, no relevant group differences were found with respect to estimated number of sexual partners over the last year, lifetime number of one-night stands, or experience with vaginal intercourse. In addition to these sociosexual variables, Santilla et al. (2009) found that there were no group differences in age of first intercourse. Finally, contrary to the fifth prediction of the Balanced Polymorphism Hypothesis as stated above, there were no group differences in the number of children produced.

A number of studies exist that have not been conducted with the explicit goal of testing the Balanced Polymorphism Hypothesis but which nonetheless furnish relevant data because they examined offspring production in the uncles of androphilic and gynephilic males. Using an Italian sample, Camperio-Ciani et al. (2004) found that the maternal and paternal uncles of androphilic males did not differ from those of gynephilic males in terms of their offspring production. Iemmola and Camperio Ciani (2009) replicated these results for maternal uncles, but found, in contrast to theoretical predictions, that the paternal uncles of gynephilic males had significantly more children than those of male androphiles. Using a British sample composed of Caucasians, Rahman et al. (2008) found no differences in offspring production between the maternal or paternal uncles of gynephilic versus androphilic males. Likewise, the authors found no significant group differences in offspring production for maternal uncles when a British sample of non-Caucasian gynephilic and androphilic males was employed. They did, however, find that paternal uncles of non-Caucasian gynephilic males had significantly more children than those of androphilic males in contrast to theoretical predictions (Rahman et al., 2008).

To date, one study relevant to testing the Balanced Polymorphism Hypothesis has been conducted in a population where transgendered male androphilia predominates. VanderLaan et al. (2012) found that the maternal and paternal uncles of Samoan *fa'afafine* did not differ from those of Samoan gynephilic males in terms of their offspring production. Taken together, none of the studies that have looked at the offspring production of the uncles of androphilic males have furnished support for the Balanced Polymorphism Hypothesis.

General Concluding Remarks

Male androphilia has a genetic component, yet most male androphiles reproduce little, if at all. A heritable trait that lowers reproductive output should be selected against, but archaeological evidence suggests that male-male sexual behavior has persisted for millennia. For these reasons, male androphilia represents one of the outstanding paradoxes of evolutionary psychology.

In recent years, progress has finally been made toward understanding how male androphilia persists over evolutionary time. Research indicates that the ancestral form of male androphilia was likely to be the transgendered form. No support for the Kin Selection Hypothesis has been garnered from research conducted in Western and non-Western populations on sex-gender congruent male androphiles. However, research has repeatedly furnished support for the Kin Selection Hypothesis in Samoa where transgendered male androphiles (fa'afafine) exhibit elevated avuncular tendencies and behavior compared to women and gynephilic men. Research on Samoan fa'afafine has also furnished evidence that their avuncular cognition exhibits hallmarks of adaptive design.

Tests of the Sexually Antagonistic Gene Hypothesis have been conducted in diverse populations of transgendered and sex-gender congruent male androphiles. Overall, this research indicates that the female kin of male androphiles produce more offspring than those of male gynephiles. However, the precise categories of female kin that exhibit elevated offspring production remain unclear. Further, tests to determine whether a true maternal fecundity effect exists independent of any coexisting fraternal birth order effect have been inconsistent. No support has been garnered for the Balanced Polymorphism Hypothesis.

In light of these results, it is possible that male androphilia could be conceptualized as a by-product of an adaptation (sensu Buss et al., 1998; Gould & Vrba, 1982) for increased female fecundity that results from sexually antagonistic selection. By-products of adaptations are characteristics that evolve in association with particular adaptations because they happen to be coupled with those adaptations (Buss et al., 1998). Although they may have some beneficial effect on fitness, they did not originally evolve to solve adaptive problems, and thus, at their point of origin they did not have an evolved fitness-enhancing function, nor were they products of natural selection. In such a situation, increased avuncularity among male androphiles could potentially facilitate reproduction by female kin and thereby have positive "effects" on the genetic factors for both increased fecundity in females and, by extension, its conjectured by-product, male androphilia. Williams (1966) invoked the term "effect" to designate the fortuitous operation of a useful characteristic not built by selection for its current role.

Humans have evolved, via kin selection, to preferentially allocate altruism toward close relatives (e.g., Daly et al., 1997). Consequently, kin nepotism should characterize all individuals, regardless of their sex, sexual orientation, or gender identity. However, markedly elevated avuncularity, such as that observed among fa'afafine, might result in distinct fitness advantages that could form a unique basis on which kin selection might act. If so, then cognitive underpinnings mediating avuncularity in male androphiles may have subsequently undergone secondary adaptive modification. Such a conclusion is consistent with our findings that the avuncular cognition of androphilic males in some populations exhibits special design features (Forrester et al., 2011; VanderLaan & Vasey, 2012; Vasey & VanderLaan, 2010b).

Acknowledgments We thank Resitara Apa, Nancy Bartlett, Gardenia Elisaia, Eiji Enomoto, Vaosa Epa, Vaasatia Poloma Komiti, Anita Latai, Sarah Faletoese Su'a, Vester Fido Collins, Liulauulu Faaleolea Ah Fook, Tyrone Laurenson, Gaualofa Matalavea, Chiji Masafumi, Avau Memea, Kiyoshige Murata, Nella Tavita-Levy, Palanitina Toelupe, Trisha Tuiloma, Avalogo Togi A. Tunupopo, Ayumi and Yoshiko Sawada, Hideki Shiraume, Takashi Yanai, Ryoko Yoshikawa, the Kuka family of Savai'i, the Enomoto family of Arashiyama, the Sakami family of Tokyo, the Samoan AIDS Foundation, the National University of Samoa, the Samoan Ministry of Health, and the Government of Samoa. We are grateful to all of the individuals who agreed to participate in our studies. We extend special thanks to Alatina Ioelu. Our research on the evolution of male androphilia has taken place over the past decade and has been supported by the University of

Lethbridge and a variety of funding agencies. PLV received funding from an Alberta Provincial Government S.T.E.P. Award, an Alberta Innovates Health Solutions (AIHS) Sustainability Fund Grant, a Canadian Institutes of Health Research (CIHR) Catalyst Grant in Methods and Measures for Gender, Sex, and Health, three Natural Sciences and Engineering Research Council (NSERC) of Canada Grants, and a Social Sciences and Humanities Research Council of Canada (SSHRC) Grant. DPV received funding from an NSERC of Canada Graduate Scholarship-D3, the Sigma Xi Scientific Research Society Grants-in-Aid of Research, a Ralph Steinhauer Award of Distinction, an American Psychological Foundation Henry David Travel Grant, and a Sexual Medicine Society of North America Postdoctoral Fellowship Stipend.

References

Abild, M., VanderLaan, D. P., & Vasey, P. L. (2013). No evidence for treating friends' children like kin in Canadian androphilic men. *Journal of Sex Research, 50*, 697–703.

Abild, M., VanderLaan, D. P., & Vasey, P. L. (2014). Does proximity influence the expression of avuncular tendencies in Canadian androphilic males? *Journal of Cognition and Culture* (in press).

Ackerman, J. M., Kenrick, D. T., & Schaller, M. (2007). Is friendship akin to kinship? *Evolution and Human Behavior, 28*, 365–374.

Alvard, M. S. (2002). Carcass ownership and meat distributions by big game hunters. *Research in Economic Anthropology, 21*, 99–131.

Anderson, R., & Fetner, T. (2008). Cohort differences in tolerance of homosexuality: Attitudinal changes in Canada and the United States 1981–2000. *Public Opinion Quarterly, 72*, 311–330.

Aune, R. K., & Waters, L. (1994). Cultural differences in deception: Motivations to deceive in Samoans and North Americans. *International Journal of Intercultural Relations, 18*, 159–172.

Bagley, C., & Tremblay, P. (1998). On the prevalence of homosexuality and bisexuality, in a random community survey of 750 men aged 18 to 27. *Journal of Homosexuality, 36*(2), 1–18.

Bailey, J. M. (2003). *The man who would be queen: The science of gender-bending and transsexualism.* Washington, DC: Joseph Henry Press.

Bailey, J. M., Dunne, M. P., & Martin, N. G. (2000). Genetic and environmental influences on sexual orientation and its correlates in an Australian twin sample. *Journal of Personality and Social Psychology, 78*, 524–536.

Bailey, J. M., & Zucker, K. J. (1995). Childhood sex-typed behavior and sexual orientation: A conceptual analysis and quantitative review. *Developmental Psychology, 31*, 43–55.

Barclay, P. (2010). Altruism as a courtship display: Some effects of third-party generosity on audience perceptions. *British Journal of Psychology, 101*, 123–135.

Bartlett, N. H., & Vasey, P. L. (2006). A retrospective study of childhood gender-atypical behavior in Samoan *fa'afafine. Archives of Sexual Behavior, 35*, 559–566.

Berling, T. (2001). *Sissyphobia: Gay men and effeminate behavior.* Philadelphia: Harrington Park Press.

Binford, L. R. (2001). *Constructing frames of references: An analytical method for archaeological theory building using hunter-gatherer and environmental data sets.* Berkley, CA: University of California.

Blanchard, R. (2004). Quantitative and theoretical analyses of the relation between older brothers and homosexuality in men. *Journal of Theoretical Biology, 230*, 173–187.

Blanchard, R. (2012). Fertility in the mothers of firstborn homosexual and heterosexual men. *Archives of Sexual Behavior, 41*, 551–556.

Blanchard, R., & Lippa, R. A. (2007). Birth order, sibling sex ratio, handedness, and sexual orientation of male and female participants in a BBC Internet research project. *Archives of Sexual Behavior, 36*, 163–176.

Bobrow, D., & Bailey, J. M. (2001). Is male homosexuality maintained via kin selection? *Evolution and Human Behavior, 22*, 361–368.

Bogaert, A. F., & Skorska, M. (2011). Sexual orientation, fraternal birth order, and the maternal immune hypothesis: A review. *Frontiers in Neuroendrocrinology, 32*, 247–254.

Buss, D. M., Abbott, M., Angleitner, A., Asherian, A., Biaggio, A., & Blanco-Villasenor, A. (1990). International preferences in selecting mates: A study of 37 cultures. *Journal of Cross-Cultural Psychology, 21*, 5–47.

Buss, D. M., Haselton, M. G., Shackelford, T. K., Bleske, A. L., & Wakefield, J. C. (1998). Adaptations, exaptations, and spandrels. *American Psychologist, 53*, 533–548.

Buss, D. M., & Shakelford, T. K. (2008). Attractive women want it all: Good genes, economic investment, parenting proclivities, and emotional commitment. *Evolutionary Psychology, 6*, 134–146.

Camperio-Ciani, A., Corna, F., & Capiluppi, C. (2004). Evidence for maternally inherited factors favoring male homosexuality and promoting female fecundity. *Proceedings of the Royal Society of London B, 271*, 2217–2221.

Camperio Ciani, A., & Pellizzari, E. (2012). Fecundity of paternal and maternal non-parental female relatives of homosexual and heterosexual men. *PLoS One, 7*(12), e51088.

Cantor, J. M., Blanchard, R., Paterson, A. D., & Bogaert, A. F. (2002). How many gay men owe their sexual orientation to fraternal birth order? *Archives of Sexual Behavior, 31*, 63–71.

Cardoso, F. L. (2005). Cultural universals and differences in male homosexuality: The case of a Brazilian fishing village. *Archives of Sexual Behavior, 34*, 103–109.

Cardoso, F. L. (2009). Recalled sex-typed behavior in childhood and sports preferences in adulthood of heterosexual, bisexual, and homosexual men from Brazil, Turkey, and Thailand. *Archives of Sexual Behavior, 38*, 726–736.

Central Intelligence Agency. (2012). *The world factbook.* Retrieved November 31, 2012, from https://www.cia.gov/library/publications/the-worldfactbook/rankorder/2127rank.html

Crapo, R. H. (1995). Factors in the cross-cultural patterning of male homosexuality: A reappraisal of the literature. *Cross-Cultural Research, 29*, 178–202.

D'Augelli, A. R., Hershberger, S. L., & Pilkington, N. W. (1998). Lesbian, gay and bisexual youth and their families: Disclosure of sexual orientation and its consequences. *American Journal of Orthopsychiatry, 68*, 361–371.

Daly, M., Salmon, C., & Wilson, M. (1997). Kinship: The conceptual hole in psychological studies of social cognition and close relationships. In J. A. Simpson & D. Kenrick (Eds.), *Evolutionary social psychology* (pp. 265–296). Mahwah, NJ: Erlbaum.

Diamond, L. M. (2006). The evolution of plasticity in female-female desire. *Journal of Psychology and Human Sexuality, 18*(4), 245–274.

Dixson, A. (2010). Homosexual behaviour in primates. In A. Polani (Ed.), *Animal homosexuality: A biosocial perspective* (pp. 381–400). Cambridge, England: Cambridge University Press.

Duranti, A. (1994). *From grammar to politics: Linguistic anthropology in a Western Samoan village.* Berkeley, CA: University of California Press.

Ember, C. R. (1975). Residential variation in hunter-gatherers. *Cross-Cultural Research, 10*, 199–227.

Forrester, D. L., VanderLaan, D. P., Parker, J., & Vasey, P. L. (2011). Male sexual orientation and avuncularity in Canada: Implications for the kin selection hypothesis. *Journal of Culture and Cognition, 11*, 339–352.

Fruth, B., & Hohmann, G. (2006). Social grease for females? Same-sex genital contacts in wild bonobos. In V. Sommer & P. L. Vasey (Eds.), *Homosexual behavior in animals: An evolutionary perspective* (pp. 294–315). Cambridge, England: Cambridge University Press.

Gavrilets, S., & Rice, W. R. (2006). Genetic models of homosexuality: Generating testable predictions. *Proceedings of the Royal Society of London B, 273*, 3031–3038.

Gorer, G. (1966). *The danger of equality.* London: Cresset.

Gould, S. J., & Vrba, E. S. (1982). Exaptation—A missing term in the science of form. *Paleobiology, 8*, 4–15.

Halman, L., Inglehart, R., Díez-Medrano, J., Luijkx, R., Moreno, A., & Basáñez, M. (2008). *Changing values and beliefs in 85 countries: Trends from the values surveys from 1981 to 2004.* Leiden: Brill.

Hamilton, W. D. (1963). The evolution of altruistic behavior. *American Naturalist, 97*, 354–356.

Harrington, J. P. (1942). Culture element distributions 19: Central California coast. *Anthropological Records, 7*(1), 1–46.

Henrich, J., Heine, S. J., & Norenzayan, A. (2010). The weirdest people in the world? *Behavioral and Brain Sciences, 33*, 61–135.

Herdt, G. (1997). *Same sex different cultures.* Boulder, CO: Westview Press.

Hill, K. R., Walker, R. S., Bozicevic, M., Eder, J., Headland, T., Hewlett, B., et al. (2011). Co-residence patterns in hunter-gatherer societies show unique human social structure. *Science, 331*, 1286–1289.

Hollimon, S. E. (1997). The third gender in California: Two-spirit undertakers among the Chumash, their neighbours. In C. Claassen & R. A. Joyce (Eds.), *Women in prehistory: North America and Mesoamerica* (pp. 173–188). Philadelphia: University of Pennsylvania Press.

Iemmola, F., & Camperio Ciani, A. (2009). New evidence of genetic factors influencing sexual orientation in men: Female fecundity increase in the maternal line. *Archives of Sexual Behavior, 38*, 393–399.

Inglehart, R. (1990). *Culture shift in advanced industrial society.* Princeton, NJ: Princeton University Press.

Irons, W. (1998). Adaptively relevant environments versus the environment of evolutionary adaptiveness. *Evolutionary Anthropology, 6*, 194–204.

Jaeger, S. R. (2000). Uncovering cultural differences in choice behaviour between Samoan and New Zealand consumers: A case study with apples. *Food Quality and Preference, 11*, 405–417.

Johnson, M., Jackson, P., & Herdt, G. (2000). Critical regionalities and the study of gender and sexual diversity in South East and East Asia. *Culture, Health and Sexuality, 2*, 361–375.

Kendler, K. S., Thornton, L. M., Gilman, S. E., & Kessler, R. C. (2000). Sexual orientation in a U.S. national sample of twin and nontwin sibling pairs. *American Journal of Psychiatry, 157*, 1843–1846.

King, M. D., Green, J., Osborn, D. P. J., Arkell, J., Hetherton, J., & Pereira, E. (2005). Family size in white gay and heterosexual men. *Archives of Sexual Behavior, 34*, 117–122.

Kitayama, S., Markus, H. R., Matsumoto, H., & Norasakkunkit, V. (1997). Individual and collective processes in the construction of the self: Self-enhancement in the United States and self-criticism in Japan. *Journal of Personality and Social Psychology, 72*, 1245–1267.

Knopp, L. (1990). Some theoretical implications of gay involvement in an urban land market. *Political Geography Quarterly, 9*(4), 337–352.

Knüsel, C. J., & Ripley, K. M. (2000). The man-woman or 'berdache' in Anglo-Saxon England and Post-Roman Europe. In W. Frazer & A. Tyrrel (Eds.), *Social identity in early medieval Britain* (pp. 157–191). Leicester: Leicester University Press.

Korchmaros, J. D., & Kenny, D. A. (2006). An evolutionary and close-relationship model of helping. *Journal of Social and Personal Relationships, 23*, 21–43.

Kramer, K. L., & Greaves, R. D. (2011). Postmarital residence and bilateral kin associations among hunter-gatherers: Pumé foragers living in the best of both worlds. *Human Nature, 22*, 41–63.

Lal, B. V., & Fortune, K. (2000). *Pacific islands: An encyclopedia*. Honolulu: University of Hawaii Press.

Långström, N., Rahman, Q., Carlström, E., & Lichtenstein, P. (2010). Genetic and environmental effects on same-sex sexual behavior: A population study of twins in Sweden. *Archives of Sexual Behavior, 39*, 75–80.

Larco Hoyle, R. (1998). *Arte erotico en el antigue Peru*. Lima: Museo Arqueologico Rafael Larco Herrera.

Leung, K. (1997). Negotiation and reward allocation across cultures. In P. C. Earley & M. Erez (Eds.), *New perspectives on international industrial and organizational psychology* (pp. 640–675). San Francisco: Lexington Press.

LeVay, S. (2010). *Gay, straight and the reasons why: The science of sexual orientation*. Oxford: Oxford University Press.

Lippa, R. A. (2005). *Gender, nature, nurture* (2nd ed.). Mahwah, NJ: Erlbaum.

Mageo, J. M. (1998). *Theorizing self in Samoa: Emotions, genders and sexualities*. Ann Arbor, MI: University of Michigan Press.

Marlowe, F. W. (2005). Hunters-gatherers and human evolution. *Evolutionary Anthropology, 14*, 54–67.

McBrearty, S., & Brooks, A. S. (2000). The revolution that wasn't: A new interpretation of the origins of modern human behavior. *Journal of Human Evolution, 39*, 453–563.

McLelland, M. J. (2000). *Male homosexuality in modern Japan: Cultural myths and social realities*. London: RoutledgeCurzon.

Miller, E. M. (2000). Homosexuality, birth order, and evolution: Toward and equilibrium reproductive economics of homosexuality. *Archives of Sexual Behavior, 29*, 1–34.

Mills, J., & Clark, M. S. (1982). Exchange and communal relationships. In L. Wheeler (Ed.), *Review of personality and social psychology* (Vol. 3, pp. 121–144). Beverly Hills, CA: Sage.

Murray, S. O. (2000). *Homosexualities*. Chicago: The University of Chicago Press.

Namaste, V. (2000). *Invisible lives: The erasure of transsexual and transgendered people*. Chicago: University of Chicago Press.

Nanda, S. (1999). *Gender diversity: Crosscultural variations*. Long Grove, IL: Waveland Press.

Nash, G. (2001). The subversive male: Homosexual and bestial images on European Mesolithic rock art. In L. Bevan (Ed.), *Indecent exposure: Sexuality, society and the archaeological record* (pp. 43–55). Glasgow: Cruithne Press.

Ochs, E. (1988). *Culture and language development: Language acquisition and language socialization in a Samoan village*. Cambridge: Cambridge University Press.

Phillips, T., Barnard, C., Ferguson, E., & Reader, T. (2008). Do humans prefer altruistic mates? Testing a link between sexual selection and altruism toward nonrelatives. *British Journal of Psychology, 99*, 555–572.

Prine, E. (2000). Searching for third genders: Toward a prehistory of domestic space in Middle Missouri villages. In R. A. Schmidt & B. L. Voss (Eds.), *Archaeologies of sexuality* (pp. 197–219). London: Routledge.

Rahman, Q., Collins, A., Morrison, M., Orrells, J. C., Cadinouche, K., Greenfield, S., et al. (2008). Maternal inheritance and familial fecundity factors in male homosexuality. *Archives of Sexual Behavior, 37*, 962–969.

Rahman, Q., & Hull, M. S. (2005). An empirical test of the kin selection hypothesis for male homosexuality. *Archives of Sexual Behavior, 34*, 461–467.

Rieger, G., & Savin-Williams, R. C. (2012). Gender nonconformity, sexual orientation, and psychological well-being. *Archives of Sexual Behavior, 41*, 611–621.

Ritchie, J., & Ritchie, J. E. (1989). Socialization and character development. In A. Howard & R. Brodsky (Eds.), *Developments in Polynesian ethnology* (pp. 95–135). Honolulu, HI: University of Hawai'i Press.

Ruse, M. (1982). Are there gay genes? Sociobiology and homosexuality. *Journal of Homosexuality, 6*, 5–34.

Sanderson, S. K., & Roberts, W. W. (2008). The evolutionary forms of the religious life: A cross-cultural, quantitative analysis. *American Anthropologist, 110*, 454–466.

Santilla, P., Högbacka, A.-L., Jern, P., Johansson, A., Varjonen, M., Witting, K., et al. (2009). Testing Miller's theory of alleles preventing androgenization as an evolutionary explanation for the genetic predisposition for male homosexuality. *Evolution and Human Behavior, 30*, 58–65.

Schwartz, G., Kim, R. M., Kolundziji, A. B., Rieger, G., & Sanders, A. R. (2010). Biodemographic and physical correlates of sexual orientation in men. *Archives of Sexual Behavior, 39*, 93–109.

Seil, D. (1996). Transsexuals: The boundaries of sexual identity and gender. In R. P. Cabaj & T. S. Stein (Eds.), *Textbook of homosexuality and mental health* (pp. 743–762). Washington, DC: American Psychiatric Press.

Shear, K., Jin, R., Ruscio, A. M., Walters, E. E., & Kessler, R. C. (2006). Prevalence and correlates of estimated

DSM-IV child and adult separation anxiety disorder in the national comorbidity survey replication. *American Journal of Psychiatry, 163*, 1074–1083.

Shore, B. (1981). Sexuality and gender in Samoa. In S. Ornery & H. Whitehead (Eds.), *Sexual meanings* (pp. 192–215). Cambridge: Cambridge University Press.

Silk, J. B. (2003). Cooperation without counting: The puzzle of friendship. In P. Hammerstein (Ed.), *Genetic and cultural evolution of cooperation* (pp. 37–54). Cambridge, MA: MIT Press.

Smith, A. B. (1999). Archaeology and the evolution of hunter-gatherers. In R. B. Lee & R. Daly (Eds.), *The Cambridge encyclopedia of hunters and gatherers* (pp. 384–390). Cambridge, England: Cambridge University Press.

Smith, A. M., Rissel, C. E., Richters, J., Grulich, A. E., & de Visser, R. O. (2003). Sex in Australia: Sexual identity, sexual attraction, and sexual experience among a representative sample of adults. *Australian and New Zealand Journal of Public Health, 27*, 138–145.

Stewart-Williams, S. (2007). Altruism among kin vs. nonkin: Effects of cost of help and reciprocal exchange. *Evolution and Human Behavior, 28*, 193–198.

Tessman, I. (1995). Human altruism as a courtship display. *Oikos, 74*, 157–158.

Tooby, J., & Cosmides, L. (2005). Conceptual foundations of evolutionary psychology. In D. M. Buss (Ed.), *The handbook of evolutionary psychology* (pp. 5–67). Hoboken, NJ: Wiley.

Triandis, H. C. (1995). *Individualism and collectivism.* Boulder, CO: Westview Press.

Triandis, H. C. (2001). Individualism and collectivism: Past, present, future. In D. Matsumoto (Ed.), *The handbook of culture and psychology* (pp. 35–50). Oxford: Oxford University Press.

VanderLaan, D. P., Forrester, D. L., Petterson, L. J., & Vasey, P. L. (2013a). Offspring production among the extended relatives of Samoan men and *fa'afafine. PLoS One, 7*(4), e36088.

VanderLaan, D. P., Forrester, D. L., Petterson, L. J., & Vasey, P. L. (2013a). The prevalence of *fa'afafine* relatives among Samoan men and *fa'afafine. Archives of Sexual Behavior, 42*, 353–359.

VanderLaan, D. P., Gothreau, L., Bartlett, N. H., & Vasey, P. L. (2011a). Recalled separation anxiety and gender atypicality in childhood: A study of Canadian heterosexual and homosexual men and women. *Archives of Sexual Behavior, 40*, 1233–1240.

VanderLaan, D. P., Gothreau, L., Bartlett, N. H., & Vasey, P. L. (2011b). Separation anxiety in feminine boys: Pathological or prosocial? *Journal of Gay and Lesbian Mental Health, 15*, 1–16.

VanderLaan, D. P., Ren, Z., & Vasey, P. L. (2013c). Male androphilia in the ancestral environment: An ethnological analysis. *Human Nature, 24*, 375–401. doi:10.1007/s12110-013-9182-z.

VanderLaan, D. P., & Vasey, P. L. (2011). Male sexual orientation in independent Samoa: Evidence for fraternal birth order and maternal fecundity effects. *Archives of Sexual Behavior, 40*, 495–503.

VanderLaan, D. P., & Vasey, P. L. (2012). Relationship status and elevated avuncularity in Samoan *fa'afafine. Personal Relationships, 19*, 326–339.

VanderLaan, D. P., & Vasey, P. L. (2013). Birth order and avuncular tendencies in Samoan men and *fa'afafine. Archives of Sexual Behavior, 42*, 371–379.

VanderLaan, D. P., Vokey, J. R., & Vasey, P. L. (2013b). Is male androphilia familial in non-Western cultures? The case of a Samoan village. *Archives of Sexual Behavior, 42*, 361–370.

Vasey, P. L. (2006). The pursuit of pleasure: An evolutionary history of homosexual behavior in Japanese macaques. In V. Sommer & P. L. Vasey (Eds.), *Homosexual behavior in animals: An evolutionary perspective* (pp. 191–219). Cambridge: Cambridge University Press.

Vasey, P. L., & Bartlett, N. H. (2007). What can the Samoan *fa'afafine* teach us about the Western concept of "Gender Identity Disorder in Childhood"? *Perspectives in Biology and Medicine, 50*, 481–490.

Vasey, P. L., Parker, J. L., & VanderLaan, D. P. (2014). Comparative reproductive output of androphilic and gynephilic males in Samoa. *Archives of Sexual Behavior, 43*, 363-367.

Vasey, P. L., Pocock, D. S., & VanderLaan, D. P. (2007). Kin selection and male androphilia in Samoan *fa'afafine. Evolution and Human Behavior, 28*, 159–167.

Vasey, P. L., & VanderLaan, D. P. (2007). Birth order and male androphilia in Samoan *fa'afafine. Proceedings of the Royal Society of London B, 274*, 1437–1442.

Vasey, P. L., & VanderLaan, D. P. (2009). Materteral and avuncular tendencies in Samoa: A comparative study of women, men and *fa'afafine. Human Nature, 20*, 269–281.

Vasey, P. L., & VanderLaan, D. P. (2010a). Avuncular tendencies in Samoan *fa'afafine* and the evolution of male androphilia. *Archives of Sexual Behavior, 39*, 821–830.

Vasey, P. L., & VanderLaan, D. P. (2010b). An adaptive cognitive dissociation between willingness to help kin and non-kin in Samoan fa'afafine. *Psychological Science, 21*, 292–297.

Vasey, P. L., & VanderLaan, D. P. (2010c). Monetary exchanges with nieces and nephews: A comparison of Samoan men, women, and *fa'afafine. Evolution and Human Behavior, 31*, 373–380.

Vasey, P. L., & VanderLaan, D. P. (2012). Is female homosexual behavior in Japanese macaques truly sexual? In J. B. Leca, M. J. Huffman, & P. L. Vasey (Eds.), *The monkeys of Stormy Mountain: Over half a century of research on the Arashiyama macaques* (pp. 153–172). Cambridge: Cambridge University Press.

Vasey, P. L., VanderLaan, D. P., Gothreau, L., & Bartlett, N. H. (2011). Traits of separation anxiety in childhood: A comparison of Samoan men, women and *fa'afafine. Archives of Sexual Behavior, 40*, 511–517.

Whitam, F. L. (1983). Culturally invariant properties of male homosexuality: Tentative conclusions from cross-cultural research. *Archives of Sexual Behavior, 12*, 207–226.

Whitam, F., & Mathy, R. M. (1986). *Male homosexuality in four societies: Brazil, Guatemala, the Philippines and the United States.* New York: Praeger.

Widmer, E. D., Treas, J., & Newcombe, R. (1998). Attitudes toward nonmarital sex in 24 countries. *Journal of Sex Research, 35*, 349–358.

Williams, G. C. (1966). *Adaptation and natural selection.* Princeton, NJ: Princeton University Press.

Wilson, E. O. (1975). *Sociobiology: The new synthesis.* Cambridge, MA: Belknap.

Winkelman, M. (2010). *Shamanism: A biopsychosocial paradigm of consciousness and healing.* Santa Barbara, CA: Praeger.

Woodburn, J. (1982). Egalitarian societies. *Man, 17*, 431–451.

Yamaguchi, S. (1994). Empirical evidence on collectivism among the Japanese. In U. Kim, H. C. Triandis, C. Kagitcibasi, S. C. Choi, & G. Yoon (Eds.), *Individualism and collectivism: Theory, method, and applications* (pp. 175–188). Newbury Park, CA: Sage.

Yates, T. (1993). Frameworks for an archaeology of the body. In C. Tilley (Ed.), *Interpretive archaeology* (pp. 31–72). Providence, RI: Berg Publishers.

Zietsch, B. P., Morley, K. I., Shekar, S. N., Verweij, K. J. H., Keller, M. C., Macgregor, S., et al. (2008). Genetic factors predisposing to homosexuality may increase mating success in heterosexuals. *Evolution and Human Behavior, 29*, 424–433.

Zucker, K. J., Blanchard, R., Kim, T.-S., Pae, C.-U., & Lee, C. (2007). Birth order and sibling sex ratio in homosexual transsexual South Korean males: Effects of the male-preference stopping rule. *Psychiatry and Clinical Neurosciences, 61*, 529–533.

Zucker, K. J., Bradley, S. J., & Sullivan, C. B. L. (1996). Traits of separation anxiety in boys with gender identity disorder. *Journal of the American Academy of Child and Adolescent Psychiatry, 35*, 791–798.

Reflections on the Evolution of Human Sex Differences: Social Selection and the Evolution of Competition Among Women

20

David C. Geary, Benjamin Winegard, and Bo Winegard

In detailing the argument for natural selection, Darwin (1859) introduced another set of processes above and beyond this "struggle for life" (p. 61), namely the struggle for mates or sexual selection. Darwin's (1871) focus was on competition among males for access to mates and female choice of mating partners, and indeed this is a very common pattern in nature (Andersson, 1994). The success of sexual selection in explaining how many sex differences evolved and are expressed has resulted in a relative neglect of other evolutionary processes that can result in sex differences. Darwin (1859) was certainly aware that natural selection (e.g., if males and females foraged in different habitats) could influence the evolution of sex differences but did not greatly elaborate on these. In recent years, however, scientists are examining these processes, especially as related to social competition for resources other than mates (Tobias, Montgomerie, & Lyon, 2012; West-Eberhard, 1979, 1983). This social selection is particularly important for understanding competition among females, a dynamic that has been largely overlooked in comparison to Darwin's male–male competition. We begin by providing a brief overview of sexual and social selection and illustrate the latter in a couple of nonhuman species. We then apply the concept of social selection to research on competition among co-wives in polygynous marriages and provide some hypotheses about how this could have influenced the evolution of women's competitive strategies and how the supporting cognitive competencies may have been elaborated.

Sexual and Social Selection

In two seminal articles, West-Eberhard (1979, 1983) established the basic framework for social selection. She argued that there is an important theoretical distinction between sexual selection, where the "resource at stake" is mates, and social selection, which refers to "differential success in social competition, whatever the resource at stake" (1983, p. 158). From this perspective, sexual selection is a subset of social selection that in turn is a subset of natural selection (Crook, 1972; Lyon & Montgomerie, 2012; West-Eberhard, 1979), as shown in Fig. 20.1.

Most generally, sexual selection involves competition with members of the same sex over mates (*intrasexual competition*) and discriminative choice of mating partners (*intersexual choice*). This is most typically manifested in male–male competition over access to mates or control of the resources mates need to reproduce, such as nesting sites, and female choice of mating partners (Andersson, 1994; Darwin, 1871).

D.C. Geary (✉)
Department of Psychological Sciences, University of Missouri, 210 McAlester Hall, Columbia, MO 65211-2500, USA

Interdisciplinary Neuroscience Program, University of Missouri, Columbia, MO 65211, USA
e-mail: GearyD@Missouri.edu

V.A. Weekes-Shackelford and T.K. Shackelford (eds.), *Evolutionary Perspectives on Human Sexual Psychology and Behavior*, Evolutionary Psychology, DOI 10.1007/978-1-4939-0314-6_20,
© Springer Science+Business Media New York 2014

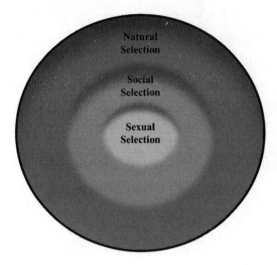

Fig. 20.1 Sexual selection is a subset of social selection that in turn is a subset of natural selection. *Note*: Sexual selection is defined as competition over mates and discriminative choice of mating partners; social selection is competition with conspecifics over any type of resource, including mates; natural selection refers to differential survival and reproduction resulting from all the forces of nature (e.g., drought). The boundaries are deliberately fuzzy emphasizing that it is often impossible to precisely separate these categories (adapted from Tobias et al. (2012))

The pattern of male–male competition and female choice arises from fundamental sex differences in the potential rate of reproduction (Clutton-Brock & Vincent, 1991) and in investment in offspring (Trivers, 1972). The sex with the slower rate of reproduction and higher investment in offspring (typically females) is a resource over which the lower investing sex (typically males) competes. Internal gestation and postpartum suckling, for instance, result in a slower potential rate of reproduction for female than male mammals and a sex difference in parental investment. The predicted pattern of intense male–male competition, with little male parenting, and discriminative female choice is found in at least 95 % of mammalian species (Clutton-Brock, 1989).

Darwin's (1871) traditional definition of sexual selection inspired and guided the study of sex differences in hundreds of species of mammal, fish, insect, and plant (Andersson, 1994; Shuker, 2010). At the same time, the success of this traditional approach resulted in a relative neglect

of female–female competition and male choice, with the exception of "sex-role-reversed" species; the latter are species in which males have a slower rate of reproduction and invest more in parenting than females (e.g., they brood eggs) and, as predicted, females compete intensely for access to mates and males are choosy (e.g., Amundsen & Forsgren, 2001). It is now clear that males can be choosy if females differ in fertility or parental behavior, even when these males provide little or no investment in parenting (Kraaijeveld, Kraaijeveld-Smit, & Komdeur, 2007). Likewise, in many species in which females do not compete for access to mates, they are nevertheless highly competitive with one another over access to other resources (Clutton-Brock, 2009; Stockley & Bro-Jørensen, 2011).

The recognition of male choosiness and female–female competition that is largely unrelated to parental investment and access to mates, respectively, has led some scientists to question whether the traditional view of sexual selection is too narrow in scope (Clutton-Brock, 2009; Kraaijeveld et al., 2007; Tobias et al., 2012). Carranza (2009), for instance, suggested any pressures that act differently on males and females, including but not restricted to intrasexual competition and intersexual choice, be regarded as sex-dependent selection. Following West-Eberhard (1979, 1983), other scientists have argued that within-species social dynamics are partitioned into sexual selection, as traditionally defined, and social selection (Lyon & Montgomerie, 2012; Tobias et al., 2012). The latter involves competition for access to resources other than mates that can affect reproductive success. Whether a distinction between sexual and social selection is useful for understanding the evolution and expression of associated traits remains to be determined; for instance, sexually selected traits are often costly signals that can affect health and longevity (Zahavi & Zahavi, 1997), but it is unclear whether socially selected traits are costly signals to the same degree.

Conceptually, however, distinguishing social and sexual selection may prove helpful in

Fig. 20.2 Female and male *Onthophagus sagittarius*. 1 = Cephalic horn; 2 = pronotal horn. Photo credit: U. Schmidt, 2009. Creative Commons License

Female *Onthophagus Sagittarius*   Male *Onthophagus Sagittarius*

understanding the evolutionary importance of social dynamics beyond Darwin's (1871) intrasexual competition and intersexual choice. The distinction should be particularly useful for understanding how competition among females for resources other than mates has contributed to the evolution of sex differences.

Social Selection and Female–Female Competition

When females invest more in parenting than males and especially when males invest little in parenting, females are "in demand," and thus they do not have to compete intensely or at all for access to mates (Trivers, 1972). Parental investment however often entails considerable costs, especially for species with long gestational periods and extensive postpartum investment (Clutton-Brock, 1991). When the resources needed to support these costs, such as high-quality foods or nesting sites, are in short supply, females are predicted to compete intensely for priority access to them (Heinsohn, 2008; Tobias et al., 2012). The result is female status hierarchies and the evolutionary elaboration of behavioral and other traits that signal relative status and that enable its establishment and maintenance. In other words, even in the absence of Darwin's (1871) traditional intrasexual competition for mates, intrasexual competition for ecological resources can be a potent selection pressure that contributes to the evolution of sex differences.

Examples of Social Selection in Nonhuman Species

In many species, traits that have been elaborated by male–male competition are also expressed, though to a lesser degree, in females. One common explanation for these elaborated female traits is genetic correlation, that is, the traits are expressed in females not because females use them to compete but rather because of the expression of genes inherited from their fathers (Lande, 1980). As West-Eberhard (1983) noted, this is not a satisfactory explanation for many of these traits, as it is now known that they are often used in status-related competition with other females, in territorial defense against predators or conspecifics of both sexes, or as indicators of fertility or parental behavior in species with male choice (Clutton-Brock, 2007; Kraaijeveld et al., 2007).

As an example, in most beetle species, horns are expressed solely by males and are used in intrasexual conflict over mates—as described by Darwin (1871). However, in the genus *Onthophagus*, many females also develop horns that are physically different than those expressed by males and thus cannot be due to genetic correlation (Emlen, Marangelo, Ball, & Cunningham, 2005). For example, females of the dung beetle species *O. sagittarius* (hereafter referred to as dung beetles) possess horns that are qualitatively different in both size and shape from the male's horns (see Fig. 20.2). While the male develops two relatively small cephalic horns, the female develops one large cephalic horn and, above this, a pronotal horn. Such sex-differentiated horn development is indicative of unique selection pressures in females.

Dung beetle females, alone or in cooperation with a male, locate fresh dung that they drag into an excavated tunnel where they construct a brood chamber. The collected dung is then rolled into a brood ball where the female will lay an egg. Upon egg release, the female seals the brood ball with dung and fills the tunnel. The mating system of dung beetles consists of biparental care with facultative male investment. Males compete with each other for access to mates using their cephalic horns during such competition. Conversely, females do not use their horns for mating competition and males do not prefer females with larger horns (Watson & Simmons, 2010a). Thus, sexual selection, as traditionally defined, is unlikely to account for horn evolution in female dung beetles.

Social selection, upon the other hand, may provide an explanation for the evolution of female horns. The amount of dung in a brood ball is related to offspring fitness with larger brood balls producing more fecund and competitive offspring. Thus, females may compete with each other over access to dung and maintenance of tunnel possession. Watson and Simmons (2010b) demonstrated that all females produced significantly fewer broods when forced to compete with other females for resources. However, both females with larger bodies and females with larger horns did relatively better in competition than their smaller-horned or smaller-bodied competitors. Moreover, competitive success among females was related specifically to horn size, controlling for body size. These studies provide strong evidence that female horns in this species evolved as a result of female–female competition over ecological resources, the control of which results in the production of higher quality offspring.

The Soay sheep (*Ovis aries*) is a polygynous ungulate and provides another example of social competition among females. Male Soay sheep engage in intense competition over access to females and females mate promiscuously (Clutton-Brock & Pemberton, 2004). As with the dung beetle, its horns are a polymorphic trait: males grow either large horns (normal) or smaller horns (scurred); females grow both, but some are also hornless (polled). The males use their horns in contest competition over access to mates and engage in sperm competition. Horn length, body size, and testes size all independently predict male reproductive success (Preston, Stevenson, Pemberton, Coltman, & Wilson, 2003). As with the dung beetle, the weaponry (horns) that female Soay sheep wield seems to allow them to better compete for important ecological resources, not access to mates.

Robinson and Kruuk (2007), for example, demonstrated that the horns confer size-independent advantages to females during aggressive interactions. These interactions—and, concomitantly, female aggressiveness in general—are facultative and depend upon group density, age, and reproductive status. A high rate of neonatal death creates intense competition for food, especially when group density is high. During periods of resource strain, horned females may be better able to procure important resources like food and to protect better their offspring by intimidating or defeating same-sex conspecifics in antagonistic interactions. These results suggest that Soay female horns are socially selected weapons that allow females to compete better, not for mates, but for access to limited ecological resources.

Social Selection and Competition Among Women

Men's investment in parenting, either direct child care and protection or some form of provisioning (Geary, 2000), is predicted to result in female–female competition to partner with men who are best able to provide these resources (Trivers, 1972), and many lines of evidence indicate that this is the case (Geary, 2010). Competition over marriage partners is an aspect of sexual selection as traditionally defined, but competition among wives married to the same man does not fit neatly into this traditional definition. Our thesis is that competition among co-wives in polygynous marriages is a form of social competition that has been a potent selection pressure during human evolution and has thus contributed to the evolution of sex differences in traits that facilitate this competition (below); for a more general discussion of social selection in humans, see Nesse (2009).

Competition in Polygynous Marriages

Polygyny is common across human societies (Murdock, 1981) and has been an important feature of human evolution (Alexander, Hoogland, Howard, Noonan, & Sherman, 1979). In the vast majority of traditional societies, high-status men (often 10–20 % of men) will often marry two to four women, other men marry monogamously, and still others never marry or have children. These high-status men, often in cooperation with their male kin, have social influence or control land or other ecological resources that allow them to manipulate mating dynamics in self-interested ways (e.g., Borgerhoff Mulder, 1990, 2000; Chagnon, 1988), either through male-on-male violence (Puts, 2010), direct female choice, or more often the choice of the female's parents (Apostolou, 2007, 2010). Apostolou's finding that in nearly 90 % of traditional cultures and during much of recorded history, marriage partners are often chosen by parents or other kin indicates that unfettered mate choices, as are now commonly practiced in Western cultures, may not have been the norm for much of our recent evolutionary history (Walker, Hill, Flinn, & Ellsworth, 2011).

The combination of kin making marriage choices and polygynous marriages is important, because it lessens the role of traditional female choice and female–female competition for mates per se and increases the importance of female–female competition within the context of polygynous marriages. This is not to say that females do not have preferences in social contexts in which arranged marriages are common; they do. Scelza (2011) found that 23 % of the children of Himba women in arranged, often polygynous, marriages were sired by an extra-pair man compared to none of the children of women who chose their husbands (called "love marriages"). When unconstrained by kin preferences, female choice

and variation in male quality also result in female–female competition over mates, as traditionally defined (Geary, 2010). Our point here is that scientists' personal familiarity with Western marriage systems and the focus on Darwin's sexual selection have resulted in a neglect of the natural history of the mating dynamics in our species (see Geary, Bailey, & Oxford, 2011; Geary & Flinn, 2001; Puts, 2010), which included polygyny, families composed of multiple wives, and children of different mothers (often different fathers, with cuckoldry).

However it is achieved, polygynous marriage creates a vastly different social context for women than does monogamous marriage. Women in these contexts do not compete for a mate per se, as in traditional sexual selection, but rather compete for access to resources controlled by their husband, for social or material resources (e.g., land) that will be inherited by their children, and for the emotional and sexual attention of their husbands (Jankowiak, Sudakov, & Wilreker, 2005).

One critical result is that women have to contend with the competing interests of the other wives of their husbands, as well as their husbands' female kin if they move into his village (Strassmann, 2011). The level of competition will likely vary with whether or not a co-wife is a sister, the extent to which co-wives must cooperate to produce food, and the relative ages of the wives (Jankowiak et al., 2005; White, 1988). With regard to the latter, postmenopausal co-wives are often less engaged in competition with younger wives than are younger wives with each other, in part so that younger wives will provide some care for them in their old age (Jankowiak et al., 2005). Whatever the specifics, polygynously married women often (but not always; Borgerhoff Mulder, 1988) have less healthy offspring and fewer surviving offspring than do monogamously married women, even when the overall level of resources available to children is the same or higher in polygynous than monogamous families (Amey, 2005; Josephson, 2002; Omariba & Boyle, 2007; Strassmann, 1997; Strassmann & Gillespie, 2002). Within polygynous marriages, dominant co-wives often have more surviving children than subordinate co-wives (Gibson & Mace, 2006).

Strassmann (1997, 2011; Strassmann & Gillespie, 2002) provides one of the more thorough assessments of this pattern, with her study of the lifetime reproductive success of monogamously and polygynously married Dogon—an agricultural society in western Africa—women. For Dogon women, the reproductive disadvantage of polygyny is largely due to a sharply higher mortality rate for their children; even with increased mortality, men still benefit (reproductively) from polygyny. After controlling for children's age and sex, the number of children in the family compound, and the overall economic well-being of the family, Strassmann (1997) found that the odds of premature death were 7–11 times higher for children from polygynous than from monogamous marriages. The premature mortality was not due to diminished resources per child but may have been related to less paternal investment and competition from co-wives. "In addition to neglect and mistreatment, it was widely assumed that cowives often fatally poisoned each other's children...Cowife aggression is extensively documented in Malian court cases with confessions and convictions for poisoning" (Strassmann, 1997, p. 693).

Murdering the children of co-wives not only increases immediate resources available to a wife's own children; it also reduces the number of heirs to her husband's land. This is because sons inherit and divide the land of their father and therefore the sons of co-wives are direct competitors for the land each woman's sons will need to attract wives. This competition may explain why the mortality of Dogon boys is 2.5 times higher than that of their sisters. Short of murdering the children of co-wives, children born into polygynous families are at heightened risk for stunted physical growth in comparison to children born into monogamous families, even with control of the amount of wealth available to their mothers (Hadley, 2005; Strassmann, 2011). There is often variation among the growth of children of co-wives living in the same compound, suggesting dynamics among the co-wives and potential favoritism by husbands are contributing factors (Bove & Valeggia, 2009;

Leroy, Razak, & Habicht, 2008). Indeed, Jankowiak et al.'s (2005) review of the ethnographies of 69 cultures revealed that co-wife conflict over children and resources that will be provided to these children was common.

The historical record also provides many salient examples of women competing to ensure that their children (mostly sons) were conferred legitimacy and status. Such competition was particularly acute in monarchical, winner-take-all forms of government where illegitimate or officially unrecognized children were often brutally murdered or banished (Ogden, 1999). The high-ranking women in these societies relied on guile, social aptitude, seduction, and, if necessary, ruthlessness to increase the probability that their husbands (and other high-status men) conferred legitimacy on the women's biological offspring.

In ancient Macedon, the marriage system of the ruling family (the Argeads) was openly polygynous (see Betzig, 1986; Ogden, 1999). Philip II, king and father of Alexander the Great, married at least seven women, mostly for political reasons (Worthington, 2008). Olympias of Epirus, the mother of Alexander the Great, was his fifth wife. Olympias is described as possessing an exotic and beautiful visage and a beguiling personality. She was an avid member of a snake-worshiping cult of Dionysus (Plutarch, 2004). After giving birth to Alexander, her relationship with Philip II soured. He soon met and fell in love with the Macedonian noblewoman, Cleopatra, whom he married. The marriage between Philip and Cleopatra posed an acute threat to Alexander because, unlike Olympias, who was an Epirote (i.e., a foreigner), Cleopatra was Macedonian by birth. Attalus, a member of the Macedonian nobility, implored the gods, after Philip II and Cleopatra's wedding, "to give them a lawful [a son from a Macedonian mother] successor to the kingdom..." (Plutarch, 2004, p. 10).

Shortly after the wedding, Philip II was assassinated by one of his bodyguards in what was, on the face it, the act of a disgruntled loner. However, Plutarch (2004) notes that guilt was "laid for the most part upon Olympias..." (p. 11). Although modern scholars debate exactly who is responsible for the assassination (see Cartledge, 2004), it is clear that Olympias had ample reason to arrange the crime. If Olympias was responsible for Philip II's death, she was deft enough to leave scholars with nothing but innuendo and hearsay. In any case, by killing Philip II, Olympias ensured the succession of her son, Alexander, to the throne. To solidify Alexander's social position after Philip II's death, Olympias had Cleopatra and her infant son with Philip II killed, thus ensuring that Alexander would not contend with internal threats to his legitimacy (Pausanias, 2012). The rest is history, so to speak.

Open polygyny was not sanctioned during the early Roman Empire, but most of the Caesars took multiple wives over the duration of their lives—not to mention sexual access to many slaves (Betiz, 1992)—and this placed the wives and their sons effectively in the same situation as Olympias and Alexander, and we believe most women during a substantial part of our evolutionary history. While many of the wives of the Caesars enjoy posthumous notoriety, perhaps none enjoys the maculated reputation of Agrippina the Younger, who was the sister of Caligula, wife of Claudius, and mother of Nero; to keep the following straight, see Fig. 20.3 for a concise family tree. While Dio Cassius admitted that Agrippina was "beautiful," he shared in Tacitus' assessment that she was "immoral, infamous, and violent." (Cassius, 1914, p. 14; Tacitus, 2004, p. 242). It appears Agrippina was cold, calculating, and, at times, ruthless. A modern biographer, tabulating the ancient sources, records that Agrippina had at least 10 lovers and 11 alleged victims (Barrett, 1996), largely to survive, increase her status, and, most importantly, propel her son, Nero, to the throne (Freisenbruch, 2010); as Dio asserted, "she was very clever in making the most of her opportunities..." (p. 17). Given the numerous examples of Julio-Claudian women who met an unceremonious fate, Dio's assessment seems accurate.

Agrippina achieved the latter feat by marrying the emperor, Claudius, and convincing him to anoint her son (with a previous husband) heir to the throne. This was quite the accomplishment considering that Claudius had a *biological* son,

Britannicus, with his previous wife Messalina. Dio, impressed by Agrippina's powers, recounted how she was able to cajole Claudius into raising Britannicus "as if he were a mere nobody" (p. 17). While Agrippina succeeded for a time, Claudius eventually began to regret marrying her and began to lavish attention on Britannicus. Rumors swirled that Claudius wished to rid himself of Agrippina and make his own son heir. Agrippina could not idly allow this turn of events to unfold and, according to the ancient sources, quickly decided to murder Claudius. According to Suetonius (2011), all sources agreed that Agrippina poisoned Claudius while some even said she did so personally by offering him a poisonous mushroom (p. 226). Shortly after the death of Claudius, Agrippina arranged to have her son, Nero, hailed as emperor by his troops.

Our point here is that while the men of Rome almost always translated their status into mating opportunities (Betzig, 1992), Agrippina, the doting mother, used her status to propel her son to the pinnacle of Roman power. She was not alone among the women of Rome or among women in similar social situations in other parts of the world (see, e.g., Garland, 1999, for examples from the Byzantine Empire).

Female–Female Social Competition and Psychological Adaptations

The physical size differences between men and women, greater variation in reproductive success among men than women in modern-day traditional and in historical societies, as well as population genetic studies indicate more intense competition among our male than female ancestors (Betzig, 2012; Plavcan & van Schaik, 1997; Underhill et al., 2000). The implication is the cost–benefit trade-offs of escalating conflict to the point of risk of physical injury or death have been higher for our male than female ancestors (Campbell, 2004; Daly & Wilson, 1988), as is the case for other mammalian species in which males compete more intensely for mates than females. The descriptions above nonetheless indicate that women can be quite competitive

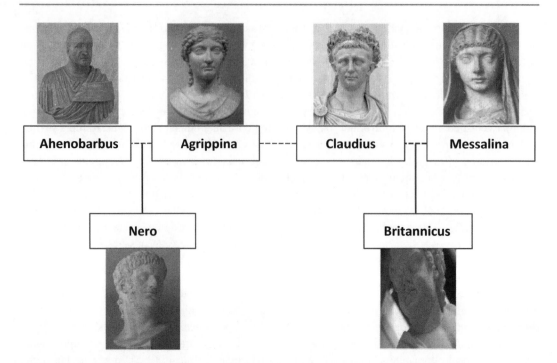

Fig. 20.3 Family tree illustrating Agrippina's relationships. All pictures from Wikimedia Commons

with one another when it comes to pursuing their reproductive self-interests, which includes the interests of their biological children (Strassmann, 2011). This competition is on average more subtle than that among men, who often resort to physical dominance or pursuit of status and prestige through competition for control of culturally important resources and social influence (von Rueden, Gurven, & Kaplan, 2011).

Poisoning one's competitor or their children aside, women typically pursue a less risky strategy of attempting to subtly organize their social world in ways that benefit them and their children (Geary, 2010). This "palace intrigue" is now called relational aggression. Although both sexes engage in it (Archer & Coyne, 2005; Card, Stucky, Sawalani, & Little, 2008; Feshbach, 1969), it is women's strategy of choice. The associated behaviors involve the use of gossip and rumors to sully the social and sexual reputation and manipulate the friendships of potential rivals (Owens, Shute, & Slee, 2000). Aggressors also use nonverbal cues, such as eye rolling and other dismissive behaviors, in their attempts to organize these relationships and to create psychological

distress in competitors. Such behaviors can of course be directed toward men—but largely they are directed toward other women— and sometimes over romantic partners (Smith, Rose, & Schwartz-Mette, 2010) but also over same-sex friends (an important source of social support; Taylor et al., 2000) and other resources (Björkqvist, Osterman, & Lagerspetz, 1994). If these behaviors have been elaborated through female–female social competition, then (a) females should be more sensitive and react more strongly to relational aggression than males, and (b) females should have advantages over males in the cognitive and affective systems that support the use and detection of social information (e.g., facial expressions) conveyed through relational aggression.

Behavioral Strategies

Both sexes engage in relational aggression, as noted, largely against same-sex competitors, but the effects of being victimized by it are more pernicious for women than men (Smith et al., 2010), in part because women appear to be more sensitive to acts of relational aggression and may react more strongly than men to these social tactics (Benenson et al., 2013).

In a prospective study of more than 2,500 adolescents, Bond, Carlin, Thomas, Rubin, and Patton (2001) found that females who are the victims of relational aggression are 2.6 times more likely to suffer from depression or anxiety than are females who are not victims or males who are victims. The risk for females is particularly high if they lack social support from friends or family. Similarly, in a qualitative study, Owens et al. (2000) documented the intense pain, embarrassment, and even suicidal feelings that victims of relational aggression often deal with. One girl in their focus group explained that expulsion from a friend group "could emotionally damage someone for life" (p. 367). The same pattern has been found in adulthood (Kendler, Myers, & Prescott, 2005). In a study of 2,319 high school students, Leenaars, Dane, and Marini (2008) confirmed higher levels of depression in victims of relational aggression and that physically attractive teenage girls, but not boys, were victimized more often than their less attractive peers; "a one standard deviation increase in physical attractiveness increased the odds of females being indirectly victimized by 35 % ... and decreased the odds of males being victimized by 25 %" (Leenaars et al., 2008, p. 410). Vaillancourt and Sharma (2011), in an experimental study, found that attractive women who were dressed in a provocative manner were especially likely to provoke negative responses from other women including rolling of the eyes, gossip, and, in one case, direct confrontation.

In other words, it does not take much to evoke relational aggression in women, including when she is a potential competitor for mates but also in competition for other resources. To be an effective evolved strategy, however, this harassment would have to undermine the reproductive potential of victims. This has not been assessed in studies of Western girls and women, but the evidence is suggestive in the context of polygynous marriages.

In a review of the mental health of women in polygynous marriages, Shepard (2012) concluded that in comparison to their monogamously married peers, these women were at increased risk of heightened anxiety and depression, as well as more serious psychiatric disorders. Although not conclusive, their findings are consistent with Jankowiak et al.'s (2005) finding of nearly ubiquitous hostility and conflict among co-wives across hunter-gatherer, agricultural, and other traditional societies. The reproductive effects of these continual stressors are not fully understood for humans, but there is some evidence that the result may be reduced fertility in some women. In a longitudinal study of 393 couples (who completed most assessments of 430 who started) who were attempting to conceive, Hjollund et al. (1999) found that heighted psychological distress (i.e., increased anxiety, depression, fatigue) in the week prior to ovulation reduced the chances of conception from 16.5 to 12.8 %, especially for women with long cycles. These women were assessed for as many as six cycles, and thus changes in the odds of conceiving as related to changes in levels of psychological distress could be determined for each woman. A decrease in the level of psychological distress from one cycle to the next was associated with an increase in the odds of conceiving, but again primarily for women with long (>30 or 35 days) cycles. Similarly, a study of 274 women aged 18–40 who were attempting to conceive found that increased levels of α-amylase, a biomarker of stress, but not cortisol, resulted in a decrease in women's probability of conception (Buck Louis et al., 2011, but see Lynch, Sundaram, Buck Louis, Lum, & Pyper, 2012). Psychological distress can also affect cycle length, often resulting in less regular or longer cycles (Coppen, 1965; Jarrett, 1984; Matteo, 1987).

On top of potential reductions in fertility, psychological harassment may be an effective strategy for undermining the psychological well-being and thus later the social competitiveness of the children of co-wives. Psychologically and socially undermining these children is less risky than poisoning them and can provide the aggressors' children with a later advantage. Unfortunately, these potential risks have not been as extensively studied as physical risks. The available evidence is mixed but suggests heighted risk of psychopathology and academic problems in children but not adolescents from polygynous as compared to monogamous families (Elbedour, Onwuegbuzie, Caridine, & Abu-Saad, 2002). Given the increased incidence of abuse and neglect of nonbiological children, it seems very likely that psychological harassment of the children of co-wives, especially those children who are potential competitors of the abusers' children, is a common feature of polygynous marriages (Daly & Wilson, 1981).

Cognitive Competencies

The evolutionary effect of physical male–male competition over access to mates, as was well documented by Darwin (1871) and supported by subsequent research (Andersson, 1994), is an exaggeration of the physical traits (e.g., antlers) that facilitate this competition, whereas behavioral competition (e.g., bird song) results in the elaboration of the supporting cognitive and brain systems. The sex differences that emerge from the latter are often more subtle relative to the differences that evolve as a result of physical competition but are nonetheless readily understood from the perspective of sexual selection. In fact, understanding how males compete for access to mates has been critical to the study of these traits, as illustrated by Gaulin and Fitzgerald's (1986, 1989) research on spatial cognition in voles. They reasoned that species in which males expand their territory during the breeding season to search for multiple, ecologically dispersed mates would have better spatial abilities than females of the same species and males of related species that do not expand their territory to search for mates. The results from a series of field and laboratory were consistent with this prediction and several recent studies have confirmed that mating-related territorial expansion is related to enhanced spatial abilities in males relative to conspecific females and males of cousin species that do not engage in territorial expansion (Jašarević, Williams, Roberts, Geary, & Rosenfeld, 2012; Perdue, Snyder, Zhihe, Marr, & Maple, 2011).

We use the same logic to make predictions about the cognitive competencies that might have been elaborated through an evolutionary history of relational aggression among women. Specifically, we propose that this form of social competition has contributed to women's advantage relative to men in language fluency, sensitivity to nonverbal cues (e.g., gestures, body posture), facial expressions, and perhaps theory of mind (Geary, 2010). Of course, these sex differences could have evolved through the advantages of being able to subtly manage opposite sex relationships, develop and maintain same-sex friendships, or through direct female–female competition over mates. In several of these domains (below), women are in fact more sensitive to these cues when expressed by other women than by men, suggesting their advantages are particularly enhanced in managing same-sex relationships. When it comes to these relationships, the current literature does not allow us to determine whether women's advantages in these forms of cognition are beneficial to maintaining friendships, in competition with other women, or most likely some combination.

Figure 20.4 shows Geary's (2005) hypothesized organization of evolved cognitive systems for monitoring and processing social information. These folk psychological systems are organized around the self, other individuals, and collections of individuals. Our focus in on sex differences in individual-level systems, because relational aggression, whether competition for marriage to a preferred mate (sexual selection) or within the context of polygynous marriages (social selection), should be facilitated by enhanced competencies in these areas. An extensive review is provided elsewhere (Geary, 2010), and thus we present a few examples to illustrate our point.

Nonverbal Behavior and Facial Expressions

A female advantage in interpreting and sending nonverbal social cues is found from childhood, perhaps infancy forward. These advantages are manifested by skill at reading emotional states conveyed in facial expressions, gesture, and body language and in generating nuance in the social use of these cues (Buck, Savin, Miller, & Caul, 1972; Hall & Matsumoto, 2004; McClure, 2000; Rosenthal, Hall, DiMatteo, Rogers, &

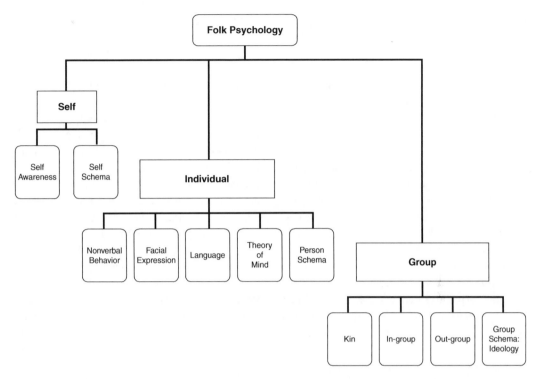

Fig. 20.4 Evolutionarily salient social information-processing domains (adapted from "The origin of mind: Evolution of brain, cognition, and general intelligence," by D. G. Geary, 2005, p. 129. Copyright 2005 by American Psychological Association)

Archer, 1979; van Beek & Dubas, 2008; Wagner, Buck, & Winterbotham, 1993). Rosenthal et al. (1979) conducted one of the most ambitious and comprehensive assessments of sex differences in this area and found that girls and women were more accurate than boys and men when judging emotion cues based on facial expressions, body posture, and vocal intonation. These differences were found in all nations in which three or more samples were obtained—Australia, Canada, the United States, Israel, and New Guinea—and were of the same general magnitude in all of these nations (see Hall, 1984). Hall concluded that the advantage of girls and women in the decoding of nonverbal messages "is most pronounced for facial cues, less pronounced for body cues, and least pronounced for vocal cues" (Hall, 1984, p. 27). When all nonverbal cues are provided—a more accurate assessment of decoding skills during actual dyadic interactions—about 17 out of 20 girls and women are more accurate at decoding the emotion cues of

another individual than is the average same-age boy or man (Hall, 1978).

Of particular importance for our thesis is the finding that females are more sensitive to the nonverbal cues and facial expressions of other females than to those of males, consistent with the evolutionary enhancement of these competencies within the context of same-sex competition. As an example, Buck et al. (1972) found that dyads of women are more effective in expressing and reading the emotion cues of the other member of the pair, as signaled by changes in facial expression, than are dyads of men (also Rotter & Rotter, 1988). Rehnman and Herlitz (2006) found that 9-year-old girls have a better memory for faces than do boys and that girls have an especially large advantage for recognizing the faces of other girls and women than the faces of boys and men. In a follow-up study, Rehnman and Herlitz (2007) confirmed this sex difference in adults. These findings appear to reflect a combination of girls and women allocating more attention to the processing of same-sex faces than boys and men, the greater sensitivity of girls and women to the emotion cues signaled by facial expressions and other nonverbal behaviors, and a greater expressiveness of the part of women than men (Hall, 1984; Herlitz & Rehnman, 2008).

A heightened social expressiveness may be helpful for initiating and maintaining friendly dyadic interactions and relationships among women but at the same time would put them at a disadvantage when it comes to relational aggression. In particular, highly expressive women would be easily "read" and thus socially outmaneuvered by competitors and would be at a disadvantage in terms of concealing relational aggression, e.g., by spreading rumors in ways that are plausibly deniable (Lee & Pinker, 2010), if confronted by the victim. We would therefore expect women to have an enhanced ability relative to men to inhibit social expressions and other behaviors in emotionally charged situations, and this is the case. In a review of sex differences in inhibitory abilities, Bjorklund and Kipp (1996) concluded that girls and women are better able to conceal nonverbal behaviors and facial expressions than are boys and men, when motivated (e.g., instructed by an experimenter) to do so. These sex differences do not appear to reflect a general advantage of females on inhibitory tasks, as there appear to be no sex differences on some other inhibition tasks including the classic Stroop task (see Bjorklund & Kipp, 1996).

Language

Women do not talk more than men (Mehl, Vazire, Ramírez-Esparza, Slatcher, & Pennebaker, 2007), but they talk about different things and have advantages over men in many basic aspects of language production, comprehension, and the pragmatics of language (Anderson & Leaper, 1998; Kimura, 1999; Majeres, 2007; Shaywitz et al., 1995).

Pragmatics refers to the use of language in social contexts. Boys and men tend to use language as part of their overall strategy to achieve status and social dominance. Boys and men use

intrusive, dominance-oriented interruptions during conversations primarily when they are in a group setting (Anderson & Leaper, 1998; Leaper & Smith, 2004). These are contexts in which dominance displays convey information to a wide audience (Vigil, 2009), and here almost 3 out of 4 men intrusively interrupt others as a means of displaying dominance (e.g., superior knowledge). When introduced to a new acquaintance, boys and men also use dominance-oriented language more frequently than girls and women, who are more accommodating (Maccoby, 1990). Although this has not been experimentally documented, the one exception might be during the initial relationship formation between co-wives. Jankowiak et al.'s (2005) review suggests that these relationships are often openly verbally (sometimes physically) hostile when a new co-wife joins the family. Over time, the open hostility tends to lessen and is replaced by simmering resentment and likely more subtle forms of aggression; the change is due in part to the husband's suppression of open hostility among his co-wives.

In any case, dominance-oriented language among men eventually has to be backed up by physical threat or aggression or by demonstrated superiority in a culturally important domain. Because women do not tend to escalate their conflicts as much as men, language itself appears to be more central to their development and maintenance of friendships and in their conflicts with other women than it is for men. Indeed, women's relational aggression is largely conveyed through language, specifically gossiping about other girls, spreading lies and rumors about their sexual behavior, telling secrets, and attempting to control other girls' social behavior. The use of language in relational aggression sets the stage for selection to elaborate basic language competencies more in women than in men.

Indeed, relative to boys and men, girls and women have advantages for many basic language-related skills, including the length and quality of utterances, the ease and speed of articulating complex words and strings of words, the speed of retrieving individual words from long-term memory, and skill at discriminating basic language sounds from one another (Block, Arnott, Quigley, & Lynch, 1989; Halpern, 2000; Hampson, 1990; Hyde & Linn, 1988; Majeres, 2007). Girls and women also show many fewer pauses (e.g., filled with "uhh") in their utterances than do boys and men (Hall, 1984), and, at the same time, boys and men manifest language-related disorders, such as stuttering, 2–4 times more frequently than do girls and women (Tallal, 1991). There is also evidence that women process the prosody (e.g., emotional tone) of language more quickly and with less allocation of attention than do men (Schirmer, Kotz, & Friederici, 2005). The relative advantage of girls and women in these areas ranges from small to very large, depending on the skill and the complexity of the task.

If women's advantages in these areas are related to female–female competition (including competition for same-sex friends; Geary, 2010), then the same-sex bias found for face processing should also be found for language processing. Specifically, we predict that women will be more sensitive to subtle variation in vocal into- nation and prosody that is socially dismissive and particularly sensitive to these variations when uttered by other women. The one area in which we do not expect sex differences or a male advantage is when the intonation contains a dominance-related component. Unfortunately, the existing studies do not provide a test of these hypotheses.

Theory of Mind and Person Schema

Theory of mind represents the critical ability to make inferences about the intentions of other peo- ple and their beliefs and to infer whether the emotions or other states signaled by social cues are or are not an accurate reflection of the actual emotional state or intentions of the individual (Baron-Cohen, 1995; Leslie, Friedman, & German, 2004). The person schema is related to theory of mind but is focused on knowledge about specific significant others, rather than the more general ability to make inferences about the internal states of others.

As a result of the subtlety of relational aggres- sion, we predict a female advantage in some

aspects of theory of mind and in the richness of personal information they are motivated to accrue about significant others. In particular, we anticipate that girls and women will have advantages when it comes to understanding other girls' and women's thoughts, intentions, and feelings about significant relationships, including same-sex friendships. We predict boys and men, in contrast, will focus on competitors' thoughts and intentions as they relate to larger-scale groups and politics and the competencies (e.g., physical skills) that would make them reliable and effective members of competitive coalitions or teams (Benenson, 1990; Geary, Byrd-Craven, Hoard, Vigil, & Numtee, 2003). Rather than a focus on what the competitor is intending with respect to a few specific relationships, the focus is on how a potential competitor intends to organize larger, competitive groups. Unfortunately, little of the theory of mind research has focused on sex differences, and the work that has done so does not address these predictions.

The theory of mind studies that have examined sex differences suggest either no difference (Lucariello, Durand, & Yarnell, 2007) or that girls and women have a small advantage (Banerjee, 1997; Bosacki, 2000; Bosacki & Astington, 1999; Charman & Clements, 2002; Walker, 2005). The tasks used in these studies are not particularly difficult, however, which will obscure any sex differences. In one study in which a relatively (for this field) complex theory of mind task was used, Bosacki (2000; Bosacki & Astington, 1999) found that 3 out of 4 adolescent girls were more skilled than the average same-age boy at making inferences about the thoughts, feelings, and social perspective of their peers. Although Benenson et al. (2013) did not design their studies to assess sex differences in theory of mind, their results are relevant to the issue. In one study they found that women were more sensitive to social cues that signaled risk of social exclusion than were men— suggesting they may make inferences about the exclusionary intentions of others more readily than men—and in a follow-up study they found that women had higher heart rate increases when reading scenarios of social exclusion, in keeping with higher risks and costs of social exclusion for women than men (Benenson, Markovits, Emery Thompson, & Wrangham, 2011).

Relational aggression is presumably most effective when it targets social and psychological vulnerabilities of the would-be victim, and thus we anticipate that girls and women will be motivated to gather more personal information about others in their social sphere than boys and men. Our hypothesis has not been broadly assessed, except in the context of friendships. In these relationships, girls and women know more personal information about their friends than do boys and men; girls' and women's relationships are generally focused on one or two best friends, whereas that of boys and men includes a larger group of friends and allies (Benenson, 1990; Mehta & Strough, 2009). In comparison to that of boys and men, girls' and women's dyadic relationships are characterized by higher levels of emotional support and more frequent intimate exchanges (e.g., talking about their problems), and they are a more central source of help and guidance in solving social and other problems (Maccoby, 1990; Parker & Asher, 1993; Rose & Asher, 1999; Savin-Williams, 1987). Girls and women also know more about their close friends than do boys and men (Markovits, Benenson, & Dolenszky, 2001; Swenson & Rose, 2003). All of these studies are consistent with girls' and women's friendships providing an important source of support that buffers them from social and other stressors (Taylor et al., 2000), which also makes them a predicted target for competitors—disrupting competitor's friendships will undermine the victim's ability to counter the social tactics of the aggressor.

In any case, we suspect that women strategically use this personal information in the context of relational aggression when friendships dissolve, as they often do. The risks here are higher than for boys and men, because girls' and women's friendships are more dependent on equality of the give-and-take of the relationship, are more sensitive to personal slights (e.g., being excluded from a social event), and are less tolerant of conflict than are boys' and men's friendships (Benenson et al., 2011; Parker &

Asher, 1993; Rose & Asher, 1999; Whitesell & Harter, 1996); Geary (2002) provides an evolutionary analysis of these patterns. The result is fragile relationships that are more likely to permanently dissolve than are boys' and men's relationships (Benenson & Christakos, 2003).

Once the relationship has turned sour, the personal information that was revealed during the friendship can now be used to socially manipulate and undermine the psychological and social well-being of their former friend. Whether or not this personal information is used in this way remains to be determined, however. Crick and Nelson (2002) found that relational aggression was common in the context of current relationships, and there is no reason to believe this aggression ceases with termination of the friendship, especially when the former friend is still a member of the larger social group.

Discussion

Over the past four decades, Darwin's (1871) sexual selection has inspired the study of sex differences across hundreds of species (Andersson, 1994). His insights have led to the discovery of how the traits that support competition for mates and that are used in mate choices have evolved and how proximate conditions (e.g., individual health, social density) influence their expression (Andersson, 1994; Emlen & Oring, 1977). The foci of the vast majority of this research have been on male–male competition for mates and female choice of mating partners, and indeed these are very common features of reproductive dynamics. Female–female competition has been studied in "sex-role-reversed" species but largely to test the hypothesis that the near ubiquity of male–male competition is related to a more fundamental sex difference in the potential rate of reproduction (Clutton-Brock & Vincent, 1991). As predicted, in species where males reproduce more slowly than females, typically because males brood eggs or protect offspring, females compete intensely for mates that will provide this parental investment and males are choosy (e.g., Amundsen &

Forsgren, 2001). These studies confirm the importance of potential reproductive rate as a driver of sex differences in reproductive strategy and more generally that female–female competition and male choice, as defined by Darwin's traditional definition of sexual selection, occur in nature.

These studies aside, female–female competition and male choice that do not fit into Darwin's (1871) traditional definition have been relatively overlooked, although it is clear that both occur in many species (Clutton-Brock, 2009; Kraaijeveld et al., 2007; Stockley & Bro-Jørensen, 2011; Tobias et al., 2012). Following West-Eberhard (1979, 1983), we focused on female–female competition in humans as an aspect of social rather than sexual selection. This is particularly important to consider for humans, because mate choices are heavily influenced by kin in traditional societies, during recorded history, and very likely during much of our recent evolutionary history (Apostolou, 2007, 2010; Walker et al., 2011). These social dynamics do not eliminate intrasexual competition (especially for males) or intersexual choice in humans (Geary, 2010), but they have the potential to modify the strength of these selection pressures. One consequence, we argue, is that kin choice of mates reduced the pressures for females to directly compete with one another for marriage partners—males generally still have to establish themselves culturally and within their male status hierarchy even with kin choice of mates. Reduced pressures for direct competition for mates combined with the common practice of polygyny in traditional societies and very likely throughout much of human evolution (Alexander et al., 1979; Murdock, 1981) resulted in a comparatively unique social context, that is, competition among co-wives.

To be sure, competition among co-wives for the emotional and sexual attention of their husband is consistent with Darwin's (1871) traditional definition of sexual selection, but other aspects of their competition are not, in particular competition for other resources (e.g., access to arable land, goats) that can influence their reproductive success and the later reproductive prospects of their children (Jankowiak et al., 2005). We suggest that

these features of female–female competition are consistent with West-Eberhard's (1983) definition of social selection. Broadening the theoretical lens to include social selection—largely overlooked by evolutionary psychologists (Buss, 2005)—as an evolutionary contributor to human sex differences allows us to more fully appreciate competition among girls and women.

This competition is largely manifested as relational aggression, specifically the use of verbal and nonverbal communication to psychologically harass competitors, disrupt their opposite sex (with the shared husband in polygynous marriages) and same-sex (friendships as a social support) relationships, to exclude them from the social group (if possible), and in some cases to psychologically harm their children (Jankowiak et al., 2005). We propose that this competition contributed to girls' and women's advantages over boys and men in the folk psychological systems that support dyadic interactions and relationships, that is, sensitivity to subtle messages conveyed by facial expressions and other nonverbal cues and in language fluency. The evidence is mixed at this point, but we predict that women are more sensitive than men to subtle cues that indicate attempts by other women to disrupt their relationships, including same-sex friendships, and exclude them from the social group (Benenson, 2013). We also predict that women are more motivated than men to accrue personal information about other people, especially other women and would-be mates, in their social group. This is information that can facilitate the formation of relationships, as well as information that can be used aggressively.

We have not addressed it here but note that social competition, in addition to traditional male–male competition, may also be an important selection pressure for men. It is clear that men compete for physical and social dominance as well as prestige—social status freely conferred by others based on accomplishment (Cheng, Tracy, Foulsham, Kingstone, & Henrich, 2012; Henrich & Gil-White, 2001)—across cultures and do so to attract and retain marriage and mating partners (Geary, 2010). Many men also use the associated social and material resources to invest in the physical well-being, social competitiveness, and later reproductive prospects of their children (Geary, 2000). Men's investment in children is especially common and relatively extensive for successful men in societies with culturally imposed monogamy (Flinn & Low, 1986). These social constraints have not only shifted male–male competition for mates from a physical-dominance strategy to a prestige-based strategy (Henrich, Boyd, & Richerson, 2012); they appear to have shifted the nature of the selection pressures acting on men's competitiveness. Darwin's (1871) traditional male–male competition over mates is still important, but West-Eberhard's (1983) social competition for resources that will be invested in offspring also needs to be considered as an important selection pressure acting on men.

References

Alexander, R. D., Hoogland, J. L., Howard, R. D., Noonan, K. M., & Sherman, P. W. (1979). Sexual dimorphisms and breeding systems in pinnipeds, ungulates, primates, and humans. In N. A. Chagnon & W. Irons (Eds.), *Evolutionary biology and human social behavior: An anthropological perspective* (pp. 402–435). North Scituate, MA: Duxbury Press.

Amey, F. K. (2005). Polygyny and child survival in West Africa. *Social Biology, 49*, 74–89.

Amundsen, T., & Forsgren, E. (2001). Male mate choice selects for female coloration in a fish. *Proceedings of the National Academy of Sciences USA, 98*, 13155–13160.

Anderson, K. J., & Leaper, C. (1998). Meta-analyses of gender effects on conversational interruption: Who, what, when, where, and how? *Sex Roles, 39*, 225–252.

Andersson, M. (1994). *Sexual selection*. Princeton, NJ: Princeton University Press.

Apostolou, M. (2007). Sexual selection under parental choice: The role of parents in the evolution of human mating. *Evolution and Human Behavior, 28*, 403–409.

Apostolou, M. (2010). Sexual selection under parental choice: Evidence from sixteen historical societies. *Evolutionary Psychology, 10*, 504–518.

Archer, J., & Coyne, S. M. (2005). An integrated review of indirect, relational, and social aggression. *Personality and Social Psychology Review, 9*, 212–230.

Banerjee, M. (1997). Hidden emotions: Preschoolers' knowledge of appearance-reality and emotion display rules. *Social Cognition, 15*, 107–132.

Baron-Cohen, S. (1995). *Mindblindness: An essay on autism and theory of mind*. Cambridge, MA: MIT Press/Bradford Books.

Barrett, A. A. (1996). *Agrippina: Mother of Nero*. London: BT Batsford.

Benenson, J. F. (1990). Gender differences in social networks. *Journal of Early Adolescence, 10*, 472–495.

Benenson, J. F., & Christakos, A. (2003). The greater fragility of females' versus males' closest same-sex friendships. *Child Development, 74*, 1123–1129.

Benenson, J. F., Markovits, H., Emery Thompson, M., & Wrangham, R. W. (2011). Social exclusion threatens adult females more than males. *Psychological Science, 22*, 538–544.

Benenson, J. F. (2013). The development of human female competition: Allies and adversaries. *Philosophical Transactions of the Royal Society, B: Biological Sciences, 368*(1631), 20130079.

Benenson, J. F., Markovits, H., Hultgren, B., Nguyen, T., Bullock, G., & Wrangham, R. W. (2013). Social exclusion: More important to human females than males. *PloS One, 8*, e55851. doi:10.1371/journal.pone.0055851.

Betzig, L. L. (1986). *Despotism and differential reproduction: A Darwinian view of history*. New York: Aldine Publishing.

Betzig, L. L. (1992). Roman polygyny. *Ethology and Sociobiology, 13*, 309–349.

Betzig, L. (2012). Means, variances, and ranges in reproductive success: Comparative evidence. *Evolution and Human Behavior, 33*, 309–317.

Bjorklund, D. F., & Kipp, K. (1996). Parental investment theory and gender differences in the evolution of inhibition mechanisms. *Psychological Bulletin, 120*, 163–188.

Björkqvist, K., Osterman, K., & Lagerspetz, K. M. J. (1994). Sex differences in covert aggression among adults. *Aggressive Behavior, 20*, 27–34.

Block, R. A., Arnott, D. P., Quigley, B., & Lynch, W. C. (1989). Unilateral nostril breathing influences lateralized cognitive performance. *Brain and Cognition, 9*, 181–190.

Bond, L., Carlin, J. B., Thomas, L., Rubin, K., & Patton, G. (2001). Does bullying cause emotional problems? A prospective study of young teenagers. *British Medical Journal, 323*, 480–484.

Bosacki, S. L. (2000). Theory of mind and self-concept in preadolescents: Links with gender and language. *Journal of Educational Psychology, 92*, 709–717.

Borgerhoff Mulder, M. (1988). Kipsigis bridewealth payments. In L. Betzig, M. Borgerhoff Mulder, & P. Turke (Eds.), *Human reproductive behaviour: A Darwinian perspective* (pp. 65–82). Cambridge, England: Cambridge University Press.

Borgerhoff Mulder, M. (1990). Kipsigis women's preferences for wealthy men: Evidence for female choice in mammals? *Behavioral Ecology and Sociobiology, 27*, 255–264.

Borgerhoff Mulder, M. (2000). Optimizing offspring: The quantity-quality tradeoff in agropastoral Kipsigis. *Evolution and Human Behavior, 21*, 391–410.

Bosacki, S. L., & Astington, J. W. (1999). Theory of mind in preadolescents: Relations between social understanding and social competence. *Social Development, 8*, 237–254.

Bove, R., & Valeggia, C. (2009). Polygyny and women's health in sub-Saharan Africa. *Social Science & Medicine, 68*, 21–29.

Buck Louis, G. M., Lum, K. J., Sundaram, R., Chen, Z., Kim, S., Lynch, C. D., et al. (2011). Stress reduces conception probabilities across the fertile window: Evidence in support of relaxation. *Fertility and Sterility, 95*, 2184–2189.

Buck, R. W., Savin, V. J., Miller, R. E., & Caul, W. F. (1972). Communication of affect through facial expression in humans. *Journal of Personality and Social Psychology, 23*, 362–371.

Buss, D. M. (Ed.). (2005). *The evolutionary psychology handbook*. Hoboken, NJ: Wiley.

Campbell, A. (2004). Female competition: Causes, constraints, content, and contexts. *Journal of Sex Research, 41*, 16–26.

Card, N. A., Stucky, B. D., Sawalani, G. M., & Little, T. D. (2008). Direct and indirect aggression during childhood and adolescence: A meta-analytic review of gender differences, intercorrelations, and relations to maladjustment. *Child Development, 79*, 1185–1229.

Carranza, J. (2009). Defining sexual selection as sex-dependent selection. *Animal Behaviour, 77*, 749–751.

Cartledge, P. (2004). *Alexander the Great*. New York: Vintage.

Cassius, D. (1914). *Roman history: VII* (E. Cary, Trans.). New York: Macmillan.

Chagnon, N. A. (1988). Life histories, blood revenge, and warfare in a tribal population. *Science, 239*, 985–992.

Charman, T., & Clements, W. (2002). Is there a gender difference in false belief development? *Social Development, 11*, 1–10.

Cheng, J. T., Tracy, J. L., Foulsham, T., Kingstone, A., & Henrich, J. (2012). Two ways to the top: Evidence that dominance and prestige are distinct yet viable avenues to social rank and influence. *Journal of Personality and Social Psychology*.

Clutton-Brock, T. (2009). Sexual selection in females. *Animal Behaviour, 77*, 3–11.

Clutton-Brock, T. (2007). Sexual selection in males and females. *Science, 318*, 1882–1885.

Clutton-Brock, T. H. (1989). Mammalian mating systems. *Proceedings of the Royal Society of London B: Biological Sciences, 236*, 339–372.

Clutton-Brock, T. H. (1991). *The evolution of parental care*. Princeton, NJ: Princeton University Press.

Clutton-Brock, T. H., & Vincent, A. C. J. (1991). Sexual selection and the potential reproductive rates of males and females. *Nature, 351*, 58–60.

Clutton-Brock, T. H., & Pemberton, J. M. (Eds.). (2004). *Soay sheep: Dynamics and selection in an island population*. Cambridge, England: Cambridge University Press.

Coppen, A. (1965). The prevalence of menstrual disorders in psychiatric patients. *British Journal of Psychiatry, 3*, 155–167.

Crick, N. R., & Nelson, D. A. (2002). Relational and physical victimization within friendships: Nobody told me there would be friends like these. *Journal of Abnormal Child Psychology, 30*, 599–607.

Crook, J. H. (1972). Sexual selection, dimorphism, and social organization in the primates. In B. G. Campbell (Ed.), *Sexual selection and the descent of man: 1871–1971* (pp. 231–281). Chicago, IL: Aldine.

Daly, M., & Wilson, M. I. (1981). Abuse and neglect of children in evolutionary perspective. In R. D. Alexander & D. W. Tinkle (Eds.), *Natural selection and social behavior* (pp. 405–416). New York: Chiron.

Daly, M., & Wilson, M. (1988). *Homicide*. New York: Aldine de Gruyter.

Darwin, C. (1859). *On the origin of species by means of natural selection*. London: John Murray.

Darwin, C. R. (1871). *The descent of man, and selection in relation to sex*. London: John Murray.

Elbedour, S., Onwuegbuzie, A. J., Caridine, C., & Abu-Saad, H. (2002). The effect of polygamous marital structure on behavioral, emotional, and academic adjustment in children: A comprehensive review of the literature. *Clinical Child and Family Psychology Review, 5*, 255–271.

Emlen, S. T., & Oring, L. W. (1977). Ecology, sexual selection, and the evolution of mating systems. *Science, 197*, 215–223.

Emlen, D. J., Marangelo, J., Ball, B., & Cunningham, C. W. (2005). Diversity in the weapons of sexual selection: Horn evolution in the beetle genus *Onthophagus* (Coleoptera: Scarabaeidae). *Evolution, 59*, 1060–1084.

Feshbach, N. D. (1969). Sex differences in children's modes of aggressive responses toward outsiders. *Merrill-Palmer Quarterly, 15*, 249–258.

Flinn, M. V., & Low, B. S. (1986). Resource distribution, social competition, and mating patterns in human societies. In D. I. Rubenstein & R. W. Wrangham (Eds.), *Ecological aspects of social evolution: Birds and mammals* (pp. 217–243). Princeton, NJ: Princeton University Press.

Freisenbruch, A. (2010). *Caesars' wives: Sex, power, and politics in the Roman Empire*. New York: Free Press.

Garland, L. (1999). *Byzantine empresses: Women and power in Byzantium AD 527–1204*. New York: Routledge.

Gaulin, S. J. C., & Fitzgerald, R. W. (1986). Sex differences in spatial ability: An evolutionary hypothesis and test. *American Naturalist, 127*, 74–88.

Gaulin, S. J. C., & Fitzgerald, R. W. (1989). Sexual selection for spatial-learning ability. *Animal Behaviour, 37*, 322–331.

Geary, D. C. (2000). Evolution and proximate expression of human paternal investment. *Psychological Bulletin, 126*, 55–77.

Geary, D. C. (2002). Sexual selection and sex differences in social cognition. In A. V. McGillicuddy-De Lisi & R. De Lisi (Eds.), *Biology, society, and behavior: The development of sex differences in cognition* (pp. 23–53). Greenwich, CT: Ablex/Greenwood.

Geary, D. C. (2005). *The origin of mind: Evolution of brain, cognition, and general intelligence.* Washington, DC: American Psychological Association.

Geary, D. C. (2010). *Male, female: The evolution of human sex differences* (2nd ed.). Washington, DC: American Psychological Association.

Geary, D. C., Bailey, D. H., & Oxford, J. (2011). Reflections on the human family. In C. Salmon & T. Shackelford (Eds.), *The oxford handbook of evolutionary family psychology* (pp. 365–385). New York: Oxford University Press.

Geary, D. C., Byrd-Craven, J., Hoard, M. K., Vigil, J., & Numtee, C. (2003). Evolution and development of boys' social behavior. *Developmental Review, 23,* 444–470.

Geary, D. C., & Flinn, M. V. (2001). Evolution of human parental behavior and the human family. *Parenting: Science and Practice, 1,* 5–61.

Gibson, M. A., & Mace, R. (2006). Polygyny, reproductive success and child health in rural Ethiopia: Why marry a married man? *Journal of Biosocial Science, 39,* 287–300.

Hadley, C. (2005). Is polygyny a risk factor for poor growth performance among Tanzanian agropastoralists? *American Journal of Physical Anthropology, 126,* 471–480.

Hall, J. A. (1978). Gender effects in decoding nonverbal cues. *Psychological Bulletin, 85,* 845–857.

Hall, J. A. (1984). *Nonverbal sex differences: Communication accuracy and expressive style.* Baltimore, MD: The Johns Hopkins University Press.

Hall, J. A., & Matsumoto, D. (2004). Gender differences in judgments of multiple emotions from facial expressions. *Emotion, 4,* 201–206.

Halpern, D. F. (2000). *Sex differences in cognitive abilities* (3rd ed.). Mahwah, NJ: Erlbaum.

Hampson, E. (1990). Estrogen-related variations in human spatial and articulatory-motor skills. *Psychoneuroendocrinology, 15,* 97–111.

Heinsohn, R. (2008). The ecological basis of unusual sex roles in reverse-dichromatic eclectus parrots. *Animal Behaviour, 76,* 97–103.

Henrich, J., Boyd, R., & Richerson, P. J. (2012). The puzzle of monogamous marriage. *Philosophical Transactions of the Royal Society, B: Biological Sciences, 367,* 657–669.

Henrich, J., & Gil-White, F. J. (2001). The evolution of prestige: Freely conferred deference as a mechanism for enhancing the benefits of cultural transmission. *Evolution and Human Behavior, 22,* 165–196.

Herlitz, A., & Rehnman, J. (2008). Sex differences in episodic memory. *Current Directions in Psychological Science, 17,* 52–56.

Hjollund, N. H. I., Jensen, T. K., Bonde, J. P. E., Henriksen, T. B., Andersson, A.-M., Kolstad, H. A., et al. (1999). Distress and reduced fertility: A follow-up study of first-pregnancy planners. *Fertility and Sterility, 72,* 47–53.

Hyde, J. S., & Linn, M. C. (1988). Gender differences in verbal ability: A meta-analysis. *Psychological Bulletin, 104,* 53–69.

Jankowiak, W., Sudakov, M., & Wilreker, B. C. (2005). Co-wife conflict and co-operation. *Ethnology, 44,* 81–98.

Jarrett, L. R. (1984). Psychosocial and biological influences on menstruation: Synchrony, cycle length, and regularity. *Psychoneuroendocrinology, 9,* 21–28.

Jašarević, E., Williams, S. A., Roberts, R. M., Geary, D. C., & Rosenfeld, C. S. (2012). Spatial navigation strategies in *Peromyscus*: A comparative study. *Animal Behaviour, 84,* 1141–1149.

Josephson, S. C. (2002). Does polygyny reduce fertility? *American Journal of Human Biology, 14,* 222–232.

Kendler, K. S., Myers, J., & Prescott, C. A. (2005). Sex differences in the relationship between social support and risk for major depression: A longitudinal study of opposite-sex twin pairs. *American Journal of Psychiatry, 162,* 250–256.

Kimura, D. (1999). *Sex and cognition.* Cambridge, MA: Bradford/MIT Press.

Kraaijeveld, K., Kraaijeveld-Smit, F. J. L., & Komdeur, J. (2007). The evolution of mutual ornament. *Animal Behaviour, 74,* 657–677.

Lande, R. (1980). Sexual dimorphism, sexual selection, and adaptation in polygenic characteristics. *Evolution, 34,* 292–305.

Leaper, C., & Smith, T. E. (2004). A meta-analytic review of gender variations in children's language use: Talkativeness, affiliative speech, and assertive speech. *Developmental Psychology, 40,* 993–1027.

Lee, J. J., & Pinker, S. (2010). Rationales for indirect speech: The theory of the strategic speaker. *Psychological Review, 117,* 785–807.

Leenaars, L. S., Dane, A. V., & Marini, Z. A. (2008). Evolutionary perspective on indirect victimization in adolescence: The role of attractiveness, dating and sexual behavior. *Aggressive Behavior, 34,* 404–415.

Leroy, J. L., Razak, A. A., & Habicht, J. P. (2008). Only children of the head of household benefit from increased household food diversity in northern Ghana. *The Journal of Nutrition, 138,* 2258–2263.

Leslie, A. M., Friedman, O., & German, T. P. (2004). Core mechanisms in 'theory of mind'. *Trends in Cognitive Sciences, 8,* 528–533.

Lucariello, J. M., Durand, T. M., & Yarnell, L. (2007). Social versus intrapersonal ToM: Social ToM is a cognitive strength for low- and middle-SES children. *Journal of Applied Developmental Psychology, 28,* 285–297.

Lynch, C. D., Sundaram, R., Buck Louis, G. M., Lum, K. J., & Pyper, C. (2012). Are increased levels of self-reported psychosocial stress, anxiety, and depression associated with fecundity? *Fertility and Sterility, 98,* 453–458.

Lyon, B. E., & Montgomerie, R. (2012). Sexual selection is a form of social selection. *Philosophical Transactions of the Royal Society, B: Biological Sciences, 367,* 2266–2273.

Maccoby, E. E. (1990). Gender and relationships: A developmental account. *American Psychologist, 45,* 513–520.

Majeres, R. L. (2007). Sex differences in phonological coding: Alphabet transformation speed. *Intelligence, 35*, 335–346.

Markovits, H., Benenson, J., & Dolenszky, E. (2001). Evidence that children and adolescents have internal models of peer interactions that are gender differentiated. *Child Development, 72*, 879–886.

Matteo, S. (1987). The effect of job stress and job interdependency on menstrual cycle length, regularity and synchrony. *Psychoneuroendocrinology, 12*, 467–476.

McClure, E. B. (2000). A meta-analytic review of sex differences in facial expression processing and their development in infants, children, and adolescents. *Psychological Bulletin, 126*, 424–453.

Mehl, M. R., Vazire, S., Ramírez-Esparza, N., Slatcher, R. B., & Pennebaker, J. W. (2007). Are women really more talkative than men? *Science, 317*, 82.

Mehta, C. M., & Strough, J.-N. (2009). Sex segregation in friendships and normative contexts across the life span. *Developmental Review, 29*, 201–220.

Murdock, G. P. (1981). *Atlas of world cultures.* Pittsburgh, PA: University of Pittsburgh Press.

Nesse, R. M. (2009). Social selection and the origins of culture. In M. Schaller, S. J. Heine, A. Norenzayan, T. Yamagishi, & T. Kameda (Eds.), *Evolution, culture, and the human mind* (pp. 137–150). Philadelphia, PA: Lawrence Erlbaum.

Ogden, D. (1999). *Polygamy, prostitutes and death: The Hellenistic dynasties.* Oakville, CT: Duckworth.

Omariba, D., & Boyle, M. H. (2007). Family structure and child mortality in sub-Saharan Africa: Cross-national effects of polygyny. *Journal of Marriage and Family, 69*, 528–543.

Owens, L., Shute, R., & Slee, P. (2000). "Guess what I just heard!": Indirect aggression among teenage girls in Australia. *Aggressive Behavior, 26*, 67–83.

Owens, L., Slee, P., & Shute, R. (2000). 'It hurts a hell of a lot. . .' The effects of indirect aggression on teenage girls. *School Psychology International, 21*, 359–376.

Parker, J. G., & Asher, S. R. (1993). Friendship and friendship quality in middle childhood: Links with peer group acceptance and feelings of loneliness and social dissatisfaction. *Developmental Psychology, 29*, 611–621.

Pausanias. (2012). *Description of Greece* (W. H. S. JONES, Trans.). Retrieved January 2, 2013, from http://www.theoi.com/Text/Pausanias8A.html

Perdue, B. M., Snyder, R. J., Zhihe, Z., Marr, M. J., & Maple, T. L. (2011). Sex differences in spatial ability: A test of the range size hypothesis in the order Carnivora. *Biology Letters, 7*, 380–383.

Plavcan, J. M., & van Schaik, C. P. (1997). Intrasexual competition and body weight dimorphism in anthropoid primates. *American Journal of Physical Anthropology, 103*, 37–68.

Plutarch. (2004). *The life of Alexander the Great* (J. Dryden, Trans.). New York: Modern Library.

Preston, B. T., Stevenson, I. R., Pemberton, J. M., Coltman, D. W., & Wilson, K. (2003). Overt and covert competition in a promiscuous mammal: The importance of weaponry and testes size to male reproductive success. *Proceedings of the Royal Society of London. Series B: Biological Sciences, 270*, 633–640.

Puts, D. A. (2010). Beauty and the beast: Mechanisms of sexual selection in humans. *Evolution and Human Behavior, 31*, 157–175.

Rehnman, J., & Herlitz, A. (2006). Higher face recognition ability in girls: Magnified by own-sex and own-ethnicity bias. *Memory, 14*, 289–296.

Rehnman, J., & Herlitz, A. (2007). Women remember more faces than men do. *Acta Psychologica, 124*, 344–355.

Robinson, M. R., & Kruuk, L. E. (2007). Function of weaponry in females: The use of horns in intrasexual competition for resources in female Soay sheep. *Biology Letters, 3*, 651–654.

Rose, A. J., & Asher, S. R. (1999). Children's goals and strategies in response to conflicts within a friendship. *Developmental Psychology, 35*, 69–79.

Rosenthal, R., Hall, J. A., DiMatteo, M. R., Rogers, P. L., & Archer, D. (1979). *Sensitivity to nonverbal communication: The PONS test.* Baltimore, MD: The Johns Hopkins University Press.

Rotter, N. G., & Rotter, G. S. (1988). Sex differences in the encoding and decoding of negative facial emotions. *Journal of Nonverbal Behavior, 12*, 139–148.

Savin-Williams, R. C. (1987). *Adolescence: An ethological perspective.* New York: Springer.

Scelza, B. A. (2011). Female choice and extrapair paternity in a traditional human population. *Biology Letters, 7*, 889–891.

Schirmer, A., Kotz, S. A., & Friederici, A. D. (2005). On the role of attention for the processing of emotions in speech: Sex differences revisited. *Cognitive Brain Research, 24*, 442–452.

Shaywitz, B. A., Shaywitz, S. E., Pugh, K. R., Constable, R. T., Skudlarski, P., Fulbright, R. K., et al. (1995). Sex differences in the functional organization of the brain for language. *Nature, 373*, 607–609.

Shepard, L. D. (2012). The impact of polygamy on women's mental health: A systematic review. *Epidemiology and Psychiatric Sciences, 1*, 1–16.

Shuker, D. M. (2010). Sexual selection: Endless forms or tangled bank? *Animal Behaviour, 79*, e11–e17.

Smith, R. L., Rose, A. J., & Schwartz-Mette, R. A. (2010). Relational and overt aggression in childhood and adolescence: Clarifying mean-level gender differences and associations with peer acceptance. *Social Development, 19*, 243–269.

Stockley, P., & Bro-Jørgensen, J. (2011). Female competition and its evolutionary consequences in mammals. *Biological Reviews, 86*, 341–366.

Strassmann, B. I. (1997). Polygyny as a risk factor for child mortality among the Dogon. *Current Anthropology, 38*, 688–695.

Strassmann, B. I. (2011). Cooperation and competition in a cliff-dwelling people. *Proceedings of the National Academy of Sciences USA, 108*, 10894–10901.

Strassmann, B. I., & Gillespie, B. (2002). Life-history theory, fertility and reproductive success in humans. *Proceedings of the Royal Society of London B: Biological Sciences, 269*, 553–562.

Suetonius. (2011). *The Caesars* (D. W. Hurley, Trans.). Indianapolis, IN: Hackett.

Swenson, L. P., & Rose, A. J. (2003). Friends as reporters of children's and adolescents' depressive symptoms. *Journal of Abnormal Child Psychology, 31*, 619–631.

Tacitus. (2004). *The annals* (A. J. Woodman, Trans.). Indianapolis, IN: Hackett.

Tallal, P. (1991). Hormonal influences in developmental learning disabilities. *Psychoneuroendocrinology, 16*, 203–211.

Taylor, S. E., Klein, L. C., Lewis, B. P., Gruenewald, T. L., Gurung, R. A. R., & Updegraff, J. A. (2000). Biobehavioral responses to stress in females: Tend-and-befriend, not fight-or-flight. *Psychological Review, 107*, 411–429.

Tobias, J. A., Montgomerie, R., & Lyon, B. E. (2012). The evolution of female ornaments and weaponry: Social selection, sexual selection and ecological competition. *Philosophical Transactions of the Royal Society, B: Biological Sciences, 367*, 2274–2293.

Trivers, R. L. (1972). Parental investment and sexual selection. In B. Campbell (Ed.), *Sexual selection and the descent of man 1871–1971* (pp. 136–179). Chicago: Aldine Publishing.

Underhill, P. A., Shen, P., Lin, A. A., Jin, L., Passarino, G., Yang, W. H., et al. (2000). Y chromosome sequence variation and the history of human populations. *Nature Genetics, 26*, 358–361.

Vaillancourt, T., & Sharma, A. (2011). Intolerance of sexy peers: Intrasexual competition among women. *Aggressive Behavior, 37*, 569–577.

van Beek, Y., & Dubas, J. S. (2008). Age and gender differences in decoding basic and non-basic facial expressions in late childhood and early adolescence. *Journal of Nonverbal Behavior, 32*, 37–52.

Vigil, J. M. (2009). A socio-relational framework of sex differences in the expression of emotion. *Behavioral and Brain Sciences, 32*, 375–390.

von Rueden, C., Gurven, M., & Kaplan, H. (2011). Why do men seek status? Fitness payoffs to dominance and prestige. *Proceedings of the Royal Society B: Biological Sciences, 278*, 2223–2232.

Wagner, H. L., Buck, R., & Winterbotham, M. (1993). Communication of specific emotions: Gender differences in sending accuracy and communication measures. *Journal of Nonverbal Behavior, 17*, 29–53.

Walker, S. (2005). Gender differences in the relationship between young children's peer-related social competence and individual differences in theory of mind. *Journal of Genetic Psychology, 166*, 297–312.

Walker, R. S., Hill, K. R., Flinn, M. V., & Ellsworth, R. M. (2011). Evolutionary history of hunter-gatherer marriage practices. *PLoS ONE, 6*(4), e19066. doi:10.1371/journal.pone.0019066.

Watson, N. L., & Simmons, L. W. (2010a). Mate choice in the dung beetle Onthophagus sagittarius: Are female horns ornaments? *Behavioral Ecology, 21*, 424–430.

Watson, N. L., & Simmons, L. W. (2010b). Reproductive competition promotes the evolution of female weaponry. *Proceedings of the Royal Society B: Biological Sciences, 277*, 2035–2040.

West-Eberhard, M. J. (1979). Sexual selection, social competition, and evolution. *Proceedings of the American Philosophical Society, 123*, 222–234.

West-Eberhard, M. J. (1983). Sexual selection, social competition, and speciation. *Quarterly Review of Biology, 58*, 155–183.

White, D. R. (1988). Rethinking polygyny: Co-wives, codes, and cultural systems. *Current Anthropology, 29*, 529–572.

Whitesell, N. R., & Harter, S. (1996). The interpersonal context of emotion: Anger with close friends and classmates. *Child Development, 67*, 1345–1359.

Worthington, I. (2008). *Philip II of Macedonia*. New Haven, CT: Yale University Press.

Zahavi, A., & Zahavi, A. (1997). *The handicap principle: A missing piece of Darwin's puzzle*. New York: Oxford University Press.

Index

V.A. Weekes-Shackelford and T.K. Shackelford (eds.), *Evolutionary Perspectives on Human Sexual Psychology and Behavior*, Evolutionary Psychology, DOI 10.1007/978-1-4939-0314-6,
© Springer Science+Business Media New York 2014

Printed by Publishers' Graphics LLC USA
CAMZ140309.20.06.88